The Dada Cyborg

The Dada Cyborg

Visions of the New Human in Weimar Berlin

Matthew Biro

University of Minnesota Press / Minneapolis • London

The University of Minnesota Press gratefully acknowledges the financial assistance provided for the publication of this book from the Office of the Vice President for Research, University of Michigan, and the Department of the History of Art at the University of Michigan.

The University of Minnesota Press gratefully acknowledges the work of Edward Dimendberg, editorial consultant, on this project.

Chapter 3 appeared previously as "Raoul Hausmann's Revolutionary Media," *Art History* 30, no. 1 (February 2007): 26–56. Portions of chapter 4 were previously published in "Allegorical Modernism: Carl Einstein on Otto Dix," *Art Criticism* 15, no. 1 (2000): 46–70; "History at a Standstill: Walter Benjamin, Otto Dix, and the Question of Stratigraphy," *RES* 40 (Autumn 2001): 153–76; and "The New Human as Cyborg: Figures of Technology in Weimar Visual Culture," *New German Critique* 62 (Spring–Summer 1994): 71–110; copyright Matthew Biro.

Published by the University of Minnesota Press
111 Third Avenue South, Suite 290
Minneapolis, MN 55401-2520
http://www.upress.umn.edu

Library of Congress Cataloging-in-Publication Data

Biro, Matthew, 1961-
    The Dada cyborg : visions of the new human in Weimar Berlin / Matthew Biro.
        p. cm.
    Includes bibliographical references and index.
    ISBN 978-0-8166-3619-8 (hc : alk. paper) — ISBN 978-0-8166-3620-4 (pbk. : alk. paper)
    1. Cyborgs in art. 2. Dadaism—Germany—Berlin. 3. Art, German—Germany—Berlin—20th century. I. Title.
II. Title: Visions of the new human in Weimar Berlin.
    N8214.C93B57 2009
    709.43'15509042—dc22

                                                                                        2009006988

Printed in the United States of America on acid-free paper

The University of Minnesota is an equal-opportunity educator and employer.

18 17 16 15 14 13 12 11 10 09   10 9 8 7 6 5 4 3 2 1

For Bev

Contents

Acknowledgments

This book has benefited from the generous support of numerous individuals and institutions. The original idea goes back to an essay that was published in *New German Critique* in 1994, and I owe a debt to the editors of that publication, Anson Rabinbach and Andreas Huyssen, for their belief in the project and their incisive responses to my initial formulations. A number of scholars, including Dora Apel, Edward Dimendberg, Ann Duroe, Geoff Eley, Barry Flood, Romy Golan, Jennifer Jenkins, Donald Kuspit, Christine Mehring, Alex Potts, and Jonathan Reynolds, read various chapters (or portions thereof) at different stages of their evolution, and I greatly appreciate their valuable comments and suggestions. Other parts of the manuscript were presented at different venues around the United States, and, for their observations and questions about the ideas treated in this book, I thank the organizers and attendees of talks that I delivered at Columbia University, Northwestern University, Swarthmore College, the Center for Advanced Study in the Visual Arts, the Slought Foundation, the College Art Association annual conference, the German Studies Association annual conference, the University of Michigan, and Bryn Mawr College. Finally, I am deeply grateful to four stalwart readers—Edward Dimendberg, Christine Mehring, Libby Otto, and an anonymous reviewer for the University of Minnesota Press—who, in the concluding phase of this project, read the entire manuscript from beginning to end and pushed me to develop my arguments to their fullest possible extent. Their contributions have been particularly invaluable.

Two important fellowships—a Helmut Stern Faculty Fellowship from the Institute for the Humanities at the University of Michigan and an Ailsa Mellon Bruce Senior Fellowship at the Center for Advanced Study in the Visual Arts at the National Gallery of Art in Washington, D.C.—allowed me to accomplish the research and to write a few early essays that eventually became part of the text. More recently, through its generous sabbatical program, the University of Michigan provided me with the remaining time off that I needed to complete the manuscript; in addition, it provided the funds for the images and publication rights for all the illustrations.

I thank the various editors of the scholarly journals listed on the copyright page for their comments and, in some cases, their permission to republish certain sections of these essays. I also thank the various anonymous readers who commented on these texts for those publications. As they will see, I continued to think about their responses to my work for a long time after it was first published.

Finally, this project would not have been completed without the love and support of my wife, Beverly Fishman, and Juliane Biro, my mother. This book is dedicated to Beverly because she, more than anyone else, sustained me both emotionally and intellectually during the time when most of the manuscript was written. Every day I am inspired by her art, her love, and the generosity and grace with which she lives her life.

Introduction

Cyborgs, Hybridity, and Identity

> By the late twentieth century, our time, a mythic time, we are all
> chimeras, theorized and fabricated hybrids of machine and organism;
> in short, we are cyborgs. The cyborg is our ontology; it gives us our
> politics. The cyborg is a condensed image of both imagination and
> material reality, the two joined centers structuring any possibility of
> historical transformation.
>
> —DONNA J. HARAWAY, "A Cyborg Manifesto" (1991)

From the photomontages of the Berlin Dadaists to certain plays by Georg Kaiser to the films of Fritz Lang and the early writings on technology by Ernst Jünger and Martin Heidegger, the cyborg played a central role in many of Weimar culture's most significant productions.[1] Within art and cinema, works by Kurt Schwitters, László Moholy-Nagy, Marianne Brandt, Alice Lex-Nerlinger, Richard Oswald, and Leontine Sagan can also be related to the concept of the cyborg, and many further examples are easily found throughout theater, literature, popular magazines, advertising, and photojournalism.[2] Because the types of cyborgs created by the Berlin Dada artists were so copious and variegated, however, this volume focuses exclusively on Berlin Dada art. It is in part the Berlin Dadaists' intense exploration of the figure of the cyborg that gives the movement its enduring interest and appeal. And by investigating the Dadaists' examination of this figure, we can better understand its continuing importance.

In part the sign of a fearful response to the destruction brought about by World War I, the cyborg was, paradoxically, also a creature on which many Weimar artists and other cultural producers could project their utopian hopes and fantasies. By tracing the origins of the Weimar cyborg in Berlin Dada art, this book expands the concept beyond its initial definition as an organic–technological hybrid to encompass a series of interrelated meanings, including the cyborg as representing hybrid identity in a broad sense and as the locus of new modes of (interior and exterior) awareness created by the impact of technology on human perception.[3] It argues that the different representations of the cyborg in Berlin Dada art can help theorists and historians today understand how new forms of human existence and society were imagined in Germany between the two world wars. In addition, it also demonstrates how these representations can help us grasp how vision, hearing, touch, and embodiment were beginning to be reconceived in the early 1920s.

Although my focus is on the cyborg in Berlin Dada art, this figure did not originate in Weimar's visual sphere. Indeed, a look at science, art, literature, philosophy, and material culture since the Renaissance, both in Germany and in other Western countries, proves this was not the case.[4] In addition, if one includes automata, chimeras, and other forms of fantastic creatures as precursors of the cyborg, then the figure's history reaches back significantly further. However, as I demonstrate, the Berlin Dada movement was central for the cyborg's development, precisely because it represented the figure with such complexity.

The Cyborg: Two Concepts

The term *cyborg* never appeared in Weimar culture and was invented much later. Yet the term is useful, because it suggests how the interwar artistic and visual cultures in Germany anticipated much of the cultural discourse around the cyborg and cybernetics in the United States and Europe since the 1940s, both theoretical and practical as well as popular. The cyborgs that appeared during the Weimar Republic did not merely foreshadow the somewhat one-sided and uncritical first definition of the cyborg, articulated by Manfred E. Clynes and Nathan S. Kline in 1960, as a self-regulating human– or animal–machine hybrid: a sentient body altered biochemically, physiologically, or electronically so that it could live in environments for which it was not adapted.[5] More significant, the Weimar cyborgs also predicted several more-critical concepts attending the "origin" and development of cybernetics through the work of the mathematician Norbert Wiener and other scientists during the 1940s and early 1950s as well as that of the feminist philosopher of science Donna Haraway and her much more heterogeneous definition of the figure in the 1980s and 1990s.

Thus the cyborg has long possessed a dual life as both an image and a concept. Although these two aspects began separately and often developed separately, they can be brought together in mutually illuminating ways. Through two somewhat opposed definitions of the cyborg from the post–World War II context—Wiener's implicit, mechanistic, and liberal humanist definition versus Haraway's explicit, unbounded, and posthumanist one—we can create a conceptual model or framework to retrospectively focus on and then synthesize disparate lines of investigation centering on Berlin Dada. These two definitions do not simply allow us to bring together different, for the most part unlinked, aspects of Weimar culture. They also reveal Berlin Dada's importance for the present day, a significance that in many ways has to do with the Dadaists' focus on the relationship between representation, technology, and human identity.

The first definition emerges from cybernetics, commonly defined as the study of feedback, communication, and control in human beings, machines, and other organized systems. Despite his pioneering role in this new field, Wiener did not coin the term *cyborg*. He did, however, think deeply about the social implications of his scientific practices, and his writings on cybernetics and society elucidate the specific effects on minds, bodies, and societies that he believed cybernetics would help bring about. For this reason, by attending to Wiener's theorization of cybernetics and the view of human beings developed there (a view that began with the assumption that, by understanding human beings and machines in terms of their functions, the investigator could discover multiple ways in which they were commensurate), we can generate an initial definition of the cyborg.

While engaged in research for the U.S. military during World War II, Wiener and his coworkers proposed cybernetics as an interdisciplinary field that would unite scientists around problems of communication, control, and statistical mechanics.[6] Central to cybernetics as both a practical and a theoretical exercise was the development of numerical computers: machines that were binary, that depended on electronics rather than mechanical gears or relays, and that were entirely automatic during the computing operation.[7] Such computers, Wiener argued, could be used to form the central control systems of larger electromechanical assemblages designed to mimic complex human functions.[8] These functions included tracking an enemy aircraft with antiaircraft artillery or reading a text out loud.[9]

By proposing that complex human functions could be supplanted by computational and mechanical systems, Wiener and other scientists discovered a key for unlocking seemingly limitless amounts of instrumental power and complex control—"slave labor," as Wiener called it, that could be made subject to human direction.[10] In contrast to Clynes and Kline, the developers of cybernetics had no illusions that technological augmentation was always beneficial. Technology, they understood, also increased human beings' abilities to kill and enslave one another.[11] Wiener argued that cybernetics was bringing about a "second industrial revolution" through automation, one that held both enormous potential and terrifying danger. Although it would unleash undreamed-of productive power, it could also increase unemployment and reduce the human labor force to the condition of slavery.[12] Furthermore, the mastery over nature promoted by cybernetics could easily turn into enslavement by it, for the more human beings modified their world, the more they had to modify themselves to exist within it.[13]

Through machines that automated human functions, human beings would become more interconnected—both within their societies and across them. Thus, as a result of the development of cybernetics in the context of World War II, a human being augmented by mechanical prosthetics and computers was a figure that bound in a new and much more closely-knit relationship the enemy "other," conceived by Wiener as the pilot in the Axis warplane, and the military "self" or "ally," conceived as the Allied antiaircraft gunner.[14] Such augmentation did not simply make humans both more powerful and more vulnerable. Despite—or perhaps because of—the division of world societies into groups of competing nations, the transformation of human beings through cybernetics also made them much more interrelated and thus less able to say where the "self" ended and "others" began.

This newfound interrelation between human beings fostered by cybernetic theory also led to new problems. Suspicious of the military direction of scientific research in the context of World War II as well the corporate and cold war concerns that directed scientific research and engineering in the United States in the early 1950s, Wiener warned that, despite the ways it had enriched human beings, technological development also possessed a semi-autonomous power and logic of its own—one that exceeded the abilities of human beings to fully control and regulate it.

> The hurrying up of the pace of science, owing to our active simultaneous search for all means of attacking our enemies and of protecting ourselves, leads to ever-increasing demands for new research. . . . This enemy may be Russia at the present moment, but it is even more the reflection of ourselves in a mirage. To defend ourselves against this phantom, we must look to new scientific measures, each more terrible than the last. There is no end to this vast apocalyptic spiral.[15]

In the cold war situation of the 1950s, the flow of scientific and military information tended to overcome all national boundaries or lines of demarcation, thereby promoting an ever-intensifying arms race.[16] It thus helped produce a situation in which whatever dangers science and technology could be imagined to create for a subject were projected onto a feared enemy, whose explicit goals then became the subject's complete annihilation.

For Wiener, a human being viewed through the lens of cybernetics was a figure that interrelated friend and enemy, self and other, because it was a form that revealed human beings to be organisms that became what they were through learning and communication. Human beings, according to Wiener, learned more and displayed more adaptive behavior than any other animal, a condition that stood as the source of their obvious strengths and position of dominance on the planet.[17] Human identity, understood cybernetically, did not consist of the matter out of which people were made—the "stuff that abides," as he put it—but the "patterns that perpetuate themselves," patterns that took the form of information that controlled functioning, memory, and development.[18] Information, the same medium that made human beings like computers and machines, also made them more like one another. To view human beings as cybernetic systems was thus to recognize their collaborative natures: they were individuals created through information exchange and implementation.

Wiener's implicit concept of the cyborg—the human being as viewed from the perspective of cybernetic theory—constitutes the first important definition of the figure to be used in the following analyses. Conceived as essentially produced through information and learning, as constantly modifying or transforming, as simultaneously more powerful and more vulnerable, as fundamentally interconnected with others and the environment, and as regularly dividing the world into friends and enemies, Wiener's cyborg constituted a radically new vision of what it meant to be human. At the same time, as N. Katherine Hayles has argued, despite its far-reaching implications for human identity, Wiener did not intend for cybernetics to dismantle the traditional concept of liberal humanist subject, understood as a free and rational subjectivity, self-aware or present to itself, and free from signs of bodily difference (and hence universal).[19] Such a subject, it was commonly believed, was autonomous; its agency, desire, and will all stemmed from itself alone, and, furthermore, it owned itself and hence could sell its labor. For this reason, there is a great tension in Wiener's writings on cybernetics and society between a vision of a new (less autonomous, less fully conscious, and less clearly bounded) form of human existence and the traditional bourgeois understanding of that existence, a conceptualization of human identity that helped foster the growth of science, technology, and capitalism since the sixteenth century. Although the consequences of Wiener's revisioning of human identity from the standpoint of cybernetics would ultimately be sweeping, Wiener refused in his writings on cybernetics and society to draw the most radical conclusions.

Some of these conclusions were drawn in the annual conferences on cybernetics sponsored by the Josiah Macy, Jr. Foundation between 1946 and 1953.[20] Others emerged after the initial Wiener-inspired phase of cybernetics drew to a close. Rather than detail the history of cybernetics, however, it seems more useful to isolate a later (explicit) definition of the cyborg, which takes the initial (and implicit) concept of human identity viewed through the lens of cybernetics to extremes that Wiener and other researchers would have rejected. Responding to Wiener's understanding of human identity, to Clynes and Kline's concept of the cyborg as an organism altered to live in space, and to the great progress of cybernetics since World War II, Haraway developed a new, more socially critical concept of the cyborg in the mid-1980s. According to Haraway, the cyborg posed fundamental political questions. A creature of both "imagination and material reality," it reflected the postwar world and offered hints as to how human beings might adapt themselves to better live in it.[21] Helping reveal what it meant to be human after Wiener's second industrial revolution, the concept of the cyborg thus allowed people to understand their complex relationships to the fundamental conflicts that characterized contemporary global societies. In addition, the cyborg also functioned as a figure for imagining new possibilities of life and interaction. Particularly as developed by science fiction writers and filmmakers, it became an important means for cultural practitioners to explore new forms of social existence, family life, sexuality, economic relations, and selfhood.[22]

For Haraway, the cyborg defined a fundamentally hybrid form of human identity that undermined traditional distinctions between gender, race, and class.[23] Furthermore, the cyborg also broke down three crucial distinctions that had previously defined the difference between humans and nonhumans. First, the cyborg broke down the boundary between humans and animals.[24] It helped, in other words, reveal that "language, tool use, social behavior, [and] mental events" were characteristics that human beings shared with certain animals.[25] Although the figure of the cyborg suggested that human beings possessed highly advanced cognitive abilities, it also implied that we were more animal-like than previously believed, more instinctual as well as more open to control and cultivation. Second, the figure of the cyborg broke down the boundary between organisms—both human or animal—and machines. Machines, too, were more like humans and animals than was previously thought. As cybernetics helped demonstrate, machines had languages, they could communicate with one another, and they could learn. And because of this newly perceived complexity and animation of machines, human beings seemed more automatic, mechanical, and "inert" than ever before. Third, the cyborg broke down the boundary between the physical and the nonphysical. The cyborg, in other words, was a creature of microelectronic devices, a function of "signals, electromagnetic waves, a section of a spectrum."[26] Like Wiener, Haraway thus emphasized that the cyborg was a creature that fundamentally functioned through receiving, transmitting, and controlling information, a "substance" that, because of the multiple media into which it could be translated, often appeared to be insubstantial or noncorporeal. And these noncorporeal aspects of the cyborg often made it seem uncanny, magical, mystical, or even monstrous.

Because the cyborg was a creature of information, it was subject to constant dispersal, transformation, and exchange. In the cybernetic societies of the 1980s and 1990s, by which Haraway meant the advanced Western world as well as the non-Western societies with which the West interacted, the

> "integrity" or "sincerity" of the Western self gives way to decision procedures and expert systems. . . . No objects, spaces, or bodies are sacred in themselves; any component can be interfaced with any other if the proper standard, the proper code, can be constructed for processing signals in a common language.[27]

The cyborg, in other words, was fundamentally defined by its ability to interface with diverse—and often contradictory—systems that had the power to radically transform it.

Corresponding to the cyborg's ability to interface in a multitude of different ways, the physical and social environments in which the cyborg operated were becoming increasingly porous—that is, designed to interrelate the cyborg with what was outside its specific physical limits.[28] The increase in environmental linkages that surrounded and enabled the cyborg was the result of the radical growth of certain forms of technology. During the twentieth century, the outside or public world had entered into the private home through the channels of the burgeoning mass media (e.g., newspapers, radio, and television) at an unprecedented rate; in addition, individual control was extended through such increasingly ubiquitous devices as typewriters, telegraphs, shortwave radios, telephones, and various forms of public and private transportation. Then, beginning in the 1980s, with personal computers and the development of digital information networks, the connections between human beings and their outside worlds were exponentially increased. These new two-way devices of mass communication and control allowed people to exercise more and more influence on their environments while bringing the world and other people into the home, thereby permitting greater and greater incursions into private life. At the same time, human beings began to be identified and quantified in terms of an increasingly variegated array of systems that defined their rights, obligations, and functions, as well as the very materials out of which they were composed, a process that simultaneously enabled and controlled them. Our "natures" as workers, citizens, consumers, family members, and medical and legal subjects, in other words, afforded us more and more power in the world (e.g., through different types of law and through specific products and information technologies designed for particular classes of consumers). At the same time, however, our increasingly differentiated natures also created a situation in which the integrity of both our bodies and our minds was destroyed. More and more, our various personal and social "roles" could intrude on one another and come into conflict, and our bodies could become subject to incompatible demands (as when, in the case of a professional athlete, the criteria for peak performance and basic human health diverged).

The cyborg's increasing ability to interface with its environment, which helped bring about the twentieth-century subject's fragmentation, also helped produce a new form of labor market, a "homework economy," in which "a strongly bimodal social structure" existed.[29] On one side were the cyborg laborers, "the masses of women and men of all ethnic groups, but especially people of color, confined to a homework economy, illiteracy of several varieties, and general redundancy and impotence, controlled by high-tech repressive apparatuses ranging from entertainment to surveillance and disappearance."[30] On the other were the highly specialized cybernetic workforces, the technological–industrial elite, located primarily in the United States and Europe. Supported by the world's entertainment industries as well as various modern governments and businesses, the homework economy "feminized" labor (in that it often put men out of work and made all its subjects increasingly vulnerable) and created ever-increasing disparities of wealth and power.

Like Wiener, Haraway emphasized the fundamentally ambivalent nature of the cyborg and the global situation that it represented. Haraway's theorization, however, went far beyond that of Wiener in her emphasis on the cyborg as the "other"—the cyborg, in other words, as a woman, as a person of color, as a homosexual, as an outsider, or as a monster. For Haraway, the manifestations of the cyborg as various forms of other stood in sharp contrast to traditional Western conceptions of bourgeois, petit bourgeois, or even worker subjects in nineteenth- and early-twentieth-century societies. Because the cyborg as other revealed the effects of patriarchal and nationalist domination as well as alternative modes of existence formed in resistance to cybernetic exploitation and coercion, it disclosed the cyborg's libratory political potential. Inspired in part by feminist science fiction, Haraway's cybernetic outsiders made "very problematic the statuses of man or woman, human, artifact, member of a race, individual entity, or body."[31] And such cyborgs became, for Haraway, important symbols of noncoercive hybrid identity, "a kind of disassembled and reassembled, postmodern collective and personal self."[32] They were figures, in other words, that suggested the collaborative nature of human identity—the fact that human self-understanding always existed in a dialectic with multiple conceptions of collective or group belonging. In addition, they suggested the "limits of identification," namely, that because of such forces as the unconscious and ideology, human self-understanding was always partial, and that to best survive as a "self" in today's societies, it was necessary to recognize one's multiple affiliations.[33] Such cyborgs revealed an understanding of both self and society that tolerated—even welcomed—difference, an understanding that did not insist on a common origin or nature, let alone a master narrative or theory.[34]

Haraway's concept of the cyborg has been extremely influential—particularly in cultural studies. Even today, as the first decade of the twenty-first century draws to a close, Haraway's conceptualization is often employed without criticism or revision; its close associations with "postmodernism" and the "posthuman," concepts ripe for critique, have obscured its possible contradictions. Perhaps the greatest problem with Haraway's nonetheless extremely insightful formulation is its level of generality or inclusiveness. Because of the way Haraway defines the cyborg, almost every creature in the contemporary world, human or animal, can be seen to embody the concept. In addition, often because of its conjunction with the idea of postmodernism, the newness of Haraway's cyborg is perhaps overemphasized by some cultural theorists. (Haraway is far more circumspect in this regard.) As Allison Muri has shown, many of the central concepts associated with the cyborg go back at least as far as the seventeenth century.[35] For this reason, it is difficult to argue that the cyborg represents a radically new form of human existence.

I take issue with the first problematic implication of Haraway's concept of the cyborg, its generality, somewhat later in this text. To overcome the second troubling implication, however, it is useful to recall another aspect of Haraway's cyborg, namely, her contention that the figure is "a condensed image of both imagination and material reality."[36] Like the various forms of (liberal humanist, bourgeois, petit bourgeois, and worker) subject mentioned above, the cyborg is a conceptual abstraction. First formulated to isolate and define what was perceived to be an important phenomenon in the material world (i.e., technologically augmented human beings and animals), it was—and remains—as much an imaginative construction as a literal image or copy of something that exists in reality. For this reason, the cyborg continues to be a concept that can be either accepted or rejected or, as is often the case with speculative concepts, criticized, debated, and accepted only with subsequent modifications. The "reality" of the concept of the cyborg is thus a function of the number of people who subscribe to it at any given time, a group that has increased during the twentieth century (which is not to say that the cyborg does not exist in reality). Just because more and more people acknowledge that cyborgs exist in the contemporary moment, however, does not entail that the figure is radically new. Earlier formulations, we could just as easily say, existed with less general acceptance even before the Industrial Revolution—a position supported by the historical record. Understood in this way, what has changed is the degree to which the cyborg is experienced as an intersubjective phenomenon. More people today accept the cyborg as a conceptual model that reveals something fundamental about both themselves and their rapidly transforming worlds than was the case in the seventeenth and eighteenth centuries. The cyborg, we are coming to realize, has been with us for a long time, but it is only today that it appears in such great numbers and with the intersubjective agreement of so many different observers.

As suggested by Wiener's and Haraway's divergent concepts of the cyborg, the cyborg today possesses a long and at times contradictory conceptual history. By isolating the cyborg's conceptual poles as defined by these two thinkers, however, the figure's intellectual range and diversity can be demarcated without a longer presentation of the concept's history. Although both Wiener and Haraway defined the cyborg as a contradictory organism, a hybrid figure that connects possibility with trauma, self with other, and friend with enemy, Wiener presented a much more liberal, mechanical, and "bounded" view than Haraway, whose view of the cyborg was much more radical, open-ended, and "networked." As I demonstrate, the Berlin Dada artists made representations that can be seen as coming closer to either view, although the chronology of the Dada cyborgs does not indicate any kind of a conceptual development from one to the other. And by using these two models as schema to examine and organize visual art in the late 1910s and 1920s, I show that the many concepts, visual precedents, and social forces that helped produce the flowering of cyborgian imagery in Berlin Dada art together formed a significant cultural trajectory focused on reimagining human identity in Germany during the first few decades of the twentieth century.

A third model is presented in subsequent chapters, one that can be easily associated with—and enrich—either one of the two initial models (as forms of hybrid identity). This third model concentrates on the cyborg as a type of perceptual locus or framework. Corresponding to the development of the concept since the mid-1990s, this model has been used to delineate and explain how our senses have been transformed through different forms of technological prostheses and through the mass media. It is a model that, for example, seeks to explain how telepresence—literally, the sense of remote presence created by means of such tele-operation systems as robot arms that allow people to manipulate objects and materials at a distance—and telerobotics, the higher-level control of proxy robotic systems to explore and manipulate environments without the wide spectrum of sensory feedback characteristic of telepresence, change our inward sense of our body's boundaries and capabilities.[37] It is also a model that attempts to define how film and radio have extended our abilities to see and hear while transforming our modes of attention and developing within us increased capacities to both attend to and synthesize multiple avenues of sensation. Since the transformation of perception in the context of modern urban experience was discussed extensively in the first three decades of the twentieth century, and certain Dadaist representations of cyborgs seem to refer to these discourses, this model of the cyborg is developed at greater length in the context of analyzing specific works.

Dada Cyborgs: Hybridity, Primitivism, and Identity

The cyborg is not a subject that is usually explored in the context of Berlin Dada art. Today, the movement is recognized primarily for its montage-based aesthetic strategies such as assemblage and photomontage, techniques that located the creation of art in juxtaposing preexisting, often mass-produced materials. Because the Berlin Dadaists are generally viewed as members of the historical avant-garde, their strategies have been primarily acknowledged for the transformative effect they had on the position and function of modern art in Europe in the early twentieth century. It is only more recently that the subjects that the Berlin Dadaists treated—and the social, political, and psychological issues that were represented—have come under scrutiny.[38]

By suggesting that a particular subject, the cyborg as a figure of modern hybrid identity, was central to the practices of the Berlin Dada artists, I do not wish to de-emphasize the tremendous critical effects of Berlin Dada art, the radical shocks that it first created through its (momentary) negations of meaning and its seeming destruction of all hitherto-existing Western conceptions of art during the early interwar period. Understood as "anti-art," Dada was recognized as "ending" modern art by revealing art's institutions and exposing the groundlessness of artists' authority. Still, by suggesting that a particular subject was also important to the Berlin Dada artists, I wish to identify a characteristic of the historical avant-garde that has yet to be given the attention it deserves: namely, its radical identity politics. Since the 1960s, the montage- and media-based aesthetics of the historical avant-garde have once again become popular in contemporary art. As I argue here, the historical avant-garde also anticipates the contemporary moment through its radical practices of imagining new forms of nonbourgeois, hybrid identity.

The terms *hybrid* and *hybridity* have been rightly criticized by postcolonial theory for their suitability to racist discourse as well for their assumption of originally "pure" or unmixed states, generally of a racial, sexual, or national nature.[39] By here arguing for linkages between the idea of hybrid identity and a cybernetic conception of the subject, however, I wish to suggest that it is possible to exclude these problematic assumptions. The cybernetic conception of (hybrid) human identity defines it as a process in which different forms of self-identification or allegiance encounter and transform one another without any one of them becoming dominant. In its more radical forms, which appear in some but not all of the Berlin Dadaists' productions, hybrid identity not only defines "race," "gender," "class," and "nation" to be nonbinding, nonessential properties but also acknowledges the broader interconnections that human beings share with animals, machines, and their environments. Although this conceptualization suggests that many—if not most—forms of human identity are ultimately hybrid (and thus that hybridity is not solely a characteristic of "minority" or "postcolonial" identities), it does not imply that a person's relationship to the various forms of "otherness" that help produce that person is the same for all human beings. As such, it acknowledges that identity is not freely chosen and that ideology and unequal positions of power play a significant role in developing specific subjectivities. This definition of hybridity accords with recent usages of the term, and I employ it here to link the Weimar cyborg with contemporary debates about human identity.[40]

Another reason why the term *hybrid identity* is used here has to do with its relationship to primitivism. As it is generally employed within the history of modern art, "primitivism" refers to the appropriation of non-Western artistic forms, styles, and subjects by European artists beginning in the last two decades of the nineteenth century.[41] Although its roots go back to romanticism, primitivism in modern visual art is often thought to begin with such artists as Paul Gauguin and Vincent van Gogh.[42] Influenced by the critique of modernity, Western rationality, and Enlightenment thought that gathered momentum during the nineteenth century, these artists—as well as Pablo Picasso and the fauvist and German expressionist artists who were in various ways influenced by the first generation of primitivists—turned to sources outside the immediate Western tradition to break with the late-nineteenth-century academic and modern traditions of visual representation. Intending to make a more direct, personal, and expressive form of art, they appropriated forms and subjects from various sources, including—depending on the artist under consideration—contemporary Asian, African, and Oceanic cultures as well as Gothic and ancient art (e.g., that of Egypt or Iberia) and the art of children. In terms of form, late-nineteenth- and early-twentieth-century primitivism distorted "realistic" color, scale, perspective, and three-dimensional space, which focused the viewer's attention on the artwork's formal and material qualities; it developed an often gestural or rhythmic handling of line and form that was understood to suggest emotional or "spiritual" states; and it adopted earlier forms of artistic and folk art media (e.g., the woodcut and "reverse-painted glass"). In terms of subjects, it led to the development of a "primitive" iconography that included rural religious ceremonies, nude figures in Arcadian landscapes, tribal artifacts, and non-European figures. In addition, traditional Western subjects such as women and children were deployed in new ways to convey primitivist philosophies.

The relationship of the Dada artists to primitivism was complex. The Berlin Dadaists were most directly influenced by the German expressionist art made by the "Bridge" *(Die Brücke)* and the "Blue Rider" *(Der Blaue Reiter)* groups. Although in many ways the expressionists' "influence" on the Dadaists consisted of the Dadaists rejecting everything that the expressionists stood for, this was nonetheless a form of influence, since a number of the Dadaists' stylistic, iconographic, and material choices were direct inversions of expressionist precedents. That the Berlin Dadaists chose to attack expressionism is not surprising. Expressionism was the most important modern art movement in Germany in the decade that immediately preceded the emergence of the Dada groups, and it appeared to many to be the dominant style in the immediate postwar context. In part influenced by the broad and contradictory tradition of "cultural criticism" in Germany, which criticized modern urban life and often valorized rural agricultural existence, the various members of the different expressionist groups sought in divergent ways to incorporate aspects of African, Indian, and Oceanic art—as well as

German folk art and the German Gothic tradition—into their works to create more direct and spiritual forms of expression.[43] In addition, as Jill Lloyd has argued in relationship to the *Brücke* group, these artists were also strongly affected by the influx of African art into Germany as a result of colonial activity as well as the representation of the primitive in various forms of popular culture, including books and magazines, cabaret performances, and other forms of urban entertainment.[44] Embodying both conservative and revolutionary aspects, the primitivism of the German expressionists criticized the dominant values of Western bourgeois society while potentially also promoting false and reified ideas about non-Western cultures.[45]

Although the Berlin Dadaists claimed to reject the German expressionists' art and philosophies in their entirety, in actual practice the Dadaists rejected only certain aspects of expressionism while continuing others. This ambivalent attitude is visible in the Dadaist attitude to primitivism. The Dadaists heaped scorn on the expressionists' desire to achieve forms of subjective or "spiritual" expression through their art, and the Dadaist recourse to nontraditional forms of art making—for example, photomontage and assemblage strategies—can be seen as rejecting the expressionists' emphasis on traditional artistic materials (e.g., painting, sculpture, and printmaking) and their valorization of the artist's "hand" or gesture as a key way to express their subjective attitudes toward what they depicted. In addition, the Dadaists' focus on mechanical imagery can also be seen as a reaction to the expressionists' stress on organic forms. At the same time, however, the Dadaists seemed to continue aspects of the expressionists' primitivism in that certain types of Dada production suggest a belief that non-Western forms could help them achieve a more direct relationship to the shapes and practices of modern life. This can be seen, for example, in Richard Huelsenbeck's incorporation of African-inspired sounds and rhythms into his poetry in the late 1910s as well as Raoul Hausmann's abstract sound poetry, which attempted to break down communicative language to achieve a more direct form of expression. In addition, it can also be seen in Hannah Höch's turn to a tribal iconography to explore hybrid forms of identity.

As Nikos Papastergiadis has argued, hybridity is intimately related to primitivism.[46] Because of its roots in nineteenth-century scientific and colonialist discourse, hybridity was initially defined in terms of a mixing between Europeans and non-European "others," an understanding later absorbed into the concept of primitivism in art. Because of their conflicted relationship to artistic primitivism, it is thus not surprising that the Dadaists would have wrestled with ideas of hybridity and, moreover, that they would have reevaluated hybridity as something positive in distinction to how it was originally assessed—namely, as weak, debased, or sick—in the discourse of nineteenth-century "scientific" racism. Like the cyborg, hybridity is a subterranean concept in Berlin Dada art. Although the Dadaists did not employ the term in their statements and writings, it seems to have informed a significant amount of their production—something that appears in their art as well as in the intellectual and cultural milieu in which it was formed.

Like hybridity, "identity" is also a problematic term. One assumption of this book is that the explosion of visual representations of cyborgs during the Weimar Republic was prepared by the vast reworking of the concept of the subject in the nineteenth and twentieth centuries. In particular, the reconceptualizations of what it meant to be human carried out by Karl Marx, Friedrich Nietzsche, and Sigmund Freud helped prepare a horizon of ideas in Germany that undermined any idea of a stable human essence. Thus, when the Berlin Dadaists presented the cyborg as representing a new form of hybrid modern "identity," they were influenced by a wide variety of conceptual systems already in place in their culture that modeled subjectivity as cyborgian, that is, as systematic, constructed, and mutable. Although the theoretical systems that various cultural practitioners cited in their works were different (as were their degrees of access to the same cultural systems), they were all fundamentally engaged with reimagining what it meant to be human in the modern world.[47]

As I use it here, the term *identity* indicates the new conceptions of human subjectivity that emerged in the twentieth century. Central to the concept of identity are the ideas that human beings are—to a greater or lesser degree—socially constructed and that people are all syntheses of individual and collective elements. One way to understand this concept of identity—as well as the relationship between identity and visual images—is to briefly approach it via aspects of Freud's conceptual system, an evolving network of ideas with which a number of Berlin Dada artists were familiar at different stages of its development. As Freud defined it in 1921, "identification" *(Identifizierung)* was, in the first place, the earliest expression of an infant's emotional tie to another person.[48] In addition, identification was also the psychological process whereby the developing ego fashioned itself after an idealized model, an open-ended activity wherein the subject adjusted to reality and learned to make sexual object choices and other forms of life-determining decisions.[49] An "ego ideal" *(Ich-Ideal)*—a concept that Freud would later subsume under the "superego" *(das Über-Ich)*—was the source of an ego's potentialities for self-observation, moral conscience, dream censorship, and repression. It arose from the child's original narcissism and feelings of self-sufficiency, and it responded to all the demands that the environment made on the ego.[50] And by creating an ego ideal on the basis of a series of identifications, the child ultimately became a developed person.

According to Freud, "identification" was thus a psychological process whereby the developing subject incorporated an aspect of another person and thereby transformed itself according to the model that this idealized other provided. The subject's personality—who and what a person was as an individual—was the result of the series of identifications that it made as it grew up. And because the subject constituted its sense of self by assimilating different aspects of others with which it interacted in its environment, its images of both itself and others were central to this process. Although the Berlin Dada artists were clearly not aware of Freud's later concept of identification when they first developed their cyborgian imagery, their focus on the body in their art and their interest in representing nontraditional forms of human existence suggest that their cyborgs were developed with something similar in mind. Dadaist representations of cyborgs, in other words, were presented as potential ego ideals—images of alternative forms of existence that could provoke their audiences to rethink who and what they were. Although they were for the most part presented to adults whose personalities were fully formed, the Dada cyborgs were designed to inspire their spectators to question both selfhood and society. In a review of the "First International Dada Fair" from July 1920, Adolf Behne, an art and architecture critic largely sympathetic to the Berlin Dada movement, seemed to acknowledge this Dadaist desire to encourage new forms of self-understanding in the context of an uncertain and inexplicable present. "'Know yourself'—this is the wisdom of Dada," he wrote. "Give up the past. Give up the future. Know your*self*. . . today!"[51] The Dada cyborg helped the Dadaists and their audiences reflect on the changes in how they thought, acted, perceived, and existed as a result of technology's impact on their bodies and minds, and it also allowed them to imagine how to cope with and integrate these alterations so as to better exist in the modern world.

This book examines the figure of the cyborg in Berlin Dada art through specific artworks. Chapter 1 introduces the Berlin Dada movement as a whole by examining its historical origins as well as the journals, performances, happenings, and media hoaxes central to its definition and dissemination. By exploring the less well-known media through which the Berlin Dadaists made art, we can better understand their fundamental engagement with questions of the body, the mass media, and everyday life—issues that subtended their development of the image of the cyborg in their photomontages and assemblages. Through its focus on their performances and literary activities, this chapter balances the account of Berlin Dada in the subsequent chapters, which concentrate primarily on visual art. In this way, it avoids an important problem that has marred some recent studies of Berlin Dada, namely, an overemphasis on the Dadaists' visual productions at the expense of their other art-making practices.

Chapter 2 presents the Dadaist representation of the cyborg through an extended analysis of a single photomontage, Höch's *Schnitt mit dem Küchenmesser Dada durch die letzte Weimarer Bierbauchkulturepoche Deutschlands* [Cut with the Kitchen Knife Dada through the Last Weimar Beer-Belly Cultural Epoch of Germany] (1919–20). In this photomontage, one of the most iconic works of the Berlin Dada movement, Höch presented her vision of the radical forces transforming postwar Germany: developments in art, politics, and the mass media that directly inspired the Dadaists' reevaluation of traditional forms of human identity. The complex signifying strategies characteristic of Dadaist photomontage, *Cut with the Kitchen Knife* reveals, were developed as a corrective to the more straightforward and propagandistic signifying strategies of the German culture industry, in particular, those employed in its illustrated books and magazines. After discussing *Cut with the Kitchen Knife* as a form of political discourse and the rise of the mass media during the Weimar Republic, this chapter concludes by analyzing the cyborg as a figure that embodies new modes of sensing and comprehending created by technology's impact on the various organs of human perception.

Chapter 3 examines Hausmann's representation of the cyborg in photomontages and caricatures. Through analyzing the "anti-Freudian" psychoanalytic theories that informed his—and perhaps also Höch's—development of the image of the cyborg as a representation of hybrid identity, I argue that Hausmann's poetry and performance practices of 1918 and 1919 prepared the ground for the cybernetic imagery that became prevalent in his caricatures, photomontages, and assemblages of 1920. Hausmann used the cyborg to create provocative portraits representing Dadaist artists with whom he felt connected as well as hated enemies whom he sought to discredit. In addition, in several self-portraits, he also presented himself as a cyborg, suggesting that he saw the figure as a means of artistic self-fashioning. Evoking Weiner's conceptualization of the cyborg, Hausmann's representations of mechanically augmented men examined the transformation of vision and hearing in the context of modern life, and they presented the cyborg as a new form of spectator who bridged the traditional separation between creators and consumers of images.

Chapter 4 investigates representations of cyborgs in the works of George Grosz, John Heartfield, Otto Dix, and Rudolf Schlichter against a backdrop of German material culture produced during World War I. If Hausmann and Höch most clearly represent the Dadaist use of the cyborg as a positive form of self-portraiture and artistic self-fashioning, then the artists treated in this chapter demonstrate how the cyborg was also used to criticize modes of identity that the Dada artists rejected. The authoritarian subject was a form of German identity that supported the war and the old authoritarian social and political order, a form of identity typically represented through photographs and photomontages of armored male soldiers. By showing how the Dada artists attempted to expose this mode of subjectivity through the figure of the cyborg, I demonstrate that they were not simply engaged in imagining new forms of identity but also involved in undermining those forms that they believed to be destructive. A central aspect of this critical or deconstructive project in Dada art was the evocation of the new forms of sensation and bodily experience produced through the trauma of mechanized conflict. To deconstruct the authoritarian ideology, these Dadaists, in other words, used their representations to attack their spectators' bodies.

Finally, chapter 5 investigates the representations of cyborgs in Höch's photomontages. Höch created the most radical representations of cyborgs to be found in Berlin Dada art. Much more than any of the other Dadaists, Höch explored how the cyborg challenged traditional notions of gender and race. As a result, her work comes closest to contemporary definitions of the cyborg such as Haraway's. By situating Höch's images of hybrid figures—cyborgs in the broad sense of the term—against a backdrop of German debates over sexuality, race, and female empowerment, the cyborg, I demonstrate, was strategically employed to promote both social and political change. By acknowledging the developing technological network in which human beings were enmeshed, Höch's photomontages, in other words, potentially promoted awareness about the new dangers and possibilities affecting human development in the interwar period.

Method

In terms of method, this book was inspired by the tradition of cultural theory and criticism that was central to twentieth-century German critical theory. The founders of this cultural tradition within critical theory were such thinkers as Georg Simmel, Siegfried Kracauer, and Walter Benjamin—theoreticians who, in various ways, attempted to illuminate the experience of modernity in urban life. All three shared an early-twentieth-century desire to define what was most characteristic of their contemporary moment.[52] Apprehensive about the triumph of Western rationality, science, social planning, and technology, they analyzed culture in terms of what it suggested about human development socially and psychologically. Through various critical studies, these thinkers argued that specifically modern, social–psychological traits and problems could be discerned in both high and popular culture: traits and problems that helped explain the social and political turmoil of their time.[53] At the heart of the critical–theoretical practice of these thinkers—particularly Benjamin and Kracauer—was an allegorical mode of reading the world: a method of analyzing fragments of modern life so that they disclosed larger oscillating networks or constellations of meaning. By rejecting all concepts of totality, that is, ideas of hierarchically organized and integrated meaningful wholes, in favor of the notion of "constellation"—"a juxtaposed rather than integrated cluster of changing elements that resist reduction to a common denominator, essential core, or generative first principle," as Martin Jay put it—these cultural theorists acknowledged the play of difference and signification that characterized all cultural analysis.[54] Thereby they recognized the fundamentally dialectical nature of all meaning and representation: the fact that all significant formulations, no matter how tightly integrated and coherent, contained inconsistencies and hence the seeds of their own overcoming and reformulation. For this reason, they maximized contradiction by analyzing both art and mass culture in a negatively dialectical fashion: namely, as simultaneous sources of social–psychological conflict and potential revolutionary newness.

Later figures in this tradition of cultural criticism were Theodor W. Adorno, Max Horkheimer, and Peter Bürger, thinkers who examined either art or mass culture in the context of a sociological and political analysis of modern consumer capitalism. In separate works, Adorno and Bürger analyzed the forms, meanings, and effects of avant-garde art, which they defined as the various types of Western visual art, literature, and music that broke radically from the traditions of the West in the first few decades of the twentieth century.[55] The "nonorganic" nature of the avant-garde work of art (its character as a set of juxtaposed—or montaged—fragments not unified or made whole by an overarching structure or meaning), they argued, potentially helped its audiences imagine new, less hegemonic modes of private and public existence. Together, Horkheimer and Adorno analyzed both art and mass culture in terms of a "dialectic of enlightenment."[56] Although art could potentially criticize the status quo, mass culture—"the culture industry," as they called it—inevitably perpetuated ideologies favorable to industrial capitalism.

Although Benjamin's thinking is the primary point of reference for this study, I also draw on the other theorists mentioned above. Simmel had a major impact on Benjamin and Kracauer, and they emulated Simmel's strategy of discovering fundamental forces and characteristics of modernity in the surface phenomena of everyday modern life.[57] Benjamin, Kracauer, Horkheimer, and Adorno, moreover, all lived through the Weimar Republic and were directly affected by its art and visual culture. Their various writings on modern culture and society are, in many ways, attempts to understand the contradictions of modern life that they experienced during the interwar period in Germany. Finally, Bürger's concept of the historical avant-garde is useful because it attempts to situate Dadaism historically.

The debt that this book owes to the cultural tradition in German critical theory is manifold. The following analyses share this tradition's overall practice of focusing on particular examples, "individual moments," and finding in them "the crystal of the total event," as Benjamin put it.[58] In addition, it shares the critical theorists' affinity for montage as their primary structuring principle: to fit one's analyses of art and culture into dialectical constellations, frameworks that extend, amplify, and begin to transform the conjoined works' various associations. Furthermore, this book has adopted one of the critical theorists' overall projects, that is, thinking through the evolving relationship between (fine) art and mass culture in the twentieth century. Similarly, its analyses—like theirs—range from the critique of ideology as embodied in particular works to demonstrating certain forms of historical truth content in others. Ultimately, however, this study draws most from Benjamin's work because, by focusing on the image of the cyborg, it aims to "brush history against the grain" in the sense of the phrase that he gave it: namely, to focus on the past through present concerns, thereby revealing forgotten aspects of cultural history that can potentially get people to rethink current social and cultural development.[59] At the same time, however, this book diverges from Benjamin's thinking and that of the others in several important ways. Unlike the tradition of critical theory, it posits no outside to capitalism, no ideal of a socialist utopia as either a possibility or a hope. In addition, it rejects any simple equation of art with truth and mass culture with ideology; instead, it seeks to understand different cultural productions nonhierarchically as works designed for specific audiences and functions.

From the perspective of art historical method, the following analyses also employ traditional art historical practices, such as formal analysis, biography, social history, and the analysis of a work's contemporaneous critical reception. Indeed, there is nothing in the critical projects of Benjamin and the other German cultural critics that would invalidate these approaches so long as they are separated from simple models of authorship and progressive historical development and exempted from the requirement—characteristic of certain forms of art historical discourse—to minimize contradiction. In addition, although the focus on the cyborg may at first glance seem like iconographic analysis, this concentration actually entails inverting traditional iconographic method. It is generally the case in art history that a textual source is sought for an image. The art historian establishes the work's "true" meaning through a written tradition that pre-dates it; without the preexisting text, the interpreter's reading is suspect. By choosing images that predate the texts, this book offers a counterexample to this problematic assumption inherent in traditional forms of iconographic method. The intention is not to suggest that iconography is invalid or problematic today—a charge frequently heard in modern and contemporary art history and criticism—but to open up the method of iconography by eliminating its most problematic assumption.[60] Furthermore, by reversing iconographic analysis, this book does not seek to create a causal argument and suggest that Weimar culture inspired the concept of the cyborg. Such an argu-ment would be patently false. Instead, this book argues that a common set of concerns existed both in art and in other fields of culture since the 1920s. These concerns grew up in multiple domains, and they developed as a result of both disciplinary and inter-disciplinary pressures. By resisting all "one-way" accounts of cultural influence, the following analyses insist that cultural historians and critics must remain open to mul-tiple avenues of transmission—a position that strict forms of iconographic analysis might seem to deny.

Finally, although this book insists on bringing the question of subject matter once again to the center of the study of twentieth-century art—an insistence that certain forms of modernist art history and criticism would find objectionable—it should be noted that subject matter is not treated here at the expense of form. Although the cen-trality of representation to twentieth-century art has to some extent been obscured by the historical dominance of formalist models of modernism in art history and criticism after World War II, it is impossible to correct this imbalance by simply inverting it. Instead, what was most significant about the representational trajectories characteris-tic of twentieth-century art were how form and content were brought into relation-ship with one another and how new modes of complex signification developed as a result. In advanced forms of representational practice, form and content merge to the extent that they are inseparable, and thus to understand representation in the twenti-eth century, neither aspect can be ignored.

Modernism, Postmodernism, and the Historical Avant-Garde

As suggested by the discussion of method above, by using the cyborg as a lens through which to interrogate Dada art, this text engages with questions of modernism, post-modernism, and the historical avant-garde, periodizing concepts that now need fur-ther clarification. In art history and art criticism today, "modernism" is generally taken to indicate the transformation in nineteenth- and early-twentieth-century Western painting and sculpture whereby various artists systematically negated their represen-tational traditions and developed new forms of abstract signification. These changes led in at least two different directions. First, modernism influenced certain artists to examine and criticize the various myths of self and world to which bourgeois society subscribed. Second, it inspired others to examine perception and later the media of painting and sculpture. Although many modern artists tended in their art toward one of these two main trajectories, a number of them performed both examinations at the same time.

Postmodernism was not recognized in art history until the 1980s, but the concept was soon retrospectively projected back into the 1960s.[61] It was generally supposed to indicate the "overturning" of modernism understood as formalism and abstraction in painting and sculpture (modernism in the second sense of the term outlined above). In practice, this meant a turn to media other than traditional painting or sculpture as well as to producing art that was once again representational and that criticized—either implicitly or explicitly—such modernist values as newness, originality, subjectivity, expression, and presence. In addition, postmodernism seemed to reject the modernist focus on interrogating the properties of specific media treated in isolation from one another. Instead, it embraced heterogeneity in art (i.e., the mixing of multiple media in a single work) and affirmed the idea of visual art's interconnectedness with other forms of modernist (and premodernist) art and mass culture, such as literature, music, poetry, theater, photography, and film. Finally, postmodernism supposedly represented an overthrow of the nationalistic and patriarchal ideals of the West, and promoted a new responsiveness to questions of multiculturalism, gender, and the environment.

Problems with these two general concepts arise when modernism and postmodernism are treated as opposites. No matter how perceptual or formalist twentieth-century modernism became, it continued to produce significant innovations in narrative and iconography. Twentieth-century modernism, in other words, continued to have representational aspects, which became more complex over time, thus perpetuating the above-mentioned first trajectory: modernism as the examination and critique of bourgeois myths. Postmodern art, moreover, never fully gave up exploring perception and the various media of artistic expression, and today, despite the explosion of representation and multimedia in art since the 1960s, important formalist art continues to be produced. Such works are significantly different from formalist works produced before World War I: first, because the artistic media being explored have become more plentiful, and second, because the materials out of which "traditional" paintings and sculptures are made have become considerably more diverse. In the twenty-first century, it is thus simply impossible to claim, as some critics do, that we have somehow entered a "postmodern" moment that has overcome "modernism."

The traditional distinction between modernism and postmodernism becomes significantly complicated by the concept of the historical avant-garde. According to this concept, developed by Bürger and others, the historical avant-garde of the second, third, and fourth decades of the twentieth century—the Dada, constructivist, and surrealist movements, for example, as well as such authors as André Breton and in certain regards Bertolt Brecht—attempted to change art's role in early-twentieth-century society.[62] Rejecting bourgeois aestheticism—modernism in the sense of formalism—and its separation of the institution of art from contemporary life, the historical avant-garde endeavored to break down the division between art and life created by the development of increasingly autonomous visual art in the second half of the nineteenth century. As a result, avant-garde art was both formally and functionally different from the modernist–aestheticist bourgeois art that preceded it. On a functional level, it drew attention to the (social) institutions that defined, supported, and legitimated bourgeois art in capitalist societies.[63] And by provoking their audiences to reflect on art in this way, the avant-garde artists hoped to get them to question the normative frameworks that governed the existence and power of art in modern societies as well as to develop innovative modes of human praxis inspired by the new art.[64]

In addition to radically transforming the conceptual basis of modern art, the historical avant-garde also fundamentally transformed its forms, materials, and practices. First, by radically widening the criteria as to what could count as art, the historical avant-garde broke down all notions of teleology in relation to the historical development of Western art.[65] Radically different styles, practices, and media became equally legitimate for the making of art, and works that combined heterogeneous styles and media became more and more prevalent. Second, the avant-garde produced a new type of artist unrestricted to a particular style, technique, or medium, who used the various forms and strategies of the mass media to produce artworks.[66] In addition, because they were critical of the bourgeois myths of individual production and reception promulgated by aestheticism, the artists of the historical avant-garde turned more and more to collaborative and collective artistic practices.[67] Third, avant-garde works tended more and more to emphasize montage.[68] Often possessing only a partial or an incomplete unity, they required, in extreme cases, an engaged spectator or reader to bring coherence to the work's heterogeneous elements.[69] And it was mainly by breaking through the appearance of totality and negating unified form or subject matter that avant-garde works got their brief and relatively ineffectual social–critical power: their ability to expose art's institutional structures and the spectator's role in constructing aesthetic and, by implication, social experience.[70] Fourth, avant-garde works were much more open to the external world than bourgeois modern art.[71] The avant-garde artists' submission to materials meant a radical loosening of art's traditional boundaries and a greater openness to both the outside world and the discourses from beyond the fine art sphere. In addition, avant-garde artists also employed strategies of chance and automatism to allow something external to imprint itself on the work: a trace of an other variously understood to be objective, natural, unconscious, or even divine.[72] Fifth, avant-garde artists focused on the singular, thereby producing melancholy representations that implied both historical loss and the belief that reality could never be fully conceptualized or shaped.[73]

As is today commonly argued, avant-garde art failed in many ways.[74] Like modern art, it did not fundamentally transform capitalist–bourgeois society as it explicitly promised to do. Instead, avant-garde techniques—among them appropriation and montage—were adapted, first, for commercial purposes by the mass media and, later, for propagandistic ends by fascist and totalitarian states.[75] After World War II, formalism once again became dominant in the United States and Europe—in part, as a reaction to the co-optation of the original avant-garde. Slightly later, beginning in the 1960s, avant-garde modes of art making again became popular in both Europe and the United States, and the new "neo-avant-garde" artworks were quickly assimilated into the contemporary art market and museum system. As suggested by the reception of the neo-avant-garde movements of the 1960s, works produced through avant-garde methods quickly came to be treated as precious, autonomous objects, and as the subsequent history of contemporary art since the 1970s reveals, neo-avant-garde art continues to flourish.

Bürger's theory of the avant-garde has been rightly criticized for devaluing "neo-avant-garde" art after World War II and overvaluing the "original" avant-garde break from aestheticism.[76] In addition, his theory does not adequately deal with how avant-garde artists attempted to develop a novel form of subject matter—one that dealt with the new forms of modern human identity and the problems of modern urban life— a failure ignored by most of Bürger's critics. However, because Bürger's theory of avant-garde art's structural and formal characteristics has numerous parallels with what art critics and historians today call "postmodern" art, Bürger's account suggests that modernism was—and is—a radically broader phenomenon than many critics and historians would have it. Although, according to Bürger, the historical avant-garde defines a break with modernism in the sense of formalism, the historical avant-garde's failure to radically change the institutional context of modern art suggests that avant-gardism actually indicates yet another trajectory within modern art, one that can be seen as modifying modernism's first trajectory, namely, the analysis and critique of bourgeois myths.

For this reason, it is better to understand avant-garde art as a mode of modernism, albeit one that transformed modern art in different ways. In addition to radically expanding the materials and media in and through which art could be made, the historical avant-garde also explicitly recognized fine art's fundamental interconnections with mass culture—something that modern art alluded to and used, but which it also attempted to disavow. The emergence of the historical avant-garde thus represented a profound loss of innocence for the modern artist as well as a more mature understanding of modern art, one that saw it in dialogue with both mass culture and ideas that came from outside bourgeois society and even outside the West. In addition, the historical avant-garde also represented a turn to identity politics in art: the representation of alternative forms of subjectivity such as those evoked by the figure of the cyborg.

Modern art, as art critics and art historians as diverse as Clement Greenberg and T. J. Clark have argued, was a form of art that represented bourgeois society in crisis. It was, as Clark so eloquently put it, an "aristocratic art in the age when the bourgeoisie abandons its claims to aristocracy."[77] Modern art, in other words, was a type of art that affirmed bourgeois values at a time when the bourgeoisie could not declare its values openly but had to affirm them surreptitiously in the form of an attack on bourgeois myths and ideals—a definition that fits modernism in both its formalist and its myth-negating modes. Avant-garde art, in turn, was a response to the perceived bankruptcy of modern art—a response to the realization that modernism only pretended to reject bourgeois culture and that it really perpetuated its ideals in the form of partial negations. As a result, avant-garde art rejected modernist formalism—albeit not completely—and, in addition to continuing central aspects of modernism's first trajectory (i.e., deconstructing bourgeois concepts of subjectivity and ideal forms of selfhood through negating bourgeois myths), it added something new: the project of imagining nonbourgeois forms of subjectivity more adequate to the modern world. As this book argues, the imagining of new forms of human identity in response to the perceived bankruptcy of the bourgeois ideology was a central aspect of the avant-gardism of the Berlin Dada artists. And by examining this aspect in some detail, we can come to a better understanding of the significance of the avant-garde and the neo-avant-garde today.

Moreover, because the historical avant-garde to a large extent anticipates the emergence of postmodernism after World War II, focusing on the historical avant-garde from the perspective of the present reminds us that the roots of the contemporary moment lie in the early twentieth century. Instead of revealing a series of radical breaks—between modernism and the historical avant-garde, between the historical avant-garde and the neo-avant-garde, and between modernism and postmodernism—the development of modern art since the nineteenth century demonstrates a cyclical and variegated character. Not only does modern art develop along multiple, sometimes interacting routes, but its various "negations" of past styles, strategies, and practices were often achieved by returning to those of a slightly earlier moment. Despite the rhetoric of radicalism and decisive rupture characteristic of most modes of modern art from the nineteenth century to today, continuities exist that suggest a plurality of overlapping trajectories as opposed to a single linear development. These trajectories can perhaps best be understood as strands of a rope that sometimes appear prominently on the surface and sometimes remain hidden yet still necessary for the existence of the structure as a whole. Such a model of modern art does not do away with the possibility of innovation but suggests that artistic development must be understood apart from overarching historical narratives (whether accounts of continuous progress toward a final goal or end state, or descriptions of movement founded on the idea of radical epistemological shifts).

In addition, the influence of mass culture on the avant-garde and vice versa shows cultural historians that the ever-intensifying dialectic between "high" and "low" culture that characterizes the present day is nothing new—a fact that has important implications. If, in other words, the emergence of the "historical avant-garde" manifests many parallels with the subsequent emergence of "postmodernism," then the initial history of the avant-garde, the help it gave to the development of both consumer culture and the techniques of fascist and totalitarian propaganda and spectacle, should signal what is at stake today. Although it was not achieved, the promise that the avant-garde made to transform society is something that remains in the present. So, too, is its eventual failure—the fact that the techniques that it developed served coercive rather than libratory ends.

In light of these two possibilities, my overall purpose in using the concept of the cyborg to examine the art of the Berlin Dadaists is to reveal what I believe was most promising about the avant-garde's project in the early part of the twentieth century: the faith that new forms of modern identity could be constituted through representation, modes of existence that would bring about social and political change. By bringing to light a visual history leading to such contemporary concepts as the "divided subject" or "hybrid identity," this study shows how radical artists grappled with the powerful forces of total war, the burgeoning mass media, and new forms of social and political organization, and how they imagined ways in which human beings could best reconstruct themselves in response to these forces. And by tracing out their creative rejoinders as well as the social, visual, and intellectual traditions that fed into them, we may be able to better understand today how art and other forms of visual culture can help us—both conceptually and ethically—to evolve new and more balanced modes of being and acting in a rapidly transforming, technologically mediated world.

1. Berlin Dada

Origins, Practices, and Institutions

Dada shows the world of 1920. Many will say: even 1920 is not so horrible. This is how it is: the human being is a machine, culture is in shreds, education is arrogance, spirit is brutality, stupidity is the norm, and the military is sovereign.

—ADOLF BEHNE, "Dada" (1920)

Like most studies of Berlin Dada to date, this book focuses on its visual productions. Although this is to some extent to be expected—some of Berlin Dada's most important contributions are indeed its heterogeneous forms of visual art—this focus unfortunately de-emphasizes Berlin Dada's many magazines, performances, interventions into everyday life, and disruptions of the public sphere. To balance the focus on visual material in the subsequent chapters, here I introduce these various practices that— taken together with the more famous photomontages and assemblages—help us see the movement in a more balanced and accurate way. Examining the Berlin Dadaists' journals, performances, happenings, and media hoaxes sets the stage for discussing their representations of cyborgs. Not only did these practices predate many (if not most) of the movement's best-known photomontages and assemblages, but they also demonstrate the Dadaists' long-standing engagement with issues of the body, the mass media, and everyday life—issues central to the cyborgian understanding of human identity that subtends their visual practices.

The cyborg evokes the idea of a networked human being. It suggests, in other words, that who and what we are have no organic limits; instead, the "self" extends into—and is distributed throughout—the world. Our essential natures, according to this view, do not consist merely of our minds and bodies but, in addition, comprise the various physical supplements through which we externalize aspects of our thinking, sensing, communicating, and acting. This understanding of the cyborg has two vital implications. First, it means that human beings were always, in Andy Clark's words, "natural-born cyborgs." Since before the beginnings of recorded history, we have always been "thinking and reasoning systems whose minds and selves are spread across biological brain and nonbiological circuitry."[1] Second, this understanding of the cyborg as a networked human being means that the mass media has played a central role in transforming what it means to be human during the nineteenth and twentieth centuries.[2] By changing how we perceive others, the world, and ourselves, in other words, the mass media also changes our identities. It makes us better multitaskers for one, better able to attend to and synthesize multiple and discontinuous data streams, but also perhaps more desensitized, colder and harder, on the one hand, and more manipulable, excitable, and instinctive, on the other. For these reasons, an account of the Berlin Dada movement that demonstrates its intense engagement with mass communication is an important preliminary step when it comes to demonstrating Berlin Dada's development of the image of the cyborg as an embodiment of hybrid identity. By examining the Dadaists' use of various physical media to create art, I demonstrate that, even before they turned to actually representing cyborgs in their photomontages and assemblages, they were extremely cognizant of how (external) cultural productions both produced and transformed a sense of self.

Another reason why the following general discussion of Berlin Dada helps set the stage for discussing its cyborgian representations involves the cyborg's relationship to embodiment. Whether the cyborg ultimately needs a body has for several years now been a topic of intense debate. While some accounts suggest that embodiment is not central to the figure, others argue that the cyborg can never transcend its embodiment.[3] For various reasons that will subsequently become clear, I agree with the latter position, and an account of the body's centrality in Berlin Dada performance helps reveal that the Berlin Dada cyborg was an embodied cyborg. As suggested by both their public performances and their more impromptu interventions into everyday life—their living out a Dada lifestyle designed to help change both themselves and others in their lifeworlds—the Berlin Dada artists understood the body to be a seat of appetite, instinct, and passion. Because they sought to confront, examine, and criticize their nonrational aspects through various forms of performance, a notion of the unconscious is central to their understanding of what it meant to be human. For some, this idea of the unconscious was derived from Freud. For others, it most probably came from a reading of Nietzsche or through general cultural diffusion. At the same time, however, it is important to recognize the centrality of the body to Berlin Dadaists and the way it affected their understanding of what it meant to be human.

Origins

Berlin Dada was a loosely knit group of German artists, active between 1918 and the early 1920s, whose members included Raoul Hausmann, Richard Huelsenbeck, George Grosz, John Heartfield, Hannah Höch, and Johannes Baader. (In addition to this core group, other figures associated with Berlin Dada included Wieland Herzfelde, Franz

Jung, Walter Mehring, and, more tangentially, Otto Schmalhausen, Carl Einstein, Jefim Golyscheff, Otto Dix, Georg Scholz, and Rudolf Schlichter.) The Berlin Dadaists were not the first group of Dada artists—although Huelsenbeck, perhaps their most prominent poet and theorist (and later a psychoanalyst in New York), was also a central member of Zurich Dada, the collective that initially developed the term *Dada*.[4] In addition, the Berlin Dadaists did not originate the Dada themes of the mechanization of art, the body, and consciousness, all of which go back to the proto-Dada activities of Marcel Duchamp, Man Ray, and other artists in New York during the 1910s, which have retrospectively been given the name "New York Dada."[5] The Berlin Dadaists, however, were the first group to fully appreciate the possibilities that Dadaist strategies held for transforming art's relationship to the mass media, and they were the first group to apply these strategies to the practice of politics.

Berlin Dada's extremely political nature was a consequence of the fact that it was the first Dada group to be formed directly at the end of World War I, the world's first full-scale mechanized war, a conflagration, moreover, that had ended with the collapse of the German monarchy.[6] The war's effects were much more apparent in Berlin than they were in either New York or Zurich, and the question of Germany's future as a political and a social entity dominated both public and private discourse.[7] For these reasons, the Berlin Dadaists, who believed that their art had to orient itself toward modern life, could not help but react to the political issues concerning their immediate moment.[8] Their political nature also resulted from the fact that they operated amid everyday social and political violence, a period of significant street fighting, political assassinations, and mass strikes that witnessed, in 1920, a right-wing putsch against the new government that nearly succeeded.[9] Behind Dada's political activism was the perception that the German revolution had stalled—that, despite the overthrow of the monarchy and the election of a social democratic government directly after the war, the nationalistic and authoritarian forces that had led Germany to disaster in World War I still ruled German society and politics. The Berlin Dadaists were eager to correct this situation, and they desired to use art to accomplish this decidedly political end.[10]

In Berlin, the Dada response to nationalism and authoritarianism was to conduct a wide-ranging war against multiple enemies—a war that caused the Dada artists to exploit their position in the fine arts sphere by using their exhibitions in part as forums for communist and anarchist political propaganda, and also to develop more popular techniques of communication to bring their critical message to the developing German mass audience of the time. Through cabaret-like performances, incendiary lectures, confrontational poetry, noise concerts, spontaneous public happenings, media hoaxes, magazines, journal articles, books, leaflets, caricatures, printed posters, assemblages, and photomontages, as well as through more traditional forms of art such as drawings, paintings, watercolors, and lithographs, the Dada artists attempted to bring their anti-authoritarian lifestyle to a wider public audience. They thus practiced politics in a dual sense: they criticized and attacked multiple enemies, and they promoted themselves as new role models of antibourgeois existence.

According to the official histories, Dada "began" in Germany on January 22, 1918, when Huelsenbeck delivered his "First Dada Speech in Germany" as part of a literary evening at I. B. Neumann's Graphisches Kabinett in Berlin.[11] For the most part, the speech was a short account of the Zurich Dada movement. It stressed Dada's internationalism, its roots in cubism and futurism (as well as its opposition to both movements), and the various art-making strategies that it either developed or perfected. In Zurich, Huelsenbeck reminisced,

> we made a beautiful Negro music with rattles, wooden drumsticks, and many primitive instruments. . . . In the Cabaret Voltaire [the performance and exhibition venue that the Zurich Dadaists began in a bar in 1916], we first experimented with our own Cubist dances, with masks by [Marcel] Janco and homemade costumes of colored cardboard and spangles. Tristan Tzara, who today puts out Dadaist publications in Zurich, invented the performance of the *simultaneous poem* for the stage, a poem recited in various languages, rhythms, intonations, by several people at once. I invented the *concert of vowels* and the *bruitist poem*, a mix of poem and bruitist music, like that which the Futurists made famous with their *Reveille of the Capital*. Innovations came pouring in: Tzara invented the *static poem*, a kind of optical poem that one looks at as at a forest; for my part, I initiated the *dynamic poem*, recited with primitive movements, as never seen before.[12]

Provocatively, Huelsenbeck also insisted that the Dadaists were prowar, because, "collisions are necessary: things are still not cruel enough"—a statement that only makes sense in light of the Dadaist strategy of ironic provocation or "bluff."[13] (In other statements, Huelsenbeck was resolutely antiwar, and his Dadaist activities as a whole seem antinationalist and antimilitarist.) He concluded by insisting that Dadaism today wanted to be "the *Fronde* of the major international art movements," which engaged with reality, was only a step away from politics, and had superseded even the most avant-garde movements of the recent past.[14] A little later in the evening, Huelsenbeck also recited from his book of poems, *Phantastische Gebete* [Fantastic Prayers] (1916), a primitivist work that he had first performed in Zurich at the Cabaret Voltaire, often accompanying himself with a rhythmically swishing riding crop or a beating drum.[15] These fragmented and highly imagistic poems, which were influenced by the "free verse" of F. T. Marinetti and the dark reflective poetry of Georg Heym, consisted of real and nonsense words; as Huelsenbeck later recalled, they expressed "lostness" and "immense terror."[16] For the audience, they were a good introduction to the confrontational and antilogical modes of address to which much Dada performance aspired.

While it is true that Huelsenbeck's "Dada Speech" marks the moment when Berlin Dada first began to constitute itself as a self-conscious group, its roots reach back earlier into the war years to a cluster of journals, artists, and writers who, although influenced by expressionism, cubism, and futurism, were at that point in the midst of rejecting their influence. Through the journal *Neue Jugend* [New Youth], a largely prowar expressionist publication of which Herzfelde assumed control in 1916 and then completely transformed, Huelsenbeck came into contact with Grosz, Heartfield, Herz-felde, and Jung, who would eventually help him found Dada.[17] What appealed to Huelsenbeck about the *Neue Jugend* group was its interest in placing art in the service of antiwar politics, its focus on the contemporary moment, and its growing estrange-ment from expressionism. The Herzfelde-edited *Neue Jugend* appeared intermittently between 1916 and 1917, and its circle of artists and writers also published an almanac of antiwar writings in 1916 as well as two portfolios of lithographs by Grosz in 1917.[18] It was in *Neue Jugend* that some of the ideas and visual strategies of Berlin Dada were first developed—most notably, in the later numbers, Dada's heterogeneous typogra-phy and its provocative strategies for laying out text and image. These included the mixing of type of different styles, colors, and sizes; nonhorizontal line arrangements; and the overprinting of text with additional text or images.[19] In addition, it was in response to the banning of *Neue Jugend* by German censors in 1917 that Herzfelde founded Malik Verlag, the publishing house responsible for nearly all of the Berlin Dada publications, and later one of the main communist publishers in Germany. It was under the Malik imprint that *Neue Jugend* became a "weekly edition"—a two-colored and then a four-colored, oversized newspaper in which Heartfield's perplexing layout and design played a major role. The *Neue Jugend* circle also staged authors' evenings, which, as they became more and more radical, took on Dadaist overtones.

Through another journal, *Die freie Strasse* [The Free Street], which was founded in 1915 and edited by Jung, among others, Huelsenbeck came into contact with Haus-mann.[20] Hausmann, in turn, was associated with Höch and Baader, figures who—through Hausmann's influence—would also become central members of the Berlin Dada movement. At that time, Hausmann was primarily a painter and still enamored of abstract art as well as cubism and futurism. He had also been writing texts on aes-thetics and politics for a number of journals since 1917, and by 1918 he too was becom-ing disaffected with expressionism—at least on a conceptual and literary level. The circle of artists and writers around *Die freie Strasse* was strongly influenced by anar-chism as well as the radical psychoanalytic thinking of Otto Gross, a dissident student of Freud—an orientation that, as Hausmann stressed, offered Dada an "anti-Freudian" "psychological base" from which to work.[21] Central to Gross's theories were the ideas that the structures and contradictions of capitalist societies were directly related to the repressive nature of the patriarchal bourgeois ego and that a sexual revolution had to take place before a true social revolution could occur. Through Hausmann, these ideas became important aspects of the Berlin Dada ideology. Like *Neue Jugend, Die freie Strasse* became more typographically experimental as it developed, and in its last issue, which was edited by Huelsenbeck, Jung, and Hausmann, it became a full-fledged Dada publication, titled *Club Dada: Prospekt des Verlags freie Strasse* [Club Dada: Prospectus of the Free Street Press].

As Huelsenbeck tells it, his "Dada Speech" came as a surprise to the others partic-ipating in the event at Neumann's gallery.[22] Some of them—in particular, the expres-sionist poets Theodor Däubler and Max Hermann-Neisse (who were also contributors to *Neue Jugend*), as well as Neumann himself—reacted quite negatively and attempted to distance themselves from the evening. Other artists and writers, such as Grosz, Heartfield, Herzfelde, and Jung, were aroused by Huelsenbeck's speech, which motivated them to unite as a group and develop a unique set of practices and activities inspired by Zurich Dada but also particular to the new situation in Berlin. What became apparent in the wake of Huelsenbeck's "Dada Speech" was the popular interest that the term *Dada* generated in Germany. The audience clamored for the performance to continue after Däubler and Hermann-Neisse expressed reservations about going on, and, after the event, a number of Berlin newspapers ran accounts of the evening—something that caused Däubler and Hermann-Neisse to publish a public statement against it.[23] Encouraged by the publicity, despite—or perhaps because of—the fact that it was for the most part negative, the artists and writers associated with *Neue Jugend* and *Die freie Strasse* joined Huelsenbeck in founding "Club Dada" in the weeks that followed the "Dada Speech." Introduced to the new movement through his connections with both circles, Hausmann, too, soon became a member of Berlin Dada.[24] The new group then staged its first "official" evening of lectures, performances, and poetry readings at the Berlin Sezession on April 12, 1918.

If the "Dada Speech" was somewhat unplanned, this cannot be said of the evening at the Berlin Sezession, which took place in a large hall only a few doors down from Neumann's gallery. Announcements publicizing the evening were sent to major newspapers, and copies of the new group's collective manifesto—largely written by Huelsenbeck—were available for purchase at the event.[25] In a room hung with nationalist and prowar paintings by Lovis Corinth (which, according to a few newspaper accounts, were threatened by the violent audience reactions to the Dadaists' presentations), Huelsenbeck, Hausmann, and Grosz, among others, performed.[26] Huelsenbeck began with a long speech titled "Dada in Life and Art," which included—or perhaps consisted solely of—a recitation of the manifesto. Grosz recited poems and danced. Else Hardwinger read poems by Marinetti, Tristan Tzara, and others, most probably accompanied by Huelsenbeck with a little drum and a baby's rattle. And Hausmann closed the evening with his manifesto, "The New Material in Painting," which was later published as the "Synthetic Cinema of Painting."[27]

Huelsenbeck's manifesto sharpened the points made earlier in his "Dada Speech."[28] Through violent images that alluded to World War I, he emphasized Dada's separation from earlier art movements, and he once again singled out expressionism for particular critique. In addition, he recommended the same literary techniques as he did a few months earlier—namely, bruitist, simultaneist, and static poetry—as ways to make new forms of art. (He also mentioned the "new materials in painting," but did not spell them out in any way.) More important, however, Huelsenbeck emphasized that Dada was not so much an art movement as it was a lifestyle or (a somewhat inchoate) ideology, a way to live that sought a much more direct—or primitive—relationship to reality. Stressing Dada's internationalism as well as its ability to incorporate all forms of contradiction, he concluded by insisting, "To be against this manifesto is to be a Dadaist!"[29] He then read the names of the manifesto's cosigners. Following Huelsenbeck's presentation, Grosz recited his telegraphic lyric poems, performed a jazz-inspired tap dance, and quite possibly pretended to urinate on Corinth's canvases. He drew a strong negative reaction from the audience.[30]

Hausmann's speech was delivered at the end of the evening when the audience was in such an uproar that the management felt forced to switch off the lights midway through his performance, thereby concluding the evening.[31] Echoing Huelsenbeck's emphasis on Dada as a way to discover a more direct relationship to reality, Hausmann likewise separated Dada from previous movements. More strongly than Huelsenbeck, however, Hausmann stressed the contradictory nature of human identity as a key tenet of Dadaist thinking: "Man is simultaneous, a monster of own and alien *[Eigen und Fremd],* now, before, after, and concurrently—a Buffalo Bill bursting with an Apache Romanticism."[32] He emphasized Dada's ability to help people recognize their mixed-up natures: "Everyone who works out his salvation through his innermost inclination is a Dadaist. In Dada you will recognize your true situation: marvelous constellations of real materials, wire, glass, cardboard, fabric, organically agreeing with their own sheer perfected brittleness, and hammered out appearance."[33] In addition to calling attention to the contradictory nature of human identity, Hausmann's speech thus also implied that the subject was an assemblage of organic and industrial parts. And by proposing the idea of human–technological interface, it may have helped set the stage for the representations of the cyborg that were to come.

Although the press gave a mixed assessment of the Dadaists' performances, the attention that the Dadaists garnered caused them to expand their activities.[34] In addition to the manifesto, their first magazine, *Club Dada: Prospekt des Verlags freie Strasse,* was also published that month. A sixteen-page magazine, edited by Huelsenbeck, Jung, and Hausmann, *Club Dada* featured confusing, mocking texts by Huelsenbeck and Jung, broken and superimposed typography, woodcuts by Hausmann, and advertisements for other publications by Berlin Dada writers as well as an upcoming performance. In terms of form, its fragmented, jumbled, and superimposed contents seemed to mirror the disjunctive perceptual experience of urban life discussed by German sociologists and cultural critics in the first quarter of the twentieth century.[35] In addition, "Club Dada" was also given an address—118 Kantstrasse, No. 3, in the Charlottenburg district of Berlin—to which interested parties were encouraged to apply. The movement was underway, and over the next two years Berlin Dada made its presence known in various ways. Although the group members took hiatuses from "Club Dada" to pursue other activities, they created enough manifestations under their collective name to keep Dada in the public consciousness. It was only in 1920, after the "First International Dada Fair," that Dada was finally considered over in Berlin, although several group members continued to create Dadaist works under different rubrics and appellations well into the decade.

The Berlin Dada Journals and Other Publications

The primary ways through which Berlin Dada made its presence known in Germany between 1918 and 1920 were books and magazines, various forms of public performance, public and private "happenings," and diverse types of visual art, most notably photomontage and assemblage. *Club Dada,* the final edition of *Die freie Strasse,* was the first in a series of five different magazines associated with the Berlin Dadaists. On February 15, 1919, *Jedermann sein eigner Fussball* [Everybody His Own Soccer Ball], an "illustrated semimonthly," appeared under the Malik imprint.[36] Edited by Herzfelde and Heartfield (who was at that point still calling himself by his given name, Helmut Herzfeld), it featured texts by Herzfelde, Mynona (Salomo Friedlaender), and Mehring; satirical line illustrations by Grosz; and on the cover the first two Dada photomontages (by Heartfield and Grosz) for which a visual record survives (Figure 1.1).[37]

The first photomontage, created by Heartfield and which appears in the top left-hand corner, consists of a photograph of Herzfelde's head attached to an oversized soccer ball that serves as the figure's trunk. Wearing trousers and tie, carrying a cane in one hand, and doffing a bowler hat in a gesture of polite greeting with the other, Herzfelde would appear to be an orderly bourgeois figure, if not for his monstrous body. The photomontage thus literalizes the journal's absurd title (and makes it even funnier) while representing the Weimar Republic as an uncertain and radically transformative time—a context in which human beings were metamorphosed into playthings to be buffeted by external forces. In addition, because it represents a human being as a synthesis of living flesh and a mass-produced commodity, it evokes the theme of the cyborg that would intensify around 1920.

The second photomontage, which was created by Grosz (and discussed at greater length in chapter 4), consists of a crudely cut silhouette of a woman's fan on which portraits of various Weimar political figures and military leaders have been glued. Above the photomontage, a title appears, "Prize Question: 'Who Is the Most Beautiful?'" and directly below it, a caption reads, "German Manly Beauty 1." Through these simple juxtapositions, the photomontage suggests that the recent elections were as much a beauty contest as a competition of social and political ideas and, furthermore, that the Weimar Republic's new leaders were not as masculine as they would have liked to believe. Also typical of the mordant humor for which the Dada artists became known was a small fake advertisement on page 3 that announced, "Attention Citizens! For a film pantomime, *Wilhelm's Return,* approximately 2000 sturdy men are wanted immediately. Preferably adorned (bring medals along!) Ebert-Film Co., Café Fatherland." Referring to the deposed German monarch, Wilhelm II, as well as the current head of government, Friedrich Ebert, the first president of the Weimar Republic, the ad playfully enjoined the public to engage in counterrevolution.[38] After supposedly selling out its first run of 7,500 copies in a single day, *Jedermann* was banned by the new Social Democratic Party (SPD) government.[39]

The successor to *Jedermann* was *Die Pleite* [Bankruptcy], the first issue of which

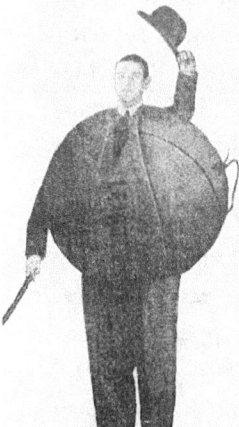

Durch Post u. Buchhandel à Nummer 40 Pf.
Abonnement: Quartal (6 Nummern incl.
Zustellung) 2 Mark. Vorzugs-Ausgabe:
100 numm. Exemplare 1-20 sign. auf echt
Zanders Bütten à 10 M., 21-100 à 3 M.

Preis 40 Pf.

Anzeigenpreise: 1 Quadratzentimeter 0,50 Mark, einmal wiederholt 10%
Rabatt, zweimal wiederholt 20% Rabatt.
Exzentrischer Satz: 1 Quadratzentimeter
1,00 Mark, bei gleichen Rabattsätzen.

"Jedermann sein eigner Fussball"

Illustrierte Halbmonatsschrift

1. Jahrgang   Der Malik-Verlag, Berlin-Leipzig   Nr. 1, 15. Februar 1919

Sämtliche Zuschriften betr. Red. u. Verl. an: Wieland Herzfelde, Berlin-Halensee, Kurfürstendamm 76. Sprechst.: Sonntags 12—2 Uhr

Preisausschreiben!
Wer ist der Schönste??

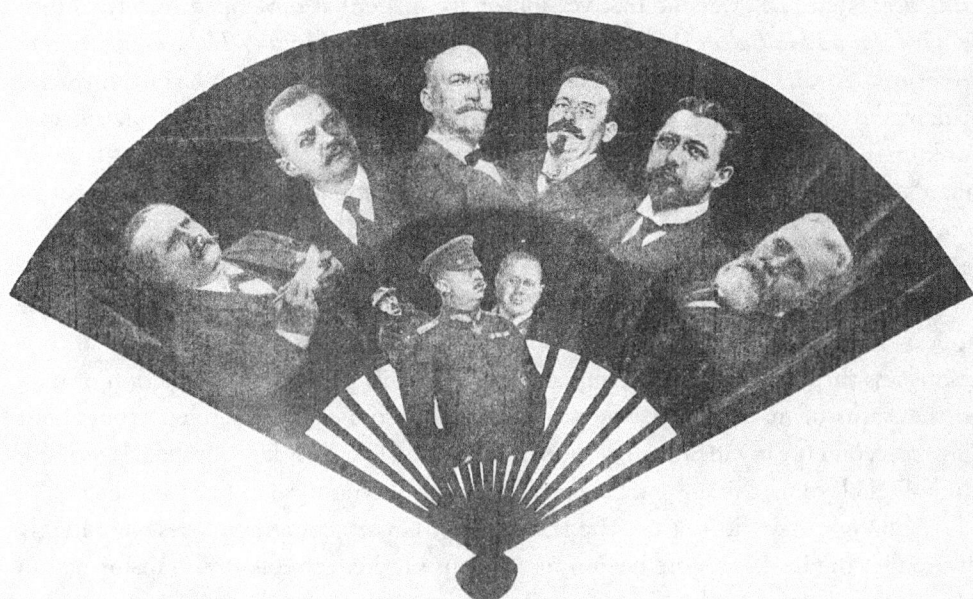

Deutsche Mannesschönheit 1   (Vergl. Seite 4)

Die Sozialisierung der Parteifonds
Eine Forderung zum Schutze vor allgemein üblichem Wahlbetrug

(Diese Ausführungen sollen den Unfug unserer Nationalversammlung selbst vom Gesichtspunkt der Demokraten aus illustrieren, jener Leute, die meinen, ein Volk dürfe keine Regierung besitzen, deren Niveau dem seines eigenen Durchschnitts überlegen ist.)

Man mag Demokrat sein, deutsch-sozialistischer Untertan oder Kommunist, man mag mit Schiller sagen: Verstand ist stets bei wenigen nur gewesen oder behaupten auf jede Stimme komme es (sogar mit Recht) an, die Tatsache wird man nicht bestreiten: Wahlen gehören zu den ge-

Figure 1.1. Cover of *Jedermann sein eigner Fussball* [Everybody His Own Soccer Ball] 1 (Berlin and Leipzig: Malik Verlag, February 1919). Illustrations by John Heartfield *(top)* and George Grosz *(bottom)*.

appeared one month later in March 1919.[40] Like *Jedermann, Die Pleite* was an "illustrated semimonthly." Although it primarily featured reproductions of line drawings and paintings by Grosz, its sixth issue also contained a photograph of war dead with the title "Hindenburg Breakfast."[41] *Die Pleite*'s editors included Heartfield, Herzfelde, and Grosz, and it presented texts by Einstein, Mehring, Herzfelde, and Hausmann, among others. More explicitly communist than *Jedermann*, a number of its issues were banned during its first year, and it finally ceased publication as an independent magazine in January 1920. It subsequently appeared as a satirical section of *Der Gegner: Blätter zur Kritik der Zeit* [The Adversary: Notes toward Criticism of the Time], edited by Karl Otten and Julian Gumperz, an appearance that caused Otten to leave *Der Gegner* as a result of *Die Pleite*'s inclusion. In 1923 and 1924, *Die Pleite* appeared again, extending its print run for another four issues.

During its first two years, *Die Pleite* reproduced some of Grosz's most incendiary illustrations on its covers, including *Maifeier in Plötzensee* [May Day Celebration in Plötzensee Prison] (1919)[42] and *Kapital und Militär wünschen sich: "Ein gesegnetes Neues Jahr!"* [Capital and the Military Wish One Another: "A Blessed New Year!"] (1920).[43] *Maifeier* (Figure 1.2) was the first version of an image that developed into the lithograph *Licht und Luft dem Proletariat—Liberté, Egalité, Fraternité—The Workman's Holiday* (1919–20) in Grosz's portfolio of prints, *Gott mit uns* [God with Us] from 1920.[44] It depicts a group of nine prisoners, their hands apparently tied behind their backs, walking in a circle in a barren prison courtyard under the eyes of two brutal-looking guards. The image's various titles all use irony to emphasize the poor treatment of working-class revolutionaries imprisoned by the new government. Instead of healthy exercise, the activity of the prisoners, who all cast their eyes downward, seems mindless, repetitive, and perhaps even compulsive. As depicted by Grosz, their exercise appears to presage a descent into madness or, at the very least, the obliteration of consciousness through senseless activity and, through this process, the reduction of men to the status of machines. As the writer and philosopher Friedlaender wrote about Grosz's second (nearly identical) version of the image: "Penitentiary-mechanics. A hard, durable circle of machine-men, between electrodes of tyrannical military mustaches."[45]

Although they did not use the term *cyborg*, Grosz's contemporaries were highly aware that the Dadaists were beginning to focus on the technological transformation of human beings in modern life, a transformation that is here shown to be deadening to both sensation and cognition. *Kapital und Militär* (Figure 1.3) depicts two grotesque figures, caricatures of the capitalist and the general, hung from facing gallows. Despite the fact that their feet hover above the ground, they extend their hands to one another in greeting, thus belying the fact that they should be dead. An ironic literalization of the fact that the left wing's hope that the German military–industrial complex would be overcome by a socialist or communist revolution had been largely dashed by that time, the drawing does not depict cyborgs per se. It does, however, evoke the idea of human beings with strange, supernatural powers and thus, once again, leads to the idea that human "nature" was at that time being radically transformed.

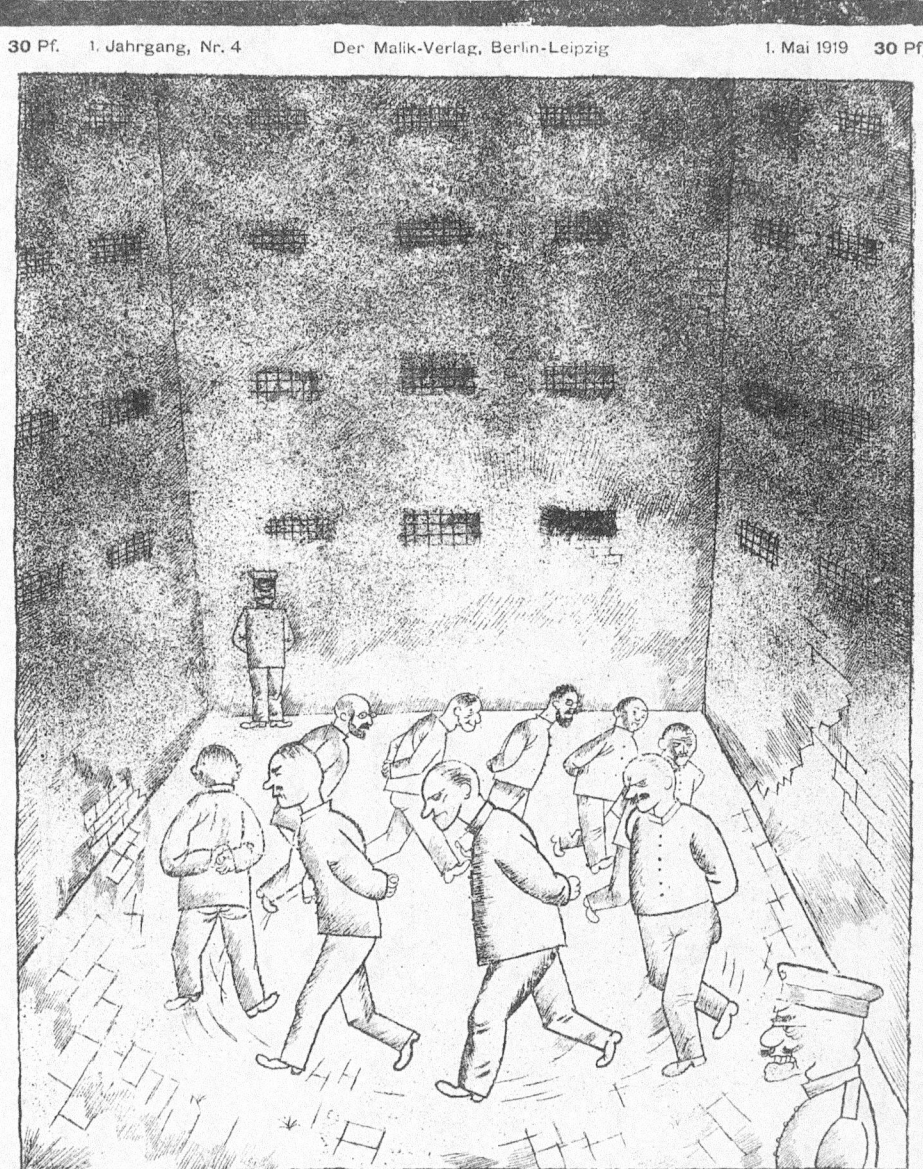

Maifeier in Plötzensee.

Figure 1.2. Cover of *Die Pleite* [Bankruptcy] 1, no. 4 (Berlin: Malik Verlag, May 1919). Illustration by George Grosz.

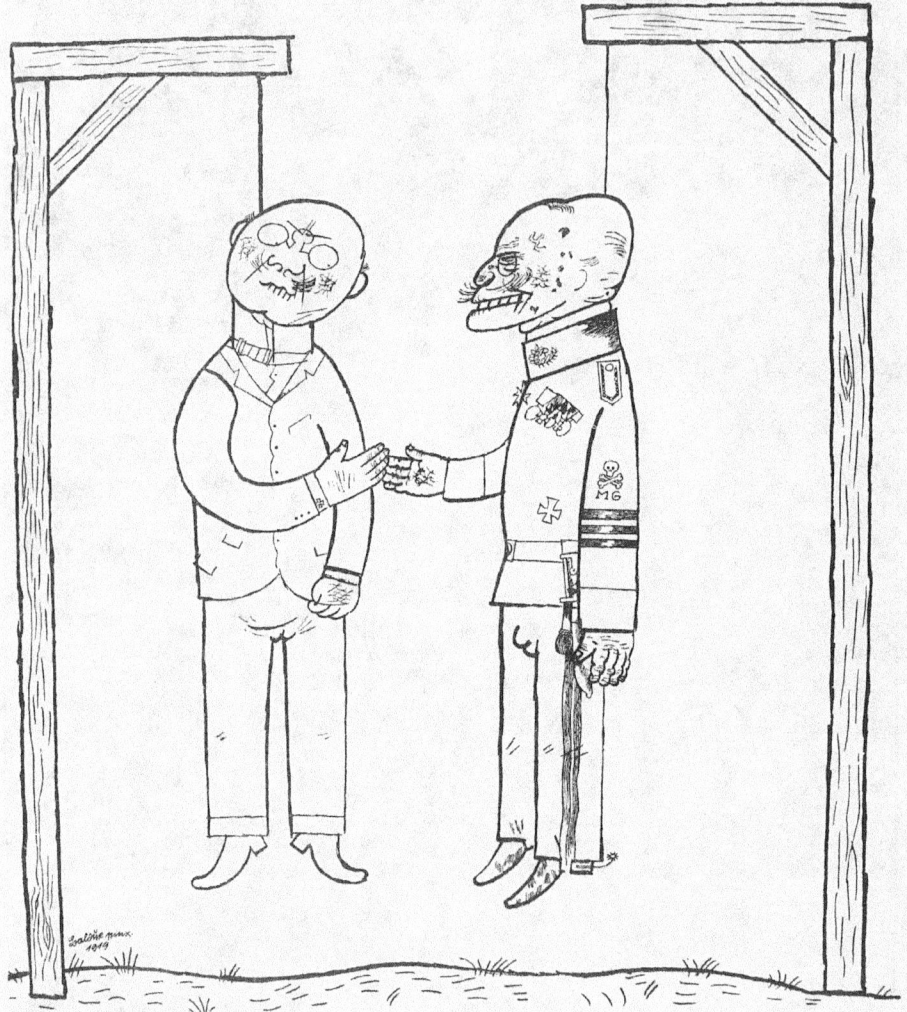

Figure 1.3. Cover of *Die Pleite* [Bankruptcy] 1, no. 6 (Berlin: Malik Verlag, January 1920). Illustration by George Grosz.

Despite its overt politics (and the fact that it almost never mentioned the Berlin Dada movement by name or advertised its creations), *Die Pleite,* as suggested by Grosz's illustrations, did not eschew the Berlin Dadaist strategy of biting irony—something that distinguished it from other communist-sympathizing publications and linked it to the Dada movement. In its sixth issue, to cite another example, it presented an outrageous collection of fake telegrams supposedly written by Wilhelm II, Ebert, Paul von Hindenburg, Philipp Scheidemann, Matthias Erzberger, and Pope Benedict XV, among others. Typical of the collection was a message from the deposed kaiser—signed "Willy"—to the "Club Dada Berlin," ordering the members to send him Dadaist drawings of himself as "Dictator of the World Proletariat at the Head of the Peoples of Europe." The Dadaist response to the supposedly positive reception of their work on the part of the former monarch was unequivocal: "As a result, Club Dada has dissolved. It could endure everything. But a dispatch from Wilhelm II was unbearable."[46] By representing themselves as involved in specious relationships with the political figures of the day, the Dadaists tarred their own attempts at social and political criticism with the same brush that they used to mock contemporary politics. Their strategy was to criticize contemporary events and actors through distortion, outrageousness, and humor, without at the same time setting themselves up in a morally superior position. Furthermore, by referring to a major instrument of mass communication that sent information rapidly around the globe (the first commercially successful transatlantic cable was completed in 1858, and radiotelegraphy became possible by the mid-1890s), the absurd collection of messages suggested how technology was extending human perception and making the world a smaller place.

In June 1919 the first issue of *Der Dada* appeared—probably the most famous and iconic of the Berlin Dadaist publications and certainly the journal that attempted to represent the movement most directly (Figure 1.4).[47] *Der Dada* 1 was edited and published by Hausmann, with contributions by Hausmann, Baader, Huelsenbeck, and Tzara. Illustrated with reproductions of Hausmann's woodcuts, which still showed the influence of expressionism and cubism, it featured mocking and confusing articles on current events, advertisements for both real and spurious Dada performances and products (as well as a macabre exhortation to "Sell your corpse for the improvement of the German fat supply"),[48] a manifesto by Hausmann ("Alitterel-Delitterel-Sublitterel"), poems by Hausmann and Tzara (including an early version of Hausmann's sound poem "kp'erioum"), and parodic religious texts by Baader. Written primarily in German, it also featured the Hebrew word for kosher on the cover and a poem (by Tzara) in French. For the most part the articles on current events parodied concerns about the contemporary revolutionary moment: Germany's signing of the Treaty of Versailles and its possible effects on the economy, the growth of communism in German society, and the nature and role of the masses. Baader's contributions lampooned religious announcements: they proclaimed the immaculate conception to be the new state religion and announced Baader's divinity as well as his (spurious) contributions to current political events. Throughout the issue, Dada was represented as a contradictory force in

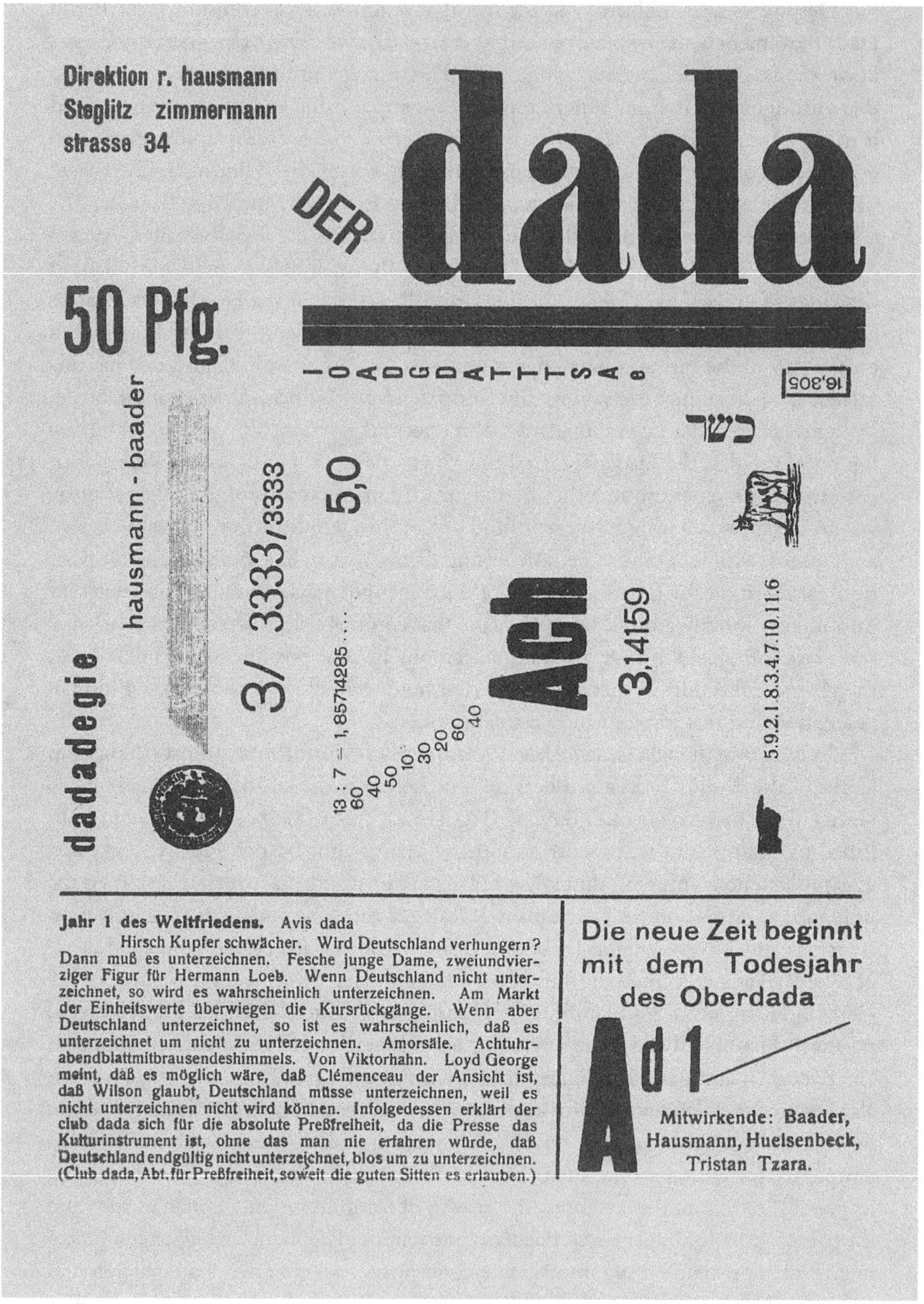

Direktion r. hausmann
Steglitz zimmermann
strasse 34

DER **dada**

50 Pfg.

16,305

dadadegie

hausmann - baader

3/ 3333/3333

5,0

13 : 7 = 1, 85714285 . . . .

60
50
40
10
30
20
60
40

Ach

3,14159

5.9.2.1.8.3.4.7.10.11.6

Jahr 1 des Weltfriedens. Avis dada
    Hirsch Kupfer schwächer. Wird Deutschland verhungern?
Dann muß es unterzeichnen. Fesche junge Dame, zweiundvier-
ziger Figur für Hermann Loeb. Wenn Deutschland nicht unterzeichnet, so wird es wahrscheinlich unterzeichnen.   Am Markt
der Einheitswerte überwiegen die Kursrückgänge.   Wenn aber
Deutschland unterzeichnet, so ist es wahrscheinlich, daß es
unterzeichnet um nicht zu unterzeichnen. Amorsäle. Achtuhr-
abendblattmitbrausendeshimmels. Von Viktorhahn. Loyd George
meint, daß es möglich wäre, daß Clémenceau der Ansicht ist,
daß Wilson glaubt, Deutschland müsse unterzeichnen, weil es
nicht unterzeichnen nicht wird können. Infolgedessen erklärt der
club dada sich für die absolute Preßfreiheit, da die Presse das
Kulturinstrument ist, ohne das man nie erfahren würde, daß
Deutschland endgültig nicht unterzeichnet, blos um zu unterzeichnen.
(Club dada, Abt. für Preßfreiheit, soweit die guten Sitten es erlauben.)

Die neue Zeit beginnt
mit dem Todesjahr
des Oberdada

Ad **1**

Mitwirkende: Baader,
Hausmann, Huelsenbeck,
Tristan Tzara.

Figure 1.4. Cover of *Der Dada* [The Dada] 1 (Berlin: Malik Verlag, June 1919).

politics, religion, and aesthetics. It was also presented as an advertising bureau and a savings bank. And by assuming the roles of club, bank, and advertising agency, the Berlin Dadaists emphasized their connections to everyday life, their embrace of commerce and the mass media, and their paradoxical incorporation of multiple antithetical positions into the movement's ideology.

The second issue of *Der Dada* appeared in December 1919 (Figure 1.5).[49] Once again Hausmann was the editor and publisher, with contributions by Hausmann, Baader, Huelsenbeck, Grosz, and Heartfield. The journal was illustrated with collages, woodcuts, and early photomontages, or "glue pictures" *(Klebebilder)*, as they were designated in the text. A collage of fragments from different Dada publications appeared on the front cover. Consisting of a confusing montage of truncated texts and geometric forms, it announced the Dadaists' embrace of mass-reproduction and their related practice of constantly cutting up their works and recycling them in new formats. On page 2, Hausmann's article "The German Philistine Gets Upset" appeared: a manifesto that attacked both the German bourgeoisie and the German expressionists and that characterized the Berlin Dadaists as advocates of constant movement, contradiction, and ironic nonsense. Like the first issue, *Der Dada* 2 thus defined Dadaism as an open-ended and contradictory philosophy. Across from Hausmann's article was an advertisement for *Dadaco,* the anthology of Dadaist art and writing that was to be published by Kurt Wolff in Munich, but which ultimately never appeared. The advertisement was illustrated by a reproduction of a woodcut, which, although it seems to be attributed to "M Höch," is similar in form to the woodcuts by Hausmann that appeared in the first issue. A portrait photograph of Hausmann and Baader illustrated the next uncredited article, "Join Dada," which has been attributed to both Hausmann and Baader, and which called on all readers sixteen and older to join the "exoteric" side of "Club Dada" and thereby gain access to the club's various institutes and departments, including its graphological institute, medical department, detective agency, advertising department, and central bureau for male and female welfare, among other divisions. By representing Berlin Dada as a gigantic conglomerate with multiple professional departments, the author or authors mocked Dada's social–political ambitions and undermined its character as an "autonomous" artistic movement separate from the German economy and society.

Following a poem reprinted from the second edition of Huelsenbeck's *Fantastic Prayers,* Baader's "Advertisement for Myself" appeared. Illustrated with a photomontage of Baader's head surrounded by newspaper text, the article recounted Baader's attempts to free the world from war. Juxtaposing Baader's (imaginary) rise to political prominence with an account of Germany's military and political mistakes since 1914, it emphasized Baader's central role in creating an "entirely new world order" and establishing 1919 as the "first year of world peace." (Although not attributed in the original text, the photomontage *Das ist die Erscheinung des Oberdada in den Wolken des Himmels* [This Is the Appearance of the Superdada in the Clouds of Heaven] is a self-portrait by Baader from 1919.)[50] In the margins of this pseudoreligious and seemingly

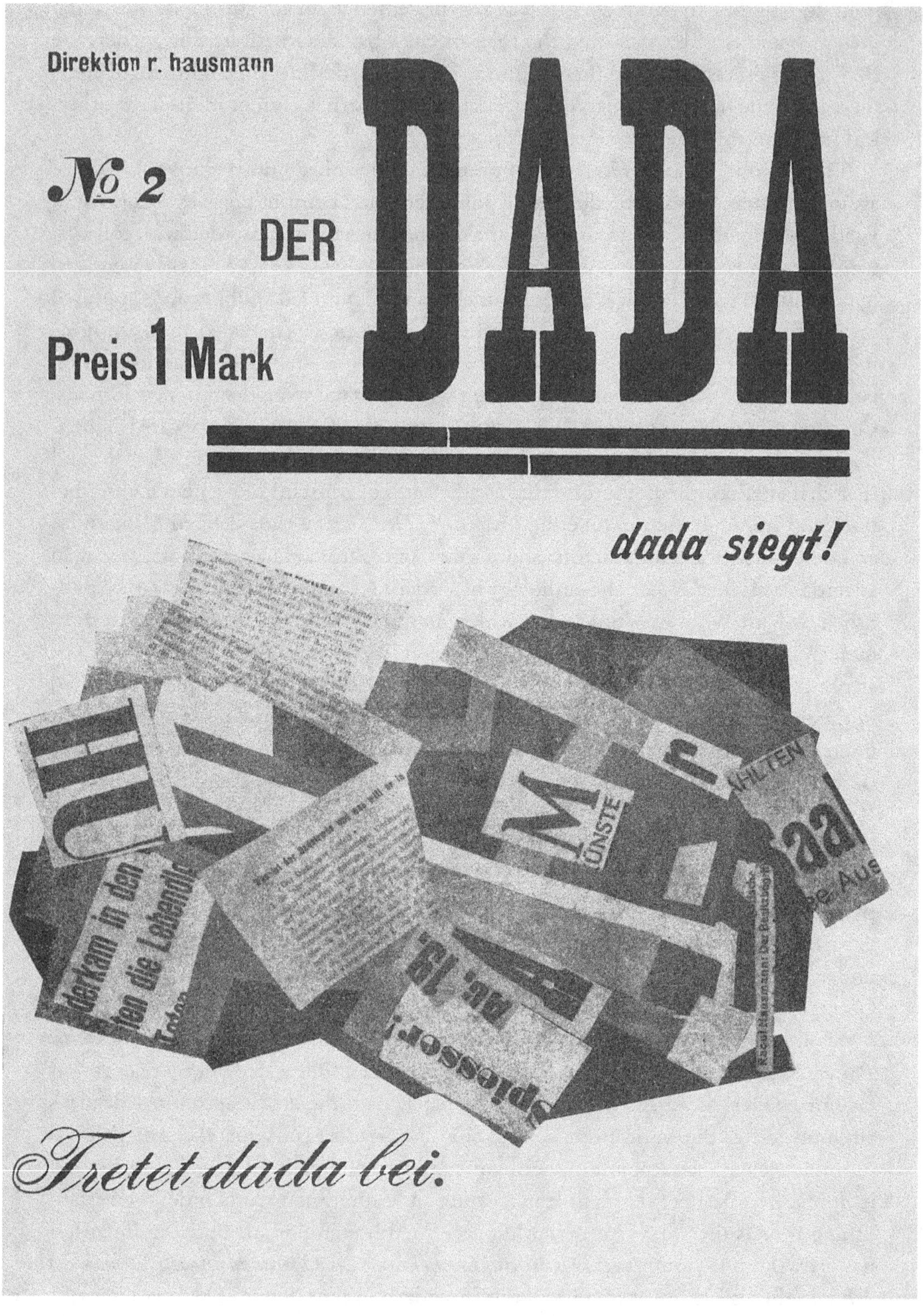

Figure 1.5. Cover of *Der Dada* 2 (Berlin: Malik Verlag, December 1919).

spurious account of Baader's encounters with various political, military, and religious figures, a linear self-portrait by Grosz was also reproduced. Below this image of Grosz as a dandy—complete with top hat, cane, and a dog—appeared a brief set of captions that summed up the Berlin Dadaists' confusing presentation of their movement: "What is Dada? An art? A philosophy? A politics? Fire insurance? Or: State religion? Is Dada actual energy? Or is it nothing, that means, everything?" Hausmann's early glue picture, *Gurk* (1919), depicting a face made from woodcut fragments, newspaper text, and a single newspaper photograph, appeared on the back cover along with an advertisement for the Dada Advertising Company, a spurious institution alluded to earlier in the issue in the article "Join Dada." The Dada Advertising Company was also the subject of a leaflet handed out at a Dada performance on July 12, 1919, where Hausmann, Huelsenbeck, and Mehring performed a sketch of the same name.[51] By emphasizing the movement's role in commercial promotion (and, by implication, self-promotion), the Dadaists used parody to undermine the bourgeois and aestheticist notion of the artist standing outside the market while emphasizing their enthusiasm for the new means of communication transforming German society. Given this enthusiasm, which was genuine, despite the fact that it was consistently intermixed with criticism, it is therefore not surprising that Hausmann's friend and later collaborator, Kurt Schwitters, the Hanover Dadaist, actually founded an advertising agency, Merz Werbezentrale, in 1924.[52]

The third and final issue of *Der Dada* appeared in April 1920.[53] Published by Malik Verlag, it was slightly smaller in size than the previous two issues, but, at sixteen pages, it was twice as long. The editors were Hausmann, Grosz, and Heartfield, and its contributors included Hausmann, Grosz, Heartfield, Herzfelde, Huelsenbeck, Mehring, and Francis Picabia. Appearing slightly more than two months before the "First International Dada Fair," which was the final important group manifestation by the Berlin Dadaists, *Der Dada* 3 presented Berlin Dada in its fullest and most developed form. Dadaist photomontages—often with cyborgian subjects—are reproduced throughout. On the cover, which was created by Heartfield, an untitled photomontage portrait of Hausmann appears (Figure 1.6). As a whole, the photomontage suggests Dadaist aggression as well as the group's confrontational performance practices. Wearing a monocle, Hausmann screams at the spectator. He is surrounded by text and advertising imagery, including tires, toothbrushes, irons, and bicycles. Hausmann's monocle, along with the mechanized and mass-produced commodities that encircle his head, combine with the other appropriated elements to suggest a vision of human identity as an assemblage of organic and technological parts. The word *dada,* moreover, which is repeated in numerous fonts and sizes, suggests the repetition—and thus the mechanization—of human speech. Evoking Hausmann's sound poems, it also suggests an infantile advertising jingle or, because the same word keeps repeating, the skipping of a record. The mechanization and mass-reproduction of sound, the photomontage perhaps implies, makes speech emptier and more persuasive at the same time—an implication that anticipates the melancholy conclusions of Max Horkheimer and Theodor W. Adorno, among others.[54]

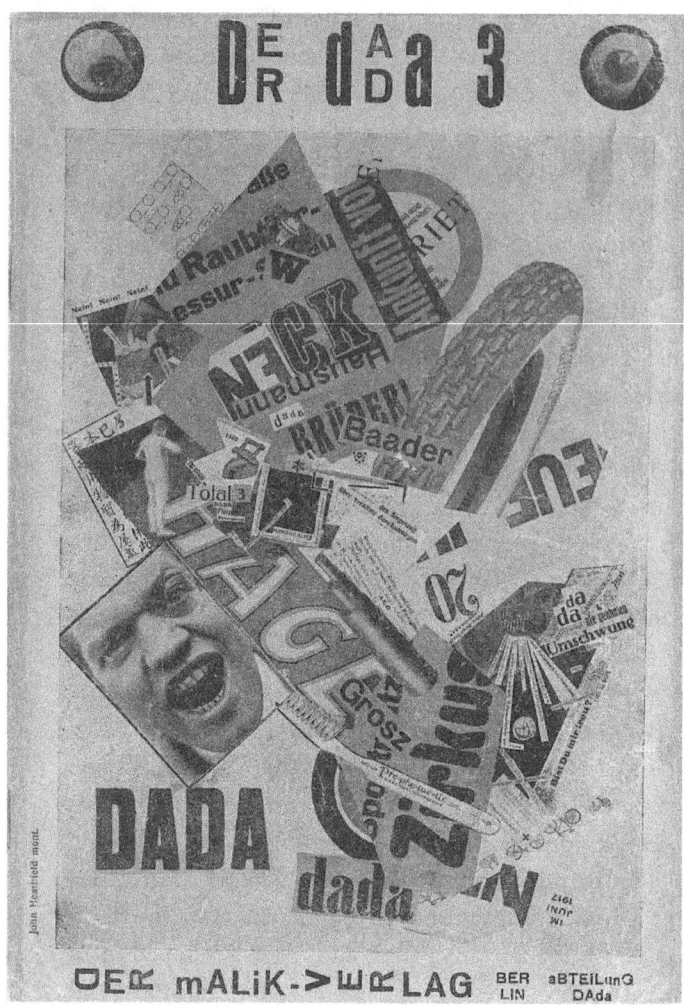

Figure 1.6. Cover of *Der Dada* 3
(Berlin: Malik Verlag, April 1920).
Illustration by John Heartfield.

Inside, an even more explicitly cyborgian photomontage by Grosz is featured: *"Daum" marries her pedantic automaton "George" in May 1920. John Heartfield is very glad of it. (Met.-mech. Constr. after Prof. R. Hausmann)* (1920), its exclusively English title emphasizing Grosz's abhorrence of German nationalism (Figure 1.7). In this "self-portrait," which is set in a space that suggests the uncanny cityscapes of the Italian metaphysical painter Giorgio de Chirico, Grosz presents himself as a streamlined, half-human, half-mechanical figure, juxtaposed with a drawn, painted, and much more organic image of the Berlin designer and model Eva Peter, who would shortly become his wife. This ironic wedding announcement suggests the mechanization of both love and sexuality as a result of the modernization of everyday life. In addition, because of the adding machine that Grosz clutches to his chest, the image evokes the *Angestellten,* or salaried masses, that Siegfried Kracauer was to describe ten years later.[55] These urban white-collar workers, Kracauer argued, constituted a new, modern class, one

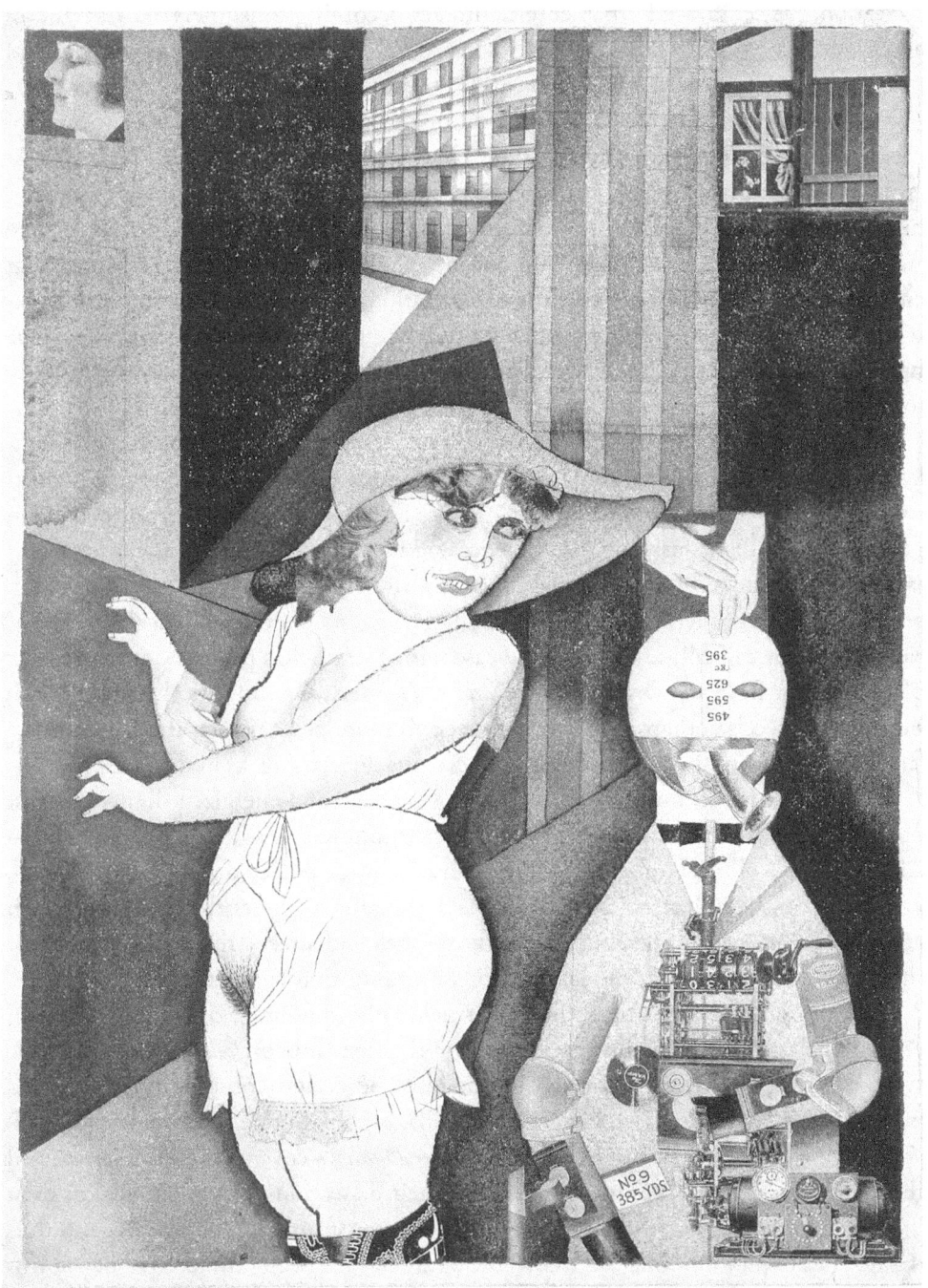

Figure 1.7. George Grosz, *"Daum" marries her pedantic automaton "George" in May 1920. John Heartfield is very glad of it. (Met.-mech. Constr. after Prof. R. Hausmann)* (1920). Watercolor, pencil, and ink on paper with photomontage and collage. 42 × 30.2 cm (16⁹⁄₁₆ × 11⅞ inches). Berlinische Galerie, Landesmuseum für Moderne Kunst, Photographie, und Architektur, Berlin. Copyright 2009 Estate of George Grosz. Licensed by VAGA, New York, NY.

divorced from custom and tradition. As a result of their bored, rootless, and overworked condition, they embraced urban entertainment, becoming consumers of mass culture and—eventually—Nazi ideology. Grosz's ironic self-portrait, which seems anxious and potentially powerless in the face of his bride's overt sexuality, anticipates this new mass figure while hinting at the transformation of the mind and the body as a result of modern technologies. In particular, the ribbon of numbers fed into his head by disembodied female hands suggests that Grosz's cyborgian augmentations have made him highly susceptible to outside suggestion and, furthermore, that his thinking has become standardized and programmed. In addition, the phonograph-horn-like funnel that emerges from his lips implies that the routinization of his cognition also possibly extends to his speech and, because of the direct line and close proximity between the number ribbon and the funnel, that the artist–bridegroom has become a mouthpiece for messages composed by others.

A few pages later, Hausmann's line drawing *Heimatklänge* [Sounds of the Homeland] is reproduced: a disturbing amalgam of a human head and a phonograph, emitting the cheers "hurra! hurraa! hurraaa!" (Figure 1.8). Typical of Hausmann's cyborgian portraits, it simultaneously suggests violence and metamorphosis. Although the presentation of the human head evokes decapitation, the organic–mechanical construction seems to live and function, and thus the image suggests the technological augmentation of human capabilities. As was the case with Heartfield's photomontage portrait of Hausmann from the cover of *Der Dada* 3, *Heimatklänge* implies that the mechanization of speech perhaps makes it emptier and more persuasive at the same time, a suggestion accomplished here not through evoking advertising, as in the case of Heartfield's photomontage, but through suggesting the wild and energized shouts of a vast body of Germans forming themselves into an emotional mass at a patriotic rally. In addition, by evoking a mode of address aimed at—or reflected by—a large crowd, *Heimatklänge,* like Heartfield's portrait of Hausmann, suggests that technology can amplify human speech, thereby allowing it to touch and affect a much larger audience than it could in a "normal" nonamplified communication context.

Toward the end of the magazine, Heartfield's photomontage of his brother's head on top of a large soccer ball is reprinted from the first issue of *Jedermann*—an ironic symbol of the Dadaist transformed by modern sports and commodity culture and buffeted by modern life. Two images of eyeballs, both with one side evenly sliced off, appear on the top left and right corners of *Der Dada* 3's cover as well as interspersed through the first few pages of text. Because their dissections appear surgical or even industrial in nature, they suggest the mechanical transformation of vision—and thus the practice of photomontage as well as the figure of the cyborg as a locus of new forms of perception. (This image of the violently altered eye was popular with the Dada artists as well as with the surrealists. Höch and Hausmann often altered the eyes of the figures in their photomontages by adding additional photomontage elements, and Hausmann also used the image of the sliced eyeball from the right corner of the cover of *Der Dada* 3 on the front of his visiting card.[56] Because of the violence it suggests,

daß nach sechstausend Jahren vergeblicher geistiger Anstrengung die Philosophie kläglich versagte und daß Ihnen die Naturwissenschaften ebensowenig ein festes Programm bieten können, so müssen Sie einsehen, daß DADA, geboren aus der Unerklärbarkeit eines glücklichen Augenblicks, die einzig praktische Religion unserer Zeit darstellt. **Sagen Sie sich von allen Hemmungen los, vergessen Sie Ihr Kartenspiel und die Wärme Ihrer Familientraulichkeit** — und Sie werden des Schwindels, den die Künstler, die Dichter mit Ihnen treiben, inne werden; Sie werden begreifen lernen, daß diese Dinge nur einer besonderen Technik bedürfen, Eigenverkehrsprobleme sind, die durch DADA aller Prahlerei und Ambition entkleidet werden: werden Sie Dadaist und Sie erwerben sich Angriffslust und die unbesiegbare Macht der Ironie!

RAOUL HAUSMANN.

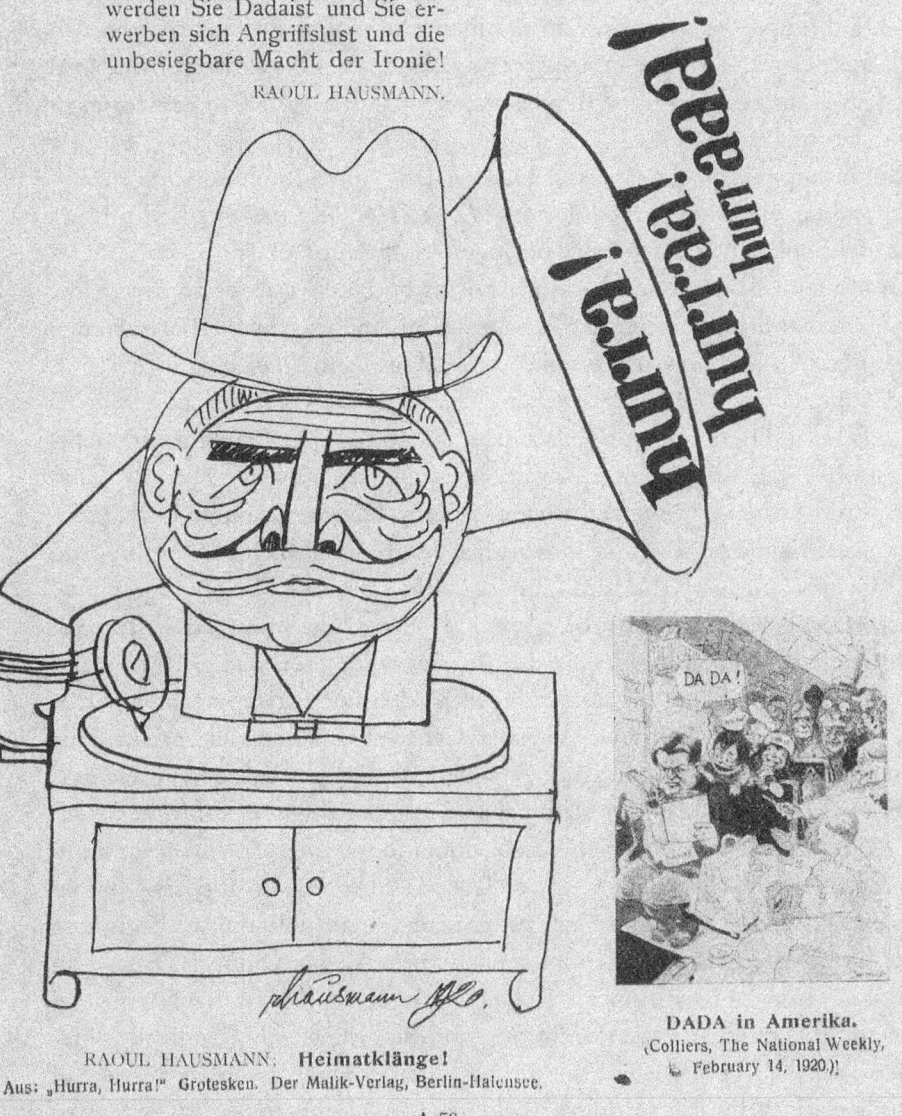

RAOUL HAUSMANN. **Heimatklänge!**
Aus: „Hurra, Hurra!" Grotesken. Der Malik-Verlag, Berlin-Halensee.

DADA in Amerika.
(Colliers, The National Weekly, February 14, 1920.)

A 50

Figure 1.8. *Der Dada* 3 (Berlin: Malik Verlag, April 1920), 7. Illustration on left by Raoul Hausmann.

the dissected eye implies a great deal of ambivalence about the transformation of vision under the conditions of mass-reproduction. As was the case with the technological modification of speech, the Dadaist cyborgs that evoke these radical changes in human perception suggest both benefits and risks.) In addition to the images of dissected eyes, numerous photographs of the Berlin Dadaists are presented throughout the magazine—including a single image of Gerhard Preiss, dubbed the "Music Dada," kissing the hand of what appears to be a manikin and, three pages later, a three-image sequence of Preiss dancing the "Dada-Trott," a "wood puppet dance," in black tights and a bowler hat (Figure 1.9). While the former image suggests an uncanny relationship between a living and a nonliving figure, the latter sequence evokes the mechanical reproduction of human life through the new medium of cinema as well as the way that human movement, once captured by the motion picture camera, can be slowed down, sped up, reversed, and otherwise replayed in ways that make it susceptible to new forms of analysis and control.

In addition to presenting the various Dada artists—often in photographic, photomontaged, and explicitly cyborgian forms—*Der Dada* 3 also presents Berlin Dada through its philosophy and performance practices. "Soul Automobile," another sound poem by Hausmann, is reproduced—as are poems by Huelsenbeck and Herzfelde. (Lending an international character to this issue, poems and texts by Picabia in French are also featured.) In addition, a short sketch by Hausmann, "Spirit in a Jiffy, or a Dadaology," is presented. Consisting of an abusive conversation between the Monteur-Dada (Heartfield) and the Dadasoph (Hausmann), it parodies the contemporary political situation while suggesting an ironic rivalry between the various members of "Club Dada." (As was the case with Preiss, the various Berlin Dadaists adopted Dada pseudonyms to create public personas, to loosen their inhibitions when performing, and to present the appearance of a unified, almost cultlike group.) The photographs of Preiss dancing in a spastic and disturbing way also suggest the provocative nature of Dada performances—something that is also the case with "You Banana Eaters and Kayak People!" a polemical and nonsensical text by Mehring, which unfolds as a diatribe against his readers. Furthermore, "A Visit to Cabaret Dada," an account of a Dada performance by "Alexis" (most probably either Huelsenbeck or Baader), presents a grossly caricatured vision of a Berlin Dada cabaret, emphasizing the performers' nonsensical activities as well as the audience's confrontational, even violent, reaction to the various acts. Finally, Hausmann's article "Dada in Europe" also appears—probably his clearest account of the Berlin Dada movement and its philosophy.[57] Beginning with a brief history of Dada in Zurich, he quickly turns to an account of Dada as an ideology and its vision of what it means to be human. "Dada," Hausmann writes, in what seems to be a conscious inversion of the expressionist Wassily Kandinsky's prewar manifesto on the importance of the spiritual in art, "is the complete absence of what man calls spirit. Why have spirit in a world that runs mechanically?"[58] The human being, moreover, is "a sometimes silly, sometimes sad affair, played and sung by its production and surroundings."[59]

DADA-TROTT

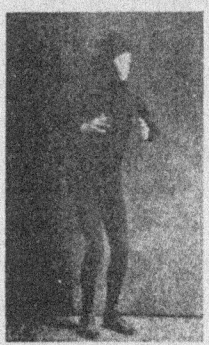

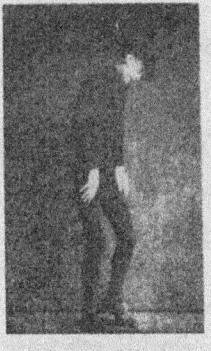

Der dadaistische
Holzpuppentanz,
vorgeführt vom
Musikdada PREISS.

DADA-TROTT

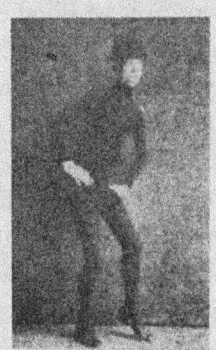

Wenn Hausmann die unangenehmste Fresse des Dadaismus hat,
so hat Picabia die angenehmste Dada-Visage. George Grosz

sodann
hui
scheel   X
war
Hai

; aufatmen
Dalypi   abbh
Daripi   Selter

oder

Das Dadalyripipidon.

*Johannes B. Krystuus,
der erste ungarische Dadaist.*

Den Dadalyden lotselt Pipikotzmos,
    Die Pipiratten späheln nach dem Dadalon.
Sieh! Da & Pi, Dapi, Pida, Pidadapi.
Auch der Mestrieze Dapidapi frosig bahreln.
Zuvörderst darfst dem Daad du fröhnen,
Junger Pipi (so pipida und dapipi dada).
Dem Dadaphon entströmeln sanfte Jamben.
Wer könnte — ohne Dadanent des Pipidroms zu sein.
Darob: Das Ganze stillgestanden (Mittelding),
Datater: dat!
Sprecht Dadamuden.
Der Laubfrosch säugelt euch mit Pipirin?
Der du die Dha von Daad stets peinlich weißt zu scheiteln,
Auf, auf, an's Dadapult, sag's nicht dem Gnömmel-Bömmel.
Gewissenlose Pipidranten flöteln,
Zumal Fritz Friedrich Sunlight (v. Sonderscheunochzagen),
Die mistverpichten Präpipister töteln.
Deromaleinst Milliarden Dadaisten ragen.

PROGRESS-DADA
WIELAND HERZFELDE.

1 mm

Figure 1.9. *Der Dada* 3 (Berlin: Malik Verlag, April 1920), 11.

People, in other words, are produced by the social and material conditions in which they exist. Although, Hausmann asserts, we believe that we are original and have free will, we are in reality "victims" of our viewpoints and educations. For this reason, the Dadaist rejects the past and is stretched by his living present. He uses all of his means to destroy the bourgeois world and to organize reality according to his own criteria. One central strategy is the "bluff," the exaggeration of the absurdity of the external world, which the Dadaist can use to transcend his own need for sensation and his own gravity. "The bluff is not an ethical principle, but rather a practical self-detoxification. Since Dada and bluff are equivalents, bluff is truth—because Dada is exact truth. Consequently, Dada is more a condition of life, more a form of inner movement, than it is a direction in art."[60] To become a Dadaist is to recognize that neither science nor philosophy can offer a true account of the world. It means to reject all inhibitions and to acquire a "desire for battle and the unconquerable power of irony."[61] As suggested by this essay, Hausmann saw human beings as socially constructed—and thus "mechanized" in the sense that they were produced by their modern, industrial environments.[62] It was only by parodying the constructive forces of the external world, he implies, that the Dadaists could expose the conventional constraints governing human identity and thus work to achieve a more liberated mode of existence.

The last two journals used as platforms by the Berlin Dadaists were *Der Blutige Ernst* [The Bloody Earnest] and *Der Gegner* [The Adversary].[63] In both cases, these were originally non-Dada magazines taken over by the Dadaists. In 1919 six issues of *Der Blutige Ernst* appeared. It was originally edited by John Höxer, an expressionist poet and painter with close ties to the Dada movement, and published by Trianon Verlag in Berlin. Throughout its publication history it featured contributions by the Berlin Dadaists. Einstein and Grosz took over as the editors with the third issue, and they continued to publish the journal until issue number six. Although the contributors became more and more exclusively Dadaist, the journal was more like *Die Pleite* than *Der Dada* in that it concentrated on political satire rather than Dadaist ideology. Its pages prominently featured line drawings and collages by Grosz satirizing contemporary German society. Edited by the expressionists Otten and Gumperz, *Der Gegner* first appeared in 1919. As mentioned earlier, the journal, which was originally published in Halle, incorporated *Die Pleite* as a satirical section in the spring of 1920. Shortly thereafter, Heartfield joined Gumperz as editor, and Malik Verlag became the publisher—a situation that continued until the journal ceased publication in September 1922. Like *Der Blutige Ernst* and *Die Pleite, Der Gegner* was less directly focused on promulgating Dada as an ideology, although it certainly accomplished this task also. Instead, it gave the various Dada artists and writers yet another forum to express themselves, and thus it contributed to creating a sense of the pervasiveness of Dada in Germany around 1920.

In addition to these journals, the Berlin Dadaists were also responsible for several other publications. The *Dada Almanac,* edited by Huelsenbeck, appeared in 1920. A 160-page book published by Erich Reiss Verlag in Berlin, it featured photographic portraits of the various Berlin Dadaists and texts by Mehring, Baader, Hausmann, and Huelsenbeck (in addition to contributions by Picabia, Hugo Ball, Philippe Soupault, Hans [Jean] Arp, Tzara, and Vincenté Huidobro, among others).[64] Huelsenbeck also published two other short books in 1920 dealing directly with Dada: *Dada Triumphs! A Balance-Sheet of Dadaism* and *Germany Must Perish! Remembrances of an Old Dadaist Revolutionary,* both published by Malik Verlag.[65] Furthermore, the Dadaists put out a four-page catalog for the "First International Dada Fair," which included reproductions of photomontages and an account (by Herzfelde) of the concepts behind Dada visual art (Figure 1.10). Finally, they also produced a host of Dadaist leaflets, performance programs, and performance posters. Combined with the portfolios of lithographs by Grosz as well as the less explicitly Dadaist publications by members of the Berlin group, these various published works helped establish Berlin Dada's presence in the literary and artistic spheres in Germany in the late 1910s and early 1920s. In addition, the centrality of these various forms of publication to the presence of Berlin Dada as an art movement in Germany also demonstrates its cyborgian roots, by which

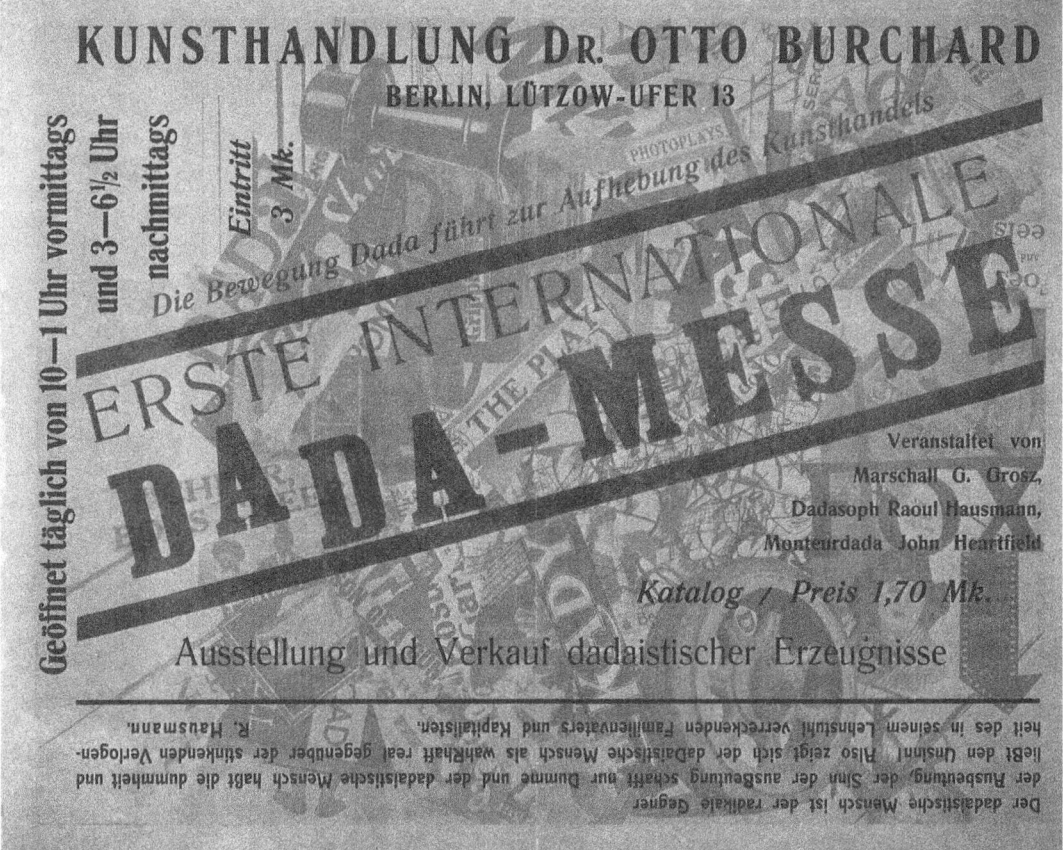

Figure 1.10. Cover of the catalog *Erste Internationale Dada-Messe* [First International Dada Fair] (Berlin: Malik Verlag, 1920). Designed by John Heartfield.

I here mean its partial origins in an artistically motivated transformation of the organs of the mass media.

The Berlin Dada Performances

In addition to their various publications, the Berlin Dadaists also put on twelve "official" public performances between 1918 and 1920.[66] These performances helped the Dadaists define themselves as a movement and make their presence known throughout Germany. As suggested by Huelsenbeck's "Dada Manifesto" as well as the first Dada evening in 1918 at the Berlin Sezession, the Berlin group was influenced by the performance practices of the Zurich Dadaists and, to a lesser extent, the Italian futurists. Accordingly, the matinees and evenings staged by the Berlin Dadaists featured simultaneous poetry (poems with many poets speaking at the same time), bruitist poetry (mixtures of poetry and noise), and other forms of avant-garde poetizing that either broke down sense, juxtaposed different languages, or combined poetic speech with dance or music.[67] In addition, if the accounts of Ben Hecht, then a reporter for the *Chicago Daily News,* and "Alexis" have any basis in fact, the Berlin Dadaists also followed the Zurich group's example in that they sometimes garbed themselves in outlandish masks, costumes, and makeup, and also performed silly, jazz-inspired dances.[68] Like performers in popular cabarets, the Dadaists evoked foreign cultures—particularly those of the United States and Africa—in some of their performances to suggest alternative lifestyles and modes of being in the world. If the United States stood for pragmatism, energy, and untrammeled modernity, then Africa stood for a more natural integration of spiritual and material life.[69] Moreover, through the efforts of the Russian Golyscheff, who was briefly a member of the Berlin group in the spring and summer of 1919, the Dadaists also appear to have put on at least one full-fledged bruitist concert: the three-part *Antisymphony,* which recalled the performances of the futurists and which the Dadaists characterized as a "musical war guillotine."[70] Soon, however, the Berlin Dadaists began to branch out, developing strategies particular to their own movement and context.

First, the Berlin Dadaists added absurd satirical sketches to their performance repertoire. Grosz and Mehring, for example, staged various versions of "Contest between the Sewing Machine and a Typewriter," as well as "Private Conversation of Two Senile Men behind a Fire Screen."[71] Hecht describes the former sketch as follows: "There was a race between a girl at a sewing machine and a girl at a typewriter. Grosz fired a starter's gun. The girls began sewing and typing at top speed. The sewing machine operator was pronounced the winner. She received a set of false whiskers, and went off the stage, proudly wearing them. There was no applause."[72] Grosz recalls a different version of the skit: "Walter Mehring would pound away at his typewriter, reading aloud the poem he was composing, and Heartfield or Hausmann or I would come from backstage and shout: 'Stop, you aren't going to hand out real art to those dumbbells, are you?'"[73] Mehring gives an account of the skit similar to that of Grosz—only in Mehring's version, there is no direct attack on the audience: Grosz runs the sewing machine while Mehring types, and both he and Grosz speak nonsense for the most part.[74] Other group sketches included "The Dada Advertising Agency Bum-Bum-Dada,"[75] in which at least eight of the Dadaists took part, and a "Recital for the Eye of Modern Music," which Hecht describes as follows: "Three girls in tights appeared. They placed a dozen large canvases, one by one, on an easel. Each canvas contained the drawing of a single musical note."[76]

As the various accounts of these performances suggest, one reason that Berlin Dadaist performances have been de-emphasized in the standard histories of the movement is that it is impossible to reconstruct them accurately. The lack of clear and unconflicting accounts points to the acts' partially unscripted nature and to the fact that the Dadaists did not focus on the performances themselves but on the complex interactions that these performances created between the artists and their audiences. It is clear, however, that the Dada performances were both ironic (in that they parodied numerous targets) and nonsensical (in that their ultimate meaning could not be resolved). Their typical targets included (fine) art, popular culture, bourgeois morality, and the notion of stable identities, and they were pervaded by a fascination with both modern technology and the chaos of everyday life.

The absurdist Dadaist sketches became somewhat popular with Berlin audiences, and in 1919, Max Reinhardt, the innovative and enormously successful Austrian-Jewish theater director, who worked in Berlin between 1902 and 1933, commissioned Mehring to contribute to a cabaret titled *Schall und Rauch* [Sound and Smoke] in the basement of Das Grosse Schauspielhaus, where Reinhardt was the director between 1919 and 1920. Mehring wrote songs for Reinhardt's cabaret and, eventually, contributed an entire evening of entertainment titled *Conférence provocative* [Provocative Discussion].[77] In addition, the group was also invited to contribute to the left-wing theater Die Tribüne, an invitation that resulted in two performances.[78] Although these performances at Die Tribüne drew mixed reviews, they were successful on a popular and an artistic level, revealing as they did the full range of the Berlin Dadaists' performance strategies.[79] In addition, the performances marked the Dadaists' first collaboration with Erwin Piscator, perhaps the greatest experimental theatrical director of Weimar Germany.[80] These collaborations can thus be read as signs that the Berlin Dadaist performance strategies were quickly recognized and accepted by at least some important members of the German artistic avant-garde.[81] Finally, between their first and second performances at Die Tribüne, the Dadaists returned to *Schall und Rauch* to perform *Simply Classical—an Oresteia with a Happy Ending*. Written by Mehring and incorporating puppets designed by Grosz and executed by Heartfield and Waldemar Hecker, *Simply Classical* cited Aeschylus's tragedy cycle to satirically comment on the events that led to the founding of the Weimar Republic.[82] Mehring's play was divided into three parts, "The War," "The Dawn of Democracy," and "The Classical Absconding of Funds," which respectively parodied World War I, the November Revolution, and the kaiser's flight to Holland after his abdication. *Simply Classical,* as Mel Gordon notes, contained many technical and thematic innovations that would later appear as stock devices in the theaters of Piscator and Brecht. An alienating Gramophone/Greek chorus interrupted the action of the play with political songs like "The Oratory of War, Peace, and Inflation." There were anti-military and anti-American themes— Electra as a Salvation Army worker. Film was incorporated into the staging—a movie entitled "Henny Pythia," parodied the film star, Henny Porten.[83]

Although unsuccessful from the viewpoint of the artists (who supposedly attacked the spectators after the performance), the play reveals the Dadaists' scathing political satire as well as the innovative nature of their sketches. In addition, it also suggested their admiring—but by no means uncritical—attitude toward popular culture. Although their works expressed an appreciation for film, cabaret, dance, popular music, and sports events, they felt compelled to simultaneously parody these different forms of mass culture and to interweave their forms with elements drawn from fine art (e.g., in the case of their second *Schall und Rauch* performance, the classical tradition).

In addition to the satirical sketches, Hausmann and Baader also developed an ironic form of lecture: a pseudoserious discourse on aesthetic, religious, or philosophical topics. Some of these lectures had extremely strange titles, while others seemed perfectly normal. In addition to "The New Material in Painting," Hausmann delivered "On the New Free Germany" and, on several occasions, "Classical Relations to the German Middle-Class Kitchen," an extremely curious discourse on aesthetics. Baader's topics seemed more megalomaniacal. They included "On Intertelluric [Interterrestrial] Insanity" and "My Last Funeral." Often beginning in a stern and dignified way, these various lectures would get stranger and more out of hand as they progressed. By parodying rational discourse, the Dadaists insulted and unnerved their audiences. As Huelsenbeck put it, audiences were "confronted with people who deliberately severed the process of communication. . . . We asked about the necessity of the transmission of values when we removed all content from what we did."[84] And by evoking and then breaking with rational discourse, these lectures provoked their listeners to examine the conventions that governed cultural production—as well as those that governed their lives.

Also unique to the Berlin Dadaists' performances was Hausmann's particular form of sound poetry, which he developed in 1918 and 1919, and which he used with devastating success over the following years. Hausmann's "optophonetic poems" were short "texts" created out of randomly combined typesetter's letters. The resulting strings of letters or "letter rows" were printed on posters that Hausmann displayed and that he also used as springboards for live performances. Repeating and improvising on the letter rows of his poster poems, Hausmann created two- to four-minute performances that eschewed all sense or meaning. Read at different speeds, pitches, and volumes, these poems focused attention on Hausmann's voice as a carrier of emotion or affect, and, in addition, they suggested the breakdown of all rational meaning or sense. This poetry, as Hausmann later stated, was "based on the necessity of finding a new form of linguistic expression" in the second decade of the twentieth century.[85] And perhaps even more than the irrational lectures, these poems were extremely confrontational and disturbing for their audiences to hear—something that I examine in more detail in chapter 3.

Another characteristic of the Berlin Dada performances that distinguished them from those of the Zurich group was a much greater emphasis on improvisation. Although aspects of the Berlin group's performances were scripted, and there was generally a printed program, the Dadaists wanted to remain open to their immediate situation. For this reason, they went onstage not fully knowing what they were going to do next. As Huelsenbeck put it,

> The one thing in common to all our performances was that we never knew in advance what we were going to say. I usually read the *Phantastische Gebete,* and Hausmann, as far as I remember, always had his sound-poems on hand. But this material naturally couldn't fill out an evening. So from the very start, we had to make the audience realize that it shouldn't expect very much.[86]

Grosz offers a similar account: "Sometimes these skits were prepared, but by and large they were improvised. Since we usually did a bit of drinking beforehand, we were always belligerent. The battles that started behind the scenes were merely continued in public, that was all."[87] And Höch concurs with this general picture:

> Mostly they [the performances] were imaginative and impromptu, broadly ranging over the intellectual terrain, and sometimes breaking down into chaos. The course these raucous presentations took basically depended on the audience's attitude. The ending was never planned. I always had terrible anxiety about the ending. But the participants and their supporters always ended up quite satisfied and relieved, while the squares *[Spiesser]* would get furious, which exposed who they were.[88]

The emphasis on improvisation allowed for a significant degree of chance to be incorporated into the performances, making each iteration a unique event. In addition, improvisation fit with the Berlin group's interest in being open to the forces and the contingencies of modern life. Moreover, as suggested by their partially unscripted and confrontational character, these performances allowed the Dadaists to explore their emotional and physiological reactions to stressful forms of public exposure. Not knowing the outcome in advance, the performances tested the fortitude and the preconceptions of the Dadaists themselves—not just those of their audiences.

Finally, the Dada performances were also distinguished by a strong emphasis on audience engagement, which the Dadaists provoked through the irrationality of their subject matter as well as actual verbal and physical assaults on their spectators. As Grosz, who remembered the group in some of the most nihilistic terms of any of the Berlin Dadaists, put it, "We insulted the people roundly," and, as a result, "fights were always breaking out."[89] Having come expecting a conventional poetry reading or a serious lecture on art, the audience grew upset because "we simply mocked everything."[90] Hausmann recalls throwing firecrackers at his audiences during his "Dada Tour" with Huelsenbeck and Baader in 1920, a traveling show that brought their absurdist humor to new audiences in both Germany and Czechoslovakia.[91] Huelsenbeck also insulted and provoked the audience, and used other techniques to break down the barriers between performers and spectators:

> One of my tricks was to propose a discussion of Dada. My suggestion was usually taken, and a whole bunch of panelists wanted to have the floor. They were understandably and comically serious about trying to grasp the phenomenon of Dada. The impossibility of defining Dada only added to the general chaos, which in turn deepened the sense of frustration; and often, when we thought we had already won the battle, forgotten complexes burst to the surface.[92]

Yet Huelsenbeck concurs with Grosz that often their intention was simply to make their audiences angry: "To sum up our reading circuit in a single sentence: we annoyed and bewildered our audiences."[93] And by provoking anger and confusion, the Dadaists hoped to liberate their audiences by getting them to express—and thus face—deep-seated emotions and concerns, another strategy whereby the Dadaist performances encouraged both the audience and the performers to explore their physical natures as seats of instinct and emotion.

The Berlin Dada Happenings: Interventions in Everyday Life

In addition to making Dada known through performances, the Berlin Dadaists also staged impromptu public "happenings." As it is used here, "happening" refers to the Dadaists' semiplanned—as well as their seemingly completely spontaneous—performances that took place in the context of everyday life. There are continuities between these happenings, the Dada performances discussed in the last section, and the Berlin Dadaists' media hoaxes, the generally spurious accounts of activities and events that they managed to get published in the German press, that I discuss in the next section. Yet another means by which the concept of Dada as a lifestyle and a nonbinding ideology was formed and transmitted to the public in the late 1910s and early 1920s, the Dadaist happenings existed in many forms.

Although the Dada happenings were different from the American happenings of the 1960s, the term is useful nonetheless. This is the case not only because a number of the American artists and critics involved in the 1960s happenings recognized a loose debt to Dada art but also because significant formal and conceptual parallels exist between the two.[94] These parallels include disregard for traditional plot or story structure, compartmentalized action (in that a performance's parts or "scenes" often bear little or no relationship or connection to one another), the attempt to transform the traditional (largely one-way) relationship between actors and audience, the use of non-traditional or "found" environments for presenting the work, the move away from language as the primary carrier of meaning, and the presence of what Michael Kirby calls "nonmatrixed behavior" (in that the actors often do not create an artificial character, as is the case in a traditional dramatic work, but simply perform actions, much like athletes in a competition).[95]

What made the Berlin Dada happenings different from the performances described above was the following: the happenings were generally even less structured than the performances, they took place in the context of everyday life, and at times their "audience" was limited to other Berlin Dadaists. For these reasons, the Dada happenings came closest to what Allan Kaprow, in his typology of happenings from 1967, identified as the sixth and last kind of happening, the "activity type." According to Kaprow, this type of happening

> ignores theaters and audiences, is more active than meditative, and is close in spirit to physical sports, ceremonies, fairs, mountain climbing, war games, and political demonstrations. It also partakes of the unconscious daily rituals of the supermarket, subway ride at rush hour, and tooth brushing every morning. The Activity Happening selects and combines situations to be participated in, rather than watched or just thought about.[96]

And like the American activity happenings, the Berlin Dadaist happenings were motivated by a desire to liberate their audiences through actions that would inspire reflection on the nature of human identity and behavior in the context of everyday life.

There were different types of Berlin Dadaist happenings. Shortly after the first Dada evening, Grosz, for example, began to roam Kurfürstendamm, the popular Berlin shopping boulevard, dressed as an allegorical figure of Death.[97] Although none of the Dadaists described this happening in any detail, a photograph of Grosz in his outlandish costume remains.[98] In it, Grosz stands erect, wearing a grinning skull mask and a long overcoat. Between his teeth he clenches a cigarette in a holder, and under his right arm he holds a cane. Parodying the attire of a well-dressed gentleman, Grosz could, in this particular garb and context, possibly have been taken for a street hawker or a sandwich-board man attempting to draw people into a nearby store. At the same time, no products are visible, and Death is an unlikely brand for inspiring the consumption of most commodities. Thus, by introducing a representation of trauma into the shopping experience of everyday Berliners (one made all the more disturbing by the recent war), Grosz's action might have provoked his unwitting audience to reflect on how Germany was attempting to forget the carnage of World War I through mindless consumption.

In addition, also in the weeks following the first Dada evening, Grosz started plastering the streets and locales of Berlin with sarcastic stickers advertising the group.

> I was very proud of some of the slogans I invented. There was "Dada today, Dada tomorrow, Dada forever"; the little political parody "Dada, Dada *über alles*"; "Come

to Dada if you like to be embraced and embarrassed"; "Dada kicks you in the behind and you like it." We had these slogans printed on small stickers which we plastered all over the shop windows, coffee-house tables, and shop doors of Berlin. They were alarming little stickers, particularly since the slogans were so mystic and enigmatic. Everyone began to wonder who we were. The popular afternoon paper, *BZ am Mittag*, devoted a whole editorial to the Dada menace.[99]

The Dadaist happenings, as Grosz's memoir suggests, did not simply shock their on-lookers. They left mysterious traces in the world, and, in addition, they had a way of making the papers.

Mehring, on the other hand, remembers a publicity stunt that they used to sell the first issue of *Jedermann sein eigner Fussball*. As he recalls, the Dadaists rented a charabanc, or open-topped bus, and a small band to advertise their publication. With the editorial staff walking behind the bus, they traversed Berlin—from the rich districts in the metropolis's western part to the lower-middle-class and working-class districts in the northern and eastern sections. As the band played military tunes, the Dadaists hawked *Jedermann*—something that drew scorn in the western districts and delight as they entered the capital's poorer areas, where the predominantly working-class population responded positively to the cynicism of the left-wing publication and its pseudopatriotic sales pitch.[100] Like Grosz's appearances on the Kurfürstendamm, the happening that Mehring recalls both embodies and parodies an advertising campaign. By creating actions that both fit into the everyday context and at the same time seemed nonsensical or ironically intended, the Dadaists transformed the urban environments through which they passed. They thus introduced uncertainty, potential discomfort, and humor into the everyday world, thereby possibly helping their onlookers examine their time-honored and conventional expectations.

Huelsenbeck, for his part, recalls another more spontaneous series of events that began in a bar near the Bahnhof Zoo in Berlin. These events were not so much directed toward an outside public but toward other Dada artists. Dissatisfied with merely drinking, Huelsenbeck, along with Jung, Herzfelde, and Heartfield, began to publicly snort cocaine. Despite their noise and aggressiveness, they managed to convince the establishment to allow them to continue all night.

> When the cleaning women came in the morning, we were all sitting or lying at the table, drinking, and swallowing cocaine. John Heartfield . . . became so unruly that we had to hold him back forcibly. We finally dragged him off to a taxi and drove to Wieland Herzfelde's studio on the *Kurfürstendamm*. . . . Here, among publishers' crates, rolls of paper, books, manuscripts piled up around the walls like bottles of wine, we continued our revels. John Heartfield was tied to a chair, and we teased him with words and poked him the way people bother an animal in a zoo.
>
> I was so drunk that I suddenly thought of setting the whole place on fire. I ignited a small torch and headed for the manuscripts. My friends leaped upon me and grabbed

my firebrand. After that I must have passed out for a while. But I still had a good deal of energy left in me. My friend Klapper, whose medical practice I covered and in whose apartment in Steglitz I was rooming, suddenly showed up. . . . It was about six a.m. Klapper hailed a horse-drawn cab. . . . Nobody could get me to climb in. Klapper sat in the old leather cushions. I trotted alongside the cab for three miles without getting out of breath, one, two, one, two.[101]

As suggested by these various accounts, the Dadaists used spontaneous actions, aggression, absurdity, and chance to challenge the expectations of the everyday person on the street. By setting up bizarre and sometimes confrontational situations, they hoped to shock people in their environment, drawing their attention to the conventional rules of behavior promulgated by German society and possibly getting them to reconsider their ways of living and acting in the world. In addition, as suggested by Huelsenbeck's account, the Dadaists also extended their confrontational challenges to one another. By using drugs and alcohol to unfetter their behavior, and by actively opposing and threatening one another, they hoped to reveal aspects of human comportment that were smothered by the traditional rules of social interaction. Although their descriptions of these events are quite possibly exaggerated or sometimes even fabricated, they nonetheless point to the Dadaists' desire to use half-thought-out or even spontaneous activities to transform daily life.

Hausmann remembers a somewhat different form of happening that he created with Baader sometime during the early days of the Dada movement. One day, on a Berlin street at twilight, they began an impromptu outdoor performance, which involved reading excerpts from *Der grüne Heinrich* [Green Henry], the Swiss author Gottfried Keller's famous quasi-autobiographical novel. Originally written in 1854–55, and thoroughly revised in 1879–80, *Green Henry*, which tells the story of a young man's attempts to become an artist, was long considered to be a classic bildungsroman, or "novel of personal development."

> We took turns to open the book at random and read scraps of sentences with no beginning and no end, changing our voices, changing the rhythm and the meaning, leafing backward and forward, spontaneously, without hesitation and without a pause. This gave the whole thing a new meaning and produced some remarkable juxtapositions. We did not notice the passersby; we certainly noticed no sign of public interest. Zealously we stuck to our task for at least a quarter of an hour. The words of the book, illuminated by our exalted mode of speech, born up on the wings of our elation, tormented by new associations, took on a meaning beyond meaning and beyond comprehension.[102]

As Hausmann's account suggests, the two Dadaists used montage and chance procedures to reconfigure Keller's novel of self-discovery, thereby creating a radically new work. An action both exploratory and improvisational, their happening generated new meanings out of very traditional material. Significantly, according to Hausmann's account, the happening failed on a collective level. Unlike the "official" Dada performances, the pedestrians did not notice the duo's activities. Although the happening brought art into the context of modern life, the people on the street refused to form an audience. Thus, although the experience of Dada art could produce engaged audiences, this was by no means a foregone conclusion.

More significant for understanding the Dadaist happenings, however, is Hausmann's description of the barroom conversation that followed their impromptu reading.

> All at once we had had enough, and, closing the book, we set off to the forecourts of a little bar somewhere near (I think it was on the corner of the *Kaiserallee*) and there, over a *Grätzer* beer, we passed an enjoyable hour talking a psychoanalytic nonsense-language we had invented ourselves, with hardly a normal, straightforward word in it. Our unconscious was in a state of excitation which led it to pour out its secrets at every turn.[103]

As Hausmann suggests, the postperformative participants continued to "live" in a Dada fashion by defamiliarizing their own speech through nonsense words in an attempt to reveal the more instinctual or unconscious drives that helped produce their lives. By editing, transforming, and recombining a literary text, an "objective" part of the German cultural canon, Hausmann and Baader hoped to reconstruct themselves, first, through a performance for an unwitting audience and, then, through everyday conversation. And this focus on the construction of art and identity through dialogue and collaboration characteristic of the Dada lifestyle appears to have been another central subject that the Dadaist happenings attempted to convey.

The Berlin Dada Media Hoaxes: Interventions in the Public Sphere

Although the solo and group actions created by Grosz, Huelsenbeck, Mehring, and the others hint at the nature of the Dadaist happenings, it was Baader—and to a lesser extent Hausmann—who developed the Dadaist intervention into everyday life to the greatest degree. In addition, it was also Baader's activities that demonstrate how porous the line was between the happenings and the media hoaxes. Because of the mass media's rapid growth during the late nineteenth and early twentieth centuries, public actions were often reported and elaborated on by the newspapers and other forms of mass communication. For this reason, an intervention in everyday life might quickly become a more widespread communicative act in different commercial media.

To some extent, Baader's role in Berlin Dada has been de-emphasized. There are several reasons for this. Huelsenbeck harbored a great antipathy toward Baader; Baader's most important contributions left few material objects; and Baader largely dropped out of sight after 1921 (although he did have a successful career later as a cultural journalist).[104] Born on June 21, 1875, in Stuttgart, Baader studied structural engineering and architecture, then worked as an engineer and architect for various architectural firms in Zurich, Hanover, Magdeburg, and Dresden between 1896 and 1905.[105] Having established a reputation as a mortuary architect in Dresden, Baader came to Berlin in 1905, where he met Hausmann in the fall of 1906.[106] In Berlin Baader began to turn more and more toward writing as well as to develop visionary architectural projects. Among the most famous of these was the *Monument for Mankind* (1906), also known as the *World Temple,* which Baader described in three separate documents.[107] This completely impractical project, for which Baader solicited money as well as architectural designs, was envisioned as a pyramidal structure made from reinforced concrete about 1,000 meters wide at the base and 1,500 meters high.[108] A monument to a utopian world community (and thus a construction that implicitly criticized German nationalism), the *Monument for Mankind* was to synthesize various styles of ancient and modern architecture and to contain totally free libraries, universities, museums, archives, sports arenas, theaters, parks, concert halls, welfare centers, and, it seemed, a whole microcosm of the outside world.[109] In addition to subtly propagandizing against nationalism and war, its function was to elevate the spirit of the human community by expressing a mystical communal sentiment that went beyond the definitions of all organized religions. In 1914 Baader published *Fourteen Letters of Christ,* a treatise that explained his particular vision of monist philosophy through fourteen pseudonymous letters to different public figures.[110] A response, in part, to Nietzsche's notion of the "death of God," Baader's treatise argued that by recognizing that traditional forms of Christianity had collapsed, one was forced to conclude that the spiritual realm existed not in heaven but on earth. Unlike Nietzsche, who was suspicious of the revival of alternative forms of spirituality in the modern world, Baader advocated a new, individual-centered form of religiosity. And among the pseudonyms that Baader used to sign the various parts of *Fourteen Letters* was "Christ." Soon after, Baader began to contribute essays to *Die freie Strasse;* through Hausmann, he was eventually drawn into the circle of the Berlin Dadaists.

As Huelsenbeck reminisced, Baader "was a kind of itinerant preacher, the Billy Graham of his time, a mixture of Anabaptist and circus owner. While we wavered between inhibition and lack thereof, Baader was imbued with psychotic exhibitionism and impulsiveness. I still can't figure out whether he was fighting for a renewal of Christianity, an improvement in public schooling, or Dada."[111] Richter, for his part, called Baader "a sack of dynamite."[112] And Hausmann remembered Baader as "often possessed by his religious-paranoid ideas," "a mixture of well-regulated character and simultaneous obstinacy."[113] As Stephen Foster has argued, Baader made manipulating the mass media a main subject of his art.[114] Through ironic self-promotion and self-aggrandizement, as well as by getting the media to publish and report on various Dada hoaxes, Baader exposed the mechanisms of print journalism and advertising during the Weimar Republic's early years, announcing his divinity as well as his struggles for world peace by all available means. In both word and deed, he presented himself as a kind of surreal messiah. And through his focus on disseminating his self-constructed divine image, he suggested the rather postmodern notion that media representations had more reality than the actual events. As Baader provocatively put it, "The World War is a war of the newspapers. It never existed in reality."[115] The same might be said of his own image. More than any of the other main Berlin Dadaists, the actuality of Baader's life has been occluded, and what remains of the man are the representations of himself that he constructed in his art, his writings, and the press.

In addition to presenting various performances in collaboration with Hausmann, Huelsenbeck, and the other Dadaists, Baader represented the Berlin Dada movement through media interventions. These involved sending mock press releases to numerous Berlin newspapers on "Club Dada" stationery. Although the total number of such documents remains unknown, it is likely that many more announcements were sent than ever appeared in print or survive in the archives of the various Dada artists. Baader had more freedom to intervene in the public sphere than the other Dadaists. As a result of a letter that he wrote to Prince Friedrich Wilhelm of Prussia, the kaiser's eldest son, Baader was certified insane in 1916. At this time, Baader was a soldier in the German army, having volunteered in the fall of 1914.[116] Although he was discharged in the same year because of a preexisting medical condition (possibly appendicitis), Baader was recalled to active duty two years later.[117] Despite his initial patriotism and enthusiasm for the war, Baader's pacifism and antiauthoritarianism quickly won out during his second tour of duty, and in that fall he wrote his famous letter, which (perhaps mistakenly) refers to the kaiser as the crown prince's grandfather.

> My dear Prince! I am currently a soldier in the army of your grandfather *[sic]*, who has become the monarch of the kingdom of violence. As I am the monarch in the kingdom of the spirit, I cannot be put under the order of an inferior master. I ask you please to inform your grandfather *[sic]* of the following: I order him to stop every warlike undertaking and to start peaceful negotiations under my leadership. With fond greetings to your grandfather *[sic]* and you, Johannes Baader, Pioneer.[118]

Through this letter, Baader recalls, "I gave the regional headquarters in Berlin a closer look at my inner psyche; and directly thereafter, by return mail, I was again designated 'permanently unfit for service,'" by reason of insanity.[119] After four additional months of service in Flanders as a member of a unit patrolling a section of the Bruges-Ghent canal, Baader was permanently discharged; he returned to Berlin in April 1917.[120]

Baader's insanity, which today is still not fully understood, appears to have been a complex phenomenon. Baader clearly suffered a good deal of mental distress during his lifetime as a result of either emotional or organic factors. He was institutionalized seven times between 1899 and 1932,[121] and his diagnoses ranged from "depression" as a result of the collapse of his Protestant religious views to "paranoid schizophrenia," with cyclical patterns of manic behavior.[122] Hausmann claimed, however, that at times Baader had himself committed to sanitariums as a way to deal with his financial difficulties,[123] a contention not entirely implausible, since the asylums where Baader stayed were not overcrowded state-run institutions but private facilities where the conditions were fairly comfortable.[124] Finally, in part because of the famous examples of Nietzsche and Friedrich Hölderlin, insanity was romanticized in German artistic culture at the time as both antibourgeois and creative. Baader was clearly influenced by Nietzsche, and thus Baader's insanity might have also contained an element of artistic self-fashioning.[125] At any rate, his certification as a result of his letter to the crown prince meant that he could not be prosecuted for his statements. Because of this status, Baader could create a public uproar free from the threat of being jailed for his inflammatory utterances and disruptive public behavior. As a result, he was at the center of almost every public controversy that involved the Berlin Dadaists.

Among the more famous events were the following.[126] On July 30, 1918, Baader sent his short text "Die acht Weltsätze" ["The Eight World Statements"] to the *BZ am Mittag,* along with a letter demanding all five of the Nobel Prizes for that year, both of which the newspaper published.[127] Beginning with the statement that "People are angels and live in heaven," "Die acht Weltsätze" deified all human beings, asserting, "Their chemical and physical transformations are magical processes, more mysterious and greater than any extinction or creation of a planet in the realm of the so-called stars." Drawing simultaneously on scientific and religious imagery, it emphasized that human consciousness was always intertwined with the world that it experiences; furthermore, both consciousness and reality were as multiple as the viewpoints that grasp them. Emphasizing that the idea of a transcendent God had been overcome (a theme Baader took over from Nietzsche), the text asserted that now the "earth" was a "part of heaven" (a monist belief that Baader developed under the influence of Ernst Haeckel).[128] It thus exhorted its readers to change their everyday perspective and to see the value of a new heavenly or spiritual life on earth. Baader's demand for the Nobel Prizes—signed by "Club Dada"—cited the "Die acht Weltsätze" as the reason. This text, the letter stated, fulfilled the Nobel Prize committee's criterion of having "the greatest idealist tendencies regardless of its length"; furthermore, it contained "the seed of the new world tree that will emerge from this bloody earth."[129] Baader's contributions were greeted with a great deal of amusement by the editors of the *BZ am Mittag*[130]—something that did not stop other newspapers from also reporting on the demand.[131] It was also as a result of this hoax that Baader received his title of *Oberdada* (Super Dada), a somewhat critical nickname given to Baader by Siegfried Jacobsohn, the influential cultural critic and editor of *Die Weltbühne,* in an unfavorable response to the article in the *BZ am Mittag.*[132] Although it was coined sarcastically as a way to point out Baader's megalomania, Baader eagerly adopted the title, using it in numerous announcements and articles over the next few years—a practice that apparently exacerbated Huelsenbeck's hostile feelings toward him, since it implied that Baader was the leader of the Berlin movement.

On September 7, 1918, Baader and Hausmann mailed a press release announcing the *Oberdada*'s candidacy as a Reichstag representative for Berlin, District One.[133] On September 8, a press release was issued that the *Oberdada* would temporarily step down as a candidate in order for the Dadaists to hold an independent election.[134] On September 10, it was announced that the Dadaists had officially nominated the *Oberdada* for the General Assembly;[135] and, on September 18, they announced that Scheidemann, the SPD politician who would proclaim the new republic on November 9, 1918, and then serve as its (second) chancellor between February 13 and June 20, 1919, had been offered and accepted a membership in "Club Dada."[136] Through the figure of the *Oberdada,* whose name carried strongly hierarchical connotations, Baader parodied Germany's pompous and authoritarian military and political leaders and added a note of uncertainty to the press's reports of current events. An even more famous event occurred on November 17, 1918, when Baader interrupted a sermon by Pastor Ernst von Dryander in Berlin Cathedral, crying out "Jesus Christ means nothing to you!" An expression of his disgust with the German church for supporting World War I, Baader's public outcry resulted in his arrest and a brief incarceration before he was acquitted by reason of insanity.[137] The press reported the events,[138] and Baader published a response to what he perceived to be misunderstandings of his action in *Die freie Strasse* the following month.[139] On February 6, 1919, the day that the First National Assembly opened in Weimar, Baader was declared "President of the Earth" at a Dada assembly in the "Emperor's Room" at Haus Rheingold on the Bellevuestrasse in Berlin.[140] A repeat of the announcement on the first page of *Die freie Strasse* from December 1918, the action parodied earlier attempts (since November 1918) on the part of various political groups and actors in Germany to form a new government. (Ebert was elected president of the new republic five days later on February 11, 1919.) Although the event did not make it into the press, it has entered numerous histories of Dada, perhaps because Baader mentions this "Dada Putsch" in an undated press release, and a flyer was printed, "Dadaists against Weimar," which later became part of a more famous Dadaist action.[141]

Other pseudopolitical actions quickly followed. In early March 1919, Hausmann and Baader decided to proclaim that a "Dada Republic of Berlin-Nikolassee" would be formed on April 1, 1919.[142] Using a typewriter and a telephone book, they planned to create lists of random names, along with fines, and post them throughout the suburb to agitate the citizenry. On the day of the fake putsch, they would then telephone the fire department at regular intervals to create even more panic, and, finally, they would enter the town hall and inform the mayor that an army of two thousand men was ready to take the suburb by force if he did not surrender immediately. A grim parody of the various left- and right-wing attempts to either radicalize or roll back the revolution and circumvent the ultimately successful actions on the part of Ebert's majority Social Democrats to form and lead a new government, the Dadaists' fake putsch announcement underlined the precariousness of the new parliamentary democracy. Furthermore, as Hausmann put it, they would show the world "how one could found a republic without violence, bloodshed, or weapons, armed with nothing but a typewriter."[143] In response to the announcement, the new government supposedly readied troops to quell the imaginary insurrection.

On March 12, 1919, Baader proclaimed the founding of the "Anational Council of Unpaid Workers" in Berlin at a Dada performance at Café Austria. This spurious group, which seemed to burlesque both capitalist and communist attempts to speak for German workers, also appeared to lampoon the attempts of postwar artists to form themselves into groups to further the revolutionary transformation of German society. (The group's name seemed to be a direct parody of the artists' organization, "Council of Intellectual Workers," founded by the expressionist Kurt Hiller.) Then, in mid-May, Baader donated a large picture of Friedrich von Schiller to the Weimar National Assembly with a statement that the Weimar Republic would be destroyed for scorning spiritual rights. A response to (then) Chancellor Scheidemann's recent citation of Schiller before the National Assembly, it underlined the political uses to which culture was being put in German society at that time.[144] On June 28, the same day that the Treaty of Versailles was signed, Baader released a pamphlet publicizing *HADO (Handbook of the Superdada)*, a scrapbook that he made from fragments of newspapers, posters, and other reproduced material.[145] This book, which became one of his main artworks, expressed his understanding of the recent history of the Weimar Republic and the central social, political, and religious role that he had come to play within it. Perhaps Baader's most famous political action, however, occurred on July 16, when he dropped a leaflet, which he had used once before in his "Dada Putsch" of February 6, onto the Weimar National Assembly.[146] Among other things, it asked: "Are the German people ready to give the Superdada a free hand? If the plebiscite says yes, Baader will ensure order, freedom, and bread."[147] Once again, Baader proclaimed himself "President of the Globe," and once again, the press reported the incident.

Other actions by Baader parodied religious events. On April 1, 1919, for example, the same day that he and Hausmann were supposedly going to carry out their putsch in Berlin, Baader sent an announcement—signed "Club Dada"—to the German press, proclaiming his own death as a result of a stroke. His announcement was quoted in full in the *Berliner Achtuhr-Abendblatt* of April 2, 1919, and reported widely in other newspapers as well.[148] In part intended as a device to publicize an upcoming Dada soirée planned by Tzara for April 9 in Zurich, the announcement was also a jibe at Huelsenbeck, who continued to complain about Baader's alleged attempts to claim the leadership of the Berlin Dada movement through his use of the appellation *Oberdada*.[149] Then, on April 2, Baader announced his resurrection; to mark that event, he began a new calendar and system for recording times and dates, one that he used consistently from April 1919 through the late 1920s and then again in the 1940s.[150] As was the case with his publication of "Die acht Weltsätze" and his interruption of the sermon in the Berlin Cathedral the previous year, these actions reveal Baader using the public sphere to disrupt traditional Christian thinking and affirm a much more universal notion of the divine. Because his actions were invested with a seriousness and an intensity that belied their absurdist character, the press responded to—and reported on—his interventions, even if it did not take them entirely seriously. As a result, Baader's provocative media interventions promoted the Berlin Dada movement at the same time as they potentially inspired the German public to rethink the role of politics and religion in everyday life. Like the happenings, they were devoted to exposing the assumptions that subtended everyday existence—the assumptions about society, identity, and behavior that ordinary Germans took for granted. And like the happenings, they were intended to promote reflection and self-examination through humor, shock, and ambiguity.

Conclusion

As suggested by the various ways in which Berlin Dada made its presence known to the German (and international) public between 1918 and 1920, actual works of art were only a small part of its overall production. This was the case, as I have already suggested, because the Dada artists were interested in promoting a reexamination of human identity at the beginning of the Weimar Republic, in which interrogating the performing body—in life, on the stage, and in the newspapers—played a central role. Through their publishing activities, performances, happenings, and media hoaxes, the Dada artists examined human nature and promoted their movement as a lifestyle and an ideology devoted to reconsidering what it meant to be human in a new revolutionary moment. The following chapters focus on the Berlin Dadaists' photomontages, assemblages, and other forms of visual art that they produced. These works, which were for the most part created during the second half of the group's official existence (i.e., in 1919 and 1920), frequently employed the cyborg as a form for imagining new modes of identity slowly emerging in German society. The Berlin Dadaists saw certain types of cyborg as logical extensions of their earlier avant-garde artistic practices; for this reason, they used this figure to retrospectively synthesize the various meanings and associations inherent in their earlier activities. In addition, the Dadaists also saw other forms of cyborg, with which they shared far less sympathy, emerging in German society from a multiplicity of different social, psychological, political, and technological forces. By representing the cyborg in various ways, they hoped to influence this figure's development, encouraging the forms that they found beneficial and attacking the other types that they believed were highly destructive. They sought, in other words, to use representation politically—and the record of their attempts continues to have relevance today.

2. Hannah Höch's *Cut with the Kitchen Knife*
Photomontage, Signification, and the Mass Media

Why can't we paint pictures today like those of Botticelli, Michelangelo, Leonardo, or Titian? Because human beings have completely changed in terms of their consciousness. This is the case not simply because we have the telephone, the airplane, the electric piano, and the escalator, but rather because these experiences have transformed our entire psychophysical condition.

—RAOUL HAUSMANN, "Présentismus" (1921)

The first stage of Walter Benjamin's critical practice aims to "carry over the principle of montage into history. That is, to assemble large-scale constructions out of the smallest and most precisely cut components. Indeed, to discover in the analysis of the small individual moment the crystal of the total event."[1] I begin, therefore, with two fragments, or "details," from Hannah Höch's photomontage *Schnitt mit dem Küchenmesser Dada durch die letzte Weimarer Bierbauchkulturepoche Deutschlands* [Cut with the Kitchen Knife Dada through the Last Weimar Beer-Belly Cultural Epoch of Germany] (1919–20). These two related images of cyborgs, as I shall show, are both wired into more-encompassing networks constituted by the photomontage as a whole as well as the work's position in its specific field of cultural production.

In the first example (Figure 2.1), Raoul Hausmann—Höch's lover and collaborator—appears in the form of a slightly hunched cyborg. The creature is composed of a frontal and cropped photographic portrait of Hausmann, wearing a monocle and yelling directly at the spectator, as well as two mass-reproduced photographs of manufactured elements, a metallic screw form that covers the top of Hausmann's head and a deep-sea diver's suit out of which his body is made. "My years with Hausmann, 1915–1922," wrote Höch more than thirty years later, "took in war, the peace settlement, revolution, hunger, and inflation. Through Hausmann I got to know Herwarth Walden's *Sturm,* the Futurists, *Die Aktion,* the Franz Jung circle (Georg Schrimpf,

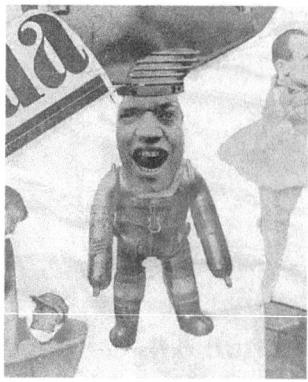

Figure 2.1. Hannah Höch, *Schnitt mit dem Küchenmesser Dada durch die letzte Weimarer Bierbauchkulturepoche Deutschlands* [Cut with the Kitchen Knife Dada through the Last Weimar Beer-Belly Cultural Epoch of Germany] (1919–20) (detail). Photomontage and collage with watercolor. 114 × 90 cm (44⅞ × 35⁷⁄₁₆ inches). Staatliche Museen zu Berlin, Nationalgalerie, Berlin. Photograph from Bildarchiv Preussischer Kulturbesitz/Art Resource, NY. Copyright 2009 Artists Rights Society (ARS), New York/VG Bild-Kunst, Bonn.

Maria Uhden, Richard Öhring), the Mynona-Segal circle, and, finally DADA."[2] And this sense that Höch had of her beer-belly cultural epoch as one that combined both trauma and possibility—a moment in which war, social revolution, economic catastrophe, and radical cultural production were intimately and inextricably bound— seems present in her cyborgian representation of her lover, the Dadasoph.

As a whole, Höch's depiction of Hausmann exudes both positive and negative associations. The hunched posture, overly long arms, cropped face, and covered and fingerless hands connote aggression and violence, and Hausmann's appearance as a whole suggests simultaneous processes of arming and dismembering that evoke the cyborgian soldiers and war cripples depicted in the paintings, photomontages, and assemblages of such Berlin Dada artists as George Grosz, John Heartfield, and (the Dresden-based) Otto Dix. Like them, Höch developed a type of imagery in this portrait that responded to and represented the existence of soldiers and cripples in German urban centers during and after the war. Yet the cyborg also projects a critical humor and energy. Hausmann's grinning and gaping mouth (emphasized by Höch's cropping of his cheeks and chin) and his slightly squinting eyes are subtle signifiers referring—both iconically and indexically—to a vital irony, a humor in the face of adversity, that Hausmann attempted to embody in his artistic practices.

Hausmann described his idea of hybrid modern identity in "The New Material in Painting," a text that he initially read at the Berlin Sezession on April 12, 1918, perhaps a year before Höch's photomontage was made. There he described the human being as "simultaneous, a monster of own and alien," that encompassed different cultures and moments of time.[3] Slightly earlier that year, in a notebook entry written in late January, he characterized the new form of humanity that he was seeking to bring about in different, but related terms:

The new man: community, the dissolution of the I, of the individual, into the force, the truth, of the We; the sublation of alien power as violent authority into the innermost personal authority as boundless responsibility: because We will exist when I am at the same time the other, [and] I, the other, am at the same time another I.[4]

And something of Hausmann's vision of human beings as provisional combinations of contradictory elements, mixtures of "I" and "we," can perhaps already be glimpsed in Höch's tiny representation of him.

We recognize Hausmann's vision of the new man—a vision influenced by Mynona (Salomo Friedlaender), Otto Gross, and Friedrich Nietzsche—in Höch's photomontage portrait of him, because the hybrid figure clearly combines "own" and "alien" elements. Hausmann's face, taken from the cover of *Der Dada* 3, sits on top of the diver's body in a "new iron diving suit" from the *Berliner Illustrirte Zeitung* [Berlin Illustrated Newspaper, or *BIZ*] of January 18, 1920, at that time Germany's most popular illustrated weekly newspaper.[5] The visage of Höch's intimately known collaborator and significant other, whose portrait in its original context evoked the Berlin Dadaists' aggressive performance practices, is thus here linked to an anonymous deep-sea diver, dressed in a suit that can go to twice the depth of previous suits, as the *BIZ* caption tells us. Thereby the head of the athletic and confident Hausmann—who despite his physical prowess was so nearsighted as to be exempted from military service—is paired with a body that seems awkward and childlike despite its ability to plumb greater depths than ever before. (In the original photograph, the diver hangs like a puppet from a cable, something that adds to its apparent clumsiness.) The figure thus conjoins intimate and external associations. It is simultaneously lover and stranger, performer and explorer, living flesh and obdurate metal. Furthermore, the same play between own and alien, intimacy and anonymity, operates on a formal level as well. On the one hand, the image is uniquely Höch's. She created the bizarre and evocative figure by selecting appropriately sized components, cutting them out of their original contexts, and gluing them together to communicate an original and idiosyncratic vision of what it means to be human. On the other hand, the image's various components are not directly connected to Höch in the ways that artistic elements have traditionally been joined with their creators. She did not create them (i.e., sketch, paint, or even photograph them) but simply appropriated them.[6] Thus, as a whole, the portrait of Hausmann combines Höch's unique vision of him as well as (a small amount of) her particular handwork with mere mass-produced and anonymous imagery. Through both subject matter and form, it suggests that human identity is a product of the interaction between subjective and objective elements, aspects of the personality both private and unique as well as general or intersubjective.

In the second image (Figure 2.2), which includes the first (Figure 2.1), Höch represents one of her (and Hausmann's) "enemies" or "opposites," the deposed German kaiser, Wilhelm II of Prussia. Like Hausmann, the former German monarch appears as a cyborg, a figure that is constituted by an even more heterogeneous constellation of fragments. The kaiser's head and body are composed of a black-and-white photomechanical reproduction of a painted portrait of the monarch overlaid with a montage of machined elements including—as one's eye moves down Wilhelm's trunk—a wheel with metal spokes and a rubber tire, a ship's motor, and the motor's screw-tipped metal housing (which, in turn, terminates toward the top of Hausmann's head, bisecting his

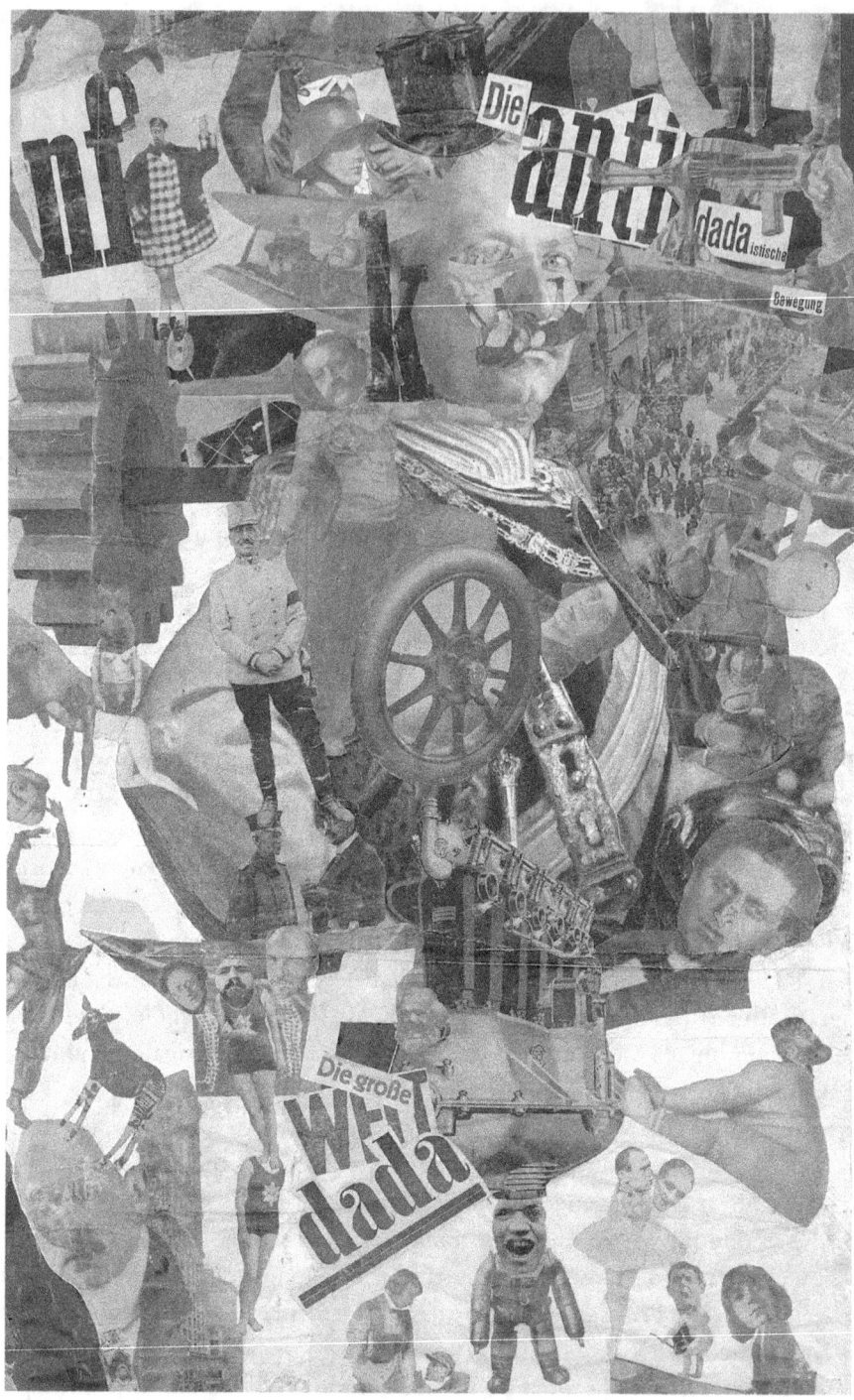

Figure 2.2. Hannah Höch, *Schnitt mit dem Küchenmesser Dada durch die letzte Weimarer Bierbauchkulturepoche Deutschlands* [Cut with the Kitchen Knife Dada through the Last Weimar Beer-Belly Cultural Epoch of Germany] (1919–20) (detail). Photograph from Bildarchiv Preussischer Kulturbesitz/Art Resource, NY. Copyright 2009 Artists Rights Society (ARS), New York/VG Bild-Kunst, Bonn.

forehead slightly above his eyebrows). A montage of two inverted wrestlers wearing leotards replaces the kaiser's trademark mustache, and an image of a newborn baby in a tray is superimposed on his right eye. An undersized, black top hat, set at a jaunty angle, crowns the kaiser's head, an allusion, perhaps, to his recent lost status as emperor of the German Empire and king of Prussia and new identity as an upper-class German *Bürger* in exile in the Netherlands. (Although he did not eschew wearing civilian headgear during his tenure as German monarch, Wilhelm's preferred form of head adornment— at least in the bellicose years leading up to his abdication—appears to have been the Prussian *Pickelhaube,* the spiked helmet characteristic of the German military after 1842, which was discontinued for its lack of protective qualities during World War I.)

Because of the mismatches between its various photomontage fragments, the kaiser's body appears monstrous—truncated or deformed at the waist or the hips. The royal cyborg also sprouts multiple appendages in the form of other figures and heads, including, dangling below the kaiser's groin, Hausmann, the cyborg on which the whole "anti-Dada" kaiser edifice perhaps rests. Further accentuating the cyborg's inhuman nature, other appendages include important conservative government and military figures as well as left-wing thinkers and artists.[7] Dr. Wolfgang Kapp, who unsuccessfully attempted to overthrow the Social Democratic Party (SPD) government in March 1920 and subsequently fled to Sweden, sits in an airplane that emerges from the kaiser's right ear. Field Marshal Paul von Hindenburg is attached to the front of the kaiser's right shoulder, his head montaged onto the body of a popular female dancer, Sent M'ahesa, in a harem outfit. Hindenburg's right arm touches the left shoulder of the Austro-Hungarian General Karl von Pflanzer-Baltin, another hero of the monarchy, whose body partially occludes Wilhelm II's right arm. Von Pflanzer-Baltin's feet rest on the heads of Ulrich Graf von Brockdorff-Rantzau, the so-called Red Count and SPD foreign minister in 1919, and Gustav Noske, the SPD's infamous minister of defense from 1919 to 1920 (and former master butcher), who was best known for employing right-wing paramilitary troops to suppress communist and left-wing uprisings throughout Germany in early 1919. These two figures appear to emerge out of the top of the kaiser's forearm. Below them, the heads of the Bolshevik Karl Radek, Johannes Baader, and Vladimir Ilyich Ulyanov Lenin, the Bolshevik leader and first head of the Soviet Union, appear like parts of a large decorative cuff. The bodies of female acrobats in checkered suits hang below the heads of Radek and Lenin and suggest further ornamentation, while the bodies of two female gymnasts dangle below Baader's head, suggesting elongated fingers emerging from beneath the kaiser's cuff. To the left of a large wheel, which projects from the kaiser's chest like an oversized nipple, the head and upper body of Else Lasker-Schüler, the expressionist poet with whom the Dada artists were friendly, grows from the deposed monarch's sternum, like a cancer or a decorative medal. Below and to the right of Lasker-Schüler, the kaiser's left hand cups the head of Max Reinhardt. The famed theater director, who collaborated with the Dadaists on the cabaret *Schall und Rauch,* seems to grow out of the kaiser's stomach. (In official portraits, the kaiser often kept his left arm slightly crooked to conceal the

fact that it was withered as the result of a birth defect. Because of this history, Reinhardt's head perhaps takes on some of the associations of the kaiser's characteristic white
gloves or sword, objects that he would sometimes hold in his left hand to mask his
infirmity.) Finally, Marx's head protrudes from Wilhelm's lower back, like another
strange growth that is possibly disturbing its host. The kaiser, as Höch represents him,
is thus both individual and collective, a radically hybrid human–machine organism
composed of contradictory and mismatched elements. Not only does the deposed
monarch incorporate different genders and different class positions (as suggested by
his inclusion of counts as well as communists, generals as well as "lowly" Dadaists),
but, as suggested by the harem costume worn by his Hindenburg appendage, he possibly incorporates different racial types as well (a type of montage juxtaposition that
became more and more ubiquitous in Höch's work as the decade developed).

Like the cyborgian image of Hausmann, the Wilhelm II cyborg connotes both
violence and energy, trauma and regeneration. A number of his appendages seem only
loosely attached to his body, and he appears to be frozen in a process in which he is
either incorporating or expelling heterogeneous parts. In addition, although the cyborg
looks monstrous and deformed, his upright and regal posture suggests both power
and control—something also emphasized by his technological enhancements. Moreover, as implied by the technological interface between the kaiser and Hausmann, the
cyborg appears as a figure through which Höch—anticipating a conceptual opposition that would intensely occupy the conservative legal theorist Carl Schmitt during
the second half of the Weimar Republic—could reimagine the relationship between
friend and enemy in a new and more densely connected way.[8] Although it is unclear
whether Hausmann is dreaming up the kaiser or the kaiser is excreting Hausmann,
they are scarcely separate beings anymore.

Cyborgian Subjects

Despite the fact that artists and other cultural producers during the Weimar Republic
posed questions about the nature of human identity in the context of modern industrial
societies, the hybrid and interconnected nature of modern existence—a phenomenon
that the concept of the cyborg would later be used to identify and analyze—was difficult to speak or write about. Instead, in the context of Germany between the wars, it
could largely only be shown. However, as suggested by the first two examples analyzed
in this chapter, the antithetical yet interrelated cyborg constellations excised from Höch's
Cut with the Kitchen Knife, the Weimar cyborg—at least as it appears in Dada art—
exhibits numerous correspondences with post–World War II concepts of the cyborg.
Already by 1920, in other words, more than forty years before the term's invention,
the cyborg appears as a figure of hybrid modern identity that undermines clear divisions between gender and class while interrelating the individual with the collective,
friends with enemies, and trauma with regeneration.

By analyzing the cyborgs in such photomontages as Höch's *Cut with the Kitchen*

Knife—by paying attention, in other words, not only to how the cyborgs are represented but also to the interrelationships that appear between them, and how they are shown to interact with their environments—we can better understand several issues now associated with Berlin Dada art. They include the innovative nature of the Berlin Dadaists' montage-based strategies of signification; Berlin Dada's relationship to the rise of the mass media in Germany after World War I; and, finally, the group's links to new discourses about transforming human perception in the modern world. These issues, I will show, help to explain why the Berlin Dadaists were so drawn to the image of the cyborg.

When taken as a (somewhat loosely organized) whole (Figure 2.3), Höch's *Cut with the Kitchen Knife* suggests that its creator saw the cyborg as fundamentally interconnected with a rapidly transforming technology-driven society. Broadly speaking, the large photomontage presents a turbulent image of Germany's postwar revolutionary moment of 1918 and 1919. It was mostly constructed from mechanically reproduced photographic fragments that Höch clipped from the *BIZ,* which appeared once a week on Thursdays, and which had the largest circulation of any illustrated weekly newspaper in Germany. Published by Ullstein Verlag, the same publisher for whom Höch worked—primarily on women's magazines—between 1916 and 1926, the *BIZ* was for Höch an illustrated record of her moment, which she drew on time and time again.[9] Against what must originally have been a white background of undefined space (now both wrinkled and browning), Höch pasted an array of photomechanically reproduced fragments that suggested Germany's wartime and immediate postwar history.

These monochromatic reproductions, with primarily sepia and olive-green coloration, consist of five main types of image. Most prominent are the figures of cyborgs: sutured-together images of Wilhelmine and Weimar personalities, including government, military, and political leaders; artists and writers; dancers and actresses; and scientists. These collaged, hybrid, and (sometimes) hermaphrodite figures represent recognizable individuals while suggesting—through their fragmented and recombined structures—a radical transformation of these modern individuals through war, revolution, and technological development. And although the photomontage contains more male cyborgs than female ones, numerous cyborgian women are also represented, thus suggesting that neither gender was immune to technological change.

Also prominent are images of metropolitan buildings and crowds, drawn primarily from New York and Berlin, which evoke the urban contexts—the sites of interface—within which Höch's revolutionary-period cyborgs exist. As suggested by the main crowd scenes—the first, in the photomontage's bottom left corner, which juxtaposes images of demonstrating masses, delegates in the Weimar National Assembly, and bourgeois concertgoers with public architecture taken from Wall Street and royal Berlin (the Berlin City Palace), and the second, in the top right, which presents a mass of jobless proletariats waiting for work in front of a Berlin unemployment office—German society was strongly stratified in the early postwar years. At the same time, because of the jumbled and intermixed character of the various crowd and architecture fragments,

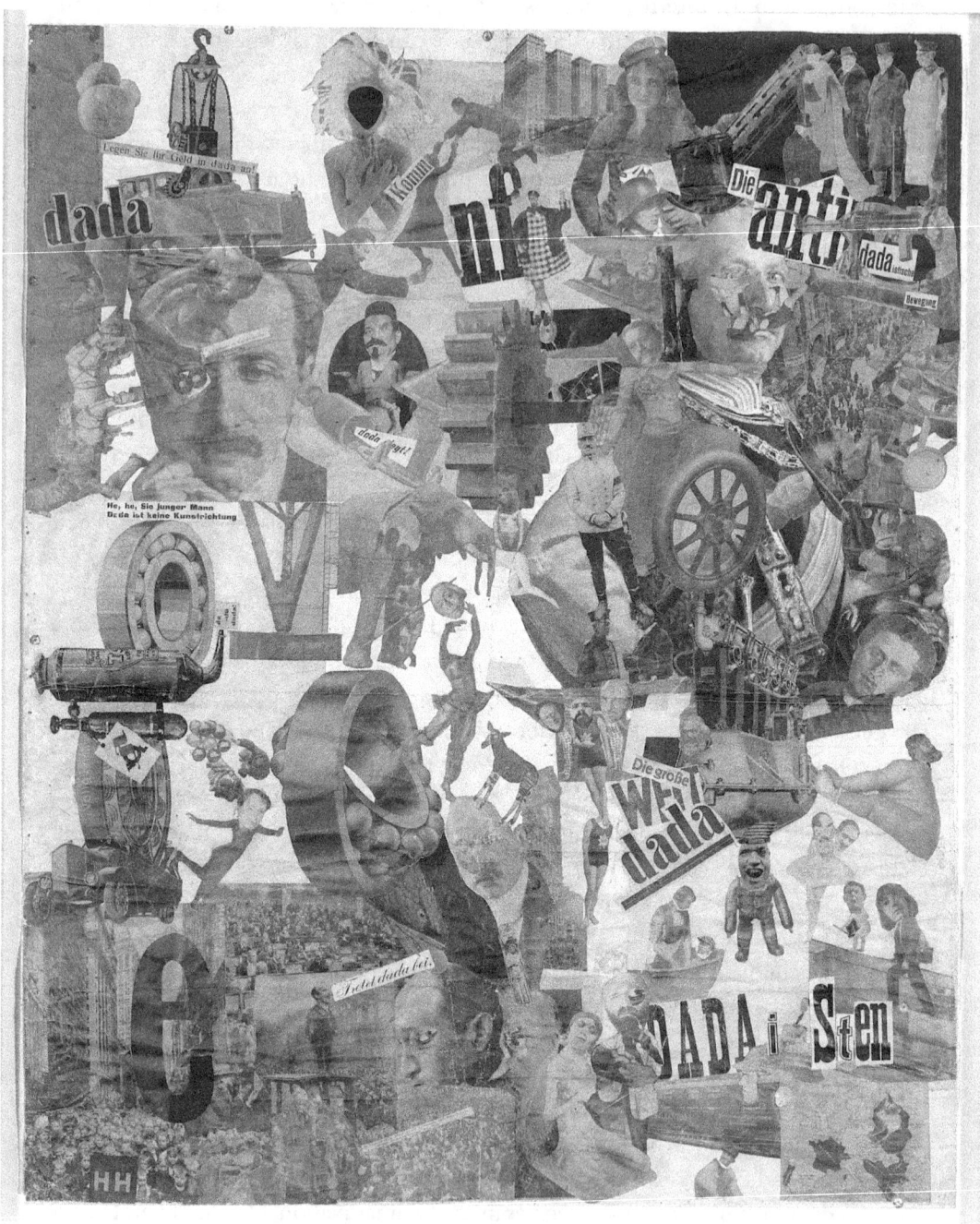

Figure 2.3. Hannah Höch, *Schnitt mit dem Küchenmesser Dada durch die letzte Weimarer Bierbauchkulturepoche Deutschlands* [Cut with the Kitchen Knife Dada through the Last Weimar Beer-Belly Cultural Epoch of Germany] (1919–20). Photograph from Bildarchiv Preussischer Kulturbesitz/Art Resource, NY. Copyright 2009 Artists Rights Society (ARS), New York/VG Bild-Kunst, Bonn.

the photomontage suggests that the new society is also a place where different classes interact. The Weimar Republic, Höch's photomontage implies, is a site of class struggle and conflict.

Although fewer in number, images of technology are also prominent—primarily because of their larger size and occasional greater separation from the other montage clusters. Here, images of turning and locomotion predominate. Five great gears or tires dominate the photomontage's middle and extend to its left side. The wheel motif, with its associations of turning, evokes the November Revolution and the resulting social and political transformation of German society.[10] In addition, it also connects Höch's photomontages to Kurt Schwitters's collage paintings, which used circular motifs to evoke similar associations of technology, movement, inversion, and social revolution.[11] Furthermore, the central foreshortened gear is connected by a dark axle to the kaiser's back, thereby suggesting that he is some sort of monstrous windup puppet. Closely related to the pictures of wheels and gears, images of such vehicles as trucks, trains, ships, and planes also appear. Evoking the early stages of a rapidly globalizing society, they connote travel, speed, and the early-twentieth-century conquest of space and time. In addition, these depictions bring to mind flying and road races, modern activities that had recently captured the public imagination and achieved significant representation in the press and in mass culture in general.[12]

Individual letters, words, and the occasional full sentence also appear throughout the picture field. Among the more legible are "Hey, hey, you, young man, Dada is not a direction in art," "Invest in Dada," "Dada," "Dada triumphs," "come," "nf," "k," "The anti-Dada movement," "The great world Dada," "Dadaists," and "Join Dada." These textual fragments, primarily taken from Dada publications, evoke the practices of sound poetry and the Dada artists' parodic advertising campaigns and media stunts. In addition, other texts, printed on the objects depicted within the montaged image fragments, suggest the realm of brand names and trademarks, additional forms of information that circulate within Höch's rapidly changing world. A few of these texts also orient the viewer by labeling different groups that inhabit the confusing picture space.

Finally, representations of animals, babies, and "primitive" people also appear. These stereotypical signs for concepts such as "nature," "origin," and "innocence" have their meanings inverted by Höch's hybridizing montage juxtapositions. Because of their proximity to images of technology and urban spaces, the natural signs come to suggest the interpenetration of nature and culture through an expanding set of increasingly powerful technologies. As a result, they evoke the debates about science and technology's impact on nature and traditional modes of life that agitated German society since the late nineteenth century.[13]

The turbulent, crisis-prone character of *Cut with the Kitchen Knife*'s subject matter is further emphasized by its formal structure. The photomontage is divided by a diagonal axis that partially runs along the bottom of the kaiser's right arm. This axis moves downward, through the machinery that constitutes the back of his torso, and along a baby's backside, then upward, along an elephant's head, until it seems to exhaust itself in the left ear of a cyborgian portrait of Albert Einstein. Above and to the right of this diagonal axis "the anti-Dada movement" appears, identified as such by Höch's appropriated texts, the Wilhelm II cyborg, and various other political and military figures, including Wilhelm of Prussia, the crown prince, dressed in an oversized checkered dress, and two representations of Friedrich Ebert. Emerging in profile from the side of Einstein's head, the first Ebert strikes a classic speaker's pose with his right arm extended in front of him as if he were exhorting a crowd. The second Ebert consists of his head montaged onto a female gymnastic artist's body. The figure is positioned to the right of Einstein's head and to the left of the central gear that seems to wind up the kaiser's body. Below this axis, the Berlin Dada artists—Hausmann, Baader, Richard Huelsenbeck, Grosz, Wieland Herzfelde, Heartfield, Walter Mehring, and Höch—appear in various hybrid forms. Grouped mainly on the bottom right, their coalition extends through Einstein on the upper left, who is identified with Dada through the various bits of text that surround him. Below and to the left of the Dada artists, the Weimar Republic's stratified social world is represented through the images of crowds and architecture. The photomontage's overall diagonal articulation—as well as its compartmentalization or clustering of figures into semidistinct groups—connotes both dynamism and struggle. Prompted by the overall compositional structure, one can envision two competing strata in German society, with the Dada artists inhabiting a more open "buffer zone" between these two groups—a position that seems to find support in Hausmann's contention from 1918 that, "besides exact photography, Dada is the only valid pictorial means of communication and equilibrium in collective experience."[14] As the composition suggests, the Dada artists at times envisioned themselves as mediators between different extremes, and this idea of mediation—of possessing the ability to translate between opposites and perhaps also to translate opposites into one another—is, as Donna Haraway reminds us, also central to the concept of the cyborg.

The fragments that make up *Cut with the Kitchen Knife* are also juxtaposed in a way that emphasizes their heterogeneity. Not only does Höch allow gaps or white spaces to show between many of the montage elements, but she also cuts them together with a disregard for exact matches in scale and perspective. To further emphasize the heterogeneous and conflict-permeated nature of her world, Höch has also sometimes accentuated the edges of her fragments with paint to make them appear even more separate. Höch thus represents her world as one of omnipresent crisis and conflict that has no overarching script or master narrative—a place where the old formulas for structuring experience no longer seem to apply. "Even before the war ended in 1918," Höch wrote in 1958, "Berlin's young people had become politically rebellious and were searching for new intellectual orientation. . . . Dada here was probably above all else a kind of negative eulogy for a form of government and life whose time and past and world view had gone up in flames."[15] And this sense of conflagration and the decisive but incomplete destruction of the previous social and conceptual orders are mirrored in her technique's violent and disjunctive forms.

As Höch's photomontage begins to suggest through both its form and its subject matter, the cyborg became a central figure in Weimar visual culture precisely because this period constituted a moment of modernity in which competing concepts of the self and society clashed in German society. Höch attempted to emphasize the conflict-ridden character of her contemporary moment through her title: "Cut with the Kitchen Knife Dada through the Last Weimar Beer-Belly Cultural Epoch of Germany." By mixing past and present in her title, Höch suggests that the old and the new live in unresolved competition. Indeed, numerous traces of the war and the deposed Wilhelmine regime remain in Höch's representation of the early years of the Weimar Republic. The steel-helmeted soldier's head, the machine gun, the airplane, and the military leaders that surround the kaiser all suggest the previous four years of fighting, and the mismatches between the heads and the figures of Höch's hybrids evoke the transformations of the human body under the conditions of mechanized warfare during World War I. In addition, the kaiser's large figure suggests the lingering presence of the German monarchy in the postmonarchal world. Despite the destruction of the old order, its loss of hegemony, the ghosts of the past are curiously alive and vital in Höch's representation. Although these specters are not portrayed as dominant figures, they do appear to be vigorous participants in the contemporary spectacle.

Because the question of what constituted the new German citizen was posed at this moment in such a forceful yet undecided way, it is perhaps not surprising that the image of the cyborg would thus emerge as it did. As Höch's photomontage implies, the figure embodied a sense of modernity that appealed to actors on all sides of the political landscape. Although it was popular with the (communist and anarchist) Dada artists who welcomed modernization, it also addressed antimodernists of all political stripes in that its freakish or uncanny qualities evoked that which they most feared. Even the most ardent traditionalists and cultural conservatives believed that they were being changed by the modern world; the figure of the cyborg, which could equally suggest both willing and unwilling mechanization, might thus also become a point of identification for the detractors of modernization. Although I am here tracing the cyborg's articulation in the work of a left-wing artist, it is significant that Höch, already at this early moment in the Weimar cyborg's history, represents the figure as appearing on all sides of the social and political spectrum.

Photomontage and Signification

As Jula Dech notes, "Every beholder can see a different picture in Hannah Höch's *Cut with the Kitchen Knife*" (Figure 2.3).[16] Maud Lavin, for example, interprets *Cut with the Kitchen Knife* as "a Dadaist manifesto on the politics of Weimar society," one that "assigns women a catalytic role in the opposition between a revolutionary Dada world associated with Karl Marx and the anti-Dada world of the politically compromised President Friedrich Ebert."[17] For Lavin, the various images of new women in the photomontage, its different and specific representations of female dancers, film stars, and artists, signify "female pleasure" and "liberation" and function as "utopian elements" that dissolve the Weimar Republic's traditional hierarchies.[18] Because of the fragmentation of its source images, however, as well as certain rather sinister juxtapositions, *Cut with the Kitchen Knife* also signifies violence.[19] Thus, as a whole, *Cut with the Kitchen Knife*—like Höch's other Weimar photomontages—focuses largely on the new woman to create a dialectic between "anger and pleasure and, for the [female] viewer, an oscillation between ironic distance and intimate identification."[20]

Central to Lavin's reading of Höch's photomontage is the pairing of the leaping body of the dancer Niddy Impekoven, her hands extended above her, with the head of Käthe Kollwitz, the left-wing artist and political activist, who, at the age of fifty-two, had just become the first female professor at the Prussian Academy of Arts, at that time one of the most important art schools in Germany (Figure 2.4).[21] For Lavin, this pairing, in an open area of space slightly below and to the left of the photomontage's center, suggests an ironic tribute to both figures—the older expressionist artist and the fragile, childlike dancer, whose lithe, androgynous body was quickly becoming a new ideal of feminine beauty.[22] By linking the young dancer, with her associations of female corporeal pleasure, to the mature artist, who had broken the gender barrier that kept female professors out of the German art academy, this hybrid figure suggests the revolutionary power of women's actions in the new republic. In addition, however, the pairing, which leaves Kollwitz's head clearly separated from Impekoven's body, also evokes anger and violence. Because of this separation, the hybrid figure can be read as a critique of Weimar German society, which, the figure implies, continues to separate a woman's mind from her body, emphasizing the latter at the expense of the former.

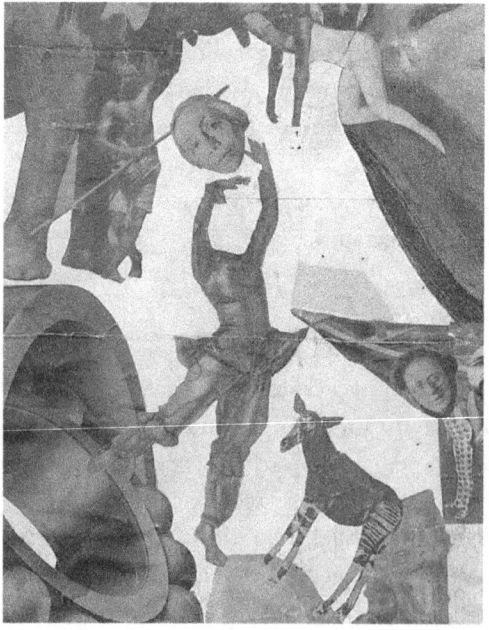

Figure 2.4. Hannah Höch, *Schnitt mit dem Küchenmesser Dada durch die letzte Weimarer Bierbauchkulturepoche Deutschlands* [Cut with the Kitchen Knife Dada through the Last Weimar Beer-Belly Cultural Epoch of Germany] (1919–20) (detail). Photograph from Bildarchiv Preussischer Kulturbesitz/Art Resource, NY. Copyright 2009 Artists Rights Society (ARS), New York/VG Bild-Kunst, Bonn.

For Hanne Bergius, on the other hand, *Cut with the Kitchen Knife* is not specifically focused on the new woman. Rather, its themes are more general: human hybridity,[23] the transformation of social bonds through the mass media,[24] and the metamorphosis of the physical world into a shifting play of forces[25]—all subjects, one might add, that have been associated with the cyborg, despite the fact that Bergius never uses the term. Although Bergius emphasizes that there is no dominant fragment or "initial image" in the photomontage, and that the "viewer's first impression is that of an unconnected mass of numerous images and quotations," her eye quickly fixes on the "striking" head of the young Einstein in the photomontage's top left quadrant.[26] For the Dadaists, Bergius argues, Einstein's theory of relativity, which dissolved matter into a sequence of events, was a primary point of reference for the photomontage's overall structure as a vast and complex "simultaneous montage," a constellation of photomechanically reproduced photographic fragments that represent the physical world as a dynamic play of forces. Characteristic of the simultaneous montage of *Cut with the Kitchen Knife* are the various disproportions or mismatches in size and viewing angle between the different photomontage fragments. As a result of these mismatches and the overall nonhierarchical composition, every person and object represented seems "to be the function of another thing," the relation between things becomes "a fundamental component of their existence," and reality becomes "a relative, energetic quantity of many possibilities."[27] Not only does the play between empty spaces and clusters of photomontage elements create a sense that the composition might fluctuate or move, but natural and mechanical motions are shown to intermingle, and traumatic experience is suggested.[28]

Interestingly, for Bergius, Höch's representations of new women in *Cut with the Kitchen Knife* are largely critical. Noting a key fragment that Lavin cites very positively—namely, a map of Europe in the photomontage's lower-right corner that delineates the countries in Europe where women had gained the right to vote—Bergius argues that the map instead signifies Höch's sense of "the contradictions between women's newly won right to vote, their politicization during the war, and the fact that they afterwards faded back into privacy during demobilization."[29] Instead of representing female liberation, the photomontage emphasizes the fact that women's "real integration into the work process failed to come."[30] Nor, for Bergius, is the new woman the dominant focus of the photomontage. In contrast to Lavin, Bergius holds that the work's central theme is the transformation of both people and the world into a play of forces that constantly reconfigures itself, a new state of being that the photomontage suggests is intimately bound up with the development of the mass media and which is reflected by the work's formal structure as a simultaneous montage.[31]

As suggested by these two interpretations of *Cut with the Kitchen Knife,* the early Berlin Dada photomontages had multiple meanings that fluctuated depending on which clusters of fragments the viewer engaged. Works like *Cut with the Kitchen Knife* are so filled with different recognizable objects, and the groupings permit so many divergent configurations, that they cannot but support a multiplicity of distinct, sometimes conflicting readings. Furthermore, because they are so obviously edited and reassembled, they impel their viewers to go beyond merely identifying and cataloging fragments to constructing overall interpretations that spell out the creator's possible "take" on his or her various subjects. Thus *Cut with the Kitchen Knife* simultaneously signifies the November Revolution, the revolutionary and repressive potentials of the new woman, the hybridization of human beings under the conditions of mass-reproduction, the capabilities of the mass media to both dissolve and reconstruct social reality, the trauma of World War I, and the new understanding of nature brought about by Einstein's theory of relativity. In addition, it is also "about" the various other interpretations that can be generated by linking different photomontage fragments in the image together. Because their component parts are so numerous and their compositions are without a main focus, the Berlin Dadaists' early photomontages necessitate constructing multiple interpretations and rejecting any sense of totality or the end of interpretation. Their all-over, nonhierarchical compositions empowered their original viewers to identify the elements that mattered the most to them, and by bringing them together, to reimagine their contemporary world.

Both the richness of and the disparities between the different interpretations supported by *Cut with the Kitchen Knife* also suggest quite strongly that Höch consciously composed her photomontage to create ambiguity and encourage multiple readings. By drawing the spectator's attention to the artificial and constructed nature of *Cut with the Kitchen Knife,* Höch underscored the perspectival nature of her representation—the fact that it represented one particular viewpoint in a potentially much larger discursive field—thereby inviting dialogue. Other artists, Höch's photomontage suggests, could have used the same source materials to create radically different perspectives on the same people and events; for this reason, the viewer should not uncritically accept Höch's representation but analyze its various implications. Finally, the multiple and conflicting combinations of text and image that characterize Höch's strategy of composition destabilize the everyday and instrumental meanings of the worldly objects that *Cut with the Kitchen Knife* contains. After viewing Höch's photomontage, we perhaps see everyday objects in a different light. In these diverse ways, Höch's photomontage helps promote a "negative dialectics" between its photomontage fragments: a nonhierarchical relationship between elements that actively undermines any single reading or overarching interpretation.

As Adorno later defined it in relation to philosophy, negative dialectics is a method of associating concepts and the particulars that fall under them to show that the conceptual order does not exhaust the natures it subsumes. According to Adorno,

> The matters of true philosophical interest at this point in history are those in which Hegel, agreeing with tradition, expressed his disinterest. They are nonconceptuality, individuality, and particularity—things which ever since Plato used to be dismissed as transitory and insignificant. . . . A matter of urgency to the concept would be what it fails to cover, what its abstractionist mechanism eliminates, what is not already a case of the concept.[32]

As it functions visually in Höch's photomontage, negative dialectics results from juxtaposing photographic and textual fragments to produce ambiguity and, very importantly, to prevent reducing reality to the level of either photographic or written representation. By creating contradictory chains of metaphoric association to prevent the discovery of a single dominant reading, Höch's photomontage juxtapositions not only produce divergent interpretations but also preserve nature's difference from both photography and language. In other words, because the photographic and textual elements do not mesh seamlessly or constitute well-known concepts or objects, it is difficult for the photomontage's various spectators to think the combinations of fragments apart from the conflicting particulars they represent. In this way, the ambiguity and multivalence of reality is retained—a sense of the world as exceeding the various definitions that human beings bring to it.

A comparison to other photomontage strategies can make this point clearer. Although created somewhat earlier, the cabinet card advertisement for *Chrl. Tichy, Anotomisches Wunder* [Chrl. Tichy, Anatomical Wonder], probably from the 1880s or 1890s (Figure 2.5), presents a good example of the (more direct and clear) commercial photomontage strategy used since the second half of the nineteenth century. In this sepia-toned albumen print mounted on heavy cardstock, sixteen separate images of the subject, a professional contortionist, are presented in a stable, symmetrical, and vaguely pyramidal composition. A bust-length portrait of Tichy in a suit and tie appears in the lower center of the image, surrounded by fifteen shots of the costumed performer in action against a painted backdrop. While the central portrait suggests Tichy's normalcy and—through his costume and dignified bearing—intimates a proper bourgeois standing, the surrounding images, which depict him in a series of mostly frontal and side poses all shot from the same vantage point, reveal his unique talents. Blocks of text serve as titles and captions, thus helping explain or interpret the composite photograph. Tichy's name and profession appear in the center just above his portrait, and three additional rectangles of text, presenting two captions, are added toward the photograph's peripheries. The first reads "medical abnormality" and suggests the rareness or uniqueness of Tichy's act; the second states "doctor examined," which helps reassure the viewer that Tichy's strange contortions are not dangerous (and thus that it is not immoral to watch his act).

Designed to function as both an advertisement and a souvenir photograph for a circus or variety act, the cabinet card differs from Höch's photomontage in several important ways. First, the various images out of which *Chrl. Tichy, Anotomisches Wunder* is composed are all the same size and shape: they have not been cut up or fragmented in any way, and they are all of roughly the same type (i.e., they are all full-figure portraits). Unlike *Cut with the Kitchen Knife,* the Tichy cabinet card does not divide or break up its subject, represent him as a hybrid figure by adding additional photomontage elements to his face or body, or cut together incongruous photographic material. In addition, the photographic elements are symmetrically arranged. They do not suggest an unstable and potentially shifting image field, as is the case with Höch's

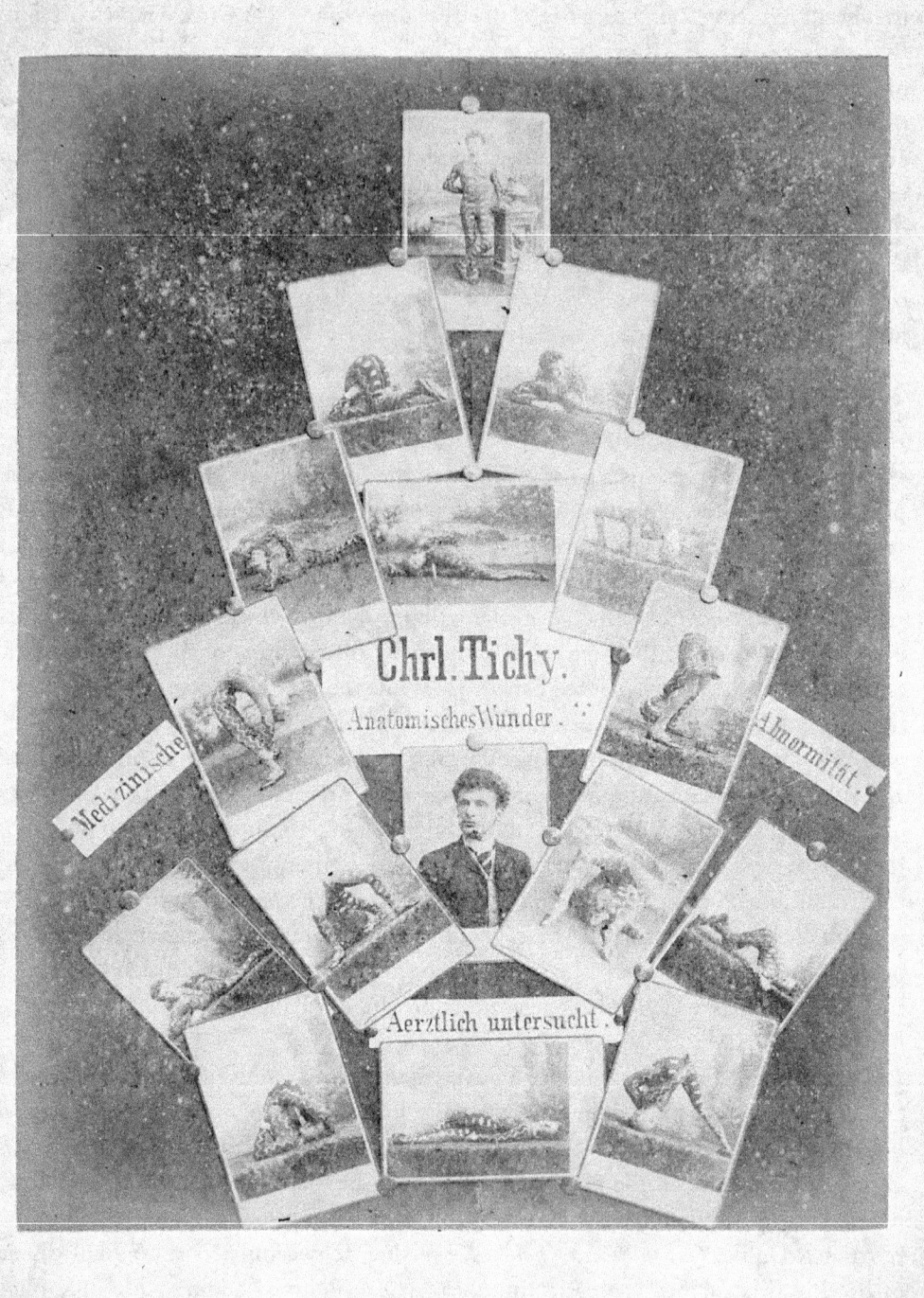

Figure 2.5. *Chrl. Tichy, Anotomisches Wunder* [Chrl. Tichy, Anatomical Wonder] (ca. 1880–1900). Cabinet card (albumen print). Photographer unknown. Private collection.

representation. Second, the text in the Tichy card explains the photographic material and supports a fairly clear message as to the performer's identity and the nature of his act. A discernable difference in typeface distinguishes the title—the performer's name— from the various captions, which list his attributes. These characteristics stand in clear contrast to the use of text in *Cut with the Kitchen Knife*, where the partial sentences, words, and letters are ambiguous and multiply interpretations. Third, the Tichy card is seamless. Instead of emphasizing its cuts, which is the case with Höch's photomontage, the mode of construction characteristic of the Tichy card covers over the disruptive aspects of its montage structure. Rather than paste together separate images, the creator of the Tichy photograph simply rephotographed a collection of existing photographs that had been affixed to an undifferentiated background (the tacks can still be seen throughout the image). And because it was produced through a less-disturbing strategy of photomontage construction, the Tichy image calls much less attention to its mode of making.

Downplaying the self-reflexivity of its photomontage medium, the Tichy card strives for strong impact and clear communication. The juxtapositions of photographic elements, though striking, do not call into question the nature of the subject that they represent, and the text, likewise, bolsters Tichy's identity instead of undermining it. Rather than challenge the spectator's assumption that his or her everyday understandings of "the human body," "contortionists," "variety acts," "medical abnormalities," and "doctor examined" can adequately comprehend and categorize the images and texts combined in the composite representation, the cabinet card instead confirms and mobilizes these everyday concepts to incite a desire to consume what is represented (by, in this case, either patronizing Tichy's act, reliving the experience through the memory, or buying the card and experiencing his act in a mediated fashion through a photographic representation). Obeying the fundamental principles of effective advertising, *Chrl. Tichy, Anotomisches Wunder* helps stabilize an existing conceptual horizon to derive profit from it—a strategy that Höch's photomontage clearly eschews. As the Tichy card thus reminds us, although Höch's photomontage technique was influenced by print advertising, it remained fundamentally at odds with its overall strategies and goals.

Rosalind Krauss's distinction between Dada photomontage and surrealist photography helps further clarify Höch's negatively dialectical compositional strategies. For Krauss, the fundamental difference between Dada photomontages such as *Cut with the Kitchen Knife* and surrealist photographs such as those created by Man Ray, Hans Bellmer, André Kertész, and Jacques-André Boiffard among others has to do with how each group respectively mobilized the indexical aspects of their photographic source material, that is, the photograph's causal connection to that which it represents or, to put it another way, its nature as an imprint taken from the real, like a fingerprint, a footprint, or a water ring left by a cold glass on a table.[33] The obvious cuts and jarring juxtapositions of the Dadaist photomontages, on the one hand, robbed their photographic sources of their compelling reality or presence, and demonstrate the Dadaist strategy of employing photographs like parts of language to construct obviously artificial (and readable) interpretations of reality. By thus injecting writing into reality through photomontage, the Dadaists revealed, to use Sergei Tretyakov's terms, not the simple social facts depicted in the photographs but the social tendencies expressed by those facts. The surrealists, on the other hand, tended to eschew photomontage, preferring instead other photographic manipulations such as radical cropping, the staging of people and objects, negative printing, multiple exposure, mirror manipulations, solarization (the inversion of photographic values through light exposure during processing), photograms (the contact printing of objects on photographic paper to create abstract and semi-abstract images), and *brûlage* (the burning of the photographic emulsion). They did this to preserve the presence of their photographic representations and thereby to employ the indexical power of photographs to present reality as a shifting representation or written sign.[34] In other words, instead of constructing an obviously artificial interpretation of reality (which argued for a particular truth) as did the Dadaists, the surrealists attempted to represent the world as permeated by the same shifting play of presence and absence that characterized the experience of the meaning of written language. Surrealist photographs, as Krauss puts it, "are not *interpretations* of reality, decoding it, as in Heartfield's photomontages. They are presentations of that very reality as configured, or coded, or written," and thus "what unites *all* surrealist production is precisely this experience of nature as representation, physical matter as writing."[35]

As suggested by Krauss's distinction, photomontages such as *Cut with the Kitchen Knife* employed montage to construct obviously artificial interpretations of the world. The Dadaists were less concerned than the surrealists with using photography to evoke an actual experience of the uncanniness of reality (which was accomplished by altering photographs while preserving a strong sense of their indexical character) and more concerned with using photography to produce a legible statement about the multiple and changing nature of the real. In short, Dadaist photomontage, in Krauss's view, was more didactic than poetic. Although Krauss's distinction between Dadaist photomontage and surrealist photography is important, it misses, I think, certain central characteristics of Dadaist practice. In the first place, Krauss does not distinguish between different forms of Dadaist photomontage—the early all-over form, for example, from the later, more hierarchical and focused compositional strategy or, for that matter, both these forms from the much clearer and more propagandistic strategy Heartfield used after 1920 (a strategy that still distinguished itself from contemporaneous advertising through its greater irony and ambiguity). In addition, Krauss's theorization does not examine the type of message that the Dadaists were attempting to communicate. For the most part, their strategies of photomontage juxtaposition were radically ambiguous and thus, in distinction to Heartfield's later photomontage work, not always (or even generally) politically didactic. In addition, as I have already shown, they did not so much eliminate the photograph's indexical character as de-emphasize it to play the photograph's indexical aspects off its iconic and symbolic characteristics, a dialectic designed to provoke viewers to compare the world as the mass media depicted it to both the realities they experienced in their lives and the possibilities they could imagine. The Dadaists, in other words, did not get rid of the photograph's indexical qualities so much as integrate them into a dialectic with both reality and human imagination. And the reason that they did this was because of their interest in depicting their contemporary moment and their focus on the burgeoning mass media.

The Weimar Republic

As numerous historians have argued, the Weimar Republic, although lasting only fourteen years, is a tremendously difficult period to describe or evaluate.[36] Beginning with Germany's defeat at the end of World War I and the abdication of the German kaiser, the Weimar Republic remained a compromise solution for most Germans throughout its existence, a much-maligned social, political, and economic settlement between ideologically opposed parties of the left, right, and center. Initially, it held tremendous promise. Germans developed their first dual-system parliamentary democracy as well as a surprisingly farsighted constitution that defined the basic rights and obligations of a modern and democratic welfare state. Women achieved the right to vote, a few advances were made in the material conditions of the working class, and while the modernization of both society and industry was allowed to proceed, some of its worst consequences were avoided or at least mitigated. In addition, progressive ideas about gender, sexuality, education, and race gained some influence in the public sphere, and there was a genuine flourishing of both "high" and "mass" culture.

But these years were also a time of great instability and dislocation. Periodic economic crises resulted from substantial foreign debt, runaway hyperinflation, and massive unemployment. Political crises developed in the form of party polarization and frequent shifts in government, the rise of political violence (with the concomitant growth of paramilitary armies linked to the various parties), foreign occupation, and the Right's eventual takeover of the democratic government through legal and extra-legal means. There were also frequent complaints about the growth of nihilism and consumerism in the population. With the continuing migration of German citizens from the countryside into urban centers, traditional social ties loosened, and, with the added pressures of cyclical unemployment and inflation, a cynical "dog eat dog" attitude emerged that undermined the social fabric from within. As the economy deteriorated, the old forms of racism and discrimination became more prevalent and virulent again, bringing fear and instability in their wake. For these reasons, by the time Adolf Hitler and the Nazi Party took over the reins of power, a significant number of Germans were not unhappy that the existing system was coming to an end.

It is thus not difficult to see why the cyborg was frequently used by the Berlin Dadaists (and, later, other German cultural producers) to represent and analyze the unique time in German history in which they lived. A contradictory figure evoking the great possibilities and dangers that characterized the Weimar Republic as well as the interconnection of even the most opposed areas of society in an overarching and only imperfectly understood technological network, the cyborg mirrored its violent, innovative, and rapidly modernizing moment. Moreover, because it could also be used as a framework to examine how the rise of mass media was transforming human perception, it could also serve as an "aggregator" for the various discourses on how human sense perception was changing in the contemporary moment.

As Detlev J. K. Peukert argued, Weimar Germany represented "the crisis of classical modernity": the culmination of a moment between the 1890s and the 1930s, when the main modern ideas and movements achieved their breakthrough and, almost immediately, became uncertain.[37] Writing in 1987, Peukert defined classical modernity as

> the form of fully fledged industrialized society that has been with us from the turn of the century until the present day. In an economic sense, modernity is characterized by highly rationalized industrial production, complex technological infrastructures and a substantial degree of bureaucratized administrative and service activity; food production is carried out by an increasingly small, but productive, agricultural sector. Socially speaking, its typical features include the division of labor, wage and salary discipline, an urbanized environment, extensive educational opportunities and a demand for skills and training. As far as culture is concerned, media products dominate; continuity with traditional aesthetic principles and practices in architecture and the visual and other creative arts is broken, and is replaced by unrestricted formal experimentation. In intellectual terms, modernity marks the triumph of western rationality, whether in social planning, the expansion of the sciences or the self-replicating dynamism of technology, although this optimism is accompanied by skeptical doubts from social thinkers and cultural critics.[38]

As a paramount figure fitting this view of "classical modernity" as a time of radical and ongoing crisis, the cyborg appealed to the Berlin Dadaists and, eventually, Weimar cultural producers of all political stripes. In it they saw the outlines of their increasingly specialized, bureaucratized, and technologically mediated society. Furthermore, the cyborg's violent and monstrous connotations confirmed and possibly also assuaged their deepest fears by suggesting that the constant appearance of the unnatural was a "normal"—potentially everyday—aspect of modern life. The cyborg potentially taught the Dadaists to live in hope despite violence or, perhaps, to live in hope through and because of violence. And the cyborg's eventual ubiquity in Weimar culture was a function of the fact that it became a figure onto which many different Germans could so resolutely project themselves.

The Rise of the Mass Media in Weimar Germany

Another reason why the cyborg was so common in Dada art was that it was the perfect reflexive figure: a type that allowed the Berlin Dadaists to think formally and critically about the new montage media out of which they often constructed their cyborgian images. As suggested by *Cut with the Kitchen Knife,* Höch's appropriative de- and reassembling of her social and cultural moment, photomontage introduced new kinds of reflexivity into German art. By promoting institutional critique, photomontages encouraged Germans to question and investigate the roles that art played in their society. In addition, photomontages, because they were created through appropriating mass-reproduced images, also provoked Germans to examine the new forms of the mass media as well as the messages transmitted. The Weimar Republic, after all, was that moment of German history in which a truly modern mass culture was initially developed. It was here that film, radio, illustrated books, newspapers, and magazines first achieved a mass breakthrough; although spending levels could never match those of the United States, there was also a developing consumer and leisure culture, particularly in advertising and the media.[39] A figure through which the Dadaists could examine the growth of Germany's society of the spectacle, the cyborg became increasingly the choice in this highly self-conscious moment.

There are many ways in which the cyborg represented the new mass subject—the consumer and target of the new modes of communication and entertainment—that developed during the Weimar Republic. Because it revealed how technologies could function as prosthetics that augmented human perception, for example, the cyborg can be seen as a figure that announces the rise of radio broadcasting. Radio developed rapidly during the 1920s. The first radio broadcast in Germany took place on October 29, 1923, between 8:00 and 9:00 p.m., when the Berlin Funk-Stunde transmitted a mixture of recordings and live recitals, consisting of instrumental solos and vocal performances, to what was at most a few thousand radios.[40] The following year, there were more than a half million registered radio subscribers, and the number of registered sets rose by nearly a half million each subsequent year: over one million by 1925, more than two million by 1928, above three million by 1929, and in excess of four million by 1932.[41] The amount of time radio stations spent on the air also increased rapidly, and by 1931 the various stations were broadcasting an average of fifteen hours per day.[42] Consisting of eight regional companies (which began operating between October 1923 and October 1924) and one national company, the Deutsche Welle, which started transmitting in January 1926, German radio was not a private enterprise, as it was in the United States, but a curious mixture between a capitalist business and a profit-restricted public enterprise, controlled by the state.[43]

Dominated as it was by the state, German radio was, unlike the German press, above party politics, and in distinction to German film production, not subject to foreign influence. In addition, because each station was granted a monopoly in its particular area, there was no competition between producers as was the case in the other media.[44] As a result, radio broadcasting was much more strictly and powerfully controlled by public authorities than any other mass medium of the time, and its programming—which included classical and popular music; lectures and readings; radio plays; social, political, cultural, and sports reportage; and specialized programming directed toward women and children—was much more uniform.[45] As Karl Christian Führer has argued, because of the bourgeois pedagogical philosophies of its most important leaders, German radio operated according to a strategy of "defensive modernization."[46] Its leaders, in other words, sought to employ modern technologies to stabilize the status quo by using radio programming for aesthetic education; thereby they hoped to educate German listeners to become better subjects and citizens through an audio diet of high culture and uplifting programming.[47] As a result, German radio was dominated by bourgeois taste throughout the Weimar Republic and its consumption remained a largely middle-class phenomenon.[48] In addition, because of the high cost of radio sets (particularly those required to pick up long-distance airwave signals) and the placement of radio transmitters in large population centers, radio listening was primarily confined to urban milieus.[49]

Although these state-dominated, urban, passive, and bourgeois-reformist characteristics of radio programming might have inspired the creative critical resistance of the Berlin Dadaists had they heard it, radio was too much in its infancy during Dada's heyday for this to be the case. At the same time, although no official German radio station existed in 1920, when Höch had (largely) finished *Cut with the Kitchen Knife*, there was a significant group of amateur "ham radio" operators *[Funkbastler]*, who reportedly numbered in the tens of thousands.[50] In retrospect, this subculture, which represented a much more active form of radio listener, stands in sharp contrast to the official and passive population of radio listeners that would soon form, and in 1920, the *Funkbastler* might have suggested to Höch that radio could be an interactive and creative phenomenon, something that the existence of the wireless telegraph might also have implied.[51] As I have already shown, Hausmann used the figure of the cyborg as early as 1920 to imagine the synthesis of human beings with audio technologies. His line drawing *Heimatklänge,* a disturbing combination of a human head and a phonographic body that shouts "hurra! hurraa! hurraaa!" and was published in *Der Dada* 3 (Figure 1.8), demonstrates that the Dadaists acknowledged the nationalistic uses of the new means of audio mass communication, applications that began during World War I. In addition, in light of Hausmann's drawing, it may not be too far-fetched to suggest that the aerial views that Höch included in many of her photomontages—as well as the figures that she depicts floating through or hovering in space—suggest the transmission of the human voice and consciousness through the air in a manner reminiscent of radio waves. Although these aerial views and floating figures connote flight as much as they do radio transmissions, radio's growing presence, with both positive and negative connotations, can perhaps be found in a number of her representations.[52]

Cinema, it seems, had a greater impact on the Dadaists. Not only did Hausmann compare photomontage to cinema in his writings, but a cinematic iconography also began to appear in the works of several of the Berlin Dadaists.[53] Heartfield, moreover, is reported to have worked as a set designer for "trick" or special effects films at Grünbaum-Film in Berlin-Weissensee between 1917 and 1920, and Heartfield and Grosz also appear to have collaborated on propaganda, advertising, cartoon, and trick films for Universum Film A.G. (UFA, which was then known as BUFA) from 1917, during the first year of the company's existence as a propaganda machine controlled by the Army

High Command, until the beginning of 1919—projects that, despite the fact that they are no longer extant, all speak to the importance of cinema for the Berlin Dadaists.[54] Among the reasons for their interest in film were no doubt the speedy artistic and technical advances made by the new medium as well as its rapid growth after about 1910. (The number of movie theaters in Germany, for example, grew from around 1,000 in 1910 to 2,446 in 1914.)[55] Furthermore, by the time Berlin Dada began at the end of World War I, German cinema was entering one of its most exciting moments.[56] During the war, a ban was imposed on foreign films, depriving German theaters of their primary product, and, in the wake of this prohibition, several major German film production companies were formed, including Deutsche Lichtbild-Gesellschaft (DLG), to produce educational and advertising films extolling Germany industries, and UFA, which became the most significant German film company of the Weimar Republic, a massive "vertically integrated" conglomerate that controlled production, distribution, and exhibition.[57] As a result of these transformations and the attraction that the new industry held for many creative Germans, German film flowered both commercially and artistically in the immediate postwar period. By 1918 there were 2,299 movie theaters in the Reich; by 1919 the number was 2,836; and by 1920, 3,731.[58] New major film companies were founded, including Emelka, Terra, Decla-Bioscop, Deulig (a transformed DLG), and National.[59] By 1919, Germany, which imported most of its films prior to 1914, had become the major film producer in Europe and was second only to the United States in terms of the quantity of its productions.[60]

From its very beginnings, Weimar cinema was extremely heterogeneous and stylistically eclectic. Despite today's scholarly image of German film in the 1920s as authorial, highbrow, psychological, and artistically complex, only a few of the feature films made in Germany at the time conform to this model of classical Weimar cinema.[61] While significant works were produced, in general much more light entertainment and kitsch appeared on German screens, and, in addition, beginning in the early 1920s, German motion pictures had to once again compete for their audience with foreign products, in particular American slapstick comedies. Adding to the heterogeneity of German film in the 1910s and 1920s was the fact that German filmmakers developed and worked in various genres, including horror (for which Weimar cinema is perhaps best known), the historical pageant (whose historical narrative was often used to comment on the contemporary moment), the "educational film" (which treated sexuality and other tabooed topics), the literary adaptation (which was based on a preexisting literary work), the "chamber drama" (which used a small cast and limited setting to dramatize psychological conflicts), the "mountain film" (which pitted man against nature), the "street film" (which explored the working-class milieu), the "silent musical comedy" (to which popular music was played as an accompaniment), as well as a host of other generic types such as comedies, romances, melodramas, detective films, adventure serials, science fiction movies, and even fake westerns.[62] Industrial and advertising films were also produced, and, in terms of style, Weimar cinema appropriated several different artistic forms including expressionism, *Neue Sachlichkeit,* and socialist realism. In addition, the realism and compelling narrative qualities of classical Hollywood cinema also had an important effect on German filmmaking—and not simply because American film companies began to establish a presence in Germany after 1925. For these various reasons, it is thus difficult to determine which characteristics of Weimar cinema attracted the Dadaists the most—or, for that matter, how uncritically enthusiastic they were about the new medium. Because Weimar cinema was a mass medium that required huge amounts of labor and capital, German filmmakers were under pressure to remain politically neutral so as to appeal to the greatest number of moviegoers. As a result, the German film industry tended to eschew politics or at least to hide it, a practice that tended at the very least to support the status quo and that often resulted in various forms of camouflaged conservatism.[63] As Siegfried Kracauer's well-known analysis of German film reminds us, even the masterpieces of Weimar cinema can be read as revealing a hidden authoritarianism—a social and psychological tendency that the Dadaists attempted to combat through their art.[64]

To generalize from what the Dadaists wrote about film, cinema was one of the inspirations for their development of photomontage.[65] In particular, it helped them understand the power and possibilities of photographic montage, which, as Hausmann argued in 1931, was a strategy that allowed the Dadaists "to use the material of photography to combine heterogeneous, often contradictory structures, figurative and spatial, into a new whole that was in effect a mirror image wrenched from the chaos of war and revolution, as new to the eye as it was to the mind."[66] Cinema, in other words, revealed the power of photographic montage to fragment and reassemble reality—a process that not only mirrored the revolutionary postwar moment but also allowed its practitioners to comment on their new reality and to imagine new forms of individual and collective existence emerging within it. In addition, it is probable that the Dadaists appreciated cinema for its working-class associations, its anarchic aspects (especially as revealed through the films of Charlie Chaplin and Buster Keaton), and perhaps also for its burgeoning ability to constitute a spectator by evoking points of view through narrative identification and subjective camerawork. Finally, because films sutured together divergent viewpoints, the Dadaists also probably appreciated cinema as a training ground for a new type of perceptual consciousness, one that could tolerate—even appreciate—competing perspectives. Thus, in general, as suggested by their photomontage practices, they valued cinema's possibilities for fantasy and criticism, for disrupting the social and political status quo, and for creating new modes of visual perception—as opposed to its more univocal, authoritarian, and (classically) narrative aspects. As I argue in the next chapter through analyses of Hausmann's *Self-Portrait of the Dadasoph* (1920) (Figure 3.2) and other photomontages, the cyborg was a figure that allowed the Dada artists to imagine how cinema affected representation and perception. This photomontage, which uses the iconography of film ambiguously, suggests that the Dada artists were well aware of cinema's potential to both expand and control consciousness.

Despite the impact of cinema on the Dadaists, however, it was print journalism—in particular the illustrated newspapers and magazines from which they made their photomontages—that probably had the biggest influence on their work. Newspapers and magazines were still the dominant form of mass communication in Germany throughout the 1920s, reaching a larger audience than either film or radio.[67] In 1866 there were about 1,500 newspapers, of which 300 were dailies. By 1900 their number had risen to 3,500; by 1914 there were more than 4,200 papers, of which slightly less than half appeared at least six times a week.[68] The number of newspapers had dropped slightly to 3,689 by 1919–20, although it rose again by the mid-1920s.[69] According to one contemporary source, in 1928 there were 3,356 daily political newspapers in Germany as well as 10,297 periodicals, a number that included fashion magazines, political and literary reviews, almanacs, professional and trade journals, scientific publications, and the like.[70] In terms of specialization, there were newspapers for every region and every political orientation throughout the nineteenth century, and, during the second half of that century, mass circulation newspapers—which emphasized mass tastes and local news, and which contained extensive advertising sections to keep subscriptions low— became more and more popular.[71] Around the turn of the century, tabloids began to appear: newspapers geared toward street sales, which broke with the subscription-based sales model followed by the majority of nineteenth-century German newspapers.[72] These papers, which increased rapidly in popularity before World War I, were even more sensational and declamatory than the mass-circulation newspapers, and, like their predecessors, they were heavily dependent on advertising.[73]

As Modris Eksteins has argued, "The most striking features of the German press on the eve of the First World War were its abundance, its decentralization, and its growing commercialization and politicization"—features that, despite certain changes, also characterized the press during the Weimar Republic.[74] The experience of World War I created a public hungry for breaking news, and, as a result, more and more high-circulation special editions were sold on the street.[75] Although papers that sought a mass audience began to renounce their explicit political allegiances during the Weimar Republic so as not to alienate their advertisers, the much-heralded "depolitization" of the press during that time was actually something of a misnomer. In the 1920s German papers remained political in that journalists were encouraged to express opinions and make judgments in their stories,[76] and papers began to support political tendencies as opposed to parties.[77] Because the majority of these "nonpolitical" Weimar newspapers tended to express the popular dissatisfaction with the current situation as well as a longing for an ideal national community (sometimes projected onto an idealized past), depolitization often resulted in a political shift to the right.[78] Only the Social Democrats, the Communists, and (later) the National Socialists possessed a centrally directed party press, and these papers suffered in terms of circulation because they emphasized national politics over local issues and were also far less entertaining.[79]

The addition of photographs also radically transformed the mass appeal of newspapers and magazines. Although the first illustrated magazines in Europe date from the late eighteenth century, it was the nineteenth century that witnessed the rise of the popular illustrated periodical—initially fashion magazines and, by midcentury, weekly pictorial newspapers such as *The Illustrated London News* (1842), *L'Illustration* (Paris, 1843), the *Illustrirte Zeitung* (Leipzig, 1843), *Frank Leslie's Illustrated Newspaper* (New York, 1855), and *Harper's Weekly* (New York, 1857).[80] Generally illustrated by means of end-grain woodcuts (produced from drawings and, slightly later, photographs), these papers and newsmagazines proved immensely popular, and they helped engender a mass audience made up of a range of social classes as well as enfranchise a new group of working-class readers. Before the development of the halftone process between the late 1870s and the 1890s, newspaper and magazine illustrations were created through several different methods including lithography, woodcut engraving, and copper plate engraving. New techniques, such as photogravure, photolithography, collographic printing, and the Woodburytype, became popular in the 1870s and 1880s for printing photographs in magazines and books; however, these techniques, like the ones mentioned above, could not be used with type and thus required that image and text remain on separate pages or for the page to be printed twice in order to combine them.[81] With the advent of halftone engraving, however, photographs and texts could finally be printed together; as a result, printing time was reduced, as were printing costs.[82] Daily newspapers started regularly publishing photographs around 1900, and rotogravure, the printing of text and image in massive rotating presses, which was introduced in the early 1900s, allowed halftone illustrations to be printed at an extremely rapid rate. As a result of these developments, illustrated newspapers proliferated during the first decades of the twentieth century.[83]

The late nineteenth and early twentieth centuries also witnessed rapid changes in photographic technologies. The dry plate process of Dr. Richard Leach Maddox, celluloid negatives, orthocromatic film, exposure calculators, anastigmatic lenses, hand-held cameras, new forms of shutters, new types of printing papers, flash powder, and the science of sensitometry, which were all developed by the early 1900s, allowed for photographs to be taken more easily and rapidly as well as in places where it was previously too difficult to obtain an image. These innovations, along with the burgeoning of amateur photography since the 1880s, led to the increased production of—and demand for—instantaneous photographs of life: candid images of fleeting events (everyday and historical) that prepared the ground for photojournalism.[84] In addition, phototelegraphy, the telegraphic transmitting of photographic images, was first put into use in 1907, thus making photographs even more readily (and quickly) available for publication.[85] For these various reasons, after World War I, press illustration became largely photographic.[86]

The interwar period was the beneficiary of these various developments. As scholars have noted, the Weimar Republic represents a moment in which the modern language of photojournalism was first developed, where newspaper and magazine layout became a significant form of creative endeavor, where the photograph became a primary mode of communication (as opposed to merely an addendum to the text), and where much thought was devoted to analyzing these transformations.[87] Magazines and illustrated newspapers, it was argued, promoted a new form of reading that was impatient, distracted, and tailored to a life on the go.[88] This was a mode of reception in which, for better or for worse, bits of reading time were snatched amid other activities—on the tram, for example, during a lunch break, or after dinner. As a result, reading materials became more visual, fragmented, and emphatic, thereby beginning a development in which changes in reading habits and changes in material culture mutually reinforced one another and contributed to lasting transformations in how ordinary Germans received and processed information. Periodical covers, for example, were changed to address the new, supposedly less attentive reader. Whereas before the war they had featured tasteful (often drawn) illustrations, single posterlike photographs began to be used more and more during the Weimar Republic, with a prominent series title above the image to lodge the periodical brand in the reader's consciousness and a caption below it to explain its significance. Articles, moreover, were becoming shorter and increasingly broken up by illustrations, photographs, and captions. In addition, there was less pressure to ensure that the images were always closely connected with the texts. Now, instead of directly illustrating something that was written, it was considered sufficient if the images at times functioned as amplifications of the article and represented aspects of the subject to which the text only alluded. Images, furthermore, became the primary means of communicating meaning—although few believed that they could function easily without some text—and it was argued that more and more a predominantly visual mode of understanding the world was coming to the fore.

As I argue over the next three chapters, the Dada artists associated the cyborg with this new more "distracted" consumption of conjunctions of images and texts that characterized the experience of reading the illustrated magazines and newspapers—a mode of perception that was strongly debated. Kracauer, for example, argued in 1927 that the illustrated newspapers, whose aim was "the complete reproduction of the world accessible to the photographic apparatus," promoted a profound loss of historical understanding.[89] Because they merely represented topical subjects wrenched out of their original contexts and juxtaposed without being given a new, historically informed significance or structure, "the flood of photos sweeps away the dams of memory. . . . Never before has a period known so little about itself. In the hands of the ruling society, the invention of illustrated magazines is one of the most powerful means of organizing a strike against understanding."[90] Benjamin, on the other hand, argued in 1936 that the distracted mode of perception that characterized the experience of film, illustrated magazines, and architecture was potentially revolutionary.[91] It was a mode of perception that was tactile (as opposed to optical), habitual, and collective, and as such it was much more suited to the new tasks that confronted human awareness at turning points of history such as Benjamin believed his own moment to be. Although Benjamin never explained how this not-fully-conscious form of perception allowed human beings to achieve revolutionary consciousness, he clearly defined how distracted perception helped mobilize the masses and condition human beings to the increased threats to life and limb characteristic of modern life, a conditioning that it achieved by exposing human beings to the shock effects of montage. For the Dadaists, it seemed, the distracted mode of viewing promoted by modern media was a mixed bag, a mode of perception that could be used for both revolutionary and reactionary ends.

But how, specifically, did the Dadaists conceptualize this experience of distracted perception? And how did this understanding affect their practices of photomontage? The *BIZ* provides a good example of the reading experience to which the Dadaists were in part reacting through their photomontages—and not simply because it was the illustrated newspaper from which a few of them, and in particular Höch, appropriated photomontage fragments. First started in 1892, and taken over in 1894 by the Ullstein Verlag, the publishing company for which Höch worked in the late 1910s and the early 1920s, the *BIZ* was the most popular weekly illustrated newspaper in Germany during the Weimar Republic.[92] Since the late nineteenth century it regularly published photographs of a wide variety of subjects including contemporary political and social events, the lives of politicians and celebrities, war and other forms of social and political unrest, natural catastrophes, foreign lands and people, scenes from popular films and theatrical productions, new technologies (particularly those of flight and other forms of modern transportation), and, very importantly, all forms of modern life (and, in particular, those appearing with increasing frequency on the streets of large German cities). Its articles were generally short and interspersed with photographs, illustrations, and captions that broke up and amplified the blocks of printed text. It also published poetry and serialized novels, and it had regular advertising and humor sections. Although it is commonly thought to be a newsmagazine, it did not present an overall account of the news of each week; rather, its coverage was determined by the interest and appeal of its visual materials. As Kurt Korff, the editor in chief from 1905 to 1933, explained, "The *BIZ* adopted the editorial principle that all events should be presented in pictures with an eye to the visually dramatic and excluding everything that is visually uninteresting. It was not the importance of the material that determined the selection and acceptance of pictures, but solely the allure of the photo itself."[93] Moreover, according to Ullstein's own promotional literature, the press emphasized the contemporaneousness or up-to-dateness of its pictures, the need to retouch nearly all its photographs to strengthen their visual impact, and the importance of mixing different forms of visual media to promote variety and reader interest.[94] The *BIZ* was thus in many ways a central medium through which the German public was exposed to the new and developing practices of photomontage—here understood in a broad sense as juxtaposing photographs with texts and other forms of illustrative materials. Despite its emphasis on visual communication, juxtaposing words with images, and breaking up and shortening blocks of text, however, the *BIZ* layout was for the most part designed so as to smooth over the dislocations produced by its strategies of montage. The experience of simultaneously viewing and reading was intended to be new and exciting, but, like the *BIZ*'s advertisements, it was also expected to be easily intelligible and not radically transformative of the status quo.

Significantly, as suggested by the following brief inventory of articles and photomontages that appeared in 1919, the *BIZ* also published features that were self-reflexive, that promoted visual literacy, and that taught its growing audience about the new forms of optical communication being introduced by the mass press. The cover of the February 16 issue, for example, stressed the new speed of information delivery. It depicted newspapers being unloaded from a two-cockpit biplane, with a caption that noted that the *BZ am Mittag,* another Ullstein publication, was the first newspaper to be delivered regularly in this way.[95] An article from August 17, on the other hand, instructed readers on "the art of instantaneous photography," detailing all the considerations that went into creating successful candid images of modern life.[96] Underwater lights and observation tools were featured in a November 9 article on new technological developments; the profession and technical tricks of newspaper photographers and their contributions to "a change in our way of thinking away from abstract speculation and towards the 'scientific objectivity' of concrete observation" were discussed on December 14; and a brief history of newspapers' roles in fostering crime prevention, world exploration, technological advance, economic growth, political engagement, democracy, bureaucratic reform, and public works was printed on December 28.[97]

Contests for cash prizes were also used to promote visual literacy, their puzzles designed to encourage readers to engage with and comprehend the new ways to combine photographs and texts. A Christmas contest announced on December 28, 1919, for example, awarded cash prizes to viewers who could identify six people or objects photographed from above (Figure 2.6).[98] The answers—a photographer hunched over his camera, a soldier wearing an assault helmet, a fireman wearing a smoke helmet, a coffee mill, a lantern, and an arc lamp—were all cyborgian or technological subjects. A contest announced on July 5, 1925, on the other hand, rewarded its viewers with cash prizes if they could successfully identify photographic fragments depicting partial faces of famous celebrities, including Chaplin, Dr. Hugo Eckener, Gerhard Hauptmann, Jack Dempsey, and Benito Mussolini (Figure 2.7).[99] This contest is particularly significant since it implies that—as photomontage developed during the Weimar Republic—an expectation arose in the popular press that at least a few readers could and would recall the identity of a represented person or object from a fragmentary image presented in a photomontage. It thus suggests that the Berlin Dadaists could assume that some of their viewers might remember the original subjects, meanings, and contexts depicted in the cut-up printed photographs used in the Dada photomontages and, furthermore, that they would call on these memories when interpreting the Dadaists' complex appropriationist works—an issue that has been vigorously debated in recent years.[100]

A somewhat earlier discussion of Dada art, published in the *BIZ* in October 1919, confirms this assumption. In an analysis of the new ". . . isms" or contemporary directions in painting, C. Sehn argued that

"Dadaism" is the gallows humor of a perverse and confused epoch. The Dadaist does not paint everything in the picture, he also pastes in catalog clippings and labels, or hammers slices of bread or prunes onto it. He only wants these things for their mood values, as symbols, and as indications of his feelings and thoughts. The Dadaist may

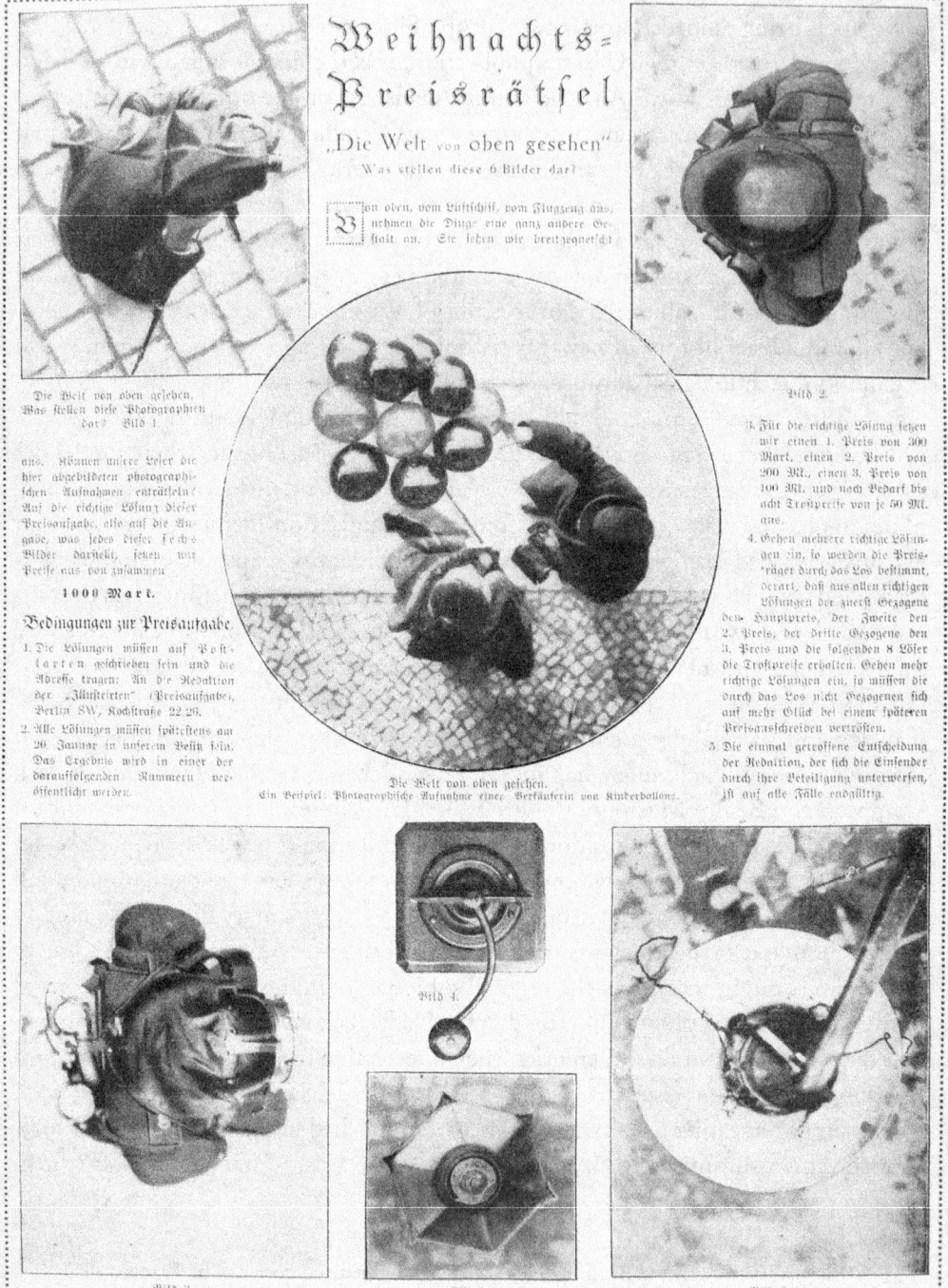

Figure 2.6. *Berliner Illustrirte Zeitung* [Berlin Illustrated Newspaper] 28, no. 52 (December 28, 1919): 544. Title: "Christmas Prize Puzzle: The World as Seen from Above."

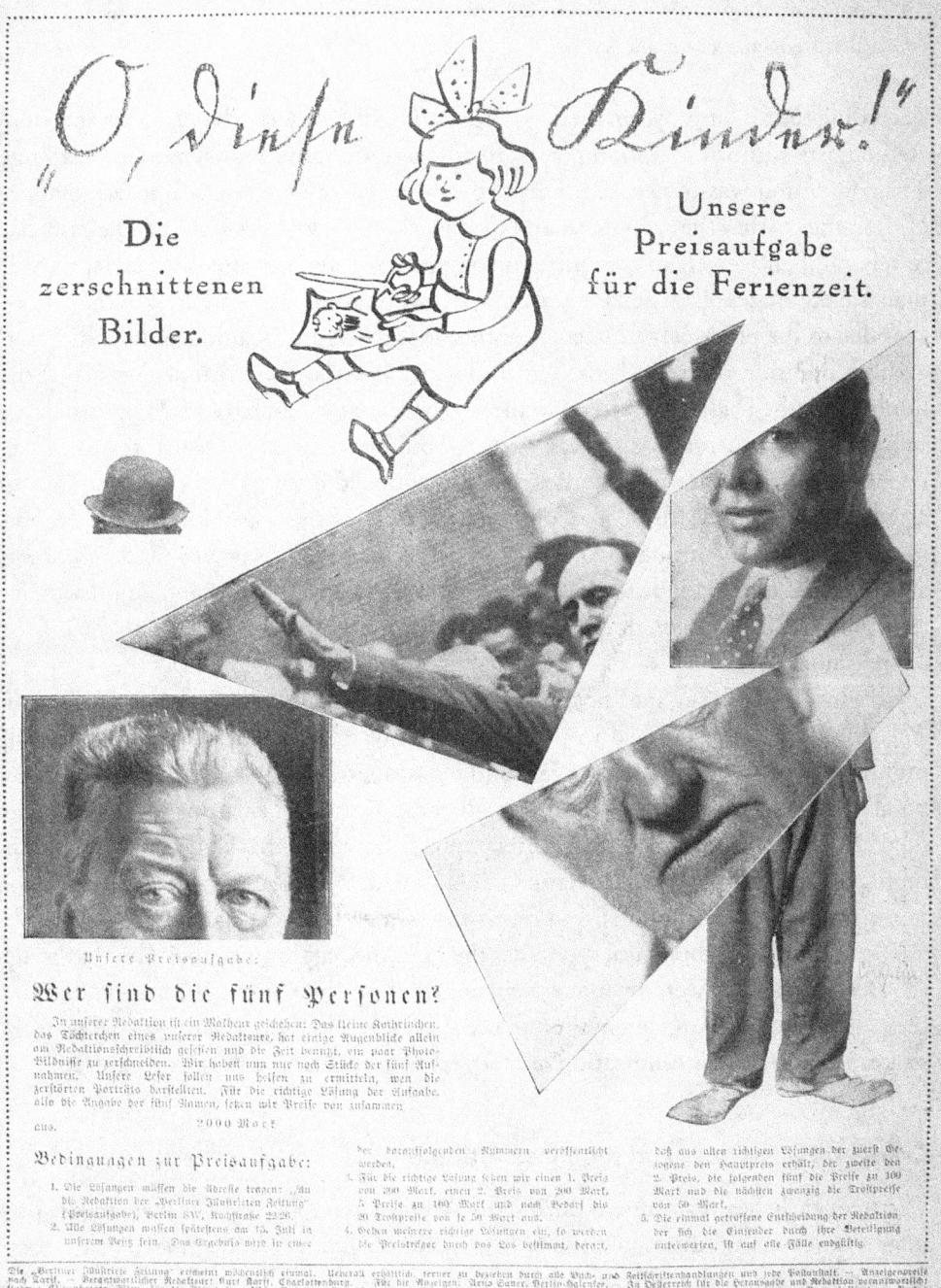

Figure 2.7. *Berliner Illustrirte Zeitung* [Berlin Illustrated Newspaper] 34, no. 27 (July 5, 1925): 846. Title: "Oh, These Children!"

care to awaken in us the idea of a definite, possibly political reading. The suggestion of this atmosphere is achieved just as well, indeed perhaps better, by a pasted clipping from a certain newspaper, than by a painted copy. The Dadaist is in many instances a sharp-edged accuser and satirist.[101]

According to this fairly sympathetic interpretation of Dada art, the Dadaists appropriated objects and printed photographs for their connotative and symbolic meanings. Their intention was to accuse, to satirize, and to encourage political interpretations of the subjects that they represented. For this reason, Sehn suggests, the Dadaists had to rely on their viewers to recognize the fragmentary subjects and objects depicted in their source materials. The *BIZ*'s art critic thus does not indicate that audiences responded to the potential of Dada photomontage to negate meaning and the hitherto-existing tradition of art and, thereby, to inspire institutional critique. Instead, Sehn implies that the Dadaists' contemporaneous spectators would have read the Dada photomontages in much the same way as they would have read traditional forms of representational art. In terms of audience expectations, the component parts of Dadaist artworks still represented people, places, and ideas. At the same time, Sehn's emphasis on connotation through words like *mood, atmosphere, suggestion,* and *indications* also indicates that Dadaist forms of representation were less direct and emphatic than traditional forms of depiction (and thus perhaps targeted at a more distracted form of spectator).

As suggested by the specific montage strategies and self-reflexive tendencies of the *BIZ,* the Dadaists responded to the new modes of simultaneous seeing and reading promoted by the illustrated magazines and newspapers, and to some extent they incorporated forms and strategies derived from these new types of print journalism into their art. Contrary to the establishment press, however, the Dadaists used photomontage to encourage their spectators to employ their distracted modes of perception to dismantle the status quo and to reveal the hidden political agendas, social ideologies, and "ideal" psychological types that the mass media promulgated. Thus, although the Berlin Dadaists were in many ways inspired by the German culture industries, they also remained fundamentally opposed to them, seeking as they did to turn the strategies of mass communication and advertising against the mass media itself.

Cyborgs, Distraction, and the Blasé Attitude

The frequently heard argument during the Weimar Republic that the mass media promoted a new, more-distracted mode of perception points to an important protocyborgian concept of the subject developed in the years preceding World War I, which linked changes in the subject as a locus of perception to changes in the subject's overall identity understood as his or her personality, consciousness, fundamental values, unconscious desires, and attitudes toward life. Although he did not emphasize the term *distraction,* Georg Simmel's account of the reserved and blasé metropolitan type has several parallels with these later characterizations of the new perceptual subject produced through the mass media.[102] In "The Metropolis and Mental Life" (1903), perhaps his most widely read essay, Simmel argued that a new mode of consciousness was evolving in urban contexts, a form of awareness that he distinguished from a rural mode of consciousness that it was displacing. Rural consciousness was characterized by deep emotional connections and regular patterns of thought resulting from a slow and uniform pattern of life as well as great familiarity with the same people and contexts over a long period of time. Given the regularity of the environment in which it existed as well as its firsthand knowledge of the habits and opinions of its everyday community, its mental life was consistent and predictable, characterized by a steady flow of impressions, customary and habitual contrasts, and sensations of fairly long duration. As a result, rural consciousness was also narrow and conformist—because of the dominance of community values and the regular and tradition-bound character of existence in the countryside, it was difficult for individuals who lived there to act or think idiosyncratically.[103]

In contrast to the countryside, modern cities were contexts in which the individual was likely to experience a much broader range of phenomena, rapid changes in perceptual stimuli, unfamiliar concepts and events, and daily interactions with strangers.[104] To shield itself from the mental shocks, contradictions, and feelings of dislocation and anxiety produced by the city's intensification of nervous stimulation, the metropolitan subject developed its intellectual capacities, namely, its abilities to reason, calculate, and conceptually interrelate all forms of distinct interior and exterior impressions.[105] Like the phenomenon of money, the intellect reduced all qualities and individual attributes to common and interchangeable characteristics; as a result, the development of the urban subject's intellectual capacities made it less emotional, "harder," as well as more objective, precise, and "reserved" in its relations to others.[106] The metropolitan type evolved, in Simmel's words, a "blasé" attitude—a blunting of sensitivity in relation to new sensations—through which it protected itself from the overwhelming stimulation of modern life, "the rapid crowding of changing images, the sharp discontinuity in the grasp of a single glance, and the unexpectedness of onrushing impressions."[107] Its protection against sensory overload, however, created a situation in which no one object was preferred over any other—a feeling that even extended to itself and at times produced profound feelings of worthlessness.[108] Thus the impact of city life on human consciousness was a mixed bag. On the one hand, the metropolitan subject was spiritually more free than the rural subject; a broader range of behaviors were permitted to the city dweller; and he or she could develop his or her personality in much more individual ways. On the other hand, urban consciousness was also a much more alienated and artificial consciousness, a type that was distanced from its inner emotional core.

Significantly, Simmel's account of the blasé, calculating, and emotionally alienated mode of urban consciousness demonstrates several parallels with the new, more-distracted mode of synthesizing disparate avenues of perception that Kracauer, Benjamin, and other cultural critics argued developed during the Weimar Republic through the influence of the German mass media on its subjects' viewing and reading habits. These parallels include the at times dialectical combination of optimism and pessimism that greeted the perceived transformations in human consciousness, the characterization of the new type of consciousness as possessing a mode of perception designed to synthesize radically divergent sensations and types of sensory phenomena, the connection of the new mode of perception to modern urban life, a sense that modern consciousness was becoming "colder," more distanced, and more objective, and a belief that the visual mode of perception was becoming an increasingly dominant part of that consciousness. In addition, we see in the various theories an understanding of vision as a medium through which the new form of perceptual consciousness did not simply apprehend the external world but, instead, read and interpreted it. Although there is no direct evidence linking Simmel's thinking to the work of the Berlin Dadaists, his influence on the theoretical models of both Kracauer and Benjamin is clear and well documented.[109] More important, however, is the fact that Simmel's formulation, which synthesizes diverse strands of thought from Immanuel Kant, G. W. F. Hegel, and others, represents a protocyborgian understanding of the subject. As such, it helps isolate trajectories in German thought that prepared the ground for the subsequent embrace of images and concepts of cyborgs, and thus it reveals how the intellectual milieu in which the Berlin Dadaists operated contained a number of the central ideas that make up our present-day understandings of cyborgs.

As William J. Mitchell has suggested, central to the protocyborgian aspects of Simmel's concept of metropolitan consciousness was his characterization of the urban subject as a "connecting creature," inextricably entangled with the networked environment in which it existed.[110] This idea of the urban subject as a function of a broader network of objects, ideas, and institutions followed from Simmel's understanding of all human beings as syntheses of individual and intersubjective elements. Borrowing a concept from the Hegelian tradition, Simmel argued that the subject was fundamentally produced through appropriations of "objective spirit" that occurred during its socialization, education, and everyday development. As Simmel put it, "In language as well as in law, in the technique of production as well as in art, in science as well as in the objects of the domestic environment, there is embodied a sum of spirit."[111] By learning, using, or otherwise appropriating these preexisting objectifications of human reason, emotion, and labor, the individual developed mentally and, in its particular development, underwent a growth based on the intellectual evolution of the human species as a whole. Although Simmel no longer believed, as did Hegel, that "ontogeny recapitulates phylogeny" in a spiritual sense—namely, that when we grow up, we pass through a mental development that repeats the intellectual evolution of humanity in general—Simmel still subscribed to the idea that cognitive development and learning in human beings was the result of their appropriation of cultural artifacts embedded in their environments.[112]

Simmel's understanding of human beings as connecting creatures also helps explain the particular problems that he saw threatening the metropolitan type in his contemporary moment. In the modern metropolis, with its dominant capitalist system, its proliferation of goods and services, and the radical occupational specializations that it tended to force on its occupants, there developed a tremendous preponderance of objective spirit with which the subject had to grapple. "Here," as Simmel put it,

> in buildings and educational institutions, in the wonders and comforts of space-conquering technology, in the formations of community life, and in the visible institutions of the state, is offered such an overwhelming fullness of crystallized and impersonalized spirit that the personality, so to speak, cannot maintain itself under its impact. On the one hand, life is made infinitely easy for the personality in that stimulations, interests, uses of time and consciousness are offered to it from all sides. They carry the person as if in a stream, and one needs hardly to swim for oneself. On the other hand, however, life is composed more and more of these impersonal contents and offerings which tend to displace the genuine personal colorations and incomparabilities. This results in the individual's summoning the utmost in uniqueness and particularization, in order to preserve his most personal core. He has to exaggerate this personal element in order to remain audible even to himself.[113]

It was for this reason that the metropolis became a site wherein the struggle between one's nature as a "general human being" and one's nature as a "unique individual" reached its greatest degree of tension.[114] And only by understanding and grappling with the problems produced by the preponderance of objective spirit in metropolitan life could urban Germans avoid the myriad problems—including alienation, anxiety, despair, desensitization, and the reduction of all human values to those of the market—that affected their identities in the modern world.

Because he understood human beings to produce themselves through their appropriations of objects embodying human thought, labor, and feeling, Simmel anticipated the concept of the cyborg in several different ways. First, he saw such central aspects of human beings as cognition, personality, and agency as "distributed"—namely, as extending beyond the physical limits of our bodies and lodged in part in the objects, tools, and individuals situated in the environments that sustain and enable us. Second, Simmel recognized information's central role in the development and functioning of human beings as well as the fact that information was often stored objectively in artifacts; for these reasons, his concept of the subject approaches Wiener's thesis that mechanical and computational systems could take over central aspects of human activity. Third, Simmel saw linkages between the concept of the subject as a locus of perception and the concept of the subject as human identity. Changes in perception would bring about changes in the psyche, understood as one's overall conscious and unconscious orientation toward life. Because we are all in part functions of our surrounding contexts, and because we take these contexts in through our various avenues of perception, changes in either our environments or our perceptual apparatuses fundamentally affect who and what we are.

Simmel's prescient account of mental life in the metropolis, which linked a model of the subject as a locus of multiple and fragmented modes of perception to a model of the subject as a form of socially constructed identity with particular values and tendencies, helps explain the conceptual underpinnings of the various accounts, developed after the mid-1920s, of distracted perception produced through the mass media. It thus reveals a conceptual system, potentially accessible to the Berlin Dadaists even before they began to develop their strategies of photomontage and their representations of human–machine hybrids, that had already formulated—albeit in a still somewhat inchoate way—a model of the cyborg as both a locus of perception and a form of hybrid identity produced through assimilating objective culture. Even if the Dadaists did not derive their inspiration from Simmel's theories, his sociology of city life reveals that protocyborgian thought existed in prewar German culture. And as such, it suggests that—as the Dadaists developed their critique of the mass media through photomontage while employing the image of the cyborg in their representations of modern life—there were resources available to them in contemporaneous German culture that would support, and even interrelate, both such moves. Although Berlin Dada emerged at an early stage of mass culture's development in Germany, the example of Simmel proves that a conceptual system was already in place that could justify the Dadaists' focus on the interrelationships between identity, perception, and the mass media.

Identity Politics

As the above excursus on the rise of the mass media in Germany suggests, Berlin Dada stood at a crossroads between two different types of cultural sphere. The first one, which existed prior to the end of World War I, was characterized by fairly clear separations between the realms of (autonomous) fine art and mass culture, while the second one, which began with Dada, and which emerged in part because of its example, was a context wherein the traditional distinctions between fine art and mass culture were beginning to break down. As a result, from today's perspective, the heterogeneous and category-confounding art of the Berlin Dadaists appears to fit into a multiplicity of cultural trajectories or traditions. Höch's *Cut with the Kitchen Knife,* for example, in many ways confirms the model of avant-garde art outlined in the introduction, an authorization to be expected, given the general scholarly agreement that Dada was part of the historical avant-garde. The photomontage's avant-garde tendencies can first of all be seen in its focus on social and political issues, something that suggests Höch's openness to her contemporary world as well as her desire to break down the aestheticist division between art and life. In addition, the work's avant-garde tendencies are also evident in its photomontage form, which introduces elements drawn from mass culture into a work of fine art, thereby potentially promoting criticism of the institution of art as well as other institutions of society and the state. Furthermore, *Cut with the Kitchen Knife*'s photomontage form also emphasizes the work's nonorganic character, and the lack of formal cohesiveness that results from its strategies of montage not only shocks the work's various spectators but also provokes them to engage with and "complete" the photomontage's conflicting strands of association. Moreover, although the work is not collaborative in the sense of being a creation of two or more Dada artists, it is collaborative in the sense that Höch used fragments of images produced by others to construct her work. Finally, because of its focus on violence through both form and subject matter as well as its depictions of real people and events in revolutionary and postrevolutionary Germany, it suggests historical loss.

At the same time, however, *Cut with the Kitchen Knife* also demonstrates continuities with past trajectories of modernism while anticipating some of the concepts and strategies of postmodernism. Its modernist tendencies can be seen in its interest in undermining bourgeois myths associated with art such as the importance of the artist's hand, the artist's individuality and the uniqueness of his or her vision, and the idea that a work of art was somehow a precious and autonomous object. In addition, through its comic and satirical treatment of the former kaiser, the current German government, and other pillars of Weimar society, it suggests a modernist interest in attacking bourgeois social and political ideals. *Cut with the Kitchen Knife*'s postmodernism, on the other hand, can be seen in its critique of originality through its strategy of appropriation, its emphasis on the interconnection of fine art and mass culture, and its undermining of the traditional formal "presence" of the artwork though its use of common, everyday materials. In addition, its postmodernism can also be seen in its raising of questions of multiculturalism and gender through some of its photomontage depictions—its hermaphrodite figures, for example, as well as its examples of cultural and racial mixing.

One reason why Dada art seems suspended between traditional and contemporary spheres of cultural production and central to several different models of artistic practice has to do with its radical cultural politics, a tendency that throughout the twentieth century has helped unite the spheres of fine art and mass culture. Through its fixation on the image of the cyborg, *Cut with the Kitchen Knife*, as I have shown, promotes a politics of "hybrid identity" that encourages its spectators to imagine new, more-networked and distributed modes of human existence. In the next chapter, to further understand the Dadaists' conception of hybrid identity, I explore in greater detail the relationship between Freudian psychology and Dada art. Although Dada artists like Hausmann were highly critical of Freud's thinking, which he deemed too bourgeois, Freud's paradigms still influenced Dadaist practices. Before turning to Hausmann's art and thought, however, it is useful to examine another example of a cyborg drawn from *Cut with the Kitchen Knife* to further investigate how such cyborgian figures inspired their audiences to reexamine the nature of human identity. Standing on the right shoulder of the kaiser, a strange hermaphrodite appears (Figure 2.8). The figure consists of the head of Field Marshal Paul von Hindenburg, chief of the general staff of the German army, and probably the most famous German military leader of World War I, sutured to the body of Sent M'ahesa (Elsa von Carlberg), a modern dancer active in Germany in the 1910s and 1920s, who was known for her dances based on Egyptian and other ancient and exotic cultures.[115] Wearing a harem costume, the figure stares at the viewer, stretching out its arms and cocking its head in a flirtatious posture of display. Although the cyborg does not reveal mechanical or prosthetic parts, its character as a cyborg is suggested by its strange, stitched-together appearance and the fact that it blends attributes of different sexes (and thereby anticipates Haraway's definition).

Examining this figure, Höch's original audiences would most probably have made a series of different associations. In the first place, the conjunction of Hindenburg's head with M'ahesa's body would for many have been seen as an attempt to undermine the powerful and noble associations attached to the military ideal embodied by Hindenburg. During World War I, for example, Hindenburg was the subject of an enormous personality cult; his image, in multiple forms, was used to symbolize German military might and to raise money for military causes.[116] As I discuss in the next two chapters, the Berlin Dada artists used the figure of the cyborg as a war cripple to lampoon and emasculate the heroic images of armored male soldiers, photomontage portraits popular in pre- and interwar German visual culture that in part inspired the development of Dadaist photomontage. In Höch's image of Hindenburg, a similar intention appears to operate. Although the field marshal is not presented as a cripple, his scantily clad female body destabilizes his authority and power. On another level, the blending of male and female attributes in the image of Hindenburg, who is represented in the act of tickling the kaiser under his chin, might have suggested same-sex desire—a topic that was gaining attention in Weimar culture.[117] Confronted with this hybrid figure, the photomontage's spectators might have been inspired to link it

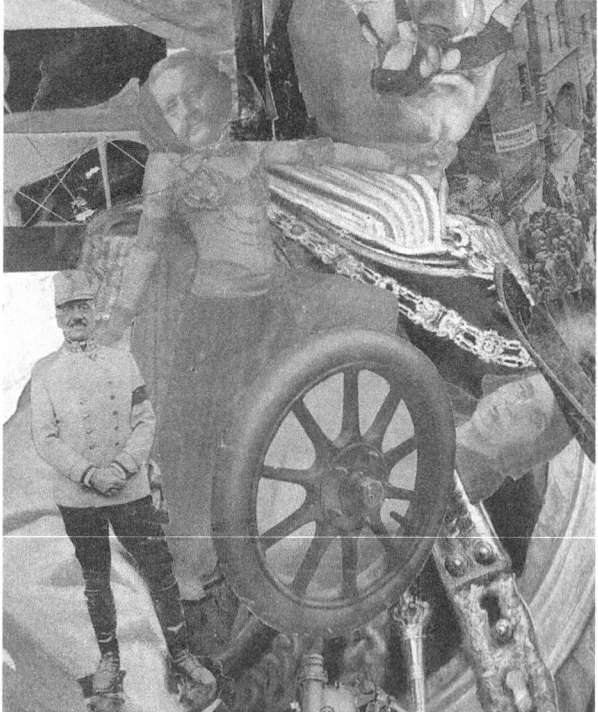

Figure 2.8. Hannah Höch, *Schnitt mit dem Küchenmesser Dada durch die letzte Weimarer Bierbauchkulturepoche Deutschlands* [Cut with the Kitchen Knife Dada through the Last Weimar Beer-Belly Cultural Epoch of Germany] (1919–20) (detail). Photograph from Bildarchiv Preussischer Kulturbesitz/ Art Resource, NY. Copyright 2009 Artists Rights Society (ARS), New York/VG Bild-Kunst, Bonn.

to the various conceptualizations of homosexuality that were discussed in the medical (and later the popular) press since the mid-nineteenth century or with the increased visibility of gay subcultures in Berlin since the late nineteenth century. Developing this chain of associations, someone might have extrapolated that, if even the macho Hindenburg could have had a female side, then perhaps the typical German man was less masculine and heterosexually identified than he appeared to be. Finally, some of the work's more erudite spectators might also have connected the image to issues of cross-dressing or to contemporary ideas in psychology about human beings synthesizing aspects of both sexes in their psyches. Beginning in the 1910s, Carl Jung argued that, over the course of human development, both men and women acquired characteristics of the opposite sex, which became part of their internal psychological makeup. Each man, according to the Swiss psychoanalyst, possessed an anima archetype—his inherited and unconsciously held feminine ideal—that determined his attraction or aversion to particular women that he met. Each woman, conversely, possessed an animus archetype—her inherited and unconsciously held masculine ideal—that conditioned her relations with the various men in her life.[118] By presenting Hindenburg as a hermaphrodite, Höch's photomontage could potentially have triggered an investigation of such concepts in the minds of some of its spectators.

Of course, in the absence of any contemporaneous critical commentary on this particular figure in *Cut with the Kitchen Knife,* it is impossible to reconstruct with absolute certainty the precise chains of association that went through the minds of the photomontage's contemporary spectators. However, given the circulation of these concepts in the intellectual sphere of the Weimar Republic—and, more important, the particular interests of the Berlin Dadaists and the cultural producers and intellectuals with whom they associated—these connotations would not be surprising. As artistic works suspended between different spheres of cultural production, photomontages such as *Cut with the Kitchen Knife* demanded to be read in terms of a multiplicity of often incommensurate sets of expectations. And to specify more concretely the horizon of ideas that enabled the "invention" of the Berlin Dada cyborg, the form that more than any other embodied the Dadaists' attempts to create an identity politics that was both artistic and practical, it is now necessary to turn to the development of the figure in the heterogeneous work of the "Dadasoph" Raoul Hausmann.

3. Raoul Hausmann's Revolutionary Media

Dada Performance, Photomontage, and the Cyborg

> The Dadaist exploits the psychological possibilities inherent in his faculty
> for flinging out his own personality as one flings a lasso or lets a cloak
> flutter in the wind. He is not the same man today as tomorrow, the day
> after tomorrow he will perhaps be "nothing at all," and then he may
> become everything.
>
> —RICHARD HUELSENBECK, *En Avant Dada: A History of Dadaism*
> (1920)

Hannah Höch's *Cut with the Kitchen Knife* was probably first shown at the "First International Dada Fair," the controversial art exhibition that took place between June 30 and August 25, 1920, in the Berlin gallery of Dr. Otto Burchard, an expert in Chinese Sung ceramics.[1] At that time the largest presentation of Dada art in Germany, the show, according to the catalog, consisted of 174 works by twenty-seven artists, although some of the names appear to have been fabricated. Filling two rooms and a corridor of Burchard's gallery from floor to ceiling with a jarring constellation of heterogeneous "products" *[Erzeugnisse],* as the Dadaists called their artworks, the fair was also, as the Dada artist, filmmaker, and historian Hans Richter notes, the "climax" of the public activities of the Berlin group.[2] After the exhibition ended, the loosely affiliated movement slowly dissolved.

The "Dada Fair" was the Berlin Dada artists' swan song as well as their eventual triumph. It is regarded as one of the central events that defined Dadaism in Germany, and several Dada artists—for example, Hausmann and Höch—are perhaps best remembered for the photomontages, assemblages, and other forms of artwork that they showed there. In addition, the exhibition is significant because it was here that the cyborg was first presented in Weimar visual culture in all its complexity. A central figure used by the Dadaists to criticize their various "enemies"—the types of human being from which they were supposedly the most different—the cyborg was also the predominant figure of Dada self-portraiture. It was, in other words, an extremely adaptable figure, one that could serve both critical and constructive projects.

As previously demonstrated, the Dadaists used photomontage to create open-ended representations that called on audiences to use their knowledge of contemporary personalities and events to generate a series of often conflicting interpretations. Depending on which constellations of fragments the viewer chose to interpret, the meanings of the photomontages fluctuated, a movement that promoted a negative dialectics between the different photomontage elements. This negative dialectics forestalled the complete reduction of reality to either the level of the photographic image or that of the written word—diminutions encouraged by the more univocal and propagandistic photomontage strategies employed by the mass press. And by playing the printed photographic fragment's indexical characteristics off its iconic and symbolic aspects, the Dada photomontages provoked viewers to compare the world as it was depicted through the media to the realities they experienced in everyday life and to the alternatives they could imagine. For these reasons, photomontage was for the Berlin Dadaists a way to encourage spectators to employ their new and evolving modes of distracted perception to dismantle the status quo and to question the mass media's subterranean social, political, and psychological stereotypes. The cyborg was thus used by the Dadaists to constitute a new type of spectator: an interpellated subject position produced by their heterogeneous artworks that investigated connections between transforming perception under the conditions of mass-reproduction and developing new forms of hybrid identity.[3]

To better understand this interpellated spectator, I turn to Raoul Hausmann, the "Dadasoph" and the Berlin Dadaists' primary theorist, who used his art to explore technology's impact on the mind and body. Hausmann's poetry and performance practices of 1918 and 1919 prepared the ground for the cyborgian imagery that dominated his caricatures, photomontages, and assemblages of 1920 and continued to be featured prominently in his work well into the 1930s. From Hausmann's poetry and performances, his concept of human identity, and his understanding of the relationship between sexuality and social revolution, I develop a new understanding of Hausmann's visual concerns. In particular, I investigate why his portraits often undermined their sitter's identity; why he sometimes emphasized sexuality in his representations; and why, in addition to reminding viewers of mechanized war, his images of the human–machine interface anticipated many of the ideas inherent in late-twentieth-century concepts of the cyborg.

From the very beginning of the movement in Germany, Hausmann was at the center of the Berlin Dadaists' political agitation and their development of new forms of nonorganic works designed to challenge and transform the spectator. Born in Vienna on July 25, 1886, Hausmann moved with his family to Berlin in 1900. His primary art education came from his father, Victor Hausmann, an academically trained Hungarian painter, although the future Dadaist also received formal training in anatomy and figure drawing between 1908 and 1911 at the Atelier for Painting and Sculpture in

Berlin-Charlottenburg, led by Arthur Lewin-Funcke.[4] In 1912 Hausmann met several Berlin expressionists, including the *Brücke* painters, Erich Heckel, Max Pechstein, and Karl Schmidt-Rottluff, as well as Herwarth Walden, whose *Der Sturm* [The Storm] journal and gallery were among the most important expressionist forums of the time. These influences, among others, caused Hausmann to reject his academicism and explore expressionist, cubist, and futurist styles of representation in traditional media such as oil, watercolor, drawing, woodcut, and lithography. After the outbreak of World War I, Hausmann—who, as an Austrian-born citizen living in Germany, was not drafted— remained in Berlin, where he continued to create modernist figure studies as well as town and street scenes. In 1915 he met several individuals who would shape his life and artistic formation leading up to the founding of the Berlin Dada movement in 1918: his lover and collaborator, Hannah Höch; Salomo Friedlaender and Franz Jung, both left-wing writers; and Otto Gross, a psychoanalyst whose thinking and practices diverged radically from those of Freud.

Influenced by Gross, Jung, Friedlaender, and Ernst Marcus, a neo-Kantian philosopher whom Hausmann met in 1916, Hausmann began in 1917 to publish short theoretical tracts on politics and art in such journals as Franz Pfemfert's *Die Aktion* [The Action], Jung and Richard Oehring's *Die freie Strasse*, Paul Westheim's *Das Kunstblatt* [The Art Paper], Anselm Ruest and Friedlaender's *Der Einzige* [The Only One], and Walther Rilla's *Die Erde* [The Earth].[5] (Previously, in 1912, Hausmann published two essays in *Der Sturm*.)[6] Hausmann was also in the audience when Richard Huelsenbeck read his controversial "First Dada Speech in Germany" in I. B. Neumann's Graphisches Kabinett in Berlin on January 22, 1918, and, in Huelsenbeck's loosely defined Dada aesthetic program, Hausmann found what he believed to be an art that suited his modernist and anarchist aesthetic theories. He enthusiastically responded to Huelsenbeck's call for a new, international, and anti-expressionist art, and, over the next three years, he devoted himself to Dada, spreading it throughout Germany not only as a set of practices but also as an ideology and a lifestyle. During this time, Hausmann wrote and published more than forty texts, both theoretical and poetic; coedited, designed, or produced several Dada publications; contributed to three exhibitions of Dada visual art;[7] planned or instigated a number of the group's most important media hoaxes; and performed at all twelve Dada "matinees" and "evenings" held primarily in Berlin but also in Dresden, Hamburg, Leipzig, Teplitz-Schönau, Karlsbad, and Prague.

Hausmann, Höch, and the Dada Lifestyle

As indicated by a publicity photograph depicting Hausmann and Höch posing in front of *Cut with the Kitchen Knife* at the "Dada Fair" (Figure 3.1), the Berlin Dada artists distinguished themselves in everyday life through several strategies. As suggested by the way they presented their bodies in public, the Dadaists saw themselves as living out a nontraditional, radically modern, and collaborative form of life. Hausmann and Höch imply this new and contradictory lifestyle through their stylish clothing and

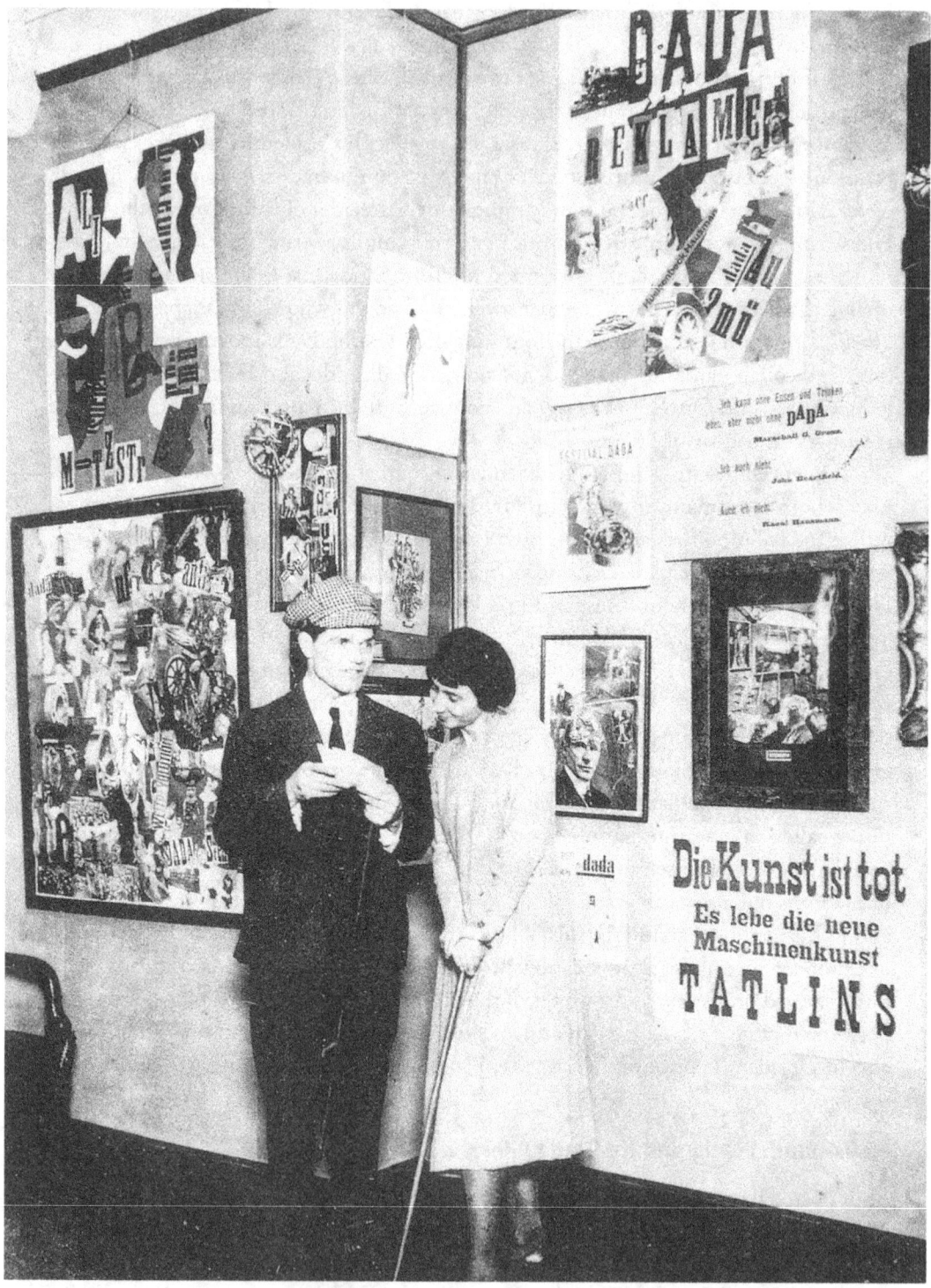

Figure 3.1. Raoul Hausmann and Hannah Höch in front of their works at the "First International Dada Fair" in Berlin, 1920 (photographer unknown). Photograph from Berlinische Gallerie, Berlin. Copyright 2009 Artists Rights Society (ARS), New York/ADAGP, Paris.

haircuts, which indicate both a modern fashion sense and a certain technological stream-lining, and the sporty cap that Hausmann wears with his suit, a weird combination of tradition and newness. This lifestyle is also suggested through the cane and fashionable stockings that Höch displays, which insinuate gender ambiguity and sexuality. Through their self-presentation, Höch and Hausmann identify themselves as part of a modern subculture at odds with traditional Wilhelmine society—something confirmed by their everyday lives, in which they experimented sexually and cultivated modern interests including fashion, sports, cinema, music, and dance.

Huelsenbeck's "Dada Manifesto" (1918), signed by Huelsenbeck, Hausmann, Jung, George Grosz, and others, helped define the Dada lifestyle that Hausmann and Höch sought to embody. The manifesto reveals the collaborative nature of Berlin Dada by representing Dada as an ideology and as a set of artistic strategies. Using violent metaphors, the manifesto's signatories argued that the highest form of art in their day should focus on the present as a nexus of traumatic contradictions, an art that "has been visibly shattered by the explosions of last week, which is forever trying to collect its limbs after yesterday's crash."[8] This art, they asserted, would achieve a new, more "primitive" relationship to reality, in which "life appears as a simultaneous muddle of noises, colors, and spiritual rhythms, which is taken unmodified into Dadaist art, with all the sensational screams and fevers of its reckless everyday psyche and with all its brutal reality."[9] Although such art was challenging and thus dangerous—both to its makers and to its viewers—it would finally break down the separation between art and life that, in the Dadaists' eyes, had made most contemporary art completely irrelevant.[10]

Because it attempted to reveal the modern world's chaos before it was given shape by concepts and conventions, Dada art, as the manifesto (loosely) defined it, promoted strategies of representation that defamiliarized everyday objects and pushed their communities to question the structure and nature of the everyday world. For these reasons, Dada was an ideology, a program that exhorted contemporary audiences to live in a state of revolutionary openness.

> Dada is a CLUB, founded in Berlin, which you can join without commitments. In this club every man is chairman and every man can have his say in artistic matters. . . . Under certain circumstances to be a Dadaist may mean to be more a businessman, more a political partisan than an artist—to be an artist only by accident—to be a Dadaist means to let oneself be thrown by things, to oppose all sedimentation; to sit in a chair for a single moment is to risk one's life.[11]

Although far less detailed than that of a political party, the Dadaist program resembled a political ideology in that it defined both a vision of the human being that its revolution was supposed to help create and antagonists or enemies whose grip on the contemporary world had first to be overcome. It also called for specific individual and collaborative practices, which included creating bruitist, simultaneist, and static poetry—defined by the Dadaists as concerts of human and machine sounds, multiple poems read simultaneously by different speakers, and poetry that renounced narrative connections between words, respectively—and it promoted "the new medium of painting," a strategy that the manifesto left undefined.

By delineating the Berlin Dada artists' intellectual framework and performative and collaborative roots, the manifesto points to their shared interest in reworking individual and collective identity in the context of group activity. Neither a style nor a movement, Dadaism, according to the manifesto, was an ideology of experimental self-transformation in the context of a nonbinding and open-ended group. And by dethroning art to produce a revolution in everyday life, the signatories of the "Dada Manifesto" invited their original audiences to join in. They believed that by changing themselves, and by suggesting new forms of interpersonal affinities and relationships, they could inspire others to do the same and in this way collectively develop new styles of living to radically alter their society.

Because it represents the Dadaists as an attractive, if slightly bizarre vanguard of a new lifestyle, the Hausmann–Höch publicity photograph helps dramatize the Dadaists' message and performative address to their audiences. "Classical Relations to the German Middle-Class Kitchen" (1920), a performance text by Hausmann that unfolds as a confusing stream-of-consciousness narrative about a conflict between a Dadaist and an expressionist artist, elucidates their message and performance strategies still further.[12] A story told for the most part in the third person, it was designed to introduce the Dada ideology and its self-fashioning lifestyle through dialogue with others in one's environment. When performed, as Hausmann did on two occasions, it allowed him to literally act out what it was to be a Dada artist at certain moments of the performance while suggesting how human beings produce themselves through appropriating culture and interacting with others in everyday life.

The narrative initially focuses on the bourgeois artist, a figure that appears to represent everything that the Dadaist will reject. The bourgeois artist is a "cleric" [Geistlicher] who "became an intellectual [Geistiger] and thus received free coupons for the noonday meal at the middle-class kitchen, which was opened in Berlin by a Mr. Abraham at the outbreak of the war."[13] In this milieu, which was supposed to suggest the social as well as intellectual impoverishment of Germany during the war years and immediately after, the intellectual eats his daily free lunch while pondering his economic and spiritual state and observing the surroundings. Hausmann presents the intellectual as his favorite caricature of an expressionist poet: namely, as an amalgam of romantic, bourgeois, Nietzschean, Christian, and nationalist elements. "For many long years he had used Wilhelm Meister as his morning prayer, Zarathustra or the Will to Power as grace for meals, and 'Above all Tree-Tops there is Peace' as his evening psalm."[14] As such, the expressionist artist is both the most extreme and the most debased form of the bourgeois—representing, as he does, "classical relations" to a grotesquely caricatured middle-class aesthetic tradition.

One day, while contemplating the decline of his financial situation, the intellectual reads graffiti that challenge his beliefs and his view of the milieu that supports him.

> On the walls of dingy eateries, on the soup-smeared tables and on the metal spittoons in which they served one's portion of turnip or dried codfish there were slogans like the following: the old God, who allowed iron to grow, did not want any Nietzsche. Or: the German middle-class kitchen is the birth of tragedy from the will to impotence. Or: Germany did not begin this war on account of Goethe.[15]

This experience of viewpoints that contradict his own not only drives him to despair but also causes him to flee the middle-class kitchen.[16] On the street and hungry, the intellectual steals a pear from a fruit store and is almost apprehended. To escape, he runs to the nearest cellar door, throws it open, and again finds himself back in the middle-class kitchen. Recognizing that his struggle to find a more spiritually congenial location is doomed to failure, he gives up his rebellion and finds a table. He decides that, from then on, he will simply eat and make observations.

As he studies his milieu, the intellectual begins to notice certain guests who are not middle class. He calls these figures "Scheidemänner"—a compound noun that could mean either "men who stand apart" or "vaginal men." These figures, who apparently come from the lower classes, are even more impoverished and in need of sustenance than the intellectual. According to the intellectual, the *Scheidemänner*

> would walk through an eatery with eagle eyes, swooping like animals onto any leftover plate of turnip, in order to devour it in some corner. . . . And later on he made the observation that these men were called "bus boys." They had never known Goethe or Nietzsche, and they were equipped with metal bowls, which they filled with the leftover food that even these men themselves no longer wanted to devour. They probably took it home to fatten a little pig, or they sold their turnip slop at night to the Spartacists.[17]

And from the class of the *Scheidemänner,* the intellectual meets a Dada artist: a man whose name and characteristics keep shifting and whose political allegiances appear to belong to the Far Left.

As Hausmann describes him, the Dadaist is a protean and contradictory being characterized by a curious combination of abjection and power, a

> man whose appearance made one think alternately that he was Kerr or Shakespeare, but it was just Leonor Goldschmidt. He looked like a corpse who had drowned in turnip water, and he had learned a lot. He bragged about his relationship with the German poet Huelsenbeck, about whom there was a rumor that he consumed dinners for three hundred marks.[18]

With his strange ideas, the Dadaist is a purveyor of radical and seemingly painful insight. In addition, he is a reminder to the intellectual of the disregard that some in his milieu have for the bourgeois aesthetic tradition in which the intellectual still believes.

The Dadaist sells the intellectual a book, *The Drama of Anti-Violence,* that he begins to read and then throws down in horror, declaring it to be "unclassical, un-Nietzschean," and anti-German.[19] Not comprehending the intellectual's dismay, the Dadaist responds to his outburst with a performance of a poem that closely resembles one of Hausmann's own.[20] (Indeed, when Hausmann recited these lines, it must have been at this moment in his narrative when he merged most seamlessly with the subject position of one of his characters.)

He [the Dada artist] wiped his soupy fingers in the gray-red hair on his head and began to recite with pathos:

The Auto of My Soul

O lullewulle weileimei
O meimeideidei bommdei
O deiedommbei parr
O parrere o parreree E E E
O o o o o o o!!![21]

After this brief interlude, Hausmann returns to third-person narrative, noting that, in response to the experience of Dada sound poetry, the intellectual grows so furious that he physically attacks "Goldkerr," as the Dadaist is called at this juncture in the action.

Hausmann now begins to describe the expressionist intellectual's state of mind in a language that makes it sound like a self-justifying internal monologue. The intellectual, Hausmann explains,

had so little self-control because it was all about the highest good of the nation. And furthermore turnips are an insidious, completely character-spoiling food. Our intellectual was less responsible for his fit of furious anger than some psychoanalysts would later have us believe, for in addition, the plump sausage-legs of the female waitresses had long provoked him. What was one to make of all those round behinds, those (sometimes slightly pendulous) bosoms, those calves above little patent leather shoes with cloth inserts, those ironed curls above tempting blue eyes—when one fed only on barley, barley, and barley![22]

And by here merging momentarily with the intellectual's subject position, Hausmann manages to increase the shock and humor of what transpires next. To the aroused intellectual's great horror and chagrin, the waitresses take the Dadaist's side, rushing to his aid and violently turning against the intellectual. The serving staff, however, cannot hurt the intellectual, because the experience of sound poetry as well as his physical attack on the Dadaist have changed him. The intellectual's eyes glow with an inner light, and, in response to the outcry against his actions, he begins to address the assembled staff and patrons of the kitchen with a brief disjointed speech in which he extols the virtues of classicism, religion, and middle-class cuisine in general. He ends with an impassioned paean to the greatness of Germany.

In the narrative development of Hausmann's allegory of artistic struggle, every action produces an even greater reaction—an intensifying dialectic that becomes extremely pronounced as the story enters its climax. After the intellectual's outburst, it is the entire group of people around him that now loses control: a response that elicits an even more astonishing one.

> The women shed tears of emotion—they are always susceptible to flights of fancy. But the men grumbled. At first softly, then loudly, and finally they were caught up in the Teutonic fury. They picked up the legs of chairs—but at this point our intellectual flew like the prophet up through the ceiling, and to this day the German spirit still is the worse for it.[23]

"For this reason," Hausmann concludes, ascribing the tastes of his fictitious bourgeois intellectual to his various listeners, "you should purchase Goetheschiller's works, published in one volume by Schmelzle and Butterfass, for 50 pfennig. But let me consume my veal cutlets undisturbed."[24]

Ending on a sudden, perplexing, and quasi-mystical note, Hausmann's performance text—an allegory about his contemporary aesthetic situation—remains obscure as to its ultimate meaning. Although he vividly describes the middle-class kitchen, its emotional and potentially dangerous clients, and the increasingly violent encounters between its grimy walls, the story's overall symbolism and ultimate allegiances are never clearly resolved. Since Hausmann at times plays each of the main characters, he seems to identify with both the Dadaist and the expressionist figure. He thereby renders his "message" to his audience ambiguous: the Dada artist, he suggests, is never entirely separated from the supposedly more traditional artists he is trying to supplant. Moreover, the expressionist seems to triumph at the end, something that also implies a mixed and heterogeneous artistic situation, one in which artists with different styles and philosophies compete. By playing both sides, as it were, Hausmann suggests that the new human is a combination of individual and collective elements—a particular synthesis of values and behaviors selected from a larger set of intersubjective possibilities circulating in German culture. The main thing that distinguishes the Dada artist from his opponent is that the Dadaist seems to be at home with constant change and self-development.

Hausmann's performance text promotes critical reflection on the institutions and the forms of modern art. Through its setting, the soup kitchen, which parodies a café where artists and intellectuals gather, Hausmann points to the literary and artistic circles that flourished in Berlin during and after the war, groups in which he had formed his identity as a cultural producer. In this way, Hausmann's text could have provoked his audiences to envision artists as dependent on multiple networks for informational and material resources. Not only does café culture feed and sustain the budding artist, but—as suggested by Hausmann's ironic metaphor of (spiritual) culture as food—by appropriating objective culture, people also produce and change themselves. However base or admirable, the cultural context, in other words, provides essential resources that make artists who and what they are, and that also help determine both the forms and the meanings of their works. In addition, through its biting irony as well as its switching of subject positions, Hausmann's text potentially gets its audiences to reflect on many related issues, including the functions of artistic competition, how artists and artworks help produce one another, and how artists can affirm, criticize, and transform their social and material contexts.

Hausmann's performance text also promotes critical reflection on human identity. The narrative's focus on nourishment, sexuality, and violence suggests a corporeal and partially unconscious play of forces motivating the story's protagonists and their strange, sometimes impulsive actions. In addition, both protagonists are extremely active, and thus they are shown to define their characters through actions, reactions, and interchanges. Furthermore, the story's subtle references to ethnic differences—created by the contrast between the intellectual's German nature and the Jewish character of the kitchen's proprietor and at times the Dadaist—might also have prompted the spectator to think about the roles that cultural or possibly even genetic forces played in determining human identity.[25] Finally, as was also the case with Hausmann's sound poems, the text's confusing and confrontational character could potentially have caused audience members to become angry, and, as a result, a situation might have arisen where they became aware of their own emotional and libidinal natures.

"Classical Relations to the German Middle-Class Kitchen" shows that Hausmann understood human identity to be a function of a person's interactions with cultural artifacts as well as others in his or her environment. A consideration of the forms and subjects of a few of Hausmann's most famous Dadaist artworks allows us to better understand the types of identity that he attempted to promote. In addition, such a consideration will also help us comprehend why exploring spectatorship became such an important component of his visual productions.

Anti-Auratic Art

As suggested by the works that surround Hausmann and Höch in their publicity photograph (Figure 3.1), the Berlin Dada artists also attempted to differentiate themselves from other modern artists by making heterogeneous and montage-based forms of art—a set of practices that probably began in early 1919. Above *Cut with the Kitchen Knife* hangs Höch's now-destroyed poster *Ali Baba Diele, Berlin* [Ali Baba Hall, Berlin] (1919–20), which juxtaposes irregularly cut letters of different typefaces with asymmetric abstract shapes. It can be read as either a street poster—presumably an advertisement, or parody thereof, promoting an institution named "Ali Baba," on "Motz Street"—or, perhaps, an abstract urban street scene of a road between two rows of buildings viewed from a high angle. To the far right of Höch's poster is Hausmann's

Dada Poster (1919–20), which, under the title of "Dada Advertisement," presents a shouting self-portrait of the Dadasoph, who is juxtaposed with irregularly cut fragments of his poster poems and sound poetry texts. Like Höch's *Ali Baba Hall,* Hausmann's *Dada Poster* appears to be printed. It is thus different in auratic status from Höch's *Cut with a Kitchen Knife* because it is not an "original" photomontage but one of potentially many reproductions.

"Aura," as Walter Benjamin argued, was the appearance of all those qualities of an artwork that conveyed its uniqueness and authenticity, those characteristics that made it a little like a person or some other type of complex natural being. To experience a work's aura was to perceive its originality, its "distance" from the everyday world as an object of respect or reverence, a phenomenon linked to art's historical origins in the practices of magic and religion.[26] Aura, according to Benjamin, was literally an artwork's "presence" as something outside the ordinary, as shaped materials imbued with meaning and significance. It was experienced through the signs that a work bore of its beginnings or causes in individuals, cultures, and societies as well as through the marks of change and the accretions that a work carried, the indices of transformation that indicated its duration in time and history.[27] In the nineteenth and twentieth centuries, the development of mass-reproduction and especially the mass media helped destroy people's abilities to perceive the aura of both art and nature.[28] And because of the seductive nature of the representations circulating since the invention of photography, human beings tended less and less to look to art as a source of normative forms or values.

By presenting such "anti-art" creations as photomontages and printed posters as works of art—as well as by playing with subtle auratic differences between the different types of work—Hausmann and Höch appear to have acknowledged the disintegration of aura under the conditions of mass-reproduction and the mass media. Directly below and parallel to the left side of Hausmann's *Dada Poster* appear two of his framed photomontages, both of which depict cyborgs: *Self-Portrait of the Dadasoph* (1920) and, below, *Tatlin Lives at Home* (1920). To the right of *Tatlin,* another framed photomontage is hung, *A Bourgeois Precision Brain Calls Forth a World Movement: Dada Triumphs* (1920). This photomontage presents what appears to be a profile portrait of Huelsenbeck, his brain partially exposed, positioned in the very front of a strangely angled room, filled with adding machines, typewriters, and wall-mounted machine parts. As the frames around the three cyborgian representations suggest, like *Cut with the Kitchen Knife,* they are much more clearly "original" photomontages than the photomontage-based posters above them. Unlike the Dada posters, the cuts and splices of the photomontages are not rephotographed and printed, and thus they seem more auratic than the posters. Despite the fact that they are primarily composed of photomechanically reproduced elements appropriated from the mass media, the photomontages appear as constellations made by hand, touched and shaped by the artist who selected them.

Finally, two printed signs, the first to the right of Hausmann's *Self-Portrait* and the second below *Dada Triumphs,* add to the play of different art forms with differing degrees of aura. The first sign reads,

"I can live without eating or drinking, but not without **DADA**."

> Marshal G. Grosz.

"I can't either."

> John Heartfield.

"Neither can I."

> Raoul Hausmann.

The second sign states:

Art is dead
Long live the new
machine art of
TATLIN

As is the case with the posters, traces of the artist's physical presence are absent from these printed signs.

In comparison with the "authentic" photomontages, these signs appear much less handmade and unique. And even in comparison to the posters, the signs seem more anonymous, more like mass-produced products—perhaps because of their less visual, more purely linguistic nature. At the same time, their irony and unconventional typography make them distinct and artistic and, thus, slightly auratic. In addition, although they do not depict cyborgs directly, like the Dada posters, they exude a cyborgian aesthetic. Not only are they made by mechanical means, but they also evoke familiar cyborgian subjects: collective military activity, the experience of violence and trauma, and a sense that technology is transforming both art and human consciousness.

In addition to acknowledging the waning of aura in the context of modern industrial societies, the Berlin Dada artists' playful attacks on the signs of art's presence, uniqueness, and authenticity through photomontage, assemblage, and signage were motivated by their rejection of all past modern art movements and their interest in bringing their audiences face-to-face with modern life's brute realities. Hand in hand with their recognition of the diminishment or loss of art's aura in the twentieth century was an awareness that art had to develop new social and political functions. One function was to reacquaint modern audiences with the realities of the modern world. As Wieland Herzfelde wrote in the introduction to the "Dada Fair" catalog, photography had supplanted the traditional purpose of painting—to allow people to see things that they could not see with their own eyes—and, as a result, modern painting had gradually liberated itself from reality. "Dadaism," in turn, was "the reaction to all those attempts to deny the factual, attempts which were the driving force of the Impressionists, Expressionists, Cubists, and also the Futurists (in that they did not want to capitulate to film)."[29] Instead of competing with photography, however,

> the Dadaist[s] say: if at an earlier time, love and effort were expended on the painting
> of a body, a flower, a hat, a shadow, etc., we only have to take the scissors and cut out

all these things we need from among the paintings, photographic reproductions; if it concerns something smaller we don't even need a depiction at all, but can take the objects themselves, for example pocket-knives, ashtrays, books, etc., all things which have been quite beautifully painted in the museums of old art, but painted just the same.[30]

Dada photomontage and assemblage were thus developed to allow modern subject matter to return to visual art in a new and provocative way.

The return of subject matter in Dada art was, moreover, a provocative gesture because it was accomplished through appropriation, a strategy that undermined the artist's traditional authority—his or her claim to privileged insight into the human condition.[31] As Herzfelde put it,

> Today the young person who does not want to give up all claim[s] to education and to the broadening of his native talents has to submit to the thoroughly authoritarian system of artistic education and the artistic public judgment. In contrast, Dadaists are saying that production of pictures is not important, and that at least one should not assume a position of authority when one does make pictures. In this way, the pleasure the masses may take in the creative activity would not be ruined by the professional arrogance of a haughty guild. For this reason the contents and also the media of Dadaistic pictures and products can be extraordinarily varied. By itself any product is Dadaistic which is created without influence from and regard for public authority and criteria of judgment. And it remains Dadaistic as long as the image works against illusion, out of the need to subversively assist the contemporary world, which obviously is in a state of disintegration and metamorphosis. . . . The only program the Dadaists recognize is the duty to make current events, current in both time and place, the content of their pictures.[32]

For the Dada artists, the loss of art's aura in their contemporary moment produced a situation in which creating and appreciating art could become more democratic. Art, they believed, could now be made both by and for a greater cross section of the public—a situation that they attempted to foster through their own statements and artistic productions. Moreover, as suggested by the anti-auratic artworks that they presented at the "Dada Fair," the figure that best embodied the new more democratic modes of art making and art reception seemed to be the cyborg. It was a motif tailor-made to represent a new type of less authoritarian and more communal artist as well as an engaged, distracted, and technologically savvy mass audience.

Three Cyborgs

As suggested by two works that he exhibited at the "Dada Fair," the photomontage *Selbstporträt des Dadasophen* [Self-Portrait of the Dadasoph] (1920) (Figure 3.2) and the ink drawing *Der eiserne Hindenburg* [The Iron Hindenburg] (1920) (Figure 3.3),

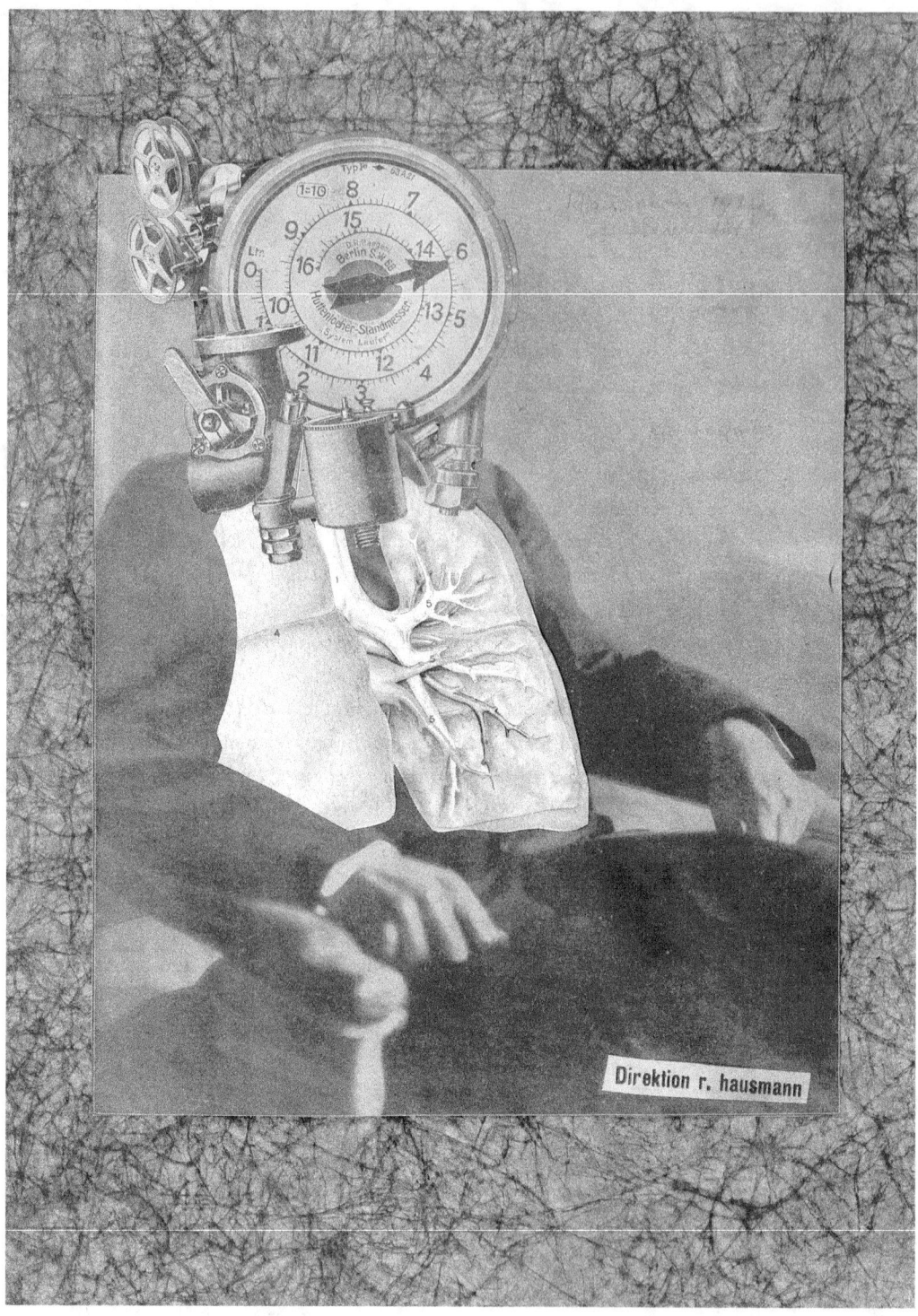

Figure 3.2. Raoul Hausmann, *Selbstporträt des Dadasophen* [Self-Portrait of the Dadasoph] (1920). Photomontage and collage on handmade Japanese paper. 36.2 × 28 cm (14¼ × 11 inches). Private collection. Courtesy of Annely Juda Fine Art, London. Copyright 2009 Artists Rights Society (ARS), New York/ADAGP, Paris.

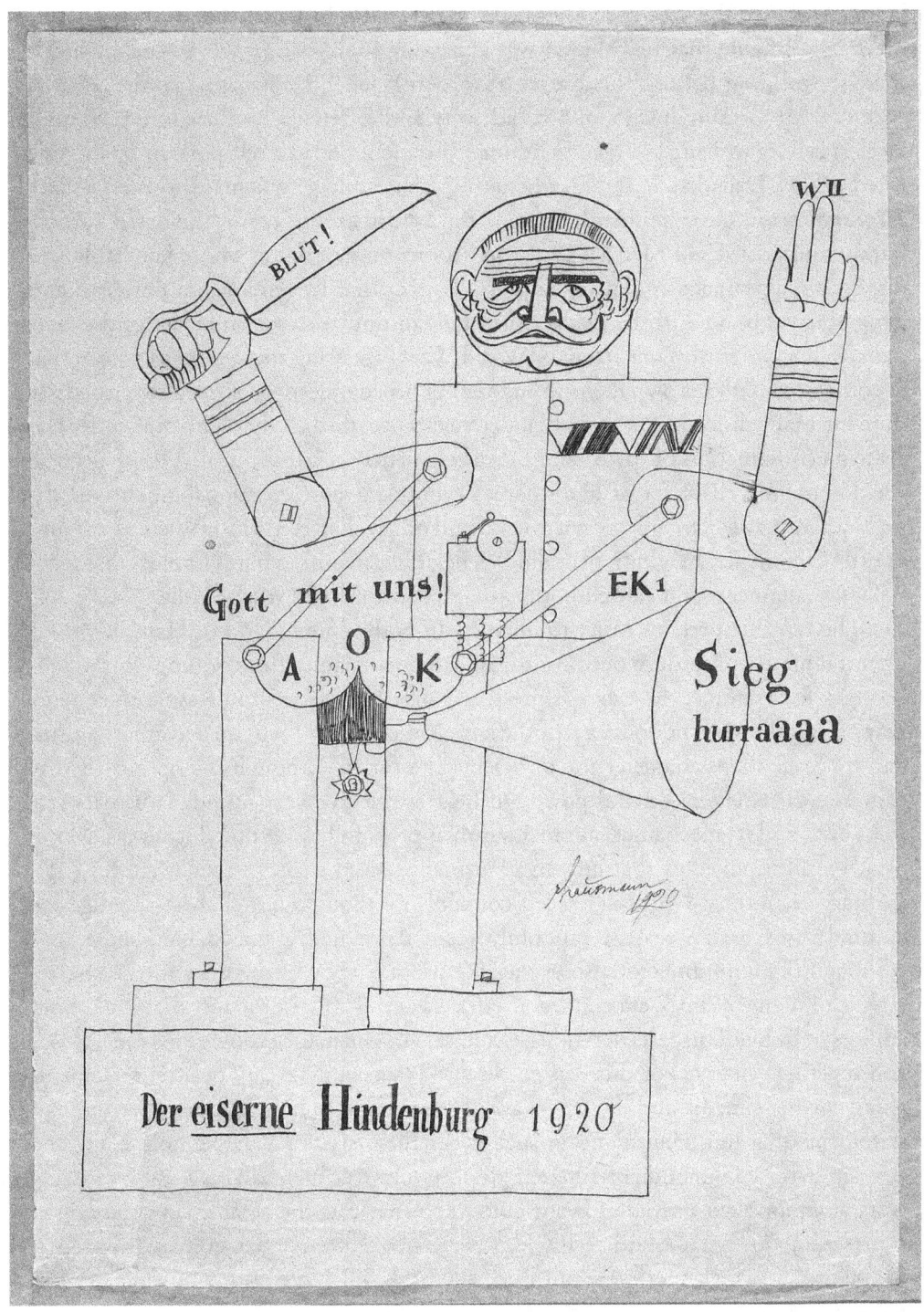

Figure 3.3. Raoul Hausmann, *Der eiserne Hindenburg* [The Iron Hindenburg] (1920). Ink on paper. 40.6 × 33.2 cm (16 × 13 inches). Musée national d'art moderne, Centre Georges Pompidou, Paris. Photograph from CNAC/MNAM/Dist. Réunion des Musées Nationaux/Art Resource, NY. Copyright 2009 Artists Rights Society (ARS), New York/ADAGP, Paris.

Hausmann used the cyborg to represent the new hybrid human: a half-organic, half-mechanized figure that he believed was appearing with ever greater frequency in his modern world. As became the case with Norbert Wiener, Hausmann saw the cyborg's potential for forming images of both identity and difference. *Self-Portrait* presents a faceless cyborg wearing bourgeois clothing. It is identified as a self-portrait by the title listed in the "Dada Fair" catalog, where the photomontage was first shown. *The Iron Hindenburg,* on the other hand, presents the cyborg as the enemy, the hated authoritarian militarist, Field Marshal Paul von Hindenburg, a figure whose laughable and disgusting appearance could not disguise the fact that he remained a powerful and dangerous "antipode" of the Dada artists and continued to act on behalf of the German military after the conclusion of World War I. By using the cyborg as a form that encompassed both his own identity and that of his enemies, Hausmann suggested the fundamentally dialectical nature of modern existence, the fact that human identity was always a combination of "own" and "alien" elements, as Gross put it. This dialectical yet overarching character of Hausmann's cyborgian representations anticipated the uneasy play between friend and enemy, self and other, characteristic of Wiener's account of early cybernetics. In addition, as did Wiener, Hausmann's cyborgs implied that technological augmentation carried both extreme benefits and extreme risks.

The risks are perhaps easier to identify. In both representations, Hausmann sets up a traumatic continuum between organic and mechanical functioning. In the self-portrait, for example, the cyborg's pressure-gauge head seems to measure the energy that pumps through his body: a parodic anticipation of the focus on servomechanisms and feedback loops characteristic of Wiener's research. Although the figure's rigidity expresses extreme tension and power, its head is put to a very mundane use, its face lacks eyes, and its mechanical augmentation appears to have exposed its lungs. Moreover, the film projector that crowns Hausmann's head suggests that whatever rudimentary brain the cyborg still has left contains not thought but clichés—predigested cultural signs that the artist randomly recirculates in his reified consciousness.[33] Although the film projector also evokes the utopian view of the mass media characteristic of many Weimar-era cultural producers and theorists, the fact that the cyborg appears to be blind suggests that—here, at least—its cinematic thoughts flow in a closed and repetitive circuit. For this reason, despite Hausmann's many positive statements about the mass media and the new ways of seeing created by science and technology, statements that link Hausmann to such other theorists as László Moholy-Nagy and Benjamin, the conjunction of different photomontage elements in his *Self-Portrait* suggests an ambivalent attitude toward cinema.[34] The fears that Hausmann sometimes expressed about science and technology, anxieties that emerged from his awareness of the uses to which they were put during World War I, are clearly apparent in this representation.[35]

In early 1922 Hausmann criticized films like Robert Wiene's *Cabinet of Doctor Caligari* (1920) and Carl Boese and Paul Wegener's *Golem* (1920) for making practical life too "interesting" and "spiritual," thereby covering up the conventional and quotidian aspects of the everyday world.[36] And while not all of his elliptical references to cinema are negative, it seems clear that Hausmann is to some extent in agreement with the idea, already strongly articulated before World War I, that film had tremendous potential to distort and lie about reality. Thus, in addition to the prewar attack on cinema by bourgeois critics, who argued that through their nonliterary and entertaining qualities, films were helping destroy German culture, we also discover attacks on cinema from left-wing spectators, who argued that motion pictures distorted and denigrated the workers' movement.[37] As I demonstrated through my analysis of *Heimatklänge,* Hausmann was suspicious of the nationalistic uses to which the new means of mass communication could be put, in which audio and film technologies were used to arouse the emotions of large groups of German citizens and bend them to the political will of the ruling powers. In this regard, Hausmann's implied criticisms of the mass media in *Heimatklänge* and *Self-Portrait* partially echo the statements of reformers such as Victor Noak, who distinguished between different types of movies and argued that certain forms had a pernicious effect on the German public. As Noak wrote in *Die Aktion* in 1912, five years before Hausmann published an essay in the very same journal, "The producers of film smut do not seek 'simply to confuse people'; they appeal to their lowest instincts, promote meanness, nurture brutality, poison the souls of young people, and destroy social values. People must resist these producers, just as they resist bad education, which is the precondition of everything loathsome."[38] And for these reasons, it is not hard to envision that the eyeless cyborg wearing a projector atop its head in Hausmann's self-portrait suggests at least a partial critique of cinema.

The portrait of Hindenburg, moreover, goes even further to emphasize the cyborg's dysfunctional nature. Expressing his hatred of German militarism, Hausmann presents the field marshal as a rigid, half-mechanized puppet, spouting clichéd military jargon, waving a sword, and propping up the kaiser's initials. A conservative monarchist and hero of the eastern front, Hindenburg was, for many Germans, the living incarnation of the Prussian "iron will" and martial spirit that had unified their country a scant half century before. As noted previously, he was the subject of an enormous personality cult during World War I, and his image was plastered on ashtrays, neckties, flags, and other forms of consumer kitsch to symbolize German military might and stimulate the patriotic spirit of ordinary Germans. In addition, in 1915, homemade wooden statues of Hindenburg were created all over Germany to raise money for military causes. The largest of these figures was a twenty-eight-ton, twelve-foot-high statue erected in Berlin's Königsplatz; in return for donations to the National Foundation of War Widows, Berliners could hammer iron, silver, and gold nails into the wooden effigy, an extremely popular practice that netted approximately one hundred thousand donations in a single week.[39] As suggested by the two nails that anchor the feet of Hausmann's representation to its base, Hausmann was most probably well aware of this phenomenon, and his caricature might even be a direct reference to these popular practices, which conflated politics with economics.

Influenced by Grosz's scathing political satire as well as the burgeoning field of popular cartoons, Hausmann's representation transforms Hindenburg, traditionally regarded as an authoritarian yet aristocratic father figure, into an obscene and violent monstrosity: a patchwork horror whose empty phrases and comic dysfunctionality do not completely mask an atmosphere of danger and menace. In this way, Hausmann expresses intense hatred of German militarism through caricature—a standard form of political and social propaganda. To emphasize the cyborg's dysfunctional nature, Hausmann displays its body split in two, its arms linked to its buttocks, and its voice emerging from its genitals. Contrasting with its human face and hairy backside, the cyborg's body displays prominent mechanical grafts—for example, the loudspeaker and military medal combination that replaces its reproductive organs. Through these grafts, Hausmann implies ambivalence about the ultimate benefits of technological enhancement; since, in addition to military capabilities, the speaker and medal amalgam also connotes castration. And in this way, Hausmann also suggests some of the dangerous authoritarian characteristics of the military leadership of World War I—a leadership that he represents as both highly aggressive and sexually dysfunctional.

The fragmented and composite character of Hausmann's Hindenburg portrait recalls Höch's undermining representation of Hindenburg in *Cut with the Kitchen Knife*. In the same way, Hausmann's representation reveals the "newness" of the patriarchal figures that live on in the postwar context. Like Höch's transgendered Hindenburg, Hausmann's castrated field marshal has been transformed by his circumstances. His laughable and disgusting appearance, however, does not disguise the fact that he remains powerful and dangerous, a figure that continues to represent—and act on the behalf of—the old and authoritarian German political order.[40] In addition, the caricatured form of *The Iron Hindenburg* and the specific political message that it expresses belie the representation's status as art. Also published as part of his print portfolio, *hurra, hurraa, hurraaa!* in 1920 by Malik Verlag, *The Iron Hindenburg* was exhibited in Room One of the "Dada Fair." By elevating "common" caricature to the status of art through its positioning in the gallery context, Hausmann carried out an avant-garde expansion of the materials out of which art could be made. In this way, he attempted to connect modern art to the long-standing and diverse traditions of political, social, and children's caricature, which were already beginning to be collected and anthologized before the war.[41] Exemplified by such figures as Honoré Daumier, Heinrich Zille, and Heinrich Christian Wilhelm Busch, respectively, these traditions were both profoundly moralizing and focused on current events. Hausmann thus incorporated caricature's topical and moralizing strategies into *The Iron Hindenburg* to make a fundamentally political form of modern art; like his photomontages, this work undermined the distinction between fine art and popular culture, and thereby attacked art's autonomy and the distinction between art and life.

By presenting Hindenburg as a traumatized and patched-together figure, Hausmann also alludes to the practice—carried out much more extensively in the photomontages, paintings, and assemblages of Grosz, John Heartfield, and the Dresden-based Otto Dix—of employing the figure of the cyborg as a "war cripple" and thus as a counter to the idealized image of the armored male soldier, a figure that became popular during World War I. Nearly all the Berlin Dada artists point to wartime visual culture as—at least in part—inspiring their photomontage practices.[42] (Cubist collages as well as the collage practices of the Italian futurists and the Zurich Dada artists were the other influences that some of them acknowledged.) For Grosz and Heartfield, their development of photomontage as a fine art strategy in the late 1910s was motivated by their earlier practice of sending collaged postcards and care packages with antipatriotic messages to one another during wartime. In these early works, none of which have survived, the ambiguity of the photomontage technique was employed to evade military censors. In addition, this strategy also evoked the practices of wartime advertising and the organized production and sending of "care packages" by female volunteers to frontline soldiers.[43] Hausmann and Höch, on the other hand, directly referred to their contact with soldier portraits in the summer of 1918 as the experience that made them realize the possibilities of photomontage as an artistic strategy.[44]

Produced by the thousands in the late nineteenth and early twentieth centuries, soldier portraits were idealized images of armored male soldiers (Figure 4.7).[45] Images that commemorated wartime service in both word and likeness, soldiers purchased them to send home to loved ones, to celebrate a comrade's retirement from active duty, or for themselves after they returned from the war. To have a portrait made, a soldier would sit for a photographer, who would shoot a likeness of the soldier's head. The photographer would then cut and paste the finished photograph into a mass-produced lithographic image or some other form of ready-made framework that depicted idealized uniformed bodies that were often positioned against military or heraldic backgrounds. Ideologically, these materially hybrid images affirmed nationalist and militarist ideals. They were produced and consumed by individuals interested in glorifying and ennobling the military subject. For the most part, this meant conforming the soldier's unique physiognomy and ready-made body to the values of the Prussian state, which wanted him to fight an enemy and possibly die, "with God for King and Fatherland," as the popular saying went. Although the soldier portraits supported the interests of the German monarchy, they were not state propaganda. Instead they were mass-market commodities that catered to the psychological needs of a majority of Germans while helping legitimate the political, economic, and military status quo.

Klaus Theweleit has analyzed the psychology of the German soldier of this period in his monumental *Male Fantasies,* a study of the memoirs of various *Freikorps* officers, veterans who served in the right-wing armies that fought the Left in Germany during the first few years of the Weimar Republic.[46] Many of these soldiers ended up serving the Nazi movement, and Theweleit's study, since its publication in the mid-1970s, has come to be interpreted as one of the paradigmatic accounts of the psychology of the fascist male subject.[47] According to Theweleit, the typical *Freikorps* officer possessed an undeveloped ego. He was afraid of his own desires as well as anything else that would cause his fragile sense of corporeal and psychic identity to be overcome. To shore up his ego, the fascist subject fortified his body through physical drill, armor, and weapons, and through exterminating all forms of otherness that threatened his inchoate and shaky sense of self: in particular, women, Bolsheviks, Jews, and the un-regimented mass. Afraid to acknowledge the personal, intimate, and desiring aspects of his being, he furthermore sought solace in abstract concepts of the community—the troop, the army, the nation, and the people *(das Volk)*—in whose name he destroyed what he perceived as different from himself and thus a threat. It was only in acts of mobilization (as part of a hierarchically organized and disciplined mass with a strong leader) and killing that he could experience his own desires—acts that not only pre-vented him from recognizing these desires for what they really were but also shored up the rigid distinctions through which he understood his world.

The soldier portraits that inspired Hausmann and Höch's development of pho-tomontage as a Dada practice fit well with Theweleit's analysis of the early-twentieth-century German military subject. As suggested by numerous examples, the soldier portraits glorified the fighting man's figure by armoring it and making it look power-ful.[48] They accomplished this by building up the soldier's body through his idealized, mass-produced uniform; by equipping him with weapons; by representing him with an erect and vigilant posture; and by often situating him amid a troop or set of iden-tically dressed comrades in arms, ideologically committed "brothers" who shared a single cause. Given this conjunction between the soldier portraits and the Wilhelmine and fascist military ideals, it is easy to see why the Berlin Dada artists favored both photomontage and the image of the cyborg as a war cripple in the early 1920s. Together, the strategy and the specific image type referred to and undermined the military ideal as represented by the soldier portraits. Typically, the Dada images of war cripples broke down the armored male body, portraying it as shattered, dysfunctional, and uncontrollable, seething with instinct and unchecked desires. And although *The Iron Hindenburg* certainly embodied this aspect of the Berlin Dada artists' practices—their attempts to use the cyborg to undermine the duplicitous military ideal that helped lead Germany to ruin—the representation of war cripples was only one part of Haus-mann's visual practice, and a small one at that. Unlike Grosz, Heartfield, and Dix, who all saw military service, Hausmann avoided the war, and afterward he rarely used the cyborg to attack the figure of the armored male soldier. Instead, in Hausmann's work, the cyborg—particularly as configured through photomontage—was far more fre-quently used to explore the positive aspects of the technological enhancement of human beings, albeit not without a consistent admixture of ambivalence.

Self-Portrait, for example, also generates positive associations about the technolog-ical transformation of vision. In the first place, the figure's pressure-gauge head, which seems to measure the energy that its body produces, could have evoked the new inter-est in measuring how the human body expended energy. As Anson Rabinbach has argued, by the 1890s, German and other European scientists were immersed in inves-tigating the physiology of labor power. Conceiving "the working body as a system of economies of force and as the focal point for new techniques that could eliminate social conflict while ensuring productivity," they redefined the human body through functional and structural analogies to machines in much the same way that Wiener would approximately a half century later; furthermore, they developed new ways to measure a person's energy expenditure to make factory work more efficient.[49] By establishing the exact caloric values of all nutritive substances, for example, they hoped to predict the precise amount of labor power that could be produced by ingesting specific types and amounts of food.[50] In addition, by constructing "ergographic" devices to measure fatigue—or how an individual's capacity to produce particular motions decreased over time through repetition—they hoped to isolate the other major factor that affected a human being's ability to produce labor power.[51] Other fatigue studies, as Rabinbach notes, quickly followed, and, after 1900, "ergonomic studies investigated the influence of weight, rhythm, heat, cold, anemia, blood chemistry, and other factors on the fatigued body."[52] Hausmann's self-portrait, which gives the impression that the cyborg is paying attention to internal senses such as thermoception (our sense of temperature), nociception (our sense of pain), equilibrioception (our sense of balance and acceleration), and proprioception (our bodily awareness or perception of the positions of our body parts to one another), reminds us of how much the metaphor of human beings as machines has refined our modes of self-awareness. Furthermore, as suggested by the history of scientific investigation of the processes of energy, heat, motion, and fatigue in the human body to which the photomontage possibly alludes, such a focus on the individual as a human motor led directly to Germany's engagement with F. W. Taylor's system of industrial management in the 1910s and 1920s.[53]

Hausmann's self-portrait could also have potentially reminded its spectators of the long invention of autogenic training by the German psychiatrist Johannes Schultz beginning in the 1910s.[54] Influenced by yoga and meditation, Schultz's technique was a method for influencing the autonomic nervous system, which has control over heart rate, circulation, digestion, respiration, and other involuntary processes that help maintain the body's homeostasis. By learning a set of simple exercises in bodily awareness and relaxation, Germans trained in Schultz's method could begin to control stress, anxiety, and tension, and, in this way, lead happier, healthier lives. Because it caused its practitioners to focus on the body's various internal processes and then to use passive concentration techniques to begin to control them, autogenic training anticipated biofeedback, which developed in the 1960s and which used various forms of electrical activity sensors to provide its practitioners with information about their bodily states. And because of its depiction of a half-human, half-mechanized creature possibly focused on its own interior processes, *Self-Portrait* evokes the trajectory of alternative medicine that—both with and without technological feedback devices—helps human beings to mentally affect their physical states.

Finally, in addition to suggesting criticisms about how cinema was affecting consciousness, Hausmann's photomontage also evokes optimistic readings having to do with how film was transforming human perception in the first few decades of the twentieth century. Embodying a position antithetical to this chapter's argument about Dada photomontage and film, Kristin Jean Makholm argues in her well-researched and informative study on Höch that the concept of montage did not become associated with film in the Weimar Republic until the late 1920s, when the theories of Russian filmmakers such as Sergei M. Eisenstein, Vsevolod I. Pudovkin, Lev V. Kuleshov, and Dziga Vertov became known in Germany; as a consequence, "the concept of filmic montage was not operative in the Dada years of 1918–21, and its predecessor, editing or cutting, was hardly a 'tactile' or 'ballistic' force at that time."[55] Although Makholm's point about the reception of Russian montage theory is well taken, to argue on that basis that Dada artists did not see film as a medium that created new meanings through juxtaposing visually disparate shots is mistaken. First, it ignores the fact that, in the case of cultural producers such as visual artists and filmmakers, actual practices often predate the development of the theories that codify and explain these practices. Second, it overlooks the important uses of shot juxtaposition in prewar German cinema—for example, how cutting and mise-en-scène were used together to create different forms of look or gaze on the part of different characters—as well as issues of internal montage, defined as meaning-producing juxtapositions within a single shot.[56] Third, and most important, this argument ignores the actual Dadaist photomontages, which clearly did juxtapose photographic fragments to create new meanings and which were understood to be doing so by at least some of their original spectators.[57]

Given these various reasons why cinematic montage could have been an operative concept in Germany during the late 1910s and the early 1920s, the cyborg's film projector headpiece and other discontinuous photomontage elements that make up his body in *Self-Portrait* could have inspired viewers to think about film's power to transform perception. Commenting on Russian filmic art, collectivist art, and film technique in general, Benjamin noted in 1927 that

> with film there truly arises *a new region of consciousness*. It is, succinctly put, the only prism in which the immediate environment—the spaces in which he lives, goes about his business, and takes his pleasures—reveals itself intelligibly, sensibly, and passionately to the contemporary observer. In themselves these offices, furnished rooms, bars, city streets, train stations, and factories are ugly, unintelligible, and hopelessly sad. (Rather they were and they appeared to be that way until the advent of film. Having discovered the dynamite of tenths of a second, film exploded this old world of incarceration, leading us into adventurous journeys among the scattered ruins.) The compass of a house or a room suddenly contains dozens of the most surprising points of arrival, the strangest of station names. It is not so much the continuous changing of the images but the sudden switch of perspectives that overpowers a milieu, ruling out any disclosure but its own and forcing from a petit-bourgeois apartment the same beauty one admires in an Alfa Romeo.[58]

As Benjamin suggests, filmic montage, which can create sudden changes in perspectives, transforms the world and allows the spectator to see it anew. Although the power of this technique can be tamed by making editing obey a narrative objective, the conjunction of different viewpoints in cinema potentially produces a revolutionary consciousness. Thus, in addition to being able to accurately represent the rush of discontinuous sensations characteristic of modern life, film, as Benjamin suggests in his essay, can transfigure the everyday by making it both intelligible and "adventurous." Benjamin thereby alludes to the idea that, by cutting reality into pieces and suspending its traditional interconnections, cinema suggests that the world as it exists is only one possibility out of many and, moreover, that if the spectator does not like the existing world, he or she is free to reimagine and remake it. In addition, Benjamin also alludes to the idea that, by combining multiple perspectives, movies can potentially interpellate their spectators as collective rather than individual subjects. Together, these two associations, both of which are produced by the technique—as opposed to the content—of filmic montage, help foster a critical attitude toward the status quo.

Self-Portrait contains numerous signs that suggest the impact of mass media on vision. In the first place, because it depicts a cyborg, it suggests the transformation of human beings through modern technologies. In addition, because the photomontage fragments that compose the Dadasoph's body evince different scales, they together imply different perspectives or viewpoints. Furthermore, because the self-portrait juxtaposes image fragments that depict the exterior of a human body with fragments that represent its interior, the photomontage alludes to the myriad ways in which new modes of seeing can dissect and analyze the body. Moreover, because the juxtapositions that make up the image are bizarre and to some extent discontinuous, Hausmann's work as a whole draws attention to its strategy of montage construction, and thus to the artist's ability to explode and recombine the everyday world. Finally, the film projector that crowns the cyborg's head implies that cinema is in certain ways responsible for these changes in human perception. For these various reasons, although Hausmann's photomontage was created approximately seven years before Benjamin wrote his essay on how filmic montage could help create new revolutionary modes of perception, a similar concept of cinematic montage could plausibly inform Hausmann's representation, thus making it, according to one reading that it generates, an optimistic and anticipatory image about film's revolutionary potential.

Another example of Hausmann's more positive representation of human–technological interface can be seen in the photomontage self-portrait *ABCD* (1923–24) (Figure 3.4). Here Hausmann presents himself more directly through a fragmented and frontal photographic portrait with an irregular and quasi-gear-like "monocle" sutured over his left eye. Pasted around his truncated visage on all sides are various photographic and photomechanically reproduced elements, including numbered tickets, letters and letter rows evincing different typographic forms, pieces of maps, photographic fragments of a starry sky, an anatomical cross section of a woman's pelvis, an upside-down Czech banknote, and (cutting off the bottom of Hausmann's chin) a fragment of an announcement designed by El Lissitzky for an optophonetic performance by Hausmann and Kurt Schwitters in Hannover in 1923.[59] A profusion of equally arresting mass-reproduced elements, these photomechanical fragments create larger constellations of

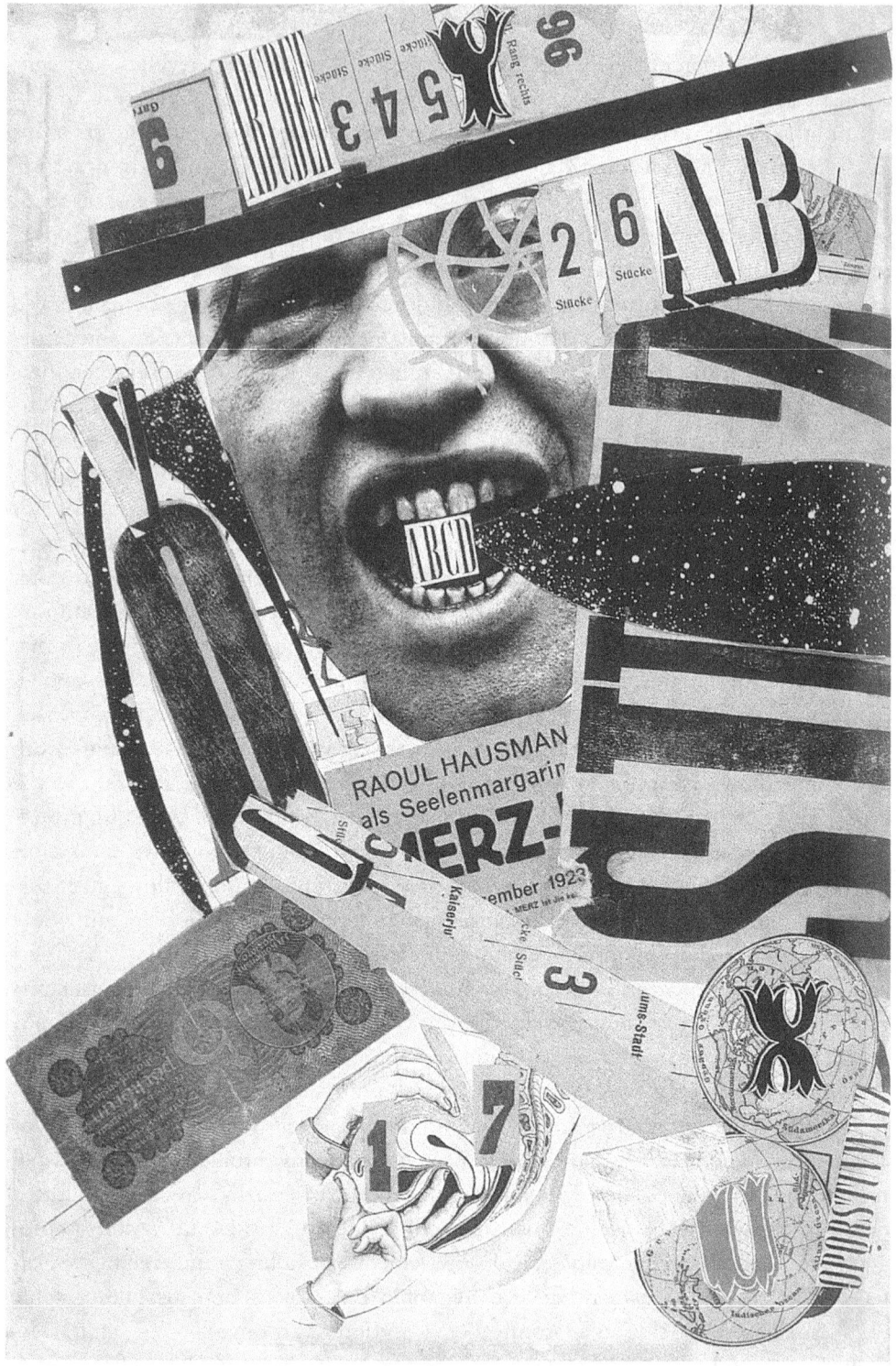

Figure 3.4. Raoul Hausmann, *ABCD* (1923–24). Collage and photomontage on paper. 40.4 × 28.2 cm (15⅞ × 11⅛ inches). Musée national d'art moderne, Centre Georges Pompidou, Paris. Photograph from CNAC/MNAM/Dist. Réunion des Musées Nationaux/Art Resource, NY. Copyright 2009 Artists Rights Society (ARS), New York/ADAGP, Paris.

meaning through which the transformative power of Hausmann's technologically augmented vision is suggested.

The power that Hausmann ascribed to cyborgian vision can first be seen at the level of the subject matter that is represented. It is implied by the emphasis and radiating motion that he gives to his left eye in conjunction with the various viewpoints implied by the image: the penetrating (male) gaze evoked by the cross section of the woman's body as well as the more neutral scientific gaze evoked by the starry sky. When connected with the profusion of tiny map elements, these iconic fragments suggest viewpoints that tend to control the things they represent—that can see below the surfaces of things, that can objectively document an important phenomenon for further study, and that can abstract from reality to better navigate and build within it. In addition, however, in conjunction with the number and letter rows (which can be read as signs of classificatory practice that have been severed from their original context and thus rendered almost meaningless), Hausmann suggests that his cyborgian vision is also one that can confound or mix up all documentary and classificatory systems, and hence a gaze that is potentially revolutionary. He thus represents his cyborgian vision as one that can fragment, transform, and synthesize multiple realities and viewpoints, a vision that is powerful and potentially exploitative, but also potentially liberating.

This sense of transformative, controlling, and liberating vision—vision as a constant process of analysis, synthesis, and reanalysis—is further emphasized by the cyborg's photomontage form. A strategic counter to both formalist and expressive abstraction in the first two decades of the twentieth century, photomontage was, as I have already shown, a much-emphasized signifier of Berlin Dada's radicalism or newness. As suggested by Herzfelde's introduction to the "Dada Fair" catalog, it represented the Dadaists' rejection of abstract painting as a subjectivist project and their affirmation that art had to take politics and modern life as its subject. In addition, as Hausmann later argued, because Dada photomontage produced a form of sensory derangement—"an explosion of viewpoints and a whirling confusion of picture planes," as he put it—photomontage was particularly well suited for examining dialectical relations between form and content.[60] By assembling both appropriated and self-made fragments so that they could be read in terms of different constellations, Hausmann's photomontages formally provoked an experience of visual and linguistic ambiguity and engaged their audiences by encouraging them to free-associate. Photomontage was thus potentially empowering, suggesting, as it did, that how one saw could potentially affect and transform what one saw. It could, in other words, make its various audiences recognize their own contributions to their aesthetic experiences, and thus it could potentially influence them to take a more reflexive and critical attitude to both life and politics. Moreover, by simplifying the process of artistic representation and by suggesting that the artist was as much a recycler as a creator of images, photomontage also made the artist and the spectator more alike. Long before Joseph Beuys or Andy Warhol, Dada photomontage implied that everyone was, indeed, an artist. Hausmann's cyborgs were thus designed to represent more than just a new Dada self and other: they also attempted to constitute a new spectator—an audience whose growing desire for the play of meaning was to result in new modes of perceiving and acting in the world.

Hausmann's Optophonetic Poetry and Performance Practices

Because they refer to Hausmann's poetry and performance practices, *ABCD*'s second major constellation of fragments, the number and letter rows, provide insight into the new form of spectator that Hausmann was attempting to create through his cyborgian photomontages. An acknowledgment of the cyborg's poetic and performative roots, these number and letter rows anticipated the focus in cybernetics in the 1940s and 1950s on exploring electrical, mechanical, and biological communication.[61] Hausmann clearly refers to his practice of optophonetic poetry through the letter and number rows. Not only does he present himself with his mouth open and a string of letters emerging from his lips, but he also directly advertises his collaborative performances with Schwitters through the Lissitzky poster.[62] In addition, the large letter row amputating the left side of his face recalls the typeface of his poster poem *fmsbw* (1918) (Figure 3.5), a text that formed the basis of some of his performances.[63] In accordance with Dada ideology, poster poems like *fmsbw* were generated both by chance and collaboratively. As

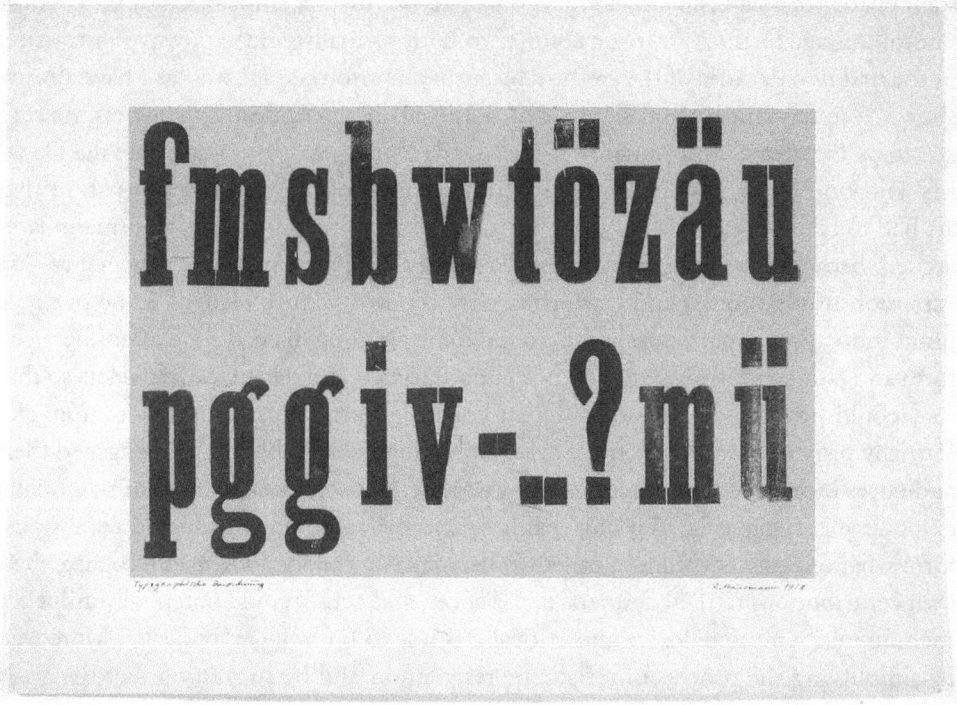

Figure 3.5. Raoul Hausmann, *fmsbw* (1918). Poster poem. Typography on orange paper. 33 × 48 cm (13 × 18⅞ inches). Musée national d'art moderne, Centre Georges Pompidou, Paris. Photograph from CNAC/MNAM/Dist. Réunion des Musées Nationaux/Art Resource, NY. Copyright 2009 Artists Rights Society (ARS), New York/ADAGP, Paris.

Hausmann tells it, he worked with a Berlin printer, Robert Barthe, who pulled the letters in a semirandom fashion until he filled up two horizontal rows.[64] The letter rows were then printed on poster board, and the resulting artworks were both exhibited and used as springboards for performances.

Like many other German artists and intellectuals at the time, Hausmann believed that the German language had degenerated and could no longer express authentic human experiences. Hausmann's optophonetic poetry was thus motivated by a utopian intention: it was designed to free language of what he perceived to be its rational and conceptual straightjackets and to broaden his audiences' understandings of its multivalent potentials. Although his poetry was developed in a context in which numerous experiments with language were being carried out, it differed significantly from other contemporary explorations.[65] First, Hausmann's use of chance and the brevity of his unit of selection—the single letter—eliminated all or almost all semantics. Hausmann's poster poems thus differed from the work of such Zurich Dada sound poets as Hugo Ball and Tristan Tzara as well as the expressionist *Wortkunst* poet August Stramm, because Hausmann's poster poems no longer used words, let alone phrases.[66] For the same two reasons (the use of chance and the emphasis on the single letter), Hausmann's poetic texts were also different from the works of such other important precursors as the Russian *zaum* poets, Velimir Khlebnikov and Alexei Kruchenykh, and the Italian futurist poets such as F. T. Marinetti and others, all of whom demonstrated greater semantic content in their poems.[67] Viewed in relation to his contemporaries, Hausmann's innovation was his treatment of letters—as opposed to words or syllables—as the basic units of language. Poetic metaphor was thus avoided, although the voice's expressive significance was retained. In addition, the bunching up of consonants and the inclusion of pictographs and punctuation symbols that could not in themselves be spoken out loud created vocalization and articulation problems. In this way, gaps or breaks were made part of the performance, and the possibility of slips of the tongue was increased. Finally, the letter was simultaneously treated as an optical and an acoustic sign. "Different sizes," Hausmann insisted, "receive different intonations."[68]

By exploring the basic materials of human language—letters and sounds—in a way that sought to establish new affinities, Hausmann believed that he was helping his audiences overcome the constrictions placed on language through its increasingly efficient and rationalized development. Montages of instantly readable forms, Hausmann's poster poems were generated automatically and collaboratively in such a way as to deny almost all semantic content. Hausmann's poetry thus undermined the individuality of the poetic "author" and negated many of poetry's traditionally "subjective" aspects. Instead, it potentially focused its audiences' attentions on affect and instinctual content as well as the highly conventional, complex, and almost unrecognizable aspects of everyday life, namely, basic forms of communication.

Hausmann re-created his optophonetic performances in several recordings between 1956 and 1966—recordings that indicate what Hausmann's original performances must have been like. These performances are generally short (under four minutes), waver between song and speech, and, as one critic put it, appear to nourish themselves "out of an unconscious condition."[69] Sometimes accompanying himself with rhythmic beats from a wooden box or cardboard tube, Hausmann sings and speaks in short repetitive phrases. As suggested by his recordings of *fmsbw* and other poems, which merge phrases or letter rows from different posters, Hausmann improvised on his poster poems when performing them out loud. And as the transformation of the poster poems from the written to the spoken word indicates, Hausmann employed montage and chance procedures on multiple levels in his poetic works, thereby increasing their cut-up and fragmented character. Like Schwitters—who appropriated the primary theme of his *Ursonate* (1922–32), "Fümms bö wö tää zää Uu, pögiff, kwii Ee," from *fmsbw* and *OFFEAH* (1918), another poster poem by Hausmann—Hausmann edited and recombined his various letter rows, repeating them with different rhythms, tones, and other variations.[70] During his recitals, Hausmann's voice changes in loudness and pitch and evokes different vocal qualities, including stuttering, throat clearing, hissing, snarling, whispering, and wheezing. In the more speechlike passages, the associative qualities of Hausmann's performances change radically. At times it seems as if Hausmann is speaking rationally in some unknown foreign language; at other times it seems as if his speech expresses the more instinctual drives of a deranged or childlike mind. At still other moments, Hausmann sounds as if he is speaking in tongues. In contrast to Schwitters's more classically musical approach, Hausmann's performances demonstrated a greater interest in improvising and exploring psychological content.

As suggested by his poster poems and the recordings of his optophonetic performances, Hausmann's original Dada performances shocked and confronted their audiences by combining formalist and reflexive concerns with psychological ones.[71] By breaking down spoken and written language into their smallest components and by evoking associations of madness and religious ecstasy as well as childhood states and conflicts, his performances could—and sometimes did—inspire his audiences to examine their own psychic construction through linguistic and social forces. Of course, it is difficult to ascertain how close Hausmann's reconstructions came to his original performances. At the same time, the historical record indicates that strong continuities existed. One contemporary observer, Hans Richter, described Hausmann's performative technique as extremely shocking and confrontational: "Hausmann always gave the impression that he harbored a dark menacing hostility to the world. His extremely interesting phonetic poems resembled, as he spoke them, imprecations distorted by rage, cries of anguish, bathed in the cold sweat of tormented demons."[72] In addition, many of the original performers and audience members have written that emotional, often violent audience reactions were common at the Dada performances.[73]

Influenced by diverse sources including the Italian futurists, Paul Scheerbart, Christian Morgenstern, Huelsenbeck, August Stramm, and Wassily Kandinsky, among others, and anticipating French *dictature lettriste* after 1945, as well as concrete and Fluxus poetry, Hausmann's compositional and performance strategies were fundamentally interrelated.[74] At the heart of these strategies lay Hausmann's avant-garde interest in opening up the historical and expressive potential of his artistic materials and exploring the formal and psychic contexts in which human beings develop their identities. As *ABCD* suggests, the figure of the cyborg—especially as configured through photomontage—continued this confrontational challenge from artist to audience to collectively reflect on the linguistic, social, and libidinal construction of subjectivity and alterity, identity and difference. It was only by collaborating with his audiences to break down traditional forms of identity through poetry and performance during the first year and a half of the Berlin Dada movement that Hausmann could later arrive at the cyborg as a dialectical figure in which self and other, friend and enemy, artist and audience found new forms of connection, interrelation, and comparison.

Hausmann's Understanding of Human Identity

That Hausmann would eventually develop the cyborg as a dialectical figure interrelating self and other, artist and spectator is not surprising, given the parallels between Hausmann's understanding of human identity and that of Wiener. According to Wiener, both humans and machines were essentially gatherers, manipulators, and producers of information. Their actions were based on received messages that programmed their activities—albeit in a manner that could potentially be altered by further learning.[75] For these reasons, machines and humans were fundamentally commensurate, and they could be combined with one another in an ever-expanding number of ways.[76] As a closer look at Hausmann's thinking on the subject reveals, creating, transmitting, and reproducing information was also central to Hausmann's understanding of what it meant to be human.

Hausmann's concept of human identity was strongly influenced by Gross and the anarchist thinking of *Die freie Strasse,* the journal edited by Jung, among others, to which Hausmann contributed in the late 1910s.[77] Gross, a renegade student of Freud, believed that psychoanalysis could provide humans with a way to dismantle once and for all the ossifying bourgeois social and family orders, and to build a new anarchist society based on individual liberty and sexual freedom. Like Freud, Gross traced individual neuroses back to the suppression of unresolved conflicts between a person's drives and what Freud eventually called his or her "superego," the representative of the social order within the individual psyche.[78] And like Freud, Gross saw childhood and adolescence as the crucial times during which the psyche and an individual's sexuality were formed. Unlike Freud, however, Gross did not uphold the traditional path of establishing sexual identity in the context of the patriarchal bourgeois family—a path that constrained the infant's original polymorphous perversity by training it as a child and as an adolescent to pursue only heterosexual and monogamous relationships. Instead, Gross argued that the patriarchal family structure was itself the source of all individual and social neurosis and that the psyche's original heterogeneity had to be rediscovered. Psychoanalysis had to be used to rethink the relations between "own" *[das Eigene]* and "alien" *[das Fremde]*: between an individual, heterogeneous, and shifting instinctual core and social role models imposed by the family and the larger social context.[79]

Hausmann adapted Gross's theory of human identity in a series of articles on social revolution published in the radical journal *The Earth* in 1919.[80] In "On World Revolution," for example, he argued that despite the partial breakdown and seeming bankruptcy of the old monarchical and bourgeois social orders in the wake of World War I, the transformation of human sexuality was a necessary precondition for developing new nonhegemonic modes of communal life.[81] Hausmann identified the old bourgeois world order with a radically hierarchical and dominating form of ideology, which he saw as characteristically male. Reinforced by the family, the economy, and the state, this essentially individualistic, hyperrational, capitalist, and heterosexual ideology repressed alterity or difference and attempted to regulate everything and everyone in its environment. Because it related to all things by trying to dominate them, the patriarchal ideology, Hausmann believed, was ultimately suicidal. In the short run, however, it possessed tremendous power, and it caused reality to submit to its rigid concepts and distinctions.[82]

In Hausmann's account, bourgeois subjectivity was fundamentally defined not through its class structure and economic relationships of ownership and production (as was the case in Marxist and communist theory) but through its sexuality. For this reason, in order for the new human and community to develop themselves, the heterosexual male system of values had first to be overcome. Homosexuality, which Hausmann viewed as a natural drive present at all stages of human libidinal development, was one way to overcome the heterosexual male drive to secure property, order, and the subjugation of others.[83] Promiscuity, the surmounting of monogamy, was another way in which this dominant system of individual and social values could be overturned. It was, however, ultimately women and their sexual practices who would define the new human and the new society.[84] Although Hausmann never developed these insights into anything resembling an elaborated theory—and, indeed, although his own personal actions sometimes seemed to contradict his more progressive statements—it is clear that he believed that human beings could transform themselves by paying greater attention to their instinctual drives and by emulating nondominant forms of gender identity.[85]

As suggested by his writings for *The Earth,* Hausmann conceptualized modern identity according to social-constructionist and psychological models. He appears to have understood the modern subject to be a semi-autonomous ego, produced through and then eventually directing the interaction of social and instinctual forces. The subject was both socially constructed—taught by the family, social and educational groups, the state, and the media—and transformable: that is, it did not simply have to repeat the roles that it had learned but could creatively vary its practices and thus change itself. Even a person's sexuality, Hausmann argued, was potentially subject to alteration, nor did it need to remain stable over time. In contrast to Wiener's more-mechanistic understanding of human identity as essentially a function of received and manipulated information, Hausmann's conceptualization tended to emphasize the corporeal and instinctual aspects of human beings to a much greater degree. In addition, because he also emphasized the slips and gaps in interhuman information exchange far more than Wiener did, Hausmann's model of identity also seems to allow for a concept of subjectivity that involves a moment of misrecognition, an identification of the self with a partially imagined ideal that, instead of reproducing the same, introduces novelty.

It is easy to envision this understanding of human identity underlying Hausmann's description of artistic competition in "Classical Relations to the German Middle-Class Kitchen," as well as his disturbing representations of both himself and others as cyborgs. If identity was in part determined by one's appropriations of culture as well as one's interactions with significant others in everyday life, then the possibilities for individual development were potentially nearly limitless. At the same time, however, it is important not to forget the somewhat fixed and mechanistic view of subjectivity inherent in the Freudian models of the human psyche from which Hausmann developed his own concepts. Although he radically criticized and reformulated Freud's account of identity under Gross's influence (whose theories he later characterized as "a new kind of anti-Freudian psychoanalysis"), Hausmann consistently stressed the importance of psychoanalytic concepts for the development of Dada art.[86] Thus, although aspects of Hausmann's model of identity anticipate the radical critique of the subject characteristic of post-Freudian psychoanalysis—as, for example, can be found in Jacques Lacan's writings—the idea of the subject as completely fictional is absent from Hausmann's writings, a result perhaps of Hausmann's very limited understanding of the processes of identification. Moreover, as was to become the case for Wiener, information, for Hausmann, was key. The identity of human beings depended on how their instinctual energies were expressed, and the expression of these energies, in turn, depended on the scripted behaviors learned from their parents and from others—even if those behaviors could be misread and thus learned improperly. As was the case for Wiener, human beings for Hausmann had machinelike aspects because they were fundamentally shaped by such messages. And it was probably for this reason that Hausmann emphasized childlike states in some of his performances—thereby evoking the period in human existence during which the majority of human behavior is programmed—for it was in this way that he could provoke his audiences to reflect on the developmental contexts in which their personalities were first formed. It was also probably for this reason that Hausmann focused on the fundamental components of written and spoken language in his sound poetry, for it was in this way that he could get his audiences to examine two of the primary media that encoded and passed on their behaviors.

The Cyborg and Portraiture

As the parallels between Wiener's theories and those of Hausmann suggest, Hausmann's Dada cyborgs were intended to represent the radically hybrid and collaborative nature of human identity in modern societies. They revealed that modern subjectivities were socially and collectively produced, and that the communal scripts they followed came from a multiplicity of conflicting sources. As has already been suggested through the analysis of *The Iron Hindenburg* (Figure 3.3), Hausmann saw his enemies or antipodes as radically hybrid like himself. Moreover, as suggested by self-portraits such as *Self-Portrait of the Dadasoph* (Figure 3.2), Hausmann recognized his kinship with the modern personalities that he most opposed.[87] Through this image, Hausmann identified himself with two of the main postwar types that he attacked in both his writings and his visual art: the bourgeois and the militarist. First, were it not for the title that identifies the cyborg as a self-portrait, the figure could easily be interpreted as an ironic symbol of reified bourgeois consciousness—the proper and obedient German "Spiesser," whose hierarchical, middle-class, and capitalist values had been rendered bankrupt by the brutality and horror of World War I.[88] Portrayed seated, in a three-quarter-view portrait, the cyborg can be read as a complacent bourgeois because of his respectable frock coat and comfy armchair, which evokes the emphasis that the bourgeois places on the private sphere. In addition, some of the photomontage's spectators would also have been aware that the cyborg's body was that of Gustav Noske, the Weimar Republic's first minister of defense, who ordered the bloody suppression of the Sparticist uprising on January 10, 1919, and therefore a figure that for Hausmann represented the brutal militarism of the first SPD government. By identifying himself with symbols of the German *Spiesser* and a fairly well-known image of Noske, which had appeared on the front cover of the *Berliner Illustrirte Zeitung* [Berlin Illustrated Newspaper, or *BIZ*] in March 1919 (Figure 3.6), Hausmann thus alluded to bourgeois and militarist aspects within his own personality.

Because they represented an extremely decentered or hybrid form of human identity, Hausmann's cyborgian portraits often undermined the standard functions of portraiture.[89] By Hausmann's time, the portrait had long been used—both in painting and in photography—to celebrate the uniqueness of human identity. Often used to signify status, convey personality, or mark a moment in a particular life, many forms of photographic and painterly portraiture claimed to present a truth both ontological and subjective. They claimed, in other words, that a particular individual existed and that the particular forms that the portrait depicted were signs revealing the sitter's specific personality, psyche, or fate.[90] And in this way, despite the representational conventions that were observed to creep into all forms of portraiture (conventions that suggest that the sitter was, in certain ways, like a number of others), the portrait subject's "individuality"—his or her specific existence and character—has often been stressed by the genre of portraiture. However, as suggested by two more cyborgian portraits by Hausmann, images of artists with whom he clearly identified, this stabilizing and individualizing effect that is often produced by painterly and photographic portraiture is much less pervasive in the portraiture that appears in Dada art.

As can be seen in both *Tatlin lebt zu Hause* [Tatlin Lives at Home] (1920) (Figure 3.7), a close-up "portrait" of the Russian artist Vladimir Tatlin, with whom the Dada artists connected the progressive and aesthetically liberating tendencies of what they called the new "machine art,"[91] and *Elasticum* (1920) (Figure 3.8), Hausmann's ironic

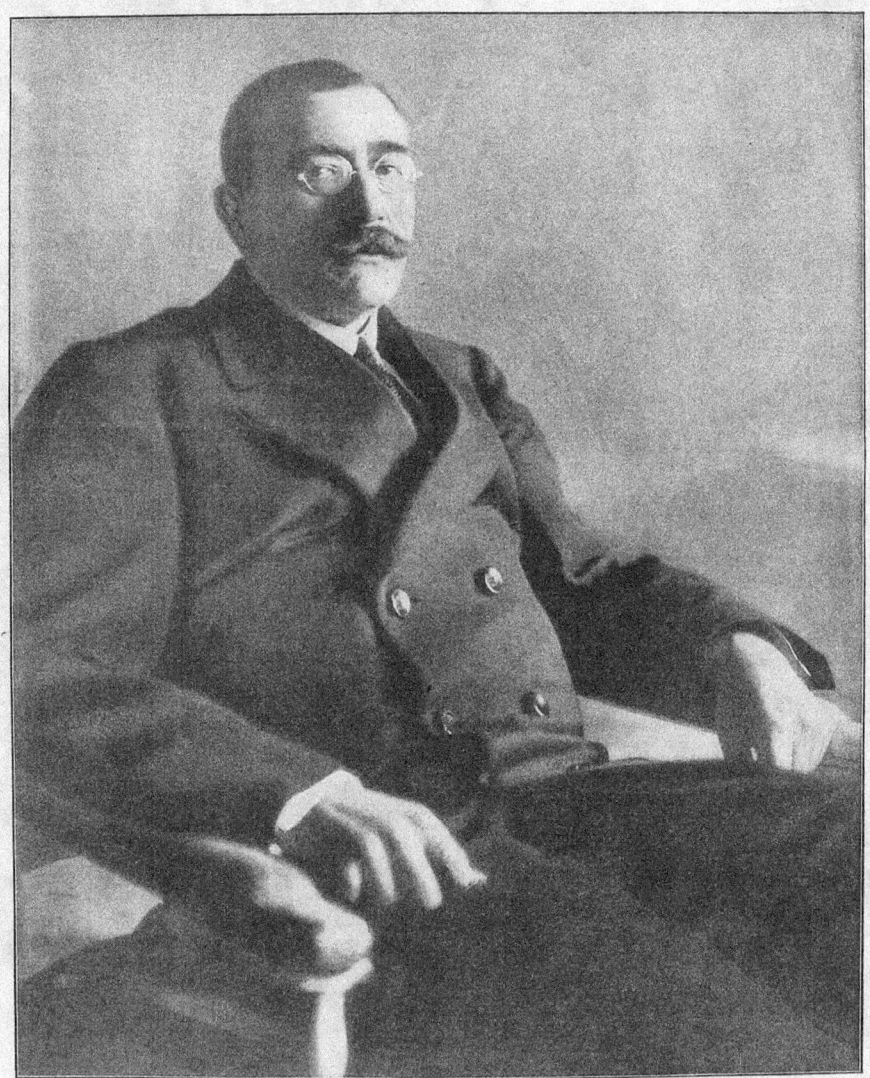

Figure 3.6. Cover of *Berliner Illustrirte Zeitung* [Berlin Illustrated Newspaper] 28, no. 9 (March 2, 1919).

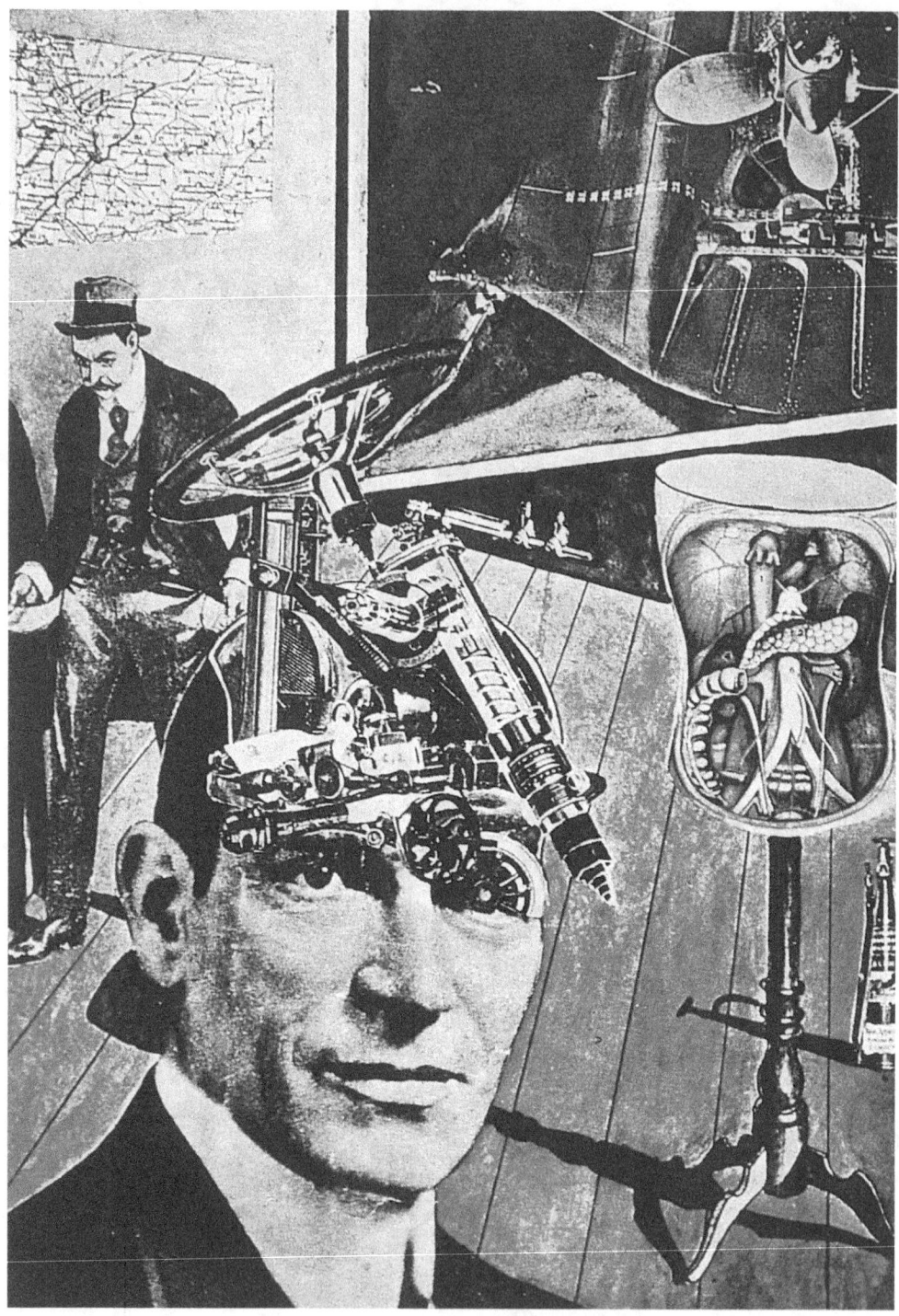

Figure 3.7. Raoul Hausmann, *Tatlin lebt zu Hause* [Tatlin Lives at Home] (1920). Photomontage. 41 × 18 cm (16⅛ × 7 inches). Missing since 1968. Photograph from Berlinische Gallerie, Berlin. Copyright 2009 Artists Rights Society (ARS), New York/ADAGP, Paris.

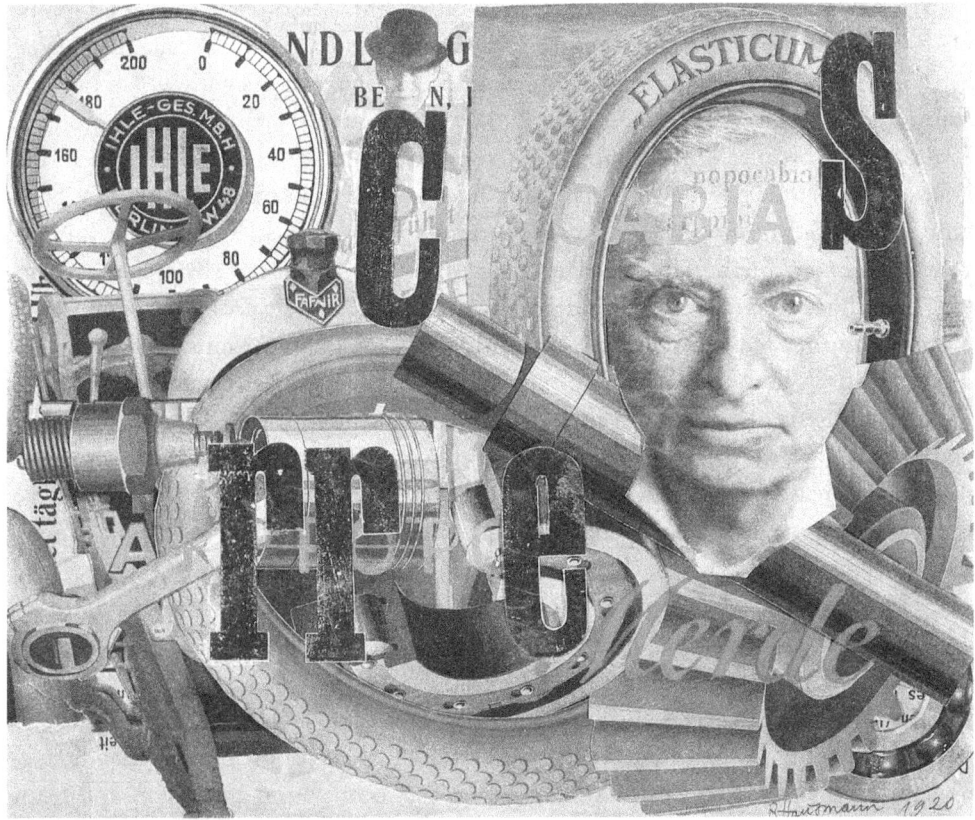

Figure 3.8. Raoul Hausmann, *Elasticum* (1920). Photomontage and collage with gouache on the cover of the "First International Dada Fair" exhibition catalog. 31 × 37 cm (12³⁄16 × 14⁹⁄16 inches). Galerie Berinson, Berlin/UBU Gallery, New York. Copyright 2009 Artists Rights Society (ARS), New York/ADAGP, Paris.

homage to the Dada artists Francis Picabia and Hans (Jean) Arp, the cyborg also was a positive role model for Hausmann—something that he was later able to represent more directly in his self-portrait *ABCD*. Significantly, neither of these two works contains photographic representations of the named artists—and, thus, unlike *ABCD*, they are not portraits in the sense of iconically representing their subjects. According to Hausmann, *Tatlin*, which was hung directly below *Self-Portrait of the Dadasoph* at the "Dada Fair," received the head of an "unknown man" that Hausmann found in an American magazine and whose features he associated with the Russian artist for reasons he could never explain.[92] The source of the head in *Elasticum* has never been revealed, although its features are definitely not those of either Picabia or Arp. Indeed, the unknown head looks much more like Henry Ford, the world-famous American inventor and businessman, whom the Dada artists associated with the assembly line and mass-production techniques.[93]

Rather than reproduce the features of their professed subjects, *Tatlin* is identified by the title of the photomontage listed in the "Dada Fair" catalog and "Picabia" and

"Arp" by textual puns situated within the image field. Hausmann thus renders the Dada artists' identities unstable, and the spectator is encouraged to associate the "Dada-ism" of the two figures with the machinery and the other objects with which they are connected as well as the fragmented and dialectical way in which they are composed. And precisely because of their anonymity, they can represent Hausmann or the other Dada artists as much as they do their ostensible subjects. These portraits are thus both individual and collective; they represent particular artists as well as more general pro-totypes of a new collaborative human—figures constructed out of elements transmit-ted through the mass media. Although, historically, not all forms of portraiture relied on physiognomic likeness to represent identity, these Dadaist portraits are nonetheless different from the (nonphysiognomic) portraits of medieval noblemen, for example, which used coats of arms to symbolize their subjects' identities, because the photo-graphic nature of the Dadaist portraits evokes physiognomic resemblance only to deny it.[94] For this reason, the Dadaist portraits perform an exemplary function—using the individual to express more general human qualities of either a noble or a base nature—in a fairly nontraditional way.[95] Instead of conforming the individual's features and body to socially established forms of posture, expression, and dress as was generally done to give a photographic portrait an exemplary character, the Dadaist portraits cre-ate exemplarity—another traditional role of portraiture—through emphasizing dis-sociative montage strategies and the collective production of images.[96]

Both photomontages present allegorical representations of the Dada artist who rec-ognizes his or her social construction and who uses both sound and vision to disrupt reality in an effort to imagine new modes of existence. As was later the case with *ABCD,* the contradictory associations produced by these images attempt to elicit a new, more-engaged spectator who is aware of humanity's power to turn reality into information. In *Elasticum*'s wildly oscillating image field, for example, repeating circular forms, some parallel with the picture plane, some rotated into depth, set off a chain of metaphoric associations, linking the cyborg's human head to a complex network of mechanical extensions: gears, tires, a steering wheel, a pipe, and a speedometer. Complicating and reinforcing this state of free association produced by the photographic materials, the fragments of text and nonsense words that Hausmann uses are juxtaposed in a way that violates all normal forms of syntax and sentence structure. Recalling Hausmann's various forms of sound poetry, as well as his interest in childhood states (suggested by the scatological "pipicabia," "popocabia" juxtaposition), the letters and letter strings help evoke a reflexive and critical investigation of both sight and sound in terms of their social and psychological characteristics.

Elasticum's self-reflexive overtones, created by the nonsense texts and Hausmann's complex montage of images, letters, and words, are further emphasized by the image's photomontage form, which potentially provokes a questioning attitude on the part of the portrait's audiences as to why *Elasticum* should be considered a work of art and—through this questioning attitude—the development of a reflexive awareness of the various institutional structures that allowed the photomontage to be perceived as a work of art in Germany in 1920.[97] In addition, the photomontage's self-reflexivity is also strengthened by Hausmann's appropriation of a human head with pronounced eyes, which, because they meet the viewer's gaze, evoke a type of heightened self-conscious attentiveness that characterizes intimate communication. In this way, *Elasticum*'s multiple forms of self-reflexivity potentially promote a meditation on selfhood, the portrait's "self-consciousness"—its various references to itself and to the idea of human subjectivity—inspiring its spectators to take up a similarly self-analytic attitude toward themselves. Suggesting the activities of driving, turning, babbling, urinating, defecating, and producing vast energies, Hausmann's photomontage thus shatters reality into disconnected fragments while suggesting—through the fixed composition into which the multiple bits of reality are then placed—that such fragments can be reassembled to create new forms of hybrid identity better able to exist in the modern world. "DADA," as Hausmann wrote in *Der Dada* 3,

> developed into the vast elasticity of the time, which took its measure from the bourgeoisie: as they grew stiffer and more senile, so DADA grew more mobile, until today it has spread across the whole world. Because, as you must know, DADA is the truth, the only proper practice of real people, as they are today, always in motion because of the simultaneity of events, of advertisements, markets, sexuality, community affairs, politics, the economy; with no room for superfluous thoughts that lead nowhere.[98]

Although this new mode of elastic and mobile identity suggested by *Elasticum* remains radically dissonant—an unwieldy composite of linguistic signs, mechanical parts, and human bodily forms—it oddly seems to function as a viable totality: an image of a new form of human existence whose components can be freely selected from the ceaseless flow of modern life.

In addition to undermining a fixed sense of its subject's identity and promoting reflection on our social construction, *Elasticum* also undermines a fixed sense of the identity of its author or creator. To make the photomontage, Hausmann began by appropriating the "Dada Fair" catalog cover, which was itself a reproduction—with additional text—of Heartfield's photomontage *Life and Times in Universal City at 12:05 Noon* (1919), which is sometimes identified as a collective creation of Heartfield and Grosz. (Parts of the "original" cover can still be seen peeking out from behind the "new" photomontage fragments that Hausmann used to assemble the image of the collaborative artist–cyborg.) By constructing his hybrid portrait of a Dada artist out of an earlier photomontage that had a clear history of transformation and reuse in different contexts, Hausmann evoked a notion of authorship both collaborative and based on multiple forms of mechanical transmission and reproduction. Suggesting that art is the product of citation and effacement, *Elasticum*'s appropriations thus reinforce the idea of the mobile, elastic, and interactive nature of human identity as well as its transformations through mechanical reproduction.

The idea that modern forms of identity result from the technologically mediated interaction of instinctual and social forces also seems to be the explicit theme of *Tatlin*

Lives at Home (Figure 3.7). Staring directly out at the beholder, a steering column aggressively extending from its mechanized brain, the artist–cyborg's mind appears to radiate a series of shardlike planes containing a set of loosely associated appropriated images: a full view of a man turning out his pockets, a map of Pomerania with the island village where Hausmann and Höch allegedly discovered the technique of photomontage, a ship's stern with a propeller, a tailor's dummy, internal organs from a human body, and a fire extinguisher.[99] Through this compositional device, the appropriated fragments can be read as the contents of the artist–cyborg's perception, at the same time as their associative qualities suggest that they could also be emblems representing his psyche, character, or standing in society. As is the case with *Elasticum,* the portrait of Picabia and Arp, the spatial discontinuities, the conflicting scales and multiple viewpoints, the strange juxtapositions of maps, diagrams, and cutaway pictures all seem to relate to the central figure's mechanically grafted eye. Together, the work's photomontage form and its representational elements thus suggest that the cyborg uses its perception to transform the world into different forms of information and thereby into messages out of which new forms of existence may be produced. *Tatlin* can thus be read as composed of—or even "scripted" by—the elements that encircle his inquiring gaze. In addition, as is also the case with *Elasticum,* the various photomontage juxtapositions that constitute the representation of *Tatlin* inhabiting his room create contradictory chains of metaphoric association—chains that do not permit the discovery of a single dominant reading. In this way, the ambiguity and multivalence of reality is retained—a sense of the world as exceeding the various representations that human beings make of it. And by evoking this state or condition, *Tatlin Lives at Home* suggests that modern human identity cannot be reduced to a single type or a unified mode of being.

In various ways, Hausmann's cyborgian portraits and self-portraits all present an image of the technologically transformed human being as a locus of new forms of perception. *Self-Portrait of the Dadasoph* suggests new modes of internal perception, ways to monitor one's own bodily processes so that one can better control them. As a result, the photomontage evokes autogenic training and other forms of self-hypnosis that developed during the Weimar Republic as well as the more technologically complex later practices of biofeedback. *Elasticum,* moreover, emphasizes multiple forms of self-reflexivity, which generate a sense of the "elastic" (or flowing, multiple, and socially constructed) character of human identity and connect it to questions about the work's status as an art object and its nature as a collectively produced representation created through multiple acts of appropriation and effacement. As such, it raises questions as to how our perceptions of artworks and other forms of representation affect and help produce our developing identities or senses of self. In addition, the figure's loosely composed "body"—the constellation of letters and machine parts that surround its human head—also suggests the physical extension of touch. Examining the work, one could plausibly envision the cyborg's physical avenues of perception extending through the gears, tires, and other mechanical parts that run to the edge of the image field—

an evocation of the much more contemporary idea of telepresence or remote presence created through mechanical prosthetics, an idea that is also suggested by the disembodied hand that tickles the bride-to-be's right breast in Grosz's cyborgian wedding announcement, *"Daum" marries her pedantic automaton "George"* from the same year (Figure 1.7). Furthermore, because of their emphasis on the mechanical augmentation of the cyborg's vision (through gearlike monocles that in both cases cover the figure's left eye) in conjunction with a presentation of image fragments that suggest different viewpoints, both *Tatlin Lives at Home* and *ABCD* imply that the cyborg possesses a type of vision that can penetrate the surface of things, select and magnify details, and then reassemble them in new ways. Particularly because both photomontages present cutaway views that disclose the insides of the human body, they suggest a powerfully invasive and controlling mode of apprehension. And finally, because most of the photomontages examined here juxtapose different forms of representational systems, they suggest a new more integrated synthesis of sound, vision, touch, and thought.

During the 1920s and 1930s, many thinkers in Weimar Germany and elsewhere began to explicitly discuss and model the changes in perception created by the new media of mass communication. Several examined the visual characteristics of photography and film, arguing that both these media radically extended human vision. In his much-cited essay on the history of photography from 1931, for example, Benjamin argued,

> It is another nature which speaks to the camera rather than to the eye: "other" above all in the sense that a space informed by human consciousness gives way to a space informed by the unconscious. Whereas it is a commonplace that, for example, we have some idea what is involved in the act of walking (if only in general terms), we have no idea at all what happens during the fraction of a second when a person actually takes a step. Photography, with its devices of slow motion and enlargement, reveals the secret. It is through photography that we first discover the existence of this optical unconscious, just as we discover the instinctual unconscious through psychoanalysis. Details of structure, cellular tissue, with which technology and medicine are normally concerned—all this is, in its origins, more native to the camera than the atmospheric landscape or the soulful portrait.[100]

By arguing that photography enhanced human vision by allowing us to freeze and analyze movement, see small objects with greater detail, perceive large expanses more comprehensively and accurately, penetrate the surfaces of objects and reveal their underlying components and structures, and filter out the interpretive aspects of our vision and thus perceive the world more truthfully, Benjamin aligned himself with a good deal of thinking since the 1920s on photography's role in modern life, which emphasized these and similar benefits.[101] Hausmann, moreover, would explicitly side with this position in a published conversation with Werner Gräff in 1933, when he argued that "like technology, photography is playing a historical role in the education of human consciousness."[102]

Many of these German theorists of perceptual transformation went farther, however, postulating that photography and film were also fostering a revolutionary consciousness in both art and politics. Beginning in the early 1920s, Moholy-Nagy, in
particular, stressed the new media's "productive" potential, arguing that, in the hands
of artists, technologies developed to mass-reproduce sound and vision could be used to
"create new relationships between familiar and as yet unfamiliar data, optical, acoustic or whatever."[103] By experimenting with new media and developing its potentials,
human beings would slowly change how they perceived and understood their worlds.
As Moholy-Nagy wrote about photography in 1927, "Just one of its features—the
range of infinitely subtle gradations of light and dark that capture the phenomenon
of light in what seems to be an almost immaterial radiance—would suffice to establish a new kind of seeing, a new kind of visual power."[104] Benjamin, in his characteristically enigmatic fashion, stressed the photograph's revolutionary potential, which in
addition to revealing the world more fully also sometimes disclosed "a magical value"
that compels the spectator "to search such a picture for the tiny spark of contingency,
of the here and now, with which reality has (so to speak) seared the subject, to find
the inconspicuous spot where in the immediacy of that long-forgotten moment the
future nests so eloquently that we, looking back, may rediscover it."[105] Recalling his
conceptualization of revolutionary "now time" [Jetztzeit] in such late writings as his
posthumously published "On the Concept of History," this passage suggests that Benjamin believed that certain photographs could simultaneously reveal objective social
facts, traces of the present in the past, and dialectical "principles" on which new, nonhegemonic communal orders could be founded.[106]

Siegfried Kracauer, no unwavering friend of photography, also recognized its revolutionary potential when he argued in 1927 that "a consciousness caught up in nature
is unable to see its own material base. It is the task of photography to disclose this previously unexamined *foundation of nature*. For the first time in history, photography
brings to light the entire natural cocoon; for the first time, the inert world presents
itself in its independence from human beings."[107] In this way, photographic technology forces human consciousness to confront "the reflection of the reality that has slipped
away from it" and thus realize that it must reject its traditional concepts and define
the world anew. Through photography (and, as he would shortly argue, film),

The images of the stock of nature disintegrated into its elements are offered up to
consciousness to deal with as it pleases. Their original order is lost; they no longer
cling to the spatial context that linked them with an original out of which the memory image was selected. But if the remnants of nature are not oriented toward the
memory image, then the order they assume through the image is necessarily provisional. It is therefore incumbent on consciousness to establish the *provisional status*
of all given configurations, and perhaps even to awaken an inkling of the right order
of the inventory of nature.[108]

Like Benjamin, Kracauer thus acknowledged that mass communication could potentially foster new, socially critical forms of perception—a position Hausmann also articulated. In his conversation with Gräff, he argued that "photography, photomontage, and film sharpen and develop the senses of the stirring masses. To see—and to know what you are seeing and what is the purpose of your seeing—is one of the most important matters, particularly in our time; that is why the development of photography as an art is beginning just now."[109] Thus, like Kracauer and Benjamin, Hausmann believed in the mass media's revolutionary potential.

A much more disturbing line of thought about mass media's transformation of perception was pursued by Ernst Jünger during the late 1920s and early 1930s. According to Jünger, film and photography had numerous effects on human consciousness that were ultimately helping change people into a newer, less empathetic, more organized, and less-individualized type of human being, which he called "the worker" *[der Arbeiter]*.[110] In the first place, film and photography acted like a "filter," magnifying and casting certain aspects of reality in a positive light while showing other aspects of the world to be lacking or outmoded. What photography glorified, according to Jünger, were those aspects of reality that most reflected the new technological age—planes, submarines, lunar landscapes, aerial shots of foreign lands, and technology-wielding humans in uniforms and protective clothing—in short, those aspects that most reflected humankind's growing involvement with the forces making the world a smaller, faster, more organized, and, ultimately, far more dangerous place.[111] Film and photography, in other words, helped people perceive—and thus select—the tools, contexts, forms of existence, and political ideologies best suited to the modern world. Thus the new media of technological perception were facilitating an "age of labor," whose dawn was signaled by World War I and the destruction of the remaining European monarchies. Characterized above all by a "total mobilization" of peoples and resources (their systematic interrelation in a global economy of instrumental transformation and exchange), this new age found its most appropriate expression in a transnational military–industrial complex.[112]

In addition to acting like a filter, film and photography were altering human physiology and ethics, producing people with a "second, colder consciousness." As Jünger argued,

> The photograph stands outside the realm of sensibility. It has something of a telescopic quality: one can tell that the object photographed was seen by an insensitive and invulnerable eye. That eye registers just as well a bullet in midair or the moment in which a man is torn apart by an explosion. This is our characteristic way of seeing, and photography is nothing other than an instrument of this new propensity in human nature.[113]

By developing a second consciousness, human beings would learn to see themselves as objects, stand "outside the sphere of pain," and, finally, evolve an objectified—that is, more pragmatic and less feeling—worldview.[114] In addition, they would come more and more to use the new means of mass communication as a weapon. Like many of the Weimar theorists, Jünger stressed that film and photography expanded human perception, making it more precise, comprehensive, and calculating. More than the others, however, he emphasized how expanding human perception through technology made us better able to locate and kill one another as well as more practiced in the arts of political persuasion. Film and photography, Jünger argued, were also propaganda tools par excellence.[115] Since the same photograph or film clip could be used to make two diametrically opposed points, the new media of mass communication could agitate and mobilize the masses.[116] Moreover, because film and photography for the most part transcended specific languages and did not require viewers who could read or write, they were particularly effective for transnational communication.[117]

As suggested by the various theorizations of the effects that the new modes of technological perception were having on human consciousness and the various avenues of human sensation, the Weimar Republic was a moment in which people were struggling to come to terms with the perceptual and ideological changes wrought by the tools of the mass media. And while it would be incorrect to assume that Dadaists like Hausmann anticipated all the various arguments articulated above about the changes in human perception created through new technologies, it is clear from his images of cyborgs that he intended to promote thinking about these developments in general. By representing the cyborg as a locus of new forms of technologically enhanced perception, Hausmann and the other Berlin Dadaists thus marked an important moment in the development of human thought about spectatorship in the age of mass-reproduction, standing as they did between the ideas about the social and linguistic construction of sound and vision that were already a part of their cultural horizon and the new thinking on the impact of technology on perception that would develop in a few short years.[118]

Cyborgs and Sexuality

Hausmann's representations of cyborgs and the theoretical and performative practices out of which they sprang in many ways confirm the model of avant-garde art developed by Peter Bürger and others since the mid-1970s.[119] In accordance with the concept of the historical avant-garde, Hausmann's art was montage-based (or "nonorganic"), appropriative, and at times collaborative. In addition, Hausmann's individual works were frequently heterogeneous (composed of a mixture of disparate materials), and his oeuvre as a whole demonstrated a wide variety of styles, techniques, and media. Furthermore, on one level, Hausmann's works clearly negate meaning and refer to the processes of their own construction. They thus challenged their spectators to examine the institutions that defined, supported, and legitimated bourgeois art in capitalist societies, provoking what Bürger and others have called "institutional critique."[120] More specifically, Hausmann's cyborgian photomontages, poster poems, and Dada performances were doubly reflexive: they helped inspire a simultaneous examination of art as an institution and representation as both a visual and a linguistic process. In addition, because of their nontraditional materials, their recourse to various forms and strategies derived from the mass media, their undermining of traditional signs of artistic originality, and their biting irony, they potentially provoked reflection on art's relative impotence in the modern world. Moreover, because of its representational aspects and its employment of strategies of chance and automatism, Hausmann's art seems radically open to the world in which it was made. Finally, because of the violence they evoke, Hausmann's works also seem profoundly mournful, that is, aware of—and attempting to work through—recent destruction, trauma, and loss, a legacy of modern German society in general and World War I in particular.

At the same time, the concept of the historical avant-garde also obscures an important aspect of Hausmann's project: namely, his practice, through his representations of the cyborg, of imagining new forms of hybrid identity, a practice much more closely associated with certain forms of postmodernism. For Bürger, avant-garde art continued aestheticism's emancipation of art from subject matter.[121] Inspired by Benjamin's concept of allegory, Bürger argued that avant-garde art negates the original contextual meanings of its various appropriated parts.[122] Instead of drawing the viewer's or the reader's attention to what is actually represented, the parts of the avant-garde artwork put the focus on the conceptual principles behind the work's construction.[123] As a result, there is no room for subject matter in Bürger's account of the historical avant-garde—a position taken over by even some of Bürger's staunchest and most articulate critics, for example, Benjamin H. D. Buchloh.[124]

As I showed in chapter 2, however, to have a critical effect, the Berlin Dada photomontages had to be read in light of the subjects depicted in their fragmentary source materials. This approach to Dadaist photomontage, which sought to identify the various figures and situations represented in the works, was one that the Dadaists appear to have intended and at least some of their original audiences expected. In addition, such an approach also helped empower the spectator. Because the clusters of elements were so diverse and the viewer tended to focus on certain fragments more than others, the Dadaists' photomontages supported a multiplicity of diverse, sometimes conflicting readings. And because they were so artificial and tendentious, they provoked their spectators to go beyond the mere identification and cataloging of the photographic fragments and construct overall interpretations of the author's possible "take" on his or her various subjects. As a result, these photomontages encouraged spectators to employ their social and political knowledge to reimagine themselves, others, and their contemporary situations. And for these various reasons, the spectator that Dadaist photomontage attempted to interpellate was thus one that was active, creative, and aware of his or her own necessary role in producing the work's meaning.

As suggested by "On World Revolution," Hausmann believed that homosexuality was a practice for overcoming traditional forms of identity and society. It thus comes as little surprise that some of his cyborgian self-portraits hint at alternative forms of sexuality. *Doppelportrait Johannes Baader und Raoul Hausmann* [Double Portrait Johannes Baader and Raoul Hausmann] (1919–20) (Figure 3.9), a print of a photo-montage, presents a good example of this subterranean homoeroticism that was part of Hausmann's politics of hybridity. The last in a series of at least three "double por-traits" created jointly by Hausmann and Baader during 1919 and early 1920, *Double Portrait* brings together two separate photographs of the artists, each nude from at least the waist up. As it is normally positioned, Hausmann appears right-side up, reclining slightly and staring directly at the spectator with an ironic smirk on his lips and a monocle over his left eye. Baader, noticeably older and more grizzled than the youth-ful Hausmann, hangs upside down next to his comrade, their cheeks touching. Baader sports a beard, a more serious expression, and a less direct—more abstracted—stare.

The figures' cyborgian aspects are downplayed but still present. Hausmann's mon-ocle once again suggests technologically augmented vision. Furthermore, the position-ing of the two figures violates traditional notions of the "nature" of the human body; namely, its obedience to the laws of gravity as well as the fact that, when vertical, human beings generally appear with their heads raised above the level of their feet. The positioning thus makes Baader seem like he has strange, supernatural powers; in addition, because of their proximity to one another, it allows them to be read as parts of a larger collective organism. Baader seems to sprout from the side and top of Haus-mann's head, and the double portrait as a whole can be interpreted as a partial view of some strange, hybrid creature. Given what appears in the image, it could be easily imagined that, if the edges of the print were extended, the two Dada artists would appear enmeshed within an even larger collective of unnaturally merged bodies.

The double portrait also evokes a certain homoeroticism that goes beyond the homosociality suggested by many of Hausmann's works. As Eve Kosofsky Sedgwick argues, in modern patriarchal societies, male homosociality—male bonding or, more generally, men promoting the interests of men—is opposed to male homosexuality. Unlike female homosociality, which is generally perceived to be more continuous with female homosexuality, male homosociality is radically distinguished from male homo-sexuality. This is the case because compulsory male heterosexuality is necessary for maintaining patriarchal societies, while female homosexuality is generally perceived as far less disruptive.[125]

In light of Sedgwick's definitions, Hausmann's portraits in *Tatlin* and *Elasticum*, which suggest shifting identities, also evoke male homosociality. They hint, in other words, that the male Dada artists are like one another and thus have common inter-ests. In addition, Hausmann's use of his comrades' names and earlier creations in these portraits also implies that his art is made with the help of other men. *Double Portrait*, on the other hand, goes much further than the portraits discussed above in that the figures' nakedness, their proximity to one another, and the emphasis placed on Haus-mann's nipple (an erogenous zone) by its positioning along the image's bottom edge together create erotic—even sexual—connotations. Moreover, by presenting the two artists as a couple, and by playing off a traditional homosexual trope of an older man

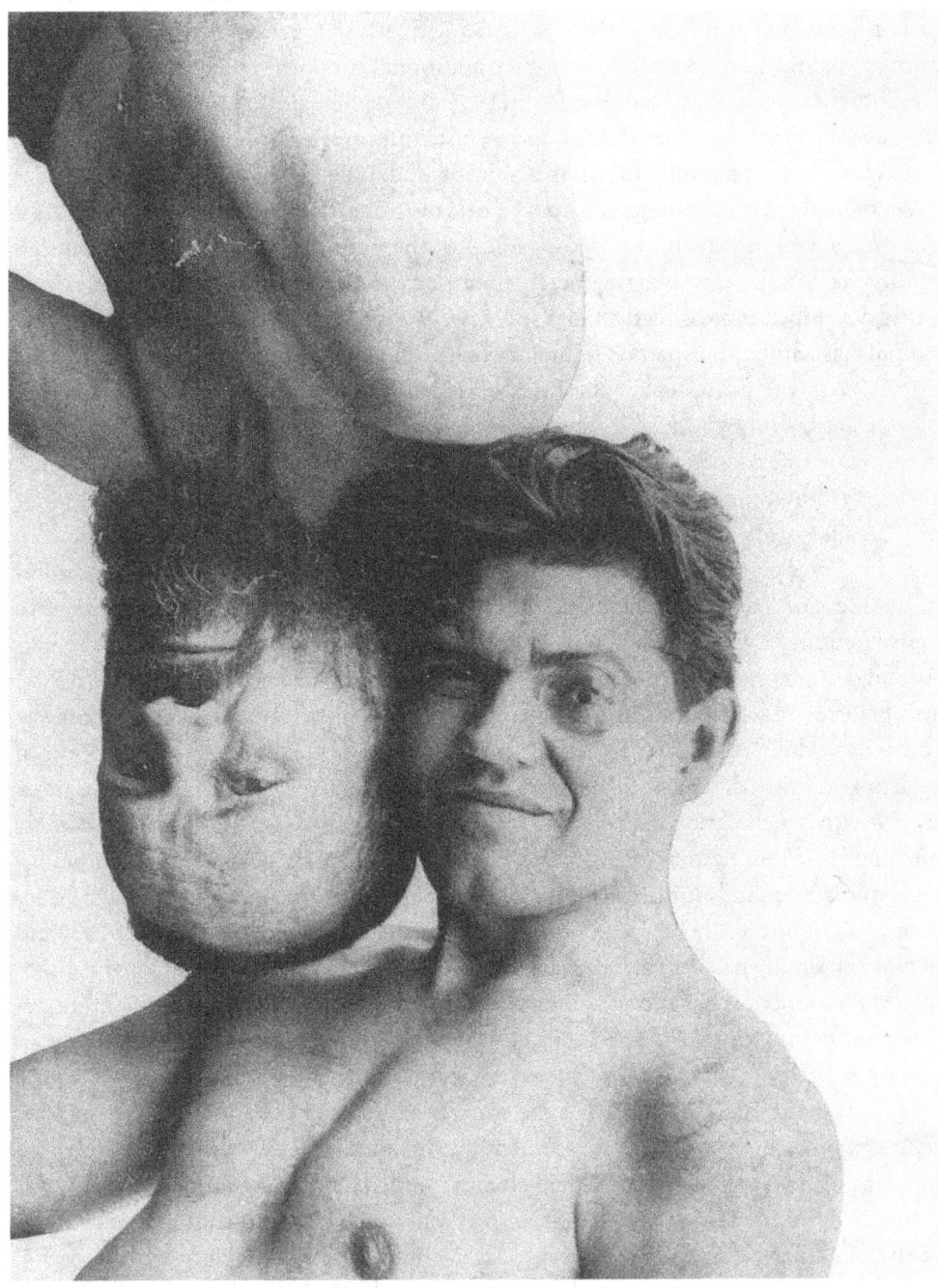

Figure 3.9. Raoul Hausmann and Johannes Baader, *Doppelportrait Johannes Baader und Raoul Hausmann* [Double Portrait Johannes Baader and Raoul Hausmann] (1919–1920). Print of photomontage. 25.4 × 15.8 cm (10 × 6¼ inches). Kunsthaus Zürich, Zurich. Copyright 2009 Artists Rights Society (ARS), New York/ADAGP, Paris.

taking a younger man as his lover, the double portrait reinforces its implied homo-eroticism,[126] something to which Hausmann's writings on the revolutionary potential of homosexuality—and thus the discursive network that he created that allows for homosexual readings of this image—gave additional support.[127] Finally, the increased attention being paid to homosexuality in the public sphere during the Weimar Republic—as well as the fact that Baader and Hausmann presented themselves in intimate contact with one another in all three of their double portraits—would also have strengthened the photomontage's homoerotic overtones.[128] Given these connotations, *Double Portrait* thus seems the most radical of the photomontage portraits discussed in this chapter, since, unlike the merely homosocial portraits, it threatens a patriarchal worldview much more directly. Finally, *Double Portrait* is also reversible around its horizontal axis; either Hausmann's figure or Baader's figure could be positioned right-side up. As such, the print evokes the form of another mass-produced object: namely, a playing card. And by recasting their conjoined images as an element in a larger game, Hausmann and Baader reinforce a sense of the mutability of human identity, a sense also created by the signs of both cyborgian augmentation and same-sex desire.

Because of its homoerotic significance, Baader and Hausmann's *Double Portrait* also manifests parallels with Donna Haraway's concept of the cyborg, which undermines ideas of fixed sexual identities and of sexuality necessarily being connected to reproduction. "Cyborgs," as Haraway notes, "might consider more seriously the partial, fluid, sometimes aspect of sex and sexual embodiment," a consideration that Baader and Hausmann's *Double Portrait* might have raised as well.[129] Moreover, as Haraway continues, while "organisms and organismic, holistic politics depend on metaphors of rebirth and invariably call on the resources of reproductive sex," "cyborgs have more to do with regeneration and are suspicious of the reproductive matrix and most birthing."[130] Thus, because the coauthored photomontage suggests issues of both non-reproductive sex and monstrousness (by conjuring up an image of a collective entity composed of uncannily merged bodies), *Double Portrait* also evokes a vision of a world in which radically new forms of human propagation are possible, a world in which biological reproduction has been augmented by a host of other possibilities, including regeneration, cloning, genetic engineering, and prosthetic replacement and enhancement.

By suggesting that *Double Portrait* evokes aspects of Haraway's concept of the cyborg, I do not wish to argue that the concept of identity that inspired Hausmann's representations of cyborgs was as radical as the one that Haraway developed. However, in terms of his view of sexuality, Hausmann's understanding of human identity was certainly more advanced than that of Wiener and much closer to contemporary views of the mutability and diversity of subjectivity. Indeed, as I demonstrate in chapter 5, the Berlin Dada artist whose works dovetail most closely with Haraway's thinking is Höch, who, throughout the 1920s and early 1930s, made photomontages that explicitly undermined clear distinctions between different genders and ethnicities as well as the divide between human and animal.[131] At the same time, however, it is important to locate Hausmann's visualization of the cyborg as a central moment in the development of the cyborg as a form of hybrid identity that, from the vantage point of today, seems conceptually situated between Wiener's more mechanistic view of the cyborg and Haraway's radically postmodern view. Although Hausmann remains closer in most regards to Wiener, his understanding of sexuality was explosively radical for his time.

Conclusion

As I have argued, after breaking down language and fixed notions of human identity through poetry, performance, and theory during the early years of the Berlin Dada movement, Hausmann reconstructed the new man as a cyborg on the level of spectacle between 1919 and 1924. Visual figures that recalled Dada's nature as an ideology supporting a collaborative and self-transformative lifestyle, Hausmann's cyborgs expressed both pleasure and anxiety about human hybridity and the constantly transforming nature of modern subjectivity. Evincing their creator's awareness of the multiple social, political, and artistic networks in which modern identity was always enmeshed (and, thus, the conventional aspects of human subjectivity), Hausmann's cyborgian new men also acknowledged the libidinal and unconscious aspects that defined them as particular individuals. In addition, Hausmann's cyborgian representations also helped interpellate a new type of spectator by combining an innovative photomontage technique, which necessitated the viewer's active and self-conscious engagement with the artwork, with a strategy of constantly depicting the cyborg as a locus of new forms of technologically enhanced perception. Influenced by anarchism and psychoanalysis, Hausmann used the cyborg to explore new ways of living in a world that no longer appeared to have any fixed rules or values, and, thereby, he employed this uncanny figure as a springboard to reimagine himself through interrogating the mutually determining interrelations between self and other, friend and enemy, artist and spectator. Although Hausmann's work remained limited by the fact that he never envisioned the cyborg as incarnating a form of female identity, his subject matter and formal strategies were extremely significant and innovative for his time.

4. The Militarized Cyborg

Soldier Portraits, War Cripples, and the Deconstruction of the Authoritarian Subject

Each individual is a component part of numerous groups, he is bound by ties of identification in many directions, and he has built up his ego ideal upon the most various models. Each individual therefore has a share in numerous group minds—those of his race, of his class, of his creed, of his nationality, etc.—and he can also raise himself above them to the extent of having a scrap of independence and originality. Such stable and lasting group formations, with their uniform and constant effects, are less striking to an observer than the rapidly formed and transient groups from which Le Bon has made his brilliant psychological character sketch of the group mind. And it is just in these noisy ephemeral groups, which are as it were superimposed upon the others, that we are met by the prodigy of the complete, even though only temporary, disappearance of exactly what we have recognized as individual acquirements.

—SIGMUND FREUD, *Group Psychology and the Analysis of the Ego* (1921)

In art history and criticism, Berlin Dada has traditionally been described as dedicated to destroying all hitherto-existing forms of bourgeois modernist art and annihilating multiple social, aesthetic, and political enemies through satire and other forms of negation.[1] These enemies included, most famously, the bourgeois, the expressionist, the militarist, and the Christian, social–psychological types that the Dada artists perceived as hindering both personal and social development in their contemporary moment. As I argued in the previous chapters, however, the Berlin Dada artists also pursued a constructive or positive project, one devoted to artistic self-fashioning and the imagining of new forms of hybrid modern identity in different media. Before I return to analyzing the positive side of Berlin Dada art in the next chapter, I deal here with the aspect of the movement that condemned and attacked multiple enemies. As was the case with the Dadaists' self-fashioning and identity-positing activities, this critical undertaking also relied quite heavily on the figure of the cyborg.

This chapter examines the Dadaists' attack on the authoritarian subject as epitomized by the patriotic militarized cyborg. Although this technologically augmented soldier—trained, equipped, and organized by his society to produce violence—was not the only figure that the Dadaists attacked, it was one of their primary targets, and it represents in many ways the most extreme form of the identity types that they opposed. The Dadaists, however, did not attack every soldier who had fought in World War I. Indeed, perhaps because several Dadaists had served in the military, they seemed somewhat sympathetic to the plight of the ordinary working-class soldier who ultimately saw through the government's nationalist myths and who came to reject war in service of the nation-state.[2] On the other hand, as suggested by their statements as well as their visual productions, the Dadaists did attack the figure of the soldier who was still willing to fight, kill, and die for such abstract ideas as the "people," "nation," "state," or "country," concepts that because of their abstraction seemed outmoded and destructive to the new forms of existence that the Dadaists were hoping to help bring about.[3] As suggested by the quotation from Sigmund Freud's famous analysis of group psychology from 1921 that begins this chapter, the soldier was often conceived as a "mass subject" during the Weimar Republic, an immature or weak personality that subordinated his individual will and desires to the goals and ideals of an organized group. Because he was less rational and less repressed than people who retained their independence from groups, and since he was easily led, the military subject was understood to be authoritarian: that is, favoring strict rules, established hierarchies, and rapid and unquestioning obedience. The antipode of the shifting and anti-authoritarian identity type favored by the Dadaists, the soldier was singled out for particular critique because he so directly contradicted the Dadaist ideology and lifestyle.

The method of deconstruction, of course, was not part of the intellectual horizon in which the Dadaists worked. The concept is still useful, however, because it helps illuminate how the Dadaists went about toppling the military ideal that they believed still determined the development of certain individuals in the postwar period. Deconstruction arose in France in the 1960s and 1970s at a moment when Western philosophy—understood broadly as the purification and systematic articulation of the principles of Western rationality—was felt to be highly problematic, because of its instrumental connections to social repression and domination, and ultimately impossible, because of the constantly reconfiguring nature of all conceptual systems. As conceived and articulated by Jacques Derrida, deconstruction was a method of reading philosophical and, later on, other types of texts to show how and what they excluded.[4] One central strategy characteristic of Derrida's technique was a focus on "undecidable" words, terms that bound together different, often contradictory meanings. By showing how a philosophical text both generated and attempted to limit the multiple meanings connected to its central concepts, the deconstructive method demonstrated the repressive aspects of a particular conceptual system and revealed significant implications that the system had attempted to deny. Another central strategy of deconstruction was to focus on fundamental binary oppositions that structured a text (such as speech–writing, sensible–intelligible, presence–absence, existence–essence, subject–object, mind–body, nature–culture, and the like), showing how the text's system privileged one side of the opposition and excluded the other. Rather than simply reverse or invert the opposition, however, deconstruction sought to bring the two terms into relation, thereby once again connecting the text's conceptual network as a whole to the meanings that it attempted to exclude. Fundamental to both strategies of deconstructive analysis was the idea of inscribing the conceptual system under investigation within a larger play of signification. Thus, in all its forms, deconstruction was geared toward opening up a text's meaning at carefully chosen sites through a mode of immanent analysis that would allow a given conceptual system to go beyond itself and to generate new ideas.

In light of this definition, the Dadaists can thus be said to have "deconstructed" the authoritarian subject in that they employed their art in specific ways to undermine this figure from within. As I briefly discussed in the previous chapter, one inspiration for the Berlin Dadaists' photomontage practices was the countless photographic soldier portraits produced during the nineteenth and early twentieth centuries. Sometimes employing photomontage strategies, these portraits were a central part of the patriotic visual culture that supported World War I. For this reason, because the Dadaists made images that both criticized the military ideal and evoked the technique and the genre through which the ideal was originally celebrated and disseminated, their approach can be considered deconstructive, in that they proceeded immanently, turning popular military propaganda against itself. Furthermore, not only did they employ photomontage to undermine the military subject, but the representations that they created referred directly to the traumatic disorders of the mind and body that were most damaging to it—disorders that the military ideal was designed to conceal. Their depictions of traumatized soldiers thus reinscribed the military subject into a larger system of concepts and historical phenomena that strongly altered its significance. Finally, the Dadaists did not simply use photomontage strategies to destabilize this form of authoritarian identity; they also employed a host of other popular practices—including field postcards and popular care packages—that were originally used to support the war. They thus reworked the media, images, and values used to promulgate wartime patriotism in Germany, exposing their strategies and opening them up to a much larger play of associations that seriously impeded their ability to function as pure propaganda. Through cyborgian representations of damaged, traumatized, and technologically altered soldiers, in other words, the Dadaists attempted to educate the spectator about how soldiers had been formed in the past and, thereby, to help the viewer avoid identifying with dangerous role models in the present.

This Dadaist education, as I show, helped focus attention on the perilous aspects of the technological augmentation of human beings. First, the militarized cyborg revealed how technology placed all people in greater danger than before, irrespective of their military or civilian status. Because of the proliferation of weapons, instruments of detection, and new modes of transportation and communication, not only were humanity's capabilities and propensities for violence intensified, but all living beings were made more vulnerable to attack and destruction. In addition, because of the instrumental networks that were shown to help create authoritarian military identities, the cyborgian soldier also revealed technology's potential to dehumanize individuals: to make them less empathetic and more able to commit violence against others. Since technologies both increased human power and helped produce a second, "colder" and less empathetic consciousness, as Ernst Jünger was to note in 1934, they combined with human goals and projects in ways that encouraged a far greater general destructiveness than ever before. Technology, as the Dadaist representations of mechanized war cripples already suggested by 1920, could thus be viewed as a suprahuman force with an internal logic and development of its own and not necessarily focused on the best interests of humanity as a whole.[5] As a paramount figure revealing this new, more autonomous and destructive understanding of technology, the cyborgian soldier became a way for the Dadaists to investigate the dangerous aspects of their postwar situation.

Allegory

Before analyzing the wealth of visual materials used by the Berlin Dadaists to combat the military ideal in postwar Germany, I investigate Walter Benjamin's notion of allegory, another important concept from the middle years of the Weimar Republic. Because its most significant articulation follows the creation of the Dada cyborg by about five years, Benjamin's concept of allegory cannot be said to have directly influenced the Dadaists. However, like many of the ideas about perception, identity, and technology developed during the interwar years in Germany, "allegory" illuminates aspects of the Berlin Dadaists' achievement, since it helps define certain problems with which they— like Benjamin—were grappling. Allegory helps explain how the negative dialectics created by the Dadaists' photomontage strategies could be used to mobilize the spectator's consciousness of history—a consciousness particularly important in the case of images of traumatized soldiers, which dealt with specific social and historical events. In addition, the use of the term *allegory* also helps us remember that the Dadaists understood the cyborg as a particular type of visual figure that—despite its specific forms—always represented a set of more general concepts and historical issues.

In his complex, sometimes contradictory cultural criticism and theory written in Germany and abroad in the 1920s and 1930s, Benjamin used the term *allegory* to signify the representational practices most commensurate with the experience of modern life, thereby redefining the term to mean something quite new. During the time that Benjamin wrote his major works, allegory already had an extremely wide range of meanings in German.[6] From the Greek, *allēgoría,* speaking otherwise than one seems to speak, it stood for multiple forms of imaginative spoken, written, and visual representation—forms of extended metaphor that encouraged their beholders to look for multiple meanings hidden beneath the work's literal surface. Although Benjamin adopted freely from the term's wide-ranging historical meanings, he also attributed to allegory a much more specific constellation of significance. For him, allegory was a mournful, modern, and secular mode of representation that was essentially violent, historical, and weakly redemptive.

Benjamin initially devised his theory of allegory in the mid-1920s to explain the principal characteristics of the German *Trauerspiel,* or royal "mourning play."[7] For Benjamin, this baroque dramatic genre, which presented the intrigues of courtly life as a metaphor for the battle between primordial forces of good and evil, also revealed the modern world's growing secularization as well as its separation from the past.[8] Secularization involved a set of interrelated processes whereby human beings transformed their concept of the natural world from a place of mythical or spiritual forces to a source of material to be shaped and formed according to subjective human intentions. Christianity contributed to the world's disenchantment by either banishing or reinterpreting the pagan gods and by shifting the place of all spiritual power to a supersensible or transcendental realm—a domain slowly taken over by reason and science beginning in the sixteenth century.

During the time of the *Trauerspiele* in the sixteenth and seventeenth centuries, secularization had progressed to where not only the pagan gods were viewed as fictional and in need of corrective reinterpretation but the strength of the Christian worldview was also beginning to be questioned.[9] For this reason, the representations of the baroque allegorists were both melancholy and retrospective; they recognized their separation from the time of myth and religion and sensed that, as human history developed, both nature and human beings were being devalued and destroyed. Since they saw human beings and nature as "eternal transience" or constantly in decay, and because they longed for a past in which the world was still "whole," the Baroque allegorists, Benjamin argued, constructed representations for a mournful audience—representations in which their loss of religious certainty was dramatized, and secular sorrows and anxieties could find satisfaction.[10]

The German mourning plays indulged the beholder's desire to consume suffering and destruction on multiple levels. The plays' main protagonists were absolute rulers, who, as tyrants, caused suffering and, as martyrs, suffered the violence of others in various horrible forms. The plays were filled with scenes of death and destruction, and their dialogues were highly emotive, in terms of both their subject matter and their language, which was packed with overextended and overdetermined metaphors and analogies. By focusing on the figure of the sovereign, the baroque allegorists represented the fate of both the fallen individual and the now secular or profane human community. In this way, they attempted to revitalize the Christian worldview by propping up traditional examples of human goodness and evil with references to multiple systems of knowledge drawn from cultural traditions that were beginning to be treated as nonabsolute. Interludes were used to introduce foreign figures, gods, moral exemplars, and personifications of abstract concepts, who commented on and interpreted the main action, thereby multiplying the systems of meaning in which the story and characters were to be understood. At numerous points in the drama, the mourning play's action was brought to a standstill, and its parts dissected and reassembled to form static tableaus that suggested both literal and underlying significance.[11]

Because of its relatively equal or evenhanded treatment of the cultural systems of the past (its tendency not to elevate one system over another), baroque allegory, for Benjamin, revealed an experience of fundamental crisis—a sense of fragmentation, loss, destruction, and impending disaster—that, nonetheless, still offered its beholders a few weak signs of redemption. Both the violence and the weakly redemptive power of the German mourning plays were connected to the fact that these plays represented human beings as creatures *[Kreaturen]*, a dialectical term that signified both God's creation and a living being that was instinctive, base, and passionate.[12] The mourning plays thus emphasized their protagonists' natural dignity and connections to an earlier time pervaded by God's grace while also revealing their "animality" and passionate natures. Through the extreme emotions and violence experienced by its "instinctive" or "material" side, the subject was first shown to be destroyed and then redeemed.[13] The sovereign—and, with him or her, the secular community—had to be torn into pieces by the allegorist to be reconstructed as a constellation of signs, the precondition for the sovereign's, and humanity's, eventual redemption.[14]

By representing the human creature dialectically—namely, as radically material, guilty, and demonic as well as possessing dignity and worth during his or her suffering and annihilation—the baroque allegorists attempted to banish absolute evil from their world.[15] The pure evil that the baroque allegories revealed in the human creature was shown to be a "subjective" projection and not an inherent quality.[16] In this way, the *Trauerspiele* attempted to redeem their audiences by directing them toward a less absolute conception of human existence: one that criticized modernity's anthropocentrism but neither demonized nor deified the subject. Because they ultimately implied that the sovereign was neither god nor devil, the baroque mourning plays suggested that, although viewed suspiciously, the systems of belief and knowledge that traditionally produced multiple forms of sovereign and enslaved existences still affected human identity in the early modern era. The "break" with the Christian world assumed by these early modernists did not mean rejecting the past and its traditions, just a different, less obedient relationship to them.

Although developed out of an analysis of baroque theater, Benjamin's theory of allegory soon began to define for him the fundamental experiences of modernity in his own time. The mourning plays, he noted, shared numerous characteristics with twentieth-century literature and art, including a concern for violence, decadence, and figurative expression as well as a highly alienated and pessimistic sense of political engagement.[17] In addition, like the *Trauerspiele,* Benjamin's contemporary culture was constantly citing the past and appropriating its forms and themes. As was also the case during the baroque period, the "spirit of the present age," he noted, "seizes on the manifestations of past or distant spiritual worlds in order to take possession of them and unfeelingly incorporate them into its own self-absorbed fantasizing."[18]

In addition to being violent and weakly redemptive, allegories, according to Benjamin's model, were historical because they sought to represent the newness of their contemporary moment—the direction in which their world was evolving—in terms of forms and concepts drawn from a multivalent past. As "ruins," or collections of fragments torn from multiple traditions, allegories proclaimed their own artificiality and attempted to extinguish the false appearance of totality.[19] In this way, they also announced their "modernity"—their separation from the past and convention—while attempting to represent the new situation taking form around them: a heterogeneous world of increasing hybridity and transformation. By isolating certain figures and actions in the profane world and commenting on them from a multiplicity of historical perspectives, allegories undermined all readings of history as a linear narrative and, instead, promoted a rethinking of the relationship between the past and future. In Benjamin's famous phrase, through allegory, "history becomes part of the setting," and the passage of historical or narrative time becomes frozen and arranged in space.[20] By stopping narrative movement, and examining actions from more than one sociohistorical perspective, allegories attempted to remind their readers of all that they had lost through modern, rational progress. Ambivalent about tradition (because they saw it as not quite appropriate to their "fallen" time), but condemned to using it (through recontextualizing appropriations of canonical forms and concepts), allegories represented their world as permeated by conflicting systems of meaning and knowledge. Thus, despite modernity's rhetoric of "break" and "separation" from the past, allegories suggested that the new world could be understood only by remembering the pasts and traditions that had been lost.

As this chapter demonstrates, the Berlin Dada artists created allegorical works in the sense that Benjamin gave the term: as mournful representations that cited a diverse array of past historical sources and that were violent and weakly redemptive. Not only do the Dadaist representations of cyborgian war cripples evoke the trauma of mechanized war, but many of these works also suggest the brutal and repressive nature of the pre-Weimar German establishment. Among the enemies targeted by the Dada representations were the Wilhelmine government and the institution of the army as run by the Army High Command, which destroyed an entire generation through its conduct of an unnecessary war; the German medical establishment, which attempted to cure traumatized soldiers through coercion; German business and industry, which profited from the carnage and even commodified patriotism and the exchange of wartime sentiments; the church, which sanctified barbarism and dressed it in a cloak of moral superiority; and the bourgeoisie, whose repressive lifestyle and values helped stifle dissent and demonized difference. By allegorically representing these various enemies, the Dadaist cyborgs denounced their contemporary moment. In addition, the various Dadaist deconstructions of the military subject were also historical in that they referred to—and attempted to comment on—specific historical circumstances: World War I, the November Revolution, protests on the streets by disenfranchised war veterans, the elections of 1919, and other social and political events. Although they cited a multivalent past, the Dadaist military cyborgs were also precisely rooted in their contemporary moment.

The redemptive nature of the Dadaist representations of traumatized soldiers can be seen in how some of the works hint at new powers given to the crippled fighting men by technological augmentation, something that is emphasized by the care with which the photomontage or assemblage elements are integrated into the work as a whole, which implies that their prosthetics are well integrated and functional. Their depictions, moreover, were redemptive in that they were radically critical of contemporary politics. By attempting to deconstruct the body of the male soldier—to show how it was both formed and destroyed, the contexts in which it functioned, and the values that it supported—these Dada representations sought to redeem their historical present by advocating change within it.

"Forty-five Percent Fit for Work"

As I showed in chapter 3, a publicity photograph of Raoul Hausmann and Hannah Höch taken at the "First International Dada Fair" was a useful point of entry into how the Dada artists often used the cyborg to suggest the new forms of hybrid modern identity that they found progressive (Figure 3.1).[21] For this reason, it should not be too surprising that a second publicity photograph taken to promote the "Dada Fair" is an excellent springboard for analyzing the critical aspects of the Dadaists' art (Figure 4.1). This photograph shows another part of Room One of the exhibition—an area contiguous with the space revealed in the Hausmann–Höch photograph; here, Hausmann stands against the wall on the far left and Höch is seated, also on the left. Other Dada artists and supporters are also present. Hausmann, now wearing black gloves, talks animatedly with Dr. Otto Burchard, the gallery's owner, who sports a light suit and a bow tie, while Johannes Baader, Hausmann's occasional collaborator, looks on and smokes a pipe. Behind and to the right of this group stands Wieland Herzfelde flanked by his wife, who like Höch sports a stylish *Bubikopf*. Framed in a doorway, they gaze intently at the art on the walls. Otto Schmalhausen, a lesser-known Dada artist and George Grosz's brother-in-law, sits in the right-most armchair, with his hands clasped. He smokes a cigarette and wears fashionable white puttees on his shoes. Behind Schmalhausen stand Grosz—with a homburg, pipe, and cane—and the diminutive John Heartfield. Like the Herzfeldes, they too contemplate the show, Grosz with a decidedly alert expression on his face and Heartfield with a rather more introspective one. Surrounding these figures, more examples of the parodic advertising signs that the Dada artists presented as works of art appear on the walls. Because they all use the same typeface, they help unite the exhibition by injecting a note of continuity into the heterogeneous collection of "products" on display. The more prominent signs read as follows: "Take DADA seriously. It pays off." "Everyone is capable of DaDa." "Dada is against the art-swindle of the Expressionists." "Dilettantes, rise up against art." "Dada is the conscious subversion of the bourgeois system of concepts." In addition, a real political poster is

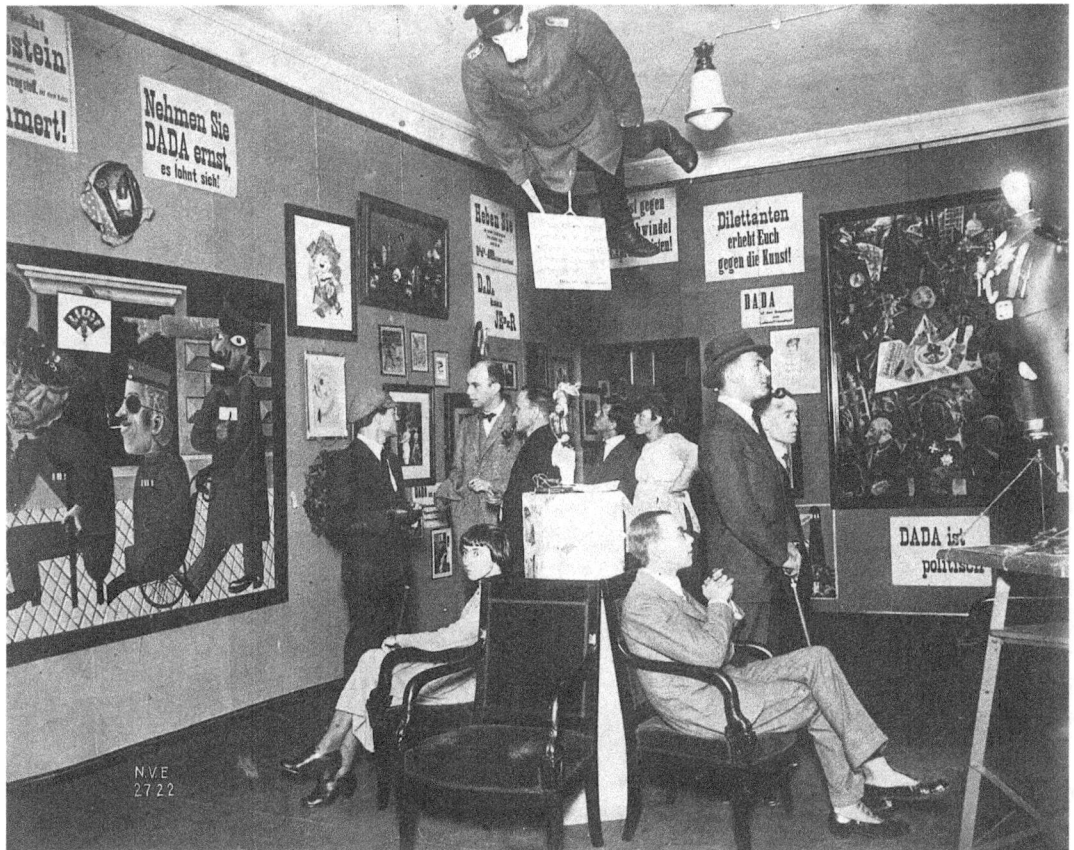

Figure 4.1. Opening of the "First International Dada Fair" in Berlin, 1920. Standing *(left to right)*: Raoul Hausmann, Otto Burchard, Johannes Baader, Wieland Herzfelde, Margarete Herzfelde, George Grosz, John Heartfield. Seated: Hannah Höch and Otto Schmalhausen. Photographer unknown. Photograph from Bildarchiv Preussischer Kulturbesitz/Art Resource, NY.

also presented—a color lithographic election placard from 1920 for the national–liberal German People's Party designed by Alexander W. Cay.[22] Depicting a lighthouse illuminating a turbulent sea, the party's name prominently displayed in its beam of light, the placard emphasizes the turbulent nature of the contemporary election scene and presents the party's image of itself as a force uniting the bourgeoisie and steering the German ship of state to safety. This poster, whose political sentiments the Berlin Dada artists definitely did not share, is cut off by the standing figures of Grosz and Heartfield.[23] Hung just above the floor on the far wall, it is situated next to another Dada sign, one that affirms that "DADA is political."

Significantly, almost all of the major works that can be identified in this image depict cyborgs. On the far left, Otto Dix's *45% Erwerbsfähig* [Forty-five Percent Fit for Work] (1920) appears, a large oil on canvas that for a time hung in the Dresden City Museum and that has often been referred to in art historical texts as *Die Kriegskrüppel* [The War Cripples] (Figure 4.2). (The canvas was later prominently exhibited in

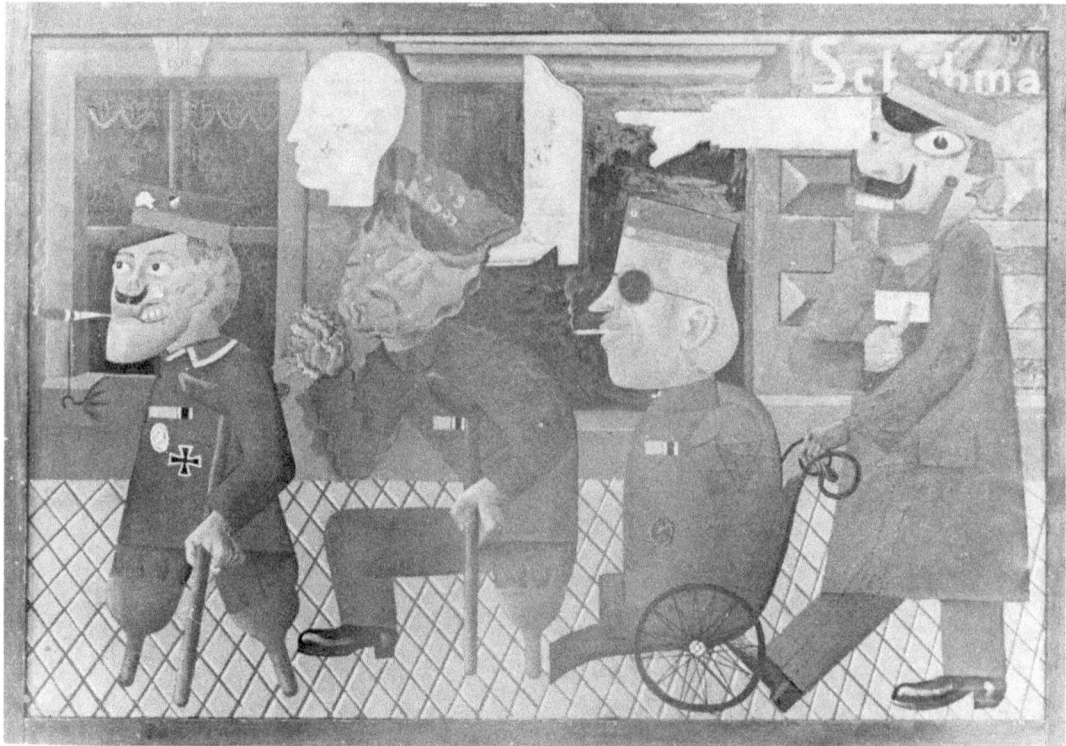

Figure 4.2. Otto Dix, *45% Erwerbsfähig (Die Kriegskrüppel)* [Forty-five Percent Fit for Work (The War Cripples)] (1920). Oil on canvas. Destroyed. Photograph from Bildarchiv Preussischer Kulturbesitz/Art Resource, NY. Copyright 2009 Artists Rights Society (ARS), New York/VG Bild-Kunst, Bonn.

Room 3 of the Nazis' infamous "Degenerate Art" exhibition in Munich in 1937, where the catalog condemned it as "painted military sabotage." It subsequently disappeared and was probably destroyed.)[24] Dix's original title referred to the concerted efforts in postwar Germany to rehabilitate disabled soldiers.[25] During World War I, regional governments and private charities assumed most of the responsibility for physically impaired veterans. This situation changed radically in February 1919, when the Weimar state took over primary responsibility for the care of disabled veterans and their dependents by setting up a national network of welfare bureaus dedicated to serving the needs of German citizens directly affected by the war. The Military Pensions Law, which was passed in 1920, codified these changes, providing support for the disabled men but emphasizing rehabilitation for at least partial reemployment. Disability pensions were meager, supplemented by "superior" welfare payments only if the veteran was truly unemployable. Dix's title, which refers to the new system's practice of defining veterans in terms of fitness percentage, alludes to this type of calculation, which goes back to the Weimar government's original decree from 1919. Depending on their degree of impairment, wounded veterans were given physical rehabilitation and job training, and a great deal of effort was made reintegrating them into the workforce.

The retraining of war amputees, which was begun as a local and private enterprise during the first years of the war, was understood to be for the benefit of the individual as well as the collective. As Anson Rabinbach argues, "The effort to reintegrate war-cripples into the workforce was necessary because of the 'degradation' suffered by individuals having to rely on public assistance—not to mention the great cost spared the nation by removing dependents from the welfare rolls."[26]

In Dix's painting, four prosthetically augmented ex-soldiers march in rigid formation down a paved street in what appears to be a shopping district, identified as such by the large display window and signs in the background. All the figures are disabled in some way—they have lost either arms or legs, one trembles with shell shock, and others are depicted as missing eyes, ears, jaws, or noses. At the same time, they all show signs of technological reconstruction in the form of grafts and mechanical replacement parts—the stumps, hooks, and crutches of the two figures in the lead; the wheelchair carrying the third figure from the left; and the prosthetic jaw, eye, arm, and leg of the standing figure bringing up the rear. In addition, the objects that float above the veterans—the transparent head that hovers over the second soldier from the left, the boot that hangs between the two middle figures, and the arm with the pointing hand that extends between the two ex-fighters on the right—evoke thought balloons, actual commodities, and street signs all at the same time. As such, they suggest dreamed-for solutions to the miseries of these cripples, means of conceptualizing and orienting themselves to their new diminished conditions, and replacement parts produced by the scientific, medical, and industrial establishments of Weimar Germany.[27]

As a whole, Dix's painting suggests little sympathy for his disabled military cyborgs. He depicts them in a simplified and caricatured style that emphasizes their ugliness and travesties their plight. Because of their uniforms and medals, their linear formation, and their lockstep quasi-military gait, it appears that they still uphold the anti-individualistic martial values in service of which they were crippled. These disabled military cyborgs, Dix's canvas suggests, have not been enlightened by their tragedies. Despite their suffering, they remain loyal to both the German state, which demands that they remain productive, and German medical and fashion industries, which, the canvas implies, emptily promise to relieve their suffering through modern prostheses as well as cosmetics, salves, and clothing. Furthermore, as Hanne Bergius suggests, the painting seems to parody traditional representations of triumphal processions in Western art, thereby transforming the march "into a procession of shame," publicly presenting lawbreakers on their way to punishment.[28] And by referring to and inverting a past artistic tradition designed to honor its subjects, the painting seems to criticize the figures that it depicts by emphasizing how little they play the part of heroes.

Finally, by partially undermining its status as fine art, *Forty-five Percent Fit for Work* also criticizes its subjects by suggesting that the German soldiers who sacrificed themselves in World War I do not deserve a respectful and artistic form of memorialization. As was the case with Hausmann's drawing *The Iron Hindenburg*, Dix's mode of depiction is to some extent derived from popular culture—namely, the modes of caricatured portraiture that were a staple of nineteenth- and early-twentieth-century German illustrated books and magazines. As such, the cartoonlike representational style of Dix's canvas distinguishes it from expressionist paintings, which possessed a much more direct and gestural manner of representation, as well as from the much more abstract forms of cubism and futurism. In addition, Dix's handling of representation is also radically different from the traditional style of nineteenth-century German history painting as exemplified, for example, by Anton von Werner—the realistic and academic mode of depiction favored by the German monarchy before the war for commemorating important subjects and events. Instead of tribute or remembrance, *Forty-five Percent Fit for Work* suggested a critical attitude toward its subjects and toward bourgeois art in general—something that it achieved by the overall ugliness of its forms as well as its resort to caricature, with its connotations of scorn and disparagement.[29] Although Dix's paintings, even during the artist's Dadaist phase, were never as radically anti-art as some of the other Berlin Dadaist productions—for example, Grosz and Heartfield's "corrected masterpieces," which used photomontage to deface reproductions of modern and traditional artworks—the grotesqueness of *Forty-five Percent Fit for Work* seems to question the efficacy of both traditional and modern forms of art in the postwar world.[30] Despite their radical critique of the artistic tradition, however, the Berlin Dadaists never produced such extreme forms of anti-art as Marcel Duchamp's "readymades," appropriated mass-produced objects that fundamentally called into question all hitherto-existing forms of artistic production and reception. Instead, as Dix's painting suggests, the majority of the Berlin group's works were attempts to make new forms of art commensurate with their transformed (postwar) historical situation. Despite their over-the-top rhetoric, the Dadaists, in other words, did not destroy the institution of art in their actual practices but instead criticized how art was used in the past and engendered new forms of creation and reception.

The ways in which other Dada artworks were displayed in relation to *Forty-five Percent Fit for Work* help reveal the new understanding of art promoted by the Berlin Dadaists. When Dix's canvas was installed at the "Dada Fair," Grosz's *Ein Opfer der Gesellschaft* [A Victim of Society] (later renamed in English *Remember Uncle August, the Unhappy Inventor*) (1919), a canvas with oil, pencil, buttons, and photomontage elements, was hung over the face of the lead cripple in Dix's painting (Figure 4.3). In addition, Grosz's photomontage, *Galerie deutscher Mannesschönheit, Preisfrage "Wer ist der Schönste?"* [Gallery of German Manly Beauty, Prize Competition: "Who Is the Most Beautiful?"] (1919), previously published on the front cover of the Dada journal *Jedermann sein eigner Fussball* (1919), was placed directly over the boot floating between the middle two cripples, the "shaker," whose spastic motions suggest one of the symptoms of shell shock, and the smoker in the wheelchair, whose demeanor suggests a cool, perhaps imbecilic composure that even his horrible injuries cannot obliterate (Figure 1.1). By installing other works directly over Dix's canvas, Grosz, Heartfield, and Hausmann, the exhibition's curators, made the multiple meanings supported by *Forty-five Percent Fit for Work* even more diverse while turning the spectator's attention to

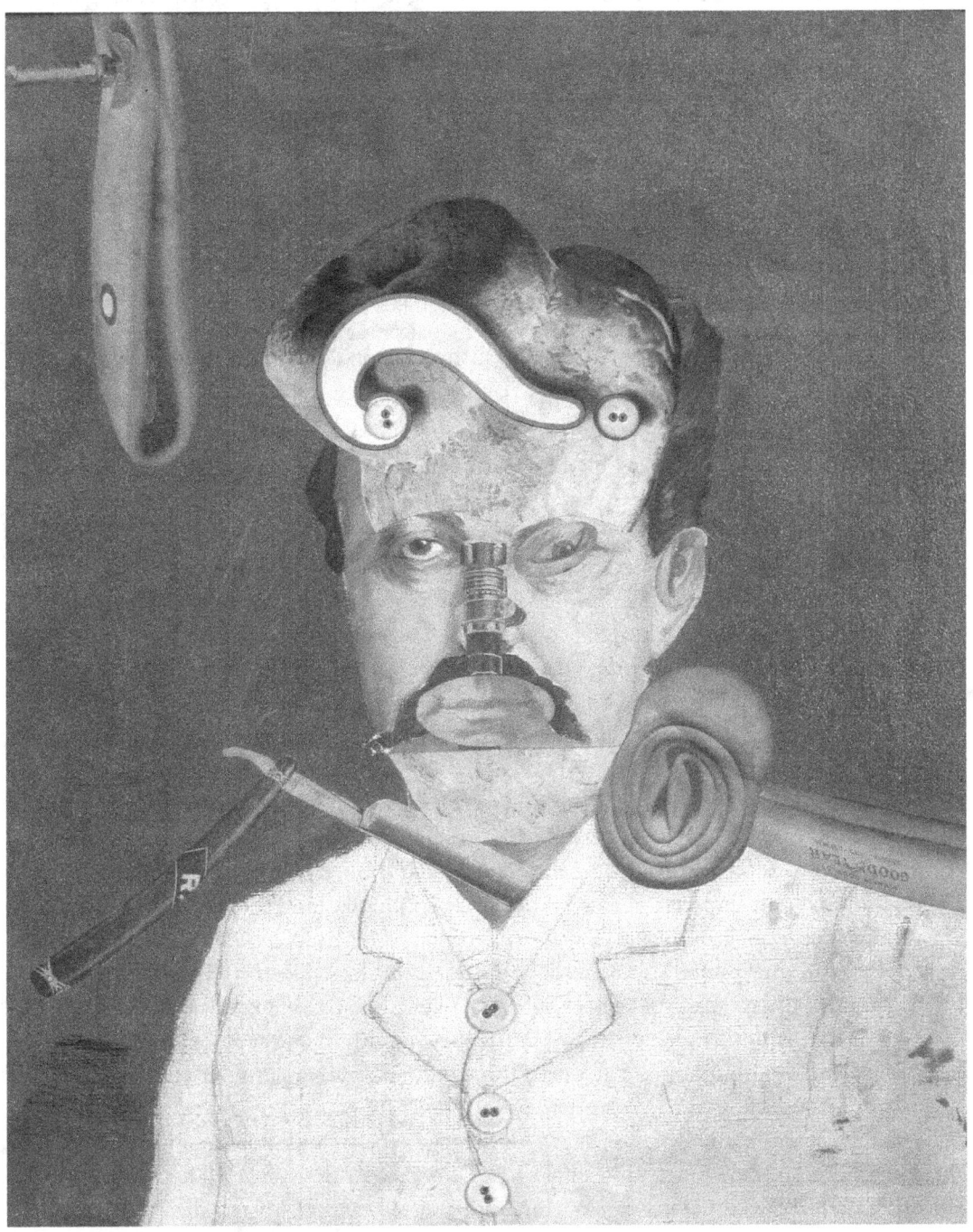

Figure 4.3. George Grosz, *Ein Opfer der Gesellschaft (Remember Uncle August, the Unhappy Inventor)* [A Victim of Society (Remember Uncle August, the Unhappy Inventor)] (1919). Oil, pencil, photomontage, and buttons on canvas. 49 × 39.5 cm (19 ⁵⁄₁₆ × 15⁹⁄₁₆ inches). Musée national d'art moderne, Centre Pompidou, Paris. Photograph from CNAC/MNAM/Dist. Réunion des Musées Nationaux/Art Resource, NY. Copyright 2009 Estate of George Grosz. Licensed by VAGA, New York, NY.

the installation as a whole. In this way, they expanded the montage principle that governed the production of specific works to the exhibition in general, and they perhaps also suggested that the audiences' experience of the interaction of the various representations in relation to one another was more important than their contemplation of the individual artworks.

The Dadaists used montage to create a multiplicity of sometimes conflicting interpretations of their art, interpretations that prevented the full reduction of reality to either the level of the photographic image or that of the written word. In this way, they empowered their audiences by making them aware of their contributions to their aesthetic experience of the various photomontages and assemblages. Through their exhibition practices at the "Dada Fair," the Dadaists intensified this characteristic of their art. The additional works hung on top of *Forty-five Percent Fit for Work* helped "allegorize" Dix's painting; namely, they provoked the spectator to interpret the work as a constellation of signs referring beyond the literal situation that they depicted. The spectator was thus encouraged by these supplemental works to add their meanings to the loose constellation of elements that constituted Dix's representation. These additional chains of signification generated in the spectator's mind as he or she contemplated the hybrid ensemble led to areas of meaning that would not have been readily connected with *Forty-five Percent Fit for Work* if it was perceived separately from the representations that were hung on top of it.

A Victim of Society presents a portrait of a disfigured man, cut off at the chest and positioned so that his left side projects slightly toward the viewer. He wears a white suit or lab coat with real buttons, which, because they are sewn directly along the suit's opening, appear to be stitched into his body as well. A rolled-up hose or blanket and an inner tube with a Goodyear logo are situated on his left shoulder, and a straight razor is balanced under his chin, its handle extending to his right. The unknown victim's forehead is horribly distended as if he had suffered some traumatic brain injury and his skull was only imperfectly reconstructed. To emphasize his disability, his hat hangs on a metal bar above him as if it will no longer fit on his head. Two buttons are sewn directly into the flesh of his forehead, and a question-mark-like form is anchored between them like a substitute lock of hair. The man's nose has been replaced by a spark plug or a series of threaded pipes and nuts, a new mouth has been pasted over his old one, partially cutting off his drooping mustache, and an irregular flesh-colored lump now substitutes for his chin. His left eye has been supplanted by a new one, which looks like it was partially screwed into his damaged socket and then left in an upside-down position. Finally, an additional eye, oriented at a ninety-degree angle from the norm, is fitted into his left ear. A grotesque constellation of mismatched elements, Grosz's anonymous portrait is characterized by a style of caricatured depiction that harmonizes with Dix's canvas beneath.

Like the wounded veteran that he partially occludes, Grosz's victim appears to be a disabled soldier. This is suggested by his facial disfigurements, which resemble contemporary photographs of wounded soldiers published in the independent socialist weekly *Die freie Welt* [The Free World] in 1920, which also published caricatures and photomontages by Grosz (Figure 4.4).[31] Other similar photographs had already been published during the war in medical journals, advertising brochures for prosthetics and other forms of restorative treatment, and pamphlets put out by veteran's relief organizations; such imagery would soon become much more widely disseminated through Ernst Friedrich's classic antiwar book, *Krieg dem Kriege* [War against War] (1924), which published numerous photographs of bodily- and facially-disfigured veterans, as well as through Friedrich's International Antiwar Museum, founded in Berlin in 1924, which also exhibited photographs of traumatically injured soldiers.[32] (Dix appears to have based an image in his famous etching series *Der Krieg* [The War] from 1924 on a similar photograph.)[33] The victim's status as a war veteran is also suggested by his hat, which appears to have a circular military insignia sewn on its side, as well as by the hose or blanket and inner-tube combination that rests on his shoulder and suggests an epaulet. At the same time, the disabled figure's scientific garb (the unpainted white coat), as well as his positioning in a dark interior space, possibly implies a different social location than that of the cripples marching on the street. And the painting's later title, "Remember Uncle August, the Unhappy Inventor," also evokes a somewhat different—perhaps higher—social standing.

In his entry on Grosz's photomontage in the "Dada Fair" catalog, Herzfelde reads the image as a representation of a disabled person sick of living an irreparably damaged life. Citing the question mark, Herzfelde suggests that the victim questions his situation, but, because of his debilitated state, he has forgotten exactly what he is puzzled about. Furthermore, the photomontage elements on his left shoulder, which prop up his head, suggest physical exhaustion. The razor, on the other hand, implies that he contemplates suicide, and the buttons and suit suggest that, despite all this, he remains the proper German bourgeois, who, despite his adverse circumstances, attempts to look proper. As Herzfelde concludes, "All the first signs of development have come to a standstill, only the pedantic habit of buttoning himself up has remained—'simple, but orderly.'"[34] More recently, Brigid Doherty has suggested that the victim's head is that of Friedrich Ebert, the first president of the new republic; in addition, because of the violent disfigurement of the subject's features, the inclusion of photomontage elements, and the lack of paint on the figure's jacket, Grosz's painting implies a critique of painted portraiture in general.[35] "Seen that way," as Doherty puts it, "*A Victim of Society* proposes that Ebert cannot be painted; or, that he can only be painted if painting incorporates its own impotence and disfiguration—in the form of montage."[36] Although there is not enough visual evidence to conclusively prove that the visage is indeed that of Ebert, it is certainly possible.[37] And if the painting's spectators found this to be so, it would add an additional set of associations to the constellation of works as a whole, one that would inspire the audience to investigate parallels between Ebert—who, as the party chairman of the SPD, had supported the war since its very beginnings—and the disabled yet patriotic veterans, who had returned from the war as broken shells of their former selves. Furthermore, another spectator could potentially add

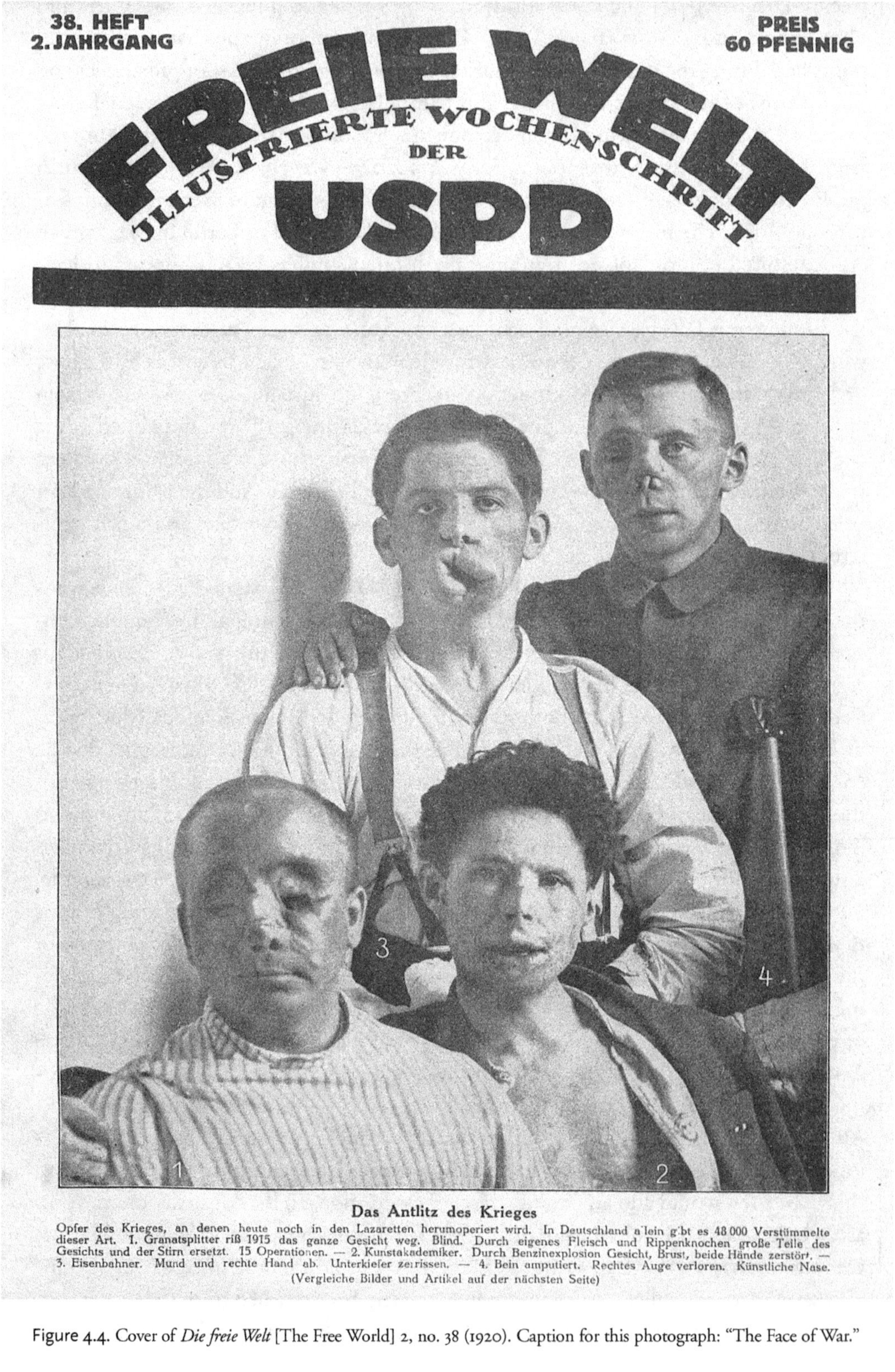

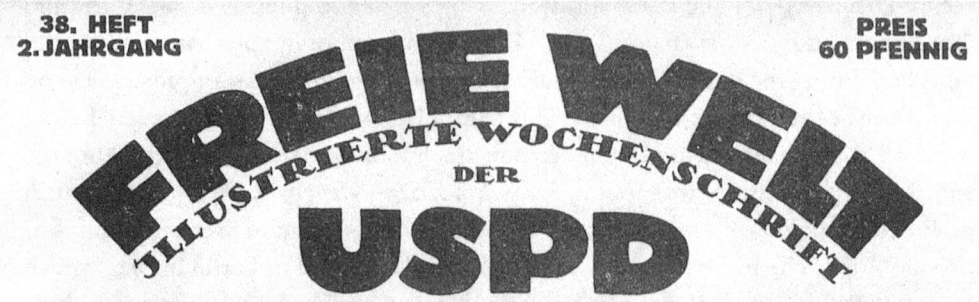

38. HEFT
2. JAHRGANG

PREIS
60 PFENNIG

FREIE WELT

JLLUSTRIERTE WOCHENSCHRIFT DER

USPD

Das Antlitz des Krieges

Opfer des Krieges, an denen heute noch in den Lazaretten herumoperiert wird. In Deutschland allein gibt es 48 000 Verstümmelte dieser Art. 1. Granatsplitter riß 1915 das ganze Gesicht weg. Blind. Durch eigenes Fleisch und Rippenknochen große Teile des Gesichts und der Stirn ersetzt. 15 Operationen. — 2. Kunstakademiker. Durch Benzinexplosion Gesicht, Brust, beide Hände zerstört. — 3. Eisenbahner. Mund und rechte Hand ab. Unterkiefer zerrissen. — 4. Bein amputiert. Rechtes Auge verloren. Künstliche Nase.
(Vergleiche Bilder und Artikel auf der nächsten Seite)

Figure 4.4. Cover of *Die freie Welt* [The Free World] 2, no. 38 (1920). Caption for this photograph: "The Face of War."

to Herzfelde's and Doherty's interpretations of Grosz's portrait—which read the representation as despairing, social critical, and self-reflexive—by arguing that the figure's steel "nose" also suggests protection and strength, and that the extra eye on his ear implies that he has gained new powers through his surgical reconstruction. Once again, it could be claimed, the figure appears to have been transformed into a cyborg, one whose stitched-together features suggest both past trauma and new powers. Importantly, given the great ambiguity of Grosz's representation, this more positive reading does not contradict the interpretations offered earlier so much as supplements them, thereby adding to the work's rich network of significations. As is characteristic of the Berlin Dadaist approach to representation in general, the overall goal is to create an image that supports multiple readings and thus involves the audience by inspiring debate. Although creating an image with a clear and unambiguous message leads to the most comprehensible message—and thus to what is possibly the best form of propaganda—it is the Dadaist strategy that leads to the greatest amount of engagement on the part of viewers and thus to their empowerment through the work of art.

Victim thus allegorizes *Forty-five Percent Fit for Work* by suggesting—through the Ebert association and the victim's resemblance to a scientist or an engineer—that the figures' continuing patriotism may have something to do with their class identifications. Because Dix's painting appears for the most part to depict petty officers, the addition of *Victim* emphasizes the notion that, despite their abject conditions, the patriotic war cripples continue to identify with the middle and upper classes, groups that largely supported the war. Despite their horrifying wounds, which link them to the ordinary working-class soldiers who made up the majority of the frontline troops, they refuse to acknowledge their connections to the exploited proletariat. In addition, because of its scientist or engineer associations, Grosz's canvas also suggests that the victims of war may have been actively involved in transforming themselves into new forms of life through technology. And because of this latter association, *Victim* seems to invert one of the original meanings of Dix's canvas. As implied by the biting irony of its original title, Dix's *Forty-five Percent Fit for Work* criticized the government's attempts to rehabilitate German veterans through new and better prostheses to enable them to rejoin the workforce. The overlaying of Grosz's canvas onto Dix's representation, on the other hand, points to a hope that these promises were perhaps not entirely false and that disabled veterans might be partially—or even fully—restored through the inspired application of medical technologies.

The promises made by German medical science at this time were extremely idealistic and utopian. Influenced by the German science of work as well as Taylor's system of scientific management, many of the physicians and technicians involved in treating amputees believed in the ability of modern technologies to overcome even radical disabilities.[38] Central to the healing process was the development of prostheses designed for specific, work-oriented functions—initially the idea of the French hygienist and fatigue expert, Jules Amar, who created a comprehensive program of physical rehabilitation for disabled veterans during the war and whose ideas were quickly adopted in Germany. Amar's "working arm" was an industrial prosthesis to which several different types of tool—often designed for specific jobs—could be attached. These included a "one armed punch" for marking railway tickets as well as "a complex mechanical hand that could be used to type or play the violin."[39] As it was developed in Germany, the working arm "typically consisted of a custom-fitted truss that was strapped or mounted onto the stump and equipped with a variety of interchangeable metal attachments—including hooks, rings, rods, drills, claws, gouging blades, eating utensils, hammers, files, wrenches, screwdrivers—that could be either inserted, clamped, or screwed onto the base."[40]

Both during and after the war, numerous books and pamphlets were produced extolling the power of work, the working arm, and the German prosthetics industry in general to rehabilitate disabled veterans and industrial workers.[41] Positive accounts were also printed in illustrated newspapers, extolling the benefits of technological enhancement.[42] As a general rule, prostheses were represented as making German men whole and virile again. In light of this tendency, Dix's canvas seems like a clear protest against the overwhelmingly optimistic representations of prosthetic men *[Prothetiker]* in the mass media. Not only does Dix's canvas make its veterans seem rather weak and emasculated, it evokes the protest marches by disabled German soldiers against what they perceived to be public and government indifference to their plight.[43] At the same time, as the weak positive associations produced by *Victim* suggest, rehabilitating German soldiers through work was not as horrible as it is sometimes depicted as being. Although there were certainly excesses and problems, many German veterans stated that their postwar employment made them feel human again and no longer useless.[44] Thus, despite the fact that Germany's support of its disabled veterans was remembered negatively (something reflected in numerous histories of this period), new research has suggested that the problem was not reintegrating disabled German soldiers into the workforce but the German government's inability to take the disabled veterans' psychological needs into account. Through its policies of cutting off private aid to former soldiers after the war, it created a situation in which they felt they were denied the "thanks of the Fatherland." And by evoking contradictory associations about reintegrating disabled veterans into the workforce, the hybrid work formed by the combination of Dix's and Grosz's canvases inspires inquiry into the nature of prosthetic augmentation after World War I.

The other work that was hung on top of *Forty-five Percent Fit for Work,* Grosz's photomontage *Gallery of German Manly Beauty* brings a different set of associations to the underlying canvas (Figure 1.1). Generally acknowledged to be one of the first published photomontages by a Berlin Dada artist that can be dated precisely,[45] *Gallery of German Manly Beauty* was published on February 15, 1919, in the first—and only—issue of *Jedermann sein eigner Fussball,* the early Dada periodical banned by the government for supporting the Bavarian communist revolution.[46] Herzfelde, the editor (with Heartfield) and publisher, was arrested and imprisoned a month later for *Jedermann*—a two-week incarceration that he described in his text *Schutzhaft* [Protective

Custody], published shortly after his release on March 20.[47] In Grosz's photomontage, the original of which is now lost and presumed destroyed, portrait photographs of the central figures of the new Weimar government—including Ebert, Philipp Scheidemann, Gustav Noske, and Matthias Erzberger—as well as Erich Ludendorff, are arrayed across a crudely cut silhouette of a woman's fan.[48] By turning the recent election into a beauty contest, the photomontage feminizes the politicians while suggesting the growing importance of the mass media in politics since the mid-nineteenth century. Recalling the representation of movie stars in contemporary German illustrated magazines and the tradition of celebrity galleries in nineteenth-century photography, Grosz's photomontage suggests that, through photography and mass reproduction, electoral politics has been turned into an emotional and image-driven process. In its original context on the *Jedermann* cover, rows of text below the photomontage stated, "The Socialization of Party Funds," "A Call for Protection in the Face of the Generally Usual Election Fraud," and, "This commentary should illustrate the nonsense of our National Assembly from the point of view of the Democrats, namely, those people who believe that a nation should not have a government whose level is superior to their own average."[49] As suggested by these captions, the message of Grosz's photomontage in the context of *Everybody His Own Soccer Ball* was that the German nation's sorry state had resulted in the election of inferior politicians who regularly cheated the people whom they were supposed to represent. And when mounted on *Forty-five Percent Fit for Work,* as the original was at the "Dada Fair," Grosz's fan suggested that the insanity of contemporary electoral politics was connected to the nationalistic veterans who marched in the streets, a suggestion that strengthened the political associations of the hybrid work as a whole.

The inclusion of the photomontage not only suggested that the veterans' vote could be manipulated for electoral ends but also hinted at the important role that the *Dolchstosslegende,* or myth of the "stab in the back," was coming to play in German politics.[50] According to this pernicious belief, initially created by the Army High Command, the Germany military had been betrayed by the "home front" and the new republican politicians, the ones who signed the peace treaty and, eventually, the Treaty of Versailles, which determined Germany's moral and financial responsibilities for the war. Were it not for the German Jews, communists, trade unions, war profiteers, and new civilian government (dubbed the "November Criminals" by its most vehement critics), the German nation, the *Dolchstosslegende* implied, would ultimately have been victorious in battle. A mainstay of the propaganda of numerous right-wing and conservative parties, the legend of the backstab contributed to the new Weimar government's rapid loss of legitimacy in the eyes of the German public as well as to the assassination of a number of its most important politicians. And by connecting Dix's representation of damaged yet patriotic veterans to the idea of the German electoral process as a media-driven popularity contest, Grosz's *Gallery of German Manly Beauty* implied that representations that depicted military sacrifice as well as the new government's supposed shabby treatment of its former soldiers played an important role in the contemporary political scene.

The ways in which the Dada artists encouraged their spectators at the "Dada Fair" to interrelate the various images of cyborgian war cripples and feminized male politicians suggest a fairly novel attitude toward art. Although their heterogeneous works revealed a critical stance toward traditional forms of art making, the Dadaists, despite their rhetoric, did not produce anti-art. Instead, the works at the "Dada Fair" evoked an interest in encouraging their viewers to develop new ways to appreciate the creative act and its various productions. In addition to provoking their viewers to develop multiple interpretations of their ambiguous allegorical representations, the Dadaists pushed their audience to interrelate the various works displayed in the gallery. In this way, the play of meanings generated by the cyborgian paintings and photomontages was increased, and the idea of a unique and significant work was allowed to take second place to the open-ended activity of producing multiple interpretations and dialogue.

Prussian Archangel

Halfway across the room from *Forty-five Percent Fit for Work,* Heartfield and Rudolf Schlichter's *Preussischer Erzengel* [Prussian Archangel] (1920) was hung, a work that suggested its subject's cyborgian nature not by blurring the distinction between man and machine (as was the case with Dix's painting) but by undermining the separation between human and animal (Figure 4.5). In the publicity photograph, this now-destroyed assemblage of objects is suspended from the ceiling as if floating above the gallery's main seating area. Constructed from a stuffed soldier's uniform to which officer's epaulets have been applied, the assemblage was a work—along with Grosz's portfolio of lithographs *Gott mit Uns* [God with Us] (1919)—for which a number of the people responsible for the exhibition were brought to trial in 1921, charged with insulting the German army.[51] (Of the five who were indicted, three—Burchard, Schlichter, and Baader—were acquitted, and two, Herzfelde and Grosz, were let off with modest fines.) Instead of a human face, a pig's visage juts out from underneath the officer's cap. His arms are held rigidly at his sides, his legs are unnaturally twisted, and his tall black army boots appear to be spit shined. In addition, two signs decorate his body. The first sign, wrapped around his midsection, presents a quotation from a Protestant choral written by Martin Luther: "From heaven high, I come down here." The second sign gives the beholder instructions on how to view the work: "To fully grasp this work of art, one must exercise each day for twelve hours on the Tempelhof field armed for battle and carrying a fully-loaded knapsack."[52]

Like Dix's painting of the disabled petty officers, *Prussian Archangel* seems extremely critical of its subject. Not only does the figure appear physically damaged through its military affiliations—in this case, its twisted legs and missing hands suggest previous war trauma—but, in addition, its pig's head also suggests both brutality and uncontrolled appetites. Furthermore, the sign that hangs below its body—which states that only the physically exhausted participants of a sadistic military drill can appreciate the artwork—implies that the creature is a merciless and authoritarian taskmaster. This latter association is further reinforced by the assemblage's ironic title, its Luther-inspired belt, and its positioning just under the ceiling, which suggest that—at least in its own brutish mind—the Prussian archangel is a "divine" personage whose position is higher than that of mere men and, for this reason, is not subject to the same laws. In this way, Heartfield and Schlichter express their hatred of the Prussian militarist ideology in which Christian piety, nationalism, and a desire for war were deeply intertwined. As a whole, the assemblage suggests that the cyborgian officer has degenerated or de-evolved through his military elevation to leader of a fighting unit. Singled out as a commander by the military hierarchy that he represents, the officer seems to feel entitled to drill his men mercilessly. Because he floats from the ceiling, however, there is also a suggestion that the cyborg has gained mysterious nonhuman powers—abilities that in this case make it appear threatening.

Like *Forty-five Percent Fit for Work*, *Prussian Archangel* is "citational." In other words, its broken, sutured-together appearance is echoed by its references to other traditions and other historical moments. Its title, for example, provokes chains of association linking Heartfield and Schlichter's grotesque representation to the Archangel Michael in the Hebrew and Christian traditions: as the protector of Israel, as the captain of the host of the Lord, as the vanquisher of Satan, as a heavenly physician, as the patron saint

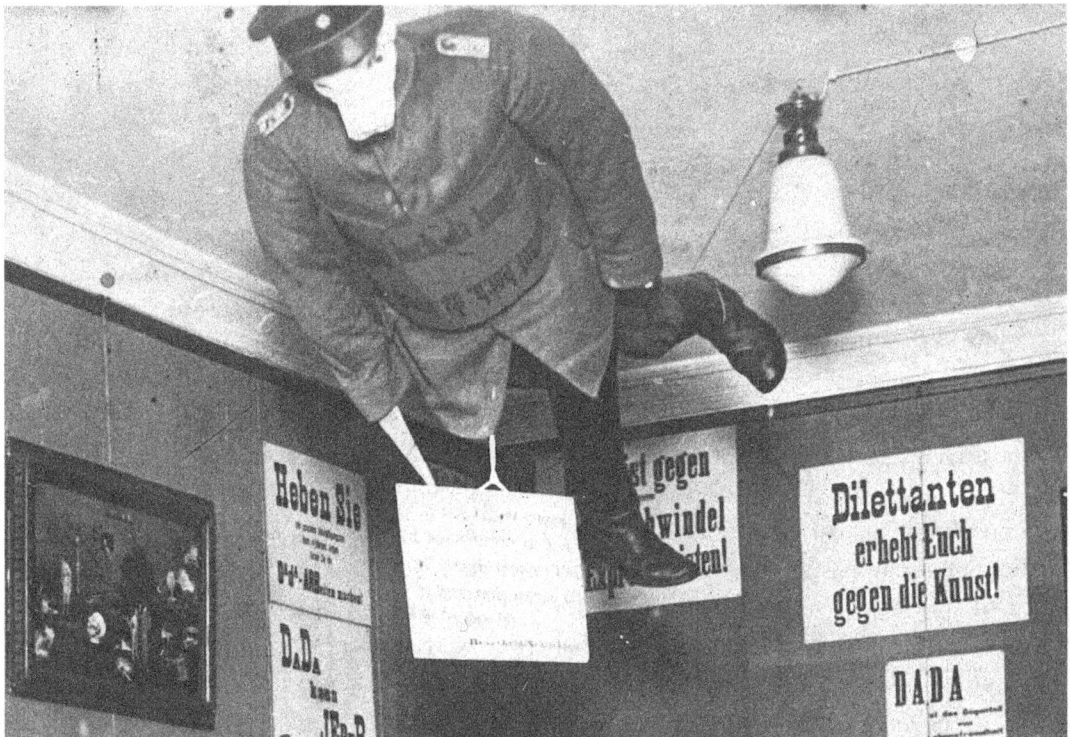

Figure 4.5. Opening of the "First International Dada Fair" in Berlin, 1920. Detail of photograph showing John Heartfield and Rudolf Schlichter's *Preussischer Erzengel* [Prussian Archangel] (1920). Mixed media. Destroyed. Photographer unknown. Photograph from Bildarchiv Preussischer Kulturbesitz/Art Resource, NY.

of the Holy Roman Empire of the German Nation, as an angel of death, as a patron of war, and as the one who weighs souls on Judgment Day.[53] Consequently, audience members might have been inspired to think about connections between the military and the church, to raise questions about whether the army had healed or destroyed Germany, or to compare the current state of the German nation to the union of medieval states in Central Europe during the Middle Ages and early modern period, a union that many spectators might have thought represented a much more exalted time in German history. Other viewers might have developed the archangel associations by asking themselves how the Prussian officer might appear to some as an angel of death, as a figure battling the devil, or as a divine judge of men. In each instance, however, the meanings produced by citing the Archangel Michael would have created a historical comparison, one that could have inspired the visitors at the "Dada Fair" to reflect on the various directions in which their contemporary moment might have been heading.

The citation of Luther could also have brought to mind additional lines of inquiry having to do with the connections between the Prussian officers, who had so recently been defeated, and the famed German theologian and religious reformer, who had translated the Latin Bible into the German vernacular and whose ideas had helped inspire the Protestant Reformation. Historically, Luther loomed large in German consciousness. Not only did the spiritual reformation that he helped inspire divide the Holy Roman Empire along religious lines, but his legacy was also mixed. Although Luther's teachings transformed Christian notions of salvation, faith, and the role of the church and priesthood in profound and powerful ways, his preaching was virulently anti-Semitic, and, when confronted with a peasant rebellion that his doctrines to some extent inspired, he came down decisively on the side of the secular nobility.[54] By the time of the "Dada Fair," German Protestantism had long been associated with the conservative values of the Prussian monarchy and the German middle class. Since the nineteenth century, Protestant intellectuals had given Germany's various European wars a religious sanction, thereby providing German nationalism with spiritual underpinnings.[55] There was thus widespread Protestant support for World War I, the kaiser, and the army in the years leading up to the November Revolution; during the entire Weimar era, with a few important exceptions, German Protestants aligned themselves decisively against the republican cause and the men and parties that supported it.[56] Spectators at the "Dada Fair" would have undoubtedly recognized the *Prussian Archangel*'s monarchist, antirevolutionary, and antisocialist connotations, created in part by the assemblage's reference to Luther—as well as, perhaps, an undertone of anti-Semitism (which would have been reinforced by the officer's decidedly nonkosher visage). As a result, they might have felt challenged to think about the long and complex historical connections in Germany between religion and authoritarianism as well as to ponder the role of spirituality in their own contemporary moment.

The references to the Archangel Michael and to Luther created by different aspects of the *Prussian Archangel* thus situated it within a larger network of meaning with the potential to inspire its original spectators to engage with issues of German history.

Moreover, Heartfield and Schlichter's provocative assemblage might also have inspired its audiences to compare the "fallen" context of postwar Germany to a religious past in which the earth seemed permeated with the "divine," or to think about World War I as the end point of a long history marking humanity's gradual fall from grace (an association much more likely). In addition, however, this cyborgian figure, which emphasizes the danger of technology by suggesting how it increases and extends human barbarism, also perhaps counters thoughts of religious pessimism with a ray of hope. Since the figure seems so ridiculous and idiotic, the representation as a whole implies that the *Prussian Archangel* is by no means all-powerful. And by depicting the authoritarian subject they both hated and feared in such a derogatory way, the Dadaists perhaps suggested that its influence could be overcome—and that technological augmentation, which amplified the destructiveness of war to undreamed-of levels, could also be used to stop those individuals who would misuse science and industry.

Heartfield Gone Wild

In the publicity photo that contains the *Prussian Archangel,* part of Grosz and Heartfield's assemblage, *Der wildgewordene Spiesser Heartfield (Elektro-mech. Tatlin-Plastik)* [The Petite-Bourgeois Philistine Heartfield Gone Wild (Electro-Mechanical Tatlin Sculpture)] (1920), appears on the right (Figure 4.1). This assemblage, which stands directly opposite from *Forty-five Percent Fit for Work,* was, like Dix's canvas, subsequently destroyed, and it can be seen more clearly in another publicity photograph from the "Dada Fair," where it is flanked by its two creators (Figure 4.6). Here, Grosz, on the left, and Heartfield, on the right, grasp the same sign praising the "machine art" of Tatlin found to the right of Höch in the Hausmann–Höch publicity photograph analyzed in chapter 3 (Figure 3.1). As was also the case in the Hausmann–Höch photograph, the Tatlin sign helps the viewer interpret the nearby artworks by emphasizing their distance from traditional forms of modern art as well as the partially mechanized nature of their creation. The assemblage depicts Heartfield as a half-human, half-mechanized cyborg, a synthesis of organic and mechanical parts—in this case, the organic side suggested by the more natural forms and materials of the tailor's dummy. Furthermore, as the sign implies, the assemblage's dual creators can also be considered cyborgs because of the way they have made the representation. Instead of sculpting *Heartfield Gone Wild,* they have assembled it like factory workers, as they often emphasized in their statements and writings.[57] Thus, as was the case with the *Prussian Archangel,* they used new forms of technology to create their artwork and also merged their artistic practices and collaborated—signs that function as signifiers not only of avant-garde practices but also of a cyborgian aesthetic as well.

To represent Heartfield "gone wild," Grosz and Heartfield chose a miniature tailor's dummy as their subject's body. To this childlike form they then added several objects as metaphoric replacements for the missing body parts: a working lightbulb for the head, a revolver for the right arm, an electric doorbell for the left arm, and a full set

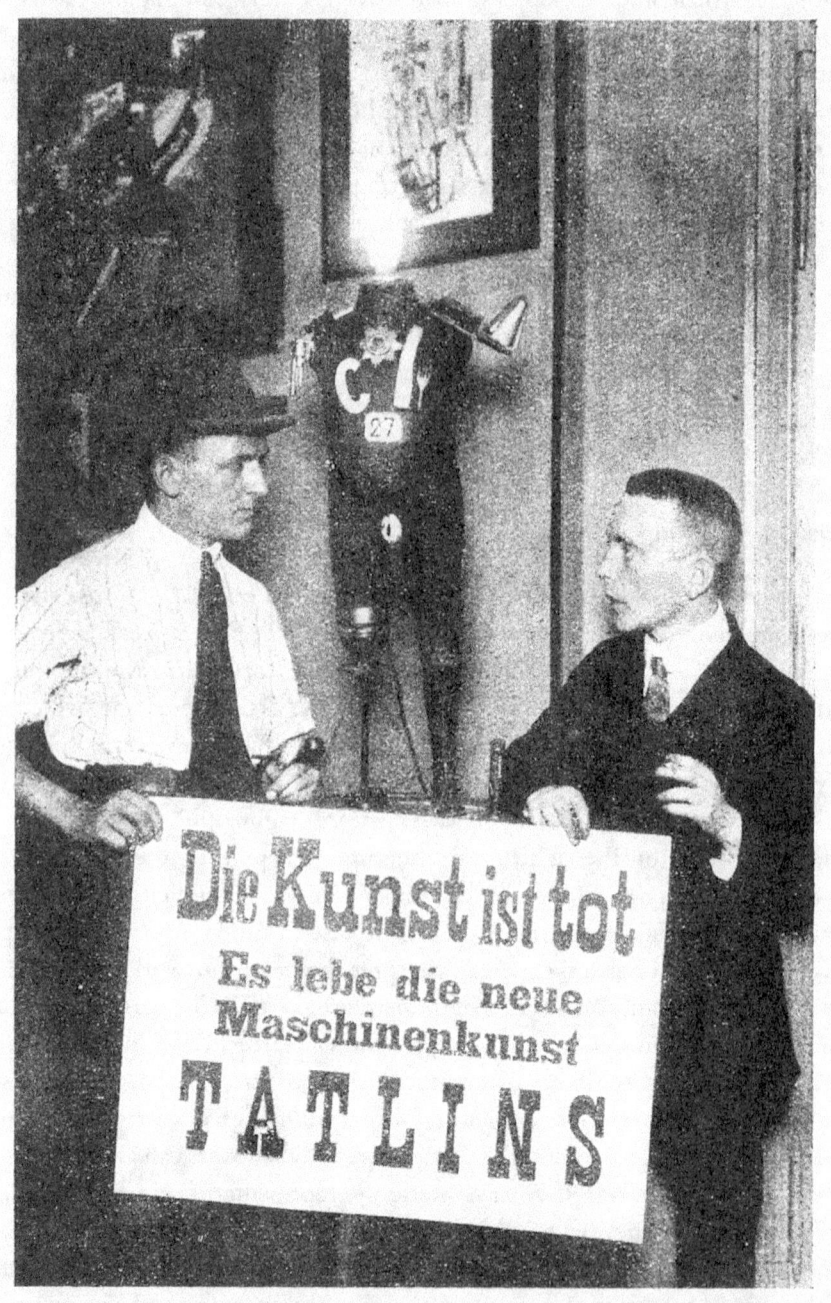

George Grosz (links) und **John Heartfield** (rechts)
demonstrieren gegen die Kunst zugunsten ihrer Tatlinistischen Theorien
(anläßlich der Dada-Ausstellung im Juni 1920).

Figure 4.6. Richard Huelsenbeck, *Dada Almanach* [Dada Almanac] (Berlin: Erich Reiss, 1920),
unpaginated page between pages 40 and 41, reproducing a photograph by an unknown photographer
depicting George Grosz and John Heartfield at the "First International Dada Fair" in Berlin, June 1920.

of plaster teeth for the genitals. The right leg has been replaced by an object that looks like a lamp stand from which an electrical wire—the conduit for the power that allows the head to illuminate—trails. Finally, a knife, a fork, numbers, letters, and military medallions were pasted to the trunk, and, according to newspaper reports, an iron cross, obtained from an unknown source, was pinned to the backside.[58]

Like the other images of cyborgian soldiers, Grosz and Heartfield's representation of the veteran Heartfield emphasizes the violent and dysfunctional nature of some Germans who returned from the front. The mismatched character of Heartfield's replacement arms suggests war trauma, literally the loss of limbs, an association reiterated by the figure's prosthetic right leg. Likewise, the plaster teeth evoke both castration and feminization through their simulation of a vagina, and the figure's childlike body suggests regression under the stress of war. The lightbulb head, furthermore, implies rote and mechanized cognition and the loss of independent thinking. The gun, letters, numbers, and military medallions help identify the figure as a former soldier and also intimate the loss of the figure's individual nature, the elimination of its various "personal" qualities in favor of its limited but defined functions as a member of a larger military force. In a related way, by evoking an obsession with food, the knife and fork worn as insignia hint at a hypertrophy of Heartfield's instinctual (or creaturely) aspects and a corresponding loss of higher, more intellectual abilities. Finally, the electric doorbell and lightbulb—as well as the wire running from the figure's leg—recall the use of electricity to treat war neuroses by German doctors both during and after World War I.[59] Although Heartfield, as the title ironically suggests, has attempted to form himself into a "good" petit bourgeois German subject, obedient, orderly, respectful, and above all clean, his endeavors to better himself have failed. Instead, his war experiences have transformed him into a cyborg, and the lingering residues of shock and trauma have caused him to lose control of his instincts and emotions.

In addition to creating a strange combination of criticism of and identification with the disabled soldier, the assemblage also evokes a sense of the fighting man as a cog in a much larger technologically interconnected system. As implied by, among other phenomena, the *Dolchstosslegende,* World War I marked a moment in modern warfare during which the army and the general population became more closely integrated than ever before. Because the war ran on the basis of a vast industrial economy, soldiers and civilians could no longer be clearly distinguished—just like the frontline soldier, the worker in the munitions factory helped advance the war, as did the train engineer, postal worker, and the German housewife, who maintained the soldier's family and helped elevate frontline morale through her letters and other contributions to the conflict. In the new armed conflicts of the twentieth century, everyone was either helping further the war effort or considered as possibly undermining the national cause. Remembering his wartime experience, Jünger made this point quite explicitly in 1930 when he argued that,

> in addition to the armies that meet on the battlefields, originate the modern armies
> of commerce and transport, foodstuffs, the manufacture of armaments—the army of

labor in general. In the final phase, which was already hinted at toward the end of the last war, there is no longer any movement whatsoever—be it that of the home worker at her sewing machine—without at least indirect use for the battlefield. In this unlimited marshaling of potential energies, which transforms the warring industrial countries into volcanic forges, we perhaps find the most striking sign of the dawn of the age of labor.[60]

In light of this description, Grosz and Heartfield's *Heartfield Gone Wild* presents a powerful personification of Jünger's age of labor in which war involved the "total mobilization" *[totale Mobilmachung]* of a country's citizens and resources. Not only is the Dadaist figure a synthesis of domestic and military components, but the assemblage also suggests that human limbs and organs can be replaced—although perhaps not perfectly—by mechanical prosthetics. And as such, the half-humorous, half-terrifying construction could have reminded its spectators of the networked character of the military cyborg—the fact that people can be changed into cyborgs only through a preexisting (albeit developing) system of technical knowledge that interrelates human beings with one another, with their environments, and with machines.

Jünger hinted at the existence of a broader system of technical knowledge supporting total mobilization when he argued that the phenomenon really only began in the war's final stages and that the various revolutions that had toppled the remaining European monarchies at the conclusion of the hostilities were continuations of this process.[61] The (incomplete) instances of total mobilization apparent before 1918, in other words, were simply the harbingers of a much broader transformation occurring in the 1920s, one that would bridge war and peace.[62] It would also unify formerly distinct nations into one gigantic authoritarian world order, as Jünger was to argue slightly later in his book, *Der Arbeiter* [The Worker], from 1932.[63] More important than actual mobilization was the "readiness for mobilization": a mental attitude that allowed human beings to see the various possibilities for mobilization and technological interface and that prepared them to freely and willingly accept becoming part of a rapidly forming biological–technological totality. For Jünger, as I showed in chapter 3, the repeated experience of film and photography would foster this attitude in which the good of the whole would be recognized to supersede all individual aspirations and desires, and thus, for him, the ultimate acceptance of total mobilization was essentially linked to the new technologies of mass communication. By making the system of culturally encoded knowledge that defined the new interrelationships between humans and machines seem desirable as well as impossible to resist, the mass media facilitated the development of a cyborgian world order.[64]

As Benjamin correctly argued, however, the understanding of war embodied in Jünger's theory of total mobilization was "nothing other than an uninhibited translation of the principles of *l'art pour l'art* to war itself."[65] War, in other words, had no purpose beyond its own mere existence; in Jünger's eyes, it became "eternal," "cultic," "metaphysical," and an end in itself. For this reason, although Jünger's positing of a network of technical knowledge supporting the mobilization of a country's entire re-sources for the waging of war could be taken as valid, his argument that humanity needed to uncritically submit to this system did not need to be accepted. Technology, as a system of cultural knowledge, could be resisted as well—or, better yet, it could be judged by other more human-centered criteria, its positive potentials embraced and its negative effects opposed. *Heartfield Gone Wild* seems to imply this latter (Benjamin-ian) position. Although the technological network for total mobilization is suggested by the assemblage, it does not convey the message that humanity must necessarily— and completely—submit to this intersubjective system of concepts. Instead, the vio-lence inscribed on the figure, the trauma and dysfunctionality that it evokes, implies the opposite: while recognizing the fact that human identity can be partly constructed through a system of technological knowledge that supports the military conduct of war, human beings must do everything in their power to resist being caught up in this network. The militarized cyborg, in the hands of Heartfield and Grosz, thus invites its spectators to distinguish between the positive and negative aspects of technical knowledge, and, implicitly, it proposes that we consider how human reason has over the past centuries become more and more instrumental.

Soldier Portraits

Dix, Heartfield, Schlichter, and Grosz were all ex-soldiers, and, as suggested by both their published statements and the art that they made that dealt most directly with the war, they were all radically disillusioned by their experiences. Dix was probably the most committed. Like many of his generation, he enlisted voluntarily in August 1914. That fall, at the age of twenty-three, he received training as an artillerist and machine-gun operator, and subsequently fought for almost four years in the trenches along the western and eastern fronts, eventually being promoted to the rank of vice sergeant major. For his service, Dix, who was wounded in battle, received the Iron Cross, Sec-ond Class, and the Friedrich-August Medal; in 1918, when the war was coming to an end, he reenlisted in the German air force and began training as an aerial observer.[66] As Dix's military history suggests, although Dix was repelled by war, he was also fas-cinated by it. "The war was a hideous thing," he remarked years later, "but there was something tremendous about it, too. I couldn't afford to miss it. You have to see human beings in this uninhibited condition in order to know something about them."[67] Dix's war experiences terrified him, maiming him psychologically by giving him wounds that even his art could not heal. "For years," as he noted in another late interview, "at least ten years, I kept having these dreams in which I would have to crawl through de-molished houses, through corridors that barely permitted me to pass. The ruins were constantly in my dreams. . . . Not that painting was a release for me."[68]

Unlike Dix, Heartfield did not volunteer for service, and, as his brother recounts, he remained aloof from the conflict for as long as possible. Heartfield was, however, finally drafted into an infantry regiment in the fall of 1915, whereupon he reported himself unfit for military service because of mental illness.[69] Although his company commander initially dismissed his claims, Heartfield eventually flew into such a rage that, instead of being ordered to the front, he was sent to a Berlin hospital instead. A few months later, he was released as fit for civilian work duty and was for a time employed as a mail carrier, a job that he reputedly carried out by throwing the mail he was supposed to deliver down a storm drain.[70] War, as he remembered it throughout his life, was a force of overwhelming destructiveness. "Wilhelm II," he wrote in 1961, "the Kaiser of Peace, as he called himself, already rattled the atomic bomb before it was even invented."[71]

Like Dix, Grosz volunteered for service—albeit in November 1914 when he most certainly would have been drafted if he had not volunteered.[72] Assigned to an infantry regiment, he nevertheless gained little if any direct experience of battle. Instead, in the winter of 1914–15, Grosz was assigned first to a reserve unit and later to a military hospital because of a severe sinus condition; then, in early May 1915, he was released on medical grounds because of his sinus disorder. In early January 1917, Grosz was recalled; the next day, he was admitted to a mental hospital in Guben and, shortly thereafter, to a mental hospital in Görden, both near Berlin.[73] In April of that year, Grosz was discharged from the army on the grounds that he was mentally unfit to serve. As he put it years later, "For me, war represented horror, annihilation, and mutilation. . . . It came to mean filth, lice, idiocy, disease, and deformity," and he claimed that he used his drawing as an outlet for his pent-up emotions and disillusionment.[74] Moreover, as a result of his wartime experiences, he developed a hatred for authority that became strongly apparent in his work. "I had been bellowed at for so long that I finally developed the courage to bellow back. I defended myself as best I could against vicious stupidity and brutality."[75] As a result, during his Dadaist phase, he "considered all art useless unless it could be employed as a political instrument in the battle for freedom. My art was to be my arm, my sword."[76] In addition, his war experiences also led him to develop a skeptical attitude about mass solidarity and the proletariat's role in contemporary life, something that is surprising, given Grosz's membership in the German Communist Party (KPD) in the late 1910s and early 1920s.[77] Finally, like Dix, Grosz's memories of the war haunted him for years afterward: "I thought the war would never end," he wrote in 1946, "and I think it never really did."[78]

Like Heartfield, Schlichter was not enthusiastic about the war, and he did not enlist like so many young men of his generation. The war, he noted later, was provoked to satisfy an "imperial desire for expansion" on the part of rulers who had "long since degraded moral postulates into tools of merciless exploitation."[79] Because of his nearsightedness, Schlichter was not drafted for nearly two years; instead, he was allowed to continue his art school education in Karlsruhe until 1916. Once called up, however, he was quickly mobilized and sent to the western front, a situation that did not last long. "When I came after various stages to the French front in 1916 [to serve] as a munitions driver," Schlichter remembered, "I secured my exclusion from active service through a hunger strike."[80] Like Heartfield and Grosz, Schlichter had an extremely negative reaction to military service, and like them, he secured his release through actions that placed him in the category of "unfit for service," that is, war resisters or the physically or mentally ill.

Given Dix's, Heartfield's, Grosz's, and Schlichter's military backgrounds, works like *Forty-five Percent Fit for Work*, *Prussian Archangel*, and *Heartfield Gone Wild* can thus perhaps be partly understood as attempts to remember and communicate personal wartime experiences. This can be seen on the level of form, where the works' montage structures recall the dissociating experiences of battle, violence, and trauma—either directly experienced, witnessed at close quarters, or perceived through the effects of war trauma on others behind the lines or in military hospitals. Significantly, however, most of the representations of soldiers or ex-soldiers that were exhibited at the "Dada Fair" were not self-portraits, although, as suggested by *Heartfield Gone Wild*, the Dada artists also recognized their connections to the individuals and social groupings that they most opposed. Instead, when choosing to memorialize the war through the military cyborg, the Dada artists largely embodied wartime experiences in figures that they also criticized and disagreed with. But the Dada artists did not simply represent the war in their scathing artworks; they also attempted to engage with the German visual culture that disseminated the image of war—a visual culture both patriotic and one-sided in that it tended for the most part to cover up the violence and sheer destructiveness of mechanized combat.

The soldier portrait *Musketier Podolski* (1915) (Figure 4.7), by the commercial photographer Albert Pfeifer, presents a good example of the type of imagery that the Dada artists were consciously attempting to evoke and at the same time attack.[81] A color photolithographic print with a photographic head of its young male subject montaged on the central figure's body, this soldier portrait is a characteristic example of the celebratory cyborgian soldier imagery produced during World War I. Podolski is depicted realistically, in a manner that merged the photomontage's graphic and photographic elements, and that suggested the image's truth or veracity as well. He stands erect, helmeted, and vigilant, grasping both a rifle and a flare gun, flanked by two companions in a forest of sturdy oaks. Wearing the uniform of the German infantry, he either guards or advances along a road, while to his rear a bucolic village appears, resting in a mostly flat pastoral landscape and watched by a German Zeppelin patrolling overhead. Podolski's cyborgian nature is stressed by his weapons, his symmetric and articulated uniform, and his similarity to—almost interchangeability with—his unknown companions. In addition, the field glasses around his neck, along with the Zeppelin and the flare gun, stress the new technologically enhanced powers of observation on which his battle effectiveness now depended.

Musketier Podolski is typical of the thousands of soldier portraits produced in Germany in the late nineteenth and early twentieth centuries, cyborgian imagery that served commercial as well as ideological functions. As I showed in chapter 3, soldier portraits, which combined cutout photographic portrait heads of real individuals with ready-made lithographic or photolithographic backgrounds depicting soldiers' bodies

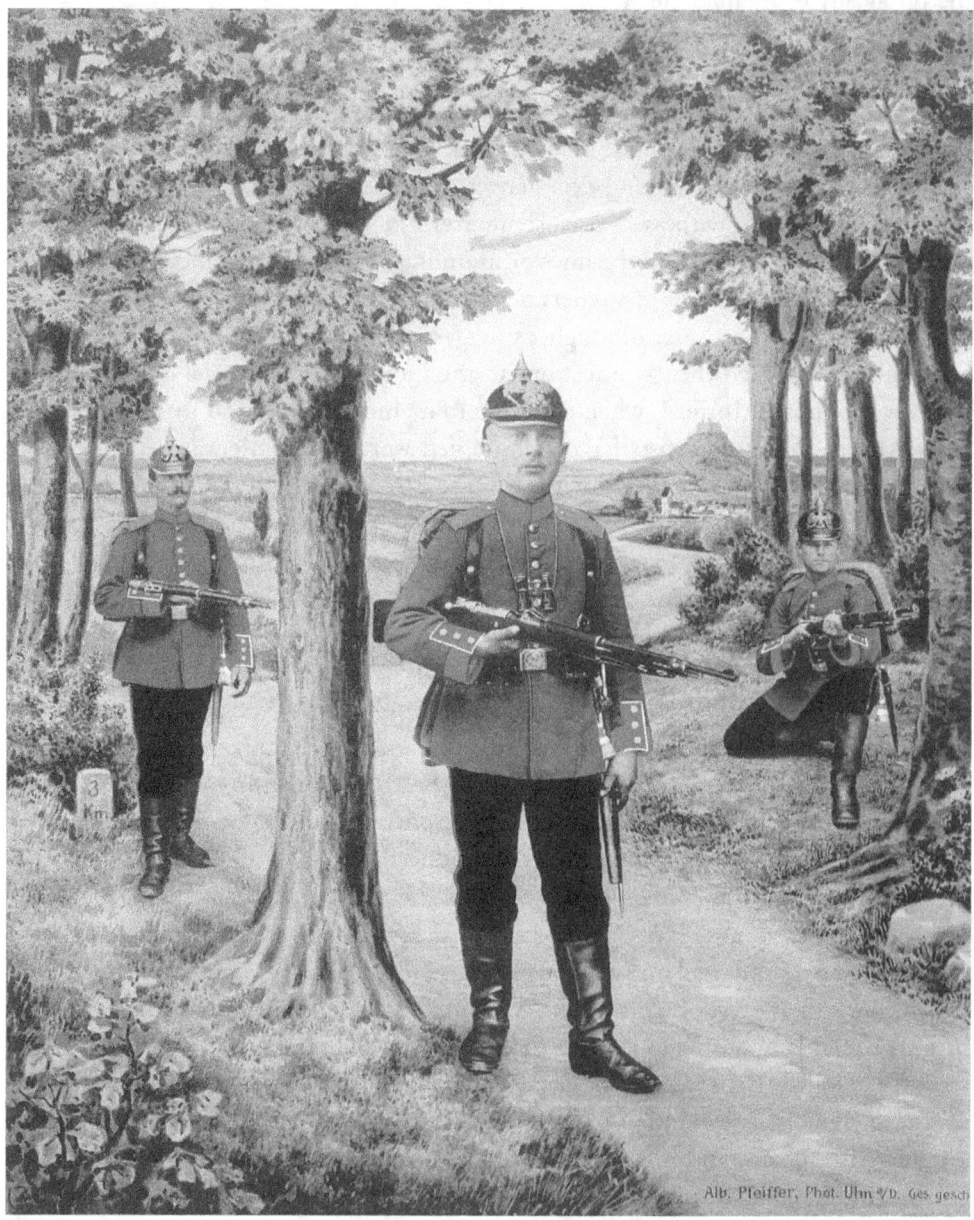

Figure 4.7. Albert Pfeifer, *Portrait Musketier Podolski, 7. Companie, 2. Unter Elsässer Infantrie-Regiment Nr. 137, Hagenau* (1915). Gelatin silver bromide print multicolored lithograph, montage. 45 × 32 cm (17¾ × 12½ inches). Museum Folkwang, Essen. Photograph from Museum Folkwang, Essen. Copyright 2009 Museum Folkwang, Essen.

in military contexts, were one source that inspired the Dada artists to develop photo-montage as an artistic strategy. As *Musketier Podolski* suggests, promilitary visual culture glorified the fighting man's body by armoring it and making it look superhumanly strong. Podolski's body is built up in several ways. First, he is given multiple weapons that he holds in readiness. Second, his body is literally built up through his uniform and through his erect and vigilant posture. Third, his "backup," his identically dressed comrades in arms, represents a unified force that Podolski maintains at his command. He is not a single entity but the leader of an elite fighting unit. Podolski's integration into his environment, which bears the same technological stamp that he does, also empowers the figure. The domesticated wood, even road, distance marker, flat plain, and clear recession into depth suggest the previous technological appropriation of nature as well as the fact that more technological change is possible.

Soldier portraits like *Musketier Podolski* are some of the purest examples of ideology analyzed in this book, defined here in its second primary sense as false consciousness. Ideology as false consciousness means an epoch's ruling ideas, the ideal expressions of the dominant material relationships, the concepts and spectacles that legitimate and serve the status quo. As false consciousness, ideology is an upside-down version of reality. It obscures a society's true material conditions—a people's actual relationships of production, ownership, and control—by creating representations both false and convincing. Such representations work to inspire consumption, politics, and other forms of mass behavior, and they do so by creating needs and fulfilling fantasies. Soldier portraits like *Podolski* served the German monarchy by representing the ideal German soldier: a technologically enhanced being that was powerful, attractive, and destined to win. For the soldiers who commissioned them, these portraits acted as inspirations, ideal self-images, or visual records to encourage them to fight and possibly die for their country. For the noncombatants, they were similarly ideal; they were images of manhood to be respected, emulated, or loved, and symbols that Germany would triumph in the war.

The material conditions that the soldier portraits concealed were the actual conditions of mechanized warfare in the early twentieth century. For the majority of soldiers, the new technologies of warfare did not make them safe from harm, although they did make them more powerful. With their increased abilities to kill, however, came the growing likelihood that they would be killed themselves. As Jünger, then a lieutenant in the Seventy-third Hanoverian Fusilier Regiment and by no means a foe of modern war, describes leading frontline troops at the close of World War I, mechanized warfare typically destroyed many of the men who waged it.

> I had men posted at the block and the trench cleared of the dead. At 11:45, without any warning having been given us, our artillery opened out on the position in front of us with the utmost fury. The result was more casualties for us than for the English, and it was not long before the tale of woe opened. The cry for stretchers came along the trench from the left. Hurrying along, I found what was left of my best platoon

commander, a shapeless mass, in front of the block in the hedge trench. He had had a direct hit in the loins from one of our shells. The fragments of his uniform and clothing, torn from his body by the force of the explosion, were hanging above him on the splintered remnant of a thorn hedge. I had a ground sheet thrown over him to spare the men the sight. Immediately after three more men were wounded at the same spot. One of them had both hands severed at the wrist. He staggered to the rear, covered in blood, both arms resting on the shoulders of a stretcher-bearer.[82]

Unlike Podolski's soldier portrait, Jünger's war memoir covers up neither the soldier's vulnerability nor the fact that in the twentieth century war technologies made the world increasingly dangerous. In addition, the specific images that Jünger remembers, which either literally or figuratively suggest castration, are reminders of the perversely uncanny effects that war technologies have on their subjects.

The material realities that soldier portraits like *Podolski* disguised were both economic and demographic. The first year of the war, 1914, marked the end of nearly thirty years of uninterrupted industrial expansion in Germany. After 1914 Germany experienced "virtually three decades of crisis, stagnation, and, frequently, falls in production."[83] Germany's national debt went from 5 billion marks in 1914 to approximately 157 billion by 1918, and at the immediate end of the war there were acute shortages in food and material.[84] Contrary to what *Podolski* suggests, the technologization of war actually helped bring about economic crisis and disaster because of the incredible waste of human beings, supplies, manufactured goods, and nature that it created.[85] In addition, the casualties produced by mechanized warfare contradicted the Podolski portrait's emphasis on the wholeness and perfection of the cyborgian soldier's armored body. By the end of World War I, there were 2,037,000 German soldiers either killed or missing in action; another 5,687,000 soldiers were wounded; and there were approximately 700,000 German civilian deaths.[86] Germany's casualties were the highest of any of the combatants, and only France suffered proportional losses. Although more powerful than ever before, the new cyborgian soldier was also much more likely to be killed, a truth that the soldier portraits attempted to hide.

War Neuroses

As suggested by the works just analyzed, Dix, Schlichter, Grosz, and Heartfield used numerous strategies to deconstruct the image of the invincible armored soldier circulating in German visual culture in the years leading up to the "Dada Fair"—strategies that included the literal representation of the symptoms and effects of war trauma, as well as much more complex formal evocations of the same. The Dadaist representations were thus not simply embodiments of the artists' own (perhaps dimly remembered, perhaps reconstructed) war traumas but self-conscious attempts to deal with the patriotic myths that helped support the interdependent systems of capitalism, nationalism, and militarism in Germany in the 1910s and 1920s. In the first place, the

Dadaists' canvases and assemblages reproduced the trauma and violence of war through "cutting" and "suturing." Even when they did not employ photomontage directly, the majority of their works reveal a montage-based principle of construction in that they were at least partially assembled out of components severed from their real-world contexts and then recombined into new loosely organized configurations. (*Forty-five Percent Fit for Work,* which does not initially seem to fit this description, nonetheless also suggests a montage-based principle of construction as a result of its nonnaturalistic combination of elements—the floating head, boot, and arm, for example, which hover above the cripples. In addition, as suggested by the hanging of other artworks on top of Dix's canvas, the show's organizers attempted to increase the painting's fragmented and cut-up character through nontraditional installation strategies.) Furthermore, as Doherty has demonstrated, the Berlin Dada artists attempted to evoke the various symptoms associated with war neuroses in their representations of cyborgian soldiers and cripples—what the German medical establishment at the time called "male hysteria," "traumatic neurosis," and "shell shock," among other appellations.[87] For Germans in the 1910s and 1920s, the symptoms of war neuroses, Paul Lerner shows, were understood to include such physical manifestations as persistent shaking, stuttering, tremors, and nervous tics; functional disorders such as muteness, deafness, and the paralysis of different bodily parts (which, despite their reality for the affected soldiers, could not be traced to a clear form of organic pathology); and mental conditions such as insomnia, depression, and uncontrollable emotionality.[88] And these symptoms, which were variously argued to have either physical or psychogenic causes,[89] were represented in the Dada soldier portraits, which, because they were often photomontages or assemblages, also formally evoked the traumatic physical shocks that were sometimes the cause of the various hysterical symptoms.[90]

The physical manifestations of war neurosis, for example, are embodied in the trembling figure in *Forty-five Percent Fit for Work* as well as the facial grimaces of his companions, which, in addition to depicting horrendous facial scars, possibly suggest the nervous tics and twitches that affected mentally traumatized soldiers. In addition, the repetitive syndromes associated with shell shock and hysteria, the fact that traumatized soldiers would sometimes repeat the same actions or gestures over and over again as a way to ward off or come to terms with their past traumas, are evoked by the signs of marching and drill in both *Forty-five Percent Fit for Work* and the *Prussian Archangel*—the mindless formation into which Dix's figures group themselves as well as the obsessive lengths to which the archangel's sign enjoins its viewers to exercise. Uncontrollable emotional outbursts are implied by the various figures' diverse intimations of angry intensity, the convulsed position in which the archangel holds its legs, as well as the extremely rigid postures of nearly all the figures. Furthermore, the regressive tendencies that the Freudian psychoanalyst Sándor Ferenczi associated with war neuroses—the soldier's "lapse into atavistic and infantile methods of reaction"—are hinted at by the childlike nature of the soldiers' bodies; for example, the cartoonlike figures of *Forty-five Percent Fit for Work* with their overly large heads, the child-mannequin's body of *Heartfield Gone Wild,* and, in a somewhat different way, the de-evolved head of the *Prussian Archangel.*[91]

Finally, in addition to evoking the various symptoms of war neuroses, contemporary German treatments for war neuroses were also suggested by the various Dada representations.[92] The electrical wire attached to *Heartfield Gone Wild,* for example, could have called to mind the practices of electroshock therapy used at the time.[93] Developed by Dr. Fritz Kaufmann, who called his therapy a "surprise attack method," electrotherapy was designed to forcibly cure shaking, paralyzed, and otherwise nonfunctioning soldiers. According to Kaufmann, the therapy consisted of four basic elements: "suggestive preparation," in which the doctor convinced the patient that the treatment would be successful; the application of strong measures of alternating current on the nonfunctioning body part along with physical exercise by the patient and a great deal of verbal suggestion by the doctor; the maintenance of strict military discipline during the entire procedure; and the continuation of the therapy until the patient was cured. As suggested by Lerner, although this painful and sometimes deadly therapy was successful, "the key to the Kaufmann method lay not in the nature of the electric treatment but rather in its suggestive force."[94] The jolts of electricity did not cure the patient, but by forcing him to move and by making the cure more painful than the malady, they convinced him that his afflictions could be overcome. In addition, the bell on Heartfield's shoulder could have suggested the less violent but nonetheless coercive "startle" method developed by Dr. Robert Sommer to cure psychogenic deafness and deaf-muteness.[95] Sommer would distract the patient by hooking him up to a vise-like apparatus that held his arm and measured his hand movements. Then Sommer would startle the patient by ringing a loud bell behind his head, something that generally produced an unintended movement by the disabled soldier. In this way, Sommer demonstrated to the soldier that his deafness was psychogenic rather than somatic, and, as a result, he was generally cured. In addition, the dark interior space depicted in Grosz's *Victim of Society* possibly suggested the isolation therapies used to calm nervous exhaustion.[96] Through compulsory inactivity and lack of stimulation, it was believed, the traumatized soldier would be shielded from the shocks that created his hysterical condition, and thereby, he would slowly recover. By sometimes housing veterans in asylums with actual mental patients, however, and by regulating their food and contact with the outside world, the doctors in effect coerced their patients to get better. They suggested, in other words, that unless their patients renounced their neurotic symptoms, they would essentially remain prisoners of the medical establishment.

By evoking the specific mental states produced by traumatic war experiences as well as the precise—and often brutal—"cures" used to "heal" them, the Dada artists attempted to make concrete the experience of shell shock, thereby undermining the ideological effects of the powerful images of male fighters presented in the soldier portraits. As suggested by Jünger's account of battle, trench warfare was savage, unpredictable, and hierarchical. It made the world seem meaningless and threatening, and it caused the soldiers to feel helpless by robbing them of control over their lives. Wartime cures for the psychic damage suffered by soldiers were similarly disempowering and authoritarian. As Lerner argues,

> Despite the wide variation in the methods of active treatment, most techniques functioned in essentially the same way. Whether it was based on deception, startling, isolation, or persuasion, whether it utilized hypnosis, electric current, or a faux injection, active treatment operated through suggestion. It targeted the patient's will and aimed to convert the will to remain disabled into the will to recover. It sought to restore the patient's control over his own body, but paradoxically, in doing so it demanded that the doctor wield full control and authority over the patient's mind and body. The goal, then, was to create healthier wills through subordination to medical power, which stood in as a representative of the state and the national cause. Indeed, by using these methods, doctors attained a great deal of influence and even control over a whole category of patients and integrated the exercise of medical power into the core of the therapeutic procedure. With the trappings of science and the seductions of magic, medical power operated in the treatment room to forge functioning bodies and patriotic subjects.[97]

And by evoking the irrational, authoritarian, violent, and mechanistic factors that led to war neuroses as well as the similarly deceitful, hierarchical, dangerous, and technological methods devised to overcome them, the Dada images of disabled soldiers went beyond the simple critique of ideology by provoking analysis of the psychological forces that undermined the military subject and the "scientific" techniques by which the German medical community attempted to rebuild him. In this way, the Dadaist representations of militarized cyborgs placed the military ideal as depicted in patriotic visual culture into a broader horizon of meaning that the nationalistic representations had attempted to conceal. They thus opened up the ideal military subject to a range of associations that would undermine and transform it, and, by so doing, they potentially provoked ordinary Germans to reexamine their identifications with authoritarian types of role models.

The Mass Subject

The Berlin Dada artists also deconstructed the military ideal by emphasizing their subjects' bodily aspects over their rational aspects, thereby indicating another horizon of meaning that the military ideal attempted to suppress. As I have already demonstrated, Dadaist images of cyborgian soldiers emphasized signs of sexuality, aggression, consumption, digestion, and elimination. And by pointing their spectators toward the libidinal, instinctive, or corporeal side of human beings, the Dada artists used the representations of war cripples to direct attention to central aspects of the military psyche. Long before Klaus Theweleit's theorization of the fascist male subject, the type of ego that made an ideal member of a military group was the subject of investigations by such psychologists as Gustave Le Bon and Sigmund Freud in the late nineteenth and early twentieth centuries.[98] For Freud in particular, the ideal military male subject was best understood through mass psychology, an approach that began with observing and theorizing about crowds and mass behavior. Viewed from this perspective, the mass subject, the type of modern individual most susceptible to the lure of the crowd, was discovered to be less rational and less repressed than individuals who retained more autonomy from defined social groups. When made a part of a multitude, in other words, such a person, according to Freud, grew impulsive, changeable, and suggestible—in the grip of simple and extreme feelings and responsive to exaggerations and repetitions. The mass subject became unable to reason critically or separate truth from falsehood when ensconced within the crowd: it began to think in images, and it became unconcerned with contradictions, all attributes that allowed it to submerge its individual interests within collective ones. Furthermore, to survive, the mass subject was necessarily conservative and intolerant: it was afraid of thinking for itself and thus wanted desperately to be led.[99]

For Freud, the mass subject was immature and weak, and fundamentally dissatisfied with itself. By belonging to a group, however, the mass subject could overcome its feelings of dissatisfaction, because group belonging promoted strong relationships of identification between group members. These ties were initially created by the mass subject's primary identification with the group leader, which the mass subject took as its ego ideal or general model to which it attempted to conform its psyche. Bolstered, as it were, from the outside, mass subjects in groups exhibited regressive behavior. By becoming part of the mass, in other words, they were allowed to succumb to weakness of intellect, a lack of emotional restraint, a dearth of independence, and an inability to moderate or defer appetites.[100] The pleasure that the mass subject felt when part of a group arose from the fact that it was no longer bothered by feelings of guilt, failure, and powerlessness, something that would have been the case if it had to confront the fact that its ego and its ego ideal were radically separate.[101] As opposed to an individualistic and inactive state of melancholy brought on by a perceived separation between ego and ego ideal, group experience promoted a highly active state of collective mania and feelings of intense power.[102]

Despite its strong emotions and lack of reliance on rational calculation, the military subject was not disorganized or prone to heedless behavior. This was the case because, in Freud's formulation, the military subject was understood to be a particular form of mass subject. Like the religious subject to which it was compared, the military subject was the product of an "artificial group," a group held together by external forces.[103] Artificial groups were hierarchically organized and thus behaved more like rational individuals with long-range plans. Through specialization, rationalization, and a clear chain of command, artificial groups avoided a primary difficulty faced by spontaneous crowd activities, namely, the irrational consequences of a mass's generally regressive behavior.[104] Thus, despite its infantile and antirational tendencies, the military subject was highly functional—albeit within a limited range of behaviors.

Although there is not a one-to-one correspondence between Freud's account of the military subject and the Dada artists' creations, clear parallels seem to exist that suggest that the Dada artists were working with similar ideas about military identity. They emphasized the instinctual side of their military cyborgs by depriving them of their human heads or by showing them engaged in mindless group activities, for example, marching.[105] In addition, as intimated by the transparent head, the army boot, and the outstretched arm with the pointing finger above the heads of the war cripples in *Forty-five Percent Fit for Work*, these damaged soldiers possibly think in images, or, at the very least, because of their coordinated military formation and the fact that they all move in the direction suggested by the finger, they are extremely susceptible to being led.[106] Moreover, because of their seeming acceptance of their montaged or sutured-together forms, the various military cyborgs produced by Dix, Schlichter, Heartfield, and Grosz appear untroubled by their contradictory attributes.[107] Finally, the Dada representations of cyborgian soldiers attacked precisely those things that tied the mass subject to the group. As suggested by the *Prussian Archangel,* they denigrated the group leader and thus made it hard to identify with him. In addition, as implied by the negative ways in which they represented military formation and drill, they also attacked the physical processes through which military groups were brought together and made to cohere as organized, rationally controlled units. And by undermining the ties of group authority, the Dada artists attempted to further deconstruct the military ideal.

Postcards and Care Packages

Highly aware of the various forms of visual culture and communicative practices that helped produce patriotic military subjects, the Berlin Dada artists used their art to evoke these forms and practices, thereby reminding their audiences of how identity was constructed through warfare. In this way, they kept their spectators aware of the broad network of cultural knowledge that supported mobilizing people and resources for militarized action, one that—because it depended on a multiplicity of different interconnections between human beings and various forms of technology—was cyborgian. This network, they suggested, did not simply consist of the technical knowledge that supported the increased interrelation of human beings with one another and machines. As I have already shown, it also consisted of a "colder," more objective way to look at things created through technological modes of perception that allowed human beings to better tolerate both violence and danger. Furthermore, as implied by the Dadaists' wartime creations, patriotic military subjects were also partially produced through communicative practices whereby emotional bonds were manufactured and transmitted between the German home and the battlefront. [108]

Another one of the many "origins" of photomontage lay in the wartime creation and exchange of "care packages" and altered postcards between Grosz, Heartfield, and others.[109] As Herzfelde noted in 1962,

[Grosz] had specialized in sending care-packages to annoy soldiers at the front. As far as he was concerned, they weren't annoyed enough. In late 1916, while I was stationed on the Western Front for the second time, I received one of his packages. I took great pleasure in the graceful way the field address was written, in the care with which everything was packed, and above all in the irony with which he had selected the gifts. It contained two starched shirt fronts, one white and one with a floral pattern; a pair of black sleeve protectors; a dainty shoe horn; a set of assorted bags containing samples of tea, which, according to their individual handwritten labels, were to evoke patience, beautiful dreams, respect for authority, and loyalty to the ruling house. Haphazardly glued to a cardboard were advertisements for hernia belts, fraternal song books, and fortified dog food, labels from schnapps and wine bottles, photos from illustrated papers—all clipped at will and irrationally assembled. Soon Grosz and John [Heartfield] began to use similarly hand-finished postcards for their correspondence. Decades later my brother spoke of postcards which were sent back home from the front, and on which photograph clippings had been assembled in a way that they said in pictures what would have been censored had it been said in words. Some of our friends, among them [Sergei] Tretyakov, created out of that story the legend that the anonymous masses had thus invented photomontage. The truth is that many who received the aforementioned cards took pleasure in them and attempted to make something similar. That encouraged Heartfield to develop a conscious technique out of what had originally been a politically inflammatory playfulness. . . . Indeed photomontage was discovered rather than invented.[110]

As suggested by Herzfelde's reminiscences about photomontage's origins, a diverse array of visual and material culture developed during World War I to serve—as well as to profit from—the war effort.[111] In addition to the personalized soldier portraits discussed above, numerous other types of photographic materials were made and purchased in the field or behind the lines. These included nonphotomontage portraits taken by professional photographers or by the soldiers themselves as well as mass-produced photographic postcards depicting various subjects—war heroes and military leaders, individual fighters and troops, satirical and otherwise critical images of the enemy, idealized love scenes between soldiers and their beloveds, children dressed in military uniforms, allegorical representations of the German nation, scenes of women and children praying for the fighters at the front, militarized holiday scenes, and pictures of occupied villages and cities (Figure 4.8).[112] As the conflict progressed, more-realistic postcards were also produced depicting incidents from everyday life in the trenches and actual scenes from the war, including ruined buildings and landscapes, prisoners, troops outfitted for battle, corpses of the enemy, weapons, graves, and other images of wartime verisimilitude (Figure 4.9).[113] Purchased by soldiers along with tobacco, writing supplies, newspapers, and other goods at stationery shops sanctioned by the German military, these mass-produced postcards often affirmed the ideals of military service—brotherhood, heroism, piety, joie de vivre, and self-sacrifice—although,

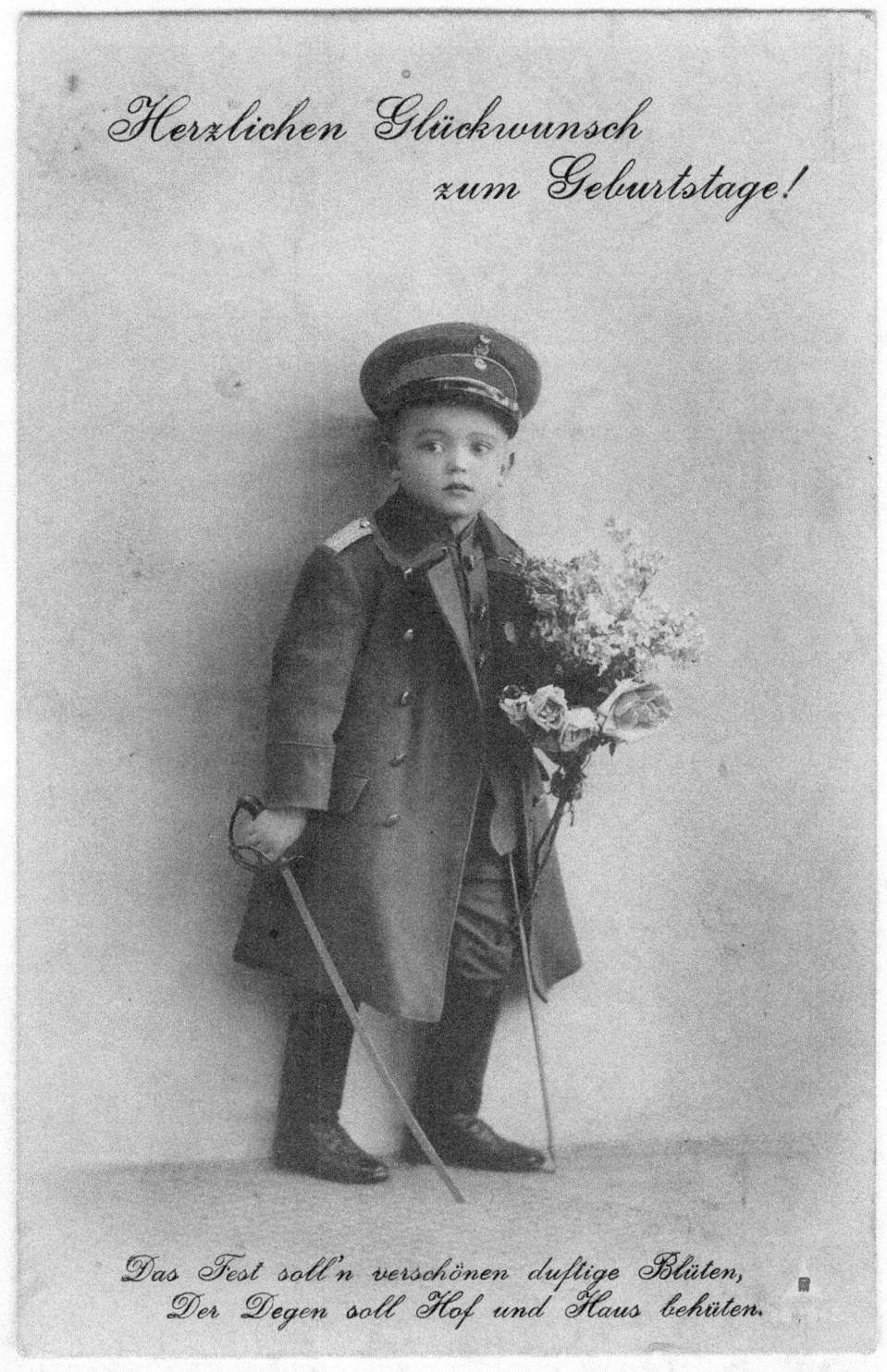

Herzlichen Glückwunsch zum Geburtstage!

*Das Fest soll'n verschönen duftige Blüten,
Der Degen soll Hof und Haus behüten.*

Figure 4.8. World War I field postcard: child soldier birthday card (1916). Photographic postcard; photographer unknown. 13.5 × 8.5 cm (5⁵⁄₁₆ × 3⅜ inches). Private collection. Text on the card: "Heartfelt good wishes for your birthday." and "May fragrant blossoms beautify the celebration, May the sword protect house and home."

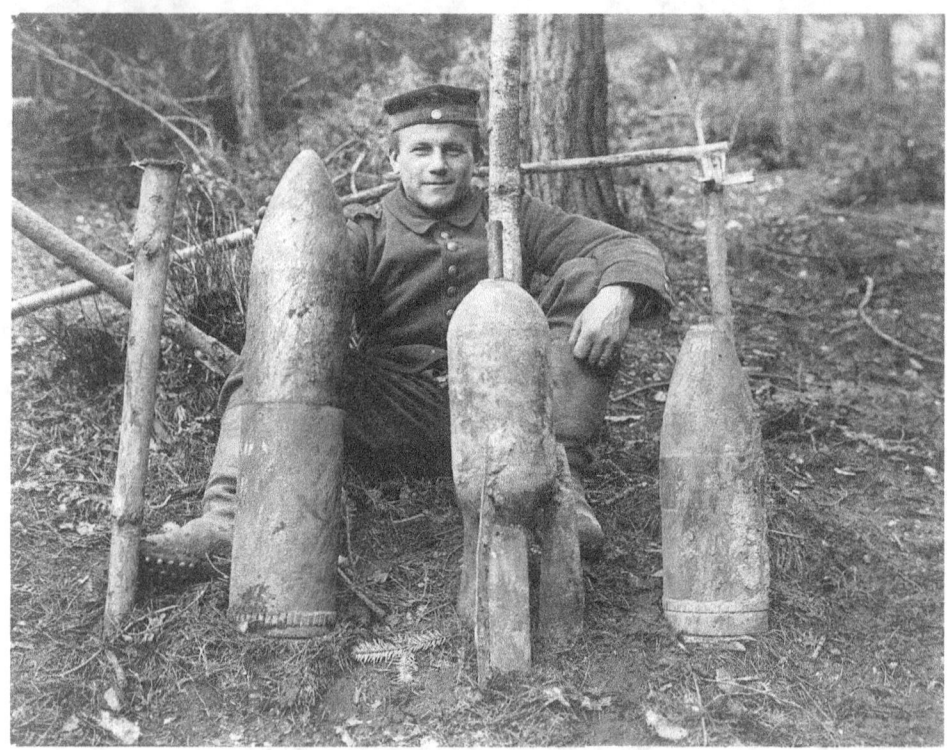

Figure 4.9. World War I field postcard: soldier posing with shells (1916). Photographic postcard; photographer unknown. 8.7 × 13.9 cm (3½ × 5½ inches). Private collection.

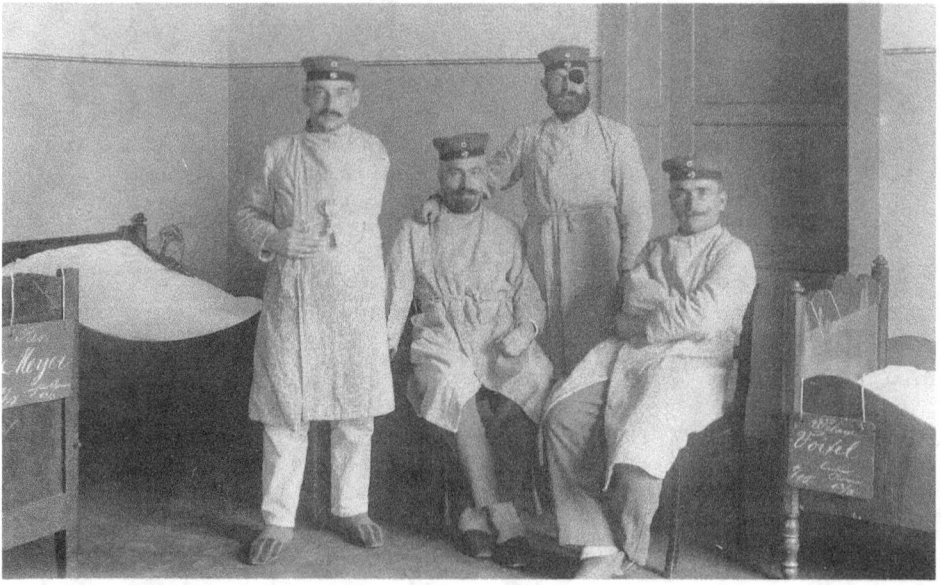

Figure 4.10. August Bies, World War I field postcard: soldier amputees in hospital (ca. 1914–18). Photographic postcard. 8.4 × 13.8 cm (3⁵⁄₁₆ × 5⁷⁄₁₆ inches). Private collection.

particularly with the increase in their realism as the war progressed, they also revealed the growing horror of mechanized slaughter. Thus, for example, in a less frequently seen but still ordinary postcard depicting four wounded soldiers in a hospital, most probably commissioned by one or more of them to inform family or friends of their recovery and life in rehabilitation, one can discover the same shocking signs of the destruction of the fighting man's body employed by the Dadaists in their representations of war cripples (Figure 4.10).[114]

Typically, however, the postcards were less undermining of the German cause than this last example, and they were sent back home to inform friends and loved ones and to reassure them that all was well. Psychologically, they helped provide the soldiers with a small sense of normalcy in their otherwise extremely stressful existences; for the families waiting at home, they offered proof that a loved one was still alive, or, if it turned out that he had recently perished, a memorial image touched by their fallen hero. The postcards thus connected the soldiers with the people for whom they fought, and through their specific imagery, the postcards helped justify the war, demonize the enemy, and reassure their writers and recipients that family, God, and nation were watching over them. Finally, because they required less literary skill than regular mail from the field, the field postcards, with their limited space for writing, also possibly contributed to the loss of the soldiers' abilities to communicate their wartime experiences.[115]

Given this exchange in patriotic postcards that supported the war, it is thus not surprising that Heartfield and Grosz used altered photographic postcards sent from the field to avoid military censors. Although the postcards were read and censored along with the regular mail to and from the front, ironic visual commentary seemed to evade detection more easily than written criticism—perhaps because the regular field postcards already had to pass a military censorship board before they were published.[116] And given the significant amount of mail that was sent back and forth every day, the German military's ability to censor the soldiers' correspondence was limited. Interestingly, Herzfelde employed a related technique when he first began to publish antiwar periodicals during the war. Discussing *Neue Jugend [New Youth]*, his first antiwar publication, which came out in the summer of 1916, he reminisced,

> The title *Neue Jugend* didn't mean a thing: a school magazine with this name had existed before the war in Charlottenburg; founding new papers during the war without special permission was forbidden; so we bought the name and to fool the censors we began with Number Seven at page 127. On this first page a poem *To Peace* by J. R. Becher, which was revolutionary rather than pacifistic, was printed.[117]

As was the case with the early photomontage postcards of Heartfield and Grosz (all, unfortunately, now lost), Herzfelde appropriated an existing means of communication and surreptitiously adapted it to antiwar ends. And this strategy of "refunctioning" existing forms and means of mass communication became a central strategy of the Berlin Dada artists—one to which they would return again and again.

Furthermore, as Herzfelde's reminiscence suggests, the wartime exchange of souvenirs went far beyond the circulation of photographs and postcards. In addition to the newspapers and popular books that reported on the war and that were also carefully censored, there was an energetic trade in commodities directed at soldiers, an economy that took the form of "care packages" filled with food, spirits, clothing, books, tobacco, chocolate, and other items sent from home.[118] Heavily promoted in the newspapers, these care packages, or *Liebesgaben*—literally "gifts of love"—were used by German women to show their "devotion" to the men fighting at the front and to help the war effort.[119] (Other forms of feminine devotion included serving in the Red Cross and giving direct financial support for the war through gifts of money and other valuable items; "gold for iron," as the old expression went.)[120] Unique to World War I, the *Liebesgaben* were sent by friends, families, and loved ones, but also quite often by women who did not know the soldiers personally.[121] Means of boosting morale at the front as well as involving nonmilitarized German women in the war effort through an intense but nonspecific emotional bond, the *Liebesgaben* were officially sanctioned yet supposedly personal forms of support. They also created a new need for particular forms of commodities, a desire that the German industry was quick to notice and exploit. Already in the second month of war, German illustrated papers began to promote subscription deliveries to soldiers as a way to boost morale, and their advertising sections offered a wide variety of products that could be sent directly to loved ones on the frontlines. Tobacco, alcohol, patent medicine, and books were the most heavily promoted items, but the papers also encouraged the sending of socks, underwear, earmuffs, gloves, medical trusses, stationery, candy, and food.[122] So popular did *Liebesgaben* become that the supply roads to the front became clogged with nonmilitary transport services, and the German government was forced to prohibit the private transport of care packages in early November 1914.[123] By 1915 significant criticism was being directed against the unrestrained promotion of questionable "restorative tonics," such as Sanatogen, Leciferin, and Amol, which advertised themselves as essential components of any gift sent to the front—another indication of the care packages' popularity as well as the dubious involvement of German industry in their promotion.[124]

Related to the wartime *Liebesgaben* phenomenon were the "glue rooms" *[Klebestuben]*, which emerged in Hamburg in the beginning of 1914. Here, female volunteers made photomontage books—literally *Klebehefte,* or "glue books"—to include in the care packages. The glue rooms were the brainchild of Ida Dehmel, the second wife of the poet Richard Dehmel and a liberal bourgeois reformer in Hamburg.[125] Since the first decade of the twentieth century, Ida Dehmel's feminist reform efforts focused on creating women's clubs to encourage German women to become involved in social and political issues and to allow women from different social classes to meet and interact. The glue rooms, in turn, were offshoots of the women's clubs and responses to the new circumstances brought about by World War I. They were designed to orient German women toward modern life and the war effort, which, Dehmel believed, it was their social and moral duty to support. Established at different sites in Hamburg during 1914 and 1915, the glue rooms housed female volunteers, who assembled booklets of clippings and photographs culled from contemporary newspapers and magazines. Sitting at wide wooden tables in brightly lit rooms with newspapers and magazines piled in front of them and scissors and glue pots ready at hand, the women cut and reassembled texts into large albums.

According to a contemporary newspaper account, the volunteers' function was to edit, compile, and illustrate inspiring reports, organizing them according to subject.

> Everything that refers to a particular topic is clearly arranged and glued together. Thus, for example, everything that had to do with the exploits at Emden and their illustrious end; or the last, brilliant parliamentary assembly of the war, along with the commentaries of the various papers. Pretty pictures of the day were always pasted in between for relief, and to finish it well, a beautiful title page on the cover.[126]

These photomontage books were then assembled with other products into larger care packages and sent to soldiers fighting at the front and recovering in German field hospitals. Made for soldiers whom the creators would never meet, the *Klebehefte* were designed for an anonymous readership that most probably consisted of more than one person, since the soldiers frequently shared the photomontage books. At the same time, the *Klebehefte* were designed to mimic personal gifts so as to better inspire their addressees; in language and tone, they often adopted a personal—almost romantic—mode of address.[127] Although it is impossible to determine how far the *Klebehefte* phenomenon extended beyond the glue rooms of Hamburg, more than five hundred women were engaged in their production during the height of Dehmel's project, and the demand became so great that German children were even recruited to help with creating additional photomontage books for the soldiers.[128]

Analyzing the care packages and letters the soldiers wrote back to their benefactresses, Doherty argues that the soldiers and their supporters at home learned to objectify their bodies through the exchange of gifts. They were taught, in other words, to perceive their physical as well as emotional needs in terms of commodities and thus to become "both consumers and objects of consumption" through a socially sanctioned set of processes that were partially commercial and partially private.[129] The "official" care packages contained reified expressions of desire—expressions that the soldiers avidly consumed, but with which they also expressed dissatisfaction because the exchange also revealed that the desired person was absent and perhaps the gift was ultimately of less emotional significance than it would have been if it had come from a wife, girlfriend, or family member.[130] And the proto-Dada care packages that Grosz sent to his friends—as well as the later Dada photomontages and assemblages that emerged from this practice—were designed to draw attention to and satirize this process by revealing *Liebesgaben* to be empty mass-produced commodities that disclosed but did not satisfy important emotional needs and desires. They were intended, in other words, to temporarily defetishize wartime commodities through irony and by exposing their ideological functions.[131] It is unclear whether the Dada artists were aware of the Hamburg *Klebehefte,* which seemed in certain ways to anticipate their own later practices of photomontage. However, as suggested by Herzfelde's description of Grosz's now lost care package, they were clearly familiar with the *Liebesgaben* phenomenon of which the *Klebehefte* were the most extreme expressions. Emphasizing the fragility of the human body by showing how easily it could become sick or in need of repair, the proto-Dada care packages reminded their recipients of the realities that the wartime exchange of sentiments attempted to conceal.[132] Thereby, the proto-Dada care packages mocked the exchange of feelings in times of war and emphasized the physical states and the emotional desires that the *Liebesgaben* sought to satisfy. By exposing their false promises, Grosz's care packages and the photomontages and assemblages that developed out of them suggested the loss of experience, the lack of connections between people, and the reification of desire produced by World War I.[133]

Conclusion

The various Dada photomontages and assemblages that deconstructed the military subject were thus extremely significant. Embodying as they did the officially sanctioned wartime practices of soldier portraits, *Liebesgaben,* and the exchange of propagandistic postcards, they recalled Germany's various techniques of inspiring wartime patriotism while radically inverting the message. For this reason, these mordantly satirical works also revealed the specific media, practices, and institutions for both constructing and contesting militaristic, nationalistic, and consumerist ideologies. The paintings, assemblages, and photomontages that Dix, Schlichter, Grosz, and Heartfield exhibited at the "Dada Fair" thereby fostered awareness of how new forms of perception, communication, and warfare helped produce militarized forms of identity; furthermore, they suggested that through humor, an awareness of history, and a willingness to face the hard facts and trauma of Germany's military defeat, people could begin to avoid such dangerous forms of identification in the future.

Like the examples of Dadaist portraiture and self-portraiture treated in earlier chapters, the works examined here that deconstructed the military subject used the cyborg as an allegorical figure indicating the technological system, a complex network of concepts, people, material culture, institutions, and technologies in which human identity in the twentieth century was always enmeshed. Instead of emphasizing the positive aspects of this more distributed, powerful, perceptive, and interconnected vision of human existence, however, the military cyborg brought out its dangerous and dehumanizing aspects. The intellectual, human, material, and infrastructural conditions for the possibility of total mobilization, in other words, were shown by this figure to be some of the greatest threats to human development in the contemporary moment. In this way, Dadaists such as Dix, Schlichter, Grosz, and Heartfield emphasized that technology also had a menacing side, that Germany's headlong rush toward modernization should be slowed, and that no simple embrace of mechanization and mass communication could be affirmed. Although the horror of the war that had partially destroyed Germany perhaps contained the seeds of a better future, there was no possibility, their works suggested, of redeeming all that had been lost. Despite the fact that the cyborgian future was quite possibly inevitable, the developing symbiosis between human beings and their technologies could be allowed to move forward only with great caution and forbearance.

5. The New Woman as Cyborg

Gender, Race, and Sexuality in the Photomontages of Hannah Höch

The peculiar characteristics of photography and its approaches have opened up a new and immensely fantastic field for a creative human being: a new, magical territory, for the discovery of which freedom is the first prerequisite. . . . Whenever we want to force this "photomatter" to yield new forms, we must be prepared for a journey of discovery, we must start without any preconceptions; most of all, we must be open to the beauties of fortuity.

—HANNAH HÖCH, "A Few Words on Photomontage" (1934)

Hannah Höch was the only woman to play an active role in the Berlin Dada movement. While she was initially relegated to the peripheries—by the original participants and critics and, later on, by curators and art historians—her status as a Dada artist has changed radically in Germany and in the United States since the 1980s.[1] This is in part because of the growth of feminist perspectives in art history and the concomitant interest in reexamining female artists who were only sketchily treated in the historical record. More important, however, this has been the result of both the quality and the quantity of Höch's work. Although she neither wrote nor performed extensively, Höch developed the photomontage medium between the late 1910s and the early 1930s far more than any other Berlin Dada artist, with the possible exception of John Heartfield. In addition, Höch also produced a substantial body of painting, which incorporated compositional insights gained from her photomontage works, anticipated surrealist painting, and remains largely unexplored even today.

Despite her bourgeois origins, Höch led a fairly unconventional life for the time.[2] Born Anna Therese Johanne Höch on November 1, 1889, the eldest of five, whose father was a senior insurance company employee, she entered the School of Applied Arts in Berlin in 1912, where she studied design and calligraphy, and then briefly worked for the Red Cross and other charitable organizations at the beginning of World War I. In 1915 Höch began to study graphic design with Emil Orlik—as well as figure drawing and calligraphy at night—at the State Museum of Applied Arts in Berlin, a mixed fine and applied arts academy, where she remained enrolled until 1920. Also in 1915, Höch met Raoul Hausmann, with whom she began a seven-year relationship, despite the fact that he was already married and had a young daughter. Höch's relationship with Hausmann, who lived, worked, and traveled with Höch extensively between 1915 and 1922, was the source of great turmoil for her, in part because, despite his professed love for Höch, Hausmann refused to leave his wife. In 1916 Höch began working three days a week at the Ullstein Verlag, where she remained employed until 1926, and for which she primarily made embroidery, lace, and dress designs for various women's magazines. She also sometimes provided Ullstein publications with illustrations, lettering, layouts, advertising vignettes, composite photographs, and articles on crafts.[3] When the Berlin Dada movement formed in early 1918, Höch became a Dadaist, contributing photomontages, objects, and other works to their various exhibitions in Berlin, and occasionally performing at their events.[4] After breaking up with Hausmann in 1922, she went on to form a variety of long-standing artistic relationships, including associations with Kurt Schwitters, Sophie Taeuber, Hans (Jean) Arp, Theo van Doesburg, and László Moholy-Nagy.[5] In 1926 Höch met Til Brugman, a Dutch poet and language teacher who wrote for *Merz* and *De Stijl,* and with whom she had a lesbian relationship that lasted until 1935. In 1935, while hiking in the Alps, Höch met Heinz Kurt Matthies, a German businessman and pianist, who was twenty-one years younger than Höch. They were married in 1938 and divorced in 1944.

Höch's early artistic influences were *Jugendstil,* expressionism, and so-called primitive art (the arts of Africa and Asia), enthusiasms that she shared with Hausmann. Perhaps because of her design background and her work with wallpaper patterns, Höch was interested in abstract art throughout her life, and this enthusiasm surfaced from time to time in her art in different media. Furthermore, as Peter Boswell has noted, as her art developed in the 1920s, it suggested additional influences including orphism, constructivism, futurism, metaphysical painting, and cubist collage.[6] Like the other Berlin Dadaists, Höch was drawn to photomontage because of its topicality, its realism, and the possibilities it offered for social and political commentary. Unlike many of the other Berlin Dadaists, however, she was also drawn to photomontage for its ability to go beyond critique and to transform the real into something new and fantastic—a tendency that appears most strongly in her photomontages made after the Weimar Republic.[7] Höch also distinguished herself from the other Berlin Dadaists by her interest in traditional women's crafts, which continued unabated during her time in the Berlin Dada movement, as well as by her enthusiasm for traditional forms of painting. It is significant that, after the "First International Dada Fair," Höch did not exhibit her photomontages again until 1929. Instead, she preferred to show her paintings, works in which she explored both autobiographical and metaphysical themes, and which have over time received much less critical acclaim and attention.[8] Although she continued to make photomontages throughout the Weimar Republic (and, indeed, until her death in 1978), she appears to have regarded photomontage as a more private pursuit during most of the Weimar years. It was only at the landmark "Film und Foto" [Film and Photo] exhibition in Stuttgart in 1929 that she once again began to show the photomontages for which she has rightly become famous.

Höch both experienced and represented many of the most important issues affecting the "new women" of the Weimar Republic—those women forging modern roles and new places for themselves in what was in many ways still a very tradition-bound German society. Influenced by Hausmann's concept of human identity as socially constructed and transformable, she developed the figure of the cyborg in dialogue with Hausmann and the other Dada artists to explore the mutable characteristics of human— and often female—identity in modern technological societies.[9] To a greater degree than Hausmann and the others, however, Höch investigated the implications of the cyborg, examining in her various photomontages how it broke down divisions between races, genders, species, and generations. For this reason, Höch seems to have created the most radical visual representations of cyborgs of any of the Dada artists, images that anticipate, in many ways, the concept of the cyborg formulated by Donna Haraway and other cultural theorists since the mid-1980s.

As has already been demonstrated, Haraway's work suggests that the cyborg is more diverse than it was originally conceived to be in the work of Manfred E. Clynes and Nathan S. Kline or than was implied in the pioneering theories of Norbert Wiener and other scientists during World War II. The cyborg does not simply indicate a synthesis of the organic with the mechanical, Haraway argues, but also a crossing of the boundaries that separate the human from the animal as well as the living from the nonliving. N. Katherine Hayles puts it quite well when she summarizes the implications of Haraway's model:

> Fusing cybernetic device and biological organism, the cyborg violates the human/ machine distinction; replacing cognition with neural feedback, it challenges the human–animal difference; explaining the behavior of thermostats and people through theories of feedback, hierarchical structure, and control, it erases the animate/inanimate distinction. In addition to arousing anxiety, the cyborg can also spark erotic fascination: witness the female cyborg in *Blade Runner*. The flip side of the cyborg's violation of boundaries is what Haraway calls its "pleasurably tight coupling" between parts that are not supposed to touch. Mingling erotically charged violations with potent new fusions, the cyborg becomes the stage on which are performed contestations about the body boundaries that have often marked class, ethnic, and cultural differences. Especially when it operates in the realm of the Imaginary rather than through actual physical operations (which act as a reality check on fantasies about cyborgism), cybernetics intimates that body boundaries are up for grabs.[10]

When viewed from the perspective of this expanded definition, Höch's photomontages reveal different types of cyborgs. In addition to representations of human–machine hybrids, Höch's photomontages include syntheses between humans and animals, between people of different genders, between persons of different ethnicities and cultures, and between individuals of different ages or generations. The cyborg's eroticism is also apparent in a number of Höch's works. And, although Höch made representations of male cyborgs, this chapter for the most part examines her representations of women. Not only has the male cyborg been examined in-depth in the previous chapters, but female cyborgs ultimately become much more prevalent in Höch's art. In the end, the new woman as cyborg appears to have been Höch's primary concern.

This chapter also concerns itself with Höch's changing compositional strategies and how her photomontages signify their multiple meanings. Like other Berlin Dadaists, Höch moved from an intricate mode of composition to one simpler and more direct. Unlike Heartfield, however, Höch never developed a strongly didactic form of photomontage practice. Despite the increased compositional simplicity of her works, they remained semantically complex and open-ended. Berlin Dada photomontages were designed to produce multiple and often conflicting readings, thereby encouraging spectators to become aware of their contributions to the experience of the artwork and, in this way, to become more active, self-aware, and engaged. They also attempted to counteract photography's traditional realism by making their spectators suspicious of any direct or transparent connection between the photographic fragments that they incorporated and the real-world entities to which they were indexically and iconically related. Instead of suggesting that the photomontage fragments simply represented what they depicted, the Berlin Dadaists employed the cutting, editing, and transformative aspects of the photomontage technique to signal that they were commenting on their appropriated subjects. They produced representations, in other words, that, despite their photographic source materials, did not suggest clear mirrors of reality but conceptual reformulations of that reality—arguments about the world.

The Dadaists, as I argued in chapter 4, attempted to create modern allegories through their photomontages. They endeavored, in other words, to manufacture representations that addressed what they perceived to be the underlying causes of their contemporary moment, representations that used imagery drawn from everyday life to disclose invisible forces, overarching concepts, and underlying types. These representations were historical, violent, and weakly redemptive: they evoked the brutality, danger, and loss that were part and parcel of the historical process; they cited a multivalent tradition to create historical points of comparison for analyzing the present moment; and by reminding their viewers of the "creaturely" side of all human beings, they attempted to mourn historical loss and to suggest that, despite our destructive propensities, humanity was still worth saving. Höch used photomontage to create allegories about women's lives in the modern world. Referring to multiple cultures and different historical events, they explored the social, political, and institutional forces that oppressed women in Höch's contemporary moment as well as the new developments that could help them overcome their subjugation. And by examining how women had been forced to deny aspects of their identities in the modern world, they helped their audiences imagine new, more open-ended forms of female existence that resisted narrow definitions and one-sided role models.

Höch, as I show, used the figure of the cyborg as an allegory because she understood the developing technological network that subtended modern life to present both the greatest dangers and the most important possibilities to women living in the Weimar Republic. This developing system of technical knowledge interrelated human beings with one another, their environments, and machines, and, in addition, promoted a colder way of looking at things that enabled them to better tolerate both violence and manipulation. By inspiring meditation on the relationship of women to the modern technological system that made possible the altering, mobilizing, and interrelating of all people and resources, Höch's Weimar photomontages could have helped their original audiences better understand their contemporary situation. In addition, by allowing them to recognize their fundamentally cyborgian natures, Höch's photomontages also implicitly suggested an answer to a question raised in the introduction in relation to Haraway's extremely general or inclusive concept of the cyborg. According to Haraway's definition, almost every creature in the contemporary world can be seen to be a cyborg, and for this reason there is almost no way on the basis of Haraway's formulation to distinguish humans and animals who are cyborgs from those who are not. Although Höch's art implies that Haraway's definition is indeed true, it also stresses that such an understanding does not entail that every person or creature stands in the same relationship to technology. As intimated by Höch's photomontages, the most decisive or crucial cyborgs in her contemporary moment were those that recognized their fundamental interconnections with technology and that attempted to act on the basis of this recognition. It was only by understanding the networked and distributed nature of human identity, Höch's works seem to suggest, that women could begin to change their social and historical possibilities and thereby distinguish themselves as cyborgs in the crucial potentially liberatory sense of the term.

Finally, by using the cyborg to identify continuities that unite the photomontages that Höch made at the beginning of the Weimar Republic with those that she made at its end, I also wish to suggest that, despite many of the artists going their separate ways, Dadaism in Berlin did not somehow stop being a source of creative inspiration after the early 1920s. The fact that Höch continued a central aspect of Berlin Dada in her work—namely, the use of the cyborg to imagine new forms of hybrid identity—until at least the end of the decade implies that Dadaism was not superseded by *Neue Sachlichkeit* or international constructivism, as is sometimes thought. Rather, as demonstrated by Höch's example, it continued to function as an ideology, a lifestyle, and a set of artistic practices throughout the Weimar era—albeit with less critical and public recognition than before.

The New Woman

Like the cyborg, the "new woman" of Weimar society was a figure of both imagination and material reality.[11] The term referred to the new social roles that women increasingly adopted during the Weimar Republic as a result of changes in German work, politics, consumer culture, and entertainment. It also referred to a set of stereotypical images or "types"—created by the burgeoning mass media—that affected male and female behavior alike. On the most basic level, the new woman suggested a transformed mode of "modern" female identity, distinguished from the "traditional" types characteristic of Wilhelmine society and connected to the modernization, rationalization, and sometimes the "Americanization" of everyday life during the Weimar Republic. In addition, however, the new woman quickly became a primary sign representing the radical transformation of Germany after the war. As a result, she was lauded as a representative of new possibilities open to women at the time yet demonized as a primary force threatening the nation's social, moral, physical, and economic stability.

The actual changes that led to the development of the new woman during the interwar years are perhaps easiest to discern in politics and the workplace.[12] In the first place, women gained the right to vote and to stand for office as a result of the November Revolution. They voted for the first time on January 19, 1919, in the National Assembly elections, and, as a consequence, nearly 10 percent of the elected delegates in the first parliament were women. Although the rapid entry of women into the German political sphere augured well for women's rights and the eventual equality of women in German society, these advances turned out to be less transformative than they were initially perceived to be. The number of women's votes dropped in each successive election during the Weimar Republic—as did the number of female delegates in parliament. The organized women's movement also declined in importance during this time, perhaps as a result of the erroneous view that the necessary social and political rights for women had already been secured (a view that ignored, for example, the facts that abortion still remained illegal and that section 109 of the Weimar constitution granted men and women the same civil rights and duties only in "principle"). Still, women's suffrage and the election of female politicians was a momentous event in the new republic. It caused real and important changes in women's lives, and it radically altered public perceptions about women's roles in German society in both positive and negative ways.

With the exception of the war years, the proportion of women in the workforce did not change dramatically between the last decade of the Wilhelmine Empire and the pre-Depression years of the Weimar Republic.[13] Although it increased slightly between 1907 and 1925, the overall proportion of women working outside the home, about one-third, remained relatively constant. Still, there were important changes in the workforce's internal makeup. While the ratio of women working in family businesses remained the same, the ratio of female domestic workers and female farm workers fell during the Weimar Republic, and the ratio of female white-collar workers and civil servants increased significantly. In addition, women also entered various modern industries in significant numbers during World War I, and, although many lost their jobs to returning men, they retained a considerable presence on the factory floor after the war as these industries expanded. Women were employed in the various industries because of the lower wages they could be paid, and their wartime and postwar presence in these supposedly masculine spaces contributed to the idea that women were as capable as men in these areas as well as to the false impression that women were stealing men's jobs.[14] Finally, the proportion of women in higher education rose, as did their ratio in medicine, education, and the arts. In terms of projecting a sense of new possibilities available to women, these were important gains, despite the fact that in terms of absolute numbers, these professional women were the smallest part of the female workforce.[15]

It was, however, in the white-collar fields of civil service, clerical, and sales jobs that the increase of women working outside the home was most noticed. New jobs for German women, such as secretary, stenographer, typist, sales clerk, and switchboard operator, were created, and it was from the ranks of the female white-collar workers that the most widespread stereotype of the new woman emerged. As represented in films, newspapers, and popular literature, the new woman was generally young, unmarried, consumerist, and nonpolitical.[16] The primary customer of the mass media, she was, according to the representations produced by the German culture industry, associated with sports, fashion, cosmetics, smoking, bobbed or masculine hairstyles (the so-called *Bubikopf* and *Herrenschnitt*), and urban entertainment, such as the cinema, variety reviews, dance halls, shopping boulevards, and cafés. Athleticism and androgyny were other attributes of the new woman, and, because of a widespread perception that abortions and contraceptive use were on the rise, her sexuality was suspect. In addition, women were beginning to get married at a later age during the Weimar Republic, a result of the loss of young men of marriageable age during the war as well as personal choices to defer marriage. Furthermore, with the population shift away from agriculture and the countryside, couples were having fewer children. And for these reasons, the new woman was accused of not fulfilling her female "duty" to bear children—and thus of contributing to *Volkstod,* the death of the German nation.[17]

As was already recognized at the time, however, the new woman of the Weimar Republic was as much a media construction as she was a reality. Few female white-collar workers—let alone the female assembly-line workers who imitated them—earned enough money to indulge in fashion, recreation, and other urban entertainments in the manner in which the stereotype suggested they did. Despite the sometimes-dramatic changes in labor and politics, the new woman was in many ways also an illusion, and it was the mass media that shaped and developed the image of the new woman to its fullest degree. As feminist historians have argued, the new woman was both the subject and the object of the mass media—a very important consumer and one of its primary subjects of representation.[18] The mass media thus sold an idealized image of the new woman to a growing audience that emulated her. Female athletes, dancers, revue girls, film stars, and other celebrities were the "highest" exemplars of this type—the standard bearers of the new lifestyles and activities to which the actual new woman supposedly aspired. And related to these various forms of new woman were other media stereotypes: the "efficient" housewife, the ideal wife and mother who possessed modern ideas about nutrition, hygiene, and household organization, and the sexually ambiguous *garçonne,* a boyish figure that in certain contexts came to represent lesbianism.[19] And as suggested by these sub- or related types, the new woman was an ambiguous figure that was multivalent and mutable.

Because of her multiple connections to the mass media, the new woman was often criticized by male intellectuals during the Weimar Republic for undermining high culture and critical consciousness. Despite the trenchant character of his cultural criticisms, Siegfried Kracauer was no exception. Linking the new women to his analysis of the "homeless" and consumerist white-collar workers, or *Angestellten,* Kracauer argued that the new woman undermined distinctions between the bourgeoisie and the proletariat. Despite her often lower-middle-class or proletarian origins, the new woman identified with the bourgeoisie, and thus she supported the system of commodity capitalism that by rights she should have opposed. Thus, for example, in "The Little Shopgirls Go to the Movies," Kracauer argued that Weimar cinema hinted "at subversive points of view without exploring them. Instead, they smuggle in a respectable way of thinking."[20] Through probing analyses of different popular films, Kracauer demonstrated that in each case real social problems were represented, only to be given a false solution, one that the sentimental, largely female audience uncritically accepted. In this way, he suggested that the new female consumer helped extend and entrench the capitalist hegemony of the rationalized industrial monopolies and cartels prevalent during the Weimar Republic.[21]

Kracauer's criticisms were correct to the extent that they pointed to how the ideal of the new woman was ideological and how it helped create a situation in which a double burden was placed on women. Like German men, the majority of German women believed that they had different virtues and different roles to play in German society, and the ideal of the new woman often encouraged them to believe that they had to simultaneously play both traditional and modern roles in the contemporary world.[22] As suggested by her Dadaist photomontages, however, Höch was not—like Kracauer's shop girls—an uncritical consumer of the image of the new woman. Instead, by neither fully accepting nor fully rejecting the new woman, Höch analyzed her myth and thereby revealed both her ideological and her revolutionary potential. Like the new woman, Höch both consumed and reworked existing stereotypes in her life and art—and it is this exploratory and critical process of reworking the image of the new woman through photomontage that has become Höch's most important legacy.

Central to Höch's project of reimagining Weimar-era female identity was the revelation of the new woman's cyborgian nature—namely, her hybridity, her partial construction through a technological system that both oppressed and empowered her, and her central role as both a consumer and an object of representation within the new mass media. By showing her fundamental connections to the new systems of communication and entertainment, Höch emphasized the new woman's growing importance as a "taste maker" determining the images and narratives that Germans used to entertain themselves, as well as a popular allegorical figure that could stand in for what was both best and worst about the new social, political, and economic situation. In addition, by embodying the role of the cyborgian artist, a creator who refunctioned the new media's products, Höch also proposed a third cyborgian role for the new woman to play—namely, a technologically aware producer who revealed the pernicious ideologies promulgated by the mass media and who developed new representations that better suggested women's diverse and multifaceted natures within the new republic.

Early Dada Photomontage

Höch's early photomontages were characterized by a strategy of "simultaneous montage"—an overall compositional structure consisting of multiple photomontage clusters separated by small open spaces of blank background.[23] The nonhierarchical organization of Höch's simultaneous montage strategy—along with the fact that it juxtaposed radically disparate fragments photographed from multiple angles and viewpoints—multiplied the divergent interpretations of her representations; as a result, works like *Cut with the Kitchen Knife* supported a multiplicity of different, sometimes conflicting readings, and their interpretations changed depending on the clusters of fragments with which the viewer engaged (Figure 2.3). This open-endedness of Höch's early montage strategy also empowered the original viewers of her works by encouraging them to identify the photomontage fragments they found most important and to use their startling combination of elements as jumping-off points to reimagine their contemporary world.

Dada-Rundschau [Dada Panorama] (1919), another early work by Höch, employs the same compositional strategies as *Cut with the Kitchen Knife;* as such, it allows us to further explore the semantic implications of the simultaneous montage structure characteristic of early Berlin Dada photomontage (Figure 5.1). Like *Cut with the Kitchen Knife, Dada Panorama* presents an all-over or nonhierarchical array of photomontage fragments that encourages multiple readings. And like *Cut with the Kitchen Knife, Dada Panorama* also interpolates blank spaces between the photomontage clusters, gaps that interrupt the viewer's attempts to seamlessly associate one element with the next and that potentially start the engaged spectator off on new associative trajectories. Consisting of photomontage elements, printed text, off-white collage elements, gouache, and watercolor, *Dada Panorama* is, however, even more heterogeneous than *Cut with the Kitchen Knife.* Flashes of color enliven the composition more strongly than they do in the more famous work. In addition, because *Dada Panorama* arranges its predominantly horizontally, vertically, and diagonally oriented elements against a largely pitch-black background, the photomontage also seems more dissonant than *Cut with the Kitchen Knife.* Its images and texts contrast powerfully with the dark background, and, even more strongly than is the case with *Cut with the Kitchen Knife,* they evoke the flickering character of early cinema.

As a whole, the photomontage, which was created on the verso of a photoengraved portrait of Wilhelm II, presents a turbulent portrait of the political situation during the first eight months of the Weimar Republic.[24] Once again, Friedrich Ebert, the newly

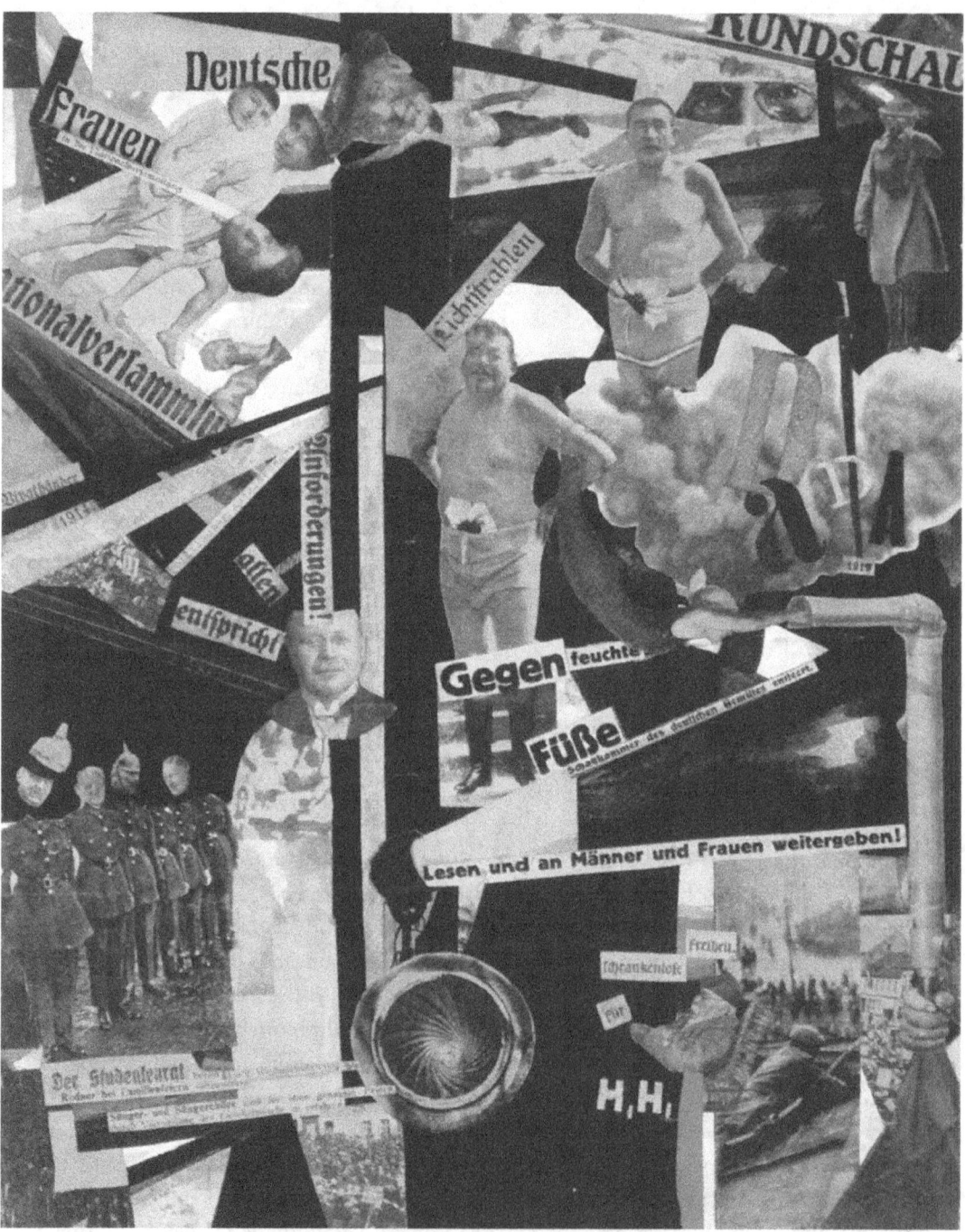

Figure 5.1. Hannah Höch, *Dada-Rundschau* [Dada Panorama] (1919). Photomontage and collage with gouache and watercolor on cardboard. 43.7 × 34.5 cm (17³⁄₁₆ × 13⁹⁄₁₆ inches). Berlinische Galerie, Landesmuseum für Moderne Kunst, Photographie und Architektur, Berlin. Photograph from Berlinische Gallerie, Berlin. Copyright 2009 Artists Rights Society (ARS), New York/VG Bild-Kunst, Bonn.

elected president, and Gustav Noske, the republic's first defense minister, appear. This time, they are dressed in bathing suits with their hands on their hips—images that Höch appropriated from the infamous cover of the *Berliner Illustrirte Zeitung* that appeared on August 24, 1919 (Figure 5.2). Around these two government figures, Höch has glued a network of images evoking a horizon of pressing social and political concerns. A constellation of photomontage fragments in the upper-left quadrant of *Dada Panorama,* which includes a portrait head of Anna von Gierke, one of the thirty-six women elected to the National Assembly, perhaps evinces optimism. Von Gierke is flanked by two other female politicians: Gertrud Bäumer, leader of the middle-class feminist movement before 1914, a prominent member of the bourgeois-liberal Deutsche Demokratische Partei (DDP) founded in November 1918, and another newly elected member of the National Assembly; and Agnes von Harnack, the important feminist organizer and DDP member.[25] The heads of both Bäumer and von Harnack are glued onto the necks of young female dancers, whose lithe moving bodies are clad in togas. This cluster of new women is associated with lines of text that read "German women in the National Assembly," words that underlined the fact that an important legal barrier disenfranchising women from politics had just been overcome. At the same time, the inclusion of von Gierke, for a time a parliamentary representative of the right-wing Deutschnationale Volkspartei (DNVP), whose nationalist and monarchist politics ran counter to those of Höch, implies that even this momentous change did not necessarily guarantee better times for Germany. (After the DNVP refused to support her second term in parliament, von Gierke withdrew from the party in May 1920.) A mixture of progressive and reactionary figures, this cluster expresses optimism about the new political potentials of women's suffrage as well as fears that the radical change in German politics they represented might turn out to be less favorable than it initially seemed.

The negative associations suggested by von Gierke's links to the DNVP are perhaps emphasized by a constellation of fragments in the photomontage's lower-left quadrant that depicts a row of German military officers who recede in formation into the distance. Like the Käthe Kollwitz–Niddy Impekoven hybrid in *Cut with the Kitchen Knife* (Figure 2.4), the officers' heads are severed from their bodies, and they float precariously above their owners' decapitated shoulders. The figure nearest to the viewer bears the visage of General Erich Ludendorff, the former commander in chief of the German army on the western front, who in 1919 was in exile in Sweden, while the figure farthest away from the spectator possibly sports the head of General Hans von Seeckt, who was then the chief of the *Truppenamt* in the Reich ministry of defense and who would become head of the German army between 1920 and 1926.[26] This separation between the soldiers' heads and their bodies creates a disruption in the spectator's viewing experience that suggests that "reality" has been cut or edited, and that allows the cluster to be read in contradictory ways. The line of generals with the floating heads suggests the destruction of the old German army; equally, because they maintain their rigid bearing and military formation, the line of generals also implies the

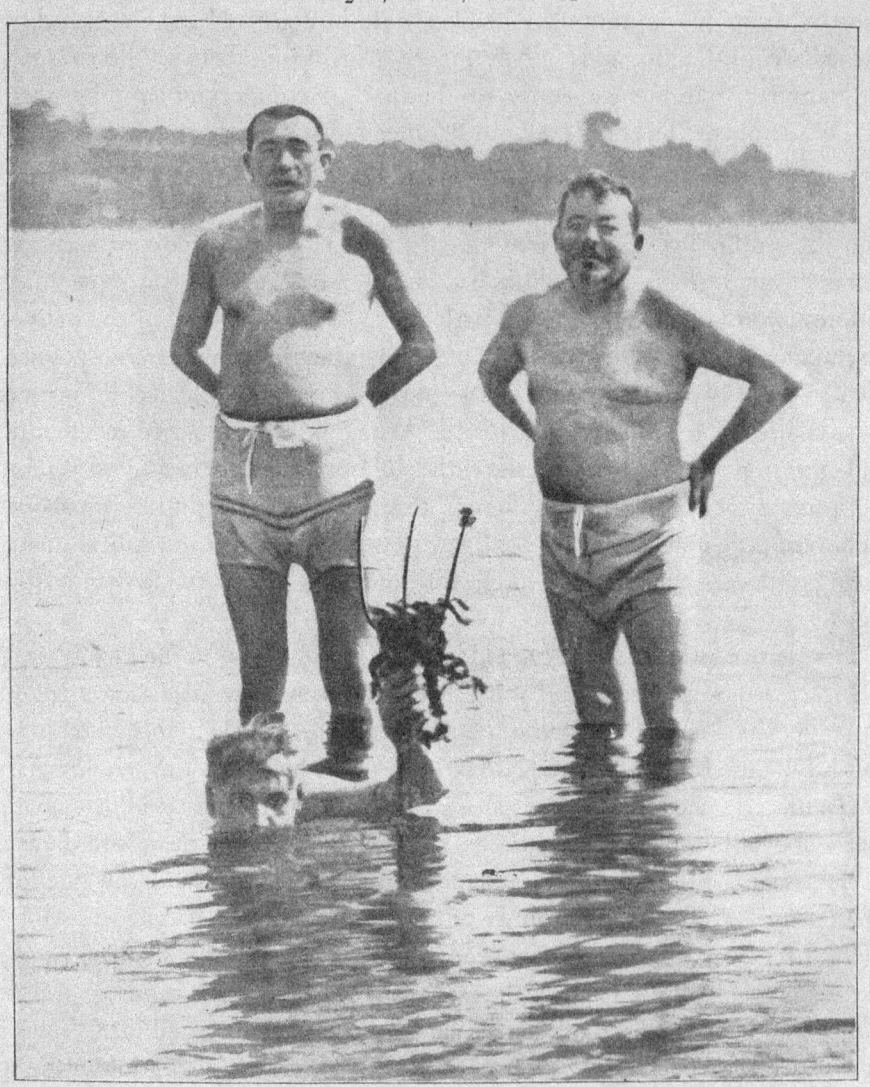

24. August
1919
Nr. 34
28. Jahrgang

Berliner

Einzelpreis
des Heftes
25 Pfg.

Illustrirte Zeitung

Verlag Ullstein & Co, Berlin SW 68

Ebert und Noske in der Sommerfrische.
Aufgenommen während eines Besuchs des Seebads Haffkrug bei Travemünde.

Figure 5.2. Cover of *Berliner Illustrirte Zeitung* [Berlin Illustrated Newspaper] 28, no. 34 (August 24, 1919).

continuation of the army as a dangerous, unstable, and disloyal "tool" of a weak social democratic state. (When Ludendorff returned to Germany in 1920, sometime after Höch completed *Dada Panorama,* he became an early supporter of Hitler and took part in the Nazis' failed "Beer Hall Putsch" of November 8–9, 1923.) This latter association is augmented by the text at the officers' feet, which evokes newspaper advertising directed at students promoting social directives and communal activities. The deposed, conservative, and nationalistic "Wilhelmine" way of life, *Dada Panorama* suggests, insidiously attempts to keep its worldview alive in the halls of academia—a fear that, as history suggests, was not so far from the truth. During the Weimar Republic, German universities became bastions of conservative thought, and they facilitated the development of the Nazi movement and Hitler's eventual rise to power.[27]

In the lower-right quadrant of *Dada Panorama,* a truncated image of Georges Clemenceau, the French prime minister and one of the framers of the Treaty of Versailles, appears. Here, despite their amputations, Clemenceau's head and upper body look comfortably "seated" in an armchair. This fragment is juxtaposed with Höch's collaged "H.H." signature, the words "unlimited," "freedom," and "for," as well as two irregularly cut images of crowds taken from a high vantage point: a famous image of government soldiers atop the Brandenburg Gate holding their guns at ready and staring down at left-wing revolutionaries during the government's brutal suppression of the Spartacist uprising in Berlin on January 10, 1919 (a military action ordered by none other than Noske), and, slightly farther to the right, nationalist demonstrations against the new government. A third fragment depicting a right-wing, antigovernment crowd appears on the image's left side, below and to the right of the headless generals, and touching the edge of some strange circular machine. These various images of revolutionary and reactionary masses from the immediate past connote the new republic's continuing instability. And because they cluster around the ambiguous image–text complex connecting a German Dada artist—as represented by Höch's signature—to a French politician and former "enemy" of the German nation, Höch's appropriations of images of different revolutionary and reactionary masses also suggest the interconnection of art and politics. Although the connections between the demonstrating masses, Höch, and Clemenceau remain obscure, the viewer is prompted to link Höch's assertion of unlimited freedom for herself to her artistic manipulation of images with highly charged political connotations. Her ability to manipulate political images, the photomontage suggests, can possibly help her change both herself and her society.

A cluster of fragments in the upper-right quadrant seems to represent the conflict-ridden contemporary political situation of the Weimar Republic. At the bottom of this quadrant, the jumbled letters "DADA" appear in a cloud that occludes Noske's legs from his bare thighs down. Behind Noske, the word "Panorama" appears, as well as a feminine-looking image of a World War I soldier—or perhaps a woman—in a trench coat and gas mask. Standing below and to the left of Noske, Ebert monopolizes the center of the composition. Above Ebert, a composite figure, consisting of the head of the U.S. president Woodrow Wilson attached to the body of a male gymnast, seems to fly across the sky. Evoking Wilson's role in setting out a peace plan for post–World War I Europe in his "Fourteen Points" speech, this figure is trailed by another fragment of Wilson's body: a second set of eyes complete with his trademark pince-nez glasses. Below and to the left of Ebert, the disembodied head and shoulders of Matthias Erzberger appear. (A representative of the Catholic Center Party in the German Reichstag since 1903, Erzberger was the politician who had actually signed the armistice ending World War I on November 11, 1918. Finance minister of the new republic between June 1919 and March 1920, Erzberger was a dominant political figure during the first two years of the Weimar Republic before he was murdered by right-wing extremists on August 26, 1921.)[28] This constellation of politicians and soldiers constitutes the largest cluster of elements in *Dada Panorama*. It seems to represent the realm of Höch's present day, pushed down on from the upper left by female forces that are at least partly identified with revolution. In addition, the cluster of politicians and soldiers also appears as a context in which revolutionary forces can be transformed into a new form of violent and reactionary mass. This latter association is suggested by the military boots that Ebert wears, which connect him to the generals below, as well as the athletic female swimmer just under Ebert's arm, who dives into a military field periscope. The power and freedom evoked by the female athlete in motion, the photomontage suggests, can possibly be channeled into a constraining "pipe" with military connotations. By surrounding Ebert and Noske with fragmented images of Wilson as well as emblems of both Dada and the war, Höch suggests that while these politicians currently stand at the center of the Weimar political panorama, this situation might be subject to change. The precariousness of both Ebert's and Noske's positions is reiterated by their feminization—an effect created, first, by the fact that Höch appropriates bathing images that depict them partially nude and thus make them a ridiculous spectacle, and second, through her addition of flower-montages sticking out of the front of their tight bathing trunks. Finally, their precariousness is also suggested by Höch's emphasis on their bodily functions: their corpulence as revealed by their nude chests and stomachs, the outfitting of Ebert's feet with a montage of images and text that suggest the need to protect them from moisture, and the enveloping of Noske's feet and legs in a cloud of gas that perhaps suggests bodily effluences.

As is the case with *Cut with the Kitchen Knife*, *Panorama* is organized into several central constellations partially separated by "blank" planes of paper and (in the case of *Panorama*) abstractly painted watercolor collage. Each cluster seems to exist separately in its own space yet connects to the others through bands of text, pieces of machinery, and occasionally through lines of human bodies. All the clusters are linked through numerous avenues of interface, and thus they suggest multiple chains of association. In addition, the appropriation of the ridiculous image of Ebert and Noske implies that Höch was very aware of mass media's power to influence politics. The image of Ebert and Noske had already garnered considerable attention before Höch appropriated it.[29] The bathing picture, taken on a mid-July visit to the Baltic Sea resort of Haffkrug near Travemünde, was originally published in an illustrated weekly, *Bilder zur Zeitgeschichte,* a supplement of the right-wing German newspaper the *Deutsche Tageszeitung,* where it was presented with a caption describing the image as "The Representatives of the New Germany."[30] Clearly intended by the *Tageszeitung* editors to humiliate and discredit the new republican government just a few days before its liberal constitution was signed into law, a cropped version of the photograph was printed again just fifteen days later, during the week of Ebert's inauguration, by the liberal mass-circulation Ullstein publication, the *BIZ.* Although generally supportive of the new government, the *BIZ* editors clearly could not pass up the picture; because of its humorous and eye-catching character, it no doubt increased circulation. The *Deutsche Tageszeitung* reprinted the photograph in 1919 as a composite postcard, in which the cropped image of Ebert and Noske was juxtaposed with photographs of Wilhelm II and Field Marshal Paul von Hindenburg and the title "Then and Now!"—a montage that suggested that the new regime had destroyed the traditional dignity of the German nation as embodied by its monarchy and its army.[31] The embarrassing image of Ebert and Noske was also republished as a fake stamp—with the title "The New German Stamp"—by the conservative humor magazine *Kladderadatsch,* which also used the photograph as the basis for a mocking cover cartoon in its subsequent issue.[32] In both cases, the point intended by the *Kladderadatsch* editors was to suggest the inadequacy of the new Germany as represented by its political leaders. Another conservative humor magazine, *Satyr,* followed suit, portraying the two politicians with bathing suits made out of the old flag of the German monarchy to imply (once again) that the new government was actively besmirching the honor of a noble German past.[33] Cartoons based on the photograph also appeared in the left-wing illustrated newspaper *Die freie Welt,* suggesting that the Left, too, recognized the image's destabilizing and antigovernmental effect.[34] As a whole, these examples, which do not in any way exhaust the various uses to which the image was put in the early years of the Weimar Republic, demonstrate the enormously embarrassing repercussions the photograph had for the new republican government as well as the allegorical uses to which it was quickly put by the mass media. Indeed, Ebert attempted to legally prevent the use of the picture on the grounds that it destroyed the honor of his governmental position and of the Weimar democracy in general. As a result of his experiences with the German press in the early days of his presidency, he lodged a series of libel suits over the next few years against journalists who represented him in a negative light.[35]

By including fragments of a photograph that had already garnered strong political resonances, Höch's photomontage evoked the new government's lack of media savvy while exposing their "beer bellies" and thus revealing them to be complacent and unheeding bourgeois figures. This was a typical Berlin Dadaist strategy, and, as suggested by the full title of *Cut with the Kitchen Knife Dada through the Last Weimar Beer-Belly Cultural Epoch of Germany,* it was a tactic to which Höch repeatedly returned to undermine her male subjects' power and dignity. Through their focus on their enemies' appetites and corpulence, Dadaists like Höch suggested that their opponents were nonrational, bestial, and out of touch with the new German world, a place that Richard

Huelsenbeck argued was one of everyday starvation and rage.[36] *Dada Panorama,* it seemed, acknowledged this situation, which had grown worse after the war, and proceeded to combat it through irony and self-reflexivity about the role of the mass media in German politics.

Central to the self-reflexivity of Höch's representation was its stress on the cyborgian character of the world and people it depicted. The cyborgian nature of many of the photomontage's figures can be seen in their mixing of genders (in the cases of Ebert, Noske, and the androgynous soldier to their right) as well as ages (in the cases of the female parliamentarians, Wilson, and perhaps the line of generals with levitating heads). It can also be discovered in the manner in which organic and mechanical parts are combined, as is the case, for example, with the figures wielding guns, gas masks, and periscopes. In addition, the environment in which the cyborgs move and stand is defined by strange machines, including a spotlight and a bizarre mechanical aperture, and a more general sense of human beings functioning as parts of a larger technological system is hinted at by the images of organized protesting masses as well as the generals who stand in formation and thus evoke the army's hierarchical organization, which, as Jünger showed, could allegorically signify total mobilization. Furthermore, the female diver about to spring into the military periscope that runs along the right border also conveys an idea of a technological system of knowledge governing human action. The fragments representing aerial shots of figures, crowds, and buildings, moreover, imply new modes of technological perception through their radical angles and scales—a connotation reinforced by the rhythmic juxtaposition of dark and light elements, which suggests the flicker of early films, as well as by the photomontage's title, which suggests a news report from a newspaper or newsreel. As a whole, the photomontage thus evokes a cyborgian world characterized by surveillance and the simultaneity of multiple actions in which human beings are technologically linked to one another and their environments, and in which different groups struggle for control. And by recognizing one's cyborgian nature, Höch's representation perhaps implies, a person could possibly avoid being merely manipulated by the technological system—as was the case for the new republican government during the bathing picture affair—and possibly gain some control over one's destiny in the modern world.

Höch's Later Photomontage Strategies

In the late 1910s and early 1920s, the compositional strategies of Höch's photomontages underwent a series of changes. Höch began to move away from the simultaneous montage of the early Dada works toward the simpler forms of composition that the other Berlin Dadaists, such as Hausmann and Grosz, were also beginning to favor. Instead of multiple figures, Höch's photomontages began to focus on a much smaller set of main characters, generally between one and three in number. More like traditional forms of painterly and photographic representation, these photomontages articulated clear centers of interest or focus, and by allowing for definite size differences between the various photomontage elements, the compositions also became more hier-archically organized. Höch also started to use colored paper and watercolor to create simple but dramatic backgrounds that often suggested shallow, stagelike spaces in which her dramatis personae stood or interacted. Furthermore, the characters that Höch represented became more general. No longer choosing for the most part to appropriate specific historical individuals, Höch instead opted to construct common social or psy-chological types, often created out of a multiplicity of carefully cut fragments that left the spectator with little or no idea of the actual person from whom the components were originally taken. At the same time, cyborgs—as defined by Haraway in the broad sense of the term as figures that embody various forms of hybrid identity—continued to populate her art. In these later works, which became somewhat smaller in size than Höch's first photomontages and lost some of their playful political irony, Höch used this figure to raise more general questions about psychology, sexuality, and the social construction of identity. Human identity, these works suggested, was a function of a broader technological network that was becoming more diverse and more densely inter-connected over time.

Two related photomontages, both representing cyborgs, reveal the early stages of the transformation of Höch's compositional strategies. In the photomontage *Das schöne Mädchen* [The Beautiful Girl] (1919–20) (Figure 5.3), Höch presents the new woman as a seemingly brainless cyborg. Although the background is still extremely busy and filled by heterogeneous elements, the relative size and positioning of the figure make her the central element and thus the focus. Here, a bathing beauty, dressed in a form-fitting black bathing suit, sits on an I-beam, her head—but not her bouffant hairdo—displaced by an electric light bulb. She is surrounded by circular motifs, which seem to stand as symbols of her desire but which also have connotations of danger or men-ace. The American boxer and heavyweight champion Jack Johnson, to whom the New York Dada artist Arthur Craven lost a boxing match in Barcelona in 1916, moves in from the left, his body penetrating a thin motorcycle tire and his gloves touching the beautiful girl's arm and parasol.[37] A subterranean reference to Dada's international his-tory, the Johnson figure also connotes sport, athleticism, and, because of his nakedness and proximity to the girl cyborg, cross-racial desire. (This latter connotation might have been amplified for spectators with knowledge of U.S. culture by the fact that Johnson was romantically linked to white women throughout his boxing career and married two of them in succession, something that incited considerable controversy among both whites and blacks at the time.)[38] To the right of the beautiful girl, a crankshaft juts aggressively outward toward the viewer, around which appear approx-imately twenty-seven BMW insignias of varying sizes. The crankshaft echoes the I-beam, which also thrusts forcefully into the spectator's space. Partially balancing this suggestion of extended space in front of the main figure, the circular BMW logos, which are superimposed on one another, suggest a similar extension behind the beautiful girl as well. In addition to the floating logos, a young woman's face stares out at the spec-tator from the upper-right corner of the photomontage. One eye has been replaced

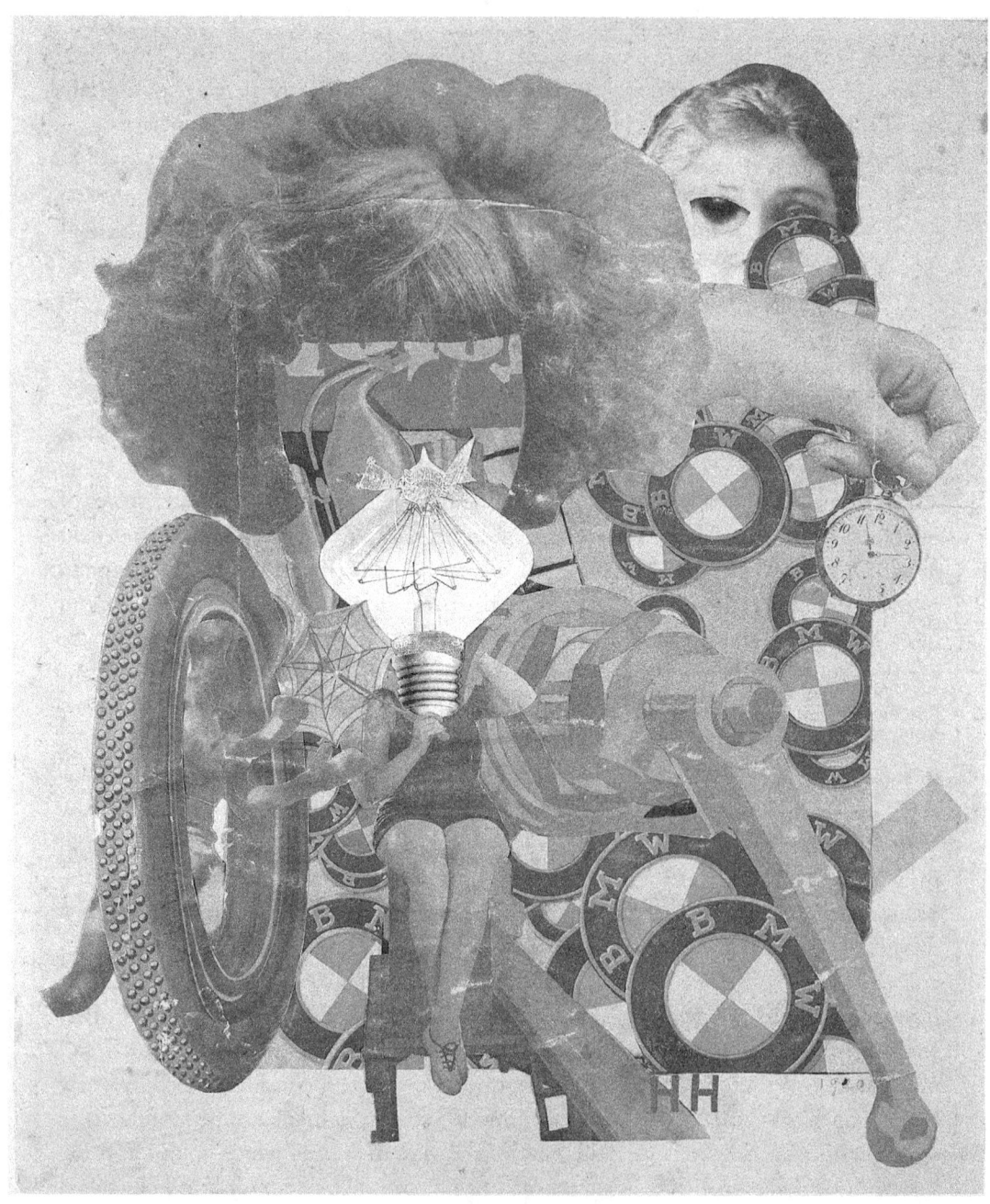

Figure 5.3. Hannah Höch, *Das schöne Mädchen* [The Beautiful Girl] (1919–20). Photomontage and collage. 35 × 29 cm (13¾ × 11⁷⁄₁₆ inches). Private collection. Photograph from Bildarchiv Preussischer Kulturbesitz/Art Resource, NY. Copyright 2009 Artists Rights Society (ARS), New York/VG Bild-Kunst, Bonn.

with a larger cropped eye, and the lower portion of her visage is obscured by a woman's hand holding a pocket watch, which extends from the side of the beautiful girl's hairdo. In conjunction with the hand and watch constellation, the clusters of BMW logos perhaps suggest the hypnotic nature of commodity culture.

In many ways, Höch's girl cyborg follows the traditional forms of allegorical representation in that it seems to present an embodied representation of an abstract concept or quality: in this case, the new ideas about beauty created by the growth of commodity culture and spectacle during the early years of the Weimar Republic. Like traditional forms of allegorical emblems, the cyborg's photomontage attributes—or in this case, her signs of desire—can be read and enumerated. Here, because they are represented through idealized depictions appropriated from the mass media, these signs of desire—beauty, sport, sexuality, travel, and status—are all shown to exist as different types of manufactured product. And because they reveal the commodification of even the most intimate aspects of human existence, they also function as indicators of anxiety, a connotation reinforced by Höch's photomontage technique, which is still characterized by disturbing physical and spatial disjunctions. At the same, however, Höch's figure also interacts with its environment and attributes in strange and heterogeneous ways that seem odd in comparison to most traditional allegorical representations. In particular, it is unclear if the countenance in the top-right corner belongs to the cyborg. On the one hand, it seems to be the correct size for her head, if not her body. If slid down and to the left, the face looks like it would just fit under the bouffant wig and above the metal screw neck of the light bulb that defines her throat. And if the visage with the montaged eye did belong to the beautiful girl, then the power of commodity culture could perhaps be seen to emanate from the cyborg, and the figure itself could be read as productive and as exercising control. On the other hand, the face of the woman with the montaged eye seems radically separate from the girl's body; furthermore, the head appears at the very back of the photomontage's fictive space. All the other photographic elements—hairdo, hand, and BMW insignias—thus seem to divide it from the body. Following this reading, one could imagine the beautiful cyborg's consciousness being left behind as she explores pleasure and consumption in the modern world. No longer the figure in control, she is, instead, a passive and gullible consumer: a woman seduced by a field of attractive, but ultimately two-dimensional, images. Mass communication and mass reproduction, the photomontage suggests, contain both possibilities and dangers.

Although composed of different fragmentary photographic images, *The Beautiful Girl* represents a type, not an individual. Unlike *Cut with the Kitchen Knife* and *Dada Panorama,* it did not for the most part encourage its spectators to identify specific historical personages and to imagine their particular histories and their implied transformations as envisioned by the artist. (In the context of *The Beautiful Girl,* the historically specific figure of Johnson seems like a remnant of Höch's earlier approach.) Thus, because it drew attention to a common type, *The Beautiful Girl* prompted its spectators to focus on the mass media and commodity culture as institutions and how they functioned to create, channel, and repress both female and male desire. Expressing both pleasure and anxiety about the identity roles offered to German women through manufactured goods and the mass media, it provoked its spectators to examine their relationship to the modern myths circulating in the early years of the Weimar Republic. Moreover, as Maria Makela notes, *The Beautiful Girl* was quite possibly related to another work of approximately the same size and format: *Hochfinanz* [High Finance], a photomontage with collage from 1923 (Figure 5.4). Although dated two years later than *The Beautiful Girl, High Finance* is closer in imagery and composition to the works that Höch created around 1920 than it is to those created after 1922. In addition, the two photomontage fragments in *High Finance* that can be dated with any accuracy appear to have been published either during or before 1920.[39] Since Höch dated her photomontages long after they were made and, in a few instances, appears to have gotten the dates wrong, it is possible that *High Finance* was made earlier than 1923.[40] For these reasons, as well as the fact that *High Finance* could easily function as a pendant to *The Beautiful Girl,* I analyze it here in relation to the earlier work.

High Finance presents two full-length male figures striding across a landscape that consists of a bird's-eye view of a fairground with ceremonial buildings and a stadium.[41] They are surrounded by other objects, including an aerial view of a factory complex hovering at the level of their shoulders, a large tire with a truck positioned at its apex, a shiny chrome nut or ball bearing that appears to prevent the tire from rolling, and two fragmentary double-barrel shotguns, each showing a stock, a trigger, and a breech broken open to receive shells. Both men clutch long metal machine parts—possibly a piston rod or a rocker arm—in their right hands as if they were clubs or canes, and to the left of the leftmost figure, two or three small fragments of what is possibly a striped flag appear. These fragments, which have been identified as the red-white-black-striped flag of the German monarchy, have also been described as orange, white, and green, and thus not associated with the German Imperial Empire at all.[42] Given the faded colors of the photomontage, however, the stripes could also be red, white, and blue, and thus they could have plausibly evoked the United States, which was an important model for German businesses and industry during the Weimar era. Both men, moreover, have had their heads replaced with new ones, which seem too large for their bodies. The carefully cropped profile head of the man on the left has not been identified, while the man on the right sports the countenance of Sir John Herschel, the nineteenth-century British chemist. Originally shot by Julia Margaret Cameron in 1867, this portrait was taken from an article on Cameron in the ladies' fashion magazine *Die Dame* published by Ullstein Verlag in May 1920.[43] Höch's photomontage is inscribed on the bottom-left margin with a dedication to Moholy-Nagy, who published it in 1925 in his book *Painting, Photography, Film.* In Moholy-Nagy's book, the photomontage was given an alternative title: *The Multimillionaire,* and a caption, *The Dual Countenance of the Ruler.*[44]

As suggested by its various titles, Höch has constructed a rather threatening image of two bourgeois cyborgs, an image that suggests connections between capitalism,

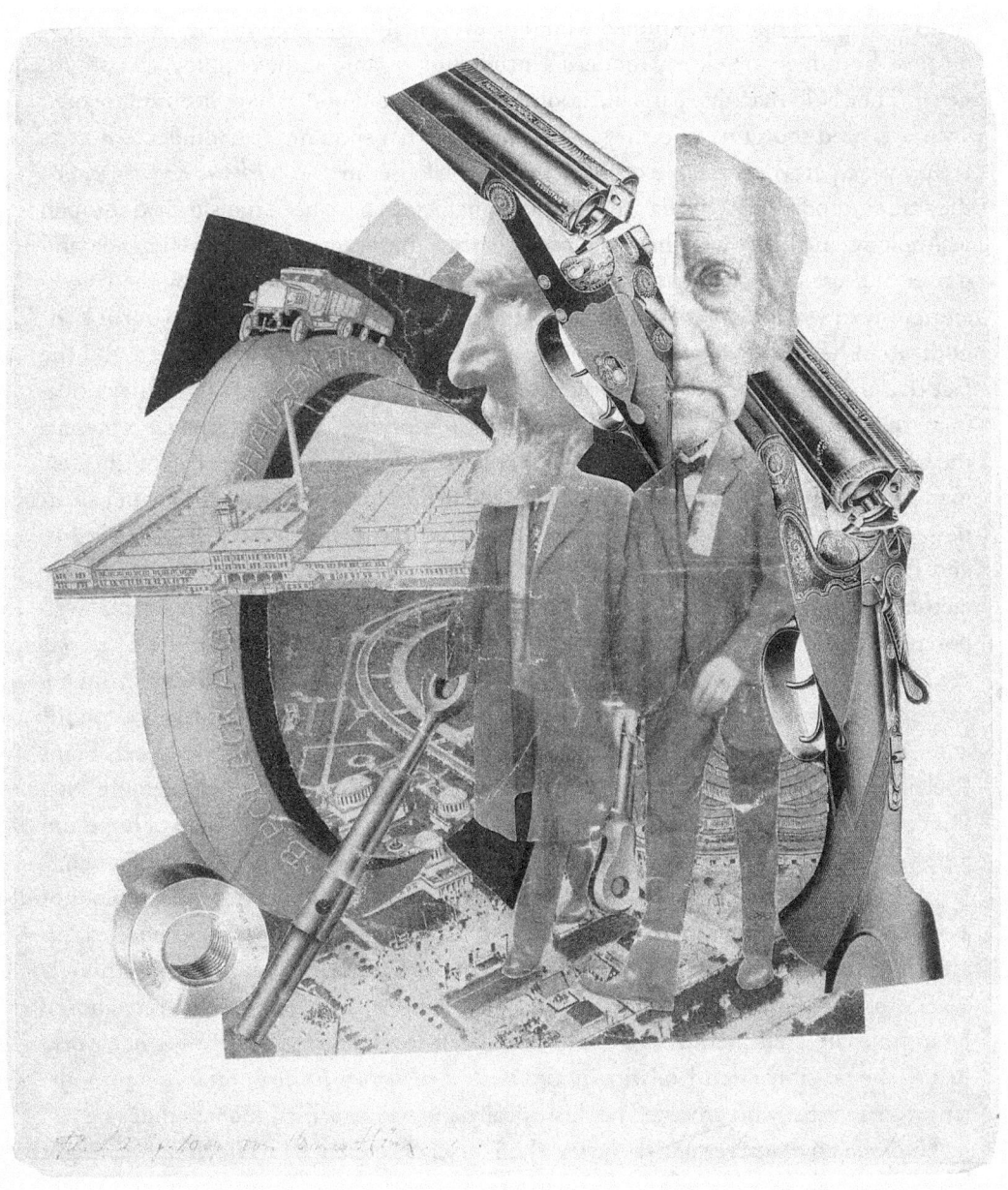

Figure 5.4. Hannah Höch, *Hochfinanz* [High Finance] (1923). Photomontage and collage on paper. 36 × 31 cm (14³⁄₁₆ × 12³⁄₁₆ inches). Galerie Berinson, Berlin/UBU Gallery, New York. Copyright 2009 Artists Rights Society (ARS), New York/VG Bild-Kunst, Bonn.

militarism, and nationalism during the Weimar Republic (and, depending on how the spectator read the colors of the "flag" in the background, perhaps monarchism and Americanism as well). Despite the fact that the two figures are representatives of a class that Dada artists like Höch hoped would be eventually destroyed by the German revolution, both men are clearly modern syntheses of organic and technological components. They hold machine parts like tools; their heads and bodies have been augmented with oversized shotguns; and they are pressed together shoulder to shoulder almost as if they were parts of the same organism. Like the kaiser in *Cut with the Kitchen Knife,* they are antipodes of the Dada artists, who, nonetheless, have been transformed through technology and thus who have adapted to their modern world. The violence and power of these two members of the economic ruling class is suggested by the threatening way in which they hold their tools, the shotguns that have become parts of their bodies and heads, the fragmented and mismatched character of their figures, and the fact that their size relative to the other elements in the image suggests that they dominate their environment. Even though the photomontage does not directly represent the German military, their weapons, their possible association with the flag of the German monarchy, and their quasi-military stride all connote militarism. The fancy business suits they wear and the beautiful coat worn by the one on the left suggest wealth, and the photomontage's various titles—as well as the photographic fragment of the factory that hovers next to them like a child's game board with which they play—also potentially imply their nature as capitalists. The flag—if read as that of the *Deutsches Kaiserreich*—and the caption given to the photomontage by Moholy-Nagy insinuate monarchist sympathies. In addition, the ground on which they walk, the Fair Grounds and Centennial Hall in Breslau, evokes their nationalism. Built by the architects Hans Poelzig and Max Berg in 1913 to commemorate Germany's defeat of Napoleon in 1813, this complex was regarded by many Germans in the early 1920s as a symbol of hope and renewal for a nation that had once again been defeated and occupied by the French.[45]

Like the beautiful girl, the capitalists of *High Finance* are portrayed as types, not as individuals. Although the figure on the right can be easily identified as Herschel, his identity seems to have more to do with self-reflexive concerns than it does with Herschel's role in German society or culture. One reason that Höch might have chosen to appropriate Herschel's visage could have been to establish a lineage for her work. Just as she possibly cited Kollwitz in *Cut with the Kitchen Knife* to refer to an important woman artist who preceded her historically and whose achievement perhaps helped make Höch's own career a little easier, the Herschel reference in *High Finance* might have been a way to acknowledge Cameron as another important inspiration for Höch. In addition, Herschel himself was an early photographer, and he made several key (and generous) contributions to the history of photography.[46] Most important, he invented the cyanotype process and discovered that sodium thiosulfate (formerly and erroneously called "hyposulphite of soda") could be used as a photographic fixative to stop the development process and make photographic images permanent—an insight that he shared with two of early photography's greatest inventors, Louis-Jacques-Mandé

Daguerre and William Henry Fox Talbot. In addition, Herschel also coined the term *photography,* and he was the first to use the terms *positive* and *negative* to describe different aspects of the photographic process. His portrait might thus have been included by Höch as a subtle way to indicate part of the history out of which her practice of photomontage emerged.

For these reasons, it seems that *High Finance,* like *The Beautiful Girl,* uses its photomontage fragments not for political satire but for exploring broader currents in Weimar society. As mentioned before, these currents were the manifold and reactionary connections between capital, the military, nationalism, and counterrevolution that characterized the Weimar Republic's early years. To emphasize the newness as well as the systematic or networked character of this dangerous amalgam of concepts, forces, and institutions, Höch makes her financiers cyborgs. Like the Dada artists, the old Wilhelmine order had been changed by both war and revolution, but, as Höch's photomontage reminded its spectators, this did not mean that these forces were now working to free the world from domination. Instead, as the photomontage implies, German capitalists were using all possible means of technological enhancement—not only new machines but also Taylor's system of scientific management—to maximize their profits irrespective of the human costs. Although the proletariat initially won concessions from employers in the early years of the Weimar Republic, their advances were fought tooth and nail during the 1920s and early 1930s.[47] And by representing its cyborgian capitalists as giants violently ruling an industrialized world, the photomontage suggests that the divisions in wealth and power would only become greater over time, perhaps as a result of the technological system's ability to reinforce and multiply itself.

In addition, when compared with *The Beautiful Girl, High Finance* implies something perhaps unexpected about differences between genders in the new "transformed world," as Ernst Jünger would call it in 1933.[48] As suggested by Höch's two photomontages, the first of a type of new woman and the second of a type of new man, the growth of technology did not seem to radically alter traditional differences between men and women but to intensify them. The beautiful girl is identified with the mass media, commodity culture, spectacle, and perhaps (because of her montaged eye) spectatorship—attributes that could all be read as rendering her passive (although this is certainly not the only interpretation). On the other hand, the financiers are associated with the means of production and with movement, activity, and violence. Although technology, the photomontages suggest, has transformed both genders in the modern world, these transformations can still be understood in terms of an active-male, passive-female dichotomy. Although this is not the only interpretation that can be derived from Höch's two works, it is certainly one of the major ones, and it raises the question whether technology—often seen as a force that overcame distinctions and linked opposites— could also be a power to increase and reify gender differences in a manner similar to how it augmented and solidified social and economic stratification. For this reason, despite their greater simplicity, these transitional works are just as ambiguous as the early works characterized by the compositional strategy of simultaneous montage. The critique characteristic of Höch's earliest photomontages has here become more general, but, like the earliest works, they do not appear to have been made to provide answers. Instead, *The Beautiful Girl* and *High Finance* provoke disturbing questions about the relationship of gender to industry, commodification, capital, spectacle, and the broader technological system that subtends them.

The Portrait Series

Based on the subtitles of a number of her photomontages as well as their formal and thematic connections, scholars suggest that the Weimar photomontages that Höch made after 1923 can be roughly divided into a "portrait" series, an "ethnographic museum" series, and a "love" series.[49] Although not without overlaps—that is, works that seem to fall into more than one series—these broad divisions in Höch's Weimar photomontages are useful, because they permit the tracing of specific themes in her art. *The Beautiful Girl* and *High Finance* stand as early examples of the portrait series, which, as mentioned before, focuses on types rather than specific historical individuals.[50] Although many of these portraits do not represent clear examples of human–machine interface, they suggest cyborgs, nonetheless, because of their radically hybrid and self-reflective character.[51]

Mischling [Half Breed] (1924), for example, presents a black-and-white, three-quarter-view portrait of a young African woman, who appears to have tears or scars running down her cheeks (Figure 5.5). Her chest and neck are bare, and she wears a beaded necklace. A cut beneath her chin defines her jawline and potentially suggests a second necklace. The woman's mouth has been occluded by a pink photomontage fragment, which depicts the red made-up lips and chin of a white (presumably European or American) lady. In comparison with a duplicate of the original photomontage fragment, which remains unidentified but can be found on page 58 of Höch's "mass media scrapbook" from 1933, Höch has carefully trimmed the woman's head and body, which, in both cases, is cut off just below her collarbone.[52] In particular, her long black hair and shoulders have been removed, and her visage and truncated upper body have been mounted on an irregularly shaped sepia collage fragment, which in turn has been pasted against a rectangular sepia background. The fragment, which extends to the image's right border, is slightly darker than the background. Although actually positioned beneath the photomontage fragment that depicts her face, it seems to surround her forehead and run down the side of her face, occluding her ear. A wavy and irregular band of lighter color that touches her forehead and the side of her head and neck heightens this effect by suggesting a head covering or perhaps blond hair.

As a whole, the image suggests sadness, ethnic mixing, violence, and eroticism. The woman's tears and the shininess of her eyes imply sorrow, an emotion emphasized by the photomontage's somber, muted colors and the lack of articulation characteristic of its collage elements. Because the blank character of the background and the collage

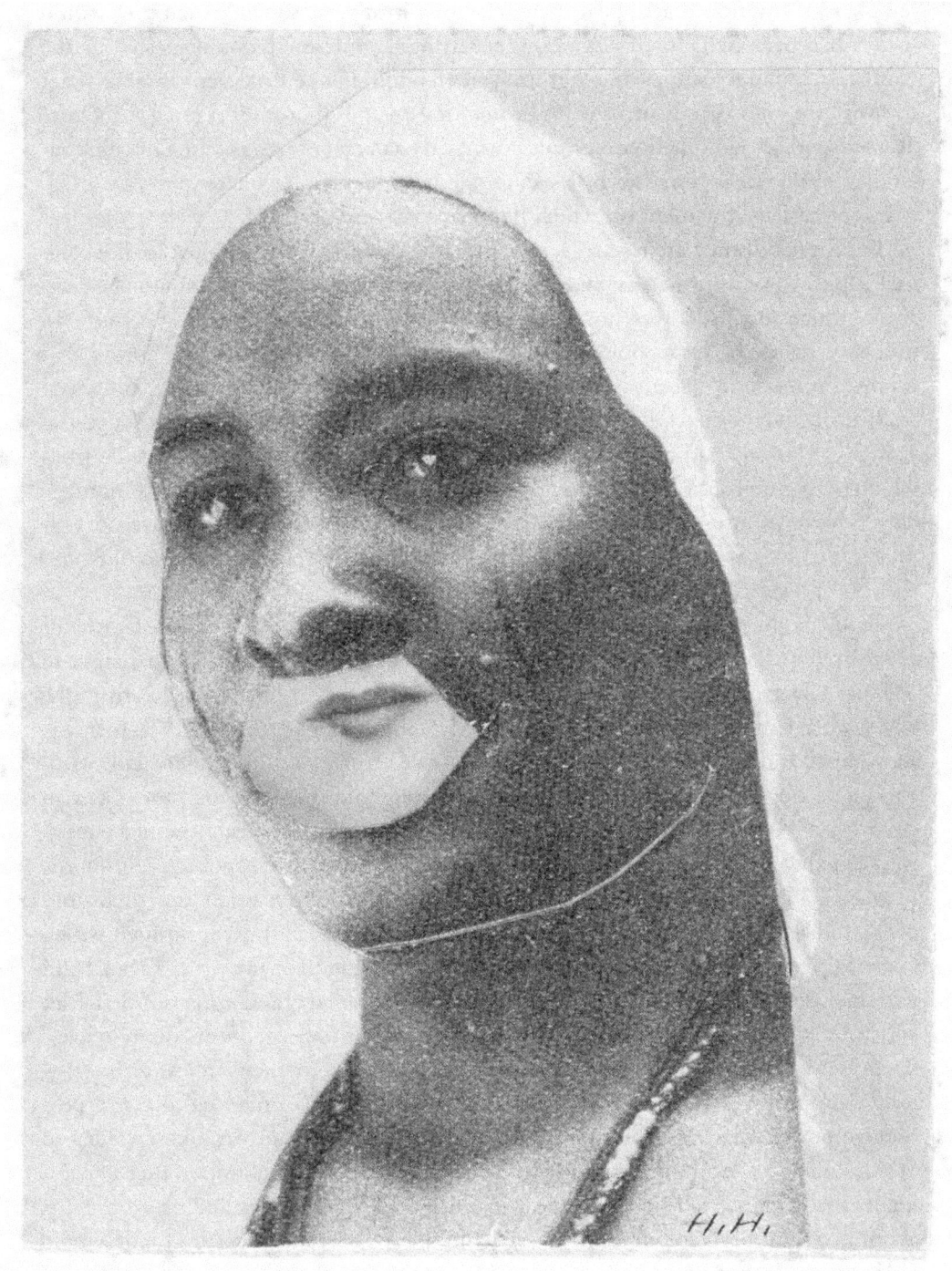

Figure 5.5. Hannah Höch, *Mischling* [Half Breed] (1924). Photomontage. 11 × 8.2 cm (4⁵⁄16 × 3¼ inches). Institut für Auslandsbeziehungen, Stuttgart. Copyright 2009 Artists Rights Society (ARS), New York/VG Bild-Kunst, Bonn.

fragment that surrounds her head encourage the spectator to focus on her face, the few signs of emotion that appear there take on a stronger resonance than they would if they had been juxtaposed with a busier setting. Ethnic mixing is suggested by the conflation of facial features drawn from women of different ethnicities. (Prior to 1926, the year she met Brugman, Höch also referred to the photomontage as the *Dutch Woman,* perhaps alluding to the ethnically mixed character of parts of the Dutch population.)[53] Violence is connoted by the cut underneath her chin, which exposes the irregular sepia collage fragment on which her face has been mounted, as well as the lines on her cheeks (if they are read as scars). Eroticism, moreover, is implied by the colonial subject's youthful beauty and the close-up character of the photomontage fragment, which reveals the texture of her skin and suggests an intimate viewpoint. (In Höch's mass media scrapbook, the woman's image is part of a two-page spread that presents examples of mostly African women and children, all young, nude, and physically attractive.) Finally, the woman's "hair" or "head scarf"—which also suggests a *hijab,* or Muslim head covering—resembles an undifferentiated mass of stone from which her figure could have been partially carved. For this reason, the photomontage also seems to comment self-reflexively on artistic creation—an association perhaps emphasized by the visible cut in her neck as well as the mismatch between her mouth and the rest of her face.

Evoking the plight of women of mixed ethnicity both inside and outside Germany, Höch's photomontage raises questions about attitudes toward race and imperialism in Weimar society. Germany had a very short colonial history, which stretched from the 1880s, when German colonies were established in South-West Africa, Togo, Cameroon, East Africa, and the Pacific, until 1918.[54] Although Germany lost its colonies at the conclusion of World War I, many groups worked throughout the 1920s to restore German colonialism, and interest in acquiring new colonies—or reacquiring the old ones— was kept alive by numerous organizations, politicians, and writers, not to mention the mass media.[55] In addition, as Susanne Zantop has argued, there was a long prehistory of "colonial fantasies" from the sixteenth century onward, narratives through which Germans redefined their desire for power and foreign conquest in terms of sexual and paternalistic scenarios.[56] During Germany's actual colonial era, German imperialism was justified by Germany's supposedly desperate need for *Lebensraum* or "room to live," by an "emigrationist" ideology that prescribed German settlement in less technologically advanced countries as a way to counter the loss of German culture and productive power occurring through emigration to Western countries like the United States, and by an "economic" argument that stressed the financial importance of colonialism to national self-determination in Europe.[57] More long-standing arguments about how European colonialism "was a 'natural impulse' to take possession of 'virgin' territory" analogous to the human reproductive drive or that it improved the lives of more "primitive" races were also used to support Germany's colonial ambitions.[58] Since the nineteenth century, German colonialism was maintained by ideas of essential biological differences between African and European "races"—ideas widely accepted in both Europe and the United States that helped make imperial conquest seem natural.[59] Observable distinctions in skin color, hair, eye color, body type, physiognomy, and skull type were argued to have a biological basis by such authors as Joseph Arthur Comte de Gobineau.[60] Although now discredited, this "scientific" form of racism, horribly linked with negative eugenics policies by the Nazi state in the 1930s and 1940s, continued to find powerful adherents until the conclusion of World War II.

In light of Germany's colonial history and the ideas used to justify and explain it, the representation of ethnic mixing in *Half Breed* seems to evoke the colonial fantasy of the white male explorer or settler "improving" the nonwhite native "stock" in a foreign context. By representing the progeny of ethnic mixing as an attractive woman, the photomontage reminds its spectators of the long-standing connection of women with the primitive in European culture,[61] and thus it plays to German assumptions that any person of mixed black–white heritage would more likely than not have a white father and a black mother. The woman's tears, however, potentially turn this colonial fantasy into a rape scenario and thus imply criticism of the colonial mission. Although Darwinist thinking could still justify rape as a part of natural selection—the fittest reproducing in whatever way they see fit—the close focus on the woman's sorrowful and distorted face encourages the spectator to empathize with her and thus to take a dim view of colonial exploitation. Also implying criticism of Germany's colonial history is the fact that the woman's ethnically different parts do not seem to match, thereby suggesting that exogamy (or "miscegenation," in racist discourse) as practiced in a colonial context leads to suffering. In addition, the figure's white mouth, with its closed lips, seems to stifle or gag her otherwise African countenance, thereby suggesting that colonialism may suppress the voices of indigenous peoples—a suggestion reinforced by the fact that in the original photographic image pasted into Höch's scrapbook, the woman's mouth is half open.

A second historical reference no doubt intended by Höch was France's occupation of the German Rhineland beginning in 1919 to force compliance with the war reparation payments mandated by the Treaty of Versailles.[62] Not only was the French military maneuver a radical affront to German nationalism, but because the French used African troops—generally of Algerian, Moroccan, Tunisian, Malagasy, and Senegalese ethnicity—to hold German soil, the occupation led to a frenzy of outrage in Germany. There was an outpouring of racist propaganda about the French troops of non-European descent infecting the German population with all sorts of tropical and sexually transmitted diseases as well as tales of assaults and of "pure" German women being raped by non-European soldiers and giving birth to biracial children. (It is estimated that between five hundred and eight hundred children were born as a result of liaisons between German women and black—or mixed black—French colonial occupation troops. The accounts of alleged rapes, however, were grossly inflated. Presumably not all or even a majority of these children were the result of forced sexual relations.)[63] Outraged accounts about the "Black horror on the Rhine" appeared in waves in both the German and the foreign press between 1919 and 1922—along with spirited denials of the German propaganda, particularly on the part of the French. These accounts sub-sided in early 1923, when the French occupied the German Ruhr region with noncolo-nial troops, and the German nationalists turned their attention to the "greater" crime of France's seizure of Germany's heartland. Colonial troops, however, would remain on German soil until 1929, although their numbers would decrease significantly after 1925.

An elegantly drawn, flat, and linear cartoon by Olaf Gulbransson in the German humor magazine *Simplicissimus* from June 9, 1920, makes the German fears of ethnic mixing—and the racist ideas on which they were based—quite plain (Figure 5.6).[64] Under the title "The Black Occupation," a dark-brown bellowing gorilla wearing the cap of a French colonial soldier strides over sloping, grassy ground. The fingers of the beast's left hand drag on the earth, thereby emphasizing its short legs and inhuman yet powerful proportions. In its right arm it carries a naked woman with long blond hair, her back to the viewer, pressing her hands against the gorilla's chest and shoul-der in an attempt to break its grip. Her left breast is silhouetted against the gigantic animal's fur, and, because she raises her outermost leg, the curve of her left buttock is also emphasized. The woman's white skin and blond hair identify her as German, her arched posture emphasizes her attractiveness and eroticism, and her nudity and the signs of her struggle define the scene as one of horrible sexual violation. To make the meaning of the cartoon even clearer, a caption below it reads, "A shame for the white race—but it's happening in Germany."

A grotesque and over-the-top representation of the fears of racial pollution grip-ping Germany at the time, the image also makes clear the racist assumptions that typi-fied the German discourse around the occupation. Because it used a gorilla to represent the nonwhite French troops, the cartoon revealed the "scientific" evolutionary assump-tions on which the popular concept of race was built in the postwar context. In addi-tion, by evoking the eighteenth-century Enlightenment construct of the "Great Chain of Being," a vertical scale that arranged all of creation from lowest to highest and that was used to justify whites' superiority to blacks,[65] it also emphasized the standard racist myths that blacks were closer to animals than whites and that they had a much greater propensity for violence and sexuality. Furthermore, because it reversed the terms of the colonialist fantasy, it suggests the continuing dominance of this metaphor for the colo-nial mission during the Weimar Republic. Finally, because the caption emphasizes that the action is a disgrace for the white race, it assumes a racial solidarity between Euro-peans that should have "naturally" trumped French political aims—a solidarity that echoes Gulbransson's (and the German propagandists') conflation of multiple (Arab and African) ethnicities into the unified and monstrous figure of the "black" colonial soldier.

In comparison with the *Simplicissimus* cartoon, *Half Breed* offers a much more sympathetic picture of ethnic mixing. Not only does the photomontage present the woman in a way that creates empathy for her, but the physiognomic details that Höch selected emphasize her youth and attractiveness. In addition, because it represents an ethnically mixed person rather than a brutal act of imaginary cross-species rape, it focuses on the uniqueness and particularity of an individual born of ethnically diverse parents,

Lieber Simpliciſſimus!

Ich kenne einen Herrn, der Fett liefern kann. Dieſer Herr erzählte mir, er habe eine Einladung zum Beſuch eines Nacktanzabends erhalten. — Erſchließung der höchſten Myſterien!! Weihevolle, göttlich reine Kunſt!! Ekſtaſe!! uſw. — Ich machte Bedenken geltend, dieſe Anpreiſungen könnten

Nepperei ſein. Der Herr wollte ſich aber mal überzeugen. Nach Tagen ſtürzte er auf mich zu und ſprach begeiſtert: „Es war überwältigend! Nich die Spur von Nepperei. Die Mädchen waren wirklich und wahrhaftig alle ſplitternackt!"

Ein Kriegsbeſchädigter bittet auf der Fürſorgeſtelle im Rathaus um eine Beihilfe zum Möbelkauf.

Bei den hohen Möbelpreiſen könne er ohne Beihilfe nichts anſchaffen. Er habe nur drei Betten und acht Kinder. Der Stadtſekretär wiegt den Kopf. „Sie hätten ſich aber ſchon damals im Frieden mehr Möbel zulegen können, da waren ſie doch billig!" — „Wieſo im Frieden?" fragt der Antragſteller. „Ich habe doch erſt vor vierzehn Tagen geheiratet."

Die ſchwarze Beſatzung

(Zeichnung von O. Gulbransſon)

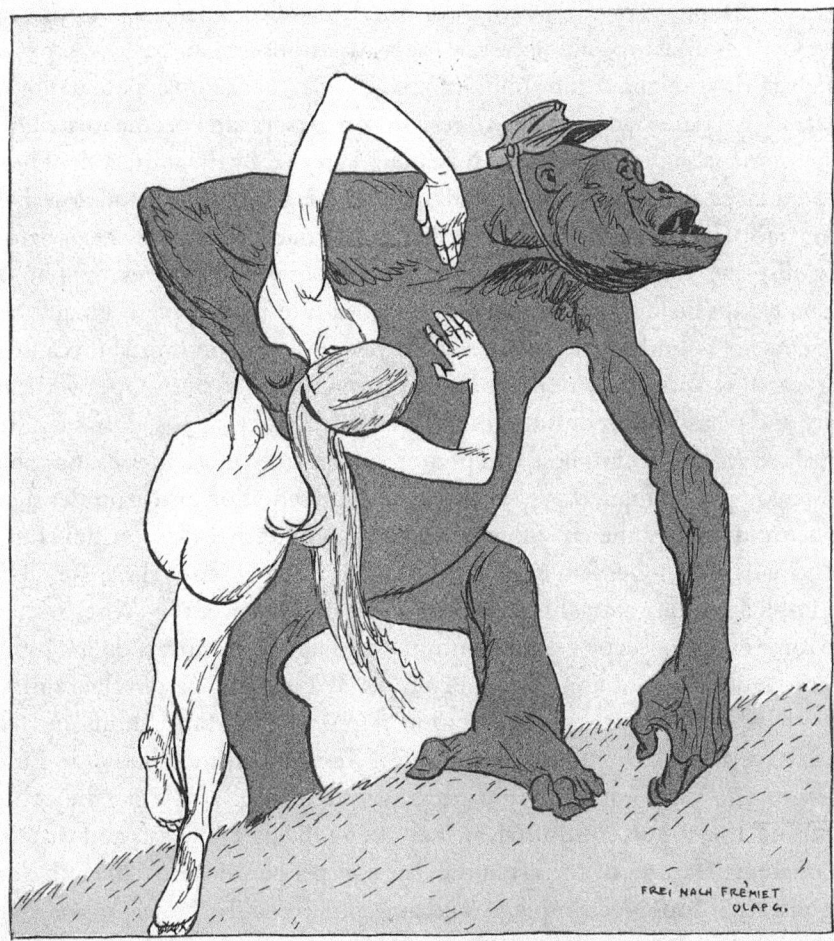

Eine Schmach für die weiße Raſſe — aber es geſchieht in Deutſchland.

Luiſe Zietz

Luiſe iſt eine gefeierte Rednerin; ſie überwältigt jeden; ſie hat eine etwas ausgeleierte aber unwiderſtehliche Gabe, zu reden.

Sie redet als kosmopolitiſche Liſe gegen den Raſſenkampf und ähnliche Dummheiten (und von den Ariern weiß der Menſch ja, wie ſie freudig auf ſolchen Steckenpferden herumreiten).

Warum ſoll Lisbeth ihre hitzige Lanze nicht für die Senegalneger und gegen uns einlegen?
Als ein kosmopolitiſches Mädchen kann ſe Sympathien für jedes ſchwarze Schwein hegen, denn für die Menſchheit ſchwärmt ſie in jedem Falle . . .

nur gegen alles Deutſche ſpuckt ſie gleich Galle.

Emanuel

Figure 5.6. *Simplicissimus* 25, no. 11 (June 9, 1920), 168. Illustration by Olaf Gulbransson. Title of illustration: "The Black Occupation."

thereby humanizing her and suggesting that she should be treated in a civilized and morally responsible manner. Furthermore, because the photomontage is constructed from preexisting images appropriated from illustrated books and magazines, it seems to reflexively point to how the mass media was used in Germany to disseminate and reify racist ideas and stereotypes, and thus it implies that the concept of race might be as much a construct of the media as it was a "biological" fact.

Despite the many ways in which it seems critical of colonialism, scientific racism, and the German mass media, however, the associations generated by *Half Breed* are ultimately fairly ambiguous. The photomontage's title, for example, potentially implies the existence of "pure" races, which, in certain contexts, could become mixed. In addition, the woman's slightly monstrous appearance, created by the mismatch of her facial features, perhaps also suggests an underlying biological basis for distinctions between different "races," a biological basis that, when violated, causes degenerate or deformed-looking offspring. Furthermore, given the woman's sorrowful features, the photomontage also perhaps insinuates that ethnic mixing leads to unhappiness. Finally, because it represents her as both erotic and in some mysterious way victimized (because of her tears or scars), Höch's photomontage also reiterates the racist stereotypes of the hypersexuality and relative powerlessness of colonial subjects.

Höch, as *Half Breed* implies, used photomontage to evoke, criticize, and transform ethnic stereotypes. In many ways, however, the representation also expresses the deep-seated contradictions inherent in even the more progressive views of non-European peoples circulating in German culture of the time. During the Weimar Republic, the racism implicit in the colonialist mission and the outrage over the French occupation were to some extent offset by German primitivism, namely, the attraction felt by numerous avant-garde artists for non-Western cultures, as a result in part of their disillusionment with aspects of European civilization. However, as Mark Antliff and Patricia Leighten have argued, the valorization of non-Western culture inherent in European primitivism was itself not without aspects of stereotyping. "Within the context of modernism," they argue, "'primitivism' is an act on the part of artists and writers seeking to celebrate features of the art and culture of peoples deemed 'primitive' and to appropriate their supposed simplicity and authenticity to the project of transforming Western art."[66] And although European primitivism reversed the devaluation of non-white peoples characteristic of the racist colonial discourse, it left other pernicious ethnic stereotypes in place. In particular, it characterized the "primitive" person as timeless and unchanging in contrast to the "civilized" human being, who was acknowledged to develop over time; as a result, while Western artists were believed to have the ability to be influenced by non-Western art, this capability was denied to non-Western artists, who were located outside history in a timeless and "infantile" past.[67] In addition, European primitivism tended to view non-Western artworks as expressing the general material needs or instinctual drives of the tribal groups that made them, and thus, in contrast to Western art, primitive artifacts were not considered to be products of highly trained and developed individuals.[68]

Although they distorted the nature of "tribal" art, the European primitivists none-theless valued it quite highly. Westerners, they believed, could learn from the sim-plicity and directness of non-Western art, which was understood to be much more direct, vital, spiritual, and natural than the West's more-developed art. The influence of primitive cultures, furthermore, would allow the West to overcome the divisions that the progress of Western civilization created between the mind and the body as well as the intellect and the instincts. And because primitive art allowed the overciv-ilized Westerner to become inspired through contact with a previous stage of human development, it could thus help emotionally and spiritually rejuvenate him or her.[69] Finally, because the European middle classes viewed primitive art as something low and grotesque, its forms were tailor-made for the avant-garde project of attacking and undermining the bourgeoisie's taste and worldview.[70] At the same time, however, when compared with colonialist discourse, primitivism projected a not entirely dissimilar view of the nonwhite, non-European other. Like the racist thinking that subtended impe-rialism, primitivism lumped numerous distinct (African, Asian, and Arab) cultures together; in addition, it associated the primitive with women, nature, irrationality, superstition, sexuality, and violence.[71] Furthermore, for many primitivists, non-Western peoples still represented an earlier developmental stage of humankind, and as such they were more childlike, passive, instinctual, and powerless in the face of Western tech-nology. Thus, although European primitivists sometimes explicitly sought to overturn colonialist stereotypes, they generally tended to simply repeat colonialist prejudices in inverted forms.[72]

Because of its contradictory associations, *Half Breed* can be seen to embody many of the paradoxes of European primitivism—paradoxes that Höch began to treat more directly by the decade's end. Although *Half Breed* seems sympathetic to the plight of nonwhite women, it also permits the generation of several rather essentialist readings. At the same time, although Höch did not appear to be aware of the sometimes prob-lematic ways in which she mobilized signs of ethnic difference, photomontages like *Half Breed* could have served an important function in Weimar culture if they were shown—something that did not occur publicly between 1920 and 1929.[73] By producing such contradictory readings, Höch's photomontage might have provoked Germans to analyze their conflicted feelings about race and, in this way, to discuss how racism and colonialism were affecting their contemporary situation. In addition, although the pho-tomontage form of *Half Breed* does not seem to accord with the more handmade, abstract, or ornamental forms characteristic of much primitivist art in Europe, the fact that several Dadaists, such as Huelsenbeck, Herzfelde, and Hausmann, referred to Dada-ism or photomontage as permitting a more "direct" or "primitive" form of expression reminds us that the Dadaists adapted and transformed modernist concepts that they inherited from the immediate past.[74] Although the Dadaists came more and more in the late 1910s and the early 1920s to reject the primitivism of the German expressionist painters and writers who were among their early inspirations and, as a result, to em-ploy the most modern means of representation available to them as strategic counters to the "soulful" and "metaphysical" forms of art making that they rejected, they also appear to have understood technology to possess a primitive side as well. The primitive, in other words, did not disappear in the Dadaist valorization of the machine and technology; instead, it returned as an archaic, irrational, and often menacing force at the core of what was most modern.

The menacing aspects of technology as a developing system of knowledge by means of which human beings understood and manipulated both themselves and their worlds can be discovered by attending to the cyborgian aspects of *Half Breed*. In the first place, Höch's photomontage depicts a cyborg, understood here as an ethnic hybrid, a figure that attempts to undermine stable concepts of race, although it does not fully succeed at this task. *Half Breed* thus suggests that in the context of the Weimar Republic, the "primitive" and the "modern" were becoming more and more intertwined. In addition, through its photomontage form as well as its subject matter, it evokes several different technological systems, all of which played a role in developing and perpetuating colonialism—long-distance transportation, advanced weapons and other forms of military technology, industry (which wanted colonies for raw materials), and the mass media (which, in more recent years, informed subjects at home about other cultures, alerted them to their nation's engagement with the world at large, and, in these various ways and others, helped produce and disseminate images of national, cultural, and ethnic difference). Finally, by evoking the "scientific" notions of race that subtended colonialism since the nineteenth century as well as by suggesting issues of human breeding through its title, the photomontage raises questions of race and eugenics.[75]

As Detlev J. K. Peukert has argued, around the beginning of the twentieth century, "the gap created by the decline of religious influence on everyday life in industrial society was so great, and the conquest of the world by secularized, scientific rationality was so overwhelming, that the switch from religion to science as the source of meaning-creating mythology for everyday life took place almost without resistance."[76] As a result, the human and social sciences attempted to assuage people's fear of death, traditionally eased by religious faith, by distinguishing between the individual, who was doomed to pass away, and the "people" or "race," which, it was believed, could potentially live on forever.[77] Although it was not an inevitable consequence, this distinction provided the Nazi state with the intellectual grounds for its barbaric negative eugenics policies, whereby it defined the national body or *Volkskörper* as that of a specific (albeit vaguely defined) "Aryan race," the "healthy" development of which was threatened by people of "lesser value" within the borders of the Third Reich: first, mentally ill or "hereditarily sick" Germans, and later, Jews, Roma, Slavs, and other ethnic groups that the Nazis saw as threatening racial "others."[78] (Male homosexuals, another group defined as dangerous to the Aryan state, also became victims of the Nazis' negative eugenics policies.) Merely by living, the Nazi argument went, the various "others" of the *Volk* threaten the racial hygiene of the German state, and in this way, the hierarchies inherent in scientific racism between people of "value" and those of "lesser value" were allowed to justify the systematic and technologically facilitated murder of millions of innocent human beings in the "Final Solution." Thus, although it would be silly to argue that Höch's photomontage anticipates the Holocaust, *Half Breed*'s evocation of issues of race, procreation, and the technological systems that support both violent and nurturing interactions between different ethnic groups is eerily prescient.

As Lavin has argued, Höch was a critical consumer of the mass media. She enjoyed the fantasies that it enabled while acknowledging the problems to which these flights of fancy gave rise: the ways, for example, fantasies could devalue reality or how ideals of femininity could encourage self-destructive behavior. Drawing on Patrice Petro's study of female spectatorship in the Weimar Republic, Lavin argues that Höch's use of close-ups in several photomontage portraits from the mid-1920s was a way to examine the conventions of melodramatic representation: the "images of excess, exaggeration, and unambiguous iconography" that rendered visible those elements of ordinary women's lives "most often ignored, trivialized, or treated as invisible."[79] *Der Melancholiker* [The Melancholic] (1925), which investigates the negative aspects of self-examination in the context of Weimar's burgeoning society of spectacle, is a case in point (Figure 5.7). Against a black, unarticulated background, it presents a close-up of a strange androgynous figure in profile. Although the title suggests the figure is male, the portrait appears to be composed of both male and female faces: the main portion of the head is quite possibly masculine; however, the lips, chin, and eyes appear almost definitely to be feminine. Höch has also distorted the melancholic's head by trimming it in an unnatural fashion; its forehead seems to bulge or distend, and its left eye and cheek appear to be sunken or missing. The figure's right eye has been replaced by a slightly larger one, which was photographed from a frontal position and thus clashes with the orientation of the rest of the face, and its lips and chin have been replaced by slightly smaller ones. Although the sides of the melancholic's face and jawline are carefully trimmed to match the two pieces, the figure's lips rest too close to its nose, and thus warp its features still further.

All and all, the face has a sinister affect, which is created by its deformed appearance. The beautiful right eye, ringed with eyeliner and mascara, engages the viewer's attention, but it does so in a disturbing way: because of the melancholic's glowering features, the figure seems to give the spectator an intense stare or perhaps an "evil eye." Furthermore, the outlines of the various photomontage fragments are sharp-edged—perhaps even jagged—and, as such, they connote violence. In addition to being sexually ambiguous, the figure appears to suffer and simultaneously to want to cause others pain. As suggested by the title, which possibly refers to Freud's distinction between mourning and melancholia, the photomontage perhaps represents a negative form of introspection: an ambivalent meditation on loss that turns into self-reproach. And as a representation of this form of depressed activity, the photomontage reveals Höch's interest in examining general psychological types as defined by her culture.[80]

Höch, it has been noted, remembered her years with Hausmann as painful ones.[81] Writing about that time in an autobiographical fragment that probably dates from the mid-1960s, Höch stated, "I was so disappointed, crushed, destroyed, that even today

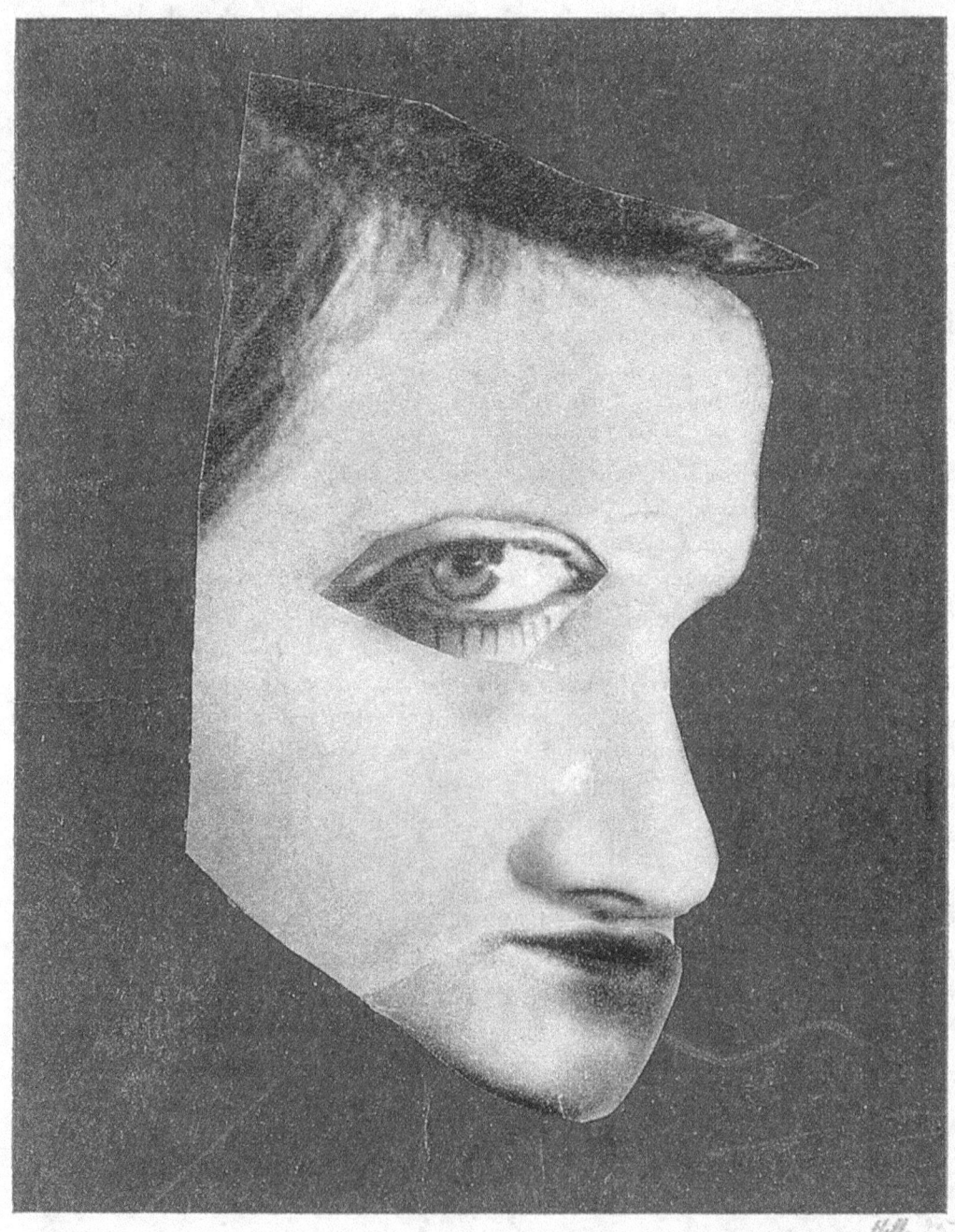

Figure 5.7. Hannah Höch, *Der Melancholiker* [The Melancholic] (1925). Photomontage. 16.8 × 13 cm (6⅝ × 5⅛ inches). Institut für Auslandsbeziehungen, Stuttgart. Copyright 2009 Artists Rights Society (ARS), New York/VG Bild-Kunst, Bonn.

it is almost impossible for me to reflect on these years."[82] According to Höch, her colleagues acted according to a double standard. Although none of them was satisfied with a conventional woman, "neither were they inclined to abandon the male/masculine morality toward the woman. Enlightened by Freud, in protest against the older generation . . . they all desired this 'new woman' and her groundbreaking will to freedom. But—they more or less brutally rejected the notion that they, too, had to adopt new attitudes."[83] And perhaps some of Höch's disappointment about the way she was treated as a woman in the Berlin Dada movement appears in the androgynous and melodramatic figure of the melancholic. In addition, however, as Petro has argued, the exaggerated expressions of the melodramatic mode of representation also had a positive effect in that they gave voice to (women's) experiences that were not always recognized by mainstream patriarchal culture; for this reason, the photomontage seems critical as well, since the figure's exaggerated expression of its inner condition could suggest a woman finally expressing what she really feels.[84] Moreover, by evoking Weimar cinema through its photomontage form and melodramatic content, *Der Melancholiker* indicates the overarching system of mass entertainment that could communicate deep-seated needs specific to women's lives and distort them. As the figure's hybrid (and thus cyborgian) features suggest, people's identities in the Weimar Republic were beginning to be influenced by the entertainments they consumed, and, perhaps for this reason, they could potentially become amalgams of male and female elements.

Höch's photomontage portraits did not simply suggest how new forms of cyborgian identity were being constructed through human interaction with the mass media during the Weimar Republic. In addition, they explored how people defined and changed themselves through interaction and dialogue with others, processes that—because they distributed identity beyond the confines of the individual—can also be considered cyborgian. It has been suggested that two paired photomontage portraits from 1928, *Englische Tänzerin* [English Dancer] (Figure 5.8) and *Russische Tänzerin (Mein Double)* [Russian Dancer (My Double)] (Figure 5.9), represent Höch and Brugman, her lesbian lover between 1926 and 1935.[85] Although the sizes and the overall colors of the two photomontages are somewhat different, they have numerous similarities. They both consist of a close-up frontal portrait of a woman's face that sprouts tiny feet or legs on which she seems to dance; in each case, the woman's visage is composed of features appropriated from at least two different people. Furthermore, both figures exist in an extremely simplified, rather barren spatial context. The English dancer, whose facial features have been compared to those of Höch, moves on tiny satin high-heel shoes toward the right frame of what is a predominantly grayish-blue photomontage. Her short hair, a single lock falling over her forehead, is ornamented with flowers, the stems of which peek out from behind the gaps that exist between the photomontage fragments that make up her face. The Russian dancer, on the other hand, moves toward the left frame of what is a predominantly sepia, gray, orange, and brown photomontage. She too has short hair, which is swept to the side, although her legs are longer and end in real ballet shoes. Adorned with flowers, feathers, and lacelike material that functions

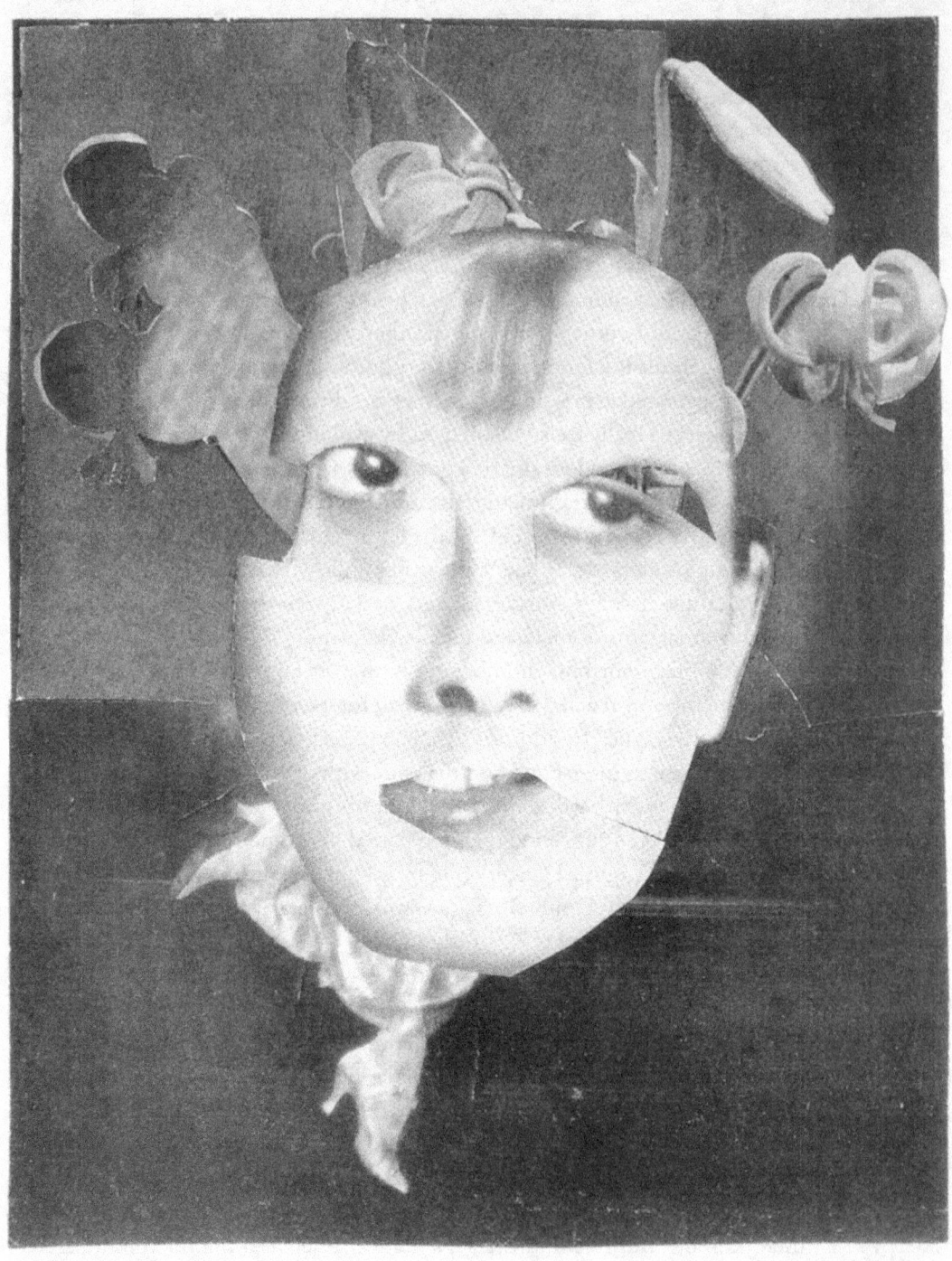

Figure 5.8. Hannah Höch, *Englische Tänzerin* [English Dancer] (1928). Photomontage. 23.7 × 18 cm (9 5/16 × 7 1/16 inches). Institut für Auslandsbeziehungen, Stuttgart. Copyright 2009 Artists Rights Society (ARS), New York/VG Bild-Kunst, Bonn.

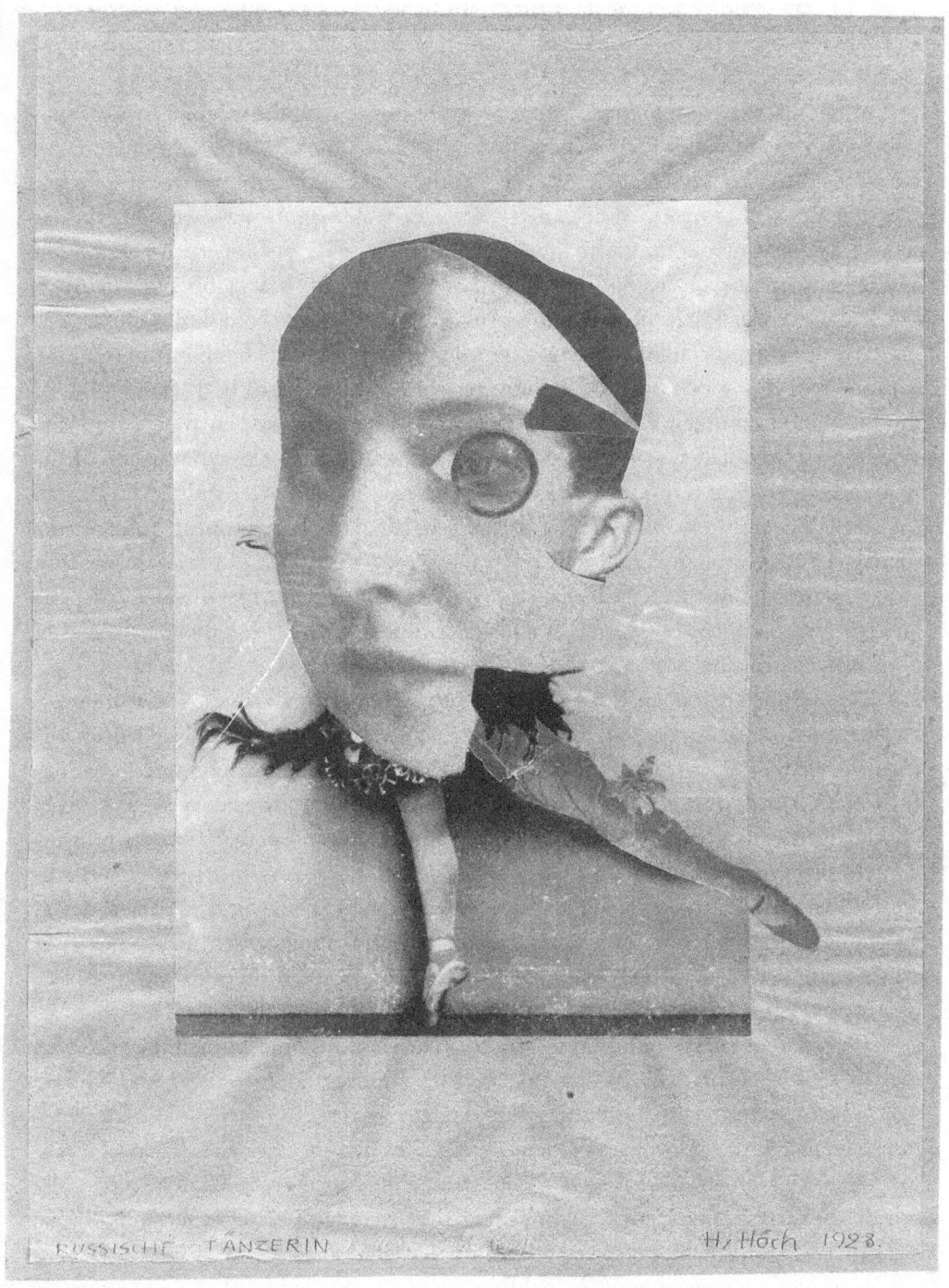

RUSSISCHE TÄNZERIN   H; Höch 1928.

Figure 5.9. Hannah Höch, *Russische Tänzerin (Mein Double)* [Russian Dancer (My Double)] (1928). Photomontage. 30.5 x 22.5 cm (12 x 8 ⅞ inches). Herzog Anton Ulrich-Museums Braunschweig, Kunstmuseum des Landes Niedersachsen. Joint property of Braunschweigischer Vereinigter Kloster- und Studienfonds. Photograph from Herzog Anton Ulrich-Museums Braunschweig. Copyright 2009 Artists Rights Society (ARS), New York/VG Bild-Kunst, Bonn.

as a skirt, she stands on point. Her tiny right hand, extended out behind her to balance her left leg, peeks out from behind her right cheek. She also sports an altered eye with a monocle.

As has already been argued, Höch used the image of the dancer in her Weimar photomontages to symbolize female empowerment and the new freedoms opening up for women in Weimar society. Not only was the dancer powerful, active, and attractive, but she also represented an athletic and desirable type of new woman, and, as such, a new role model for German women to emulate. By possibly depicting herself and her partner as dancers, figures that in various ways mirror or double one another, Höch also suggested that the formation of female identity was a complex balancing act, one that occurred through interaction with significant others. The theme of masking is prominent in the two portraits. Höch constructed the faces of both women out of multiple photomontage fragments juxtaposed so as to suggest that their composite visages have been laid over a second countenance that exists below the surface of the first one. The eyes and mouth of the English dancer, for example, seem to lie behind the rest of her features. Likewise, the face of the Russian dancer appears to cover the slightly darker visage of a man, whose left ear and tiny portions of his left brow, hair, and cheek remain uncovered. In this way, the photomontages evoke the idea of female identity as a masquerade—a socially constructed performance that models itself after dominant, patriarchal stereotypes.

As the British psychoanalyst Joan Riviere argued the following year, "womanliness" was essentially a "masquerade" that women often unconsciously created to deflect criticisms of their (real or perceived) deviations from the patriarchal feminine ideal and, thereby, to better fit into Western societies. Most apparent in the behavior of a subset of those women who diverged most strongly from the dominant image of femininity—namely, professional women and (paradoxically) some lesbians—the performance of femininity was nonetheless a characteristic of all women as a result of the usual developmental process whereby they became sexually functioning adults. All women thus possessed masculine components in their psyches that caused them to want to compete with men in patriarchal society, but their sexual development forced them to alienate and deny these nonfeminine aspects in order to become women they believed men desired (or, in the case of lesbians, to avoid criticism and attack).[86] And while it would be incorrect to attribute this specific nexus of ideas to Höch's two representations of dancers, the hybridity of Höch's figures as well as the pervasive theme of masking suggest that Höch subscribed to the idea that feminine identity was at least partially socially constructed and that actual women's lives were far more complex and diverse than they were normally perceived to be in patriarchal societies.[87]

The closely related theme of doubling—which is evoked by the various types of shadows that appear in both images and that mirror or repeat aspects of each figure—also suggests an idea of the social construction of identity. The English dancer's head, for example, is covered with both flowers and flower silhouettes, which, in relation to the "original" floral images, appear as their shades or traces. The shapely legs and skirt of the Russian dancer cast actual shadows on the wall behind her, a result of Höch's sub-tle photomontage technique, which carefully organized the photomontage fragments to mirror the photographically represented shadows that appear in the fragment of the background that also contains her right leg. When the two photomontages are juxtaposed with one another, the figures seem to mimic one another. Balancing on opposite feet and moving in opposite directions, they each strike the same pose as if they were dancing together. Finally, Höch subtitles the Russian dancer "my double," an appellation that suggests the figure is like her in many ways. For these reasons, the two dancers evoke a sense of human identity formation through emulating others. Even if the dancers were not intended to represent Höch and Brugman directly, the various signs of shadowing and doubling suggest an intimate and interactive practice in which two women mirror and change one another—that is, construct one another through different forms of intercommunication. Distributed identity, these photomontages imply, can be produced through acts of love and friendship.

The Ethnographic Museum Series

Höch's use of the figure of the cyborg during the 1920s to criticize the idea that fem-inine and ethnic identities were clear and fixed—and that they could give rise to clear typologies and rigorous classificatory systems—is significant in light of what Helmut Lethen has called the "classification mania" of the Weimar Republic, which was itself a response to the dissolution of boundaries brought about by the period's political rev-olution, social changes, and ceaseless modernization.[88] As Lynne Frame has argued, the tendency to produce taxonomies was characteristic of both the scientific literature and the popular culture of the Weimar period.[89] Including such serious studies as the psychiatrist Ernst Kretschmer's *Body Type and Character: Investigations into the Problem of Constitution and the Teaching of the Temperaments*,[90] an enormously popular clinical study of the mentally ill that developed a typology linking a person's body type to his or her temperament and character, and frivolous articles in the popular press, defin-ing different types of new women or what one's body language revealed about one's personality, the new taxonomies could be used "as both hermeneutic tools and behav-ioral guides."[91] They could be employed, in other words, to identify and define oth-ers in one's environment or as role models to regulate either one's own or someone else's behavior. In addition, because of the hierarchies that tended to creep into classificatory systems, they were potentially destructive, since they could be used to justify discrim-ination against certain classes or groups of people. Since Höch's photomontages seem intended to undermine this tendency toward constructing classificatory systems, they can thus be assigned to the great countermovement to taxonomy that Lethen also iden-tifies in Weimar culture: those cultural tendencies that sought to relax conventions, blur boundaries, and do away with clear ideological distinctions.

Höch's ethnographic museum series, which consists of approximately seventeen to twenty works made between the mid-1920s and the early 1930s, reveals her continued use of the cyborg to dissolve clear-cut taxonomies of ethnicities and gender.[92] In this series, photographic fragments representing non-European sculptures are combined with body parts of Western and non-Western figures. Generally set against abstract backgrounds, these hybrid figures are frequently placed on forms that resemble pedestals or are framed in ways that suggest museological display. Often subtitled "from an ethnographic museum" or "from an ethnographic collection," they refer quite directly to the exhibition of non-Western cultural objects in Europe during the early part of the twentieth century. As scholars have noted, Höch created this series to comment on Western attitudes about non-Western cultures, to undermine traditional stereotypes of Western beauty, and to examine the multivalent relationships between gender and ethnicity.[93] In addition, they also reveal a sophisticated understanding of primitivism, which, even more than the portrait series, stresses its entwinement with the forces of modernization.

Although it predates the series proper, *Geld* [Money] (ca. 1922) (Figure 5.10) deals with a number of the central themes of this group of works. Moreover, because it employs an appropriated image of what is probably an ancient Greek sculpture of a male face to comment on specifically German historical issues, it offers a good introduction to the series as a whole.[94] In this tiny photomontage, which measures just under 4 by 7 inches, stacks of coins appear against an empty blue background. Some of the columns stretch from the top to the bottom of the frame, suggesting an immense array of wealth. Other stacks appear to have been cut off when the coins were sliced

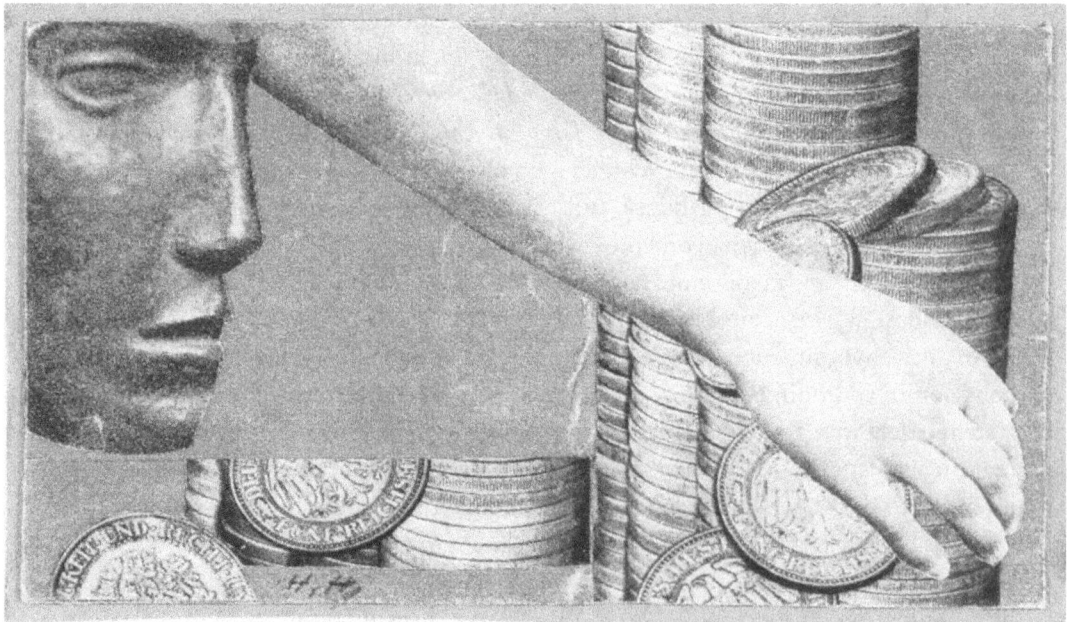

Figure 5.10. Hannah Höch, *Geld* [Money] (ca. 1922). Photomontage. 10 × 17.5 cm (3¹⁵⁄₁₆ × 6⅞ inches). Institut für Auslandsbeziehungen, Stuttgart. Copyright 2009 Artists Rights Society (ARS), New York/VG Bild-Kunst, Bonn.

from their original context, a disruption of the image's realism that reveals its construction from appropriated magazine photographs. A white female hand connected to a thin forearm reaches in from the upper left in a covetous gesture made apparent by the fact that a few coins near the hand are depicted in the act of falling. Next to the (living) arm and hand at the frame's far left side, a (lifeless) sculptural profile of a male visage appears, truncated at the eyebrows and cheekbone. Because of its size and format, the photomontage resembles some of the larger German bills or *Reichsbanknoten* from the first half of 1922, before their size was reduced by nearly 50 percent as a result of their extremely limited shelf life. (As the money-conscious German government soon realized, when the bills aged, they quickly became worth less than the materials used to make them.)[95]

The image suggests the panic of the postwar inflation and the hyperinflation, which began in late 1922.[96] The French occupation of the Ruhr at the beginning of 1923, which followed its military takeover of the Rhineland in 1919 and is evoked by Höch's *Half Breed* (Figure 5.5), resulted in a government-initiated program of "passive resistance" on the part of German workers, whereby they attempted to force the French to withdraw by bringing industrial production to a standstill. To pay the striking workers, the German government intensified its policy of printing unsecured banknotes, a practice that resulted in the complete collapse of the German mark between 1922 and 1923.[97] Although the passive resistance was not the only cause of the German hyperinflation, Germans at the time believed it to be a major contributing factor.[98] And in light of these historical associations, *Money* takes on several different connotations.

In the first place, the ancient sculptural face, the grasping hand, and the piles of money suggest that the rush to accumulate capital is like a primitive force, and by implying that irrational behaviors characteristic of a magical or a mythic worldview return in the context of a modern, rationalized, and industrial society, the photomontage evokes the critique of Enlightenment principles begun by Nietzsche in the late nineteenth century and continued in the work of Max Horkheimer and Theodor W. Adorno during World War II.[99] As the latter would argue in the mid-1940s, the "program of the Enlightenment was the disenchantment of the world, the dissolution of myths and the substitution of knowledge for fancy."[100] At the same time, however, by getting rid of animism, by substituting reason for superstition, and by developing instrumental thinking to its fullest extent, the progress of enlightenment extinguished all traces of its own self-consciousness and became a new mythology.[101] Humanity's increasingly rational development, in other words, resulted in a reified and administered world, where everything had reality only inasmuch as it could be reduced to an abstract quantity and fit into a rational system, where power became the principle of all relations, and where human thinking became enslaved by the status quo, unable to negate what factually existed and, thereby, to think beyond it to what might be better.[102] "Mankind," Horkheimer and Adorno lamented, "whose versatility and knowledge become differentiated with the division of labor, is at the same time forced back to anthropologically more primitive stages, for with the technical easing of life the persistence of domination brings about a fixation of the instincts by means of heavier repression."[103] And by suggesting that the economy had become a mythic force in everyday German life during the early 1920s, *Money* seems to present a trenchant anticipation of this most despairing midcentury formulation of the critique of instrumental reason, one that implies that Germans were being destroyed by their entwinement within the abstract system of capitalism, which reduced all reality to a set of interrelatable quantities irrespective of the human costs.

Already in the first decade of the twentieth century, Georg Simmel described the money economy as the modern world's most characteristic and fundamental sign. Although far less hopeless than Horkheimer and Adorno, Simmel too emphasized the economy as a vast network that interrelated people with one another and with things in the world. "There is no more striking symbol of the completely dynamic character of the world than that of money," he noted. "Money is nothing but the vehicle for a movement in which everything else that is not in motion is completely extinguished."[104] This supposedly ephemeral "substance," in other words, was the driving force behind the incredible flux, anonymity, objectification, and blasé-calculating attitude of modern life,[105] its power resulting from the fact that it was in essence the medium that could translate all things into one another. As Simmel put it,

> The philosophical significance of money is that it represents within the practical world the most certain image and the clearest embodiment of the formula of all being, according to which things receive their meaning through each other, and have their being determined by their mutual relations. It is a basic fact of mental life that we symbolize the relations among various elements of our existence by particular objects; these are themselves substantial entities, but their significance for us is only as visible representatives of a relationship that is more or less closely associated with them. Thus, a wedding ring, but also every letter, every pledge, every official uniform, is a symbol or representative of a moral or intellectual, a legal or political, relationship between men. Every sacramental object embodies in a substantial form the relation between man and his God. The telegraph wires that connect different countries, no less than the military weapons that express their dissension, are such substances; they have almost no significance for the single individual, but only with reference to the relations between men and between human groups that are crystallized in them. . . . Money represents pure interaction in its purest form; it makes comprehensible the most abstract concept; it is an individual thing whose essential significance is to reach beyond individualities. Thus, money is the adequate expression of the relationship of man to the world, which can only be grasped in single and concrete instances, yet only really conceived when the singular becomes the embodiment of the living mental process which interweaves all singularities and, in this fashion, creates reality.[106]

By representing money as a primitive force inspiring rapaciousness, Höch's photomontage thus obliquely referred to the great dangers inherent in the capitalist system that formed the basis for modern life in the Weimar Republic.[107] Thereby, Höch seemed to indicate once again the growing systematization of modern life: a world fundamentally characterized by a growing network of financial and technological relationships that enabled both peace and war and that affected identity by making human beings increasingly cyborgian.[108] As was the case with *Half Breed* as well as the other photomontages in the portrait series, *Money* suggests that ethnicity, gender, and the line between organic and inorganic were becoming increasingly porous because of the distributed nature of identity, that is, its inscription in a larger network that, because of its ability to find common denominators, related everything to everything else.

Also evoking threatening aspects of modernity as well as a new, more critical concept of primitivism, *Die Süsse* [The Sweet One] (ca. 1926) (Figure 5.11) presents the German new woman as a hybrid synthesis of Western and non-Western parts. Against a swirling orange, yellow, red, and brown watercolor background, a female figure appears, constructed from a set of black-and-white photomontage fragments. Her arms clasped in front of her, she seems to dance on a stage. The figure is a combination of animate and inanimate elements, including parts of two different African sculptures— a mask and a male "idol figure," both from the Congo—and an eye, lips, left hand, and legs drawn from newspaper images of various Western female figures.[109] These diverse body parts both match and clash with one another. Although her eyes and lips are proportionate to her face, her head as a whole is too large for her body; in addition, her left hand is much larger than it should be. Her left arm is missing from slightly below her shoulder to a little above her fingers, which causes her hand to float mysteriously in front of her. (The original sculpture, which is damaged, also possesses this uncanny floating hand.) Finally, her white legs, clad in fashionable dress shoes, stick out below the stumpy legs of the African statue. Emerging from the juncture between the idol's legs where, in the original photographic reproduction, the sculpture sprouted a prominent penis and testicles, these Western legs elongate her body to almost normal proportions and transform the statue's legs into a short revealing skirt. Reinforcing the African idol's symbolic castration through photomontage (observant spectators might notice that the statue's chest remains male), the woman's "female" sexuality is emphasized. Not only is the figure given a title, "the sweet one," which suggests her eroticism and desirability, but she appears to wink with her left eye, her lips are full and made up, her "skirt" shows off her shapely legs, and, by dancing, she seems to display herself as an erotic spectacle.

The Sweet One deals with several interrelated issues characteristic of early-twentieth-century German art, in particular, the relationship between women, primitivism, and modernity. Höch wrote in 1965 that the ethnographic museum series was in part inspired by the focus on tribal art by German expressionist painting during the twentieth century's first few decades.[110] As Jill Lloyd has demonstrated, the expressionist painters adapted forms and subjects from a wide variety of artworks that they deemed "primitive," including African, Asian, and Gothic sources, to develop a new artistic language to more directly express the underlying archaic forces that still permeated the modern

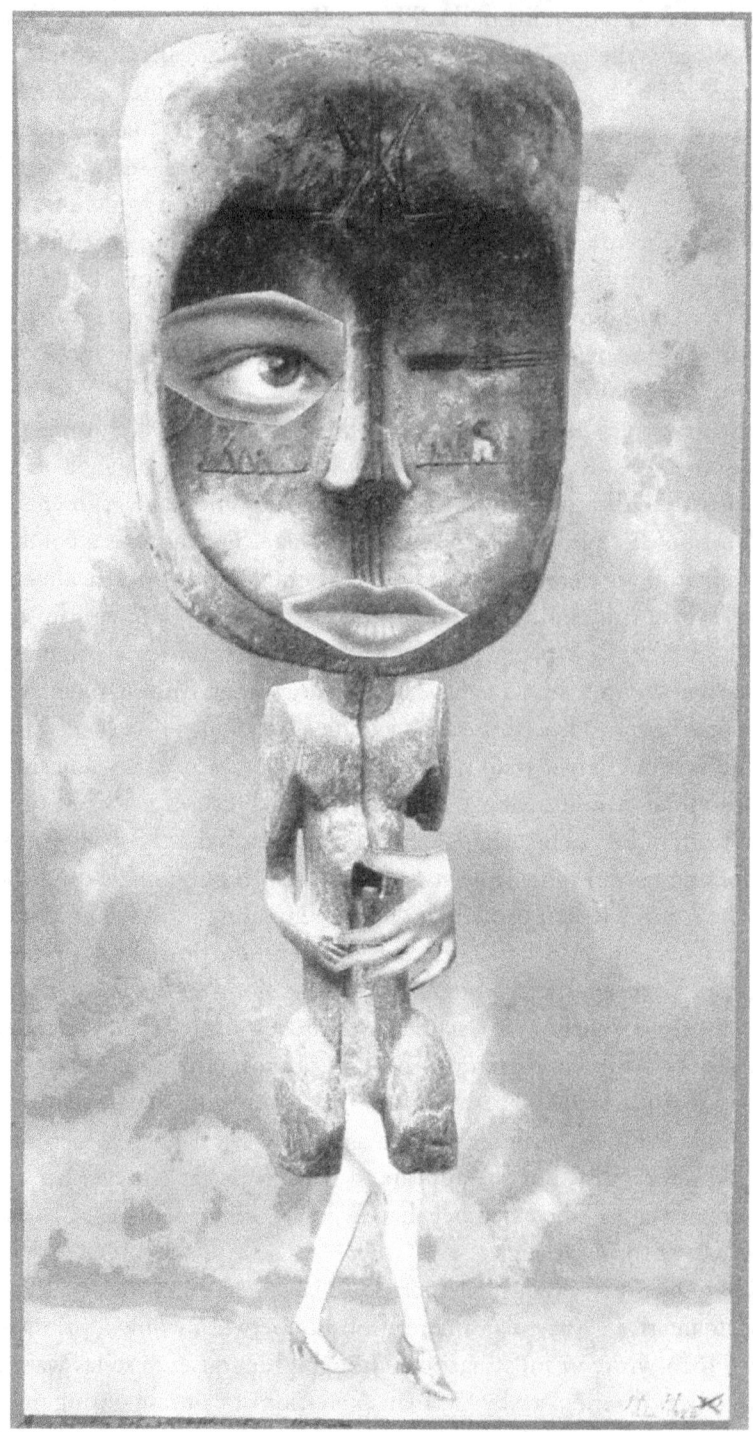

Figure 5.11. Hannah Höch, *Die Süsse* [The Sweet One] (ca. 1926). Photomontage with watercolor. 30 × 15.5 cm (11 13⁄16 × 6 1⁄8 inches). Museum Folkwang Essen. Photograph from Museum Folkwang Essen. Copyright 2009 Artists Rights Society (ARS), New York/VG Bild-Kunst, Bonn.

world as well as its subjective aspects, those contours of reality that revealed themselves to the expressionists' supposedly heightened and sensitized vision.[111] Supported by the art historian and aesthetician Wilhelm Worringer's interpretation of the abstract and transcendental character of Gothic art (its alienation from the flux of phenomena characteristic of the external world) as well as by the critic and historian of modern art Carl Einstein's understanding of the conceptual character of African sculpture (its ability to present the "pure" forms of objects as opposed to their merely visual aspects as seen from a particular perspective), expressionist artists like Ernst Ludwig Kirchner became famous for a type of painting and sculpture that eschewed fidelity to the exact contours of the external world and instead attempted to express deep interconnections between modern life and primitive, mythic forces.[112] And central to the work of the expressionists—and, in particular, to Kirchner's paintings made in the last few years before the outbreak of World War I—was the use of the modern woman to express the primitive energies at the heart of the modern metropolis.

As suggested by *The Sweet One*, Höch cited this tradition of expressionist primitivism to provoke her spectators to think about the use of the female figure as a symbol of those aspects of the modern world that seemed most threatening and out of control. By making the conflation of the modern woman and the "primitive" art object so explicit, the photomontage—once it was eventually shown in the late 1920s and early 1930s—could have potentially inspired reflection on this deep-seated convention in modern art.[113] German spectators, in other words, could have plausibly been caused to reflect on how certain sets of concepts—for example, "women," "nature," "children," and "primitive people"—were "naturally" associated in their culture by intellectuals and the general population alike. In addition, they might also have been provoked to reflect on the conventions that defined beauty in both the art and the mass media. The hybrid figure is simultaneously attractive and grotesque, an uncanny conflation of human and sculptural parts. Because of Höch's careful assembly, the figure's heterogeneous components seem to fit together, and for this reason, the image is all the more disturbing. Since the representation of the woman's body seems to "work" aesthetically, the spectator could have been prompted to ask why this was the case and, thus, to reflect both geographically and historically on the various conceptions of beauty that had circulated in human cultures up until the present day. And by comparing and contrasting different conceptualizations, he or she might have been led to recognize the relative or contextual nature of beauty—the fact that it was culturally constructed and that it changed relative to time and place.

By locating its cyborgian figure in the context of a museum (through its abstract background as well as its subtitle, "From an Ethnographic Museum"), *The Sweet One* also signaled that the concept of the primitive in Weimar culture had changed radically since the prewar moment of German expressionism. As Kristin Makholm has argued, Höch developed a highly self-conscious form of primitivism between the mid- and the late 1920s, one that recognized that European primitivism did not arise from an unmediated confrontation between artists and non-Western artifacts as was originally believed, but that it consisted of a set of beliefs and practices produced through the experience of "tribal" objects in relation to various aesthetic discourses, museum practices, and popular culture's embodiments of the primitive. By situating her figures in simulated museum settings rather than in the "wild," as it were, Höch's photomontages thus reminded their audiences that the ethnographic museum was the primary context in which European artists "discovered" non-Western art in the late nineteenth and early twentieth centuries—a place where diverse cultures were often presented in a geographically and temporally mixed fashion, and where, by the mid-1910s, modes of organization emphasizing formal similarities rather than cultural, geographic, or historical information were increasingly prevalent.[114] In addition, by using "primitive" imagery culled from newspapers and art magazines, Höch indicated that, over the past two decades, ethnographic objects as well as "tribal" lands and people had become fixtures in the German illustrated press and, thus, that the mass media also helped determine artists' conceptions of non-Western people and artifacts. Like Höch's primitivist photomontages, the popular press frequently juxtaposed primitive and modern forms; thus, for example, blacks were used to sell all forms of modern products such as shampoo and shaving cream,[115] and even more highbrow art magazines like *Der Querschnitt,* from which Höch appropriated many of her image fragments, presented non-Western people and artifacts side by side with images of Western performers.[116] By situating her primitivist works in a fictional ethnographic museum, Höch alluded to the fact that the old ideas supporting European primitivism were passé and that the primitive had become a part of the modern popular imagination. Because of their self-consciousness—as well as the fact that, no matter how carefully cropped and integrated, the various Western and non-Western parts that made up her cyborgian figures also remained distinct—Höch's photomontages suggested that a highly artificial and constructed concept of the primitive had become central to the modern world. Weimar Germany, in the words of Höch's contemporary Count Harry Kessler, who used them to describe a 1925 performance in Berlin by the African American entertainer Josephine Baker, had become a mixture of "ultramodern and ultraprimitive."[117]

Given the photomontage's highly self-conscious concept of the primitive, the spectator might also be led by *The Sweet One* to consider the artificial nature of the concept of race. As Charles Hirschman has recently argued, "Race and racism are not ancient or tribal beliefs but have developed apace with modernity over the last 400 years and reached their apogee in the late nineteenth and the first half of the twentieth century."[118] Hirschman distinguishes racism from ethnocentrism, "the nearly universal tendency to believe in the rightness of one's own group and the natural aversion to difference."[119] Ethnocentrism, as Hirschman defines it, is a common feature of most human societies, and it has remained relatively stable over time. Although it can promote xenophobia, it is also open to the cultural assimilation of people considered to be radically "other." It assumes that outsiders who give up their foreign ways can become full-fledged members of their adopted society. "Racism," on the other hand, holds that otherness is not simply a product of socialization, language, or culture, but is part of the inherent character of different groups. In modern terminology, racism is the belief that all humankind can be divided into a finite number of races with differing characteristics and capacities because of their genes or other inherited biological features. Therefore, adopted children inherit the attributes of their biological parents (and ancestors) and can never become the equals of their adoptive families or society.[120]

The modern concept of race thus presupposes that a person's outward physical appearances as defined by skin color, body size, and shape are always firmly correlated with innate characteristics such as temperament, abilities, predispositions, and propensities for certain types of behavior. Furthermore, it assumes that these characteristics are both heritable and fixed.[121]

This concept of race was a modern idea that developed since the seventeenth century,

> as a result of three transformations that created sharp divides between Europeans and other peoples: 1) the enslavement of millions of Africans in plantation economies in the New World; 2) the spread of European colonial rule across the world, especially Asia and Africa in the nineteenth century; and 3) the development of Social Darwinism—the pseudoscientific theory of European superiority that became dominant in the nineteenth century.[122]

After legitimating Western plantation slavery and European imperialism and colonialism during the seventeenth, eighteenth, and nineteenth centuries, the modern concept of race was severely attacked after World War II for its pernicious effects—for example, the role it played in perpetrating the Holocaust and other forms of genocide in the twentieth century.[123] Today, however, race is still central to the social and political definition of many—if not all—social groups in modern societies, although it has in many (but not all) cases lost its biological underpinnings. Race is now becoming to be understood as a social—as opposed to a biological—category that relies on a subject's own self-definition. As such, the new concept of race is illogical: "race," as Hirschman argues, "is whatever people think they are or whatever they think others are," and, for this reason, "race" should be replaced by the concept of "ethnicity," which is "explicitly subjective," "acknowledges multiple ancestries," and "recognizes that ethnic groups are porous and heterogeneous."[124]

Hirschman's definition and critique of the concept of race is useful because it summarizes the issues with which Höch's photomontages grappled. As suggested by the writings about race in both the scientific and the popular press during the Weimar Republic, the dominant definition of ethnicity was fairly biological and essentialist. And although Höch seems to have reversed the terms of German racist discourse in that she valorized African and other non-Western cultures as repositories of values being lost in the West, there is little in her art to suggest that she rejected a biological concept of race. Despite her sophisticated concept of primitivism, many of the stereotypes about so-called primitive people are repeated in her art. In *The Sweet One,* for example, the new woman is associated with African artifacts, sexuality, and, because of her oversized head that resembles that of an infant, perhaps also with childhood. At the same time, as the disturbing character of the various syntheses brought together in the sweet one's figure makes clear, the photomontage mobilizes the stereotypes of primitivism in such a way as to stretch them to their breaking point. If the contemporary concept of the cyborg implies a definite rejection of the idea of race in favor of a much more ambiguous notion of ethnicity, then Höch's ethnographic museum series can be seen as an important step toward this central insight. By bringing up the various stereotypes that circulated around the idea of the primitive so directly, and by showing how constructed and arbitrary primitivism's various equivalences actually were, *The Sweet One* thus began the important task of deconstructing the modern, biological understanding of race.

The Love Series

As is the case with Höch's other two series developed after the breakup of the Berlin Dada movement, the boundaries of her "love series" are porous. Certain works can fit into more than one series, and earlier photomontages—for example, *Dada-Tanz* [Dada Ball] (1922)—seem both thematically and compositionally related. Comprising at least six compositions, the love series was begun in the early 1920s, and it continued until around 1931.[125] Generally focusing on the interactions of two individuals, it examined flirtation, courtship, marriage, and sexuality. After Höch became involved with Brugman in 1926, the series also began to include representations of lesbianism. As was the case with the other sets, Höch for the most part created representations of general types as opposed to specific historical individuals. In addition, like the other groupings, the representations in the love series are ambiguous and populated by cyborgian characters that synthesize heterogeneous characteristics. Perhaps more than the works in any other series, however, the photomontages in the love series are highly psychologically charged—something that is not surprising, given their focus on human emotion and interpersonal relationships.

Die Kokette I [The Coquette I] (1923–25) (Figure 5.12) depicts a new woman—identified as such by her pearl necklace, simple bracelet, sheer stockings, pointed shoes, and short, fashionable, sleeveless evening dress—interacting with two bestial admirers. Standing directly in front of her, a baby with a dog's head raises its arms to the new women in a supplicating gesture, an object—possibly a gift—clutched between its hands. Directly behind the dog-baby hybrid stands the canine from which the head was apparently cut. Grafted to the dog's poised and (seemingly) disciplined and obedient body is the head of a man, and a photomontage fragment depicting a cloth scarf occludes the graft between the two species. All the figures are situated on simple collage pedestals—the woman sits on the highest one, while the two suitors rest on successively lower ones. They also display partial amputations: dog-baby's legs are truncated above the knees, the man-dog appears to have lost three of its four paws, and the woman has lost her thumb, neck, and the back of her head. The three pedestals rest on top of a flat raised area, and the background is a blank white void, enlivened only by a flat and oblong orange form in the upper-right corner, which suggests a sun, and across which a blackish-brown beetle flies or crawls.

Both violent and humorous at the same time, the photomontage displays numerous signs of physical transformation. The woman has been decapitated, a truncated and monstrous mask with blank eyes, a huge nose, and a grinning mouth replacing her head. Instead of possessing a full head, she seems to have only a hollow visage that hovers precariously above her neck and seems in imminent danger of falling to the floor.

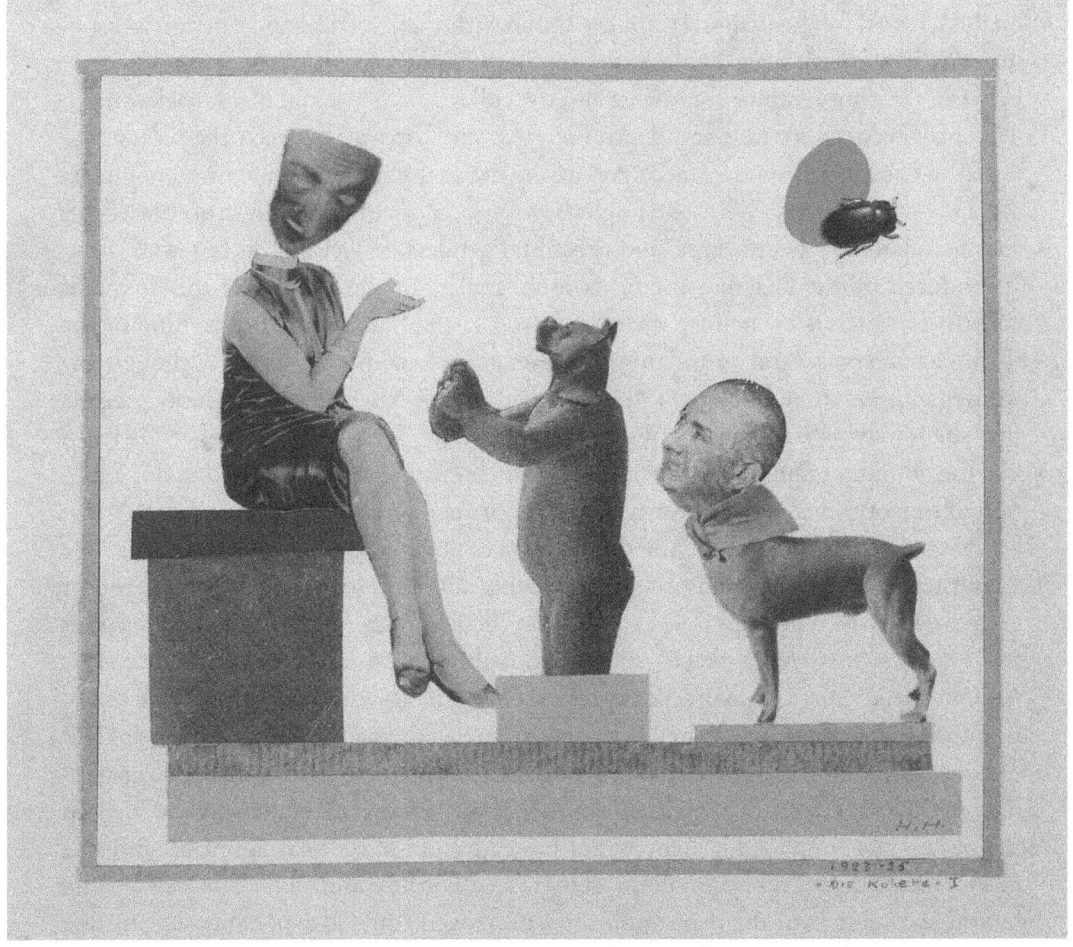

Figure 5.12. Hannah Höch, *Die Kokette I* [The Coquette I] (1923–25). Photomontage with collage. 18.5 × 20.5 cm (7⁵⁄₁₆ × 8¹⁄₁₆ inches). Institut für Auslandsbeziehungen, Stuttgart. Copyright 2009 Artists Rights Society (ARS), New York/VG Bild-Kunst, Bonn.

Despite the violence that has been done to her cranium, however, she sits on her pedestal in a casual yet confident manner, with her legs crossed and her right hand partially extended as if reaching to accept the dog-baby's gift or gesticulating while giving a lecture to her two admirers. Her two suitors, moreover, seem more comic than grotesque. The dog-baby's head appears too small for its body—something that makes it look slightly more adult. It gives the impression that it is pleading with the woman, presenting its gift as if it were a supplicant for some favor that the woman might possibly bestow. Waiting behind the dog-baby, the man-dog has the opposite problem: its head is too big for its body, a characteristic that makes it seem puny and perhaps less adult. Despite its mismatched and slightly deformed appearance, however, it stands at attention, although it is not entirely clear if it too is a suitor/supplicant or simply the dog-baby's pet or companion.

As a whole, the photomontage shows the influence of international constructivism. Not only is it extremely sparse and abstract, but it also possesses a strong rectilinear quality created by the pedestals and the frame with their vertical and horizontal articulations. The image plays between flatness and depth, a result of the strong contrast between the photographic fragments and the collage elements and blank background. This play between flatness and depth increases the disparity between the representational and abstract elements, and it potentially draws the spectator's attention to Höch's specific juxtapositions. Why, one might be prompted to ask, does the artist create this specific mixing of species, ages, and (possibly) genders, as well? (This last association is produced by the fact that the mask looks male.) In the context of the theme of courtship, which is created by the title as well as the hierarchical positioning of the three characters, several conflicting interpretations could easily arise. Although the woman appears to be in control, the fact that a mask has replaced her head suggests that she is playing a role or putting on a masquerade. Despite the fact that she looks like the dominant figure, it is possible that her elevation has also resulted in her adoption of stereotypes of female beauty and comportment created by the prevailing patriarchal culture. In addition, is the dog-baby actually trying to court her, or does the youngster plead for something else? Is it possibly adoption that the baby desires, or for the new woman to perhaps give birth to it in the first place? Höch had two abortions while she was involved with Hausmann, and, although she resisted starting a family with an already married man, she expressed her desire for children through a series of watercolors and paintings created between the late 1910s and the early 1920s.[126] In light of her personal desires—as well as the more general popular fears of *Volkstod,* or population decline, as a result of German women having fewer children during the Weimar Republic—the supplicating baby could be read as an allegorical figure begging the new woman to give up her modern lifestyle and become a mother. The strange and hybrid appearances of the two supplicants, moreover, could also possibly suggest that the activity of courtship caused formerly adult figures to regress to "earlier" infantile or animalistic states. Finally, the bug that moves across the orange collage element contributes an additional sense of unreality to the image. Because it has been appropriated as a complete image, it almost seems like a real bug walking across the photomontage's flat surface. As such, it makes the photomontage in its entirety seem more like a representation than a window on the world. And by emphasizing the photomontage's artificiality, the bug reminds the viewer that, despite its photographic source material, the work is not an objective representation of reality but a coded allegorical construction from which multiple messages can be deciphered.

Sexuality, which had increasingly become a topic of investigation and debate since the turn of the century, became even more of a flashpoint during the Weimar Republic. Debates raged about the roles of the sexes, the significance of marriage, the nature of the family, and the most appropriate forms of child rearing—arguments that were wrapped up with disputes about education, social policy, and government intervention as well as questions about population growth or decline. Among the most disputed topics was the right to an abortion, which was a punishable offense under Article 218 of the penal code.[127] Also controversial was the distribution of contraceptives, which was restricted by Articles 218 and 184.3, laws that prohibited the production, sale, and dissemination of "lewd objects."[128] There were also significant debates about legalizing homosexuality, which, according to Article 175, was illegal for men—but not, surprisingly, for women, whose potential for same-sex love was for the most part ignored. There was also a great deal of discussion about the right to divorce and whether the purpose of marriage was procreation or love.

The responses to these issues were varied—both from the right and from the left.[129] As Peukert argues, two different trajectories of thought inspired the progress toward sexual liberalization that began in the final decades of the Wilhelmine era and continued during the Weimar Republic. First, a movement for health and hygiene emerged, which viewed sexuality scientifically and tried to educate people on how to have healthy sex and prevent venereal disease.[130] Second, there was a movement associated with population policy, which was motivated by fear of a decline in the "healthy" sector of the German population as well as an increase in the number of people of supposedly "lesser value," made possible by the new state's welfare policies that mitigated the effects of "natural selection." Its proposed solutions were often eugenicist in both the positive and the negative sense; it advocated policies, in other words, that encouraged the "healthy" or "gifted" sections of the population to reproduce and that discouraged or prevented the procreation of Germans deemed "ill," "weak," "asocial," "genetically inferior," or otherwise of "less biological worth."[131] A range of political positions could be discovered in both trajectories, and, while these movements made discussing sexuality a greater part of the intellectual landscape, they also articulated new fears—about hereditary and venereal diseases, for example—while defining a new set of often-rigid sexual norms as to what was "natural," "normal," and "healthy."

Supporting these new developments in educational and social policy focusing on the scientific reform of human sexuality were new views about the nature of human eroticism and instinct. Sexuality, as Peukert suggests, was discussed during the Weimar Republic from two main perspectives.[132] There was a biological viewpoint geared toward rational intervention. Encouraged by the advances made in dealing with epidemic diseases such as cholera and tuberculosis, it aspired to define and classify all sexual behavior—both "normal" and "deviant"—in terms of clear, scientific categories that would then enable rational intervention. In addition, as has already been discussed, there was a psychoanalytic viewpoint, which was geared toward understanding the individual personality through a dialogue between an analyst and a patient that uncovered the patient's unique unconscious and developmental history. Defining the psyche as a product of both instinctual drives and socially defined mandates and prohibitions, psychoanalysis quickly attracted numerous adherents and practitioners who placed radically dissimilar emphases on different aspects of Freud's theories—a fact made clear by the unorthodox example of Otto Gross, whose thinking made such an impact on Hausmann. These new ways of viewing sexuality reached a mass audience during the Weimar Republic, where they offended traditionalist sectors of the population and led to more liberal and rational approaches to human love, eroticism, reproduction, child rearing, and family relations. Unfortunately, aspects of the biological viewpoint also led to horrifying eugenics policies during the Third Reich.

Höch's love series seems to engage with the viewpoints and debates about sexuality that characterized the Weimar Republic. As suggested above, *The Coquette I* perhaps evokes the specter of *Volkstod* by suggesting that the dog-baby begs the new woman to become its mother. In addition, the animalistic and infantile aspects of the woman's suitors seem to suggest the new ideas about the power of sexuality as an instinctual drive. The fact that two suitors stand at the feet of a single woman might also imply new ideas about open marriages such as those advocated by Hausmann.[133] Moreover, the hybridity of the figures might suggest eugenic ideas about the control of human reproduction, and, by resembling monsters, the two suitors raise fears about the propagation of the congenitally ill. Because they are so obviously chimeras formed out of different species, the two figures also imply that human beings can be radically transformed. Finally, because the images are composed out of the materials of the mass media, the photomontage as a whole formally evokes the public sphere in which these debates were happening. Sexuality, the photomontage might have suggested, was being influenced by the representations of it promulgated in films, books, magazines, and newspapers. In addition to the various organizations and schools of thought trying to influence public opinion as well as social and political policies, the burgeoning German media culture, the photomontage posits, was also having an effect on how Germans viewed and legislated the most intimate aspects of their lives.[134]

It was in its representations of female homosexuality, however, that Höch's love series revealed its most radical side. *Liebe* [Love] (1931) (Figure 5.13) depicts two hybrid female figures interacting against a yellow and beige background divided by a flat horizon line. The top figure, its back to the spectator, consists of a woman's white buttocks and thighs, another woman's calves and feet dressed in black high-heeled dress shoes, and the upper body and head of a four-winged insect. She appears to hover in the air. The second figure, its front to the spectator, consists of the crossed legs of a white woman, her feet encased in light-colored high-heeled dress shoes, the nude torso and arms of another white woman, and the head of a young African girl wearing a set of heavy necklaces. This lower figure lies recumbent on a group of "pillows," which appear to be constructed out of decorated baskets. For the most part, the photomontage elements are cut so as to integrate closely with the fragments next to them. However, in the case of the lower figure, one of her legs has been trimmed so as to suggest a second crotch, and thus the combination of photomontage elements implies that her lower body possesses three legs instead of two.

Overall the connotations of this photomontage are fairly clear. As suggested by the title, the nudity of the figures, their primarily female body parts, and their positioning

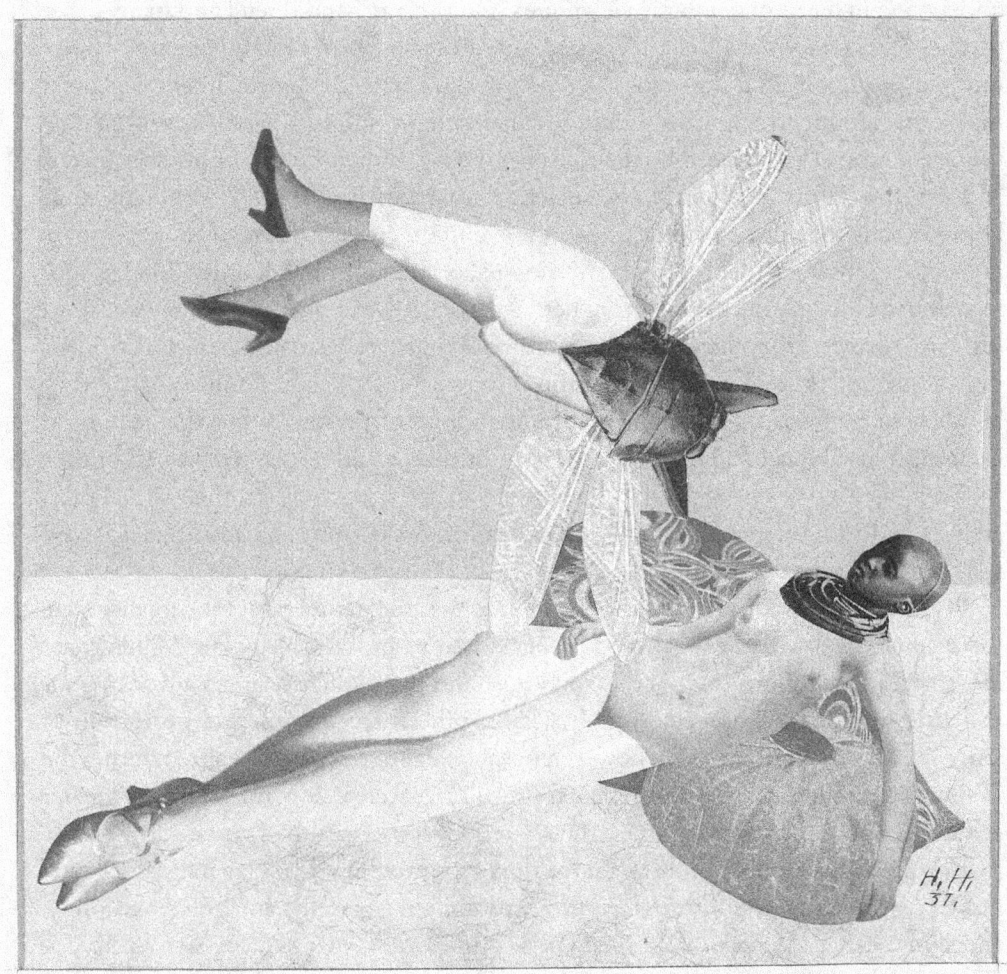

Figure 5.13. Hannah Höch, *Liebe* [Love] (1931). Photomontage. 21 × 21.8 cm (8¼ × 8⁹⁄₁₆ inches). National Gallery of Australia, Canberra. Photograph from National Gallery of Australia, Canberra. Copyright 2009 Artists Rights Society (ARS), New York/VG Bild-Kunst, Bonn.

vis-à-vis one anther, *Love* evokes lesbian sexuality. In addition, as suggested by the combination of white European and African body parts in the lower figure, the photomontage evokes ethnic mixing as well. Furthermore, because of the mixture of human and insect components in the upper figure, there is also a suggestion of the blending of different species—an implication that could equally imply an evolutionary or a devolutionary development. Finally, because of how the figures are positioned, in addition to sexuality, their interaction could also hint at the activities of feeding or dreaming. The top figure seems to hover above the bottom one like a bee about to take pollen from a flower. Moreover, because the bottom figure reclines on pillows with her eyes closed, she could also be read as asleep and dreaming of the figure above her.

What is not clear, however, is how the photomontage's various main lines of association connect with one another. During the Weimar Republic, homosexuality was understood in terms of two basic viewpoints. On the one hand, Freud and many other psychologists and sexologists understood human sexuality to be fundamentally polymorphous. Arguing that the human psyche was fundamentally bisexual, they explained that sexual identity was largely culturally constructed—and that people's eventual sexual orientations were formed by their interactions with their families, churches, peers, and other social institutions in the societies in which they lived.[135] Although adult homosexuality could not be unlearned, it was not biologically determined. Sexologists such as Magnus Hirschfeld and Otto Weininger, on the other hand, understood homosexuals to be biologically distinct from heterosexuals. Advocating the concept of a "third sex" or "intersex," they suggested that culture played a very small role in sexual identity and that one's biological predispositions were primary.[136] The homosexual, as they saw him or her, was a fundamentally different type of person.[137] For this reason, as Weininger and Hirschfeld both argued, homosexuals could not be reeducated or otherwise influenced to change and feel heterosexual desires; as a result, their sexual preferences had to be respected as natural according to their physiological makeup and thus not be criminalized by law.[138]

Paralleling the radical divergences of opinion on the nature of homosexuality were the disputes as to whether it should be permitted or proscribed by law. While some members of both the cultural–constructionist and the biologist camps advocated for its legalization, others opined strongly against official recognition and protection of same-sex desire. In point of fact, however, homosexuality was never legalized during the Weimar Republic, although homosexual subcultures were tacitly tolerated to a greater extent than before, particularly in Berlin.[139] In addition, a wealth of visual culture arose that made homosexuality more visible as the 1920s progressed.[140] Gay magazines such as *Der Eigene* and *Blätter für Menschenrecht* promoted gay rights and greater visibility, and films such as *Different from the Others* (1919), *Michael* (1924), *Sex in Chains: The Sexual Plight of Prisoners* (1928), and *Girls in Uniform* (1931) brought gay themes to an even wider audience.[141]

Love evokes this growth in the representations of homosexuality in the mass media through photomontage. By using preexisting imagery appropriated from illustrated newspapers and magazines, the photomontage suggests the diffusion of images of same-sex desire in Weimar culture through the technologies of mass reproduction and distribution. In addition, the photomontage also evokes both the biological and the social–constructionist viewpoints on the nature of homosexuality. On the one hand, the use of materials drawn from the mass media suggests the power of images to affect behavior and thus how one's sexual identity might be formed through examples that one discovers in one's culture. And by hinting at the role that representation plays in forming alternative forms of sexuality, the photomontage implies a social–constructionist point of view. On the other hand, the bottom figure's double crotch and suggestion of a third leg could be read as crudely biologizing lesbian sexuality by implying that this biracial woman possesses a penis. The blending of human and insect forms could also be interpreted as suggesting that homosexuals were biologically different from heterosexuals. Conversely, the intertwining of different ethnicities might imply equivalences between the so-called others of white, heterosexual, and patriarchal German society. The associations of dreaming, furthermore, could have suggested that unfettered homosexual love remained a utopian ideal in the still-repressive context of the Weimar Republic, and, in addition, dreaming might also imply that lovers sustain one another in spiritual as well as corporeal ways. As is the case with Höch's other photomontages, these chains of association conflict with one another in a way that potentially provokes an engaged spectator to explore these issues in his or her own life and society. Underlying the conflict of interpretations created by *Love,* however, is a fundamentally cyborgian notion of the individual. Whether biologically innate or developed through human interaction and exposure to representations of same-sex desire in the mass media, homosexuality, the photomontage implies, was a genuine and reasonable form of desire in the modern world.

Conclusion

As suggested by the photomontages that she created during the Weimar Republic, Höch employed the figure of the cyborg to explore alternative forms of human identity as well as the positive and negative implications of the overarching technological system that was rapidly changing her world. Not just a figure that represented the new, more dense interconnections between human beings and technology during the 1920s, the cyborg, in Höch's art, became a form through which she could raise fundamental questions about the "nature" of gender, race, and sexuality. Given the intentional ambiguity of Höch's representations as well as the divergent understandings of ethnic and sexual identity circulating in Weimar culture, it is impossible to identify Höch with either a purely essentialist or a purely social–constructionist position. Despite her left-wing politics and the ways in which her photomontages fit social–constructionist readings of human identity—that is, readings that suggest that gender, race, and sexuality are not immutable, biological essences but roles produced by the interactions of individuals with their families, peers, and societies—it cannot be definitively said that Höch held a social–constructionist view about all aspects of human identity. Instead, there are enough cues in her photomontages to suggest lingering traces of a biologically based and essentialist form of thinking—cues that at times, as I showed in the case of *Half Breed*, give her works disturbing quasi-racist overtones.[142]

If the cyborg in its most radical contemporary forms entails rejecting the idea of biological essences, then these analyses, by bringing the contemporary concept of the cyborg into relation with Höch's art, reveal that the Weimar Republic was a battleground for far more than just the political forces of the Left and the Right. It was, in addition, a time when radically different conceptualizations of the nature of human identity were proposed and debated. From today's perspective, which has seen so much violence result from the idea of fixed human essences, Höch's photomontages reveal the importance and power of these conflicting formulations of what it meant to be human. For it was in interwar Germany, during the crisis of classical modernity, that many of the most important definitions of human identity—both positive and negative—were not just articulated but acted on. And by attending to the conflicts embodied in Höch's photomontages as well as the personal, social, and political issues to which they refer, we can today gain insight into the range of historical effects to which these conflicts sometimes lead.

Conclusion

Dada Cyborgs in the Twenty-first Century

> Human biological brains are, in a very fundamental sense, incomplete
> cognitive systems. They are naturally geared to dovetail themselves, again
> and again, to a shifting web of surrounding structures, in the body and
> increasingly in the world.
>
> —ANDY CLARK, *Natural-Born Cyborgs: Minds, Technologies, and the*
> *Future of Human Intelligence* (2003)

By examining the Berlin Dada movement through the concept of the cyborg, a number of its characteristics previously either downplayed or ignored attain far greater
prominence.[1] Specifically, the cyborg has helped reveal the constructive side of Dadaism in Berlin: the movement's focus on using art to criticize traditional types of German subjects and to imagine and explore new forms of hybrid identity that might be
better suited to cope with the novel conflicts and possibilities inherent in postwar
modern life during the Weimar Republic. This shift in focus has, it is hoped, helped
dismiss once and for all a number of different myths that have circulated about Berlin
Dada: that it was just a critical or destructive movement; that it was simply concerned
with creating nonsensical works of anti-art designed to inspire institutional critique;
or that it was exclusively focused on the trauma of World War I. Although these sum-
mations must be recognized as revealing aspects of the movement, they should not be
overemphasized so as to obscure this movement's primary contribution: its interest in
creating new forms of nontraditional identity through cultural production. In addition,
the shift in focus facilitated by the cyborg has also helped bring out how the Berlin
Dadaists contributed to the development of a new form of spectator for modern art,
one that was engaged and highly self-conscious about the interrelationships between
making, viewing, and interpreting. By approaching their spectators through their artworks, and by suggesting commonalities between creators and interpreters, the Berlin

Dadaists hoped to transform the way art was perceived, break down the division between art and life, and inspire new modes of being and acting in the world.

The concept of the cyborg has also led this study to foreground the question of representation in Berlin Dada art to a far greater extent than has traditionally been the case. Although for the past ten or fifteen years scholars of Dada art have begun to focus more on subject matter, the idea that we should take seriously the representational strategies embodied in photomontage and assemblage was significantly undermined by mistaken perceptions about the nature of avant-garde art between the 1910s and the 1930s that have circulated in cultural discourse since the mid-1970s: that avant-garde art simply did away with the original contextual meanings of its various appropriated parts; that it caused the spectator to focus his or her attention solely on the conceptual principles behind a work's construction; and that readymade and assemblage practices could not be used representationally and critically at the same time.[2] Because this book demonstrates how complexly Dadaist works engaged with social, political, and conceptual meaning, it will put some of these misapprehensions to rest. In addition, although art historians have more recently begun to interpret Berlin Dada's subjects, they have not for the most part attempted to develop a more general theory as to how the art functions semantically. By examining how Dadaist photomontages and assemblages produce a form of negative dialectics and a conflict of interpretations, this study has attempted to fill that gap by defining the signifying mechanisms characteristic of Berlin Dada art. It thus hopes to curtail the practice of one-sided interpretation that seems particularly problematic in relation to Dada art through exhibiting how semantically open-ended the photomontages and assemblages were intended to be.

Attending to Dadaist representations of cyborgs has also allowed this book to construct a more integrated picture of the Berlin Dada movement than has often been the case. Because most of their works can be seen in terms of a project of remembering and criticizing traditional forms of identity and imagining and exploring new ones, the art objects they left behind can now be understood as part of the same creative impulse that was also responsible for their magazines, their theoretical and critical essays, their performances, their happenings, their media hoaxes, and their tendencies at times to live their lives as confrontational pieces of performance art. Seeing the continuities between Dada photomontage, assemblage, and the various artistic practices that preceded these endeavors allows us to develop a better understanding of how the Berlin Dadaists integrated art and life as well as to grasp how their art—as a coherent set of practices—lived on after the historical disintegration of the movement in Berlin.

Finally, an investigation into the Dada cyborg has also permitted us to see how artists and other cultural producers during the Weimar Republic were beginning to comprehend the tremendous changes in perception that were taking place through the growth of technology. The spectator that the Berlin Dadaists interpellated through their artworks was one sensitized to how new modes of technological perception were changing its experience of the world: how sight, hearing, touch, and various modes of (interior) perception, in other words, were being transformed through different forms of technological prosthesis. And by focusing on the various technologies through which perception was transformed during the early part of the twentieth century, human beings, the Dadaists seemed to believe, would discover the distributed nature of their identities—the fact that their subjectivities extended beyond the confines of their physical bodies and were, in fact, functions of a much broader technological network that interrelated human beings with one another, with machines, and with objective culture in their world.

I have stressed the Dadaists' anticipations of concepts like distracted perception, the waning of aura, and total mobilization because it seems to me that—in terms of both form and content—their art's most enduring legacy was its ability to evoke the technological networks in which human beings were becoming increasingly enmeshed and how these networks affected representation, perception, and identity in the modern world. The cyborg emerged during the Weimar Republic because it was here that a number of discourses—on subjectivity, the body, urban experience, the mass media, perception, and technology—first converged in such a way as to reveal how radically technologically mediated humanity had become. And the Dadaists' representations of various forms of hybrid organism constructed out of mechanically reproduced fragments appropriated from German commodity culture and the mass media, I believe, were a central part of this convergence. By emphasizing how the Dadaists' visual art anticipated textual formulations that appeared a few years later, I insist on the importance of art to conceptual thought—the fact that sometimes human beings give visual form to ideas before they become conceptualized in language. At the same time, it should be noted that I have not argued that this was necessarily or always the case. By locating Berlin Dada art in a plurality of discourses that emerged just before and just after its brief existence as an art movement, I hope to have demonstrated how art can form a part of a larger cultural conversation in which lines of direct influence play only a part and in which the creative stimuli that affect subsequent productions do not simply follow the traditional divisions between various media but—just as much—cross and subvert them.

Today, contemporary art and culture is perhaps most intensively engaged with issues having to do with hybrid identity as a function of human involvement with multiple systems of technological communication and control—an engagement so widespread that to enumerate a list of important artists and cultural producers does not seem necessary here. By reminding ourselves of how the Berlin Dadaists anticipated this trajectory of cultural activity (and, indeed, how they stand as precursors to much of the identity politics prominent in contemporary art since at least the 1990s), we can better trace the cyborgian focus on hybridity and technology in a historically specific fashion and recognize its development in a multiplicity of geographic and temporal contexts since the 1920s. In this way, we can recall the diverse individual, social, political, and technological influences that at different times pushed this trajectory in one way or another, remember the varied justifications as well as the roads not taken, and, perhaps most important, recollect the effects of and cultural responses to the various particular embodiments of this complex conjunction of issues. Thereby we may be able to envision new paths of development at the current juncture, novel solutions to a set of problems people have been wrestling with since at least the second decade of the twentieth century. That the Berlin Dada artists anticipated both the radical subject matter of hybrid identity and the cyborgian understanding of reality characteristic of many artists and cultural producers practicing today in no way diminishes the radicalism and importance of contemporary production. Instead, it simply shows that the strategies of representation that emerged in Berlin Dada art have yet to reveal their full potential.

Notes

Introduction

1. See, for example, Georg Kaiser, *The Coral: A Play in Five Acts* (1917), trans. Winifred Katzin (New York: Ungar, 1963); Kaiser, *Gas I: A Play in Five Acts* (1918), trans. Herman Scheffauer (New York: Ungar, 1957); Kaiser, *Gas II: A Play in Three Acts* (1920), trans. Winifred Katzin (New York: Ungar, 1963); and Martin Heidegger, *Being and Time* (1927), trans. Joan Stambaugh (Albany: State University of New York Press, 1996), in particular Heidegger's discussions of the "handiness" or "readiness-to-hand" *[Zuhandenheit]* of things in the world. For Jünger's photomontage account of technological modernity, which features numerous images of cyborgs, see Edmund Schultz, ed., *Die veränderte Welt: Eine Bilderfibel unserer Zeit* (Breslau: Wilh. Gottl. Korn Verlag, 1933). Although Schultz is credited as the editor, and Jünger is simply listed as the author of the introduction, the chapter titles, page headings, and captions clearly reflect Jünger's thinking of the late 1920s and early 1930s. See, for example, Ernst Jünger, "Total Mobilization" (1930), trans. Joel Golb and Richard Wolin, in *The Heidegger Controversy,* ed. Richard Wolin (Cambridge, Mass.: MIT Press, 1993), 119–39; Jünger, "War and Photography" (1930), trans. Anthony Nassar, *New German Critique* 59 (Spring–Summer 1993): 24–26; Jünger, "On Danger" (1931), trans. Donald Reneau, *New German Critique* 59 (Spring–Summer 1993): 27–32; Jünger, *Der Arbeiter: Herrschaft und Gestalt* (1932; repr. Stuttgart: Klett-Cotta, 1982); and Jünger, "Photography and the 'Second Consciousness'" (1934), an excerpt from "On Pain" in *Photography in the Modern Era: European Documents and Critical Writings,* ed. Christopher Phillips (New York: Aperture, 1989), 207–8. Fritz Lang's most cyborgian film is, of course, *Metropolis* (1927); however, the interface between human and machine looms large in many of Lang's movies from the Weimar era, including *Dr. Mabuse the Gambler* (1922), *Spies* (1928), *Woman in the Moon* (1929), *M* (1931), and *The Testament of Dr. Mabuse* (1933). On Lang's cinema and its relationship to technological modernity, see Tom Gunning, *The Films of Fritz Lang: Allegories of Vision and Modernity* (London: BFI, 2000); Thomas Elsaesser, *Metropolis* (London: BFI, 2000); Anton Kaes, *M,* rev. ed. (London: BFI, 2001).

2. For a good account of the futuristic novel in Weimar Germany, a genre of popular

literature that often treated cyborgian themes, see Peter S. Fisher, *Fantasy and Politics: Visions of the Future in the Weimar Republic* (Madison: University of Wisconsin Press, 1991). On the spectacle of modernity in metropolitan visual culture during the Weimar Republic, see Janet Ward, *Weimar Surfaces: Urban Visual Culture in 1920s Germany* (Berkeley: University of California Press, 2001).

3. My original formulation of this project appeared in print as Matthew Biro, "The New Man as Cyborg: Figures of Technology in Weimar Visual Culture," *New German Critique* 62 (Spring–Summer 1994): 71–110.

4. See the examples of human–machine and animal–machine synthesis collected in Bruce Mazlish, *The Fourth Discontinuity: The Co-Evolution of Humans and Machines* (New Haven, Conn.: Yale University Press, 1993). In addition, see the examples of nineteenth-century cyborgs collected in Friedrich Wendel, *Das neunzehnte Jahrundert in der Karikatur* (Berlin: J. H. W. Dietz Nachfolger, 1925). These examples of cyborgs in caricature include "The Pioneer of Modern Civilization," an 1898 caricature of Wilhelm II published in *Puck,* reprinted in Wendel as Plate 4. Other nineteenth-century examples in Wendel's collection include Figure 1 (page 5) and Figure 135 (page 187). Finally, Hanno Möbius connects the histories of both prosthetics and automata to the development of montage and collage in art. See Hanno Möbius, *Montage und Collage: Literatur, bildene Künste, Film, Fotografie, Musik, Theater bis 1933* (Munich: Wilhelm Fink Verlag, 2000), 104–7.

5. See Manfred E. Clynes and Nathan S. Kline, "Cyborgs and Space" (1960), in *The Cyborg Handbook,* ed. Chris Hables Gray (New York: Routledge, 1995), 29–33.

6. Norbert Wiener, *Cybernetics, or, Control and Communication in the Animal and the Machine* (New York: John Wiley and Sons, 1948), 19.

7. Ibid., 10.

8. Ibid., 13.

9. Ibid., 11, 31.

10. Norbert Wiener, *The Human Use of Human Beings: Cybernetics and Society,* rev. ed. (Garden City, N.Y.: Doubleday, 1954), 162.

11. Wiener, *Cybernetics,* 37.

12. "Let us remember that the automatic machine, whatever we think of any feelings it may have or may not have, is the precise economic equivalent of slave labor. Any labor which competes with slave labor must accept the economic conditions of slave labor. It is perfectly clear that this will produce an unemployment situation, in comparison with which the present recession and even the depression of the thirties will seem a pleasant joke. This depression will ruin many industries—possibly even the industries which have taken advantage of the new potentialities. However, there is nothing in the industrial tradition which forbids an industrialist to make a sure and quick profit, and to get out before the crash touches him personally.

"Thus the new industrial revolution is a two-edged sword. It may be used for the benefit of humanity, but only if humanity survives long enough to enter a period in which such a benefit is possible. It may also be used to destroy humanity, and if it is not used intelligently it can go very far in that direction" (Wiener, *Human Use of Human Beings,* 162).

13. Wiener, *Human Use of Human Beings,* 46–47.

14. On the dialectic between self and enemy in Weiner's thinking, see Peter Galison, "The Ontology of the Enemy: Norbert Wiener and the Cybernetic Vision," *Critical Inquiry* 21, no. 1 (Autumn 1994): 265.

15. Wiener, *Human Use of Human Beings,* 128.

16. Ibid., 129.

17. Ibid., 58.

18. Ibid., 96–102.

19. N. Katherine Hayles, *How We Became Posthuman: Virtual Bodies in Cybernetics, Literature, and Informatics* (Chicago: University of Chicago Press, 1999), 2–7.

20. On the Macy conferences, see Steve Joshua Heims, *Constructing a Social Science for Postwar America: The Cybernetics Group, 1946–1953* (Cambridge, Mass.: MIT Press, 1991); and Jean-Pierre Dupuy, *The Mechanization of the Mind: On the Origins of Cognitive Science,* trans. M. B. DeBevoise (Princeton, N.J.: Princeton University Press, 2000).

21. Donna J. Haraway, "A Cyborg Manifesto: Science, Technology, and Socialist-Feminism in the Twentieth Century" (1985), in *Simians, Cyborgs, and Women: The Reinvention of Nature* (New York: Routledge, 1991), 150.

22. Ibid., 173–81.

23. Ibid., 155.

24. Ibid., 151.

25. Ibid., 151–52.

26. Ibid., 153.

27. Ibid., 163.

28. Ibid., 163–64, 170. The remainder of this paragraph is not a summary of Haraway's position but my own interpretation of how the growth of technology and different ways of defining the subject have helped dissolve the subject's integrity. This account does not, however, contradict Haraway's model of the cyborg and the administered world in which it lives, and thus it may stand as a useful supplement to her discussion.

29. Ibid., 166–69.

30. Ibid., 169.

31. Ibid., 178.

32. Ibid., 163.

33. Ibid., 157.

34. Ibid., 177.

35. Allison Muri, *The Enlightenment Cyborg: A History of Communications and Control in the Human Machine, 1660–1830* (Toronto: University of Toronto Press, 2007).

36. Haraway, "Cyborg Manifesto," 150.

37. On the difference between telepresence and telerobotics, see Andy Clark, *Natural-Born Cyborgs: Minds, Technologies, and the Future of Human Intelligence* (New York: Oxford University Press, 2003), 89–114.

38. Since the 1990s, several good studies have been published on the subjects of Berlin Dada; "subjects" here understood as a set of characteristic figures, objects, and settings common to a group of artists and that have been invested with commonly held meanings and concepts. See, for example, Maud Lavin, *Cut with the Kitchen Knife: The Weimar Photomontages of Hannah Höch* (New Haven, Conn.: Yale University Press, 1993); Maria Makela, "The Misogynist Machine: Images of Technology in the Work of Hannah Höch," in *Women in the Metropolis: Gender and Modernity in Weimar Culture,* ed. Katharina von Ankum (Berkeley: University of California Press, 1997), 106–27; Brigid Doherty, "'See: We Are All Neurasthenics!' or, The Trauma of Dada Montage," *Critical Inquiry* 24, no. 1 (Autumn 1997): 82–132; Doherty, "Figures of the Pseudorevolution," *October* 84 (Spring 1998): 65–89; Sherwin Simmons, "Advertising Seizes Control of Life: Berlin Dada and the Power of Advertising," *Oxford Art Journal* 22, no. 1 (1999): 119–46; and Hanne Bergius, *"Dada Triumphs!" Dada Berlin, 1917–1923, Artistry of Polarities,* trans. Brigitte Pichon (New Haven, Conn.: Hall, 2003).

39. See, for example, Nezar AlSayyad, ed., *Hybrid Urbanism: On the Identity Discourse and the Built Environment* (Westport, Conn.: Praeger, 2001), esp. 1–18.

40. See, for example, Pnina Werbner and Tariq Modood, eds., *Debating Cultural Hybridity: Multi-Cultural Identities and the Politics of Anti-Racism* (Atlantic Highlands, N.J.: Zed Books, 1997), and, especially, the volume's final essay, Nikos Papastergiadis, "Tracing Hybridity in Theory," 257–81. In terms of Papastergiadis's typology of conceptualizations, the definition of hybridity articulated above shares elements with the conceptualizations of both Stuart Hall and Homi Bhabha. In the same volume, Werbner notes the connections between the concept of the cyborg and debates about cultural hybridity. See Pnina Werbner, "Introduction: The Dialectics of Cultural Hybridity," 1–26, esp. 8–11.

41. See, for example, Gill Perry, "Primitivism and the 'Modern,'" in *Primitivism, Cubism, Abstraction: The Early Twentieth Century,* ed. Charles Harrison, Francis Frascina, and Gill Perry (New Haven, Conn.: Yale University Press, 1993), 3–85. On primitivism in early-twentieth-century German art, see Jill Lloyd, *German Expressionism: Primitivism and Modernity* (New Haven, Conn.: Yale University Press, 1991).

42. Lloyd, *German Expressionism,* vii.

43. Perry, "Primitivism," 34–36, 63.

44. On the *Brücke* artists' knowledge of—and contact with—tribal art and culture, see Lloyd, *German Expressionism,* esp. 26–29, 39, 68–82, 169–85, 191–94, 199–211, and 216–34. On their contact with popular representations of the primitive, see, in particular, Lloyd, *German Expressionism,* 30–31, 86–96.

45. Lloyd, *German Expressionism,* vii.

46. Papastergiadis, "Tracing Hybridity in Theory," esp. 262–64.

47. By calling the conceptual models of Marx, Nietzsche, and Freud "systems," I do not wish to underemphasize their antisystematic aspects. Indeed, all of these thinkers conceived of modern identity as having a profoundly unconscious and material side: a side that made humans open to development and exploitation through technological systems.

48. Sigmund Freud, *Group Psychology and the Analysis of the Ego,* trans. and ed. James Strachey (New York: Norton, 1959), 46.

49. Ibid., 46–51.

50. Ibid., 52–53.

51. Adolf Behne, "Dada," *Die Freiheit* (July 1920), in *Hannah Höch: Eine Lebenscollage* vol. 1, pt. 2, ed. Berlinische Galerie and Cornelia Thater-Schulz (1919–20; repr. Berlin: Argon Verlag, 1989), 680.

52. On the concept of modernity in the work of these three thinkers, see David Frisby, *Fragments of Modernity: Theories of Modernity in the Work of Simmel, Kracauer, and Benjamin* (Cambridge, Mass.: MIT Press, 1986).

53. Benjamin was an antisubjectivist thinker in that he rejected a concept of the subject as something fully rational and conscious. In addition, he rejected the Hegelian concept of the subject—adopted by Marx and much of the Marxist tradition—as a creative and consistently self-improving "rational consciousness" that realized itself on an individual and a collective level in and through history. The subject, however, remains a part of Benjamin's thinking in its corporeal, libidinal, and emotional aspects: aspects that Benjamin theorized in the 1920s through the concept of the human being as "creature."

54. Martin Jay, *Adorno* (Cambridge, Mass.: Harvard University Press, 1984), 14–15.

55. Theodor W. Adorno, *Aesthetic Theory* (1970), trans. Robert Hullot-Kentor (Minneapolis: University of Minnesota Press, 1997); Peter Bürger, *Theory of the Avant-Garde* (1974), trans. Michael Shaw (Minneapolis: University of Minnesota Press, 1984).

56. Max Horkheimer and Theodor W. Adorno, *Dialectic of Enlightenment* (1944), trans. John Cumming (New York: Continuum, 1972).

57. See Frisby, *Fragments of Modernity*, 3, 6–9. For Kracauer's excellent analysis of Simmel's "philosophy of culture," see Siegfried Kracauer, "Georg Simmel," in *The Mass Ornament: Weimar Essays*, trans. and ed. Thomas Y. Levin (Cambridge, Mass.: Harvard University Press, 1995), 225–57.

58. See Walter Benjamin, *The Arcades Project* (1982), trans. Howard Eiland and Kevin McLaughlin (Cambridge, Mass.: Harvard University Press, 1999), 461.

59. See Walter Benjamin, "On the Concept of History" (1940), trans. Harry Zohn, in *Walter Benjamin: Selected Writings, Vol. 4, 1938–1940*, ed. Howard Eiland and Michael W. Jennings (Cambridge, Mass.: Harvard University Press, 2003), 389–400.

60. See, for example, Rosalind Krauss's widely influential criticisms of iconographic and biographical approaches to Picasso's art, "In the Name of Picasso," in *The Originality of the Avant-Garde and Other Modernist Myths* (Cambridge, Mass.: MIT Press, 1985), 23–40. On why rejecting iconography in modern and contemporary art history is problematic, see Richard Meyer, "Two on One: Richard Meyer on Robert Rauschenberg," *Artforum* 42, no. 6 (February 2004): 25–26; see also Alex Potts's convincing counterexample to a purely formalist reading of Rauschenberg's combines and his analysis of the formalism–iconography debate, "Robert Rauschenberg and David Smith: Compelling Contiguities," *Art Bulletin* 89, no. 1 (March 2007): 148–59, esp. n. 22.

61. As is the case with the concept of modernism articulated above, my definition of postmodernism is a conceptual abstraction, and, as such, it does not do complete justice to the phenomenon that it attempts to define. At the same time, the basic meanings ascribed here to both terms conform to numerous actual definitions and uses of the concepts in art history and other forms of cultural discourse, and thus provide useful heuristic models to evaluate different ways to discuss the development of advanced art in the nineteenth and twentieth centuries. Among the texts that I have found particularly useful in thinking about these definitions are the following: T. J. Clark, "Clement Greenberg's Theory of Art," *Critical Inquiry* 9, no. 1 (September 1982): 139–56; Clark, "Arguments about Modernism: A Reply to Michael Fried," in *The Politics of Interpretation*, ed. W. J. T. Mitchell (Chicago: University of Chicago Press, 1983), 239–48; Clark, *The Painting of Modern Life: Paris in the Art of Manet and His Followers* (Princeton, N.J.: Princeton University Press, 1984); Clark, *Farewell to an Idea: Episodes from a History of Modernism* (New Haven, Conn.: Yale University Press, 1999); Douglas Crimp, *On the Museum's Ruins* (Cambridge, Mass.: MIT Press, 1993); Hal Foster, ed., *The Anti-Aesthetic: Essays on Postmodern Culture* (Port Townsend, Wash.: Bay, 1983); Michael Fried, *Three American Painters: Kenneth Noland, Jules Olitski, Frank Stella* (Cambridge, Mass.: Harvard University/Fogg Art Museum, 1965); Fried, "How Modernism Works: A Response to T. J. Clark," *Critical Inquiry* 9, no. 1 (September 1982): 217–34; Clement Greenberg, "Avant-Garde and Kitsch," *Partisan Review* 6, no. 5 (Fall 1939): 34–49; Greenberg, "Towards a Newer Laocoon," *Partisan Review* 7, no. 4 (July–August 1940): 296–310; Greenberg, "Modernist Painting" (1960), in *The Collected Essays and Criticism, Vol. 4: Modernism with a Vengeance, 1957–1969* (Chicago: University of Chicago Press, 1995), 85–94; David Harvey, *The Condition of Postmodernity: An Inquiry into the Origins of Cultural Change* (Cambridge, Mass.: Blackwell, 1990); Andreas Huyssen, *After the Great Divide: Modernism, Mass Culture, Postmodernism* (Bloomington: Indiana University Press, 1986); Fredric Jameson, *Postmodernism, or, The Cultural Logic of Late Capitalism* (Durham, N.C.: Duke University Press, 1991); Krauss, *Originality of the Avant-Garde*; Donald Kuspit, *The Cult of the Avant-Garde Artist* (New York: Cambridge University Press, 1993); Kuspit, *The End of Art* (New York: Cambridge

University Press, 2004); Jean-François Lyotard, *The Postmodern Condition: A Report on Knowledge,* trans. Geoff Bennington and Brian Massumi (Minneapolis: University of Minnesota Press, 1984); and Craig Owens, *Beyond Recognition: Representation, Power, and Culture* (Berkeley: University of California Press, 1992).

62. Bürger separates Brecht from the avant-garde in that Brecht did not seek to destroy the institution of art as did the historical avant-garde, but instead sought to refunction it (*Theory of the Avant-Garde,* 88–89).

63. Bürger, *Theory of the Avant-Garde,* 22, 50–54.

64. Ibid., 49.

65. Ibid., 63.

66. Ibid., 18.

67. Ibid., 53.

68. Ibid., 56, 72–73.

69. Ibid., 56.

70. Ibid., 80–82.

71. Ibid., 64–65.

72. Ibid., 67.

73. Ibid., 69–71.

74. Ibid., 57–58, 91–92.

75. See Benjamin H. D. Buchloh, "From Faktura to Factography," in *The Contest of Meaning: Critical Histories of Photography,* ed. Richard Bolton (Cambridge, Mass.: MIT Press, 1989), 49–80.

76. See Benjamin H. D. Buchloh, "The Primary Colors for the Second Time: A Paradigm Repetition of the Neo-Avant-Garde," *October* 37 (Summer 1986): 41–52; and Hal Foster, "What's Neo about the Neo-Avant-Garde?" *October* 70 (Fall 1994): 5–32. To his credit, Bürger has over the years significantly changed his original evaluation of neo-avant-garde art. See Peter Bürger, "Letter to Jean-François Chevrier," in *Politics, Poetics: Documenta X, the Book,* ed. Catherine David and Jean-François Chevreir (Amsterdam: Cantz, 1997), 379–80; see also Peter Bürger, "Im Schatten von Beuys: Anmerkungen zum Thema Kunst und Philosophie Heute," *Kunstforum International* 90 (July–September 1987).

77. Clark, "Clement Greenberg's Theory of Art," 147.

1. Berlin Dada

1. Andy Clark, *Natural-Born Cyborgs: Minds, Technologies, and the Future of Human Intelligence* (New York: Oxford University Press, 2003), 3.

2. William J. Mitchell expresses both ideas quite well when he argues that "we are at the endgame of a process that began when our distant ancestors started to clothe themselves with second skins stripped from other creatures, to extend and harden their hands with simple tools and weapons, and to record information by scratching marks on surfaces. It picked up speed when our more recent forebears began to wire up telegraph, telephone, and packet-switching networks, to place calls, to log in, and to download dematerialized information to wireless portable devices. It is repeated whenever a child learns to do these things; for the cyborg, ontogeny recapitulates phylogeny. It is not that we have become posthuman in the wireless network era; since Neanderthal early-adopters first picked up sticks and stones, we have never been human" (*Me++: The Cyborg Self and the Networked City* [Cambridge, Mass.: MIT Press, 2003], 168). Although I am not certain that we can characterize even our contemporary moment as the "endgame" of this process, Mitchell's characterization of the long-standing human–technological symbiosis seems to me to be

correct in its strong emphasis on the centrality of various forms of human communicative media to the evolution of the cyborg.

3. The erasure of embodiment in the development of cybernetics is a central theme of N. Katherine Hayles's work on cybernetics and literature. See N. Katherine Hayles, *How We Became Posthuman: Virtual Bodies in Cybernetics, Literature, and Informatics* (Chicago: University of Chicago Press, 1999). I am indebted to Hayles's arguments as to why this erasure is problematic.

4. On Zurich Dada, see Hans Richter, *Dada: Art and Anti-Art,* trans. David Britt (London: Thames and Hudson, 1965), 11–80; Brigitte Pichon and Karl Riha, eds., *Dada Zurich: A Clown's Game from Nothing* (New York: Hall, 1996); Leah Dickerman, "Zurich," in *Dada: Zurich, Berlin, Hannover, Cologne, New York, Paris,* ed. Leah Dickerman (Washington, D.C.: D.A.P./National Gallery of Art, 2005), 16–83; and Tom Sandqvist, *Dada East: The Romanians of Cabaret Voltaire* (Cambridge, Mass.: MIT Press, 2006).

5. On New York Dada, see Richter, *Dada: Art and Anti-Art,* 81–100; Francis M. Naumann with Beth Venn, *Making Mischief: Dada Invades New York* (New York: Whitney Museum of American Art, 1996); Francis M. Naumann, *New York Dada, 1915–1923* (New York: Abrams, 1994); Amelia Jones, *Irrational Modernism: A Neurasthenic History of New York Dada* (Cambridge, Mass.: MIT Press, 2004); and Michael R. Taylor, "New York," in Dickerman, *Dada,* 274–372.

6. Cologne Dada emerged slightly later in Germany—namely, in early 1919—and it was less overtly political than Berlin Dada. Cologne was also more peaceful than Berlin, since it was occupied by British troops, and consequently it did not see the same sort of political fighting that occurred in other German cities. On Cologne Dada, see Sabine T. Kriebel, "Cologne," in Dickerman, *Dada,* 214–73.

7. When he first returned to Berlin in January 1917, Huelsenbeck was struck by the differences between the two cities: "In Zurich the international profiteers sat in the restaurants with well-filled wallets and rosy cheeks, ate with their knives and smacked their lips in a merry hurrah for the countries that were bashing each other's skulls in. Berlin was a city of tightened stomachers, of mounting, thundering hunger, where hidden rage was transformed into a boundless money lust, and men's minds were concentrating more and more on questions of naked existence. Here we would have to proceed with entirely different methods, if we wanted to say something to the people" (*En Avant Dada: A History of Dadaism* [1920], trans. Ralph Manheim, in *The Dada Painters and Poets: An Anthology,* 2nd ed., ed. Robert Motherwell [Boston: Hall, 1981], 39).

8. See Richard Huelsenbeck, "Collective Dada Manifesto" (1918), in Motherwell, *Dada Painters and Poets,* 242–43.

9. The politics of the Berlin Dada artists ranged from communist to anarchist. Heartfield, the most unambiguously "communist" Dada artist, was also the most practically engaged. His dust jackets for the German translations of novels by Upton Sinclair and Ilya Ehrenburg, published by Malik Verlag, were designed to attract the proletariat to communist thought and literature. Later, as an artist working for Willi Münzenberg's *Arbeiter Illustrierte Zeitung* [Workers' Illustrated Newspaper, or *AIZ*], Heartfield produced devastating critiques of the National Socialist Party. See Peter Pachnicke and Klaus Honnef, eds., *John Heartfield* (New York: Abrams, 1992). Baader and Hausmann are the primary examples of the more anarchist side of the Berlin Dada movement. Their anarchism was manifested by their spontaneous performances, stunts, and media hoaxes designed to provoke public uproar, as well as by their unwillingness to restrict their social criticism and provocation to a simple communist message. See Stephen C. Foster, "Johannes Baader: The Complete Dada," in *Dada/Dimensions,* ed. Stephen C. Foster (Ann Arbor, Mich.:

UMI Research Press, 1985), 249–71. On postwar political violence in Berlin, see Thomas Friedrich, Andreas Hallen, Diethart Kerbs, Tatjana Schmolling, and Karin Teske, *Revolution und Fotografie, Berlin 1918/19* (Berlin: Neue Gesellschaft für bildende Kunst/Verlag Dirk Nishen, 1989).

10. "Instead of continuing to produce art, Dada, in direct contrast to abstract art, went out and found an adversary. Emphasis was laid on the movement, on struggle" (Huelsenbeck, *En Avant Dada,* 41).

11. See, for example, Richter, *Dada,* 102–3; and Brigid Doherty, "Berlin," in Dickerman, *Dada,* 87.

12. Richard Huelsenbeck, "First Dada Speech in Germany" (1918), in *Dada Almanac,* ed. Richard Huelsenbeck (1920), trans. Malcolm Green, Derk Wynand, Terry Hale, Barbara Wright, Antony Melville, and Susan Barnett (London: Atlas, 1993), 111–12.

13. Huelsenbeck, "First Dada Speech," 112. On the concept of "bluff," see Raoul Hausmann, "Dada in Europa," *Der Dada* 3 (April 1920): 5–7; see also Malcolm Green, preface to Huelsenbeck, *Dada Almanac,* viii–ix.

14. Huelsenbeck, "First Dada Speech," 113.

15. Richter, *Dada,* 20–22.

16. See Richard Huelsenbeck, "About My Poetry" (1956), trans. Joachim Neugroschel, in *Memoirs of a Dada Drummer,* ed. Hans J. Kleinschmidt (Berkeley: University of California Press, 1974), 167–69, esp. 168–69.

17. On the history of *Neue Jugend,* see Roy F. Allen, *Literary Life in German Expressionism and the Berlin Circles* (Ann Arbor, Mich.: UMI Research Press, 1983), 211–13, 229–39; and James Fraser and Steven Heller, *The Malik-Verlag 1916–1947: Berlin, Prague, New York* (New York: Goethe House, 1984), 20.

18. For Herzfelde's account of *Neue Jugend,* see Wieland Herzfelde, "How a Publishing House Was Born," in *The Era of German Expressionism,* ed. Paul Raabe (Woodstock, N.Y.: Overlook, 1985), 219–20; see also Raabe's editorial notes, 350–51. See also Wieland Herzfelde, "On Founding the Malik-Verlag" (1927), in Fraser and Heller, *Malik-Verlag,* 10–12. On *Neue Jugend*'s complex publishing history, in which earlier numbers were reprinted and added to later numbers, and which also included an edition of 1919, see Hanne Bergius, *"Dada Triumphs!" Dada Berlin, 1917–1923, Artistry of Polarities,* trans. Brigitte Pichon (New Haven, Conn.: Hall, 2003), 378, 380.

19. For examples of early forms of Berlin Dadaist layout and typography, see the reproductions of the pamphlet to the *Kleine Grosz-Mappe* [Small Grosz Portfolio] (1917) and *Neue Jugend* [New Youth] (June 1917) in Pachnicke and Honnef, *John Heartfield,* 69–76.

20. On the history of *Die freie Strasse,* see Allen, *Literary Life in German Expressionism,* 58–59, 131, 246.

21. Raoul Hausmann, "Club Dada: Berlin 1918–20," in Raabe, *Era of German Expressionism,* 225.

22. "I told Herr Neumann I would give a brief introductory speech. . . . Then, without his or my friends' knowledge, I spoke about Dada. I said the reading was dedicated to Dada" (Richard Huelsenbeck, "The Dada Drummer" [1957], trans. Joachim Neugroschel, in *Memoirs of a Dada Drummer,* 56). "The Dada Drummer" is a translation of Richard Huelsenbeck, *Mit Witz, Licht und Grütze: Auf den Spuren des Dadismus* (Wiesbaden: Limes Verlag, 1957).

23. See the reviews collected in Karin Füllner, *Dada Berlin in Zeitungen: Gedächtnisfeiern und Skandale* (Siegen: Universität-Gesamthochschule-Siegen/MuK, 1986), 15–18. The evening, however, did not stop Däubler and Hermann-Neisse from continuing to collaborate with the Dada artists over the next few years.

24. On Hausmann's connections to *Neue Jugend,* a journal to which he never contributed, see Timothy O. Benson, *Raoul Hausmann and Berlin Dada* (Ann Arbor, Mich.: UMI Research Press, 1987), 65–66. On Hausmann's much closer relationship to the circle around *Die freie Strasse,* see Benson, *Raoul Hausmann and Berlin Dada,* 67–72.

25. Mel Gordon, "Dada Berlin: A History of Performance (1918–1920)," *Drama Review* 18, no. 2 (June 1974): 116.

26. Doherty, "Berlin," 87–88.

27. See the program and invitation reprinted in Karl Riha and Hanne Bergius, eds., *Dada Berlin: Texte, Manifeste, Aktionen* (Stuttgart: Reclam, 1977), 21. See also the newspaper reviews collected in Füllner, *Dada Berlin in Zeitungen,* 19–27. Hausmann's "Synthetic Cinema of Painting" was first published in Raoul Hausmann, *Am Anfang war Dada,* ed. Karl Riha and Günter Kämpf (Giessen: Anabas Verlag, 1972), 27–29. However, he created a print with the first two-thirds of the text and a collage of cigar bands, with the new title in 1918. See Eva Züchner, Anna-Carola Krausse, and Kathrin Hatesaul, eds., *Raoul Hausmann, 1886–1971: Der Deutsche Spiesser Ärgert Sich* (Berlin: Berlinische Galerie, Museum für Moderne Kunst, Photographie und Architektur im Martin-Gropius-Bau, 1994), 176.

28. Huelsenbeck, "Collective Dada Manifesto," 242–46.

29. Ibid., 246.

30. See Doherty, "Berlin," 88, and Gordon, "Dada Berlin," 116. Gordon, who bases his account on conversations with Walter Mehring, describes Grosz's performance as part of the literary evening at Neumann's Gallery on January 22, 1918. It is much more likely, however, that it occurred on April 12, 1918, as part of the Berlin Sezession performance, since the contemporary reviews of the Berlin Sezession performance corroborate this. See Füllner, *Dada Berlin in Zeitungen,* 22, 24, 25.

31. Hausmann, *Am Anfang,* 27.

32. Raoul Hausmann, "Synthetisches Cino der Malerei," in *Bilanz der Freierlichkeit,* vol. 1 of *Texte bis 1933,* ed. Michael Erlhoff (Munich: Edition Text u. Kritik, 1982), 15.

33. Ibid., 16.

34. Füllner, *Dada Berlin in Zeitungen,* 19–27.

35. See chapter 2.

36. Allen, *Literary Life in German Expressionism,* 246–47.

37. Reprinted in its entirety in Pachnicke and Honnef, *John Heartfield,* 81–84.

38. Ebert was German chancellor during the November Revolution between November 9, 1918, and February 11, 1919, and then president of the Weimar Republic between February 11, 1919, and February 28, 1925. See Peter D. Stachura, *Political Leaders in Weimar Germany: A Biographical Study* (New York: Simon and Schuster, 1993), 41–42.

39. Allen, *Literary Life in German Expressionism,* 247; Fraser and Heller, *Malik-Verlag,* 22.

40. Allen, *Literary Life in German Expressionism,* 247–48.

41. *Die Pleite* 1, no. 6 (January 1920): 3.

42. *Die Pleite* 1, no. 4 (May 1919): 1.

43. *Die Pleite* 1, no. 6 (January 1920): 1.

44. In English, the titles, which do not correspond with one another, read: "Light and Air for the Proletariat," "Liberty, Equality, Brotherhood," and "The Workman's Holiday."

45. Mynona, *George Grosz* (Dresden: Rudolf Kaemmerer Verlag, 1922), 21.

46. *Die Pleite* 1, no. 6 (January 1920): 3.

47. *Der Dada* 1 (June 1919).

48. Ibid., 4.

49. *Der Dada* 2 (December 1919).

50. Reproduced in Foster, *Dada/Dimensions,* 260.

51. "Dada Advertising Company," in Huelsenbeck, *Dada Almanac*, 162–63.

52. On Schwitters's work in advertising, see John Elderfield, *Kurt Schwitters* (London: Thames and Hudson, 1985), 187, 197. See also Maud Lavin, *Clean New World: Culture, Politics, and Graphic Design* (Cambridge, Mass.: MIT Press, 2001), 26–49.

53. *Der Dada* 3 (April 1920).

54. See, for example, their account of the culture industry in Max Horkheimer and Theodor W. Adorno, *Dialectic of Enlightenment: Philosophical Fragments* (1944), trans. John Cumming (New York: Continuum, 1972), 120–67.

55. See Siegfried Kracauer, *The Salaried Masses: Duty and Distraction in Weimar Germany* (1929), trans. Quintin Hoare (1930; repr. London: Verso, 1998).

56. See Raoul Hausmann, *Visiting Card* (1919), 6 × 12.5 cm (Berlin: Berlinische Galerie). Reproduced in Züchner, Krausse, and Hatesaul, *Raoul Hausmann*, 169 (fig. 265).

57. See Raoul Hausmann, "Dada in Europe," trans. Jean Boase-Beier, in *The Dada Reader: A Critical Anthology*, ed. Dawn Ades (Chicago: University of Chicago Press, 2006), 92–93, translation altered.

58. *Der Dada* 3 (April 1920): 5–6. On Kandinsky's position on the spiritual in art, see *Über das Geistige in der Kunst: Insbesondere in der Malerei* (Munich: R. Piper, 1912).

59. *Der Dada* 3 (April 1920): 6.

60. Ibid. On bluff as a strategy, see Malcolm Green, preface to Huelsenbeck, *Dada Almanac*, viii–ix.

61. *Der Dada* 3 (April 1920): 7.

62. As he puts it, "The surroundings, your somewhat dusty atmosphere, have set the soul's motor in motion, and it all runs by itself: murder, adultery, war, peace, death, shady dealings, values—it all slips from your hands, it isn't possible to stop it: you are simply being played on" (*Der Dada* 3 [April 1920]: 6).

63. Allen, *Literary Life in German Expressionism*, 248.

64. Richard Huelsenbeck, *Dada Almanach* (Berlin: Erich Reiss, 1920).

65. Richard Huelsenbeck, *Dada Siegt: Eine Bilanz des Dadaismus* (Berlin: Malik Verlag, 1920); Huelsenbeck, *Deutschland muss Untergehen! Erinnerungen eines alten dadaistischen Revolutionärs* (Berlin: Malik Verlag, 1920).

66. Richter, *Dada: Art and Anti-Art*, 129.

67. Simultaneous poems were listed on the programs for Dada performances taking place on April 30, 1919, May 15, 1919, and February 18, 1920. A bruitist poem is listed on the program for a Dada performance that took place on April 30, 1919. Dadaist dances are listed on the programs for May 15, 1919, and February 18, 1920. See the performance programs reproduced in Züchner, Krausse, and Hatesaul, *Raoul Hausmann*, 166, 168. In addition, photographs of Gerhard Preiss doing a Dada dance are reproduced in *Der Dada* 3 [April 1920]: 11.

68. Although the author obviously exaggerates, "Alexis" emphasizes the surreal costumes and appearances of the Dada performers. See Alexis, "A Visit to Cabaret Dada," *Drama Review* 18, no. 2 (June 1974): 126–28. Hecht, whose account seems much less fabricated than that of "Alexis," notes that Grosz sometimes performed in blackface. See Ben Hecht, "Dadafest," *Drama Review* 18, no. 2 (June 1974): 125. See also the program for the "Great Dada Soiree" on May 15, 1919, in the Harmoniumsaal in Berlin, which lists a "Dada Dance with Masks." This program is reproduced in Züchner, Krausse, and Hatesaul, *Raoul Hausmann*, 166. The dances performed by the Zurich Dadaists, which were informed by the avant-garde dance practices of Rudolf Laban and Mary Wigman, were probably much more sophisticated. See John D. Erickson, *Dada: Performance, Poetry, and Art* (Boston: Twayne Publishers, 1984), 4–5; and Valerie Preston-Dunlop, "Notes on Bodies

in Dada," in *Dada: The Coordinates of Cultural Politics,* ed. Stephen C. Foster (New York: Hall, 1996), 171–96, esp. 172–79. In addition, Emmy Hennings was an experienced singer, cabaret performer, and dancer in Germany before coming to Zurich. See Hubert van den Berg, "The Star of the Cabaret Voltaire: The Other Life of Emmy Hennings," trans. Roy F. Allen, in Pichon and Riha, *Dada Zurich,* 69–88.

69. On the associations that the United States conjured up in the minds of Germans in the 1920s, see Beeke Sell Tower, *Envisioning America: Prints, Drawings, and Photographs by George Grosz and His Contemporaries, 1915–1933,* with an essay by John Czaplicka (Cambridge, Mass.: Harvard University Press, 1990). See also the primary source material collected in Anton Kaes, Martin Jay, and Edward Dimendberg, eds., *The Weimar Republic Sourcebook* (Berkeley: University of California Press, 1994), 393–411.

70. See the program for the Dada evening on April 30, 1919, at Neumann's Graphisches Kabinett in Berlin, reproduced in Züchner, Krausse, and Hatesaul, *Raoul Hausmann,* 168.

71. Gordon, "Dada Berlin," 119.

72. Hecht, "Dadafest," 125.

73. Grosz, *A Little Yes and a Big No,* trans. Lola Sachs Dorin (New York: Dial, 1946), 183.

74. Walter Mehring, *Berlin Dada* (Zurich: Verlag der Arche, 1959), 51.

75. Performed at the "Dada-Matinee" on December 7, 1919; see the program reproduced in Züchner, Krausse, and Hatesaul, *Raoul Hausmann,* 168.

76. Hecht, "Dadafest," 125.

77. Gordon, "Dada Berlin," 120.

78. Ibid., 120–21.

79. Füllner, *Dada Berlin in Zeitungen,* 28–38.

80. Huelsenbeck, "Dada Drummer," 71.

81. Grosz would continue to collaborate with Piscator during the 1920s, contributing the projections for *Das trunkene Schiff* by Paul Zech in 1926 and set designs for *Die Abenteuer des braven Soldaten Schwejk* by Max Brod and Hans Reimann (based on the novel by Jaroslav Hašek) in 1928. See Stiftung Stadtmuseum Berlin, ed., *George Grosz: Zeichnungen für Buch und Bühne,* mit Beiträgen von Lothar Schirmer und Sabine Herder (Berlin: Henschel Verlag, 2001), 160–61.

82. Gordon, "Dada Berlin," 121–22.

83. Ibid., 122.

84. Huelsenbeck, "Dada Drummer," 70–71.

85. Hausmann, *Am Anfang,* 37.

86. Huelsenbeck, "Dada Drummer," 68.

87. Grosz, *A Little Yes and a Big No,* 182.

88. Hannah Höch, "A Glance over My Life," in Lavin, *Cut with the Kitchen Knife,* 212.

89. Grosz, *A Little Yes and a Big No,* 182.

90. Ibid.

91. Hausmann, *Am Anfang,* 115.

92. Huelsenbeck, "Dada Drummer," 70.

93. Ibid., 68.

94. On the perceived influence of Dada on U.S. happenings by American artists and critics, see Allan Kaprow, *Essays on the Blurring of Art and Life,* ed. Jeff Kelly (Berkeley: University of California Press, 1993), 16, 85; and Michael Kirby, introduction to *Happenings,* ed. Michael Kirby (New York: Dutton, 1965), 22–24, 29–31.

95. See Kirby, introduction, 9–42.

96. Allan Kaprow, "Pinpointing Happenings" (1967), in Kaprow, *Essays on the Blurring of Art and Life,* 84–89, esp. 87.

97. See Gordon, "Dada Berlin," 117.

98. See Bergius, *Das lachen Dadas* (Giessen: Anabas-Verlag, 1989), 13. Although Bergius dates the photo from 1919–20, it could plausibly be the same or a similar costume to the one Grosz supposedly wore in 1918.

99. Grosz, *A Little Yes and a Big No,* 185.

100. Mehring, quoted in Richter, *Dada,* 110–12. See also Mehring, *Berlin Dada,* 67–70.

101. Huelsenbeck, "Dada Drummer," 58–59.

102. Raoul Hausmann, *Courrier Dada* (Paris: Editions Allia, 1992), 76. English translation in Richter, *Dada,* 124. The happening is also described in Hausmann, *Am Anfang,* 57.

103. Hausmann, *Courrier Dada,* 76. English translation in Richter, *Dada,* 124.

104. For Huelsenbeck's criticisms of Baader, see Huelsenbeck, "Dada Drummer," 67. See also Hans Baumann, "A Personal Dada Matter," in Huelsenbeck, *Dada Almanac,* 37–43. It is generally assumed that Huelsenbeck wrote this attack on Baader. On the radically differing evaluations of Baader articulated by the original Dada artists as well as in the early historical accounts of the movement, see Foster, "Johannes Baader," 250–51. On Baader's career as a journalist in the second half of the 1920s, see Adrian V. Sudhalter, "Johannes Baader and the Demise of Wilhelmine Culture: Architecture, Dada, and Social Critique, 1875–1920" (PhD diss., New York University, 2005), 330–34.

105. Sudhalter, "Johannes Baader," 19–46.

106. On Baader's career as a mortuary architect, see Sudhalter, "Johannes Baader," 47–61, 69–76, 85–90, 138–43. On his first meeting with Hausmann, which is often dated to 1905, see Sudhalter, "Johannes Baader," 91–93. Sudhalter's arguments as to why the meeting took place in 1906 rather than 1905 seem convincing and are adopted here.

107. See Sudhalter, "Johannes Baader," 98–127. The documents were Johannes Baader, "Über private Denkmalspflege: Lose Gedanken," *Das Blaubuch* (Berlin) 1, no. 30 (August 2, 1906): 1184–87; "Bestimmungen für die Teilnahme am Wettbewerb A. in Sachen Propaganda für den Bau der internationalen Reisenpyramide," a mock competition flyer dated September 17, 1906, now in the Getty Research Institute Special Collections, Los Angeles; and "Architekt Johannes Baader (Persönliches)," a printed sheet dated October 12, 1906, now in the Getty Research Institute Special Collections.

108. Johannes Baader, "Über private Denkmalspflege," cited in Sudhalter, "Johannes Baader," 103.

109. See Johannes Baader, "Architekt Johannes Baader (Persönliches)," in *Oberdada: Schriften, Manifeste, Flugblätter, Billets, Werke, und Taten,* ed. Hanne Bergius, Norbert Miller, and Karl Riha (Lahn-Giessen: Anabas-Verlag, 1977), 9–17, esp. 9, 11.

110. See Johannes Baader, *Vierzehn Briefe Christi: Ein Geburtstagsgeschenk für seine Abteilung Ernst Haeckel vom Besitzer des Kabarets zur blauen Milchstrasse* (Berlin-Zehlendorf: Verlag der Tagebücher, 1914), reprinted in Johannes Baader, *Oberdada: "Vierzehn Briefe Christi" und andere Druckschriften,* ed. Karl Riha (Frankfurt am Main: Verlag Peter Lang, 1988), 9–54. On the matrix of ideas that informed Baader's writing of *Fourteen Letters of Christ,* see Sudhalter, "Johannes Baader," 184–90.

111. Huelsenbeck, "Dada Drummer," 67.

112. Richter, *Dada,* 108.

113. Hausmann, *Am Anfang,* 19.

114. Foster, "Johannes Baader," 249–71.

115. Baader, *Oberdada: Schriften,* 93, cited in Foster, *Dada,* 152.

116. On Baader's military service and discharge, see Sudhalter, "Johannes Baader," 209–12.

117. Johannes Baader, "Es dürfte sich empfehlen, festzustellen . . ." (1954), in *Oberdada: Schriften,* 175.

118. Johannes Baader, letter from 1916, cited in Karl Riha, "Der Oberdada im Urteil der Dadaisten," in Baader, *Oberdada: Schriften,* 194, and translated by Adrian Sudhalter in Sudhalter, "Johannes Baader," 210.

119. Baader, *Oberdada: Schriften,* 175.

120. Ibid., 175–76.

121. Karl Riha, "Anmerkung des Herausgebers," in Johannes Baader, *Das Oberdada,* ed. Karl Riha (Hofheim: Wolke Verlag, 1991), 102.

122. Sudhalter, "Johannes Baader," 29, 132.

123. Raoul Hausmann, quoted in a letter from Baader to Paul Adler, March 15, 1918, in *Hannah Höch: Eine Lebenscollage,* vol. 1, pt. 1, ed. Berlinische Galerie and Cornelia Thater-Schulz (1919–20; repr. Berlin: Argon Verlag, 1989), 351.

124. Sudhalter, "Johannes Baader," 16.

125. Sudhalter argues that Baader may have taken up the epistolary form as a result of the influence of Nietzsche's "letters of madness" that he wrote following his breakdown in 1889 ("Johannes Baader," 135–36). In addition, on January 17, 1908, Baader had himself committed to the same asylum (the University Clinic in Jena) nineteen years to the day after Nietzsche was admitted there, where he was treated by the same psychiatrist who had treated Nietzsche (134). Finally, Baader also wrote several letters to Nietzsche's sister, wherein he revealed his strong identification with the philosopher (184–90).

126. The following list of events is based on "Dada: A Chronology," in *New Studies in Dada: Essays and Documents,* ed. Richard Sheppard (Driffield, England: Hutton Press, 1981), 161–88, and is supplemented by Sudhalter's discussions of the various actions in "Johannes Baader."

127. Johannes Baader, "Die acht Weltsätze," in Riha, *Dada Berlin,* 41–43. See also "Die Dadaisten fordern die Nobelpreise," *BZ am Mittag* (July 30, 1918), reprinted in Berlinische Galerie and Thater-Schulz, *Hannah Höch,* 1:1:427–28.

128. On Baader's monism and his admiration of Ernst Haeckel, see Sudhalter, "Johannes Baader," 186–90.

129. "Die Dadaisten fordern die Nobelpreise," *BZ am Mittag* (July 30, 1918), reprinted in Berlinische Galerie and Thater-Schulz, *Hannah Höch,* 1:1:427.

130. Berlinische Galerie and Thater-Schulz, *Hannah Höch,* 1:1:427.

131. Including the *Berliner Tageblatt* (July 31, 1918) and *Die Wahrheit* (August 3, 1918). See Sudhalter, "Johannes Baader," 230. See also Hannah Höch's letter in support of Baader's demands written to the *BZ am Mittag* on July 31, 1918 (Berlinische Galerie and Thater-Schulz, *Hannah Höch,* 1:1:428–29).

132. See Siegfried Jacobsohn, "Dadaist," *Die Weltbühne* 14, no. 35 (August 29, 1918): 204.

133. As Sudhalter notes, although the announcement has not survived, it was quoted or cited in several newspapers, including the *Berliner Mittagszeitung* (September 8, 1918), the *Berliner Tageblatt* (September 9, 1918), the *Berliner Volks-Zeitung* (September 9, 1918), and the *[Württembergische] Zeitung* (September 11, 1918). See Sudhalter, "Johannes Baader," 238–39.

134. As Sudhalter notes, the press release survives in the Getty Research Institute Special Collections, and a notice appeared in the *Berliner Tageblatt* (both dated September 9, 1918). See Sudhalter, "Johannes Baader," 243.

135. Press release, September 10, 1918, reprinted in *Scharfrichter der bürgerlichen Seele: Raoul Hausmann in Berlin 1900–1933: Unveröffentlichte Briefe, Texte, Dokumente aus den Künstler-Archiven der Berlinischen Galerie,* ed. Eva Züchner (Stuttgart: Hatje, 1998), 84–85; reported in the *Tägliche Rundschau* (September 11, 1918). See Sudhalter, "Johannes Baader," 243.

136. Press release, September 18, 1918, reprinted in Züchner, *Scharfrichter der bürgerlichen Seele,* 88; reported in the *Deutsche Tageszeitung* (September 19, 1918). See Sudhalter, "Johannes Baader," 243.

137. Sudhalter, "Johannes Baader," 244–47.

138. See, for example, the report from November 18, 1918, published in the *Deutsche Zeitung,* cited in Berlinische Galerie and Thater-Schulz, *Hannah Höch,* 1:1:335.

139. See Johannes Baader, "An das B.T.," *Die freie Strasse* 10 (December 1918): 1; facsimile reprinted in Bergius, *Das lachen Dadas,* 86. See also Riha, *Dada Berlin,* 39, 144, for a compendium of various conflicting accounts of the event.

140. See the announcement reprinted in Baader, *Oberdada: Schriften,* 46.

141. See Baader, *Oberdada: Schriften,* 50–51; Sudhalter, "Johannes Baader," 250; and Sheppard, *New Studies in Dada,* 176.

142. See Hausmann's discussion of the action in *Am Anfang,* 58–60.

143. Hausmann, *Am Anfang,* 59.

144. See the editor's notes in Huelsenbeck, *Dada Almanac,* 139.

145. Central Bureau of Dada, "Hado," in Huelsenbeck, *Dada Almanac,* 137.

146. Sudhalter, "Johannes Baader," 250; and Sheppard, *New Studies in Dada,* 176.

147. Johannes Baader, "AD 19,400 Special Issue 'Green Corpse,'" in Heulsenbeck, *Dada Almanac,* 39.

148. The text in the *Berliner Achtuhr-Abendblat* is transcribed in Berlinische Galerie and Thater-Schulz, *Hannah Höch,* 1:2:553–54. Among the other newspapers that reported the event are the *Neues Wiener Journal* (April 1, 1919) and the *(Würtemburgischer) Zeitung* (April 11, 1919). The event was also discussed by Leo Heller in "Der Oberdada von Berlin," *Salonblatt Zeit Signale: Moderne illustrierte Wochenschrift* 14, no. 16 (April 19, 1919): 340–41. See Sudhalter, "Johannes Baader," 257–58.

149. Sudhalter, "Johannes Baader," 255–58.

150. On Baader's dating system, which began in 1919, and used both letters and numbers, see Sudhalter, "Johannes Baader," 262–63.

2. Hannah Höch's *Cut with the Kitchen Knife*

1. Walter Benjamin, *The Arcades Project* (1982), trans. Howard Eiland and Kevin McLaughlin (Cambridge, Mass.: Harvard University Press, 1999), 461.

2. Hannah Höch, "A Glance over My Life" (1958), trans. Peter Chametzky, in Maud Lavin, *Cut with the Kitchen Knife: The Weimar Photomontages of Hannah Höch* (New Haven, Conn.: Yale University Press, 1993), 212.

3. Raoul Hausmann, "Synthetisches Cino der Malerei" (1918), in *Bilanz der Freierlichkeit,* vol. 1 of *Texte bis 1933,* ed. Michael Erlhoff (Munich: Edition Text u. Kritik, 1982), 15.

4. "Der neue Mensch: Gemeinschaft, die Auflösung des Ich, des Einzelnen, in der Wucht, der Wahrheit des Wir; die Aufhebung der fremden Macht als Gewaltautorität in die innerste eigne Autorität als grenzenlose Verantwortung: denn Wir wird sein wenn Ich zugleich der Andere bin, ich der Andere zugleich anderes Ich bin." Entry dated January 29, 1918, in a notebook by Hausmann dated January 29–January 31, 1918, reprinted in Berlinische Galerie and Cornelia Thater-Schulz, *Hannah Höch: Eine Lebenscollage,* vol. 1, pt. 1 (1919–20; repr. Berlin: Argon Verlag, 1989), 339–40.

5. *Berliner Illustrirte Zeitung* 29, no. 3 (January 18, 1920): 28.

6. There is no evidence that Höch ever made photographs herself, although this was certainly not impossible. Hausmann, on the other hand, became a photographer in the 1920s and worked extensively in this medium during his life. See Jean-François Chevrier,

"Die Beziehungen des Körpers," in *Raoul Hausmann, 1886–1971: Der Deutsche Spiesser Ärgert Sich,* ed. Eva Züchner, Anna-Carola Krausse, and Kathrin Hatesaul (Berlin: Berlinische Galerie, Museum für Moderne Kunst, Photographie und Architektur im Martin-Gropius-Bau, 1994), 68–101.

7. On the identification of the various photomontage fragments, see Jula Dech, *Hannah Höch Schnitt mit dem Küchenmesser Dada durch die letzte weimarer Bierbauchkulturepoche Deutschlands* (Frankfurt am Main: Fischer Taschenbuch Verlag, 1989); and Brigid Doherty, "Berlin," in *Dada: Zurich, Berlin, Hannover, Cologne, New York, Paris,* ed. Leah Dickerman (Washington, D.C.: D.A.P./National Gallery of Art, 2005), 107. On the political significance of a number of these figures, see Peter D. Stachura, *Political Leaders in Weimar Germany: A Biographical Study* (New York: Simon and Schuster, 1993).

8. Carl Schmitt, *The Concept of the Political* (1927), trans. George Schwab (Chicago: University of Chicago Press, 1996).

9. On Höch's training in design and traditional women's crafts and her work for the Ullstein Verlag, see Maria Makela, "By Design: The Early Work of Hannah Höch in Context," in Peter Boswell, Maria Makela, Carolyn Lanchner, and Kristin Makholm, *The Photomontages of Hannah Höch* (Minneapolis: Walker Art Center, 1996), 49–79, esp. 50–60.

10. As suggested by Siegfried Kracauer's analysis of Weimar cinema of this time, circular motion could also represent chaos, an interpretation that Kracauer gives to the circular motifs in Robert Wiene's classic horror film *The Cabinet of Dr. Caligari* (Decla-Bioscop A.G., 1920). See Siegfried Kracauer, *From Caligari to Hitler: A Psychological History of the German Film* (Princeton, N.J.: Princeton University Press, 1947), 73–74.

11. See Dorothea Dietrich, *The Collages of Kurt Schwitters: Tradition and Innovation* (New York: Cambridge University Press, 1993), esp. 86–96, 108–14.

12. According to the Ullstein Verlag's own promotional materials, the *BZ am Mittag,* the publisher's extremely popular midday newspaper, owed a large part of its success (and its rapid growth in circulation since 1904) to its unsurpassed sports and automobile coverage. See *Der Verlag Ullstein zum Welt-Reklame-Kongress Berlin 1929: International Advertising Association Berlin Congress 1929: Congrès de Publicité de Berlin 1929* (Berlin: Ullstein Verlag, 1929), 100, 113–14, 139. On the significance of airplanes and flying for the German popular imagination, see Peter Fritzsche, *A Nation of Fliers: German Aviation and the Popular Imagination* (Cambridge, Mass.: Harvard University Press, 1992).

13. For a good example of a critique of German modernization that valorizes traditional modes of life, see Julius Langbehn, *Rembrandt als Erzieher, von einem Deutschen* (Leipzig: Hirschfeld, 1890). Both Fritz Stern and George Mosse have explored the antimodernist trajectory of thought in Germany as embodied by cultural critics such as Langbehn, Paul de Lagard, and Arthur Moeller van den Bruck, among others. See Fritz R. Stern, *The Politics of Cultural Despair: A Study in the Rise of the Germanic Ideology* (1961; repr. Berkeley: University of California Press, 1974); and George L. Mosse, *The Crisis of German Ideology: Intellectual Origins of the Third Reich* (New York: Grosset and Dunlap, 1964).

14. Hausmann, "Synthetisches Cino der Malerei," 1:16.

15. Höch, "Glance over My Life," 212.

16. Dech, *Hannah Höch,* 15.

17. Lavin, *Cut with the Kitchen Knife,* 19.

18. Ibid., 19, 23, 35.

19. Ibid., 23, 32.

20. Ibid., 29.

21. For Lavin's reading of the Kollwitz-Impekoven hybrid, see Lavin, *Cut with the Kitchen Knife,* 30–34.

22. On the "fragile" and "childlike" character of Impekoven's dance style and figure, see Karl Toepfer, *Empire of Ecstasy: Nudity and Movement in German Body Culture, 1910–1935* (Berkeley: University of California Press, 1997), 182–86.

23. As Bergius puts it, "People appear as images of the culturally uprooted European 'hybrid'" (*"Dada Triumphs!" Dada Berlin, 1917–1923, Artistry of Polarities,* trans. Brigitte Pichon [Farmington Hills, Mich.: G. K. Hall, 2003], 166).

24. The "social connection of life is replaced by the public system of communication and mass media" (Bergius, *"Dada Triumphs!"* 166).

25. Bergius, *"Dada Triumphs!"* 144–45.

26. Ibid., 120. The analysis of Einstein's head then picks up on page 142.

27. Ibid., 145.

28. Ibid., 151, 149.

29. Ibid., 175.

30. Ibid.

31. Ibid., 169.

32. Theodor W. Adorno, *Negative Dialectics* (1966), trans. E. B. Ashton (New York: Seabury, 1973), 8.

33. See Rosalind E. Krauss, "The Photographic Conditions of Surrealism," in *The Originality of the Avant-Garde and Other Modernist Myths* (Cambridge, Mass.: MIT Press, 1985), 87–118, esp. 103–12. Either directly or indirectly, most descriptions of the indexical nature of photographic representation—and Krauss is no exception here—owe a debt to Charles Sanders Peirce's theory of signs. "An index," as Peirce wrote, "is a sign which refers to the object that it denotes by virtue of being really affected by that object" ("Logic as Semiotic: The Theory of Signs," in *Philosophical Writings of Peirce*, ed. Justus Buchler [New York: Dover, 1955], 102). In reference to photography, Roland Barthes called this indexical character of certain representations, the "that-has-been," which for him was ultimately a corporeal relationship between signifier and signified that was always mediated by an awareness of death. "The photograph," Barthes wrote, "is literally an emanation of the referent. From the real body, which was there, proceed radiations which ultimately touch me, who am here; the duration of the transmission is insignificant; the photograph of the missing being, as Sontag says, will touch me like the delayed rays of a star. A sort of umbilical cord links the body of the photographed thing to my gaze: light, though impalpable, is here a carnal medium, a skin I share with anyone who has been photographed" (*Camera Lucida: Reflections on Photography,* trans. Richard Howard [New York: Hill and Wang, 1981], 80). Through its indexical characteristics, in other words, a representation potentially reminds the beholder of something that existed and that has subsequently ceased to be.

34. "The experience of nature as sign, or nature as representation, comes 'naturally' then to photography" (Krauss, *Originality of the Avant-Garde,* 113).

35. Krauss, *Originality of the Avant-Garde,* 113, 115.

36. See, for example, Eberhard Kolb, *The Weimar Republic,* trans. P. S. Falla (London: Unwin Hyman, 1988), ix. See also Detlev J. K. Peukert, *The Weimar Republic: The Crisis of Classical Modernity,* trans. Richard Deveson (New York: Hill and Wang, 1992), 3–6.

37. Peukert, *Weimar Republic,* 276.

38. Ibid., 81–82.

39. Ibid., 174–77.

40. Karl Christian Führer, "A Medium of Modernity? Broadcasting in Weimar Germany, 1923–1932," *Journal of Modern History* 69 (December 1997): 742; and Brian Currid, *A National Acoustics: Music and Mass Publicity in Weimar and Nazi Germany* (Minneapolis: University of Minnesota Press, 2006), 19, 30.

41. Führer, "Medium of Modernity?" 731.

42. Ibid., 742.

43. Ibid., 724–28.

44. Ibid., 724.

45. Ibid., 728, 743–53.

46. Ibid., 730, 753.

47. For an excellent account of the tradition of bourgeois aesthetic education in Hamburg, namely, the attempts on the part of educated liberal Germans to mold model citizens (often from the working classes) through direct contact with and instruction in German culture, see Jennifer Jenkins, *Provincial Modernity: Local Culture and Liberal Politics in Fin-De-Siècle Hamburg* (Ithaca, N.Y.: Cornell University Press, 2003).

48. Führer, "Medium of Modernity?" 737–38.

49. Ibid., 736–37.

50. Currid, *National Acoustics,* 30–31.

51. For an example of how the wireless telegraph was popularized in the mass media, see "Das Telephon in der Reisetasche," *Berliner Illustrirte Zeitung* 28, no. 44 (November 2, 1919): 446, as well as the cover photograph on 445.

52. See, for example, Höch's photomontage *Untitled* from 1921 in which a man with a bug on his head and a pipe in his mouth seems to play with machine parts in a way that suggests a telegraph or ham radio operator; reproduced in Boswell et al., *Photomontages of Hannah Höch,* 36. See also Höch's *From Above,* a photomontage with collage from 1926–27, in which two figures hover above a city landscape from which human and machine parts jut like radio towers; reproduced in Boswell et al., *Photomontages of Hannah Höch,* 92.

53. See, for example, the filmstrip that appears in the lower-right corner of Heartfield and Grosz's *Life and Times in Universal City at 12:05 Noon* (1919), reproduced in Peter Pachnicke and Klaus Honnef, eds., *John Heartfield* (New York: Abrams, 1992), 68; the film projector that crowns the head of the main figure in Hausmann's *Self-Portrait of the Dadasoph* (1920) (Figure 3.2); and a photograph on an easel that suggests a movie projection screen in Hausmann's *A Bourgeois Precision Brain Calls Forth a World Movement: Dada Triumphs* (1920) (Züchner, Krausse, and Hatesaul, *Raoul Hausmann,* 185), to name only the most obvious examples. See also Höch's frequent use of the faces and bodies of film stars in *Cut with the Kitchen Knife* (Figure 2.3) as well as other works.

54. See Jeanpaul Goergen, "Marke Herzfeld-Filme: Dokumente zu John Heartfields Filmarbeit, 1917–1920," in *John Heartfield: Dokumentation; Reaktionen auf eine ungewöhnliche Austellung,* ed. Klaus Honnef and Hans-Jürgen Osterhausen (Cologne: DuMont, 1994), 23–66.

55. Thomas J. Saunders, *Hollywood in Berlin: American Cinema and Weimar Germany* (Berkeley: University of California Press, 1994), 20.

56. During its first decade, roughly 1895 to 1905, German film was defined by the *Wanderkino,* or traveling theater. Short films, often imports from abroad, were purchased by independent producers and shown in tents to small audiences in different urban centers. Although the middle and upper classes were initially attracted to these venues because of the novelty of the new medium, the inexpensive *Wanderkino* quickly became a largely working-class entertainment. Then, between 1905 and the outbreak of the war, permanent theaters were built, and production and distribution companies were formed. Films became longer and more complex, their subjects became more diverse (so as to sustain the interests of workers while enticing the middle and upper classes to return to the cinema), and a star system began to form. See H. H. Wollenberg, *Fifty Years of German Film* (London: Falcon Press Limited, 1948), 7–11; Bruce Murray, *Film and the German Left in the Weimar*

Republic: From Caligari to Kuhle Wampe (Austin: University of Texas Press, 1990), 15–16; and Saunders, *Hollywood in Berlin,* 20–21.

57. Wollenberg, *Fifty Years of German Film,* 12; and Saunders, *Hollywood in Berlin,* 21–22.

58. Wollenberg, *Fifty Years of German Film,* 15; and Saunders, *Hollywood in Berlin,* 23.

59. Wollenberg, *Fifty Years of German Film,* 17; and Saunders, *Hollywood in Berlin,* 24.

60. Saunders, *Hollywood in Berlin,* 4–5, 10.

61. See Eric Rentschler, "Mountains and Modernity: Relocating the *Bergfilm,*" *New German Critique* 51 (Autumn 1990): 137–61, esp. 149–50. This misperception, which Rentschler criticizes, has persisted for a very long time. See Wollenberg, *Fifty Years of German Film,* 19.

62. See Wollenberg, *Fifty Years of German Film,* 10–13, 18–22; Murray, *Film and the German Left,* 25–29; and Saunders, *Hollywood in Berlin,* 24–25.

63. In addition, as Murray has argued, despite producing a number of important films, the German Left could never effectively compete with mainstream filmmakers during the Weimar Republic. See Murray, *Film and the German Left,* 233–37.

64. See Siegfried Kracauer, *From Caligari to Hitler: A Psychological History of the German Film* (Princeton, N.J.: Princeton University Press, 1966).

65. See, for example, Hausmann, "Synthetisches Cino der Malerei," 14–16, as well as the print he created with the same title using the first two-thirds of the text and a collage of cigar bands in 1918 (reproduced in Züchner, Krausse, and Hatesaul, *Raoul Hausmann,* 176). Hausmann first presented "Synthetic Cinema of Painting" under the title "The New Material in Painting" at the Berlin Sezession on April 12, 1918 (see chapter 1); in addition, he also created a second print with the same title. Although Hausmann does not discuss film directly in his text, he was, as the title suggests, interested in how cinema could be merged with traditional forms of art such as painting. Presumably under the influence of film, cubism and futurism, he notes, took steps toward representing the "fourth dimension" and the contradictory nature of human experience, which interweaves contrasts. Dada, he argued, would develop this cinematic tendency even further, thereby leading to "the true experience of all relationships." See also Raoul Hausmann, "Photomontage" (1931), trans. Joel Agee, in *Photography in the Modern Era: European Documents and Critical Writings, 1913–1940,* ed. Christopher Phillips (New York: Metropolitan Museum of Art/Aperture, 1989), 178–81. Hausmann also writes about being strongly moved by films; see the letter from Raoul Hausmann to Hannah Höch, June 4, 1918, in Berlinische Galerie and Cornelia Thater-Schulz, *Hannah Höch,* 1:1:389. Wieland Herzfelde had a somewhat different account of the importance of film for the development of photomontage. As he wrote in 1920, by taking over the representational functions of painting, photography and film caused painting to develop toward abstraction. Photomontage, which was a reaction to painting's flight from reality, was thus inspired by film but did not seek to represent reality in the same way. Instead, the significance of photomontage was its rejection of the tradition of fine art, its anti-illusionism (which was a function of its use of photographs and actual objects), and its power to further the disintegration of the contemporary moment. See Wieland Herzfelde, "'Introduction,' First International Dada Fair, 1920," in *German Expressionism: Documents from the End of the Wilhelmine Empire to the Rise of National Socialism,* ed. Rose-Carol Washton Long (Berkeley: University of California Press, 1993), 273–74.

66. Hausmann, "Photomontage," 179. This statement seems to agree with the anti-illusionism that Herzfelde stressed was an important attribute of Dada photomontage. See note 65.

67. Bernhard Fulda, "Industries of Sensationalism: German Tabloids in Weimar Berlin,"

in *Mass Media, Culture, and Society in Twentieth-Century Germany,* ed. Karl Christian Führer and Corey Ross (Basingstoke, U.K.: Palgrave Macmillan, 2006), 183–84.

68. Modris Eksteins, *The Limits of Reason: The German Democratic Press and the Collapse of Weimar Democracy* (London: Oxford University Press, 1975), 13.

69. Ibid., 74.

70. See Georg Bernhard, "Die Deutsche Presse," in *Der Verlag Ullstein zum Welt-Reklame-Kongress Berlin 1929: International Advertising Association Berlin Congress 1929: Congrès de Publicité de Berlin 1929* (Berlin: Ullstein Verlag, 1929), 70, 74–78.

71. Eksteins, *Limits of Reason,* 14.

72. Fulda, "Industries of Sensationalism," 184.

73. Eksteins, *Limits of Reason,* 14–15.

74. Ibid., 16.

75. Fulda, "Industries of Sensationalism," 185.

76. Eksteins, *Limits of Reason,* 75.

77. Bernhard, "Die Deutsche Presse," 63–64; and Eksteins, *Limits of Reason,* 78.

78. Eksteins, *Limits of Reason,* 75.

79. Eksteins, *Limits of Reason,* 84; and Fulda, "Industries of Sensationalism," 186.

80. Pierre Albert and Gilles Feyel, "Photography and the Media: Changes in the Illustrated Press," in *A New History of Photography,* ed. Michel Frizot, trans. Susan Bennett, Liz Clegg, John Crook, and Caroline Higgitt (Cologne: Könemann, 1998), 359–61.

81. Albert and Feyel, "Photography and the Media," 364.

82. Robert Taft, *Photography and the American Scene: A Social History, 1839–1889* (New York: Dover, 1938), 419–50.

83. Albert and Feyel, "Photography and the Media," 362, 365.

84. Naomi Rosenblum, *A World History of Photography,* 3rd ed. (New York: Abbeville, 1997), 244–79, 442–48.

85. Albert and Feyel, "Photography and the Media," 362, 366.

86. Ibid., 369.

87. See, for example, Tim N. Gidal, *Modern Photojournalism: Origin and Evolution, 1910–1933,* trans. Maureen Oberli-Turner (New York: Macmillan, 1973), 5–30; Fred Richin, "Close Witnesses: The Involvement of the Photojournalist," in Frizot, *New History of Photography,* 591–611, esp. 599–600; and Torsten Palmér, *The Weimar Republic through the Lens of the Press,* ed. Hendrik Neubauer, trans. Peter Barton, Mark Cole, and Susan Cox (Hagen: Könemann, 2000), 4–37. For important contemporary attempts to analyze the new practices of mass communication of text and image, see László Maholy-Nagy, *Painting, Photography, Film* (1925/1927), trans. Janet Seligman (Cambridge, Mass.: MIT Press, 1969); Jan Tschichold, *The New Typography: A Handbook for Modern Designers* (1928), trans. Ruari McLean (Berkeley: University of California Press, 1998); and the articles collected in Anton Kaes, Martin Jay, and Edward Dimendberg, eds., *The Weimar Republic Sourcebook* (Berkeley: University of California Press, 1994), 641–54.

88. See Edlef Köppen, "The Magazine as a Sign of the Times" (1925), Kurt Korff, "The Illustrated Magazine" (1927), and Johannes Molzahn, "Stop Reading! Look!" (1928), in Kaes, Jay, and Dimendberg, *Weimar Republic Sourcebook,* 644–45, 646–47, 648–49.

89. Siegfried Kracauer, "Photography" (1927), in *The Mass Ornament: Weimar Essays,* ed. and trans. Thomas Y. Levin (Cambridge, Mass.: Harvard University Press, 1995), 57–58.

90. Ibid., 58.

91. Walter Benjamin, "The Work of Art in the Age of Mechanical Reproduction" (1936), in *Illuminations,* ed. Hannah Arendt and trans. Harry Zohn (New York: Schocken, 1969), 238–41, 250.

92. See Gidal, *Modern Photojournalism,* 14. The circulation of the *BIZ,* which was small in its first few years of publication, rose to 1 million during World War I and nearly 2 million by 1930. See Christian Ferber, *Berliner Illustrirte Zeitung: Zeitbild, Chronik, Moritat für Jedermann, 1892–1945* (Berlin: Ullstein Verlag, 1983), 5–6; and Friedrich Luft, "Die Geschichte der Berliner Illustrirten," in *Facsimile Querschnitt durch die Berliner Illustrirte,* ed. Friedrich Luft (Munich: Scherz Verlag, 1965), 11–12.

93. Kurt Korff, "Die illustrierte Zeitschrift," *Fünfzig Jahre Ullstein (1877–1927)* (Berlin: Ullstein, 1927), 279–303, translated and reprinted in Kaes, Jay, and Dimendberg, *Weimar Republic Sourcebook,* 646–47.

94. Hans Weber, "Der Bilderdienst," in *Der Verlag Ullstein zum Welt-Reklame-Kongress Berlin 1929,* 189–91.

95. "Zeitungs-Flugdienst Berlin-Weimar," *Berliner Illustrirte Zeitung* 28, no. 7 (February 16, 1919): 49.

96. "Die Kunst der Moment-Photografie," *Berliner Illustrirte Zeitung* 28, no. 33 (August 17, 1919), 318–19.

97. "Interessantes aus dem Reich der Technik," *Berliner Illustrirte Zeitung* 28, no. 45 (November 9, 1919): 462–63; "Der Photograf als Journalist," *Berliner Illustrirte Zeitung* 28, no. 50 (December 14, 1919): 522–23; and "Die Zeitung als Pionier," *Berliner Illustrirte Zeitung* 28, no. 52 (December 28, 1919): 546–47.

98. "Die Welt von Oben Gesehen," *Berliner Illustrirte Zeitung* 28, no. 52 (December 28, 1919): 544; and "Auflösung unseres Preisrätzels aus Nr. 52," *Berliner Illustrirte Zeitung* 29, no. 5 (February 1, 1920): 55.

99. "O, diese Kinder!" *Berliner Illustrirte Zeitung* 34, no. 27 (July 5, 1925): 846; and "Ergebnis unserer Preisaufgabe aus Nr. 27," *Berliner Illustrirte Zeitung* 34, no. 31 (July 31, 1925): 991.

100. As Peter Nisbet has argued in relation to Höch's photomontages, identifying the photographic source material can serve several different purposes. It can help refine and correct the dating of the works; it can "shed some light on the artist's choices, by showing what was omitted, excised, transfigured; and it can, perhaps, contribute to the interpretation of the work in question." See Peter Nisbet, "A Cut-Up at the Dada Fair," *Boston Book Review* 4, no. 3 (April 1997): 8–9. As suggested by the *BIZ* contest encouraging readers to identify various photographic fragments, one could assume, at least during the middle period of the Weimar Republic, that certain newspaper readers would have been able to identify the fragmentary images that were parts of photomontages and that these identifications would become components in their interpretations. Dada photomontage, I would argue, helped cultivate this ability.

101. ". . . ismen: Die verschiedenen Richtungen in der Malerei," *Berliner Illustrirte Zeitung* 29, no. 43 (October 24, 1920): 498–99.

102. See Georg Simmel, "The Metropolis and Mental Life" (1903), trans. Kurt H. Wolff, in *The Sociology of Georg Simmel,* ed. Kurt H. Wolff (New York: Free Press, 1964), 409–24.

103. Ibid., 410.

104. Ibid.

105. Ibid., 411.

106. Ibid., 412.

107. Ibid., 410.

108. Ibid., 414–15.

109. See David Frisby, *Fragments of Modernity: Theories of Modernity in the Work of Simmel, Kracauer, and Benjamin* (Cambridge, Mass.: MIT Press, 1986), 3, 6–9; and Siegfried Kracauer, "Georg Simmel," in *Mass Ornament,* 225–57.

110. William J. Mitchell, *Me++: The Cyborg Self and the Networked City* (Cambridge, Mass.: MIT Press, 2003), 8–9.

111. Simmel, "Metropolis and Mental Life," 421.

112. For Hegel's articulation of this position, see Georg Wilhelm Friedrich Hegel, *Phenomenology of Spirit* (1807), trans. A. V. Miller (Oxford: Clarendon, 1977), preface, paras. 28, 29.

113. Simmel, "Metropolis and Mental Life," 422.

114. Ibid., 423.

115. On Sent M'ahesa, who created a number of her modern dances on the basis of her study of ancient Egyptian art and artifacts, see Toepfer, *Empire of Ecstasy,* 175–79.

116. See Peter Fritzsche, *Germans into Nazis* (Cambridge, Mass.: Harvard University Press, 1998), 40, 49–50.

117. On the growing discourse about homosexuality in Germany since the 1860s, see James D. Steakley, *The Homosexual Emancipation Movement in Germany* (New York: Arno, 1975).

118. Jung's thinking on the anima and the animus goes back to the early 1910s. See, for example, the essays collected in C. G. Jung, *Two Essays on Analytical Psychology,* 2nd ed., trans. R. F. C. Hull (Princeton, N.J.: Princeton University Press, 1966), and in particular, the original versions of the essays collected in the appendixes.

3. Raoul Hausmann's Revolutionary Media

1. On the "First International Dada Fair," see Hanne Bergius, *"Dada Triumphs!" Dada Berlin, 1917–1923, Artistry of Polarities,* trans. Brigitte Pichon (Farmington Hills, Mich.: G. K. Hall, 2003), 231–82, as well as the "Catalogue of the Exhibition and Its Reconstruction," 355, 1–67; Bruce Altshuler, *The Avant-Garde in Exhibition: New Art in the Twentieth Century* (Berkeley: University of California Press, 1994), 98–115; and Helen Adkins, "Erste Internationale Dada-Messe, Berlin 1920," in *Stationen der Moderne: Kataloge epochaler Kunstausstellungen in Deutschland 1910–1962, Kommentarband,* ed. Eberhard Roters (Cologne: Verlag der Buchhandlung Walter König, 1988), 77–94.

2. Hans Richter, *Dada: Art and Anti-Art* (1964), trans. David Britt (New York: Oxford University Press, 1965), 133. The term *Erzeugnisse* is used on the catalog's front cover.

3. On the concept of interpellation, see Louis Althusser, "Ideology and Ideological State Apparatuses" (1970), in *Lenin and Philosophy and Other Essays,* trans. Ben Brewster (New York: Monthly Review Press, 1971), 127–86. As I use it here, "interpellation" indicates the combination of processes whereby a work of art or other form of visual culture simultaneously addresses a spectator, calls out for the spectator to identify with it in one way or another, and defines its spectator in terms of a specific set of characteristics. By responding to works that address us, we engage with these works and accept the various social roles that they offer to us. In the case of advertising, this process is fairly clear: different advertisements in the mass media address us as members of a certain demographic, cultural, or subcultural group. In the case of artworks this process is much more complex, although in many ways it remains analogous.

4. On Hausmann's early life, artistic training, art, and artistic and intellectual influences, see Eva Züchner, "Quellen der Revolte," in *Raoul Hausmann, 1886–1971: Der Deutsche Spiesser Ärgert Sich,* ed. Eva Züchner, Anna-Carola Krausse, and Kathrin Hatesaul (Berlin: Berlinische Galerie, Museum für Moderne Kunst, Photographie und Architektur im Martin-Gropius-Bau, 1994), 13–32; and Timothy O. Benson, *Raoul Hausmann and Berlin Dada* (Ann Arbor, Mich.: UMI Research Press, 1987), 5–57.

5. See Michael Erlhoff, "Anmerkungen zu den Texten," in Raoul Hausmann, *Bilanz der Freierlichkeit,* vol. 1 of *Texte bis 1933,* ed. Michael Erlhoff (Munich: Edition Text u. Kritik, 1982), 204–20.

6. "Wieder Herr Scheffler" and "Die gesunde Kunst." See Erlhoff, "Anmerkungen," in Hausmann, *Texte bis 1933,* 1:204.

7. Hausmann participated in the exhibition "Für unbekannte Architekten" [For Unknown Architects] curated by the Arbeitsrat für Kunst in I. B. Neumann's Graphische Kabinett between March 25 and April 25, 1919. The first Dada photomontages were shown April 28–30 in a three-day Dada show also at Neumann's gallery. Finally, Hausmann participated in the "First International Dada Fair" between June 30 and August 25, in Kunsthandlung Dr. Otto Burchard; see Züchner, Krausse, and Hatesaul, *Raoul Hausmann,* 282.

8. Richard Huelsenbeck, "Collective Dada Manifesto" (1918), in Robert Motherwell, ed., *The Dada Painters and Poets: An Anthology,* 2nd ed. (Boston: Hall, 1981), 242.

9. Huelsenbeck, "Collective Dada Manifesto," in Motherwell, *Dada Painters and Poets,* 244.

10. Ibid., 243–44.

11. Ibid., 246.

12. Raoul Hausmann, "Klassische Beziehungen zur deutschen Mittelstandsküche," *Das Bordell* (Berlin: April 1921), 6–9, reprinted in Hausmann, *Texte bis 1933,* 1:172–75. Hausmann first read the text at a Dada performance at the *Curio-Haus* in Hamburg on February 18, 1920.

13. Hausmann, *Texte bis 1933,* 1:172.

14. Ibid.

15. Ibid.

16. Ibid.

17. Ibid., 1:173.

18. Ibid.

19. Ibid.

20. The title of the poem delivered in "Classical Relations to the German Middle-Class Kitchen," "The Auto of My Soul" closely resembles one of Hausmann's published poems, "Soul Automobile." The texts, however, are different, although they both appear to be transliterations of optophonetic performances. For the text of "Seelen-Automobil," see Hausmann, *Texte bis 1933,* 1:101.

21. Hausmann, *Texte bis 1933,* 1:173.

22. Ibid., 1:174.

23. Ibid., 1:175.

24. Ibid.

25. The ethnic identity of the anti-Dada artist is suggested by his identification with all things German. The possibly Jewish identity of other characters in the story is suggested by their names. The proprietor of the establishment, for example, is identified as "a Mr. Abraham," and, at another point in the narrative, the Dada artist is called "Leonor Goldschmidt."

26. Walter Benjamin, "The Work of Art in the Age of Mechanical Reproduction" (1936), in *Illuminations,* ed. Hannah Arendt, trans. Harry Zohn (New York: Schocken, 1969), 222–23.

27. Ibid., 221.

28. Ibid., 222–23.

29. Wieland Herzfelde, introduction to "First International Dada Fair, 1920," in *German Expressionism: Documents from the End of the Wilhelmine Empire to the Rise of National Socialism,* ed. Rose-Carol Washton Long (Berkeley: University of California Press, 1993), 273.

30. Ibid.

31. Ibid., 274.

32. Ibid.

33. For a literary description of the conventional mind, see Hausmann, "Lob des Konventionellen," in *Sieg Triumph Tabak mit Bohnen,* vol. 2 of *Texte bis 1933,* ed. Michael Erlhoff (Munich: Edition Text u. Kritik, 1982), 48–50.

34. Despite the utopian ideas connected to the mass media during the Weimar Republic, the new institution of cinema received much criticism in Germany in the decades following its invention. See, for example, the critical essays collected in Jörg Schweinitz, ed., *Prolog vor dem Film: Nachdenken über ein neues Medium 1909–1914* (Leipzig: Reclam Verlag, 1992), 55–143. Although much of the negative film criticism came from bourgeois and traditionalist critics, left-wing critics and theorists also expressed reservations. See, for example, Siegfried Kracauer's essays on film collected in *The Mass Ornament: Weimar Essays,* trans. Thomas Y. Levin (Cambridge, Mass.: Harvard University Press, 1995), 281–328, which articulate numerous criticisms of the new medium. Benjamin also notes both the benefits and the risks of the new mass media in a number of his most important essays. See, for example, Walter Benjamin, "Little History of Photography" (1931), trans. Edmund Jephcott and Kingsley Shorter, in *Walter Benjamin: Selected Writings, Vol. 2, Part 2, 1931–1934,* ed. Michael W. Jennings, Howard Eiland, and Gary Smith (Cambridge, Mass.: Harvard University Press, 1999), 507–30; as well as Benjamin, "Work of Art," 217–51. Moholy-Nagy was for the most part extremely positive about cinema, especially when it was used in an experimental and nonnarrative way. See, for example, László Moholy-Nagy, *Painting, Photography, Film* (1925/1927), trans. Janet Seligman (Cambridge, Mass.: MIT Press, 1969), esp. 33–34, 122–37, 41–45.

35. For Hausmann's worries about the scientific and technological extension of human perception, see Raoul Hausmann, "Synthetisches Cino der Malerei," in Hausmann, *Texte bis 1933,* 1:14–16, esp. 15.

36. Raoul Hausmann, "Lob des Konventionellen," *Die Pille* 3, nos. 1–2 (January 1922): 4–7, reprinted in Hausmann, *Texte bis 1933,* 2:48–50, esp. 48.

37. For an excellent account of bourgeois criticisms of cinema and the various prewar attempts to reform the film industry in Germany, see Mirian Hansen, "Early Silent Cinema: Whose Public Sphere?" *New German Critique* 29 (Spring–Summer 1983): 147–84, esp. 164–71. For examples of left-wing criticisms of cinema, which, unfortunately, were often not free of a significant admixture of sexism, see P. Max Grempe, "Gegen die Frauenverblödung im Kino," *Die Gleichheit* 23, no. 5 (1912–13): 70–72, reprinted in Schweinitz, *Prolog vor dem Film,* 120–27; and Roland, "Gegen die Frauenverblödung im Kino," *Die Gleichheit* 23, no. 8 (1912–13): 115–16, reprinted in Schweinitz, *Prolog vor dem Film,* 127–30.

38. Victor Noak, "Der Kientopp," *Die Aktion* 2, no. 29 (July 17, 1912): 905–9, reprinted in Schweinitz, *Prolog vor dem Film,* 70–75, esp. 75.

39. See Peter Fritzsche, *Germans into Nazis* (Cambridge, Mass.: Harvard University Press, 1998), 40, 49–50.

40. Hindenburg is depicted in Hausmann's written work as a creature of extreme appetites, with decidedly monarchist tendencies. See Raoul Hausmann, "Warum Hindenburg 'nen Vollbart trägt," in *Texte bis 1933,* 1:134–36.

41. See, for example, the anthologies of caricature collected by Eduard Fuchs, such as *Die Frau in der Karikatur* (Munich: A. Langen, 1907), *Illustrierte Sittengeschichte vom Mittelalter bis zur Gegenwart* 1–3 (Munich: A. Langen, 1909–12), and *Die Juden in der Karikatur: Ein Beitrag zur Kulturgeschichte* (Munich: A. Langen, 1921), among many other examples.

42. See Brigid Doherty's compendium and analysis of the Berlin Dadaists' conflicting

accounts of the development of photomontage: "Berlin," in *Dada: Zurich, Berlin, Hannover, Cologne, New York, Paris,* ed. Leah Dickerman (Washington, D.C.: National Gallery of Art/DAP, 2005), 90–99.

43. Ibid., 93–95.

44. See ibid., 90. See also note 99. As Hausmann would say in 1958, "It was like a thunderbolt: one could—I saw it instantly—make pictures, assembled entirely from cut-up photographs. Back in Berlin that September, I began to realize this new vision, and I made use of photographs from the press and the cinema" (*Am Anfang war Dada,* ed. Karl Riha und Günter Kämpf [Giessen: Anabas Verlag, 1972], 45, trans. Brigid Doherty, in Doherty, "Berlin," 90). See also Hannah Höch, "A Few Words of Photomontage" (1934), originally published in Czech in *Strediško* 4, no. 1 (1934), translated from German into Czech by Frantisek Kalivoda and from Czech into English by Jitka Salaguarda, in Maud Lavin, *Cut with the Kitchen Knife: The Weimar Photomontages of Hannah Höch* (New Haven, Conn.: Yale University Press, 1993), 219–20, esp. 219.

45. On the history and significance of the soldier portraits in Germany, see Elizabeth Otto, "Figuring Gender: Photomontage and Cultural Critique in Germany's Weimar Republic" (PhD diss., University of Michigan, 2003), 19–55; and Otto, "Uniform: On Constructions of Soldierly Masculinity in Early Twentieth-Century Culture," in *Kunst, Geschlecht, Politik: Männlichkeitskonstruktionen und Kunst im Kaiserreich und in der Weimarer Republik,* ed. Martina Kessel (Frankfurt am Main: Campus Verlag, 2005), 17–42.

46. Klaus Theweleit, *Male Fantasies, Volume 1: Women, Floods, Bodies, History,* trans. Stephen Conway, Erica Carter, and Chris Turner (Minneapolis: University of Minnesota Press, 1987); and Theweleit, *Male Fantasies, Volume 2, Male Bodies: Psychoanalyzing the White Terror,* trans. Erica Carter, Chris Turner, and Stephen Conway (Minneapolis: University of Minnesota Press, 1989).

47. See, for example, Hal Foster, "Armor Fou," *October* 56 (Spring 1991): 65–97, esp. 64, 81–86.

48. See the examples collected in Robert Bosshard, Ute Eskildsen, and Robert Knodt, *Erinnerung an die Dienstzeit: Fotografien der Jahrhundertwende aus eigenem Bestand* (Essen: Museum Folkwang, 1993).

49. Anson Rabinbach, *The Human Motor: Energy, Fatigue, and the Origins of Modernity* (New York: Basic Books, 1990), 120–21.

50. Ibid., 126–27.

51. Ibid., 133–37.

52. Ibid., 138.

53. Ibid., 123, 253–58, 271–78.

54. See Johannes H. Schultz, *Das Autogene Training: Konzentrative Selbstentspannung* (Stuttgart: Georg Thieme Verlag, 1932); and Schultz, *Die Seelische Krankenbehandlung (Psychotherapie): Ein Grundriss für Fach- und Allgemeinpraxis,* 5th ed. (1918; repr. Jena: Gustav Fischer, 1943), esp. 127–31, 191, 347. My account of autogenic training has been helped by the webpage of the British Autogenic Society. See http://www.autogenic-therapy.org.uk/index.htm (accessed December 3, 2007).

55. Kristin Jean Makholm, "Film, Portraiture, and Primitivism in the Photomontages of Hannah Höch" (PhD diss., University of Minnesota, 1999), 40–41.

56. See, for example, Heide Schlüpmann, "Asta Nielsen and Female Narration: The Early Films," in *A Second Life: German Cinema's First Decades,* ed. Thomas Elsaesser (Amsterdam: Amsterdam University Press, 1996), 118–22; and Michael Wedel, "Melodrama and Narrative Space: Franz Hofer's *Heidenröslein,*" in Elsaesser, *Second Life,* 123–32.

57. See, in particular, the sections on "photomontage and signification" and "the rise of the mass media in Weimar Germany" in chapter 2.

58. Walter Benjamin, "A Discussion of Russian Filmic Art and Collectivist Art in General," first published as "Eine Diskussion über russische Filmkunst und kollektivistische Kunst überhaupt," *Die literarische Welt* 3 (March 11, 1927): 7–8, translated and reprinted in *The Weimar Republic Sourcebook*, ed. Anton Kaes, Martin Jay, and Edward Dimendberg (Berkeley: University of California Press, 1994), 626–28, esp. 626.

59. See Züchner, Krausse, and Hatesaul, *Raoul Hausmann*, 283.

60. Raoul Hausmann, "Photomontage" (1931), trans. Joel Agee, in *Photography in the Modern Era: European Documents and Critical Writings, 1913–1940*, ed. Christopher Phillips (New York: Metropolitan Museum of Art/Aperture, 1989), 178–79.

61. Norbert Wiener, *Cybernetics, or, Control and Communication in the Animal and the Machine* (New York: Wiley and Sons, 1948), 16.

62. The Czech banknote also possibly refers to performances by Hausmann and Schwitters in Prague on September 6 and 7, 1920. See Hannah Höch, "A Glance over My Life" (1958), trans. Peter Chametzky, in Lavin, *Cut with the Kitchen Knife*, 211–15. See also Züchner, Krausse, and Hatesaul, *Raoul Hausmann*, 283.

63. The "s" and the "z" recall the typography of *fmsbw* (1918). The row of letters as a whole, however, corresponds neither to *fmsbw* nor to *OFFEAH* (1918), the other surviving example of Hausmann's poster poems. This suggests that Hausmann created additional poster poems that have been lost. See Züchner, Krausse, and Hatesaul, *Raoul Hausmann*, 162.

64. Hausmann, *Am Anfang*, 43.

65. For an excellent account of the similarities and differences between various forms of experimental poetry in the early decades of the twentieth century, see Richard Sheppard, *Modernism–Dada–Postmodernism* (Evanston, Ill.: Northwestern University Press, 2000), 101–44.

66. See John D. Erickson, *Dada: Performance, Poetry, and Art* (Boston: Twayne Publishers, 1984), 37–38, 96–98.

67. For examples of the much more coherent poetry of the Italian futurists, see Willard Bohn, ed., *Italian Futurist Poetry* (Toronto: University of Toronto Press, 2005). Sheppard also distinguishes the "revisionist" poetry of the Italian futurists from the "radical" poetry of Hausmann and other Dada poets; see Sheppard, *Modernism–Dada–Postmodernism*, 125–31. On *zaum* poetry see John J. White, *Literary Futurism: Aspects of the First Avant-Garde* (Oxford: Clarendon, 1990), 250–57. On the semantics of the *zaum* poets, see Gerald Janecek, *Zaum: The Transrational Poetry of Russian Futurism* (San Diego: San Diego State University Press, 1996).

68. Hausmann, *Am Anfang*, 43. On Hausmann's interest in synesthesia and the broadening of sense perception, see Eva Züchner, "Quellen der Revolte," in Züchner, Krausse, and Hatesaul, *Raoul Hausmann*, 286–87.

69. Jörg Drews, "Die Stellung der Zunge im Gaumen: Tonbänder mit phonetischen Dichtungen Raoul Hausmanns," in *Raoul Hausmann*, ed. Kurt Bartsch and Adelheid Koch (Vienna: Literaturverlag Droschl, 1996), 258. Hausmann's poems are available on compact disc, Raoul Hausmann, *Poèmes Phonetiques* (Rochechouart: Musée Départemental d'Art Contemporain de Rochechouart, 1997).

70. Kurt Schwitters, *Ursonate* (Mainz: Wergo Schallplatten GmbH, 1993). According to Jerome Rothenberg and Pierre Joris, Schwitters heard Hausmann's *fmsbw* for the first time in Prague in September 1921, shortly before he would begin to develop the *Ursonate*; Jerome Rothenberg and Pierre Joris, introduction *Pppppp: Poems, Performance Pieces, Proses* [sic], *Plays, Poetics*, by Kurt Schwitters, ed. and trans. Jerome Rothenberg and Pierre Joris

(Philadelphia: Temple University Press, 1993), xxvi. Richter reports that Hausmann also maintained that the *Ursonate* was based on his work; see Richter, *Dada,* 139.

71. The psychological concerns of Dada art have received significant treatment in several recent studies. Doherty discusses Berlin Dada in light of neurasthenia, shell shock, and Sándor Ferenczi's writings on war neurosis; see Brigid Doherty, "'See: *We Are All Neurasthenics!*' or, The Trauma of Dada Montage," *Critical Inquiry* 24, no. 1 (Autumn 1997): 82–132. Amelia Jones productively analyzes New York Dada's relation to neurasthenia and war neurosis in *Irrational Modernism: A Neurasthenic History of New York Dada* (Cambridge, Mass.: MIT Press, 2004).

72. Richter, *Dada,* 139.

73. See Richard Huelsenbeck, "Dada Tours," in Kaes, Jay, and Dimendberg, *Weimar Republic Sourcebook,* 486–87; Huelsenbeck, *Memoirs of a Dada Drummer* (Berkeley: University of California Press, 1991), 67–71; Hannah Höch, "A Glance over My Life," in Lavin, *Cut with the Kitchen Knife,* 211–15, esp. 212–13; and Walter Mehring, *Berlin Dada: Eine Chronik mit Photos und Dokumenten* (Zürich: Arche, 1959), 47. See also Richter's description of Schwitters performing his *Ursonate* in *Dada,* 142–43; Karin Füllner, *Dada Berlin in Zeitungen: Gedächtnisfeiern und Skandale* (Siegen: Universität-Gesamthochschule-Siegen, 1986), 21, 26, 29, 32, 33, 35, 36, 38, 39, 40–41, 43, 47–48, 49, 50, 54–55; and Bergius, *"Dada Triumphs!"* 27–29, 35–36, 64–69.

74. On Hausmann's sound poetry, see Karl Riha, "fmsbwtözäu pgiv-..?mü: Raoul Hausmanns optophonetische Poesie," in Bartsch and Koch, *Raoul Hausmann,* 31–44; and Jörg Drews, "Die Stellung der Zunge im Gaumen: Tonbänder mit phonetischen Dichtungen Raoul Hausmanns" in Bartsch and Koch, *Raoul Hausmann,* 256–59. Hausmann claims that he was not aware of Ball's abstract poetry or that of the *zaum* poets until 1920; see Janecek, *Zaum,* 210.

75. Norbert Wiener, *The Human Use of Human Beings: Cybernetics and Society,* rev. ed. (Garden City, N.Y.: Doubleday, 1954), 15–27, esp. 26–27.

76. Ibid., 57, 167.

77. On Jung, Gross, and *Die freie Strasse,* see Hanne Bergius, *Das Lachen Dadas* (Giessen: Anabas-Verlag, 1989), 66–89. On Gross's psychological theories and their influence on Hausmann, see Jennifer E. Michaels, *Anarchy and Eros: Otto Gross' Impact on German Expressionist Writers: Leonard Frank, Franz Jung, Johannes R. Becher, Karl Otten, Curt Corrinth, Walter Hasenclever, Oskar Maria Graf, Franz Kafka, Franz Werfel, Max Brod, Raoul Hausmann, and Berlin Dada* (New York: Peter Lang, 1983), 35–55, 167–75; and Sheppard, *Modernism–Dada–Postmodernism,* 191–92. See also Roy F. Allen, *Literary Life in German Expressionism and the Berlin Circles* (Ann Arbor, Mich.: UMI Research Press, 1972), 58, 131, 246.

78. In the late 1990s, Freud's concept of the ego ideal plays this role in certain respects; see J. Laplanche and J.-B. Pontalis, *The Language of Psychoanalysis* (1967), trans. Donald Nicholson-Smith (New York: Norton, 1973), 144–45.

79. See Otto Gross, "Vom Konflikt des Eigenen und Fremden," *Die Freie Strasse,* 4, 1916, reprinted in Bergius, *Das Lachen Dadas,* 71–73. See also Gross's essays, "Die Einwirkung der Allgemeinheit auf das Individuum" (1913), "Anmerkung zu einer neuen Ethik" (1913), and "Notiz über Beziehungen" (1913), reprinted in *Der Fall Otto Gross: Eine Pressekampagne deutscher Intellektueller im Winter 1913–14,* ed. Christina Jung and Thomas Anz (Marburg: Verlag LiteratureWissenschaft.de, 2002), 159–69.

80. On Hausmann's politics and his interest in synthesizing Gross's radical psychology with "anarcho-communist" thought, see Sheppard, *Modernism–Dada–Postmodernism,* 330–34.

81. "This most inner core of the revolution—the resignation of the male spirit and of the one-sided male drive for order—must lead, by means of a complete dissolution of the existing petty-bourgeois moral sexual relations, to the creation of a new community, and concurrently with the realization of the maxim, 'Everyone according to their abilities, everyone according to their needs,' eventually to a new justice and truth. The exploding point lies in the sexual as well as the economic. In the sexual, a revolution has still not begun, and we experience that, for example, in many cities in Russia, the male monogamous family is sublated, and in its stead, women are subjugated to a nearly monopoly-like concept of property. Here only a clarification of sexual relations will lead to liquidating technological developments. The Communist Manifesto promotes the female community and refers to the fact that the family—and consequently the dominant patriarchal morality—was of little value to the proletariat. It is, however, necessary that one proceeds here not only in general according to the classes but also according to the fundamentals of human existence. The child's sexual complex shows us the way to this" (Hausmann, *Texte bis 1933*, 1:51–52). See also Hausmann, "Der Besitzbegriff in Hausmann, in *Texte bis 1933*, 1:34–38, esp. 37–38.

82. Hausmann, *Texte bis 1933*, 1:50–51.

83. "In young friendships, for example, homosexuality is apparent as a natural drive of human beings. Nearly every child has homosexual tendencies—tendencies that do not derive from its strategies of accommodation to the family. The bourgeois family scorned homosexuality and directed the sexual complex toward either masculine or feminine poles. The child is a highly instinctually developed form of human being. Homosexuality is not only present simply before and during puberty. In its wavering over the authentic gender roles, homosexuality is characteristic of the human being in general. The expansion of the sexual formation of human beings through homosexuality is repressed by the Christian romantic point of view during the family upbringing. Just as the forced compression of sexuality in monogamy was invented primarily as a means to simplify male domination tactics vis-à-vis women and was for generations continued thoughtlessly, so the essence of monogamy was pushed into dissolution through this mechanization. The secret male sexual form, which was needed for the continuation of patriarchal society, crippled the female drive to organization and society in its opposition to women, so that we only know the developmental forms of the mother or the prostitute or some lesbians, which cannot be considered in the context of the species development of the female spirit" (Hausmann, *Texte bis 1933*, 1:52).

84. "The formation of a female society, which leads to a new promiscuity and, in connection with this mother's law (as opposed to the patriarchal family law of male imprint), is most intimately connected to the reconstruction of bourgeois society through communism. The property concepts, which until now have been prized as sexual fidelity, have proven to be comfortable exploitation lies on the part of men. These concepts reduce women to prostitutes in more or less calculable forms; however, these concepts do not do justice to actual female sexuality, neither in the case of the mother, nor in the case of the free woman. The expansion of petty-bourgeois anarchist individualism (which requires taking possession of things in order to be able to represent property in the first place) into communism will point to that which is inalienably characteristic of male as well as female sexuality. The family as an instrument of coercion will be transformed into groups, relationships, and elective families through the transformation of women from their hitherto only male-determined and male-oriented sexuality to a truly female one, one whose essence is able to support friendship, camaraderie, and adherents (in other forms), just like the hitherto male mode of sexual behaviour. The end of the subjugation of women will show

286 — Notes to Chapter 3

that women are perhaps more strongly qualified than men to create moral values and social organization—only they will able to do this in a less simple way than men. Law and moral concepts, the so-called truths of men, must be totally destroyed; and they will show themselves as injustice and lies—precisely because of their simplifying and exclusionary aim to subjugate everything. The evaluation of an existence in contradiction will be set up by women, because women are actual, real in opposition to the idealizing gestures of men, who have grasped only some of the laws that direct life. The so-called mendacity of women will be transformed at a new stage of development into an ability to realize, an ability that was previously forced to appear as a lie because of the male will to do violence. Today, true men stand up for the dissolution of the property rights of men over women and for a transformation of the family of little worth as much as for the economic communist society, which runs parallel with an expansion of the sexual outlook" (Hausmann, *Texte bis 1933*, 1:52–54).

85. On the contradictions between Hausmann's professed beliefs and his actions toward Höch, see, for example, Lavin, *Cut with the Kitchen Knife*, 26–29; and Karoline Hille, *Hannah Höch und Raoul Hausmann: Eine Berliner Dada-Geschichte* (Berlin: Rowohlt, 2000), esp. 130–36.

86. See, for example, Raoul Hausmann, "Club Dada: Berlin 1918–20" (1958), trans. J. M. Ritchie, in *The Era of German Expressionism*, ed. Paul Raabe (Woodstock, N.Y.: Overlook, 1985), 225–27.

87. See Brigid Doherty, "Figures of the Pseudorevolution," *October* 84 (Spring 1998): 72, 77.

88. Hausmann, "Der deutsche Spiesser ärgert sich," in Hausmann, *Texte bis 1933*, 1:82–84.

89. For an excellent account of the nature and functions of portraiture as well as the conceptual issues that surround it, see Richard Brilliant, *Portraiture* (Cambridge, Mass.: Harvard University Press, 1991). For more historically specific analyses of the characteristics and functions of portraiture in different media and at different historical moments since the Renaissance, see the essays collected in Joanna Woodall, ed., *Portraiture: Facing the Subject* (Manchester: Manchester University Press, 1997), esp. Joanna Woodall, "Introduction: Facing the Subject," 1–25.

90. Brilliant, following Hans-Georg Gadamer, discusses this ontological connection by means of the concept of "occasionality." See Brilliant, *Portraiture*, esp. 7–9, 18–19.

91. According to Timothy Benson, despite their avowed interest, the Dada artists knew little of Tatlin's art in 1920. Instead, they had received most of their information by reading Konstantin Umanski's article, "Neue Kunstrichtungen in Russland: I. Der Tatlinismus oder die Maschinenkunst," *Der Ararat* 1, no. 1 (January 1920). See Benson, *Raoul Hausmann and Berlin Dada*, 186.

92. Raoul Hausmann, quoted in Benson, *Raoul Hausmann and Berlin Dada*, 186.

93. On the Berlin Dada artists' interest in Henry Ford, see Doherty, "Berlin," 93.

94. On the role of physiognomic likeness in portraiture, see Woodall, "Introduction: Facing the Subject," in Woodall, *Portraiture*, 1, 6–7.

95. On some of the problems that emerge when an artist treats a portrait as exemplifying more general human qualities, see Brilliant, *Portraiture*, 32–40. In addition, although most exemplary portraits attempt to honor or idealize their subjects, caricature, as is well known, is a form of portraiture that generally attempts to do the opposite. See Brilliant, *Portraiture*, 69–72.

96. In comparison with the portraits by artists associated with *Neue Sachlichkeit* in Germany in the mid- and late 1920s, which also play between the personal and the typical,

the portraits of the Berlin Dadaists are much more innovative. On *Neue Sachlichkeit* portraiture, see Sabine Rewald, ed., *Glitter and Doom: German Portraits from the 1920s* (New Haven, Conn.: Yale University Press, 2006).

97. On the concept of institutional critique, see Peter Bürger, *Theory of the Avant-Garde*, trans. Michael Shaw (Minneapolis: University of Minnesota Press, 1984), 12–13, 22, 49. See also Benjamin H. D. Buchloh, "Conceptual Art 1962–1969: From the Aesthetic of Administration to the Critique of Institutions," *October* 55 (Winter 1990): 105–43.

98. Raoul Hausmann, "Dada in Europa," *Der Dada* 3 (April 1920): 5. See also the translation of Hausmann's text by Jean Boase-Beier, which has been altered here, in *The Dada Reader: A Critical Anthology*, ed. Dawn Ades (Chicago: University of Chicago Press, 2006), 93.

99. On Heidebrink, the island where Hausmann and Höch claimed to have discovered photomontage as an artistic strategy, see Eva Züchner, ed., *Scharfrichter der bürgerlichen Seele: Raoul Hausmann in Berlin, 1900–1933* (Berlin: Berlinische Galerie/Hatje, 1998), 80n1.

100. Walter Benjamin, "Little History of Photography" (1931), trans. Edmund Jephcott and Kingsley Shorter, in *Walter Benjamin: Selected Writings, Vol. 2, Part 2, 1931–1934*, ed. Michael W. Jennings, Howard Eiland, and Gary Smith (Cambridge, Mass.: Harvard University Press, 1999), 511–12.

101. See, for example, Albert Renger-Patzsch, "Aims" (1927), trans. Joel Agee, in Phillips, *Photography in the Modern Era*, 104–5; Albert Renger-Patzsch, "Joy before the Object," trans. Joel Agee, in Phillips, *Photography in the Modern Era*, 108–9; Hugo Sieker, "Absolute Realism: On the Photographs of Albert Renger-Patzsch" (1928), trans. Joel Agee, in Phillips, *Photography in the Modern Era*, 110–15, esp. 111; László Moholy-Nagy, "Sharp or Unsharp? A Reply to Hans Windisch" (1929), trans. Matyas Esterhazy, in Phillips, *Photography in the Modern Era*, 132–39, esp. 135–36; and Franz Roh, "The Value of Photography" (1930), trans. Joel Agee, in Phillips, *Photography in the Modern Era*, 160–63, esp. 161.

102. Raoul Hausmann and Werner Gräff, "How Does the Photographer See?" (1933), trans. Joel Agee, in Phillips, *Photography in the Modern Era*, 195.

103. László Moholy-Nagy, "Production-Reproduction" (1922), trans. Caroline Fawkes, in Phillips, *Photography in the Modern Era*, 80.

104. László Moholy-Nagy, "Unprecedented Photography" (1927), trans. Joel Agee, in Phillips, *Photography in the Modern Era*, 83–84.

105. Benjamin, "Little History of Photography," in Jennings, Eiland, and Smith, *Walter Benjamin: Selected Writings*, 510.

106. See Walter Benjamin, "On the Concept of History" (1940/1950), trans. Harry Zohn, in *Walter Benjamin: Selected Writings, Vol. 4, 1938–1940*, ed. Howard Eiland and Michael W. Jennings (Cambridge, Mass.: Harvard University Press, 2003), 389–400, esp. 395–96. See also Benjamin's discussion of film and photography in "The Work of Art in the Age of Mechanical Reproduction," which stresses both their analytic and their revolutionary potentials (in Benjamin, *Illuminations*, 217–51, esp. 235–37).

107. Siegfried Kracauer, "Photography" (1927), trans. Thomas Y. Levin, in Kracauer, *Mass Ornament*, 61–62.

108. Kracauer, "Photography," 62.

109. Hausmann and Gräff, "How Does the Photographer See?" in Phillips, *Photography in the Modern Era*, 196.

110. Ernst Jünger, *Der Arbeiter: Herrschaft und Gestalt* (1932; repr. Stuttgart: Klett-Cotta, 1982).

111. Ernst Jünger, "Einleitung," in *Die veränderte Welt. Eine Bilderfibel unserer Zeit*, ed. Edmund Schultz (Breslau: Wilh. Gottl. Korn Verlag, 1933), 7–8.

112. See Ernst Jünger, "Totale Mobilmachung" (1930), in *Krieg und Krieger,* ed. Ernst Jünger (Berlin: Junker und Dünnhaupt, 1930), trans. Joel Golb and Richard Wolin as "Total Mobilization," in *The Heidegger Controversy: A Critical Reader,* ed. Richard Wolin (Cambridge, Mass.: MIT Press, 1993), 122–39.

113. Ernst Jünger, "Photography and the 'Second Consciousness,'" an excerpt from "On Pain" (1934), trans. Joel Agee, in Phillips, *Photography in the Modern Era,* 208.

114. Ibid., 207–8.

115. "In politics, too, the photograph is a weapon that is being used with increasing mastery. It seems to offer our new type a particularly effective means of tracking down his enemy's individual (and hence no longer adequately defended) character; the private sphere is no match for the photograph" (Jünger, "Photography and the 'Second Consciousness,'" 209).

116. Jünger, "Einleitung," 7.

117. Ibid., 6–7.

118. On the partially linguistic construction of perception, see, for example, Edmund Husserl, *Logical Investigations,* 1–2, ed. Dermot Moran, trans. J. N. Findlay (1900, 1901; repr. New York: Routledge, 2001).

119. See Bürger, *Theory of the Avant-Garde.* Bürger's theory of the avant-garde has had a significant impact on modern and contemporary art history since its publication. In the United States alone, important historian–critics like Donald Kuspit, Benjamin H. D. Buchloh, and Hal Foster have all cited, developed, and criticized Bürger's concepts. In particular, Bürger has been faulted for his devaluation of post–World War II "neo-avant-garde" art. The argument that this book makes—that Bürger's theory of the avant-garde obscures a radical politics of hybrid identity—has not been made before, nor has Bürger altered his theory in a way that would render these criticisms invalid.

120. See note 97.

121. Bürger, *Theory of the Avant-Garde,* 49.

122. Ibid., 69. Bürger derives this argument from a particular passage in Benjamin's book on the German *Trauerspiel.* See Walter Benjamin, *The Origin of German Tragic Drama,* trans. Josh Osborne (New York: Verso, 1990), 183–84. Although the passage does suggest that the allegorist eliminates the original meaning of the allegorical fragment and gives it a new one, Benjamin's actual interpretive practices raise questions as to how closely he followed this principle.

123. Bürger, *Theory of the Avant-Garde,* 79–80.

124. Buchloh, for example, attacks Joseph Beuys for his representational use of ready-mades—that is, his use of real-world objects to stand for ideas—a use, according to Buchloh, that is a radical perversion of Duchamp's original ready-made practices, which "were viable and relevant primarily as epistemological reflections and decisions within the formal discourse of post-Cubist painting and sculpture," which changed "the state of a formal language according to given historical conditions," and which did not, when originally made, possess "psychological, emotional, [or] metaphysical meaning." See Benjamin H. D. Buchloh, "Twilight of the Idol," *Artforum* 18, no. 5 (January 1980): 35–43, esp. 39–40. A reliance on the same citation from Benjamin also underlies Craig Owens's contention that postmodern works of art replace the meanings of the fragments that they appropriate. See Craig Owens, "The Allegorical Impulse: Toward a Theory of Postmodernism," in *Beyond Recognition: Representation, Power, and Culture* (Berkeley: University of California Press, 1992), 52–87, esp. 54.

125. Eve Kosofsky Sedgwick, *Between Men: English Literature and Male Homosocial Desire* (New York: Columbia University Press, 1985), 1–5.

126. For a good example of this trope, see Plato's *Symposium* (*Plato: Symposium,* trans. Robin Waterfield [New York: Oxford University Press, 1994]).

127. On the idea of a preexisting discursive network—"gossip"—helping support a homosexual reading of a work of art, see Gavin Butt, *Between You and Me: Queer Disclosures in the New York Art World, 1948–1963* (Durham, N.C.: Duke University Press, 2005), esp. 5–9. Like Butt's discursive source materials, Hausmann's writings on homosexuality help support and legitimate a homosexual reading of some of his artworks. On Hausmann's understanding of the revolutionary potential of homosexuality, see notes 81 and 83.

128. For reproductions of the other two double portraits, see Züchner, Krausse, and Hatesaul, *Raoul Hausmann,* 50–51. On the growing discourse about homosexuality in Germany since the 1860s, see James D. Steakley, *The Homosexual Emancipation Movement in Germany* (New York: Arno, 1975).

129. Donna J. Haraway, "A Cyborg Manifesto: Science, Technology, and Socialist-Feminism in the Twentieth Century" (1991 revision of an essay from 1985), in Haraway, *Simians, Cyborgs, and Women: The Reinvention of Nature* (New York: Routledge, 1991), 180.

130. Haraway, "Cyborg Manifesto," 181.

131. On Höch's bisexuality and her use of photomontage to undermine traditional forms of gender identity, see Lavin, *Cut with the Kitchen Knife,* 185–204, esp. 188–90.

4. The Militarized Cyborg

1. This is typical of many of the histories of twentieth-century art. See, for example, Hal Foster, Rosalind Krauss, Yve-Alain Bois, and Benjamin H. D. Buchloh, *Art since 1900: Modernism, Antimodernism, Postmodernism, Volume 1, 1900–1944* (New York: Thames and Hudson, 2004), 168–73; H. H. Arnason, *History of Modern Art: Painting, Sculpture, Architecture, Photography,* 5th ed., Peter Kalb, revising author (Upper Saddle River, N.J.: Prentice Hall, 2004), 254–56; Robert Hughes, *The Shock of the New,* 2nd ed. (New York: Knopf, 1991), 66–78; and Werner Haftmann, *Painting in the Twentieth Century,* trans. Ralph Manheim, 2nd ed. (New York: Praeger, 1966), 1:186. This is also typical of many specialized studies on Berlin Dada; see, for example, Hans Richter, *Dada: Art and Anti-Art,* trans. David Britt (London: Thames and Hudson, 1965), 101–35; as well as the articles and book chapters by Brigid Doherty and Bruce Altshuler, cited below.

2. See, for example, John Heartfield and George Grosz's polemic essay, "The Art Scab," which argues in support of an armed workers' struggle against all those who would exploit them: Heartfield and Grosz, "Der Kunstlump," *Der Gegner* 1, nos. 10–12 (Berlin: Malik Verlag, 1920): 48–56, translated and reprinted as "The Art Scab" in *The Weimar Republic Sourcebook,* ed. Anton Kaes, Martin Jay, and Edward Dimendberg (Berkeley: University of California Press, 1994), 483–86. Grosz would later disassociate himself from his procommunist statements and his professions of solidarity with the masses; see George Grosz, *A Little Yes and a Big No,* trans. Lola Sachs Dorin (New York: Dial, 1946), 158, 162–63, 165–68.

3. Grosz's later statements on disabled soldiers, while fairly neutral, were not particularly positive or sympathetic. He suggested, for example, that at least some of the crippled street beggars were simulating their injuries. See Grosz, *A Little Yes,* 170.

4. Among the most useful books for understanding deconstructive method are Jacques Derrida, *Of Grammatology* (1967), trans. Gayatri Chakravorty Spivak (Baltimore, Md.: Johns Hopkins University Press, 1997); Derrida, *Margins of Philosophy* (1972), trans. Alan Bass (Chicago: University of Chicago Press, 1982); and Derrida, *Positions* (1972), trans. Alan Bass (Chicago: University of Chicago Press, 1981). This brief account of deconstruction

has also benefited from Christopher Norris, *Deconstruction: Theory and Practice* (London: Methuen, 1982); and Rodolphe Gasché, *The Tain of the Mirror: Derrida and the Philosophy of Reflection* (Cambridge, Mass.: Harvard University Press, 1986).

5. Ernst Jünger, "Photography and the 'Second Consciousness,'" an excerpt from "On Pain" (1934), trans. Joel Agee, in *Photography in the Modern Era: European Documents and Critical Writings, 1913–1940,* ed. Christopher Phillips (New York: Metropolitan Museum of Art/Aperture, 1989), 207–10.

6. For the range of meanings that allegory had in German art history in the 1920s and 1930s, see, for example, Otto Schmitt, ed., *Reallexikon zur deutschen Kunstgeschichte* 1 (Stuttgart: J. B. Metzlersche Verlagsbuchhandlung, 1937), 346–66.

7. Walter Benjamin, *The Origin of German Tragic Drama,* trans. Josh Osborne (New York: Verso, 1990).

8. As Benjamin suggested, "The three most important impulses in the origin of western allegory are non-antique, anti-antique: the gods project into the alien world, they become evil, and they become creatures" (*Origin of German Tragic Drama,* 225).

9. Benjamin, *Origin of German Tragic Drama,* 78–80.

10. Ibid., 179, 224, 119.

11. Ibid., 192–95.

12. Ibid., 85, 89. As Beatrice Hanssen notes, the meaning of the word "creature" undergoes several transformations in Benjamin's writings. See Beatrice Hanssen, *Walter Benjamin's Other History: Of Stones, Animals, Human Beings, and Angels* (Berkeley: University of California Press, 1998), esp. 103–7, 150–62. In *The Origins of German Tragic Drama,* Benjamin primarily emphasized the word's double meaning as both a sacred and a profane term. Originally a translation of the Latin *creatura* in the late Middle Ages, "creature," in German, first meant the totality of God's creation, a meaning eventually taken over in the eighteenth century by the term "nature." See J. Wiebering, "Kreatur, Kreatürlichkeit," in *Historisches Wörterbuch der Philosophie,* ed. Joachim Ritter and Karlfried Gründer (Basel: Schwabe, 1976), 1204–11. In addition, however, by Benjamin's time, "creature" had also come to mean what was "animal-like" in the sense of instinctive, base, enslaved, material, passionate, or bodily. See Hans Schulz, ed., *Deutsches Fremdwörterbuch,* vol. 1 (Strassburg: Karl Trübner, 1913), 402.

13. Or, as Benjamin so characteristically put it, even "the human body could be no exception to the commandment which ordered the destruction of the organic so that the true meaning, as it was written and ordained, might be picked up from its fragments" (*Origin of German Tragic Drama,* 216–17).

14. Through the allegorist's intervention, the "product of the corpse is life," because the "deadness of the figures and the abstraction of the concepts are . . . the precondition for the allegorical metamorphosis of the pantheon into a world of magical, conceptual creatures" (Benjamin, *Origin of German Tragic Drama,* 218, 226).

15. "Ultimately," Benjamin contended, "in the death-signs of the baroque the direction of allegorical reflection is reversed; on the second part of its wide arc it returns, to redeem" (*Origin of German Tragic Drama,* 232).

16. "Allegory goes away empty-handed. Evil as such, which it cherished as enduring profundity, exists only in allegory, is nothing other than allegory, and means something different from what it is. It means precisely the non-existence of what it presents. The absolute vices, as exemplified by tyrants and intriguers, are allegories. They are not real, and that which they represent, they possess only in the subjective view of melancholy; they are this view, which is destroyed by its own offspring because they only signify its blindness. They point to the absolutely subjective pensiveness, to which alone they owe

their existence. By its allegorical form evil as such reveals itself to be a subjective phenomenon" (*Origin of German Tragic Drama*, 233).

17. Benjamin, *Origin of German Tragic Drama*, 53–56.

18. Ibid., 53.

19. Ibid., 176–82.

20. Ibid., 177.

21. As Brigid Doherty notes, the Dadaists hired a professional photographer to document the "Dada Fair" and send pictures to newspapers and magazines. See Brigid Doherty, "'See: *We Are All Neurasthenics!*' or, The Trauma of Dada Montage," *Critical Inquiry* 24, no. 1 (Autumn 1997): 86n9.

22. See Sherwin Simmons, "Advertising Seizes Control of Life: Berlin Dada and the Power of Advertising," *Oxford Art Journal* 22, no. 1 (1999): 119–46, esp. 139–41.

23. The poster is listed as item 77 in the "Dada Fair" catalog and described as follows: "German People's Party poster glued up by workers of a Berlin cliché factory." See Wieland Herzfelde, *Erste Internationale Dada-Messe* (Berlin: Malik Verlag, 1920), 4. In addition, as Simmons notes, it could have potentially reminded its viewers of the controversy that Cay's work raised within the German advertising community that year when it was revealed that he had designed posters for five different political parties, thereby suggesting that political propaganda could—and was—being made by artists who did not necessarily support the party on whose campaign they were working. See Simmons, "Advertising Seizes Control of Life," 141–42.

24. Stephanie Barron, ed., *Degenerate Art: The Fate of the Avant-Garde in Nazi Germany* (New York: Abrams, 1991), 56–57; and *Entartete Kunst: Ausstellungsführer*, ed. Eberhard Roters (1937; repr. Cologne: Walther König, 1988), 15.

25. On the support and rehabilitation of disabled veterans during World War I and the Weimar Republic, see Deborah Cohen, *The War Come Home: Disabled Veterans in Britain and Germany, 1914–1939* (Berkeley: University of California Press, 2001), 61–97, 149–87. See also Young-Sun Hong, *Welfare, Modernity, and the Weimar State* (Princeton, N.J.: Princeton University Press, 1998), 92–97; and Detlev J. K. Peukert, *The Weimar Republic: The Crisis of Classical Modernity*, trans. Richard Deveson (New York: Hill and Wang, 1992), 137.

26. Anson Rabinbach, *The Human Motor: Energy, Fatigue, and the Origins of Modernity* (New York: Basic Books, 1990), 266.

27. In his images of war cripples, Dix often used display windows and commodities to suggest what his subjects lacked or desired. See Matthew Biro, "History at a Standstill: Walter Benjamin, Otto Dix, and the Question of Stratigraphy," *Res* 40 (Autumn 2001): 153–76, esp. 160.

28. Hanne Bergius, *"Dada Triumphs!" Dada Berlin, 1917–1923, Artistry of Polarities*, trans. Brigitte Pichon (Farmington, Mich.: G. K. Hall, 2003), 254.

29. See Richard Brilliant, *Portraiture* (Cambridge, Mass.: Harvard University Press, 1991), 19, 69–70.

30. As Altshuler notes, in addition to the two "corrected masterpieces" by Grosz and Heartfield, "the purported purity of the masterpiece was mocked throughout the show in photocollages utilizing elements of known works—Baader's image of his face over the bust of the *Venus de Milo*, Schlichter's *Improved Paintings of Antiquity* with modern heads on the *Apollo Belvedere* and, again, the *Venus de Milo*, Hausmann's doctoring of Rubens's *Bacchanal* and Grosz's attack on Botticelli's *Primavera*." One of the "corrected masterpieces" by Grosz and Heartfield was created by adding lettering and photos to a reproduction of a cubist collage by Picasso; the second was produced by gluing a photographic portrait of

Hausmann over the head of Henri Rousseau in a reproduction of one of Rousseau's self-portraits. See Bruce Altshuler, *The Avant-Garde in Exhibition: New Art in the Twentieth Century* (Berkeley: University of California Press, 1994), 109.

31. See A. N., "Die Unglücklichsten Opfer des Krieges," *Die freie Welt* 2, no. 38 (1920): cover, 2–3. On Grosz's contributions to *Die freie Welt*, see Sherwin Simmons, "War, Revolution, and the Transformation of the German Humor Magazine, 1914–1927," *Art Journal* 52, no. 1 (Spring 1993): 51–52.

32. See Ernst Friedrich, *Krieg dem Kriege* (1924) (Frankfurt am Main: Zweitausendeins, 1980), esp. 204–27. The first volume of *Krieg dem Kriege* appeared in 1924 and was followed by a second volume in 1926. Both volumes were reprinted during the Weimar Republic. On Friedrich's book and museum as well as on the photographic representation of war in general during the Weimar Republic, see Dora Apel, "Cultural Battlegrounds: Weimar Photographic Narratives of War," *New German Critique* 76 (Winter 1999): 49–84.

33. See Otto Dix, *The War = Der Krieg*, with essays by Annette Becker, Philippe Dagen, and Thomas Compere-Morel (Milan: 5 Continents, 2003).

34. Herzfelde, *Erste Internationale Dada-Messe*, 3. See also Bergius, *"Dada Triumphs!"* appendix, "First International Dada Fair: Catalog of the Exhibition and Its Reconstruction," 29.

35. Brigid Doherty, "Figures of the Pseudorevolution," *October* 84 (Spring 1998): 75–80.

36. Ibid., 80.

37. Going against this interpretation, the photographs of Ebert's face taken in 1920 show his face to be somewhat broader than that of Grosz's victim. In addition, the mustache of Grosz's subject droops down farther than Ebert's appears to in various photographs of him made during the Weimar Republic.

38. On the science of labor, psychotechnics, and Taylorism in Germany during World War I and the Weimar Republic, see Rabinbach, *Human Motor*, esp. 189–205, 228–34, 238–44, 253–70, 273–84. On reintegrating disabled veterans into the German workforce, see Rabinbach, *Human Motor*, 265–70; Mia Fineman, "Ecce Homo Prostheticus," *New German Critique* 76 (Winter 1999): 85–114; and Cohen, *War Come Home*, 149–87.

39. Rabinbach, *Human Motor*, 266.

40. Fineman, "Ecce Homo Prostheticus," 104–5.

41. See, for example, Konrad Biesalski, *Kriegskrüppelfürsorge: Ein Aufklärungswort zum Troste und zur Mahnung, im Auftrage der Deutschen Vereinigung für Krüppelfürsorge und der Deutschen Orthopädischen Gesellschaft herausgegeben von dem Schriftführer beider Gesellschaften* (Leipzig: L. Voss, 1915); Carl Hermann Unthan, *Ohne Arme durchs Leben* (Karlsruhe: Braun, 1916); Moritz Borchart, *Ersatzglieder und Arbeitshilfen für Kriegsbeschädigte und Unfallverletzte* (Berlin: Julius Springer, 1919); Karl von Kügelgen, *Nicht Krüppel—Sieger! Gedanken und Erfahrungen eines Einarmigen* (Langensalza: Hermann Beyer und Söhne, 1919); and Biesalski, *Grundriss der Krüppelfürsorge* (Leipzig: Leopold Voss, 1926). Fineman also cites a number of other texts; see "Ecce Homo Prosteticus," 85–104.

42. See, for example, Dr. Berndt, "Künstliche Gliedmassen: Ein wichtiges Gebiet der Kriegsinvaliden-Fürsorge," *Berliner Illustrirte Zeitung* 24, no. 28 (July 11, 1915): 377–79.

43. Cohen, *War Come Home*, 88–89.

44. Ibid., 157–58.

45. The other earliest photomontage that can be dated precisely was Heartfield's representation of his brother with a huge soccer ball replacing his body published on the cover of *Jedermann*, right above Grosz's *Gallery of German Manly Beauty*; see Bergius, *"Dada Triumphs!"* 105.

46. Bergius, *"Dada Triumphs!"* 52.

47. Wieland Herzfelde, *Schutzhaft: Erlebnisse vom 7. bis 20. März 1919 bei den Berliner Ordnungstruppen* (Berlin: Malik Verlag, 1919).

48. Bergius, *"Dada Triumphs!"* 105.

49. See the reproduction in Peter Pachnicke and Klaus Honnef, eds., *John Heartfield* (New York: Abrams, 1992), 81 (cat. no. 174).

50. For a good account of the *Dolchstosslegende,* including a few examples of the contemporary visual culture that represented this myth, see Rainer Sammet, *"Dolchstoss": Deutschland und die Auseinandersetzung mit der Niederlage im Ersten Weltkrieg (1918–1933)* (Berlin: Trafo Verlag, 2003).

51. Altshuler, *Avant-Garde in Exhibition,* 110–12.

52. "Um dieses Kunstwerk vollkommen zu begreifen, exerziere man täglich zwölf Stunden mit vollgepacktem Affen und feldmarschmäßig ausgerüstet auf dem tempelhofer Feld." The sign is then signed "Heartfield-Schlichter mont." See Figure 4.5.

53. See Frederick G. Holweck, "St. Michael the Archangel," in *The Catholic Encyclopedia,* ed. Charles G. Herbermann, vol. 10 (New York: Appleton, 1911), online edition (1999) (accessed December 18, 2007); and "Michael, Archangel," *New Catholic Encyclopedia,* 2nd ed., 15 vols. (Detroit: Gale, 2003), 9:595, Gale Virtual Reference Library (accessed December 18, 2007).

54. See Henry G. Ganss, "Martin Luther," in *The Catholic Encyclopedia,* ed. Charles G. Herbermann, vol. 9 (New York: Appleton, 1910), online edition (1999) (accessed December 24, 2007); and "Luther, Martin," *New Catholic Encyclopedia,* 2nd ed., 15 vols. (Detroit: Gale, 2003), 8:877–83, Gale Virtual Reference Library (accessed December 24, 2007).

55. See Hartmut Lehmann, "The Germans as a Chosen People: Old Testament Themes in German Nationalism," *German Studies Review* 14, no. 2 (May 1991): 261–73.

56. See Karl-Wilhelm Dahm, "German Protestantism and Politics, 1918–1939," *Journal of Contemporary History* 3, no. 1 (January 1968): 29–49.

57. See, for example, Hausmann's discussion of photomontage, quoted in Richter: "We called this process photomontage because it embodied our refusal to play the part of the artist. We regarded ourselves as engineers, and our work as construction: we *assembled* (in French: *monter*) our work, like a fitter" (Richter, *Dada,* 118).

58. Bergius, *"Dada Triumphs!"* 210.

59. Doherty, "See," 121–23.

60. Ernst Jünger, "Totale Mobilmachung" (1930), in *Krieg und Krieger,* ed. Ernst Jünger (Berlin: Junker und Dünnhaupt, 1930); Jünger, "Total Mobilization," in *The Heidegger Controversy: A Critical Reader,* ed. Richard Wolin, trans. Joel Golb and Richard Wolin (Cambridge, Mass.: MIT Press, 1993), 126.

61. Jünger, "Total Mobilization," 123, 130.

62. Ibid., 128, 130–31, 134.

63. Ernst Jünger, *Der Arbeiter: Herrschaft und Gestalt* (1932; repr. Stuttgart: Klett-Cotta, 1982).

64. Jünger, "Total Mobilization," 129.

65. Walter Benjamin, "Theories of German Fascism" (1930), in *Walter Benjamin: Selected Writings, Vol. 2, Part 1, 1927–1930,* ed. Michael W. Jennings, Howard Eiland, and Gary Smith, trans. Jerolf Witkoff (Cambridge, Mass.: Harvard University Press, 1999), 314.

66. On Dix's wartime experiences, see Fritz Löffler, *Otto Dix: Leben und Werk* (Vienna: Anton Schroll, 1967), 14–16; and Dietrich Schubert, *Otto Dix in Selbstzeugnissen und Bilddokumenten* (Reinbek bei Hamburg: Rowohlt, 1980), 22–28. For a full-length study of Dix's representations of war, see Otto Conzelmann, *Der Andere Dix: Sein Bild vom Menschen und vom Krieg* (Stuttgart: Klett-Cotta, 1983). Dix's wartime experience became an

important issue for German critics in 1923 and 1924; see Dennis Crockett, "The Most Famous Painting of the 'Golden Twenties'? Otto Dix and the *Trench* Affair," *Art Journal* 51, no. 1 (Spring 1992): 72–80; and Andreas Strobl, *Otto Dix: Eine Malerkarriere der zwanziger Jahre* (Berlin: Reimer, 1996), 88–97. On the political debates surrounding Dix's antiwar imagery during the Weimar Republic as well as the gender politics it evoked, see Dora Apel, "'Heroes' and 'Whores': The Politics of Gender in Weimar Antiwar Imagery," *Art Bulletin* 79, no. 3 (September 1997): 366–84, esp. 368–75.

67. "Der Krieg war eine scheussliche Sache, aber trotzdem etwas Gewaltiges. Das durfte ich auf keinen Fall versäumen. Man muss den Menschen in diesem entfesselten Zustand gesehen haben, um etwas über Menschen zu wissen" (Dix, quoted in Hans Kinkel, "Begegnung mit Otto Dix," *Stuttgarter Zeitung*, November 30, 1961; reprinted in Schubert, *Otto Dix*, 24–25).

68. "Ich habe jahrelang, mindestens zehn Jahre lang, immer diese Träume gehabt, in denen ich durch zertrümmerte Häuser kriechen musste, durch Gänge, durch die ich kaum durchkam. Die Trümmer waren fortwährend in meinen Träumen. . . . Nicht dass das Malen für mich Befreiung gewesen wäre" (Dix, quoted in Maria Wetzel, "Otto Dix— Ein harter Mann, dieser Maler," *Diplomatischer Kurier* 14, no. 18 [1965]: 731–45; reprinted in Schubert, *Otto Dix*, 25).

69. As opposed to Heartfield, Wieland Herzfelde volunteered at the beginning of the war and was discharged as "not worthy to wear the Emperor's uniform" in January 1915, although he was subsequently recalled and spent more time on the western front; on Herzfelde's military service, see Herzfelde, *John Heartfield*, 15–19; and Paul Raabe, ed., *The Era of German Expressionism*, trans. J. M. Ritchie (Woodstock, N.Y.: Overlook, 1985), 218–21.

70. Herzfelde, *John Heartfield*, 15–16.

71. John Heartfield, "Der Hass auf den Krieg," in *Land og Folk* (Copenhagen: July 8, 1961), 6, reprinted in Roland März, ed., *John Heartfield, Der Schnitt entlang der Zeit: Selbstzeugnisse, Erinnerungen, Interpretationen, eine Dokumentation,* with Gertrud Heartfield (Dresden: VEB Verlag der Kunst, 1981), 24.

72. On Grosz's wartime service and experiences, see Grosz, *A Little Yes and a Big No,* 145–46, 157–62; Hans Hess, *George Grosz* (1974; repr. New Haven, Conn.: Yale University Press, 1985), 46–48, 68; M. Kay Flavell, *George Grosz: A Biography* (New Haven, Conn.: Yale University Press, 1988), 24–27; Barbara McCloskey, *George Grosz and the Communist Party: Art and Radicalism in Crisis, 1918 to 1936* (Princeton, N.J.: Princeton University Press, 1997), 13; and Doherty, "See," 93–94n19. As Doherty notes, there are still numerous unanswered questions about Grosz's wartime experiences because of inconsistencies between various sources.

73. Grosz's account of the events is slightly different. Although he does not dispute the fact that he ended up in "an asylum for war-crazed, shell-shocked, and insane soldiers," he suggests that he spent some time training new troops and guarding and transporting prisoners of war after he was recalled. See Grosz, *A Little Yes and a Big No,* 157.

74. Grosz, *A Little Yes and a Big No,* 145, 161.

75. Ibid., 146.

76. Ibid., 162–63.

77. Ibid., 158.

78. Ibid., 161.

79. Rudolf Schlichter, undated manuscript from the artist's estate, Galerie Alvensleben, Munich, cited in Karl-Ludwig Hofmann and Christlust Präger, "Rudolf Schlichter in Karlsruhe, 1910–1919," in Staatliche Kunsthalle Berlin, *Rudolf Schlichter* (Berlin: Frölich und Kaufmann, 1984), 25a.

80. Rudolf Schlichter, "Bewerbungsschreiben" (1945), unpublished manuscript from the artist's estate, Galerie Alvensleben, Munich, cited in Gabriele Horn, "Rudolf Schlichter: Eine Biographie," in Staatliche Kunsthalle Berlin, *Rudolf Schlichter,* 7a.

81. On the history and significance of the soldier portraits in Germany, see Elizabeth Otto, "Figuring Gender: Photomontage and Cultural Critique in Germany's Weimar Republic" (PhD diss., University of Michigan, 2003), 19–55; and Otto, "Uniform: On Constructions of Soldierly Masculinity in Early Twentieth-Century Culture," in *Kunst, Geschlecht, Politik: Männlichkeitskonstruktionen und Kunst im Kaiserreich und in der Weimarer Republik,* ed. Martina Kessel (Frankfurt am Main: Campus Verlag, 2005), 17–42.

82. Ernst Jünger, *The Storm of Steel* (1920), trans. Basil Creighton (London: Chatto and Windus, 1929), 294–95.

83. Peukert, *Weimar Republic,* 12.

84. Bernadotte E. Schmitt and Harold C. Vedeler, *The World in the Crucible, 1914–1919* (New York: Harper and Row, 1984), 321–22; and Holger H. Herwig, *The First World War: Germany and Austria-Hungary, 1914–1918* (London: Arnold, 1997), 259.

85. On the other hand, the restructuring of the economy during the war also helped workers gain significantly more power than they held before 1914; see Schmitt and Vedeler, *World in the Crucible,* 320–21; and Herwig, *First World War,* 261–66.

86. John Ellis and Michael Cox, *The World War I Databook* (London: Aurum, 2001), 269.

87. Doherty, "See," 82–132.

88. See Paul Lerner, *Hysterical Men: War, Psychiatry, and the Politics of Trauma in Germany, 1890–1930* (Ithaca, N.Y.: Cornell University Press, 2003), esp. 54, 61, 72–73.

89. See Lerner, *Hysterical Men,* 61–85; and Paul Lerner, "From Traumatic Neurosis to Male Hysteria: The Decline and Fall of Hermann Oppenheim, 1889–1919," in *Traumatic Pasts: History, Psychiatry, and Trauma in the Modern Age, 1870–1930,* ed. Mark S. Micale and Paul Lerner (New York: Cambridge University Press, 2001), 140–71.

90. For a summary of the debates in the 1910s and early 1920s on whether traumatic neuroses had physical or psychogenic causes, see Sándor Ferenczi's lecture on traumatic neuroses during war in Sándor Ferenczi, Karl Abraham, Ernst Simmel, and Ernest Jones, *Psychoanalysis and the War Neuroses* (London: International Psychoanalytical Press, 1921), 5–21, esp. 6–12.

91. See Ferenczi et al., *Psychoanalysis and the War Neuroses,* 16, 18–19.

92. See Doherty, "See," 115–24.

93. Lerner, *Hysterical Men,* 102–13.

94. Ibid., 111.

95. Ibid., 116–17.

96. Ibid., 120–21.

97. Ibid., 122.

98. See Gustav Le Bon, *The Crowd: A Study of the Popular Mind* (1895; repr. New Brunswick, N.J.: Transaction Publishers, 1995); and Sigmund Freud, *Group Psychology and the Analysis of the Ego* (1921), ed. and trans. James Strachey (New York: Norton, 1959).

99. Freud, *Group Psychology,* 9–18.

100. Ibid., 62. Although Freud's description of the military subject feeling pleasure when part of an organized group might seem to contradict Theweleit's account of the *Friekorps* soldier hating the mass, this is not the case. As Theweleit argues, "The fascist has two distinct and different masses in mind, two masses that stand in mutual opposition. The mass that is celebrated is strictly formed, poured into systems of dams. Above it there towers a leader *(Führer).* To the despised mass, by contrast, is attributed all that is flowing, slimy,

teeming. (The soldier feels 'exposed to the incomprehensible, seething hatred of the corrupted masses.')" The fascist military subject, according to Theweleit, thus embraces (and is constituted by) the regulated and hierarchical mass of the armed forces, while hating and opposing himself to the amorphous and hybrid mass of revolutionary uprisings (Theweleit, *Male Fantasies, Volume 2, Male Bodies: Psychoanalyzing the White Terror,* trans. Erica Carter, Chris Turner, and Stephen Conway [Minneapolis: University of Minnesota Press, 1989], 4).

101. Freud, *Group Psychology,* 81.

102. Ibid., 82.

103. Ibid., 32.

104. Ibid., 62–63.

105. Grosz remembered the "mass intoxication" of the German people when war was first declared (*A Little Yes and a Big No,* 145). He also located part of the perpetual appeal of armed combat in the fact that it liberated men from all restraints. "War," as he put it, "freed many an individual from the environment he hated and the slavery of his everyday routine. This is one of the psychological causes and enigmas of war and that is why there is and always will be war" (Grosz, *A Little Yes and a Big No,* 146). Dix also remarked on the "uninhibited condition" in which warfare left human beings; see Otto Dix in Schubert, *Otto Dix,* 24–25, quoted above in note 67.

106. Referring to his fellow soldiers, Grosz noted that "the greatest majority did no thinking but just carried out commands" (*A Little Yes and a Big No,* 146).

107. Describing being restrained by fellow soldiers in a hospital after he attacked a medical sergeant who told him he was fit to return to active duty, Grosz noted both their mindless submission to authority in the absence of direct orders as well as their contradictory behavior toward him: "I shall never forget with what joy, yes, even passion, about seven of my sick comrades, who were permitted to leave their beds at will, jumped on me of their own accord to hold me down. . . . There was nothing personal about it since I was a matter of complete indifference to them. It was, rather, a manifestation of the unconscious principle that since they did nothing to defend themselves, neither should I. . . . Later it was all forgotten and we continued as usual to play cards, drink beer, smoke, and tell dirty jokes" (*A Little Yes and a Big No,* 157–58). Grosz also emphasized the fact that war deadened a person's feelings of empathy and made him able to tolerate—and even find humor in—the most bizarre and horrible situations. Thus, for example, Grosz described an incident where he lay in a bed in a field hospital next to a dying soldier, who had part of his abdomen shot away. "Half-unconscious because of continuous injections, he would mumble in Berlin dialect as he attempted to point to his stomach: 'Look, comrade, I had all this with me. Where are my legs? I left them somewhere. If I could only remember, comrade. If I could only remember. Now I have a way in but no way out.' He again tried to point to his midriff but neither hand nor finger permitted. He sank into sleep and died that same night without a sound, a shapeless mass" (ibid., 158). The next day, everyone felt fine as if no one had witnessed the poor man's suffering: "Since the coffee was hot, we decided that life under our checkered blankets was not so bad after all" (ibid., 158–59). Grosz also recalled the medical staff making jokes about soldiers' wounds and amputations. Referring to a man who had lost his genitals, a medic remarked, "Well, what the hell, he'll get a new one made of wood, the size will be the same anyhow" (ibid., 159). Not surprisingly, the enlisted men themselves were no better. To amuse themselves, Grosz recalled, they would throw cigars and cigarettes to a bedridden double amputee, who had lost both his arms, to see the "quarrelsome and noisy" individual catch them with his mouth (ibid., 160).

108. See Brigid Doherty, "Berlin Dada: Montage and the Embodiment of Modernity, 1916–1920" (PhD diss., University of California, Berkeley, 1996), 1–135.

109. See Douglas Kahn, *John Heartfield: Art and Mass Media* (New York: Tanam, 1985), 23–25.

110. Herzfelde, *John Heartfield*, 17–18, translated and cited by Brigid Doherty in *Berlin Dada*, 5–6. Doherty's translation has been altered. As Doherty notes, the texts of the second (1971) and third (1976) editions of the book contain significant revisions to this passage. Specifically, Herzfelde expunges the reference to "the people" having a hand in the early development of photomontage, and he distinguishes the postcards made during the war—which in the later editions of his book he insists were collages—from the photomontages made after the war. See Doherty, *Berlin Dada*, 238n13. Herzfelde is not clear if he means to draw a line between the proto-Dada works produced during the war years and the Dada photomontages created during the immediate postwar moment, or if he wants to connect the proto-Dada and Dada photomontages with one another and to separate both phases from Heartfield's later, much more cohesive strategy of photomontage. I have followed Doherty's citation of the earliest version of the story, because it was formulated nearly a decade closer to the events that it describes and because it suggests what seems to me to be convincing connections between the wartime development of new forms of proto-Dadaist communication, the politically charged Dada photomontages that followed, and Heartfield's later photomontages—connections that Herzfelde appears to have later attempted to obscure, perhaps to make Heartfield's later much more explicitly propagandistic photomontages for the *Arbeiter Illustrierte Zeitung* and the *Volks Illustrierte* more distinct from his earlier works.

111. On photography, postcards, and photographic albums in Germany in the late nineteenth and early twentieth centuries, see Ellen Maas and Wolfgang Brückner, eds., *Das Photoalbum 1858–1918: Eine Dokumentation zur Kultur- und Sozialgeschichte* (Munich: Lipp, 1975); Ellen Maas, *Die goldenen Jahre der Photoalben: Fundgrube und Spiegel von Gestern* (Cologne: DuMont, 1977); Robert Bosshard, Ute Eskildsen, and Robert Knodt, *Erinnerung an die Dienstzeit: Fotografien der Jahrhundertwende aus eigenem Bestand* (Essen: Museum Folkwang, 1993); and Klaus Honnef, Rolf Sachsse, and Karin Thomas, eds., *German Photography, 1870–1970: Power of a Medium* (Cologne: DuMont, 1997), 21–40. On photography, postcards, and "letters from the battle field" during World War I, see Rainer Rother, ed., *Die Letzten Tage der Menschheit: Bilder des Ersten Weltkriegs* (Berlin: Ars Nicolai, 1994), esp. 109–20, 137–48, 163–76; Maas and Brückner, *Das Photoalbum*, 140–46; and Maas, *Die goldenen Jahre der Photoalben*, 154–63. On war photography during World War I, see Bernd Hüppauf, "The Experience of Modern Warfare and the Crisis of Representation," *New German Critique* 59 (Spring–Summer 1993): 41–76; and Bernd Hüppauf, "Emptying the Gaze: Framing Violence through the Viewfinder," *New German Critique* 72 (Autumn 1997): 3–44, esp. 22–26.

112. This photographic postcard, with hand-painted details, depicts a young boy, wearing an officer's uniform, holding a bouquet of flowers in one hand and a sword in the other. The text on the front of the card reads, "Heartfelt good wishes for your birthday" and "May fragrant blossoms beautify the celebration, May the sword protect house and home." Dated June 20, 1916, it was sent by a soldier to his son at home. The handwritten text on the back reads: "My dear Hubert, Congratulations on your seventh birthday. Let many beautiful presents come your way. Unfortunately, I still can't give you anything. I shall give you something when I come home again. Your dear Father." Typical of the military images from the early days of the war, it is a studio image that idealizes the boy soldier by representing him as attractive, powerful, and unharmed.

113. This postcard, which depicts a soldier seated behind unexploded artillery shells, was sent to a male friend in July 1916. The handwritten text on the back of the card reads

in part, "On July 8, 1916, I received your little package for which I thank you most heartily. You can believe me that such gifts of love *[Liebesgaben]* are more welcome than those of the French, which you can see on the opposite side. These examples of ships' armament and artillery shells were found unexploded on our front. Otherwise I am well and cheerful . . ." The greater realism of the postcard, as compared with the photo of the boy soldier discussed in note 112, can be found in the fact that it was taken in the field and that it depicts the dirty and violent-looking shells that potentially could have killed the letter writer.

114. With the exception of the imprint of the photographer—"Aug. Bies, Photograph, Hannover"—this postcard has no text or date on the back.

115. See Sigrid Metken, "'Ich hab' diese Karte im Schützengraben geschrieben . . .' Bildpostkarten im Ersten Weltkrieg," in Rother, ed., *Die Letzten Tage der Menschheit,* 148. Benjamin also discusses the decrease in the ability of human beings to communicate their experiences in "The Storyteller."According to Benjamin, World War I was one of the causes that led to this situation. See Walter Benjamin, "The Storyteller: Observations on the Works of Nikolai Leskov" (1936), trans. Harry Zohn, in *Walter Benjamin: Selected Writings, Vol. 3, 1935–1938,* ed. Howard Eiland and Michael W. Jennings (Cambridge, Mass.: Harvard University Press, 2002), 143–66, esp. 143–44.

116. Metken, "'Ich hab' diese Karte im Schützengraben geschrieben . . . ," in Rother, *Die Letzten Tage der Menschheit,* 138.

117. Wieland Herzfelde, "How a Publishing House Was Born," in Raabe, *Era of German Expressionism,* 219.

118. Birte Gaethke, *Liebesgaben für den Schützengraben 1914–1918* (Hamburg: Altonaer Museum in Hamburg/Norddeutsches Landesmuseum, 1994).

119. Ibid., 13.

120. Ibid., 13, 41–44.

121. Gerhard Kaufmann, "Vorwort," in Gaethke, *Liebesgaben,* 3.

122. Gaethke, *Liebesgaben,* 29–34.

123. Ibid., 15.

124. Ibid., 31.

125. On Ida Dehmel and the glue rooms, see Johanna Poettgen, "Die Klebestuben," in Gaethke, *Liebesgaben,* 23–28.

126. *Hamburger Generalanzeiger,* December 17, 1914, cited in Gaethke, *Liebesgaben,* 26.

127. Doherty, *Berlin Dada,* 10–12, 69–70.

128. Gaethke, *Liebesgaben,* 26.

129. Doherty, *Berlin Dada,* 50.

130. Ibid., 44, 54.

131. Ibid., 78.

132. Ibid., 76–77.

133. Ibid., 80.

5. The New Woman as Cyborg

1. See, for example, Hans Richter's dismissive treatment of Höch in his history of Dada, whom he characterizes as a "lightweight": Hans Richter, *Dada: Art and Anti-Art,* trans. David Britt (London: Thames and Hudson, 1965), 130–32. On Höch being disregarded by her male colleagues, see Peter Boswell, "Hannah Höch: Through the Looking Glass," in *The Photomontages of Hannah Höch* (Minneapolis: Walker Art Center, 1996), 7–8; and Maria Makela, "By Design: The Early Work of Hannah Höch in Context," in

Photomontages of Hannah Höch, 49. Höch's exhibition schedule began to increase in the 1970s, and the art historical writing about her started to grow in the 1980s; see *Photomontages of Hannah Höch,* 211–16, 218–20.

2. On Höch's life, see Götz Adriani, "Biography—Documentation," in *Collages, Hannah Höch, 1889–1978* (Stuttgart: Institute for Foreign Cultural Relations, 1985), 8–63; Jula Dech, *Hannah Höch Schnitt mit dem Küchenmesser Dada durch die letzte weimarer Bierbauchkulturepoche Deutschlands* (Frankfurt am Main: Fischer Taschenbuch Verlag, 1989), 81–84; Cornelia Thater-Schulz, "Dada ist kein Bluff," in Berlinische Galerie, *Hannah Höch, 1889–1978: Ihr Werk, Ihr Leben, Ihre Freunde* (Berlin: Argon, 1989), 11–23; Kristin Makholm, "Chronology," in *Photomontages of Hannah Höch,* 185–210; and "Biografie," in Ralf Burmeister, *Hannah Höch: Aller Anfang ist Dada!* (Berlin: Berlinische Galerie, Landesmuseum für Moderne Kunst, Fotografie und Architektur, 2007), 160–92.

3. In the 1910s and 1920s, Höch also worked for a non-Ullstein magazine, *Stickerei- und Spitzen-Rundschau,* where she published embroidery designs and articles on crafts. See Makela, "By Design," 53–55.

4. Höch is reported to have taken part in three Dadaist performances, the first when she created percussion using pan lids and a rattle for Jefim Golyscheff's *Anti-symphony,* which was performed at Neumann's gallery in Berlin on April 30, 1919, and the second two at *Die Tribüne* on November 30 and December 7, 1919, when she took part in the reading of a simultaneous poem composed by Huelsenbeck during two Dada matinees. On February 8, 1921, Höch also participated in a reading of grotesques with Hausmann and Mynona at the Berlin Sezession; see Juan Vicente Aliaga, "A Commentated Biography of Hannah Höch," in *Hannah Höch* (Madrid: Aldeasa/Museo Nacional Centro de Arte Reina Sofía, 2004), 349–54, esp. 349–50; and Makholm, "Chronology," 188–90. For the most part, however, Höch preferred not to perform, since, as she put it, the Dada events created "terrible anxiety" for her. See Hannah Höch, "A Glance over My Life" (1958), trans. Peter Chametzky, in Maud Lavin, *Cut with the Kitchen Knife: The Weimar Photomontages of Hannah Höch* (New Haven, Conn.: Yale University Press, 1993), 212. See also Höch's own reminiscences of these events: Hannah Höch, "Erinnerungen an Dada" (1966), in Berlinische Galerie, *Hannah Höch,* 204–5.

5. On Höch's relationships with other avant-garde artists in the mid-1920s, see Peter Krieger, "Freundschaft mit der Avantgarde: Schwitters—Arp—van Doesburg—Moholy-Nagy," in Berlinische Galerie, *Hannah Höch,* 25–39; and Chris Rehorst, "Hannah Höch und die Niederlande," trans. Rosemarie Still, in Berlinische Galerie, *Hannah Höch,* 41–52.

6. Boswell, "Hannah Höch," 8.

7. See, for example, Höch's discussion of the differences between the "free-form" or artistic type of photomontage to which her work inclined and "applied" or commercial form of photomontage, in an article she wrote for the Czech journal *Stredisko* on the occasion of her one-person photomontage exhibition in Brno, Czechoslovakia, in 1934 (Höch, "A Few Words on Photomontage" [1934], trans. Jitka Salaguarda, in Lavin, *Cut with the Kitchen Knife,* 219–20).

8. Boswell, "Hannah Höch," 11. See, for example, Boswell's somewhat negative assessment of Höch's painting, in ibid., 19, 21.

9. That Höch was intimately acquainted with Hausmann's various writings is suggested by the fact that, during their time together, she served as his unofficial secretary. See Makela, "By Design," 60.

10. N. Katherine Hayles, *How We Became Posthuman: Virtual Bodies in Cybernetics, Literature, and Informatics* (Chicago: University of Chicago Press, 1999), 84–85.

11. See, for example, Atina Grossmann, "*Girlkultur* or Thoroughly Rationalized Female:

A New Woman in Germany?" in *Women in Culture and Politics: A Century of Change,* ed. Judith Friedlander, Blanche Wiesen Cook, Alice Kessler-Harris, and Carroll Smith-Rosenberg (Bloomington: Indiana University Press, 1986), 62–80.

12. On the increased political role for women during the Weimar Republic, see Ute Frevert, *Women in German History: From Bourgeois Emancipation to Sexual Liberation,* trans. Stuart McKinnon-Evans, with Terry Bond and Barbara Norden (Oxford: Berg, 1988), 168–204, esp. 168–75; and Renate Bridenthal and Claudia Koonz, "Beyond *Kinder, Küche, Kirche*: Weimar Women in Politics and Work," in *When Biology Became Destiny: Women in Weimar and Nazi Germany,* ed. Renate Bridenthal, Atina Grossmann, and Marion Kaplan (New York: Monthly Review Press, 1984), 33–65, esp. 35–44.

13. On the employment of women during the Weimar Republic, see Detlev J. K. Peukert, *The Weimar Republic: The Crisis of Classical Modernity,* trans. Richard Deveson (New York: Hill and Wang, 1992), 95–101; Frevert, *Women in German History,* 176–85; and Bridenthal and Koonz, "Beyond *Kinder, Küche, Kirche,*" 33–65, esp. 44–53.

14. See, for example, Hilde Walter's contemporaneous criticism of this pernicious belief: Hilde Walter, "Twilight for Women" (1931), in *The Weimar Republic Sourcebook,* ed. Anton Kaes, Martin Jay, and Edward Dimendberg (Berkeley: University of California Press, 1994), 210–11. See also the response of the bourgeois League of German Women's Associations, led by Marianne Weber: "Women's Work and the Economic Crisis" (1931), in Kaes, Jay, and Dimendberg, *Weimar Republic Sourcebook,* 212–13.

15. Frevert, *Women in German History,* 196–97.

16. On the image of the new woman in Weimar literature, see Barbara Kosta, "Unruly Daughters and Modernity: Irmgard Keun's Gilgi-eine von uns," *German Quarterly* 68, no. 3 (Summer 1995): 271–86. On the image of the new woman in art during the Weimar Republic, see Marsha Meskimmon, *We Weren't Modern Enough: Women Artists and the Limits of German Modernism* (Berkeley: University of California Press, 1999), 163–96. On the relationship of the image of the new woman to Höch's art, see Lavin, *Cut with the Kitchen Knife.*

17. Peukert, *Weimar Republic,* 8–9, 86–89.

18. See Meskimmon, *We Weren't Modern Enough,* 180–83; Frevert, *Women in German History,* 181–82; and, very importantly, Patrice Petro, *Joyless Streets: Women and Melodramatic Representation in Weimar Germany* (Princeton, N.J.: Princeton University Press, 1989).

19. On the lesbian associations of the *garçonne,* see Meskimmon, *We Weren't Modern Enough,* 199–229. As Lynne Frame points out, however, the *garçonne* could also carry heterosexual associations despite her "intersexual" or androgynous characteristics. See Lynne Frame, "Gretchen, Girl, *Garçonne*? Weimar Science and Popular Culture in Search of the Ideal New Woman," in *Women in the Metropolis: Gender and Modernity in Weimar Culture,* ed. Katharina von Ankum (Berkeley: University of California Press, 1997), 12–40, esp. 12, 26–27.

20. "Films are the mirror of the prevailing society. They are financed by corporations, which must pinpoint the tastes of the audience at all costs in order to make a profit. Since this audience is composed largely of workers and ordinary people who gripe about the conditions in the upper circles, business considerations require the producer to satisfy the need for social critique among the consumers. A producer, however, will never allow himself to be driven to present material that in any way attacks the foundations of society, for to do so would destroy his own existence as a capitalist entrepreneur. Indeed, the films made for the lower classes are even more bourgeois than those aimed at the finer audiences, precisely because they hint at subversive points of view without exploring them. Instead, they smuggle in a respectable way of thinking" (Siegfried Kracauer, "The Little Shopgirls

Go to the Movies," in *The Mass Ornament*, trans. Thomas Y. Levin [Cambridge, Mass.: Harvard University Press, 1995], 291–304, esp. 291).

21. See Peukert, *Weimar Republic*, 112–17; and Mary Nolan, *Visions of Modernity: American Business and the Modernization of Germany* (New York: Oxford University Press, 1994), 51–52, 70–82.

22. See, for example, Marianne Weber, "The Special Cultural Mission of Women" (1919), in Kaes, Jay, and Dimendberg, *Weimar Republic Sourcebook*, 197; and Elsa Herrmann, "This Is the New Woman" (1929), in Kaes, Jay, and Dimendberg, *Weimar Republic Sourcebook*, 206–8. See also Grossmann, "*Girlkultur*," 62–80, esp. 68, 71, 75–76.

23. On the concept of simultaneous montage, see Hanne Bergius, *"Dada Triumphs!" Dada Berlin, 1917–1923, Artistry of Polarities*, trans. Brigitte Pichon (Farmington Hills, Mich.: G. K. Hall, 2003), 142–54.

24. On the identification of the various photomontage fragments contained in *Dada Panorama* as well as the different interpretations that they generate, see Hanne Bergius, "'Dada Rundschau'—Eine Photomontage," in Berlinische Galerie, *Hannah Höch*, 101–6; Makela, notes to Plate 2, in *Photomontages of Hannah Höch*, 27; Makela, "By Design," 60–61; Lavin, *Cut with the Kitchen Knife*, 35–37; Brigid Doherty, "Figures of the Pseudorevolution," *October* 84 (Spring 1998): 82–89; and Bergius, *"Dada Triumphs!"* 151–52, 175–76.

25. On Gertrud Bäumer, see Peter D. Stachura, *Political Leaders in Weimar Germany: A Biographical Study* (New York: Simon and Schuster, 1993), 12–13.

26. On Hans von Seeckt, see Stachura, *Political Leaders in Weimar Germany*, 162–63. His official title between 1920 and 1926 was *Chef der Heeresleitung*. Bergius identifies the figure as von Seeckt; see Bergius, "Dada Rundschau," 105. Pictures of von Seeckt, however, do not seem to match the last figure in the row of German officers.

27. Despite the important role that German students played in supporting the development of the NSDAP and its eventual coming to power in Germany, the majority of German students were never Nazis during the Weimar Republic, and their numbers never even came close to constituting a majority. See, for example, Rudy Koshar, "From *Stammtisch* to Party: Nazi Joiners and the Contradictions of Grass Roots Fascism in Weimar Germany," *Journal of Modern History* 59, no. 1 (March 1987): 1–24; Stephen G. Fritz, "The NSDAP as *Volkspartei*? A Look at the Social Basis of the Nazi Voter," *History Teacher* 20, no. 3 (May 1987): 379–99; and Geoffrey J. Giles, *Students and National Socialism in Germany* (Princeton, N.J.: Princeton University Press, 1985).

28. Stachura, *Political Leaders in Weimar Germany*, 46–47.

29. Doherty, "Figures of the Pseudorevolution," 69–73. More recently, Niels Albrecht has extensively documented the publication and republication of the so-called bathing picture, as well as the public's reaction to it and the libel suits lodged by Ebert whereby the president of the Weimar Republic attempted to restore the honor of his governmental position that he felt was destroyed by the picture's publication. See Niels H. M. Albrecht, "Die Macht einer Verleumdungskampagne: Antidemokratische Agitationen der Presse und Justiz gegen die Weimarer Republik und ihren ersten Reichspräsidenten Friedrich Ebert vom 'Badebild' bis zum Magdeburger Prozess" (PhD diss., University of Bremen, 2002), Elektronische Bibliothek, Staats- und Universitätbibliothek Bremen (accessed December 30, 2007).

30. *Bilder zur Zeitgeschichte* 31, in *Deutsche Tageszeitung*, August 9, 1919; cited in Doherty, "Figures of the Pseudorevolution," 71–72. See also Albrecht, "Die Macht einer Verleumdungskampagne," 50–53.

31. Albrecht, "Die Macht einer Verleumdungskampagne," 68–69.

32. *Kladderadatsch* 36 (1919) and *Kladderadatsch* 37 (1919); see Albrecht, "Die Macht einer Verleumdungskampagne," 75–78.

33. *Satyr* 25 (1919); see Albrecht, "Die Macht einer Verleumdungskampagne," 80–84.

34. *Die freie Welt* 1, no. 21 (1919); cited in Doherty, "Figures of the Pseudorevolution," 73.

35. See Albrecht, "Die Macht einer Verleumdungskampagne," esp. 87–89, 105–6, 109–18, 121, 341–69.

36. Richard Huelsenbeck, *En Avant Dada: A History of Dadaism* (1920), trans. Ralph Manheim, in *The Dada Painters and Poets: An Anthology*, ed. Robert Motherwell, 2nd ed. (Boston: Hall, 1981), 39.

37. See Francis M. Naumann, *New York Dada, 1915–1923* (New York: Harry N. Abrams, 1994), 162–63. The photograph of Johnson, shown beating the former (white) champion James J. Jeffries in 1910 in Reno, Nevada, was taken from the *Berliner Illustrirte Zeitung* 29, no. 35 (August 29, 1920); see Makela, "Notes to Plate 9," in *Photomontages of Hannah Höch*, 34. Although Johnson had actually become champion two years before, this victory, against the long-standing champion Jeffries—who had retired undefeated and returned to the ring only to lose to Johnson—sparked race riots across the United States.

38. Al-Tony Gilmore, "Jack Johnson and White Women: The National Impact," *Journal of Negro History* 58, no. 1 (January 1973): 18–38.

39. Makela, "Notes to Plate 10," in *Photomontages of Hannah Höch*, 35.

40. On Höch's misdating of her photomontages, see Makela, "By Design," 78n94, 105.

41. On the identification and interpretation of the photomontage elements, see Makela, "Notes to Plate 10," in *Photomontages of Hannah Höch*, 35; and Makela, "By Design," 61.

42. Makela, "By Design," 61; Peter Nisbet, "A Cut-Up at the Dada Fair," *Boston Book Review* 4, no. 3 (April 1997): 9.

43. *Die Dame* 47, no. 15 (May 1920).

44. See László Moholy-Nagy, *Painting, Photography, Film,* trans. Janet Seligman (Cambridge, Mass.: MIT Press, 1969), 106.

45. Makela, "By Design," 61.

46. On Herschel, see Naomi Rosenblum, *A World History of Photography,* 3rd ed. (New York: Abbeville, 1997), 27–29, 32, 46–47, 197.

47. Peukert, *Weimar Republic,* 107–28.

48. See Ernst Jünger, "Einleitung," in *Die veränderte Welt: Eine Bilderfibel unserer Zeit,* ed. Edmund Schultz (Breslau: Korn Verlag, 1933), 5–9. This entire book of photomontage stands as a visual introduction to Jünger's theory of technological modernity as outlined in his book *Der Arbeiter: Herrschaft und Gestalt* (1932), among other works.

49. See Boswell, "Hannah Höch," 12; Makela, "By Design," 66, 69; and Lavin, *Cut with the Kitchen Knife,* 124–25, 136.

50. Although these works have not traditionally been included in the portrait series, they are assigned to it here because of their focus on a main figure (or, in the case of *High Finance,* two main figures) as well as the fact that they represent a general type as opposed to a historical individual. The same is the case for *Half Breed* below.

51. Other titles in the series include *Merry Woman* (1923), *Children* (1925), *The Singer* (1926), *Girl with a Fan* (1926), *English Dancer* (1928), *Russian Dancer (My Double)* (1928), and *The Victor* (1927).

52. On Höch's mass media scrapbook, see Lavin, *Cut with the Kitchen Knife,* 71–121; Lavin reproduces page 58 as figure 80 (ibid., 114). The entire scrapbook has been reproduced (unfortunately without page numbers); see Gunda Luyken, ed., *Hannah Höch Album* (Ostfildern-Ruit: Hatje Cantz Verlag, 2004). See also Melissa Ann Johnson, "'On the

Strength of My Imagination': Visions of Weimar Culture in the Scrapbook of Hannah Höch" (PhD diss., Bryn Mawr College, 2001).

53. Lavin, *Cut with the Kitchen Knife*, 240n38.

54. Susanne Zantop, *Colonial Fantasies: Conquest, Family, and Nation in Precolonial Germany, 1770–1870* (Durham, N.C.: Duke University Press, 1997), 1.

55. On the broadly based attempts to regain colonial territories during the Weimar Republic and the colonialist ambitions of the NSDAP, see Wolf W. Schmokel, *Dream of Empire: German Colonialism, 1919–1945* (New Haven, Conn.: Yale University Press, 1964); see also Adolf Rüger, "The Colonial Aims of the Weimar Republic," in *German Imperialism in Africa: From the Beginnings until the Second World War*, ed. Helmuth Stoecker, trans. Bernd Zöllner (Atlantic Highlands, N.J.: Humanities Press International, 1986), 297–336.

56. See Zantop, *Colonial Fantasies*, esp. 2–9, 191–201.

57. On the concept of *Lebensraum*, which was first formulated in the 1890s and justified the German conquest of territories outside its borders in terms of Darwinian natural selection, see Woodruff D. Smith, "Friedrich Ratzel and the Origins of Lebensraum," *German Studies Review* 3, no. 1 (February 1980): 51–68. On the second two justifications, see Woodruff D. Smith, "The Ideology of German Colonialism, 1840–1906," *Journal of Modern History* 46, no. 4 (December 1974): 641–62. According to the emigrationist argument, Woodruff notes, "Large numbers of Germans, displaced by economic and social changes in Germany, could settle as farmers in these colonies as an alternative to emigration to America or elsewhere. The settlement colonies would 'protect' the emigrants' culture, retain their contributions to the German economy, and recreate overseas the type of traditional peasant society which many regarded as the basis of national power and which was threatened by the process of industrialization. The expropriation of excess population would also lessen the possibility of political revolution in Germany" (Smith, "Ideology of German Colonialism," 641). Economic colonialism, on the other hand, "viewed colonies as appendages of the industrial and commercial segments of the German economy. Colonies were to exist to encourage and protect trade in raw materials not available in Europe. European presence was to be limited to government, the direction of mines and plantations, and trade with indigenous peoples. No large-scale settlement was envisioned. The economic ideology was often related to the movement to establish a central European economic area dominated by an industrialized Germany" (ibid., 642).

58. Zantop, *Colonial Fantasies*, 197.

59. As Zantop notes, even before advent of biological racism, thinking on race in Germany places the white male in a position of "natural" dominance, and the "supremacy of the white European variety, evident in its advanced civilization . . . resides in physiology and anatomy, that is, in biology" (Zantop, *Colonial Fantasies*, 79).

60. Zantop, *Colonial Fantasies*, 70–73. Gobineau's *Essay on the Inequality of the Human Races* (1853–55) is often cited as a canonical work in this regard; see Mark Antliff and Patricia Leighten, "Primitivism," in Robert S. Nelson and Richard Shiff, *Critical Terms for Art History*, 2nd ed. (Chicago: University of Chicago Press, 2003), 225–26.

61. Antliff and Leighten, "Primitivism," 220–25.

62. See Keith L. Nelson, "The 'Black Horror on the Rhine': Race as a Factor in Post–World War I Diplomacy," *Journal of Modern History* 42, no. 4 (December 1970): 606–27.

63. Susann Samples, "African Germans in the Third Reich," in *The African-German Experience: Critical Essays*, ed. Carol Aisha Blackshire-Belay (Westport, Conn.: Praeger, 1996), 53, 57–58.

64. *Simplicissimus* 25, no. 11 (June 9, 1920): 168.

65. See Henry Louis Gates Jr., *Loose Canons: Notes on the Culture Wars* (New York: Oxford University Press, 1992), 55.

66. Antliff and Leighten, "Primitivism," 217.

67. Ibid., 217–20. For an excellent account of the actual ways in which—contrary to the one-way theory of cultural transmission espoused by many European primitivists— white and black cultures mutually influenced one another in the early twentieth century, see Sieglinde Lemke, *Primitivist Modernism: Black Culture and the Origins of Translatlantic Modernism* (New York: Oxford University Press, 1998).

68. Antliff and Leighten, "Primitivism," 218.

69. Ibid., 223, 219.

70. Ibid., 230.

71. Ibid., 223–29.

72. Ibid., 229.

73. As Boswell notes, after showing *Cut with the Kitchen Knife* and several other photomontages at the "Dada Fair," Höch did not exhibit her photomontages again until 1929, when seventeen of her works were shown at the "Film and Foto" exhibition in Stuttgart. She then presented more of her photomontages at the "Kunstzaal d'Audretsch" in The Hague in 1929 and at the "Grosse Berliner Kunstausstellung" in 1930, and she continued to intermittently exhibit them in the early 1930s. See Boswell, "Hannah Höch," 10, 15. As mentioned above, however, Höch's *High Finance* was published in Moholy-Nagy's *Painting, Photography, Film* in 1925 and 1927.

74. See, for example, Huelsenbeck's claim in the Dadaists' collective manifesto that "the word Dada symbolizes the most primitive relation to the reality of the environment," one that allows the Dadaist to represent the world in an unmediated fashion (Richard Huelsenbeck, "Collective Dada Manifesto" [1918], in *The Dada Painters and Poets: An Anthology,* ed. Robert Motherwell, 2nd ed. [Boston: Hall, 1981], 244). Although seeming to distance Dada from earlier forms of expressionist primitivism, Herzfelde made a related point in his introduction to the "Dada Fair" catalog, when he stressed the directness of Dada, claiming that "Dadaism is the reaction to all those attempts to deny the factual," a type of art that rejects painting and drawing to embrace the literalism of photomontage and assemblage. See Wieland Herzfelde, "'Introduction,' First International Dada Fair, 1920," in *German Expressionism: Documents from the End of the Wilhelmine Empire to the Rise of National Socialism,* ed. Rose-Carol Washton Long (Berkeley: University of California Press, 1993), 273. (Both these texts are quoted at greater length in chapter 3.) Hausmann also stressed the primitivism (in the sense of the directness) of Dadaism; see, for example, his claim that, already in Zurich, "DADA was a creed of basic primitiveness" (Raoul Hausmann, "Dada in Europe," trans. Jean Boase-Beier, in *The Dada Reader: A Critical Anthology,* ed. Dawn Ades [Chicago: University of Chicago Press, 2006], 92–93; translation altered). (This text is treated at greater length in chapters 1 and 3.)

75. On the history of Darwinist and eugenicist thought in Germany since the late 1860s, see Richard Weikart, *From Darwin to Hitler: Evolutionary Ethics, Eugenics, and Racism in Germany* (New York: Palgrave Macmillan, 2004).

76. Detlev J. K. Peukert, "The Genesis of the 'Final Solution' from the Spirit of Science," in *Reevaluating the Third Reich,* ed. Thomas Childers and Jane Caplan (New York: Holmes and Meier, 1993), 240.

77. Ibid., 241.

78. Ibid., 242–47.

79. Lavin, *Cut with the Kitchen Knife,* 124–25.

80. Höch's interest in psychoanalysis was probably inspired by Hausmann's critique

of Freud under the influence of Otto Gross's theories. After her break with Hausmann, Höch recalls discussing Freud and psychoanalysis in the circle around Dr. Ernst Simmel in Berlin. See Höch, "Glance over My Life," 213.

81. Makela, "By Design," 64.

82. Höch, cited in ibid., 64.

83. Höch, cited in ibid., 76n64.

84. See Patrice Petro, *Joyless Streets: Women and Melodramatic Representation in Weimar Germany* (Princeton, N.J.: Princeton University Press, 1989), esp. 25–36.

85. Lavin, *Cut with the Kitchen Knife,* 146.

86. Joan Riviere, "Womanliness as a Masquerade" (1929), in *The Inner World and Joan Riviere: Collected Papers, 1920–1958,* ed. Athol Hughes (New York: Karnac, 1991), 90–102.

87. Despite his problematic view of women, Friedrich Nietzsche also emphasized the fact that they were conditioned to constantly play roles in society and that their characters were fundamentally determined by this fact. See Friedrich Nietzsche, *The Gay Science, with a Prelude in Rhymes and an Appendix of Songs* (1882/1887), trans. Walter Kaufmann (New York: Random House, 1974), esp. 125–28, 176, 208, 271–72, 316–17 (sec. 68 is particularly trenchant in this regard).

88. See Helmut Lethen, *Cool Conduct: The Culture of Distance in Weimar Germany* (1994), trans. Don Reneau (Berkeley: University of California Press, 2002), 22–23.

89. Frame, "Gretchen, Girl, *Garçonne?*" 12–40.

90. Ernst Kretschmer, *Körperbau und Charakter: Untersuchungen zum Konstitutionsproblem und zur Lehre von den Temperamenten* (Berlin: Julius Springer Verlag, 1921).

91. Frame, "Gretchen, Girl, *Garçonne?*" 13.

92. Lavin, *Cut with the Kitchen Knife,* 160, 238n6. Analyzing the photomontages, the published source materials from which they were made, and Höch's own written statements, Kristin Makholm plausibly argues that the photomontages from this series were not begun before 1928. See Kristin Makholm, "Ultraprimitive/Ultramodern: Hannah Höch's From an Ethnographic Museum," in *Hannah Höch,* 337n1; and Kristin Jean Makholm, "Film, Portraiture, and Primitivism in the Photomontages of Hannah Höch" (PhD diss., University of Minnesota, 1999), 198–202.

93. See Annegret Jürgens-Kirchhoff, "'Fremde Schönheit'—Zu Hannah Höchs Photomonagen," in *Da-da-zwischen-Reden zu Hannah Höch,* ed. Jula Dech and Ellen Maurer (Berlin: Orlanda-Frauenverlag, 1991), 127–37; Lavin, *Cut with the Kitchen Knife,* 159–82; Makela, "By Design," 70–72; Makholm, *Film, Portraiture, and Primitivism,* 194–256; and Makholm, "Ultraprimitive/Ultramodern," 331–38. Makholm's discussion of Höch's primitivism, which reveals Höch's awareness of how the mass media had changed the concept, is particularly useful.

94. Lavin identifies the fragment as "an ancient, sculptural face" (*Cut with the Kitchen Knife,* 240n38).

95. Unlike coins, which sometimes had intrinsic worth because of the materials out of which they were made, paper money displayed a frightening lack of material value. As a result, banknotes were actually used as children's toys or sold as wastepaper during the height of the hyperinflation. See Bernd Widdig, *Culture and Inflation in Weimar Germany* (Berkeley: University of California Press, 2001), 92–97.

96. Eberhard Kolb, *The Weimar Republic,* trans. P. S. Falla (London: Unwin Hyman, 1988), 160.

97. Ibid., 46–47.

98. Ibid., 160.

99. For Nietzsche's attack on the principles of Enlightenment reason, see, for example,

his criticisms of science and rationality—of which he sees Socrates as the first major representative—in *The Birth of Tragedy,* where he asks, "Could it be possible that, in spite of all 'modern ideas' and the prejudices of a democratic taste, the triumph of *optimism,* the gradual prevalence of *rationality,* practical and theoretical *utilitarianism,* no less than democracy itself which developed at the same time, might all have been symptoms of a decline in strength, of impending old age, and of physiological weariness?" (Friedrich Nietzsche, *The Birth of Tragedy or Hellenism and Pessimism* [1872/1886], in *The Birth of Tragedy and the Case of Wagner,* trans. Walter Kaufmann [New York: Vintage Books, 1967], 21–22; see also 86–98).

100. Max Horkheimer and Theodor W. Adorno, *Dialectic of Enlightenment* (1944), trans. John Cumming (New York: Continuum, 1972), 3.

101. Ibid., 11–12.

102. Ibid., 7, 9, 26–27.

103. Ibid., 35.

104. Georg Simmel, *The Philosophy of Money,* 2nd enlarged ed. (1907), ed. David Frisby, trans. Tom Bottomore and David Frisby from a first draft by Kaethe Mengelberg (New York: Routledge, 1990), 510–11.

105. Georg Simmel, "The Metropolis and Mental Life" (1903), trans. Kurt H. Wolff, in *The Sociology of Georg Simmel,* ed. Kurt H. Wolff (New York: Free Press, 1964), 411–12, 414–15.

106. Simmel, *Philosophy of Money,* 128–29.

107. As Bernd Widdig notes, money, for Simmel, formed the basis of a person's feeling of individual security as well as his or her confidence in the social-political order. In addition, it also assured people of continuity between the present and the future. Thus, in situations of hyperinflation, confidence was radically undermined on multiple levels. See Widdig, *Culture and Inflation in Weimar Germany,* 83–85.

108. The discussions on the part of German writers and critics in the 1920s and 1930s of "traffic as a perceptual model," to use Lethen's phrase, also point to the growing comprehension during the Weimar Republic of the different ways in which technological networks changed human cognition and identity (*Cool Conduct,* 26–31). The "new topos" of traffic, as Lethen argues, "redirects wartime mobilization into civilian tracks" (ibid., 26), serving to "bring to mind the superiority of the supra-individual system that directs the behavioral forms" (ibid., 29). Consider, for example, the very cyborgian conception of human beings, suggesting the distributed nature of human cognition, articulated in Siegfried Kracauer's account of traffic patterns in Berlin. "On the most important intersections in Berlin, as we know, colored signal lights regulate traffic. The red stoplight does not, however, switch immediately to green, which signals the right of way, but changes first to a glowing yellow. Yellow signals a transition from one determinate state to another. It admonishes pedestrians and drivers to pay attention and relieves them of the need to consider people and vehicles that a sudden change of signals would otherwise require. To a certain extent, the use of a transitional light objectifies consideration and takes the initiative out of human hands" (Siegfried Kracauer, "Kleine Signale" [1930], in Siegfried Kracauer, *Schriften* 5, no. 2, ed. Inka Mülder-Bach [Frankfurt am Main: Suhrkamp Verlag, 1990], 235–36, cited and translated in Lethen, *Cool Conduct,* 29).

109. As Makela notes, the African sculptures are taken from *Der Querschnitt* [The Cross Section]. The mask comes from *Der Querschnitt* 4, nos. 2–3 (Summer 1924): 136–37. The statue comes from *Der Querschnitt* 5, no. 1 (January 1925): 8–9. Makela, "Notes to Plate 50," in *Photomontages of Hannah Höch,* 104.

110. "The expansion of ethnographic research at that time only took in the 'primitives,'

especially Negro art. The German Expressionists manifested this often in their oil paintings. I enjoyed experimenting in a less serious, but always precise, way with this material" (Höch, cited in Lavin, *Cut with the Kitchen Knife*, 163).

111. Jill Lloyd, *German Expressionism: Primitivism and Modernity* (New Haven, Conn.: Yale University Press, 1991).

112. See, for example, Wilhelm Worringer, *Abstraction and Empathy: A Contribution to the Psychology of Style* (1907), trans. Michael Bullock (New York: International Universities Press, 1953); and Worringer, *Form in Gothic* (1912), trans. Herbert Read (New York: Schocken, 1957). See also Carl Einstein, *Negerplastik* (Leipzig: Verlag der weissen Bücher, 1915); and Einstein, *Afrikanische Plastik* (Berlin: Wasmuth, 1921). As noted in chapter 1, Einstein was for a time also a member of the Berlin Dada movement.

113. *The Sweet One* was exhibited at the "Film and Foto" exhibition in Stuttgart. See Berlinische Galerie, Ralf Burmeister, and Eckhard Fürlus, eds., *Hannah Höch: Eine Lebenscollage* 2, pt. 2, 1921–1945 (Berlin: Berlinische Galerie and Gerd Hatje Verlag, 1995), 361–62. It was also probably exhibited at Höch's one-person show of photomontages in Brno, Czechoslovakia, in 1934 (the various works from the ethnographic museum series are not identified by name in this checklist). See Berlinische Galerie, Burmeister, and Fürlus, *Hannah Höch* 2, pt. 2, 538–39.

114. Makholm, *Film, Portraiture, and Primitivism*, 230–32; and Makholm, "Ultraprimitive/Ultramodern," 334.

115. Makholm, "Ultraprimitive/Ultramodern," 335. See also the advertisement for *Kaloderma Rasier Seife,* which can be found in the *Berliner Illustrirte Zeitung* 34, no. 29 (July 19, 1925), 924, among other places.

116. Makholm, "Ultraprimitive/Ultramodern," 71, 334–36.

117. Graf Harry Kessler, *In the Twenties: The Diaries of Harry Kessler,* trans. Charles Kessler (New York: Holt, Rinehart, and Winston, 1971), 282, cited in Makholm, "Ultraprimitive/Ultramodern," 336. The following year, Kessler described Baker's dancing in another context as "a wonderfully stylish grotesquerie which struck a balance between what is depicted in an ancient Egyptian relief frieze and the antics of one of George Grosz's mechanical dolls." See Graf Harry Kessler, *The Diaries of a Cosmopolitan: Count Harry Kessler, 1918–1937,* ed. and trans. Charles Kessler (London: Weidenfeld and Nicolson, 1971), 284.

118. See Charles Hirschman, "The Origins and Demise of the Concept of Race," *Population and Development Review* 30, no. 3 (September 2004): 386.

119. Ibid., 388.

120. Ibid., 389.

121. Ibid., 399, 408.

122. Ibid., 392.

123. Ibid., 394–87.

124. Ibid., 408, 410.

125. Makela, "By Design," 66.

126. Ibid., 64; and Ellen Maurer, "Dadasoph und Dada-Free: Hannah Höch und Raoul Hausmann, Eine Fallstudie," in *Der Kampf der Geschlechter: Der neue Mythos in der Kunst, 1850–1930,* ed. Helmut Friedel (Munich: Städtische Galerie im Lenbachhaus/DuMont, 1995), 323–28.

127. On the abortion debates and the other issues having to do with sexual reform enumerated below, see Atina Grossmann, *Reforming Sex: The German Movement for Birth Control and Abortion Reform, 1920–1950* (New York: Oxford University Press, 1995); and Willem Melching, "'A New Morality': Left-Wing Intellectuals on Sexuality in Weimar Germany," *Journal of Contemporary History* 25, no. 1 (January 1990): 69–85.

128. Grossmann, *Reforming Sex,* 79.

129. Grossmann is particularly good at bringing out the range of positions. See Grossmann, *Reforming Sex,* 3–135.

130. Peukert, *Weimar Republic,* 101.

131. Ibid., 102.

132. Ibid., 102–3.

133. See chapter 3.

134. On the debates about the "moral" effects of early cinema on the German public, see Mirian Hansen, "Early Silent Cinema: Whose Public Sphere?" *New German Critique* 29 (Spring–Summer 1983): 147–84, esp. 164–71. Particularly debated were the *Aufklärungsfilme,* or educational films, melodramas dealing with social problems such as prostitution, venereal disease, alcohol and drug addiction, and prison reform. A number of *Aufklärungsfilme* also dealt with the issue of homosexuality. See Richard Dyer, "Less and More Than Women and Men: Lesbian and Gay Cinema in Weimar Germany," *New German Critique* 51 (Autumn 1990): 5–60.

135. See Sigmund Freud, *Three Essays on the Theory of Sexuality* (1905) (London: Norton, 1967); and Freud, "The Psychogenesis of a Case of Homosexuality in Women" (1920), in *The Standard Edition of the Complete Psychological Works of Sigmund Freud,* ed. James Strachey (London: Hogarth, 1955), 18:169–72. See also J. Laplanche and J.-B. Pontalis, *The Language of Psychoanalysis,* trans. Donald Nicholson-Smith (New York: Norton, 1973), 52–54, 418–22.

136. See Magnus Hirschfeld, *The Homosexuality of Men and Women* (1914/1920), trans. Michael A. Lombardi-Nash (Amherst, N.Y.: Prometheus Books, 2000), 365–406, esp. 372–79, 383; Otto Weininger, *Sex and Character: An Investigation of Fundamental Principles* (1903), trans. Ladislaus Löb (Bloomington: Indiana University Press, 2005); and Magnus Hirschfeld, *Sexual Anomalies: The Origins, Nature, and Treatment of Sexual Disorders: A Summary of the Works of Magnus Hirschfeld, M.D.,* rev. ed. (1948; repr. New York: Emerson Books, 1956), which presents a good summary of Hirschfeld's positions, compiled by his students.

137. Weininger, *Sex and Character,* 41–46; Hirschfeld, *Homosexuality of Men and Women,* 454–55; and Hirschfeld, *Sexual Anomalies,* 190–91, 235–36.

138. Weininger, *Sex and Character,* 45–46; Hirschfeld, *Homosexuality of Men and Women,* 1140; and Hirschfeld, *Sexual Anomalies,* 191.

139. See Peukert, *Weimar Republic,* 104.

140. For examples of the gay visual culture of the Weimar Republic, see Mel Gordon, *Voluptuous Panic: The Erotic World of Weimar Berlin,* expanded ed. (Los Angeles: Feral House, 2006), 78–129.

141. *Different from the Others,* dir. Richard Oswald; *Michael,* dir. Carl Theodor Dreyer; *Sex in Chains: The Sexual Plight of Prisoners,* dir. William Dieterle; and *Girls in Uniform,* dir. Leontine Sagan.

142. See also Höch's very disturbing photomontage, *Peasant Wedding Couple* (1931). Although the work lampoons the Nazis' celebration of the "racial purity" of the blond German peasant, it also explicitly and problematically identifies people of African descent with apes (*Photomontages of Hannah Höch,* 120 [Plate 66]).

Conclusion

1. While in the final stages of this project, I came across an essay by Craig Adcock, which, I believe, is the first publication linking the cyborg to the photomontages of the

Berlin Dada artists. Adcock argues that Dadaists like Raoul Hausmann used the cyborg to reveal the dangerous nature of their postwar German environment and the destructiveness and inhumanness of mankind. Although, as I have argued, this is only one aspect of the Dadaists' complex handling of the figure of the cyborg, I am happy to acknowledge Adcock's article as anticipating some of my arguments and, in particular, one of the major contentions of this book: namely, that images of cyborgs appeared long before the terms *cyborg* or *cybernetics* were invented. See Craig Adcock, "Dada Cyborgs and the Imagery of Science Fiction," *Arts Magazine* 58, no. 2 (October 1983): 66–71.

2. See, in particular, the discussions of theories of avant-garde art in the introduction and chapter 3. For an excellent example of how one can discover subject matter in Dada art without occluding its formal and conceptual concerns, see David Joselit, *Infinite Regress: Marcel Duchamp, 1910–1941* (Cambridge, Mass.: MIT Press, 1998).

Index

291n30; *"Daum" marries her pedantic automaton "George" in May 1920. John Heartfield is very glad of it. (Met.-mech. Constr. after Prof. R. Hausmann)*, 42–44, 143; *Galerie deutscher Mannesschönheit, Preisfrage "Wer ist der Schönste?"* [Gallery of German Manly Beauty, Prize Competition: "Who Is the Most Beautiful?"], 32–33, 170–71; *Gott mit Uns* [God with Us], 34, 172; *Kapital und Militär wünschen sich: "Ein gesegnetes Neues Jahr!"* [Capital and the Military Wish One Another: "A Blessed New Year!"], 34, 36; happenings, 55–56; *Maifeier in Plötzensee* [May Day Celebration in Plötzensee Prison], 34–35; military service, 180, 294n73, 296n105, 296n106, 296n107; *Ein Opfer der Gesellschaft (Remember Uncle August, the Unhappy Inventor)* [A Victim of Society (Remember Uncle August, the Unhappy Inventor)], 164–69, 186; performances, 30, 31, 50–51, 53–54, 268n68; represented by Höch, 74; *Der wildgewordene Spiesser Heartfield (Elektro-mech. Tatlin-Plastik)* [The Petite-Bourgeois Philistine Heartfield Gone Wild (Electro-Mechanical Tatlin Sculpture)], 175–79, 181; work in film, 86
Gulbransson, Olaf, 226–27

happenings: American, 54–55; Berlin Dada, 54–58, 64
Haraway, Donna J., 1, 2, 5–9, 150–151, 201, 203
Hausmann, Raoul: *ABCD*, 127–29, 133, 139, 143; *A Bourgeois Precision Brain Calls Forth a World Movement: Dada Triumphs*, 115; "Classical Relations to the German Middle-Class Kitchen," 110–14; concept of identity, 65, 66, 133–35, 141; "Dada in Europe," 46–48; *Dada Poster*, 115; *Doppelportrait Johannes Baader und Raoul Hausmann* [Double Portrait Johannes Baader and Raoul Hausmann], 148–50; *Der eiserne Hindenburg* [The Iron Hindenburg], 119, 120–23; *Elasticum*, 136, 139–43, 148; *fmsbw*, 130–32, 283n70; *Gurk*, 41;

happenings, 57–58; *Heimatklänge* [Sounds of the Homeland], 44–45, 86; life and artistic affiliations, 29–30, 106–7, 200, 248; media hoaxes, 58, 61–63; "The New Material in Painting," 30; "On World Revolution," 134, 285n81, 285n83, 285n84; performances, 50, 52–54, 131–33; public presentation of self, 107–9, 110; represented by Heartfield, 41; represented by Höch, 65–67, 70; *Selbstporträt des Dadasophen* [Self-Portrait of the Dadasoph], 118, 120–21, 124–25, 127, 136, 142; on sexuality and social revolution, 134, 285n81, 285n83, 285n84; sound poetry, 52–53, 112, 130–33; "Spirit in a Jiffy," 46; "Synthetic Cinema of Painting," 30–31, 267n27, 276n65; *Tatlin lebt zu Hause* [Tatlin Lives at Home], 136, 138, 139, 141–43, 148; theory of photomontage, 88, 129, 293n57; work as an editor and contributor to journals, 31, 34, 37, 39, 41, 44, 46, 107
Hayles, N. Katherine, 5, 201
Heartfield, John: corrected masterpieces, 164, 291n30; cover for the "First International Dada Fair" catalogue, 49, 141; field postcards, 123, 189–90, 193; happenings, 56; *Life and Times in Universal City at 12:05 Noon*, 141; military service, 179–80; performances, 46, 50; photomontage of Hausmann for *Der Dada*, 3, 41, 42, 44; photomontage of Herzfelde for *Jedermann*, 32, 33, 44; post-Dada photomontages, 82, 199, 202, 265n9, 297n110; *Preussischer Erzengel* [Prussian Archangel], 172–75, 181, 185, 186, 189; represented by Höch, 74; *Der wildgewordene Spiesser Heartfield (Elektro-mech. Tatlin-Plastik)* [The Petite-Bourgeois Philistine Heartfield Gone Wild (Electro-Mechanical Tatlin Sculpture)], 175–79, 181, 186; work as an editor and contributor to journals, 29, 32, 34, 39, 41, 48, 170; work in film, 86
Hegel, Georg Wilhelm Friedrich, 78, 98, 262n53
Heidegger, Martin, 1, 259n1
Herschel, Sir John, 218, 220–21

Matthew Biro is professor of modern and contemporary art at the University of Michigan.